ALSO
AVAILABLE
FROM
GRADY PUBLICATIONS, INC.:

FINAL AUTHORITY:
A CHRISTIAN'S GUIDE TO THE KING JAMES BIBLE

WILLIAM P. GRADY, PH.D.

WHAT HATH GOD WROUGHT!

A BIBLICAL INTERPRETATION OF AMERICAN HISTORY

DISCLAIMER

All quoted material is cited exactly (including misspellings) as it appears in printed sources. Within the quoted matter, including Bible verses, italicized material is emphasized by the source, bold print indicates emphasis by the author of this book.

ISBN 0-9628809-2-2
Library of Congress Catalog 96-094527
First Printing, September, 1996
Second Printing, November, 1996
Third Printing, May, 1997
Fourth Printing, November, 1997

For information, address:

GRADY PUBLICATIONS, INC.
P.O. BOX 506
SCHERERVILLE, IN 46375

Dedication

This book is gratefully and lovingly dedicated to my father in the ministry, Dr. Randy H. Carroll, forty-three years a faithful Baptist pastor, for "pulling me out of the fire" and from the clutches of Romanism, and for establishing me in the *"church of the living God, the pillar and ground of the truth."* (I Timothy 3:15)

Acknowledgments

"For I know nothing by myself."
(I Corinthians 4:4a)

T he author would like to express his deep heartfelt gratitude to the following:

Most preeminently, the precious Lord Jesus Christ for His marvelous sustaining grace.

My devoted helpmeet, Linda, who maintained her wifely support and invaluable technical assistance despite having two fledglings leave the nest during our 18-month travail.

Daniel, Sara and Paul, our three loving children, for their gracious forbearance throughout two writing projects in four-and-a-half years.

Miss Joan Lindish, a powerful prayer warrior for my wife and me who also had the initial burden for this book.

Dr. Wendell Evans for influencing me to pursue the study of history.

My senior cabinet of advisers who provided spiritual counsel on numerous occasions: Dr. Joe M. Boyd, Dr. J. Wendell Runion, Dr. Bill Boruff, Dr. J. Roy Stewart and *especially* Dr. Dallas Dobson.

Reverend Chris Stansell, Reverend Sheldon Stotmeister, Reverend Randy McAlister, Mike and Gail Riplinger, Dr. Keith Gomez, Dr. Mike Monte, Dr. Dan Woodward and Dr. Dennis Corle for their special help and encouragement.

For the second straight time, the incredible teamwork of Mrs. Linda Stubblefield's creative typesetting and Mrs. Angie Zachary's meticulous proofreading.

Tommy and Lori Ray for *another* beautiful jacket design.

Mr. Jack Minor, Mr. Daryl Whitehouse and Miss Lisa Harris for their miscellaneous research assistance.

Finally, Dr. Charles Shifflett and the Calvary Baptist Church of Culpeper, Virginia, for inspiring us all by flying the standard high in the historic center of persecution of Baptists in America.

Table of Contents

Foreword
Introduction

Foreword

BILL GRADY HAS spared no horses in his research for the source of the greatness of America and its decline physically and spiritually into the deep depression of immorality and degradation.

America is no longer beautiful in that it has plunged its righteousness into the depths of the garbage and ugliness of apostasy.

Grady points out the reason for this wicked apostasy. He rips off the cover and shows how America has denied its Pilgrim forefathers and their Bible faith.

Jesus Christ and the Bible lifted America from the miry clay and the weakness of the European political and religious quicksand only to fall into the same traps of world conspiracy which intend to overthrow all governments and all religions.

America is now in the last phase of God's wrath on wicked nations and the One World Order is now raising its serpentine head to sink its poisonous fangs into the entire world.

The memory of Jesus Christ's name and the twelve apostles is being eliminated so that the incarnate devil might appear with his false prophet to rule the world in the most cruel fashion of mass deaths on all non-supporting nations.

What Hath God Wrought! presents the true history of America and its apostasy which the slanted news media has refused to print, being ruthless companions of the so-called secret people who run the world.

Bill Grady's book is strong; theological sissies in American history would do well not to read it. But, it is a delight to those who love strong meat and not blinky milk.

Many gaps of Catholic history are filled in, revealing its wickedness, torture and demonical influence on America's political and religious life.

Baptist roots and the marvelous Baptist distinctives which formed the basis of the Constitution of the United States of America are pointed out.

What Hath God Wrought! has a pulsating soul which will glue your attention to its pages. Once you start to read it, you don't want to put it down.

– Dr. Joe M. Boyd

BIOGRAPHICAL SKETCH

Dr. Boyd was born in Jacksonville, Texas, and raised in the Dallas-Fort Worth area. He was saved at the age of 12 and called to preach at the age of 27.

Athletics came naturally to him, and he rose through the ranks of high school and college to national prominence as an All-American tackle on the Texas A&M National Championship Team of 1939 and the 1940 Sugar Bowl. He was later a first-round draft pick for the Washington Redskins. Today his name is inscribed in the Texas A&M Hall of Fame.

Dr. Boyd graduated from Texas A&M in 1940 with a Bachelor of Science degree. In 1947, Dr. Boyd graduated from Southwestern Baptist Theological Seminary, Fort Worth, Texas, with a Master of Theology degree. In 1976, he received a Doctorate of Divinity from Hyles-Anderson College, Crown Point, Indiana.

After graduation from Southwestern Seminary, he entered the evangelistic field and has conducted local, citywide and areawide evangelistic campaigns throughout the United States and several foreign countries for over half a century. Dr. Boyd has pastored three churches, served as president of a preachers' training school and operated a Christian grade school and high school.

Presently Dr. and Mrs. Boyd make their home and maintain an office in West Union, West Virginia.

Introduction

OVER THREE CENTURIES ago, the Puritan patriarch Cotton Mather, D.D., penned his influential two-volume tome, *The Great Works of Christ in America*, otherwise known as *Magnalia Christi Americana*. The opening line of his pithy introduction reads as follows:

> I write the Wonders of the Christian Religion, flying from the depravations of Europe, to the American Strand; and, assisted by the Holy Author of that Religion, I do with all conscience of Truth, required therein by Him, who is the Truth itself, report the wonderful displays of His infinite Power, Wisdom, Goodness, and Faithfulness, wherewith His Divine Providence hath irradiated an Indian Wilderness.[1]

The Lord proceeded to do *"exceedingly abundantly above"* (Ephesians 3:20) what Mather and his theonomous contemporaries envisioned, disenfranchising New England's "Holy Commonwealth" in the process and replacing it with the first government in the history of western civilization predicated on absolute religious liberty.

However, the more God blessed America, the less her citizens acknowledged their divine benefactor. In his Proclamation for a National Day of Fasting, Humiliation and Prayer, Abraham Lincoln addressed this growing spiritual amnesia, declaring at the height of the War Between the States:

> We have been the recipients of the choicest bounties of heaven. We have been preserved, these many years, in peace and prosperity. We have grown in numbers, wealth and power, as no other nation has ever grown. **But we have forgotten God.**

We have forgotten the gracious hand which preserved us in peace and multiplied and enriched and strengthened us; and we have vainly imagined, in the deceitfulness of our hearts, that all these blessings were produced by some superior wisdom and virtue of our own.

Intoxicated with unbroken success, we have become too self-sufficient to feel the necessity of redeeming and preserving grace, too proud to pray to the God that made us!

It behooves us, then to humble ourselves before the offended Power, to confess our national sins, and to pray for clemency and forgiveness.[2]

As our once-great nation approaches the end of the present millennium, her beleaguered people find themselves embroiled in a veritable war for survival. While comprising only 5% of the world's population, the United States is responsible for 55% of its total drug abuse. In this present moral stupor, the average American knows nothing of our historical Bible-centered heritage.

For instance, take the so-called separation of church and state doctrine. When the Church of the Holy Trinity in New York was accused of violating a federal immigration statute for attempting to hire a clergyman from England, the United States Supreme Court ruled in 1892:

> **Our laws and our institutions must necessarily be based upon and embody the teachings of The Redeemer of mankind.** It is impossible that it should be otherwise; and in this sense and to this extent our civilization and our institutions are emphatically Christian... This is a religious people. This is historically true. From the discovery of this continent to the present hour, there is a single voice making this affirmation... we find everywhere a clear recognition of the same truth... These, and many other matters which might be noticed, add a volume of unofficial declarations to the mass of organic utterances that this is a Christian nation.[3]

As I contemplated this nationwide epidemic of ignorance, it suddenly dawned on me that America's Christians were also losing touch with their supernatural legacy. I found myself, therefore, increasingly burdened to update an entire generation with *"the great works of Christ in America."* I began praying specifically for spiritual insights to the past. *What Hath God Wrought! A Biblical Interpretation of American History* is the result of an 18-month labor of love to help twentieth-century believers fulfill the scriptural injunction: *"Remember the days of old, consider the years of many generations: ask thy father, and he will shew thee; thy elders, and they will tell thee."* (Deuteronomy 32:7)

What you are about to read is a *spiritual* history of the United States. In the ensuing chapters, the cause for America's rise to greatness, as well as the factors contributing to her decline, will be examined in the light of Holy Scripture.

The central thesis of this volume will reveal that the foundation for our nation's unprecedented religious liberty and all subsequent and related socio-economic benefits was formed by the collective presence of America's local New Testament churches, the *"pillar and ground of the truth."* (I Timothy 3:15b) And fidelity to the King James Bible became the prime condition for the retention of these blessings.

The concluding chapters offer a critical analysis of contemporary apostasy along with a scriptural injunction to manly steadfastness.

What Hath God Wrought! does not pretend to be inspired. Only the Pope in Rome lays claim to conditional infallibility. Yet, because this book sets Bunyan's classic epic in a twentieth-century context by exposing "Pilgrim's *apostasy*," I fully anticipate the critical reviews of lost *and* saved "heathen" alike.

The eighteenth-century English revivalist, George Whitefield, once said, "The Christian world is in a deep sleep! Nothing but a loud voice can awaken them out of it."[4] With reference to the controversial American evangelist, Sam P. Jones, a century later, Reverend P. S. Henson added, "History records not the name of a single great reformer that did not wear a hairy mantle and deal blows with a bludgeon."[5]

Lord willing, a few blows from *What Hath God Wrought!* may awaken some of the brethren. It is the author's sincere prayer that this book will bring glory to God and a greater measure of discernment and burden to the body of Christ.

"Cry aloud, spare not, lift up thy voice like a trumpet,
and shew my people their transgression,
and the house of Jacob their sins."
(Isaiah 58:1)

I sought for the key to the greatness and genius of America in her harbors...; in her fertile fields and boundless forests; in her rich mines and vast world commerce; in her public school system and institutions of learning. I sought for it in her democratic Congress and in her matchless Constitution.

Not until I went into the churches of America and heard her pulpits flame with righteousness did I understand the secret of her genius and power.

America is great because America is good, and if America ever ceases to be good, America will cease to be great.

Attributed to
Alexis de Tocqueville

I

America, the Beautiful?

> *"Blessed is the nation whose God is the LORD."*
> (Psalm 33:12a)

O beautiful for spacious skies...

AFTER BRINGING TWO children into the world, a married couple suddenly decided to reverse roles and gender via joint sex-change operations. The 5' 4" wife Jean became hubby Tom while Harry, the 6' 8" husband, was transformed into the new wife, Sheila Marie.[1]

For amber waves of grain...

When a Pennsylvania man ignored his wife's demand to go out for pizza during half-time ceremonies of the 1985 Miami-New England playoffs, his infuriated spouse stabbed him five times.[2]

Enraged over his wife's new hairdo, a Florida man cut a hole in their water bed and tried to drown her by forcing her head under the water.[3]

A 30-year-old Oakland woman was so mad about her husband's gutter ball causing them to lose a bowling game to another couple that she chased his car down the freeway and shot him at point-blank range.[4]

For purple mountain majesties...

Florida authorities charged a 19-year-old woman with homicide for the fatal shooting of her own daughter. At the time of the attack, 25-week-old Brittany was peacefully snuggled in her mother's womb.[5]

Unable to secure a baby-sitter for the purpose of attending her own birthday party, a teenage mother dumped her 39-day-old daughter down the chute of the trash incinerator-compactor in her Chicago apartment rather than miss the occasion.[6]

In St. Paul, Minnesota, a woman bought two glasses of beer for a rather strange purchase price—her three-month-old daughter and sixteen-month-old son.[7]

Above the fruited plain!

While one teacher's method of discipline in Indianapolis, Indiana, called for the good students in her fifth-grade class to spit on the ill-behaved ones, another instructor in Rhode Island forced a particular second-grade boy to lick saliva off the playground during recess.[8]

A nine-year-old girl filed suit against the Chicago Board of Education stating that a twelve-year-old boy forced her under a desk and raped her while a teacher was present in the classroom. Lawyers for the board blamed the victim, surmising that the incident "...occurred as a direct result of the plaintiff's negligent failure to exercise ordinary care... [and therefore] plaintiff should be barred from any recovery."[9]

America! America! God shed His grace on thee...

An eight-year-old Chicago boy pulled a pistol out of his lunch box and shot an eight-year-old girl in the back during reading class.[10]

A nine-year-old Mississippi boy shot and killed a thirty-three-year-old off-duty policeman for arguing with his grandmother.[11]

A Houston boy, aged ten, fatally shot his forty-five-year-old father and wounded his forty-seven-year-old mother for refusing to let him go outside to play.[12]

And crown thy good with brotherhood...

School officials in Chicago were called on the carpet by a number of angry parents concerning a math test that was administered to their sixth-grade children. Two of the eight questions read as follows: "Hector knocked up six of the girls in his gang. There are 27 girls in the gang. What percentage of the girls in the gang has Hector knocked up?" "Martin wants to cut his half-pound of heroin to make 20% more profit. How many ounces of cut will he need?"[13]

From sea to shining sea!

When a five-year-old boy refused to steal candy for two juveniles, aged ten and eleven, he was dropped to his death from the fourteenth-story window of a Chicago high-rise.[14]

While a group of boys was playing soccer on a South Bronx street, a father of one of the youths became suspicious of the "ball" being used. Police were called in when it was discovered that the boys had been kicking a human head wrapped in rags.[15]

After beating his mother to death with a dozen blows from a baseball bat, a 15-year-old Richmond, Texas, youth commented during his trial, "I played a little baseball with my mother."[16]

Shortly after a 16-year-old student was informed that he owed $35.15 in overdue library fines, the account was paid in full. Unfortunately, the "conscientious" youth settled his bill with cash taken in a jewelry store heist during which he shot two people.[17]

O beautiful for pilgrim feet,

In the seventies, an appealing selection of non-traditional college courses were offered to "challenge" America's future leaders: Sandcastle Building (University of California at San Diego), Roller Coaster Riding (Bowling

Green University), and Frisbee Throwing (University of Iowa). Garbology 101 (University of Arizona in Tucson), a class on how to stack garbage, actually met at the city dump.[18]

In the nineties, "Generation X" can now choose between such classics as Relaxation Tech (University of Iowa), Movies and Malls (University of Buffalo), Comic Books in American Cultures (University of Iowa), and Am I Really What the Soap Opera Tells Me I Am? (Buena Vista College).[19]

Seventy students at the University of California at Santa Barbara earned four credits for viewing several hard-core pornographic films.[20]

For the more demanding courses, students may avail themselves of such study aids as Cheating 101: The Benefits and Fundamentals of Earning the Easy A, by Michael Moore.[21]

Any lingering stress may be relieved at the customary spring break. During one particular Ft. Lauderdale gross-out competition, where contestants were flouting national concerns over AIDS, students from Holy Cross stole the show by vomiting into each others' mouths.[22]

Whose stern, impassioned stress...

Arriving home from work, a Pittsburgh mother discovered the following suicide note signed by her twin ten-year-old sons, "We committed suicide because we are no good and no longer a part of the family. So, so long from us...Sorry about this." Although they had ingested rat poison, inhaled aerosol fumes and one had even stabbed himself in the stomach, doctors were able to save both boys.[23]

A mother and father returned to their home from a weekend trip to find their teenage daughter hanging from a basement pipe. Still dressed in her prom gown and wearing a wilted corsage, an attached suicide note read as follows: "Why the [expletive] didn't you pick me up?"[24]

Far removed from the "fun at Ft. Lauderdale," a depressed University of Oregon student jumped through a closed second story window, only to survive the fall. Determined to die, the dazed man jumped through another second-story window and was foiled once again. After an unbelievable third attempt, he was rushed to the hospital where he was pronounced dead shortly after arrival.[25]

A thoroughfare for freedom beat...

A Labrador retriever named Sadie was ordained as a minister of faith by a church in San Raphael, California. The $15.00 fee included an official certificate of ordination.[26]

An article in the *National Law Journal* revealed that there were 140 reported cases in 18 states of Catholic priests molesting children in a single year. A report by the U.S. Catholic Bishops estimated that the church's liability from anticipated litigation could exceed $1 billion.[27]

The pastor of a Unitarian Church in Texas invited an exotic dancer to take part in a Sunday worship service. Two hundred adults and children watched in fascinated silence as the woman, accompanied by recorded music, stripped down to a G-string.[28]

"Now the serpent was one bad dude, one of the baddest of all the animals the Almighty had made. And the serpent spoke to the sister and asked, 'You mean the Almighty told you not to eat of all these trees in the garden?'

"And the sister told him, 'Yeah, snake, I can eat these trees, just not the tree of knowlege or the Almighty said I'd be knocked off.'

"And that bad ol' serpent told the sister, 'Nah, sister, he's feeding you a line of bull. You won't die. The Almighty just knows that if you eat from the tree you'll be hipped to what's going down.'

"So the sister looked back at the tree and saw that things looked righteous, and she also wanted to be hipped to what was going down, so she dug in and gave some to her old man to eat."[29] (Genesis 3:1-6; *Black Bible Chronicles*)

Across the wilderness!

While the Illinois Department of Conservation received a mere $180,000 to study owl vomit, a program in the massive federal farm bill requested $19 million to study the effects of cows' belching on global warming.[30]

Believing that the ultimate solution to the environmental crisis is for the human race to die, Les Knight founded The Voluntary Human Extinction Movement. In order to set a personal example, Les castrated himself.[31]

America! America! God mend thine ev'ry flaw...

Hillary Rodham Clinton donated several pairs of her husband's presidential underwear to the Salvation Army and Goodwill Industries. They deducted the donation on their income tax return at $1.00 per pair. (She also threw in some of Chelsea's undergarments as well.)[32]

An eighteen-year-old graffiti offender caused the city of Los Angeles over $500,000 in damages by writing the word "Chaka" on 10,000 sites in Southern California.[33]

Arrested by the FBI for interstate trafficking of America's latest perversity, a diaper fetishist from Madison, Wisconsin, was caught inside a van photographing a child who was defecating into diapers. The pervert had gained the parents' confidence by passing himself off as a freelance toilet trainer.[34]

Confirm thy soul in self-control...

Based on incriminating photographs, a former employee of the San Antonio Zoo has been accused of having had sex with dogs, cats, horses, ponies, goats, sheep, cows, a pig, a duck, a gazelle, a baboon and an oryx. The 27-year-old deviate confided to an informant that he had been seeking work at Sea World so he could have sex with a dolphin.[35]

When police apprehended a suspicious 23-year-old female, she was found in the back of a hearse with the coffin lid open. Naked at the time of her arrest, the woman later confessed to having had sex with at least 40 corpses while working for a Sacramento mortuary.[36]

Jeffrey Dahmer *ate* the corpses with which he had had sex.[37]

Determining that victims such as Dahmer's shall not have died in vain, American entrepreneurs have targeted juvenile markets for two exciting product releases: "Sex Maniac" trading cards (First Amendment Publishing, Inc.) and "Psycho Killer" comics (Comic Zone Productions).[38]

Thy liberty in law!

The following solicitation appeared in the *Boston Globe* newspaper under the heading of men seeking men, Hyannis Port: "GWM, 35, quiet, romantic, sensitive, honest, looking for relationship based on old-fashioned morals."[39]

A man brandishing a syringe filled with what he claimed was his own AIDS-tainted blood, robbed an Arizona store and fled on foot with $40 in cash.[40]

San Francisco mayor, Frank Jordan, ordered flags flown at half-mast on Friday, January 8, 1993, in recognition of that city's 10,000th AIDS-related death.[41]

After devoting a lifetime to delicately nurture a large family of hemophiliacs, having lost only one son at age two, an elderly Iowa couple watched helplessly as the aftereffects of AIDS-tainted "Factor 8 Blood Clotting Agent" decimated their adult children. The eventual death toll included four sons, two daughters-in-law, and one grandson, with a fifth son testing HIV positive.[42]

O beautiful for heroes proved...

A Denver man who did not appreciate the haircut he received expressed his dissatisfaction by fatally shooting the unfortunate barber.[43]

A Pennsylvania man killed his friend by shooting him in the chest with a bow and arrow over a monopoly game. The Bucks County District Attorney stated, "The defendant wanted to be the car rather than the thimble or the hat."[44]

An Illinois man shot his own 88-year-old mother because she insisted on watching "The Cosby Show" while he preferred viewing a different program.[45]

In liberating strife...

After being shot by a sniper, a New York City mailman was ordered out of an apartment building because he was dripping blood on the floor.[46]

While walking down a stretch of I-5 near San Diego, a California man was struck by a hit-and-run driver. The injured victim spent the next four days on the highway median signaling for help as an estimated half million cars passed by.[47]

Less than six months after the *Roe v. Wade* decision, a research team at Case Western Reserve University decapitated a dozen fetuses and placed feeding tubes into the main arteries of the brains to keep the heads "alive" for experimentation. Dr. Peter Adams, associate professor of pediatrics, defended the procedure saying, "Once society's declared the fetus dead, and abrogated its rights, I don't see any ethical problem."[48]

When the partially nude body of a strangled 14-year-old rape victim was discovered in a field, at least 13 young people came out to view the corpse. While one cut a patch off the murdered girl's jeans, another said that he cared only about a marijuana cigarette he had won over a bet that the body was real. After the "show," one returned for a second look, some went to the pinball arcade, and others simply went home to bed.[49]

Who more than self their country loved...

From East to West "America's finest" have lost a lot of ground to the times. When two New York City patrolmen discovered a pair of bodies that the Mafia had dumped into their East River precinct waters, they simply dragged the corpses down river into the adjacent precinct to avoid having to investigate the case.[50]

No one at the station house felt like singing "The Twelve Days of Christmas" after Timothy Torres became the twelfth New York City police officer to commit suicide in 1994, shooting himself while on duty early Christmas morning.[51]

Police in Gary, Indiana, gave fair warning to "Enter at your own risk!" with the following billboard message in bright red letters, "Caution, you are currently in Gary, Indiana, the 1993 murder capital of America—where officers are EXTREMELY underpaid and overworked."[52]

A female motorist was pulled over on the San Francisco Bay Bridge by a motorcycle patrolman with lights flashing and issued a $28.00 ticket because her sunglasses were in violation of the California vehicle code. According to section 23120, her shades were one-half inch too wide.[53]

Another Joe Friday "wannabe" in Los Angeles ticketed an illegally parked Cadillac while the driver was seated behind the wheel. However, there was little chance that the offender would pay this ticket as he had been fatally shot 13 hours *before* the citation was issued. A sheriff's spokesman could only say, "There is no statute requiring the reporting of a dead body."[54]

And mercy more than life!

A 31-year-old Texan was given a 35-year prison sentence by a district court judge for the crime of stealing a 12-ounce, $2.00 can of Spam.[55]

After the stabbing death of his own wife and a failed suicide attempt, a 73-year-old Florida man was sentenced by a county circuit judge to watch the movie *It's a Wonderful Life*.[56]

A twenty-five-year-old man accused of sexually molesting his girlfriend's daughter was sentenced to only three years of probation. The Wisconsin judge ruled that the five-year-old victim was "unusually sexually promiscuous" and that the molester was "unable" to fend off the girl's advances.[57]

While participating in a national conference of family court judges discussing the epidemic of child abuse, an Alabama judge was arrested and charged with molesting the 13-year-old grandson of a fellow judge in attendance.[58]

America! America! May God thy gold refine...

A bank robber in Connecticut was arrested and sentenced to 80 years in prison when the get-away car he left idling outside the bank was stolen by a different crook.[59]

In one particular year, Arizona prison officials announced a new get-tough policy for incorrigible troublemakers. Opposed by the ACLU as "cruel and unusual punishment," the practice called for the offenders to be served 21 consecutive meals of meat loaf.[60]

Driven to desperation by the dangerous conditions of everyday prison life, two Missouri inmates escaped and eluded their captors long enough to file a $1.8 million lawsuit against the state for failing to provide for their security. Their suit stated that "…a person can only put up with this constant fear so long until he is forced to seek safety."[61]

Till all success be nobleness…

A man convicted of murdering his wife sued the state of Oklahoma for $60 million because he claimed he was forced to view the grisly photographs of her mutilated body. The con claimed, "I am to this date suffering from mental trauma."[62]

While hammering a 71-year-old victim senseless, a 23-year-old mugger became paralyzed from bullets fired by arriving police. After serving a three-year sentence, the streetwise ex-con filed suit against the state of New York alleging that "unjustifiable deadly force" was used in his arrest. He was awarded a $4.3 million settlement.[63]

A pervert who confessed to exposing himself between 10,000 and 20,000 times (in addition to 30 convictions for flashing) had his job application for a park attendant in Dane County, Wisconsin, denied because of his police record, but sued—*on the grounds that he had never exposed himself in a park, only in Laundromats and libraries.* Wisconsin's liberal employment officials concurred and made "an initial determination of probable cause" that the filthy animal was the "victim" of illegal job discrimination.[64]

And ev'ry gain divine!

A 61-year-old Pennsylvania man stabbed his 55-year-old wife 219 times because he didn't like the way she stacked the vegetables in their refrigerator.[65]

A 73-year-old Arkansas woman shot her 35-year-old son after he threw her Thanksgiving ham on the floor, stomped on it, and threw the pan at her.[66]

A 90-year-old Florida man murdered his bride of less than a week during an argument over whether the newlyweds should take a honeymoon cruise.[67]

While police investigated the calls of concerned neighbors over a 73-year-old California woman who had not been seen for some time, they literally uncovered more than they had bargained for. Rescue workers were not even able to locate the body until over five tons of rotting food, trash and debris were removed from the Newport Beach residence. One officer testified, "There was a minimum of three feet of trash throughout the house and drifts as high as six feet in places. She apparently walked on top of the trash to get from one room to another. There wasn't even a functioning toilet…There wasn't a bed or a chair that wasn't covered by trash. We eventually found couches and carpeting at the bottom of the pile."[68]

O beautiful for patriot dream That sees beyond the years
Thine alabaster cities gleam, Undimmed by human tears!
America! America! God shed His grace on thee,
And crown thy good with brotherhood From sea to shining sea!

"America — An insane asylum
run by the inmates."
– Dr. Lester Roloff

II

What's Really Wrong with America

> *"But if the salt have lost his savour, ... it is thenceforth good for nothing."* (Matthew 5:13b)

AMERICA'S CURRENT BLIGHT of moral bankruptcy and social disorder is epitomized by the tumultuous ethos of her own capital city. In the wake of several unprecedented frontal assaults on the White House, including a generic kamikaze mission, a sobering political cartoon appeared in a major newspaper. While two men are shown discussing some unexplained gunfire that was found to have struck the White House, the astute observation is made that the Executive Mansion may have been hit by stray bullets from any number of random D.C. shootings.

The disgraceful fact that our nation's capital holds the dubious distinction of "Crime Capital of the Planet" makes such a cartoon anything but funny. Statistically speaking, over 21,800 of the 53,500, 18- to 35-year-old males residing in the District of Columbia are in a state of perpetual motion within the city's overworked judicial system. On any given day, 42% of the community's young men are either in jail (7,800), on parole/probation (17,500) or awaiting trial (3,000).[1]

As if to illustrate the adage that "truth is stranger than fiction," many D.C. mothers were actually relieved to learn that their sons were being shipped to the Persian Gulf War. Having reared their children in neighborhoods where thin walls at bedtime made the bathtub a literal haven of rest, such battle-hardened mothers would prefer that their boys square off against Saddam Hussein rather than the local vice lord. While only 298 GI's were killed between the August 7th Desert Storm invasion and the February 27th cease-fire, a total of 404 "combat fatalities" were sustained in the killing fields of America's capital during the same period of time!

Needless to say, even the police are starting to get nervous. For one thing, a decent officer in today's liberated workplace can never be sure whom he might get as a partner. With good *morale* generated by good *morals,* the *esprit de corps* of the D.C. police department began its nosedive back in 1979. Having lost the services of undercover officer Ormus W. Davenport, a father of three, to retirement, the force gained a replacement in Miss Bonnie Sue Davenport. In case you are wondering, Bonnie Sue is not one of Ormus' grown children, *but good old Ormus himself!* The department's pioneer transsexual welcomed "its" physician's recommendation for light duty during the healing process, commenting, "After all, I'm only two months old as a woman."[2]

And where is America headed when our local police are no longer safe at their own station houses? On the afternoon of November 22, 1994, Benny Lee Lawson walked into D.C.'s block-long police headquarters. This was not his first visit, for just the week before he had been questioned by investigators for the triple slaying of an 89-year-old grandfather, the man's granddaughter and a neighbor. At approximately 3:30 p.m., the elevator doors opened at the third floor, and Benny stepped out. Moments later, he calmly entered the offices occupied by a seasoned task force of homicide detectives and FBI agents known as the "Cold Case Squad." When Detective Hank Daly, 51, a 29-year veteran, asked Benny if he needed assistance, the stranger, described as being in his mid-twenties, whipped out a TEC-9 and proceeded to take on the whole room singlehandedly. When the smoke cleared, Benny lay dead and so did two FBI agents and Officer Daly. A female FBI agent and a civilian were also wounded. Craig Floyd, chairman of the National Law Enforcement Officers Memorial Fund, stated, "You've got to be pretty crazy to do something like this."[3] No kidding!

Such tales of violence take on an added dimension when one considers that the District of Columbia just happens to have the strictest gun control laws in the nation. In true poetic justice, the bleeding-heart politician must now commute through the very jungle he has created. Although his limousine may sport a "Say No to Drugs" bumper sticker, the pious legislator will be sure to keep all of his doors locked and you can be certain he won't be picking up any hitchhiking street people. His liberal mind may prefer to believe that the Brady Bill will keep guns off the streets, but his nervous reflex at every car's backfiring betrays his true convictions. Senator

Mark Hatfield was driving home from work one evening when he inadvertently turned into a gangland shootout. The honorable congressman from Oregon put his "pedal to the metal" and never looked back one time. He declined to file an official police report stating that there seemed to be little purpose in getting involved.[4] Senator Hatfield was not alone in his pessimistic, though realistic assessment of Washington life. That very year, only 2 of his 534 congressional colleagues possessed enough ideological commitment to enroll their own children in the local public school system. In summary, Washington, D.C., has become a city on edge with its decent citizens having to rely upon the "Bonnie Sues" for protection from the "Benny Lees"!

MARION BARRY

However, for the ultimate embodiment of our capital's disgraceful character, one must discern the city's most disgraceful "character." For many, a name more revolting than either "Bonnie" or "Benny" is "Barry," as in *Marion Barry*—America's premier cocaine-smoking mayor. Hailed by some as the "Black Nixon," Barry's political comeback from crack house to city hall has afforded the nation's crime capital its most appropriate city executive. When the late Harold Washington became mayor of Chicago despite some jail time of his own, a local joke told of a plaque at the Cook County Jail which supposedly read, "Washington Slept Here." A survey of Marion Barry's public career would make even Harold appear like a Salvation Army bell ringer in comparison. Senator John Danforth assailed Barry for holding his city in double jeopardy, declaring:

> Some governments are corrupt but competent in running the city. Others are incompetent but honest. This government is scandalously incompetent.[5]

In a city where one out of every twelve residents has some kind of government job, three times the national average, absolutely nothing runs efficiently. While receiving 2.7 times the nation's per capita ratio of welfare and food stamps, D.C. is found to have a poverty level 50 % higher than the rest of the country. In 1975, the city recorded 2.3 legal abortions for every live birth. The District of Columbia School Board rakes in $5,742 per student (which is 50% more than the national average) and pays its teachers the second-highest salary in the land. Despite these exorbitant figures, the dropout rate is the highest in America at 44.5 % while SAT scores rate third from the bottom. After laying the guilt trip on Congress that a "moral responsibility" required them to send their children to the public schools, Barry yanked out his own son, placing him in Saint Albans, a private school.

Then again, who ever accused Marion Barry of having an ounce of integrity? On December 22, 1988, over 1,000 children heard the disappointing news that Santa (Mayor Barry) had to cancel his scheduled appearance with them. Area narcotics agents were even more disappointed when Rudolph and company landed on the same Ramada Inn that they had been staking out, and the "Big Guy" proceeded to visit the very pusher they were about to bust. With the embarrassing story of the scuttled raid appearing in the next morning's *Washington Post,* the mayor's days were suddenly understood to be numbered.

Although he had already lost the services of eleven aides, including two deputy mayors, to criminal convictions, Barry seemed determined to pursue his "Mayor-for-Life" campaign billing. At approximately 8:00 p.m. on January 18, 1990, only three days before he was scheduled to announce his candidacy for an unprecedented fourth term in the November municipal elections, Marion Barry visited another hotel. This time, the Feds were expecting him. Over the next 83 minutes, "Hizzoner" was secretly videotaped reclining on a bed with a former girlfriend and model named Rasheeda, inhaling twice from a pipe filled with crack cocaine, and finally surprised and handcuffed by a contingent of FBI agents who had crashed into view from an adjacent room. Within hours of the sting, most of the world got to witness the groggy mayor of America's capital repeatedly curse his predicament as he was led away in disgrace.

However, it would be the collective events of the next four years that would reveal a root problem far more threatening to the United States of America than Marion Barry, the individual. With a potential 26 years of prison facing him, the standard buck passing and scapegoat searching began immediately. In less than a week, Barry entered the Hanley Hazelden Clinic in West Palm Beach, Florida. Although busted for dope, Barry's problems were diagnosed as booze-related. He also learned that he was suffering from "repressed anger" and "overwhelming stress" due to his "worrying about people."[6] How convenient!

Feeling a little better, Barry then assured his followers that the devil made him do it, stating: "All is not well in our land. Satan and satanic forces are everywhere, trying to destroy all that which we've built up."[7]

Yet, it wasn't until the old reprobate appeared on the Sally Jessy Raphael show that we were able to learn that the *real* culprit was the "disease" of *sex*, Barry declaring:

> You get caught up in it…the ego gets into it and the grandiosity, the conquests, the women. This disease is cunning, baffling, powerful. It destroys your judgment.[8]

It is when we arrive at the trial of Marion Barry that things begin to get more than a little scary. After 11 years in office, the mayor knew his electorate well. As everything reproduces after its kind, Barry would have nothing to fear from a trial by his peers. Not only did the 18 jurors and alternates view the infamous tape of Barry taking two hits of crack, but they also learned that his blood and urine tests corroborated the deed. Furthermore, ten government witnesses testified under oath of having observed the mayor smoke cocaine on over *200* different occasions. Charles Lewis, the former city employee who received the clandestine visit from Santa, affirmed that he had personally supplied the defendant with drugs for three years. Hazel "Rasheeda" Moore, the mayor's "Mata Hari," gave testimony of sharing cocaine with Barry on at least *100* occasions. After one such encounter in her mother's basement, Moore told how the mayor floated upstairs to counsel Moore's mother on how to help her son with his own drug addiction.[9]

Despite the voluminous evidence resulting in a 14-count indictment, Barry was convicted of only *one misdemeanor*. After acquitting him on another count, the predominantly female jury claimed that they were unable to reach a decision on the other 12 charges. Outraged at such a miscarriage of justice, Judge Thomas Jackson berated the jurors for their dereliction of duty, warning them that they would now have to face both their conscience and their fellow citizens. The no-nonsense judge branded Barry as a "general who joined the enemy" in the war against drugs and gavelled him the maximum sentence of six months in jail. When defense attorneys argued that first-time offenders were usually given probation, Jackson retorted that this defendant was not a first-time offender, but had only been caught and convicted for the first time!

Another telltale sign of deterioration in our nation's capital was revealed at the mayor's official resignation. As a token of their appreciation for "a job well done," the deluded citizenry scraped their pennies together to provide the prison-bound Barry with a modest but worthy retirement gift—*a $25,000 Chrysler New Yorker.* Despite his temporary setback, the resilient Barry appeared to be living out two of his personal fantasies as captured on the FBI tape—"I'm the luckiest man in the world" and "The Lord's on my side."[10] According to Barry, his six-month jail sentence was a spiritual journey during which time he definitely saw the light. After realizing that he had a "spiritual power outage" in his life, the cokehead testified that he had finally "re-established" his relationship with God and was now "stronger than ever."[11] What he failed to mention was whether he reset his circuit breaker before or after *being busted for having sex with a female visitor in plain view of several other visitors and prison inmates.* Hoping to avoid charges of preferential treatment, Virginia officials relocated Barry and his fuse box to a stricter Pennsylvania facility. Despite his medical history of battling "Sex Syndrome," the ex-mayor protested his innocence to a local television anchor, declaring: "My character is such that I wouldn't do it. My principles are so strong I wouldn't do it."[12]

Having embraced Louis Farrakhan as his new-found spiritual adviser, the fruit of Barry's personal revival was evidenced in short order. After faithfully standing by her lying, fornicating, coke-smoking, jailbird husband through a dozen years of painful humiliation, Effi Barry was abruptly dumped by her rejuvenated mate. Marion's choice for wife number *three* was Cora Masters, a political science professor at the University of the District of Columbia. Believe it or not, Cora had also dabbled in D.C. politics, having served as the city's Boxing and Wrestling Commissioner. However, Cora was kayoed by Barry himself when a 1987 investigation confirmed that she had double-billed her expense account to the tune of $2,600.[13]

Adding insult to injury, Barry then proceeded to go on the offensive with several outrageous publicity ploys. Of course, the race card was played from the beginning with the outlandish request being made that his private stationery read "Marion Barry Political Prisoner." For their role in having forced Barry to "cool his jets," Virginia correctional officials were slapped with a $5.5 million lawsuit by the scandalized victim. And as if that 83-minute video had not caused America enough reproach on the international scene, Barry had the audacity to petition the United Nations, complaining that his civil rights had been violated.[14] He also accused his own government of having intended to kill him with a potentially lethal dose of cocaine.[15]

Finally, the phrase "only in America" took on new meaning when rumors began circulating that Marion Barry, private citizen, was considering a return to public office. In what would eventually be called his "Redemption Campaign," Barry made the ingenious stroke of transforming his personal problems of the past into political propaganda for the present. Former mayor, convicted felon, and ex-con Marion Barry sent shockwaves throughout the city by winning the first election that he entered—a seat on the city council representing one of D.C.'s poorest wards. The fact that his Chrysler New Yorker was stolen on his very first day in office was not enough to extinguish his euphoric chutzpah. After all, "easy come, easy go," and like I said, Marion has always understood his constituents.

Having gotten a foot in the door, Councilman Barry then set his eye on the real goal. Sensing the political comeback of history, Nightline's Ted Koppel compared Barry's ghoulish movements to "Dracula emerging from his coffin."[16] As the Redemption Campaign swung into high gear, Barry's mayoral bid picked up one endorsement after another from the very liberal politicians who were simultaneously vilifying Oliver North. However, it was Marion's willingness to "take his message to the people" that would make the difference on election day. Well, perhaps the word "people" is an overstatement of the fact. To illustrate the adage that "Everything rises and falls on leadership," we invite the *blood-sucking vampire* to speak for himself:

> About two or three weeks ago, I was driving down 11th and H, Northeast, and I saw these three guys were beating up this other guy, just pounding and kicking him...I stop the car and say, "Hold it brothers," and they say, "Hey, Marion Barry," and they kick him one more time. And I say, "That's not right," And they stopped and one says, "I'm going to vote for you brother." And I said, "Are you registered?" And he said, "Not yet man" and I pulled out a registration card right on the spot.[17]

On November 8, 1994, Marion Barry was elected mayor of Washington, D.C., having captured 57% of the vote. Events such as these are enough to make George Washington roll over in his grave. From a cherry tree to a crack pipe, America has surely lost her moral fiber. Could it be possible that Mayor Barry was influenced by that *other* dope-smoking Democrat across town? What's that you say? Oh, yes, I forgot. *He* didn't inhale, *did* he?

A SPIRITUAL CRISIS

In view of these and other unprecedented national calamities, more and more Americans intent on preserving their traditional liberties have resorted to a number of alternative "providers." A headline in the *Chicago Sun Times* declared, "U.S. Militia Movement Seen as Growing Danger."[18] The article proceeded to report on a foreboding phenomenon of the 1990's—the grass roots formation of armed militias by an alarmed citizenry no longer trustful of the upper echelons of government. Pointing to the Branch Davidian conflagration as a national wake-up call, one militia spokesman stated, "The militia movement in America is the biggest thing since the Revolution," while another said, "Waco was the second shot heard 'round the world."[19] Reminiscent of an earlier patriotic intolerance toward the encroachments of King George, a third commander warned, "There is one last hope to avoid armed confrontation, and that's if our state governments rise up and tell our federal government to back off. If the state does not rise up…the American people will."[20]

Although many would agree that something is frightfully wrong with the nation, an irreconcilable difference of opinion exists as to what constitutes the root cause of our present crisis hour. On the one hand, there is a large faction of conservative, patriotic Americans who work hard, pay taxes, and obey the law who view the problem as *political* in nature and consequently place their hope in a legislative reformation (i.e., kick out the Marion Barrys). Although some of these may sport bumper stickers which read, "Guns, Guts and God," a significant percentage would not profess to be "religiously inclined." While distancing themselves from Madalyn Murray O'Hair's atheism, such God-fearing "good old boys" would also be quick to point out that they can worship God in the woods as easily as they can in church. The senior representatives of this group often share a vicarious pride with the "Okie from Muskogee" while the younger generation relates more to *Forrest Gump*. And yet it needs to be said in fairness to such men (numbers of whom served their country in foreign wars) that many of these fellows would be in a church if they could find one with a real man behind the pulpit! When the famous London pastor, C. H. Spurgeon, was asked what he thought should be done when lay people fell asleep in church, he replied, "Someone should wake up the preacher."

The alternative view to a purely political cause of our nation's ills is, of course, the spiritual. Americans who espouse this approach, though likewise conservative and patriotic, would interpret current events in the light of a supernatural cause-and-effect pattern. And, whereas the activists of "Group A" may or may not profess to be "religious," the membership of "Group B" would be decidedly Christian or decidedly biblical. (This distinction between religious and biblical will become apparent in later chapters.)

Now, as to the question of, "What's really wrong with America?" I don't think my readers would be too surprised if after 22 years of active Christian service, I concluded that, *'The most High ruleth in the kingdom of men, and giveth it to whomsoever he will. "* (Daniel 4:17b) Or, to make a particular application to Group A (drawing on the experiences of my first 22 years of worldly living), why should a reader be surprised if I now choose to bypass "white lightning" for *the God Who spoke Oklahoma into existence* as *"the* greatest thrill of all"?

So to you dear folks who may, in all honesty, identify more with the political reconstructionists, I would extend to you the warmest invitation to continue with me to the concluding chapter of this book. As we are facing America's crisis hour together, I am reminded of Benjamin Franklin's timely admonition, "If we don't hang together, we will most assuredly hang separately." However, I would not ask you to give me a good hearing without being willing to earn your readership. Having pastored lumberjacks and elk hunters in the mountains of northern Idaho (80 miles from Randy Weaver's cabin), I learned quickly that the easiest way to lead a *real* man is to simply tell it like it is! Someone has rightly said that "a fact apologizes to no man."

For instance, the more we view America's growing problems as being caused by one political party and solved by another, the less likely we are to consider the possibility that the Creator of the universe might be a tad miffed at this nation for biting the hand that has fed it for so long (i.e., "In God We Trust," etc.). While Rush Limbaugh and the GOP squint at the Democrats' "mote" of *political correctness* through their own "beam" of *private enterprise,* God Almighty is calling both ideologies on the carpet in the arena of *personal righteousness.* Although Dan Rather and Connie Chung informed us that an earthquake devastated Los Angeles on January 27, 1994, they were too cowardly to tell their viewers "The Rest of the Story"—that the quake's epicenter struck in the midst of three commun-ities—Chatsworth, Northridge and Canoga Park. Would a sane man think it mere coincidence that *of the 1,400 pornographic videos produced annually in America, 95 % of them are produced by 70 companies located at that very spot?*

I contend that the patriots who have not thought to consider what *'thus saith the LORD "* has to do with things have been deceived by the devil and are unaware that such humanistic reasoning is inconsistent with the spirit of our nation's founders. Do you recall how the militia commanders kept drawing parallels to the American Revolution? Would you like to know how

Patrick Henry answered the question, "What's really wrong with America?" 200 years before it was asked?

> Bad men cannot make good citizens. It is impossible that a nation of infidels or idolaters should be a nation of free men. It is when a people forget God that tyrants forge their chains.[21]

The same patriot who said, "Give me liberty, or give me death" was also careful to identify *spiritual indifference* as the underlying cause of ultimate bondage. For that twentieth-century, red-blooded American who desires the spiritual vibrancy of his eighteenth-century forefathers, I would lovingly refer you to Paul's message to a similar crowd of burdened listeners: *"That they should seek the Lord, if haply they might feel after him, and find him, though he be not far from every one of us."* (Acts 17:27) Feel after Him through the pages of this book. What do you have to lose?

Having extended such an invitation to concerned patriots, a few observations and challenges must now be directed to the professing Christian. Although born-again believers may disagree as to exactly which spiritual problems are causing America the most harm, they do concur that the fulfilling of Bible prophecy in current events confirms that we are indeed living in the last days! However, the same Scripture makes it very clear that the end times will be characterized by widespread satanic deception. After warning, *"In the last days perilous times shall come,"* Paul declared, *"But evil men and seducers shall wax worse and worse, deceiving, and being deceived."* (II Timothy 3:13)

For instance, with all their frenzied anticipation over the Lord's imminent return, "the brethren" have apparently forgotten that the deplorable conditions of chapter one could have never enveloped our nation apart from a serious spiritual decline on the part of Christians. Jesus told His disciples in no uncertain terms: *"Ye are the salt of the earth: but if the salt have lost his savour, wherewith shall it be salted? it is thenceforth good for nothing, but to be cast out, and to be trodden under foot of men."* (Matthew 5:13)

And because God's work is always to be *"done decently and in order"* (I Corinthians 14:40b), the Lord ordained that His people be organized into local fighting units. The Saviour never said, "Upon this rock I will build my para-Christian organization," nor were such institutions promised divine perpetuity as was the church when Jesus said, *"And the gates of hell shall not prevail against it."* (Matthew 16:18b) God's remedy for evil has always called for a bulwark of vibrant, New Testament churches to lift up a standard throughout the land. The emphasis here must be on a vibrant or spiritual local assembly. "Attend the church of your choice," may look nice on the back of a semi, but a church infected with worldliness is no more of a deterrent to wickedness than a truck stop. Someone has rightly concluded that "when the church affects the world, you have revival; but when the world affects the church, you have apostasy."

Likening God's churches in this world to a ship in the sea, the nineteenth-century evangelist, D. L. Moody, used to say that the only real danger Christians faced was in "taking water on board." With the "violence" in America's high schools of only a few generations ago being limited to spit wads, throwing paper on the floors, and running in the halls, much of the blame for today's mandatory metal detectors must be traced to a faulty bilge pump. To shrink from personal responsibility for these conditions as an undesirable reality is to experience the deception of Satan.

For the Bible believer who is willing to do some deep soul searching, I would extend the same invitation I issued to the politically inclined reader—to study this book with an open mind. However, before you jump in, be forewarned that the ensuing chapters are packed full of documented material. While a truly bigoted person will eventually confirm the expression, "a hit dog yells," the sincere man will find security in the reality that "facts are stubborn things!" With America facing her crisis hour, thinking people must have no patience with theories when truth stands waiting at the door.

In conclusion, a spiritual answer to the question, "What's really wrong with America?" should startle no one for as William Penn once said, "If we will not be governed by God, then we will be ruled by tyrants." This book is based on the following premise: The solution to our present crisis hour will not be found with **politicians** making a contract with **America**, but rather in **Americans** making a contract with **Heaven**! To disregard this ultimatum brings a contract *on* America!

"The wicked shall be turned into hell,
and all the nations that forget God."
(Psalm 9:17)

III

A Nation of Providence

> *"God shall enlarge Japheth, and he shall dwell in the tents of Shem; and Canaan shall be his servant."*
> (Genesis 9:27)

P EOPLE OFTEN QUESTION whether there are any specific references to America in the Bible. When the apocalyptic passages are surveyed to identify those nations participating in end-time events, the United States is conspicuously absent from view. Given the high percentage of born-again Christians in this country, such an anticlimactic political debacle would be consistent with the paralyzing aftermath of a raptured church. (I Thessalonians 4:16, 17)

To find our nation in Scripture, one must turn from Revelation to Genesis, the book of *beginnings,* for it is not America's ignominious demise but rather her glorious conception that is magnified by the Holy Spirit. And as the number nine in Bible numerology just happens to be God's number for *fruit bearing,* we know where to find the birth announcement. In Genesis chapter 9, verse 27 (2+7=9), we read: *"God shall enlarge Japheth, and he shall dwell in the tents of Shem; and Canaan shall be his servant."*

In these verses we see the patriarch Noah uttering specific prophecies concerning the posterity of his three sons—Ham, Shem and Japheth. These pronouncements were provoked by a particularly shameful incident. Sometime after the flood, Noah became a husbandman and planted a vineyard. After he became intoxicated and fell asleep, his younger son Ham perpetrated a homosexual act on his own father (Genesis 9:21, 24; Leviticus 18:18-20; Deuteronomy 27:20). Because Ham had already been blessed in

Genesis 9:1 and because his sin was connected with his "seed," God directed Noah to place the curse on Ham's son, Canaan: *"And he said, Cursed be Canaan; a servant of servants shall he be unto his brethren."* (Genesis 9:25) The reader will note that the good Lord's indiscriminate judgment on Canaan would not be in keeping with today's humanistic reasoning. The truth is, God does what He pleases without checking with either you or me. Because Shem and Japheth *"took a garment, and laid it upon both their shoulders, and went backward, and covered the nakedness of their father,"* they received assurances of honor: *"And he said, Blessed be the LORD God of Shem; and Canaan shall be his servant. God shall enlarge Japheth, and he shall dwell in the tents of Shem."* (Genesis 9:26, 27a)

In order to appreciate the historic fulfillment of these prophecies, one must become familiar with the ethnographical table of Genesis 10 which charts the transmigration of Noah's grandchildren. The accomplished archeologist, Dr. Merril F. Unger, states:

> The descendants of Ham comprise the eastern and southern people who settled originally in lower Mesopotamia and subsequently in south Arabia, Ethiopia, Egypt and Canaan (Genesis 10:6-14). As the youngest son of Noah, Ham is regarded as the eponymous ancestor of the African peoples, as Japheth his brother is of the Indo-Europeans, and Shem of the Semites.[1]

Anytime you hear a man criticize the Bible's accuracy, you may rest assured that he is woefully ignorant of the historical record. Dr. C. I. Scofield writes:

> A prophetic declaration is made that from Ham will descend an inferior and servile posterity (Genesis 9:24, 25). A prophetic declaration is made that Shem will have a peculiar relation to Jehovah (Genesis 9:26, 27). All divine revelation is through Semitic men, and Christ, after the flesh, descends from Shem. A prophetic declaration is made that from Japheth will descend the "enlarged" races (Genesis 9:27). Government, science, and art, speaking broadly, are and have been Japhetic, so that history is the indisputable record of the exact fulfilment of these declarations.[2]

The spiritual applications are legion. Someone has said that "Judaism is the stalk on which the rose of Christianity bloomed." When we consider that the European nations, as descendants of Japheth, embraced the Semite

Christ, we stand in awe of the Bible's prediction that Japheth would one day dwell in the tents of Shem. Unger citing Coates:

> Japheth means enlargement: the grace of God has reached out, and the very fulness [sic] of God's thoughts has been brought out in connection with the Gentiles. *"In thy seed all nations shall be blessed,"* was said to Abraham, and God is persuading or enlarging Japheth now by bringing him into the tents of Shem; there is no blessing anywhere else... all blessing is connected with Christ.[3]

(One might even see a secondary application to this concept of *Shemitic shelter* in the fact that Shemites constitute a significant percentage of America's leading surgeons and health-care providers.)

The human instrument most responsible for this "Shemite tent campaign" was the great Apostle Paul, of whom the Lord declared, *"He is a chosen vessel unto me, to bear my name before the Gentiles, and kings."* (Acts 9:15b) Should we be surprised that he supported himself as a *tentmaker* (Acts 18:3) or that his providential conversion is recorded in Acts 9?

When this geo-political study is interpreted in the light of secular history, a biblical reference to America at Genesis 9:27 becomes readily apparent. As president of Yale University, Ezra Stiles emphasized the Christian destiny of America by referring to this very passage in a sermon delivered in 1783:

> Heaven has provided this country, not indeed derelict, but only partially settled, and consequently open for the reception of a new enlargement of Japheth. Europe was settled by Japheth; America is settling from Europe: and perhaps this second enlargement bids fair to surpass the first... In two or three hundred years this second enlargement may cover America with (a population of three hundred million)... The United States may be two hundred million souls, whites... Can we contemplate their present, and anticipate their future increase, and not be struck with astonishment to find ourselves in the midst of the fulfillment of the prophecy of Noah? May we not see that we are the object which the Holy Ghost had in view four thousand years ago, when he inspired the venerable patriarch with the visions respecting his posterity?[4]

In II Peter 3:8, we are reminded that *"one day is with the Lord as a thousand years, and a thousand years as one day."* This verse teaches that God Almighty is never in a hurry when working out His sovereign will.

Historian Daniel J. Boorstin comments on the late arrival of the North American theater:

> There was something extraordinary about the appearance within the European orbit of a continent which for millennia had been unknown to the civilized world. Just then North America was discovered (in DeTocqueville's phrase) "as if it had been kept in reserve by the Deity and had just risen from beneath the waters of the Deluge." What had been God's purpose in concealing the vast American continent from European eyes until so long after the Creation? Moreover, what was God's purpose in suddenly revealing this continent, in making it accessible in their particular epoch?[5]

For many old-world Christians, the purpose of America's discovery was not only to provide a haven from persecution but also to afford the prospect of unimpeded missionary activity. The Lord's challenge to Joshua was alive with fresh application: *"Every place that the sole of your foot shall tread upon, that have I given unto you."* (Joshua 1:3) Just as the Israelites crossed into the Promised Land from east to west, a distinctive *westward* pilgrimage became increasingly appealing to England's hardy believers. Boorstin writes:

> They recalled the prophecy of Jesus in Matthew 24:27, where he described the progress of the gospel as the lightning that shone from the East into the West. "God meanes to carry his Gospel westward, in these latter times of the world," declared the author of *New England's First Fruits,* "and have thought, as the Sunne in the afternoon of the day, still declines more and more to the West, and then sets: so the Gospel (that great light of the world) though it rose in the East, and in former ages, hath lightened it with his beames; yet in the latter ages of the world will bend Westward, and before its setting, brighten these parts, with his glorious lustre also." That America was West thus became a dramatic coincidence. And even the points of the compass took on a theological import.[6]

It is at this juncture that the first important lesson about our country must needs be established—*America was a special nation predestined by Almighty God to be a spiritual lightouse for all mankind.* However, before God's elected children were led to come ashore, a pair of desperate attempts at subduing the New World would be made by a different breed of Japhetic stock—one of a *monetary* persuasion.

JAMESTOWN

The disastrous results of the Roanoke and Jamestown experiments provided a sober backdrop for the subsequent spiritual victories of the Plymouth and Massachusetts Bay colonies. For nearly three decades, Elizabeth and her court had drooled with covetousness as a steady fleet of galleons transferred the plundered wealth of the Spanish Main to the coffers of Philip II. The common man was also hypnotized by such riches. So much wealth was thought to be in Virginia that the savages were rumored to use chamber pots of solid gold, encrusted with rubies and diamonds.[7]

Finally, in 1585, Sir Walter Raleigh led in the establishment of a pioneer colony on Roanoke Island off the coast of North Carolina. When these first inhabitants deserted in the throes of starvation, a second, more determined company was organized in 1587. Apparently the Indians were less than thrilled about reports that the palefaces were after their potties. The besieged prospectors persuaded their governor, John White, to return to England for emergency relief. After a two-year delay (due to the attack of the Spanish Armada), White returned to discover America's first ghost town. Nothing was astir; search teams failed to locate so much as a single human bone. All that was found were four unintelligible letters—CROA—carved into the trunk of a nearby tree. The mystery has yet to be unraveled. Perhaps it might have something to do with John 15:5c: *"For without me ye can do nothing."*

It would be 20 years before the English people were ready to even consider a return to the savage American wilderness. With the formation of the Virginia Company, an ingenious public relations scheme was launched to attract would-be investors. This time, the intended mission was "to evangelize the benighted heathen." (Of course, if they accidentally found a little gold in the process, that would be an added bonus, etc.) Even James I was persuaded by their crusading fervor. His preamble to the company charter contains these words:

> ...propagating of Christian religion to such people as yet live in darkness and miserable ignorance of the true knowledge and worship of God, and may in time bring the infidels and savages, living in these parts, to human civility and to a settled and quiet government.[8]

That the 144-odd "soul winners" who set sail in December of 1606 were, in reality, being driven by a get-rich-quick mentality could be seen by a glance at the passenger manifest. There were no women or families on board nor any heads of households intent on building a homestead. No one was planning on hanging around! Six weeks into their voyage, the three storm-tossed ships of the Virginia Company were still anchored off the English coast waiting for cooperative weather. The accompanying seasickness intensified the dissension within the crowded quarters. Little did the group realize that they were just beginning to feel the effects of a divine disenfranchisement: *"And Moses said, Wherefore now do ye transgress the commandment of the LORD? but it shall not prosper. Go not up, for the LORD is not among you; that ye be not smitten before your enemies."* (Numbers 14:41, 42)

The ominous journey took five long months compared with the Mayflower's crossing of only 65 days. Although the later New England settlers would endure untold hardships as well, there was a discernable difference between the two experiments. Whereas their northern counterparts grew accustomed to a providential interruption of their suffering, the Jamestown inhabitants knew only perpetual misery and despair. For instance, a mere 16 years after the Pilgrims landed, Harvard College was founded in Cambridge with the declared purpose being "to train a literate clergy." By comparison, a 1620 census revealed that of the 1,200 would-be colonists who sailed to Virginia that year, only 200 were still alive by the following year! In 1621, another 1,580 souls attempted the trip. Of these, 1,183 either died en route or shortly after arrival. Within weeks, the colony's adjusted population of 1,240 was reduced yet again by hostile Indians who claimed an additional 400 victims. The reader will note that, after 15 disastrous Virginia winters, it was the *Pilgrim fathers* who inaugurated the Thanksgiving holiday on their *first* anniversary in New England.

Many historians, when writing of the New England settlements, have romantically likened them to Old Testament Israel. In keeping with this typology, the Jamestown rabble would find their prefigurement in the mixed multitude who were so contagious for evil that they were positioned outside the camp. For it is only when the character of these *Virginia* opportunists is scrutinized that an uncanny correlation appears between the land's barrenness and its *"Virgin* Queen" namesake. When the "chamber pot" prospectors were confronted with the survival mandates of a howling North American wilderness, they were totally incapable of pulling together for the common good. Their destiny was sealed by Proverbs 28:22: *"He that hasteth to be rich hath an evil eye, and considereth not that poverty shall come upon him."*

The application of this Scripture to the recorded experiences at Jamestown is striking. The charter's seven-member ruling class was beset by political infighting from the start. Half of the settlers constituted a particular group of weirdos known as the "Gentleman Class" whose so-called code of conduct prohibited them from engaging in any manual labor. The shiftlessness of these professional wimps, coupled with the gold fever of everyone in general, caused the community untold misery. Rather than exert the necessary energy to secure a favorable settlement site, the majority opted to remain at their point of disembarkation despite the absence of fresh water or military advantage. It just seemed to be the easy way out. Within weeks of this decision, hordes of mosquitoes emerged from the surrounding marshlands to afflict the hapless intruders with the deadly disease of malaria.

However, it was the persistent unwillingness of these "settlers" to plant corn that revealed their true character level. The rationale for such irresponsibility was always fueled by their certainty of an imminent gold strike. When things failed to "pan out" as expected, the desperate men were reduced to "panhandling" among their Indian neighbors. In time, this expedient alternative to manly labor evolved into full-scale mooching. The compassionate savages continued to keep their starving "missionaries" alive despite the despicable actions of such ingrates as council member, John Smith. Determined to maintain his reputation as a macho explorer, Smith embarked upon a "revival campaign" of duplicity, plunder and murder.

At this point, it is important to note that the "spiritual" climate of Jamestown was simply a reflection of its own imported brand of "Anglican Christianity." With this distinctive to be elaborated upon in the next chapter, suffice it to say that the Romish practices of confession-hearing priests celebrating the Holy Eucharist around Old Testament altars constituted the very systems that the Pilgrims and Puritans were resisting.

A new sign of divine displeasure swept through the beleaguered colony in the winter of 1608. In a matter of minutes a fire reduced Jamestown to ashes. Only three buildings survived. By this time the mortality rate was a horrific 90% per year, and the following year would be even worse! In the spring of 1609, the survivors discovered that half of their emergency stash of plundered corn had rotted while the other half had been eaten by rats. The panicked stickmen took off in several directions. While some searched the rivers for shellfish and mussels, others hunted for roots, acorns and berries. By the onset of winter, all of the dogs, cats, rats, mice and snakes had been devoured. No one cared about finding golden chamber pots anymore. The deluded prospectors would pay a high price for having disregarded the literal law of sowing and reaping: *"The sluggard will not plow by reason of the cold; therefore shall he beg in harvest, and have nothing."* (Proverbs 20:4)

After boiling and eating every bit of shoe leather and every leather bookcover, the deranged wretches were driven to partake of the unspeakable. To those with sufficient strength to handle a shovel, the graveyard would impart a tough but edible *cadaver stew.* And then there was the case of that husband who couldn't wait for his mate to die a natural death. Having killed, salted, boiled and eaten her, he was summarily executed for his crime.[9]

Although the Jamestown settlers were Japhetic in stock, their unwillingness to dwell in Shemitic tents of eternal values forced them to defer the honor of enlargement to a different breed of Englishman.

IV

Popish Trash

> *"Have no fellowship with the unfruitful works of darkness."* (Ephesians 5:11a)

OF THE MANY wonderful stories concerning the founding of America, one little-known incident reveals a significant insight into our forefathers' high regard for truth. During the Pilgrims' maiden voyage in 1620, the Mayflower encountered a fierce storm in which one of her main beams was cracked. It just so happened that their teaching elder, William Brewster, had lugged his own printing press on board and its "great iron screw" was able to raise the damaged beam back to its original position. There would not have been a Plymouth landing had it not been for a preacher's burden to print Bibles and spiritual literature. By contrast, the repressive Catholic, Rowland Philips, in a sermon preached at St. Paul's Cross, London, in the year 1635 frightfully remarked, "We must root out printing, or printing will root us out."[1] Within ten years of the Pilgrims' arrival, the first textbook of American history was begun by the colony's governor, William Bradford. *Of Plymouth Plantation* would take over 20 years to complete and now constitutes the primary source for information concerning our nation's earliest days. When it came to the realistic purpose for America's founding, Governor Bradford wasted no time in getting to the heart of the matter. What you are about to read is the *first* sentence of the *first* page of the *first* history volume ever produced on American soil:

It is well known unto the godly and judicious, how ever since the first breaking out of the light of the gospel in our honourable nation of

England, (which was the first of nations whom the Lord adorned therewith after the **gross darkness of popery** which had covered and overspread the Christian world), what wars and oppositions ever since, **Satan** hath raised, maintained and continued against the Saints, from time to time, in one sort or another.[2]

One would have to be a student of history to appreciate how radical this opening statement reads when compared to any standard volume, secular or sacred. As in the account of the woman fleeing into the wilderness in Revelation 12, Bradford identified *Satan* as the age-old antagonist of God's children everywhere. Of course, such a "simplistic" assessment is rejected as a cardinal sin by the typical worldly-wise chronicler. The active presence of a literal devil taking a lively interest in the affairs of men is religiously ignored. Dr. Fenton Hort, apostate father of the modern English Bible movement (NIV, NASV, etc.), expressed his duplicity in this manner:

> Now **if** there be a devil, he cannot merely bear a corrupted and marred image of God; he must be wholly evil, his name evil, his every energy and act evil. Would it not be a violation of the divine attributes for the Word to be actively the support of such a nature as that?[3]

Bible-believing men like the governor put more stock in divine revelation than in humanistic reasoning.

With this scriptural indictment of Satan behind us, a second, even more "intolerant" remark of Bradford's may be understood more correctly. In the *first* sentence on the *first* page of the *first* history book ever written on American soil, the author makes a statement that would be branded by today's standards as politically incorrect in the extreme. In no uncertain terms, Bradford identifies "the gross darkness of *popery*" as the devil's co-defendant for evil. That this was not merely an offhanded remark can be confirmed by the fact that Bradford's "hate literature" contains five other negative references to the Papacy in the next seven pages: "popish and anti-Christian stuff," page 4; **"popish trash,"** page 5; "papists," page 6; and "popery," page 8. Bradford's opening chapter surveys the religious persecution that existed in sixteenth-century England.

Although the Protestant Reformation had displaced Catholicism as the official state religion, a determined band of Romanists was slowly but surely reinstating her diabolical tenets. As the Church of England began embracing such "popish trash" as clerical vestments, extravagant ceremony and episcopal polity, a godly remnant called for a *purifying* from within. Most of these "Puritans" felt it their duty to remain in the church; however, a few saw the handwriting on the wall and formally withdrew their membership. These "ultra-right-wingers," known as Separatists or Non-conformists, would pay dearly for their anti-Catholic convictions under the political sensitivity of Elizabeth I. And when push came to shove, an even feistier group stepped forward with a resolve to forsake all for the cause of religious liberty, including their country of birth. These believers would be known as the "Pilgrims."

Having considered the candor of America's first writing historian, as well as the politico-religious climate of the times, we now arrive at the second major lesson of this work. Not only was America's founding predestined in eternity past, but *her actual formation in time was precipitated by and occasioned as a reaction against the Vatican's Roman Catholic Church-State monstrosity.* As the later chapters will substantiate, this historical fact is absolutely germane to our earlier theme of, *"What's really wrong with America."*

At this point, I would desire to make a sincere appeal to any patriotic readers who are either Catholic themselves or who have been led to believe that it is fundamentally wrong to "attack" another man's religion. First of all, stop and remind yourself that a *real* man is not supposed to be intimidated by the truth. Will getting angry or embarrassed alter the **fact** that America was established as a haven for anti-Catholics who were fleeing from **your** oppressive forefathers? When Jesus was confronted by a mob of religious bigots, He asked them a convicting question: *"Many good works have I shewed you from my Father; for which of those works do ye stone me?"* (John 10:32) When a man is able to back up what he tells you, he has a right to ask such a question. Is it possible that **your** priests have not told you the entire truth?

The warning I am sharing with you has been born of personal experience. The concerned authority with which I speak is a result of having had my own eyes opened after spending 22 years in the Roman Catholic Church. I did not grow up on "Walton's Mountain." While others were attending Sunday school, I was serving Mass as an altar boy at St. Stephen of Hungary Catholic Church on the upper east side of Manhattan. Don Ameche and other heathen celebrities were often in attendance; ditto for my own dad and his numerous mafiosi confederates. With a population density of 36,000 people per square mile, I never saw a "little house," a "prairie," or a "Reverend Alden." My parish priest was Father James Dudley, who was also the chaplain for the New York Giants football team. I spent 12 years in strict parochial schools. The "renowned" Cardinal Spellman signed my grade-school diploma. I was married in the Catholic church. The priest who performed the ceremony started a conga line at our reception, playing "When the Saints Go Marching In" with his own accordian.

A providential encounter with a Baptist pastor who knew his Bible changed all that in 1974. Having trusted Jesus Christ as my personal Saviour, my life was transformed and my destiny altered for all of eternity. However, I can still remember how, in those early days, a number of priests kept trying to "win me back to the fold." Fortunately, I visited the local library and started finding out what *really* happened in history. I began to see how I had been as gullible as my European ancestors. I sheepishly identified with the medieval peasant whose bewilderment about *two* "authentic" John the Baptist skulls being offered at a relic sale was dispelled by the monk's assurances that "the little one was John when he was a boy."

THE DARK AGES

In his book *A World Lit Only by Fire*, William Manchester sheds a great deal of light on the repressive Dark Ages with no apologies to the Catholic League of Bishops. Manchester's credentials are impressive from an intellectual point of view: 17 books including the best-sellers, *American Caesar* and *Death of a President*. The hard-hitting author leaves no question in the minds of his readers as to the type of "church" our Pilgrim fathers detested. Take the matter of confessing sin. In the Bible, Christians are told to confess their sins to God and not to any church (much less to a priest). They are further assured that a loving Heavenly Father will in turn bestow His unconditional forgiveness. *"If we confess our sins, he is faithful and just to forgive us our sins, and to cleanse us from all unrighteousness."* (I John 1:9) With a continent of illiterate parishioners, the Catholic Church could do as she pleased. Manchester recounts the method of "forgiveness" enjoined upon a particular baron who had stolen a chalice while intoxicated:

> First he donated his entire fortune to the bishop. Then he appeared at the chancel barefoot, wearing a pilgrim's robe. For twenty-four hours he lay prostrate before the high altar, praying and fasting; then he knelt while sixty monks and priests clubbed him. As each blow fell he yelled, "Just are thy judgments, O Lord!" At last, when he lay bleeding, bones broken and sense impaired, the bishop absolved him and gave him the kiss of peace.[4]

However, what this baron experienced was mere child's play compared to the Church's ultimate penance— the *pilgrimage*. When a really bad sinner wanted to get right, he would have to shave his head and walk barefooted to a far-away destination. As the distance was determined by the degree of sinfulness, some would be sentenced to Rome while others would have to walk all the way to Jerusalem. Furthermore, if the penitent was of noble birth, he had to wear chains on his neck and wrists forged from his own armor as a testimony of how far he had fallen. At his departure, the local bishop would issue him a signed passport describing his offenses in detail and requesting that his physical needs be supplied by the merciful along the way.

Manchester records the unbelievable ordeal of a certain Count Fulk the Black of Anjou. From the looks of his penance, we would deduce that the Count had been a pretty bad boy. His experience is another illustration of the adage that "truth is stranger than fiction":

> Fulk the Black's catalog of crimes was a long one. He expected a heavy sentence, and that is what he got. He is said to have fainted when it was passed. Shackled, he was condemned to a triple Jerusalem pilgrimage: across most of France and Savoy, over the Alps, through the Papal States, Carinthia, Hungary, Bosnia, mountainous Serbia, Bulgaria, Constantinople, and the length of mountainous Anatolia, then down through modern Syria and Jordan to the holy city. In irons, his feet bleeding, he made this round trip three times—15,300 miles—and the last time he was dragged through the streets on a hurdle while two well-muscled men lashed his naked back with bullwhips.
>
> The count could have asked, though he didn't, what all this misery had to do with the teachings of Jesus of Nazareth. In fact, it had nothing to do with them.[5]

It never ceases to amaze me how even the most educated Catholics are still in the "Dark Ages." I remember sitting on an airliner next to a surgeon from Canada who told me she was a devout Catholic. Although she was smart enough to have performed several surgeries that very morning, she hadn't heard of the Spanish Inquisition. Her Catholic professors had conveniently forgotten to cover the material. She looked at me like I was crazy for stating that "her Church" had burned several thousand victims at the stake for refusing to embrace Catholicism.

From a secular standpoint, the most renowned collection of world history volumes is the 11-book set by Will Durant entitled *The Story of*

Civilization. Although Durant's standard intellectual contempt for the Bible would have led him to misrepresent true believers as "sects," his desire for academic credibility precluded any cover-up of blatant Vatican atrocities. His own Catholic credentials are impressive:

> Will Durant was born in North Adams, Massachusetts, on November 5, 1885. He was educated in the Catholic parochial schools there and in Kearny, New Jersey,...and Columbia University...He entered the seminary at Seton Hall in 1909, but withdrew in 1911.[6]

Had my Canadian friend read Durant, she would have discovered that the "Holy" Inquisition was only one of a thousand Catholic brutalities described by Bradford as, "bloody death and cruel torments" perpetrated on Bible-believing Christians. To ensure accuracy as to the purpose, scope and spirit of these heresy trials, Durant takes us to the horse's mouth, quoting a bull of Pope Nicholas III (1280):

> We hereby excommunicate and anathematize all heretics—Cathari, Patarines, Poor Men of Lyons...and all others, by whatever name they may be called. When condemned by the Church they shall be given over to the secular judge to be punished...If any, after being seized, repent and wish to do penance, they shall be imprisoned for life...All who receive, defend, or aid heretics shall be excommunicated...If those who are suspected of heresy cannot prove their innocence, they shall be excommunicated...If they remain under the ban of excommunication a year, they shall be condemned as heretics. They shall have no right of appeal...Whoever grants them Christian burial shall be excommunicated. Whoever knows of heretics, or of those who hold secret meetings, or of those who do not conform in all respects to the orthodox faith, shall make it known to his confessor, or to someone else who will bring it to the knowledge of the bishop or the inquisitor. If he does not do so he shall be excommunicated.[7]

Because most Christians desired to obey the charge of their Master to *"Be thou faithful unto death, and I will give thee a crown of life"* (Revelation 2:10d), the cruel inquisitors would often have to employ torture to elicit a confession. Durant summarizes the ordeal:

> Torture was in several cases used to force witnesses to testify, or to induce a confessing heretic to name other heretics. It took the form of flogging, burning, the rack, or solitary imprisonment in dark and narrow

dungeons. The feet of the accused might be slowly roasted over burning coals; or he might be bound upon a triangular frame, and have his arms and legs pulled by cords wound on a windlass. Sometimes the diet of the imprisoned man was restricted to weaken his body and will and render him susceptible to such psychological torture as alternate promises of mercy or threats of death.[8]

He also points out sadly that, "No limits of age could save the victims; girls of thirteen and women of eighty were subjected to the rack."[9] My friend, does this sound like the type of activity Jesus would endorse? Where do you find the rack in Titus 3:10, *"A man that is an heretick after the first and second admonition reject."* The Saviour's maximum "sentence" for an obstinate offender prescribed a verbal censure and if he would "neglect to hear the church," he was to be henceforth acknowledged as *"an heathen man and a publican."* (Matthew 18:17) The Pope, however, had "a better idea." Durant describes the ultimate punishment for rejecting the blasphemies of Rome:

> At first the procedure was simple: those condemned to death were marched to the public plaza, they were bound in tiers on a pyre, the inquisitors sat in state on a platform facing it, a last appeal for confessions was made, the sentences were read, the fires were lit, the agony was consummated. But as burnings became more frequent and suffered some loss in their psychological power, the ceremony was made more complex and awesome, and was staged with all the care and cost of a major theatrical performance... Those who were judged guilty of major heresy, but denied it to the end... were, by the intention of the Inquisition, abandoned to everlasting hell. These were led out from the city between throngs that had gathered from leagues around for this holiday spectacle. Arrived at the place prepared for execution, the confessed were strangled, then burned; the recalcitrant were burned alive. The fires were fed till nothing remained of the dead but ashes, which were scattered over fields and streams. The priests and spectators returned to their altars and their homes, convinced that a propitiatory offering had been made to a God insulted by heresy. Human sacrifice had been restored.[10]

Not even the official *Catholic Encyclopedia* can ignore these religious executions. The best they can do is to make the bizarre complaint that Protestant historians have exaggerated the total number of victims. With reference to the Spanish Inquisition under Torquemada, which constituted only one phase of the total Inquisition era of several centuries encompassing much of Europe, the *Catholic Encyclopedia* states:

> Much has been written of the inhuman cruelty of Torquemada. Llorente computes that during Torquemada's office (1483-98) 8800 suffered death by fire and 96,504 were punished in other ways... **These figures are highly exaggerated...Most historians hold...that the number of persons burnt from 1481 to 1504...was about 2,000.** The contemporary Spanish chronicler, Sebastian de Olmedo... calls Torquemada, "the hammer of heretics," the light of Spain, the saviour of his country, the honor of his order."[11]

Are you beginning to understand what our Pilgrim fathers meant by "popish and anti-Christian stuff"? And if the Canadian surgeon would take the time to go through Durant's nearly 10,000 pages of material, she would find plenty of other "popish trash" to consider. Space does not permit the uncovering of many additional Vatican attempts at genocide, such as: the St. Bartholomew's Day Massacre; the crusades against the Waldenses and Albigenses; the persecutions in the Valleys of Piedmont; the Lollard campaigns; the mass beheadings in the Netherlands; the general persecutions in Germany; the Duke of Alva's Council of Blood; the burnings of Hus, Savonarola and Tyndale; and Bloody Mary's 300 victims including Rogers, Latimer, Ridley, Cranmer and Hooper.

COLUMBUS

As the focus of this work concerns the godly heritage of *our* nation, a parting glimpse of how the "gross darkness of popery" eclipsed the lower Americas, a century before Plymouth, provides a stark antithesis to the Pilgrim's genuine piety and a sober reminder of their initial motivation for flight.

Although the name "Columbus" is practically synonymous with motherhood and apple pie, the bloody aftermath of his maiden voyage is seldom discussed. Should we have expected less from an operation that was commissioned by Ferdinand and Isabella *12 years after they inaugurated the Spanish Inquisition at Seville?* Following the establishment of colonies in San Salvador and Haiti, the inhuman behavior of these Catholic settlers would set a precedent for the conquistadors of the following century. It didn't take Columbus long to dump his original fund-raising spiel of "converting Asia to Christianity" once he was able to size up the easy pickings. Only two days after his historic landing, the gold-hungry, soon-to-be-dubbed "Admiral of the Ocean" struck an ominous note in his journal. "These people are very unskilled in arms...with fifty men they could all be subjected and made to do all that one wished."[12] In their quest for earthly riches, Isabella's "soldiers of the cross" placed an entire civilization under tribute! No less of an authority than the esteemed biographer of Columbus, Samuel Eliot Morrison, confirmed the grim statistics:

> Those who fled to the mountains were hunted with hounds, and of those who escaped, starvation and disease took toll, whilst thousands of the poor creatures in desperation took cassava poison to end their miseries. So the policy and acts of Columbus for which he alone was responsible began the depopulation of the terrestrial paradise that was Hispaniola in 1492. Of the original natives, estimated by a modern ethnologist at 300,000 in number, one third were killed off between 1494 and 1496. By 1508 an enumeration showed only 60,000 alive. Four years later that number was reduced by two thirds; and in 1548 Oviedo doubted whether **500** Indians remained.[13]

Columbus was eventually relieved of his governorship and returned to Spain as a common criminal. The deluded explorer wrote a friend, "At a time when I was entitled to expect rewards and retirement, I was incontinently arrested and sent home loaded with chains."[14]

While in New Mexico on a preaching trip, I visited the Taos Pueblo Reservation and happened onto a testimonial to the enduring infamy of the "Admiral's" atrocities. A "Wanted" poster sported the explorer's bust with an arrow sticking out of his head. The poster was worded:

WANTED:

CHRISTOPHER COLUMBUS

GRAND THEFT, GENOCIDE, RACISM
INITIATING THE DESTRUCTION OF A CULTURE
RAPE, TORTURE, AND MAIMING OF
INDIGENOUS PEOPLE AND INSTIGATOR OF THE BIG LIE
500 YEARS OF TOURISM
A NATIVE AMERICAN PERSPECTIVE
STEAL THIS POSTER—YOU'VE STOLEN EVERYTHING ELSE

The citizens of Europe would pay a high price for the evil of Columbus and company. In fulfillment of James 1:15b which states, *"Sin, when it is finished, bringeth forth death,"* Morrison adds a sober postscript:

> Evidence that syphilis existed in a mild endemic form among the American Indians before 1492 is abundant. No certain evidence of syphilis in Europe exists before 1494, although certain medical historians assert the contrary. In any case, the disease appeared in a most virulent form in Italy in 1494, and spread rapidly. By 1520 it was generally believed in Europe that syphilis came from America.[15]

The contamination was so widespread that historians have sardonically referred to this period as "the syphilization of Europe." Six months before the outbreak of this epidemic in Italy, Pope Alexander VI sent his official congratulations to Ferdinand and Isabella. Having described the culture that was about to be decimated as "multitudes of people living peaceably," he expressed his pious hope that, "if they were instructed, the name of our Lord and Saviour Jesus Christ might easily be introduced to the aforesaid lands and islands."[16] For what it's worth, 17 members of Alexander's inner circle and immediate family (including his mistress and four illegitimate children) also contracted the dreaded venereal disease.[17] Before the 72-year-old pontiff could join them, he died along with his son when his plot to poison a wealthy cardinal backfired in classic switcheroo style.

HAKLUYTUS POSTHUMUS

One of the more bizarre and rarely known episodes in the discovery of America involves the Vatican's official claim to the New World. This presumptuous act was predicated on the last clause in the fraudulent "Donation of Constantine": "Constantine gives up the remaining sovereignty over Rome..." and ending, "and of the *Western Regions*, to Pope Sylvester and his successors."[18]

Prior to the time of Columbus, the "western most" territory assigned by any pope was in 1155 when Hadrian IV "gave" Ireland to the English king. In 1493, "His Holiness" Alexander VI decided to "clear the air" with King Ferdinand as to who *really* owned the newly discovered Americas. Manhattan confirms, "The English version is from the original (englished and published by R. Eden in 1577) to be found in *Hakluytus Posthumus*,

printed by William Stansby for Henrie Fetherstone, London in 1625."[19] The
letter begins:

> Of the pope's Bull made to Castille, touching the New World.
> Alexander Bishop, the Servant of the Servants of God, to our most dear
> beloved Son in Christ, King Ferdinando, and to our dear beloved Daughter
> in Christ, Elizabeth, Queen of Castille, Legion, Aragon, Sicily and
> Granada, most Noble Princes, greeting and Apostolical Benediction... We
> are credibly informed that whereas of late you were determined to seek
> and find certain Islands and firm lands, far remote and unknown (and not
> heretofore found by any other), to the intent to bring the inhabitants... **to
> profess the Catholic Faith**... [20]

So much for the assumption by Peter Marshall and others that Columbus
was a genuine Christian. The "papal pipe dream" continues:

> You have, not without great Labor, Perils and Charges, apppointed
> our well-beloved Son Christopher Columbus (a man certes well
> commended as most worthy and apt for so great a Matter) well furnished
> with Men and Ships and other Necessaries, to seek (by the Sea, where
> hitherto no man hath sailed) such firm Lands and Islands far remote, and
> hitherto unknown, who (by God's help) making diligent search in the
> Ocean Sea, have found certain remote Islands and firm Lands, which were
> not heretofore found by any other: in the which (as is said) many Nations
> inhabit, living peaceably, and going naked, not accustomed to eat Flesh...
> We are further advertised that the fore-named Christopher hath now
> builded and erected a Fortress, with good Munition, in one of the foresaid
> principal Islands... [21]

Having dispersed the necessary "papal bull," Alexander officially gives
the New World to his Spanish minions. Here are the memorable words:

> We greatly commending this your godly and laudable purpose... We
> of our own motion, and not either at your request or at the instant petition
> of any other person, but of our own mere liberality and certain science,
> and by the *fullness of Apostolic power, do give, grant and assign to you,
> your heirs and successors, all the firm Lands and Islands found or to be
> found, discovered or to be discovered, towards the West and South,
> drawing a Line from the Pole Arctic to the Pole Antarctic (that is) from
> the North to the South;* Containing in this Donation whatsoever firm Lands
> or Islands are found, or to be found, towards India, or towards any other
> part whatsoever it be, being distant from, or without the foresaid Line,

drawn a hundred leagues towards the West and South, from any of the Islands which are commonly called DE LOS AZORES AND CAPO VERDE. All the Islands therefore and firm Lands found and to be found, discovered and to be discovered, from the said Line towards the West and South, such as have not actually been heretofore possessed by any other Christian King or Prince, until the day of the Nativity of our Lord Jesus Christ last past, from the which beginneth this present year, being the year of our Lord a thousand four hundred ninety three, whensoever any such shall be found by your Messengers and Captains...[22]

So there would be no doubts on "Ferdy's" part, Alexander reaffirms his sovereign authority:

We (continued the pope) by the Authority of Almighty God, granted unto us in Saint Peter, and by the Vicarship of Jesus Christ which we bear on the Earth, do for ever, by the tenor of these presents, give, grant, assign unto you, your heirs and successors (the Kings of Castile and Legion) all those Lands and Islands, with their Dominions, Territories, Cities, Castles, Towers, Places, and Villages, with all the Rights and Jurisdictions thereunto pertaining; constituting, assigning, and deputing you, your heirs and successors, the Lords thereof, with full and free Power, Authority and Jurisdiction: Decreeing nevertheless by this our Donation, Grant and Assignation, that from no Christian Prince, which actually hath possessed the foresaid Islands and firm Lands, unto the day of the Nativity of our Lord beforesaid, their Right obtained, to be understood hereby to be taken away, or that it ought to be taken away...[23]

Alexander concludes the historic proclamation by threatening anyone who would dare to challenge his ownership of America:

We furthermore straightly inhibit all manner of persons, of what state, degree, order or condition soever they be, although of Imperial and Regal Dignity, under the pain of the Sentence of Excommunication which they shall incur, if they do to the contrary, that they in no case presume, without special Licence [sic] of you, your heirs and successors, to travail for Merchandizes [sic]or for any other cause, to the said Lands or Islands, found or to be found, discovered or to be discovered, towards the West and South, drawing a Line from the Pole Arctic to the Pole Antarctic, whether the firm Lands and Islands, found and to be found, be situate towards India, or towards any other part....
Being distant from the Line drawn a hundred Leagues towards the West, from any of the Islands commonly called DE LOS AZORES and

CAPO VERDE: Notwithstanding Constitutions, Decrees and Apostolical Ordinances whatsoever they are to the contrary.

In Him from whom Empires, Dominions, and all good things do proceed: Trusting that Almighty God, directing your Enterprises...

Let no man therefore whatsoever infringe or dare rashly to contrary this Letter of our Commendation, Exhortation, Request, Donation, Grant, Assignation, Constitution, Deputation, Decree, Commandment, Inhibition, and Determination. And if any shall presume to attempt the same, let him know that he shall thereby incur the Indignation of Almighty God, and His Holy Apostles, Peter and Paul.

Given at Rome at Saint Peter's, in the year of the Incarnation of our Lord 1493. The fourth day of the Nones of May, the first year of our Popedom.[24]

THE CONQUISTADORS

The intervening century between the Santa Maria and the Mayflower comprised the notorious period of the Spanish Conquistadors. Despite their penchant for cruelty, a religious significance has been consistently attached to their exploits. Bernhard supplies the standard rhetoric:

> They were part of the mightiest army in the world, a fighting force honed to perfection during the wars with the fierce Muslim armies they had driven from Spain; and they were also Christian crusaders, bringing the word of Christ to "heathen" and "barbaric" civilizations.[25]

Were these mystical opportunists bona fide "ambassadors for Christ"? When Jesus warned His disciples about false prophets, He likened them to *"wolves in sheep's clothing,"* declaring unmistakably, *"By their fruits ye shall know them."* (Matthew 7:20) What kind of *fruit* did these Catholic missionaries bear? As if to substantiate the scriptural warning that, *"He that loveth silver shall not be satisfied with silver"* (Ecclesiastes 5:10a), the explorer Hernando Cortez confessed, "We Spanish suffer from a disease of the heart which can be cured only by gold."[26] How is such a philosophy to be reconciled with *"Lay not up for yourselves treasures upon earth, where moth and rust doth corrupt."* (Matthew 6:19a)

Why are these worldly reprobates depicted as Christian heroes when their worthless lifestyles could not hold up to the Bible standard for two-and-a-half seconds? For instance, when the "great" Cortez was barely 17 years of age, he was banged up pretty good in a fall while attempting to climb out of the bedroom window of another man's wife. In later years, a more distinguished-looking Hernando may have been seen erecting statues of the Virgin Mary throughout his Mexican kingdom; however, in private the old whoremonger had to be treated for the *real* "Montezuma's Revenge," along with his fellow syphilitic "ambassadors." It was enough to make Zorro roll over in his grave.

By contrast, when the orphaned William Bradford was but 12 years of age, he chose to identify himself with the despised Separatist congregation at Scrooby, *"Esteeming the reproach of Christ greater riches than the treasures in Egypt."* (Hebrews 11:26a) Although Bradford and his brethren had to endure their share of illnesses, venereal diseases would not be a problem at Plymouth. Because the Pilgrims were a Bible-literate people, they knew by experience what the Catholic "Don Juans" never learned at Mass: *"The blessing of the LORD, it maketh rich, and he addeth no sorrow with it."* (Proverbs 10:22)

This Catholic distortion of New Testament Christianity reached its apex under Francisco Pizarro, who conquered the Incan empire of Peru. The Spaniards compensated for their inferior numbers by enlisting the support of several tribes hostile to the targeted *Tawantinsuyu* empire. In the first major battle on November 16, 1532, the Incas were routed and their "god-king," Atahualpa, was taken prisoner. During the ensuing confusion, the beautiful Andes became drenched with the blood of multiplied thousands of Indian men, women and children who were shot, hacked, burned and even thrown to wild dogs.[27] Despite these atrocities, the pro-Vatican party line remains the same:

> The Spanish Conquest of Peru was made in the name of Christianity. Pope Alexander VI had conceded the right to conquer the western Americas to the King of Spain on condition that he arranged their conversion to Christianity.[28]

Without a doubt, the most sensational "conversion" of the entire "crusade" was that of the king himself. Although the pulverized Incas had initially attributed a divine origin to their light-skinned invaders, this perception began to change as they observed their new masters kneeling before Catholic priests. Another telltale sign of their mortal character was discerned from their insatiable lust for gold. The confined Atahualpa determined to capitalize on this weakness in a bid to secure his freedom. As a personal ransom, Atahualpa offered to fill with gold the very room in which he was being held if the Spaniards would ensure his release. Pizarro was astounded, as the room measured 22 feet long by 17 feet wide by 8 feet high, or 3,000 cubic feet. After a secretary recorded the chief's offer as a formal pledge, Atahualpa was promised the moon and a two-month delivery schedule of gold objets d'art was soon under way.

Having fulfilled his part of the bargain to the tune of seven million dollars on today's bullion market, the heathen king was promptly double-crossed by his "Christian" captors. Determining that Atahualpa had outlived his usefulness, Pizarro had him sentenced to death on a trumped-up charge of treason. The governor's secretary, Pedro Sancho, wrote a detailed account of the execution:

> Atahualpa was brought out of his prison and led to the middle of the square, to the sound of trumpets intended to proclaim his treason and treachery, and was tied to a stake. The friar [Valverde] was, in the meantime, consoling and instructing him through an interpreter in the articles of our Christian faith... The Inca was moved by these arguments and requested baptism, which that reverend father immediately administered to him [christening him Francisco after Governor Pizarro]. His exhortations did [the Inca] much good. For although he had been sentenced to be burned alive, he was in fact garrotted by a piece of rope that was tied around his neck.[29]

The conquistador, Lucas Vegaso, confirmed that the victim's last request was for his young sons to be committed to Pizarro's safekeeping. (The governor's clan already included four illegitimate children from two different women.) Vegaso brings our sad story to a conclusion:

> With these last words, and with the Spaniards who surrounded him saying a credo for his soul, he was quickly strangled. May God in his holy glory preserve him, for he died repenting his sins, in the true faith of a Christian. After he had been strangled in this way and the sentence executed, some fire was thrown on to him to burn part of his clothing and flesh. He died late in the afternoon, and his body was left in the square that night for everyone to learn of his death. On the following day the Governor ordered all the Spaniards to attend his funeral. He was carried to the church with a cross and the rest of the religious ornaments, and was buried with as much pomp as if he had been the most important Spaniard in our camp.[30]

Where is the New Testament precedent for such insanity? (Catholic apologists who cite Calvin's treatment of Servetus are politely headed off at the pass by the author's *Baptistic* heritage. Baptists do not kill people over doctrine.) Is it any wonder that the Holy Spirit would not allow Columbus, Cortez, Pizarro or any other killers to land on future American soil?

At this point it must be reiterated that the central premise of our present chapter is that America was founded by a group of Bible-believing Christians who were fleeing the Roman Catholic Church. The two systems are diametrically opposed and cannot be reconciled, *despite the present-day satanic efforts of Pat Robertson and Chuck Colson*! For instance, my readers have observed how the Spanish "Christians" treated their missionary prospects under the best of conditions. How does this compare to how the English Christians cared for *their* Indian neighbors under the *worst* of conditions? Which "brand" of Christianity produced the historical fruit? With reference to a smallpox epidemic, Bradford attested:

> The condition of this people was so lamentable and they fell down so generally of this disease as they were in the end not able to help one another, no not to make a fire nor to fetch a little water to drink, nor any to bury the dead. But would strive as long as they could, and when they could procure no other means to make fire, they would burn the wooden trays and dishes they ate their meat in, and their very bows and arrows. And some would crawl out on all fours to get a little water, and sometimes die by the way and not be able to get in again. But of those of the English house, though at first they were afraid of the infection, yet seeing their woeful and sad condition and hearing their pitiful cries and lamentations, they had compassion of them, and daily fetched them wood and water and made them fires, got them victuals whilst they lived; and buried them when they died...But by the marvelous goodness and providence of God, not one of the English was so much as sick or in the least measure tainted with this disease, though they daily did these offices for them for many weeks together. And this mercy which they showed them was kindly taken and thankfully acknowledged of all the Indians that knew or heard of the same.[31]

To summarize this important spiritual distinction; a Bible-believing Christian will never be found searching for a "fountain of youth." This elusive discovery has been the perpetual goal of unenlightened Roman Catholics from Ponce de Leon to Frank Sinatra (old "Blue Eyes" himself) who recently stated, "I'm getting old; God, I wish I could start over again." After all, who needs a "fountain of youth" when you already have a "fountain filled with blood drawn from Immanuel's veins"?

V

Not As Other Men

> *"They were strangers and pilgrims on the earth. For they that say such things declare plainly that they seek a country."* (Hebrews 11:13b, 14)

BEFORE THE QUESTION of *"What's really wrong with America?"* can be intelligently answered, one must first come to appreciate that which was once *right* about America. A profound interchange between the statistician, Roger Babson, and the President of Argentina sets the pace for this needed survey of America's spiritual legacy. With our previous chapter as a backdrop, Dr. Paul Tan provides the following enlightening perspective.

> Roger Babson, the statistician, was lunching with the President of Argentina. "Mr. Babson," the President said, "I have been wondering why it is that South America with all its natural advantages, its mines of iron, copper, coal, silver and gold; its rivers and great waterfalls which rival Niagara, is so far behind North America." Babson replied, "Well, Mr. President, what do you think is the reason?" He was silent for a while before he answered. "I have come to this conclusion. South America was settled by the Spanish, who came to South America in search of gold; but North America was settled by the Pilgrim Fathers, who went there in search of God."[1]

As previously mentioned, Elizabeth's approach to religious matters followed the standard route of political expediency. While allowing her

Catholic subjects to attend Mass (oftentimes attending herself), she prohibited the elevation of the host to placate her Protestant constituency. Those who rocked the boat did so at the risk of life and limb, literally. In 1513, two Separatist leaders, John Greenwood and Henry Barrow, were hanged at Tyburn while the Congregationalist, John Penry, was drawn and quartered.[2] The concept most detestable to the throne was one of ecclesiastical independence. Pastor Robert Browne wrote, "The church...is a company or number of Christians or believers, which by a willing covenant made with their God, are under the government of God and Christ."[3] In 1583, while Browne was in exile in the Netherlands, two Englishmen were executed for merely being in possession of his writings.

The nation's non-conformist minority had even less hope for civic equality under Elizabeth's successor, the autocratic James I. Although James liked the Puritans' anti-Catholic position, he strongly disapproved of their Presbyterian form of government as a threat to his royal absolutism. Having been exposed to these abuses in his previous administration as James VI of Scotland, he had no intention of subjecting his newest realm to such a confining Calvinistic theocracy, vowing to "harry them out of the land, or else do worse."[4]

FLIGHT TO HOLLAND

Such were the conditions of providence that induced the small Separatist congregation at Scrooby, pastored by John Robinson, a former associate of Robert Browne, to leave their native soil and country in 1608 for the more tolerant lands of Holland. Although free to worship God according to conscience, the new arrivals (numbering about 125) had many obstacles to overcome. Bradford describes their initial impressions of Amsterdam:

> Being now come into the Low Countries, they saw many goodly and fortified cities, strongly walled and guarded with troops of armed men. Also, they heard a strange and uncouth language, and beheld the different manners and customs of the people, with their strange fashions and attires; all so far differing from that of their plain country villages (wherein they were bred and had so long lived) as it seemed they were come into a new world. But these were not the things they much looked on, or long took up their thoughts, for they had other work in hand and another kind of war to wage and maintain. For although they saw fair and beautiful cities, flowing with abundance of all sorts of wealth and riches, yet it was not long before they saw the grim and grisly face of poverty coming upon them like an

armed man, with whom they must buckle and encounter, and from whom they could not fly. But they were armed with faith and patience against him and all his encounters; and though they were sometimes foiled, yet by God's assistance they prevailed and got the victory.[5]

Although precluded by their alien status from owning private poverty, the Scrooby refugees impressed the native population by working their landlords' fields from 12 to 15 hours per day. However, after carving out a meager existence for over a decade, the Leyden congregation (now numbering between 400 and 500 souls) was suddenly confronted by a new array of dangers. Many parents began expressing that timeless concern over would-be prodigals coming of age in a worldly environment. Bradford writes:

> But that which was more lamentable, and of all sorrows most heavy to be borne, was that many of their children, by these occasions and the great licentiousness of youth in that country, and the manifold temptations of the place, were drawn away by evil examples into extravagant and dangerous courses, getting the reins off their necks and departing from their parents.[6]

Another cause for alarm was with regard to the 12-year treaty between Spain and the Netherlands which was due to end in 1621. Over half of Leyden's 100,000 inhabitants had succumbed to disease or starvation during her last siege in 1574.

A third motivation for leaving Holland was seen in the potential for missionary activity in faraway lands:

> A great hope and inward zeal they had of laying some good foundation, or at least to make some way thereunto, for the propagating and advancing the gospel of the kingdom of Christ in those remote parts of the world; yea, though they should be but even as stepping-stones unto others for the performing of so great a work.[7]

Yet the prospect of such an undertaking being attempted by the exhausted remnants of Scrooby was viewed as hazardous in the extreme. However, after much discussion they concluded that no hardship should be avoided if it furthered the cause of Christ. Bradford's noble lines:

> It was answered, that all great and honourable actions are accompanied with great difficulties and must be both enterprised and

overcome with answerable courages. It was granted the dangers were great, but not desperate. The difficulties were many, but not invincible. For though there were many of them likely, yet they were not certain. It might be sundry of the things feared might never befall; others by provident care and the use of good means might in a great measure be prevented; and all of them, through the help of God, by fortitude and patience, might either be borne or overcome.[8]

Having settled the question of leaving the Netherlands, the next decision they faced concerned their actual choice of a destination. Their viable options were reduced to only two—Guiana and Virginia. After further deliberation, it was concluded that the combined threat of tropical diseases and lurking Spaniards made the Indian-infested coasts of northern Virginia the lesser of two evils.

Due to a limitation of resources, two of their own, Robert Cushman and John Carver, were dispatched to London with the hopes of securing a patent from the famed Virginia Company. Because such a contract would underwrite the prohibitive cost of passage, the bids were highly competitive. In a follow-up letter to Sir Edwin Sandys, signed by John Robinson, pastor of the Leyden church, and his assistant, William Brewster, a five-point outline was submitted, highlighting the strengths and convictions of the applicants:

1. We verily believe and trust the Lord is with us, unto whom and whose service we have given ourselves in many trials; and that He will graciously prosper our endeavors according to the simplicity of our hearts therein.

2. We are well weaned from the delicate milk of our mother country, and inured to the difficulties of a strange and hard land, which yet in a great part we have by patience overcome.

3. The people are, for the body of them, industrious and frugal, we think we may safely say, as any company of people in the world.

4. We are knit together as a body in a most strict and sacred bond and covenant of the Lord, of the violation whereof we make great conscience, and by virtue whereof we do hold ourselves straitly tied to all care of each other's good and of the whole, by every one and so mutually.

5. Lastly, **it is not with us as with other men**, whom small things can discourage, or small discontentments cause to wish themselves at home again. We know our entertainment in England and in Holland. We shall much prejudice both our arts and means by removal; who, if we should be driven to return, we should not hope to recover our present helps and comforts, neither indeed look ever, for ourselves, to attain unto the like in any other place during our lives, which are now drawing towards their periods.[9]

Needless to say, the Virginia Company was impressed. How long has it been since you met an American who expressed himself in such a manner? The godly character of our nation's forefathers can be summed up in that one simple phrase—*"it is not with us as with other men."* Once again, this chapter is about that which was once *right* about America.

Although John Robinson would have led his entire flock to America, in actuality only a third of the membership possessed the constitution for such a journey. And because the weaker faction comprised the majority, the pastor himself would have to forego the crossing. William Brewster, the body's teaching elder, would provide the leadership for the historic endeavor.

While Mr. Cushman was in London negotiating with Captain Christopher Jones of the Mayflower, a smaller, second vessel was purchased and fitted in Holland. The Speedwell, it was hoped, would provide invaluable service to the new colony, especially for fishing. When all was ready, a special day of prayer and fasting was enjoined, Bradford writing:

So being ready to depart, they had a solemn day of humiliation, their pastor taking his text from Ezra viii. 21: "And there at the river, by Ahava, I proclaimed a fast, that we might humble ourselves before our God, and seek of him a right way for us, and for all our children, and for all our substance." Upon which he spent a good part of the day very profitably and suitable to their present occasion; the rest of the time was spent in pouring out prayers to the Lord with great fervency, mixed with abundance of tears.[10]

We can only imagine how hard it must have been to say farewell to family and friends alike, not to mention the only pastor they had ever known. In order to lend his assistance in the needed area of leadership, Bradford left his own five-year-old son John in Holland. Many others followed suit. They had a cause that was larger than themselves. How does this compare to a bunch of American housewives knocking each other over in order to purchase Cabbage Patch™ dolls for their spoiled brats at home?

> So they left that goodly and pleasant city which had been their resting place near twelve years; but they knew they were pilgrims, and looked not much on those things, but lift up their eyes to the heavens, their dearest country, and quieted their spirits.[11]

When the group arrived in London, they were coldly informed by their sponsor's unscrupulous agent, Thomas Weston, that a glitch in their original contract required an additional payment of 30 pounds. The Pilgrims unwisely decided to allow Weston and his group of London "Adventurists," i.e., capitalists, to represent them with the Virginia Company. Although unquestionably in the right, our Pilgrim fathers esteemed their Christian testimony of far greater value than Weston's temporal mammon. Several thousand pounds of butter were subsequently sold to settle the debt.

However, of even greater concern to these sensitive passengers, especially the family heads, was with regard to the confining quarters they would be sharing with their less-than-spiritual fellow travelers—Weston's 80 opportunistic "strangers" and Captain Jones' lusty crew. The Mayflower's interior was smaller than a tennis court. And yet, these were but the beginning of a legion of trials they would encounter.

IN GOD WE TRUST

They finally set sail on August 5, 1620, but experienced a serious problem after only three days at sea. The Speedwell was taking on an excessive amount of water which forced their return to the nearby port of Dartmouth. After a week of recaulking her, they departed again only to encounter the same mysterious leaks. This time the Speedwell was pronounced unseaworthy.

Although things looked bleak, the Lord was very much at work. With the forfeited butter representing their only *surplus* food, the Heavenly Father was now removing their intended means of commercial fishing as well as their only lifeline with England, should an emergency arise. Apparently, the Pilgrims were going to have to live by the words emblazoned across the Mayflower's sails—*"In God We Trust."*

And so, another sad parting of the company occurred, as those deemed the weakest (and the most timid) limped back to London in the Speedwell. Bradford took comfort in the Scriptural precedent: "And thus, like Gideon's army, this small number was divided, as if the Lord by this work of His providence thought these few too many for the great work He had to do."[12]

On September 6, 1620, the Mayflower embarked on her epic voyage with 102 souls on board, 41 Separatists and 61 others. Unless one has personally examined a Mayflower replica, it would be difficult to appreciate the physical, emotional and psychological cost exacted in the Pilgrims' arduous transatlantic crossing. The ship was a freighter that had never carried passengers. Because Captain Jones normally hauled wine and cognac from France, his vessel was nicknamed the "Sweet Ship" for the unusual aroma of her hull. This would all change in short order.

With 45 days of disrupted travel already behind them, the Pilgrims would now endure another 65 days in the dimly lit recesses of the Mayflower's damp gun deck. For nine long weeks, they tossed and turned. The same intimidating waves that sequestered all below kept the hatches closed which caused a choking ventilation. No one could bathe or even change their clothes for the entire trip.

And then there was the food situation. Because lighted fires were prohibited, everyone ate their rations cold. The biscuits had to be smashed into pieces with a chisel. The cheese was moldy. Creepy things crawled through their peas and grain. Furthermore, it should be noted that, unlike the Jamestown rabble, numbers of women and children were on board the Mayflower, including two expectant mothers.

Now because the Pilgrims were God's chosen vessels who would be called upon to suffer greater calamities for His name's sake, it was only fitting that He would use this two-month bonding time to reveal His mighty arm of deliverance to strengthen their faith while awing the "mixed multitude" into reverential submission. Throughout the early weeks of sailing, the Pilgrims endured continuous verbal harassment from the crew. One man distinguished himself as a sort of self-appointed tormentor for the others. He delighted in calling the Pilgrims "psalmsinging puke-stockings"[13] and uttered his own prophecy that he would soon be feeding them to the fish. Bradford gives us the rest of the story:

> But it pleased God before they came half seas over, to smite this young man with a grievous disease, of which he died in a desperate manner, and so was himself the first that was thrown overboard. Thus his

curses light on his own head, and it was an astonishment to all his fellows for they noted it to be the just hand of God upon him.[14]

Another act of providence which arrested the superstitious crew was the previously mentioned incident where Brewster's iron screw secured the Mayflower's cracked beam.

On a different occasion, a young man who could no longer endure the cabin fever climbed out onto the sea-swept main deck for a breath of fresh air. In a matter of moments, John Howland got more than he had bargained for. "Man overboard," the crew members shouted with a hardened pessimism in their voices. Yet, seemingly out of nowhere, a random line found its way into the frantic, outstretched arms of one thankful, praying Pilgrim! He was hauled on board like a large flounder where he spent several days recovering from his icy ordeal.

Although one of their own, William Butten, was not as fortunate, succumbing to scurvy for his unwillingness to ingest the recommended antidotes of lemon juice and dried fruit, their numbers were offset by the miraculous delivery of a healthy baby boy to Steve and Elizabeth Hopkins. Imagine having to deliver an infant in such a filthy environment with neither heat nor warm water at your disposal. The grateful parents named him Oceanus.[15]

At daybreak on November 9, the cry of "Land Ho" was finally heard. However, it was not the coast of northern Virginia but rather the Highlands of Cape Cod which came into view. Having arrived a great distance north of where they had intended to put ashore gave them a vicarious appreciation for the Bible's original pilgrim, Abraham, who *"went out, not knowing whither he went."* (Hebrews 11:8b)

All were happy to have the sea behind them, however, and upon their entrance into Cape Harbor, Bradford informs us:

> Being thus arrived in a good harbor, and brought safe to land, they fell upon their knees and blessed the God of Heaven who had brought them over the vast and furious ocean, and delivered them from all the perils and miseries thereof, again to set their feet on the firm and stable earth, their proper element.[16]

And yet it wasn't long before a new set of concerns began to arise. What lay behind the ominous tree lines? Where would they put ashore? How much time did they have before the weather became their worst nightmare? Were they not in violation of their patent which prescribed a Virginia settlement? Would Weston's "strangers" mutiny? Bradford's pathos is moving:

> But here I cannot but stay and make a pause, and stand half amazed at this poor people's present condition; and so I think will the reader, too, when he well considers the same. Being thus passed the vast ocean, and a sea of troubles before in their preparation...they had now no friends to welcome them nor inns to entertain or refresh their weatherbeaten bodies; no houses or much less town to repair to, to seek for succour. It is recorded in Scripture as a mercy to the Apostle and his shipwrecked company, that the barbarians, showed them no small kindness in refreshing them, but these savage barbarians, when they met with them (as after will appear) were readier to fill their sides full of arrows than otherwise. And for the season it was winter, and they that know the winters of that country know them to be sharp and violent, and subject to cruel and fierce storms, dangerous to travel to known places, much more to search an unknown coast. Besides, what could they see but a hideous and desolate wilderness, full of wild beasts and wild men—and what multitudes there might be of them they knew not.[17]

But the subjects of our present chapter "were not as other men"! They identified with the words of Nehemiah 6:11a, *"Should such a man as I flee?"* These were not a bunch of gold-sick Catholics, but children of spiritual Abraham who *"looked for a city which hath foundations, whose builder and maker is God."* (Hebrews 11:10)

> What could now sustain them but the Spirit of God and His grace? May not and ought not the children of these fathers rightly say: "Our fathers were Englishmen which came over this great ocean, and were ready to perish in this wilderness; but they cried unto the Lord, and He heard their voice and looked on their adversity," etc. "Let them therefore praise the Lord, because He is good: and His mercies endure forever."[18]

MAYFLOWER COMPACT

Due to the Mayflower's late arrival and the long stretch of uncharted coastal waters to the south, Captain Jones wisely recommended that they put ashore where they were. This change of plans convinced Weston's contract laborers that they would be consigned to an unlawful servitude owing to the likelihood that their original patent stipulating a Virginia settlement would be subsequently dissolved. Thus, the Pilgrims' first order of business was occasioned by rumors of a possible mutiny by the paranoid "strangers" aboard.

However, this threat of anarchy was removed when the men were able to reach a unanimous decision to forge their own political document, authorizing a government by self-rule. William Brewster, with a personal library of over 200 books on board, was the probable framer of the now-famous Mayflower Compact. In any event, the compact followed the model of their church covenant in Leyden and read as follows:

> In ye name of God, Amen. We whose names are underwriten, the loyall subjects of our dread soveraigne Lord, King James, by ye grace of God, of Great Britaine, France, and Ireland king, defender of ye faith, etc., having undertaken, for ye glorie of God, and advancemente of ye Christian faith, and honour of our king & countrie, a voyage to plant ye first colonie in ye Northerne parts of Virginia, doe by these presents solemnly & mutually in ye presence of God, and one of another, covenant & combine our selves togeather into a civill body politick, for our better ordering & preservation & furtherance of ye ends aforesaid; and by vertue hearof to enacte, constitute, and frame such just & equall lawes, ordinances, acts, constitutions & offices, from time to time, as shall be thought most meete & convenient for ye generall good of ye Colonie, unto which we promise all due submission and obedience. In witnes wherof we have hereunder subscribed our names at Cap-Codd ye 11. of November, in ye year of ye raigne of our soveraigne lord, King James, of England, France, & Ireland, ye eighteenth, and by Scotland ye fiftie fourth. Ano: Dom. 1620.[19]

A total of 41 of the 65 males on board signed the compact, 13 of the others being represented by their fathers' signatures while the remaining 11 men were probably too sick to participate. No doubt these unassuming Christians were completely oblivious to the far-reaching consequences of their remarkable and unprecedented act. The Mayflower Compact constituted the first instance in recorded history when free men had voluntarily covenanted together to formulate their own civil government.

Today's humanist is at a loss to explain why America's political heritage begins with the words, "In ye name of God, Amen." Although James I is afforded the respect of his office, the compact affirms that his rule is solely "by ye grace of God," and that their submission as "loyall subjects" is in tacit proportion to his responsibility as "defender of ye faith, etc." That His Majesty's *Protestant* subjects perceived this function to be his highest priority is implied by their use of the subliminal "etc." to represent all of his "remaining" duties. And does not such a title constitute yet another grim reminder of Rome's relentless aggression against the church of Jesus Christ?

Consequently, this contractual document required of its signers no more than their "*due* submission and obedience." A philosophical justification for the American Revolution would be traced to a violation of this very concept of mutual responsibility.

In the meantime, the Mayflower Compact would insure that, "ye generall good of ye Colonie" would take precedence over any potential off-the-wall rights of individuals, (i.e., $2 million settlement for burns from hot coffee, etc.). A necessary Bill of Rights would eventually be drafted and yet, even this improvement is anticipated in the phrase, "from time to time."

Finally, the ultimate purpose for the founding of our great nation is spelled out in no uncertain terms: the "advancemente of ye Christian faith" (not a bad idea, given their Calvinistic theology). Soul winning is so important that it was alluded to in the Mayflower Compact.

EXPLORING THE LAND

Having settled these political matters, the time for action had arrived. While their damaged shallop was being repaired, Captain Miles Standish (their military commander) led an initial exploration party of 16 men overland. After marching about a mile up the beach, they surprised a small band of Indians who quickly disappeared into the woods. Desiring to make a friendly contact if possible, Standish and his men followed their tracks until sundown. With sentinels posted, they retired for their first night's sleep in America.

In the morning, they resumed their search but were soon lost in severe thickets. At length, they came upon fresh water which greatly encouraged their souls. Later in the afternoon, they discovered a cleared field, a huge kettle, some Indian graves and the dilapidated remains of a house. After noticing some suspicious-looking heaps of sand, Standish had his men do some digging. To their delighted surprise, several Indian baskets full of corn were unearthed. In unbelievable contrast to the conquistadors, the Pilgrim fathers (who were not as other men) agreed to take the corn only after making a solemn pledge to repay the savages at their earliest opportunity. The importance of this discovery being made only days before the same ground would have been frozen and covered by a blanket of snow cannot be underestimated:

And here is to be noted a special providence of God, and a great mercy to this poor people, that here they got seed to plant them corn the next year, or else they might have starved, for they had none nor any likelihood to get any till the season had been past, as the sequel did manifest... but the Lord is never wanting unto His in their greatest needs; let His holy name have all the praise.[20]

A scriptural parallel was readily discerned by the humble-minded Pilgrims:

So, their time limited them being expired, they returned to the ship lest they should be in fear of their safety; and took with them part of the corn and buried up the rest. And so, like the men from Eschol, carried with them of the fruits of the land and showed their brethren; of which, and their return, they were marvelously glad and their hearts encouraged.[21]

Twelve days later on November 28, Captain Jones led a thirty-man exploring expedition to the mouth of the Pamet River (later called Cold Harbor) in their newly refurbished shallop. Once again they came upon the mysterious ruins of several deserted Indian dwellings.

On the 6th of December, another detachment of men sailed away in the 28-foot launch intending to circumnavigate the cape in search of a favorable settlement site. With the Mayflower's relentless pitching and tossing straining the resolve of her perpetually drenched occupants, a new appreciation for Paul's admonition to Timothy of, *"Come before winter,"* was felt by all. (II Timothy 4:21)

As the shallop churned her way through the chilly, gray Atlantic, something in the spray-filled air whispered that this mission would be more eventful than the others.

Putting ashore toward the close of the day, they detected about a dozen Indians preoccupied with some matter on the beach. The next morning they renewed their exploring and discovered the object of the Indians' interest on the previous evening—the remains of a large "grampus" (blackfish) that had conveniently washed ashore.

At the end of this second day, they again secured their mini-log fortress called a "barricado," and posted their sentinels. Around the hour of midnight, they were suddenly awakened by a most hideous cry and the sentry's call to, "Arm, Arm." After firing a couple of muskets, the noise ceased, and they concluded that the disturbance must have been a roving pack of wolves.

While eating breakfast on the following morning, they were startled by the same dreadful noise. This time the sentinel cried, "Men, Indians! Indians!" Bradford writing:

> And withal, their arrows came flying amongst them. Their men ran with all speed to recover their arms, as by the good providence of God they did. In the meantime, of those that were there ready, two muskets were discharged at them and two more stood ready in the entrance of their rendezvous but were commanded not to shoot till they could take full aim at them.[22]

With musket balls splintering the tree bark about their ears, the savages felt led to fall back into the shadows. Because the Pilgrims "were not as other men," they pursued their antagonists so "they might conceive that they were not afraid of them or any way discouraged."[23]

Once again Bradford insisted on giving God the glory for His marvelous watchcare:

> Thus it pleased God to vanquish their enemies and give them deliverance; and by His special providence so to dispose that not any one of them were either hurt or hit, though their arrows came close by them and on every side [of] them; and sundry of their coats, which hung up in the barricado, were shot through and through. Afterwards they gave God solemn thanks and praise for their deliverance, and gathered up a bundle of their arrows and sent them into England afterward by the master of the ship, and called that place the First Encounter.[24]

Such grateful expressions were especially meaningful in light of the massacre at Roanoke. All were relieved to push away from the shore. However, after only a few hours of sailing, they seemed to be in trouble once again. A fierce tempest of both rain and storm tossed their little shallop every which way. First, the rudder broke. Next, their mast cracked in three places causing their sail to fall into the water. Why was Satan resisting them so intensely on this particular mission? Once again, the bewildered Pilgrims would have to trust the Master of the sea for direction:

> Yet by God's mercy they recovered themselves, and having the flood [tide] with them, struck into the harbor. But when it came to, the pilot was deceived in the place, and said the Lord be merciful unto them for his eyes never saw that place before.[25]

Rowing with all their might through a cove full of breakers, they finally made it to land amidst a terrible downpour. To make matters worse, it was now dark and they could hardly see a thing. The question of where they were was overshadowed by an even more important one: "Where were the *Indians?*" Although hesitant to go ashore and light a badly needed fire, an impending threat of hypothermia won out in the end. They would commit themselves to the One Who *"giveth his beloved sleep."* (Psalm 127:2b)

> But though this had been a day and night of much trouble and danger unto them, yet God gave them a morning of comfort and refreshing (as usually He doth to His children) for the next day was a fair, sunshining day, and they found themselves to be on an island secure from the Indians, where they might dry their stuff, fix their pieces and rest themselves; and gave God thanks for His mercies in their manifold deliverances.[26]

Although anxious to survey the area and return to their ship, Bradford reported, "And this being the last day of the week, they prepared there to keep the Sabbath."[27] This commitment to the Lord's day (innocently but inaccurately referred to by some as the "Christian Sabbath") was a bedrock conviction of Puritan belief throughout all of seventeenth-century New England and without question one of the important founding principles of America. The morning preaching service could last as long as four hours. After lunch everyone returned to the afternoon teaching sessions that would run another three hours.[28]

It is true that, in their zeal to please the Lord, some leaders unwisely carried a good thing too far. In 1656, a Boston man, Captain Kemble, had to sit in the stocks for two hours because of "lewd and unseemly behaviour on the Sabbath."[29] This offense consisted of kissing his wife in public; he had just returned from three years at sea. And yet the worst of these excesses could not begin to compare with those of Cortés and company.

Furthermore, the critic who is quick to pass judgment on the "rigors of Puritanism" refuses to acknowledge that the so-called "victims" had, in fact, hazarded their very lives to attach themselves to such a religious society. The reason why our spiritual forefathers held such a high regard for their "Sabbath" was because they were particularly sensitive to the *spirit* of the Old Testament. Although technically freed from the Mosaic Law by their position in Christ, the Pilgrims chose to delight themselves with the wants of their Heavenly Father.

"If thou turn away thy foot from the sabbath, from doing thy pleasure on my holy day; and call the sabbath a delight, the holy of the LORD, honourable; and shalt honour him, not doing thine own ways, nor finding thine own pleasure, nor speaking thine own words: Then shalt thou delight thyself in the LORD; and I will cause thee to ride upon the high places of the earth, and feed thee with the heritage of Jacob thy father: for the mouth of the LORD hath spoken it." (Isaiah 58:13, 14)

And so, for having discovered the secret of *how* to *"delight thyself also in the LORD,"* they gained the spiritual benefits of this "voluntary" formula— *"and he shall give thee the desires of thine heart."* (Psalm 37:4b) Can anyone argue with their track record?

PLYMOUTH ROCK

According to Bradford's journal, the Pilgrims made their discovery of and historic landing at Plymouth on the very next day after their Sabbath observance. You would "almost" think that the Word of God was true!

> On Monday they sounded the harbor and found it fit for shipping, and marched into the land and found divers cornfields and little running brooks, a place (as they supposed) fit for situation... So they returned to their ship again with this news to the rest of their people, which did much comfort their hearts.[30]

Due to the rough seas, it would be another week before the entire party would come ashore; well, most all of them that is. For it was during this time that the future governor and historian of Plymouth Colony was called to pass through some deep waters of his own.

Life had never come easy to William Bradford. Born in 1590, in Yorkshire, England, Bradford lost his father when he was only a year old and, throughout his formative years, he was shuttled from pillar to post. With his mother's remarriage three years later, he was sent to live with a grandfather. After two more years, his grandfather died and Bradford's stepfather reluctantly agreed to take him in. Unfortunately, his mother met an untimely death, and Bradford was again shipped off—this time to his father's uncles.

Throughout this turbulent period, Bradford was often very sick. However, in the providence of God, the lonely orphan of Austerfield happened upon a copy of the Holy Scriptures which he began to read with great earnestness. Soon afterwards he became acquainted with the despised congregation at Scrooby and started attending their meetings at the age of 12. Having embraced Christianity under the ministry of Richard Clifton, Bradford became a full-fledged member at age 16, much to the consternation of his scandalized uncles. Though ill a good deal of the time, he was able to master French, Dutch, Latin, Greek and especially Hebrew.

Now, because the Lord had chosen Bradford to provide the critical leadership at Plymouth (Cotton Mather in his *Magnalia* referred to Bradford as "our Moses"), his faith would have to be tested further. At some time during those last days aboard the Mayflower, Bradford's wife Dorothy "fell overboard" and drowned. With reference to her well-known fits of depression, historians are generally agreed that the poor woman probably chose to end her own life rather than face the unknown perils that lay ahead.

Although such a loss would have decimated the average husband, Bradford represented a caliber of Americans who "were not as other men"! Not only did he go on to serve the colony as its governor for 33 years, but he also declined to draw attention to his own tragedy when writing *Of Plymouth Plantation*.

And yet, one may even glean a spiritual significance from Dorothy Bradford's needless decease. Of the 102 Mayflower passengers who reached Cape Cod, a final total of 99 were able to come ashore at Plymouth.[31] In an interesting aside, we recall that the number nine in Scripture represents the Lord's number for fruit bearing (i.e., nine fruits of the Spirit, in the ninth book of the New Testament, nine-month gestation period, etc.). Consequently, as "father" Abraham was 99 years old when Isaac was conceived, the mightiest fruit-bearing nation in church history would likewise proceed from the loins of these 99 sojourners. (As with the AV 1611, add up the individual numbers in 1620; does it match the number of letters in Mayflower?)

However, before this glorious birth could occur, our spiritual progenitors had to travail through heavy labor, for Satan was not about to surrender his strategic beachhead without a fight. Bradford's spouse may have been weak, but she was not lacking in perception. Of the 17 Pilgrim wives who grieved at their sister's passing, 12 of the same would join her within as many weeks.

THE STARVING TIME

The months of January, February and March have been alternately described as the "Starving Time" or the time of the "General Sickness." Bradford relates the sober details:

> But that which was most sad and lamentable was, that in two or three months' time half of their company died, especially in January and February, being the depth of winter, and wanting houses and other comforts; being infected with the scurvy and other diseases which this long voyage and their inaccomodate condition had brought upon them. So as there died some times two or three of a day in the foresaid time, that of 100 and odd persons, scarce fifty remained. And of these, in the time of most distress, there was but six or seven sound persons who to their great commendations, be it spoken, spared no pains night nor day, but with abundance of toil and hazard of their own health, fetched them wood, made them fires, dressed them meat, made their beds, washed their loathsome clothes, clothed and unclothed them. In a word, did all the homely and necessary offices for them which dainty and queasy stomachs cannot endure to hear named; and all this willingly and cheerfully, without any grudging in the least, showing herein their true love unto their friends and brethren; a rare example and worthy to be remembered.[32]

In addition to the many precious wives who were lost, 14 of the original 26 family heads perished as well. Satan's continuous buffeting ensured that the "circle was broken" repeatedly. Only three families remained intact by winter's end.

And yet, the deaths would have been higher but for the mercy of Captain Jones who delayed the Mayflower's return to afford the Pilgrims shelter while they built their first dwellings. This was not a light decision for the afflicted captain who would leave the bodies of ten crew members behind and make his own wife a widow in less than a year. Surely the Holy Spirit had led in the decision to choose Jones over the better-known but infamous John Smith. While one would have surely opted for *profits*, the other wisely invested in *prophets*!

On Christmas Day, 1620, the Pilgrims began construction on their first building for common usage. The work went very slowly for the frostbitten laborers. Finally, the Common House was completed and became America's first hospital as many of the sick and dying were moved within the shelter of her walls.

Suddenly, on Sunday evening, January 14, Satan showed his contempt for the "Sabbath" by setting the new building on fire. The situation was especially critical due to the proximity of several open barrels of gunpowder. Bradford himself was lying sick near one of these drums. However, unlike the inferno at Jamestown, the Lord imparted supernatural strength to a few, and the structure was miraculously salvaged. A second fire on February 9 was put out as well.

Our nation's first cemetery was also located nearby, though it was unlike anything most Americans would recognize. Because of a lingering Indian threat, Captain Standish directed that the dead be interred by night in shallow, unmarked graves. The "contents" of Burial Hill became America's first military secret. On January 21st, Captain Standish buried his own wife Rose according to this stratagem.

SAMOSET & SQUANTO

However, as time went on, the "Indian problem," oddly enough, never did materialize. There were occasional shrieks from the woods and isolated sightings, but no hostile activity. This remained a great mystery to the ever-vigilant Pilgrims until one mild afternoon about the 16th of March.

With the sentry's peculiar cry of "*Indian* coming," Captain Standish and the others looked on incredulously as a tall, muscular brave, clothed only in a loincloth, boldly entered their primitive stockade and strolled down the main street. The stranger walked right to where the men were standing in front of the Common House and paused long enough for them to catch their breath. Slowly raising his hand in a friendly salute, he caught everyone off guard with the single word, "Welcome." Before they could recover from this shocking experience (i.e., Indians were supposed to say, "How!"), he asked them in broken English, "Have you got any beer?"

From where in the world did this strange guy come? Was he a spy, a vision or an agent of divine providence? Realizing that all men speak better on a full stomach, they fed their guest first and then the eager questioning began.

Samoset was his name, and he proudly attested to being a Sagamore (or chief) of the Algonquins in the country of Morattigon (present-day Pemaquid Point, Maine). However, this was not your typical "injun." Having initiated several contacts with various fishing vessels, he would exchange valued information for travel and adventure, learning English in the process.

After relating a number of minor geographic details, Samoset gave a history lesson that sent chills up their spines. Plymouth Colony was actually situated in the former territory of the Patuxet Indians. It was no accident that the Patuxets *had* been the most feared tribe in all of New England. They *were* known for having ruthlessly murdered numbers of European explorers.

Perhaps the discerning reader has noted the particular verb tense in use; the tense is past to accentuate *what had been* an intended threat of the devil. The reason why there were no Indian attacks at Plymouth was because there were no Indians at Plymouth to attack. The once proud and powerful Patuxets no longer existed. Four years before the Mayflower's arrival, the Lord allowed a mysterious plague into the region that wiped out every man, woman and child. Satan's "Atlantic Wall" had been completely obliterated.

The neighboring tribes were convinced that this had been a supernatural act. In a final act of desperation, the leading Powows (medicine men) spent three entire days in a dark swamp to place curses upon their intimidating intruders.[33] Cotton Mather wrote, "But the devils at length acknowledged unto them, that they could not hinder those people from their becoming the owners and masters of the country."[34]

Having failed to dislodge the Pilgrims, the paranoid savages took up the ancient lament of Jericho as related by Rahab: *"I know that the LORD hath given you the land, and that your terror is fallen upon us, and that all the inhabitants of the land faint because of you."* (Joshua 2:9)

As most scholars believe the American Indian migrated to this hemisphere through the Bering Strait, the vacated Patuxet lands insured that the Japhetic Pilgrims, already under Shem's *spiritual* tents, would enjoy a *literal* fulfillment of Noah's prophecy as well. The Wampanoags of Sowams (present-day Barrington, Rhode Island, about 40 miles away) were now the nearest Indians to Plymouth. According to Samoset, their chief Massasoit would be very "honored" (relieved) to establish peaceful relations with the people of the "Great White Spirit."

And yet, there was more! Because the Pilgrims were accustomed to depending upon *"him that is able to do exceeding abundantly above all that we ask or think"* (Ephesians 3:20a), Samoset informed them of a most unusual visitor who would be serving as Massasoit's official interpreter. Within a few weeks, the chief arrived in full tribal regalia accompanied by 60 painted warriors. Governor Carver wisely supplied his own "pomp and circumstance" with trumpets, drums and muskets. Following the customary refreshments and exchanging of gifts, a six-point peace treaty was promptly concluded which was to remain in force for over 25 years.

Massasoit's interpreter was another English-speaking Indian by the name of Squanto. However, unlike Samoset, his English was flawless. The Pilgrims were astounded at his explanation. Squanto had actually been a member of the Patuxet tribe but had been kidnapped by British explorers in 1605 and again in 1614. After spending nearly nine years in England, where he supplied the Council for New England with much valuable information, he was able to escape and return to his homeland. When he arrived, there was nothing but ruined buildings and skeletal remains to greet him. Of course, the experience was traumatic; but God was at work as usual. Squanto had been chosen to play the role of Joseph—kidnapped *"to save much people alive."* (Genesis 50:20b)

As Massasoit and his braves departed, Squanto surprised the Pilgrims by expressing his desire to remain with them for whatever assistance he could afford. With 50 bodies in Burial Hill, the Pilgrims embraced this kind stranger as their *"springs into the valley."* (Psalm 104:10)

Squanto taught them many valuable survival techniques, prompting Bradford to describe him as "a special instrument sent of God for their good beyond their expectation."[35] The first lesson they learned was how to catch eels with their bare feet. They soon found this strange delicacy to be "fat and sweet." In the days ahead, he also showed them how to stalk game, refine maple syrup, plant pumpkins and a myriad of other blessings.

However, it was in the area of their spring planting that Squanto's expertise would save the most lives. He taught the Pilgrims how to plant their corn "Indian style"—by using fish as fertilizer. He even showed them how to catch the valuable alewives from a nearby creek.

With the onset of April, Captain Jones readied what was left of his crew for their much-delayed return to England. In one of the greatest testimonies of Christian commitment in history, not a single Pilgrim sought to join him! After many expressions of love were exchanged, Jones and his crew steered the Mayflower slowly through the harbor and over the horizon. What a contrast to the worldly-wise Cortés having to burn his own ships. With the sea truly at their backs, they would go right on trusting their Lord.

In this same month of April, Plymouth Colony lost the services of their beloved governor John Carver. His wife also died about five or six weeks after him. William Bradford was the unanimous choice as Carver's successor and became the first government official elected on American soil.

On May 12th our nation's first wedding was celebrated and proved to be a timely diversion for all. Edward Winslow, whose first wife died during the Great Sickness, was married to Susannah, widow of William White, another victim of that first winter.

THE FIRST THANKSGIVING

The summer months sped by rapidly with everyone either working in the fields or on the new buildings. When the time of reaping finally arrived, a bountiful harvest was taken causing Governor Bradford to declare the first day of public thanksgiving to God. In a letter to a friend in England, Edward Winslow described the festivities:

> Our harvest being gotten in, our Governor sent four men on fowling, that so we might after a more special manner rejoice together, after we had gathered the fruit of our labours. They four in one day killed as much fowl as, with a little help beside, served the Company almost a week. At which time, amongst other recreations, we exercised our arms, many of the Indians coming amongst us, and amongst the rest their greatest king, Massasoit with some 90 men, whom for three days we entertained and feasted. And they went out and killed five deer which they brought to the plantation and bestowed on our Governor and upon the Captain and others.[36]

When one compares this joyous occasion to the bloody experiences at Roanoke and Jamestown, the words of Solomon come alive with new meaning: *"When a man's ways please the LORD, he maketh even his enemies to be at peace with him."* (Proverbs 16:7)

Massasoit and his braves knew from experience that their English hosts were a spiritual people. Whereas the Catholics would murder an Indian in cold blood for no particular reason, the peace-loving Pilgrims, even when legitimately provoked, were facetiously reported to have warned: "I would not hurt nor harm thee, but thou art standing where I am about to shoot."

Although it was the mercy of God that ultimately brought the Pilgrims through their first year at Plymouth, Squanto was the human instrument that had helped them so much. However, he was not to be with them long; in fact, this would be his first and last Thanksgiving celebration. Their beloved

Indian friend died of fever the following September, requesting that Governor Bradford pray "that he might go to the Englishmen's God in Heaven."[37] This may have been the first conversion in America. Compare this holy scene to the garroting of Atahualpa by Pizzaro.

Over the next 20 years, the Pilgrims would encounter many additional trials and blessings. Ships bearing new colonists would arrive without either warning or provision, forcing daily rations to as low as five kernels of corn per person. Thomas Weston would visit to cause trouble in person until the judgment of God fell upon him. Eventually, the Holy Spirit would lead the colony to abandon their unprofitable farm communes and pioneer the free enterprise system in America.

Throughout these turbulent years, the Pilgrims persevered with a resolute courage that was often invigorated by encouraging words from abroad. One such letter spoke of the many others who would be challenged by their sacrifice: "Let it not be grievous unto you that you have been instruments to break the ice for others who come after with less difficulty."[38]

In June of 1630, the vanguard of the Puritan migrations would enter Salem Harbor to the north and establish the famed Massachusetts Bay Colony. Although Governor Winthrop's initial settlement of 1,000 Puritans would eventually incorporate Plymouth and become one of the most influential colonies in New England, the Pilgrims were assured of a role that would be without parallel for both time and eternity. The above-mentioned letter concluded:

> The honour shall be yours to the world's end, etc…the same God which hath so marvelously preserved you from seas, foes and famine, will still preserve you from all future dangers, and make you honourable amongst men, and glorious in bliss at the last day.[39]

However, because the Pilgrims were "not as other men," they desired that the glory should go to another, Bradford declaring,

> Thus out of small beginnings greater things have been produced by His hand that made all things of nothing, and gives being to all things that are; and, as one small candle may light a thousand, so the light here kindled hath shone unto many, yea in some sort to our whole nation; **let the glorious name of Jehovah have all the praise.**[40]

VI

An Efficacious Experiment

> *"Who art thou that judgest another man's servant? to his own master he standeth or falleth."* (Romans 14:4a)

MUCH OF THE early colonization of America continued to be occasioned by widespread Catholic oppression in England and Europe. Following the decease of James I in 1625, his son ascended the British throne as Charles I. With both his consort and the queen mother committed to Romanism, the die was cast concerning the religious direction of Charles' realm.

In time, a pro-Vatican Anglican by the name of William Laud became the new king's chief counselor in civil and ecclesiastical matters. His dual appointments as Bishop of London and Lord Chancellor in 1628 were followed by his elevation to Archbishop of Canterbury eight years later. Describing his fanatical efforts to revive Roman Catholicism, Newman writes:

> The type of his theological teaching was throughout Roman Catholic. He attached the utmost importance to...ecclesiastical vestments and the manner of putting them on and wearing them, ecclesiastical festivals, the radical distinction between clergy and laity, the magical efficacy of priestly functions and especially of the sacraments, and could not tolerate the slightest deviation from the established forms...he did not hesitate to declare his essential agreement with the Church of Rome. "The religion of the Church of Rome and ours is one."...He promoted the restoration of religious pictures, crosses, and altars. He regarded the altar, which must

be set against the east end of the church within the chancel, as "the greatest place of God's residence upon earth, greater than the pulpit, for there 'tis 'This is my body'; but in the other it is at most, but 'This is my word.' " His idea of the Supper was the Romanist, namely, that of a sacrifice. Hence the altar.[1]

Because Laud was a typical Catholic tyrant, he was bound to be ignorant of the divine order: *"for thou hast magnified thy word above all thy name."* (Psalm 138:2)

MASSACHUSETTS BAY COLONY

Laud's impending reign of terror compelled nearly 20,000 Puritans to migrate to the New World, earning him the satirical title, "Father of New England."[2] Although their new colony at Massachusetts Bay was only 40 miles from Plymouth, the dense forest between them loomed as an impassable wilderness so that their principal intercourse with one another was occasioned by water. However, John Christian notes an important allegory here:

> But they were not so far separated by distance and physical difficulties as their general ideas and ways of looking at the great questions which were then up for consideration. So these two little confederacies, for a time, lived much to themselves.[3]

It is true that many of the Puritans showed a remarkable courage when faced with their own trials and heartaches. Whereas Governor Bradford lost his beloved Dorothy to the sea, Governor Winthrop's fifteen-year-old son, Henry, was also tragically drowned within days of their arrival. Although Reverend Cotton Mather was blessed with over a dozen children, he would be survived by only two of them. The oft-dismayed Mather would persevere to the completion of his massive 1,300-page *History of New England* only to lose his wife in the very year of its London publication (1702). The grieving minister testified:

> When I saw to what point of resignation I was now called of the Lord, I resolved, with His help therein, to glorify Him. So, two hours before my lovely consort expired, I kneeled by her bedside, and I took into my two hands a dear hand, the dearest in the world. With her thus in my hands, I

solemnly and sincerely gave her up to the Lord... When she was expired, I... prayed with her father and the other weeping people in the chamber, for the grace to carry it well.[4]

It is also correct that Winthrop's colony embraced the same Congregationalist polity followed at Plymouth, a philosophy radically different from mainstream Anglicanism. In contrast to the governmental appointment of clergymen (Charles I and Laud, etc.), Congregationalism enjoined that the *congregations* call their own ministers. Evans points out that on July 20, 1629, the first church in Salem was founded according to this maverick procedure: "About 30 heads of families, having formed a church covenant, elected... their teacher and pastor by ballot, the two ministers having admitted that they had no right to officiate without an 'outward calling' from the faithful."[5]

Another important contribution of Puritan thought advocated limitations on legislators. Although these embryonic concepts would be dramatically augmented in time (especially in the area of religious liberty), they did represent a step in the right direction. Reverend John Cotton, the chief theologian of early Massachusetts, warned:

> Let all the world learn to give mortal men no greater power than they are content they shall use, for use it they will... It is... most wholesome for magistrates and officers in church and commonwealth never to affect more liberty and authority than will do them good, and the people good; for whatever transcendent power is given will certainly overrun those that receive it... It is necessary, therefore, that all power that is on earth be limited, church power or other.[6]

Thomas Hooker, one of the most influential Puritan divines in all of New England, likewise concurred:

> We know in other countries, had not the law overruled the lust of men, and the crooked ends of judges many times, both places and people had been in reason past all relief... **The law is not subject to passion**, nor to be taken aside with self-seeking ends, and therefore ought to have chief rule over rulers themselves.[7]

That America owes its very form of Constitutional government to a puritanical promulgation of the doctrine of original sin can be confirmed by any number of historical sources. While Samuel Adams wrote that, "ambition and lust for power... are predominant passions in the breasts of most men,"[8] James Madison added, "The truth was that all men having power ought to be distrusted to a certain degree"[9] (i.e., as in Mayor Marion Barry). Alexander Hamilton asked and answered his own question: "Why has government been instituted at all? Because the passions of men will not conform to the dictates of reason and justice without constraint."[10] And in the face of the optimism of the French Enlightenment, Thomas Jefferson asserted:

> It would be a dangerous delusion were a confidence in the men of our choice to silence our fear for the safety of our rights; that confidence is everywhere the parent of despotism—free government is founded in jealousy, and not in confidence... In questions of power, then, let no more be heard of confidence in man, but **bind him down from mischief with the chains of the Constitution**.[11]

In a fair assessment of all that was noble about seventeenth-century New England Puritanism, John Christian concludes:

> Out of this civilization, with all of its defects, there came a type of life and character, self-dependent, God-fearing, industrious, capable and highly conscientious. Bishop Creighton's judgment, the judgment of a trained historian but not an ecclesiastical sympathizer, was hardly an exaggeration of the facts, when he said that this movement "stamped upon the early colonies of America the severe morality and patient industry which have trained a nation."[12]

However, notwithstanding these many positive qualities, history compels us to recognize the negative implications in Dr. Christian's earlier analogy regarding the *philosophical* woodlands which separated the two colonies. In their ecumenical, pro-Vatican distortion of America's religious foundations, entitled *The Light and the Glory* (ignorantly endorsed by many Christian schools), co-authors Peter Marshall and David Manuel express surprise at the demise of Puritan power:

> One of the greatest mysteries that we faced in our search was the question of what finally became of the Puritans. They had seemed to be prospering in every way—the hard times were behind them, there was plenty of good land and plenty to eat, spacious houses, and they were living in peace with the Indians. Spiritually, for the most part, they were deeply committed, obedient, and fulfilling the terms of the covenant. And God was blessing them beyond all measure.... Then, like a fire slowly

dying down, the spiritual light began to dim, until, by the beginning of the 1700s, what had been a blazing light of the Gospel of Christ had become only a faint glow from smoldering embers. What had gone wrong?[13]

Although Governor Bradford lamented the eventual spiritual decline of his own settlement, bemoaning, "But it is now a part of my misery in old age, to find and feel the decay and want thereof,"[14] the entrapment of material prosperity took a far greater toll on the Massachusetts Bay Colony, Boorstin writing:

> The firm establishment of a community in New England was marked by a growing sense of security, a decline of many of the fears and uncertainties which had nourished a desperate dependence on God. The second generation owed its presence in New England, not to God's happy guidance across the perils of an ocean, but to the simple accident of birth. Puritan immigrants who came after the mid-century were met, not by the Indian arrows which had greeted the first Pilgrims, but by the embrace of their countrymen. Glowing fireplaces and full storehouses were ready for them. Their welcome now seemed less from God—or from Satan—than from their fellow-Puritans.[15]

Marshall concedes this point regarding materialism by quoting Cotton Mather's contemporaneous indictment, *Religio peperit Divitias, et filia devoravit matrem:* "**Religion begat prosperity, and the daughter devoured the mother**."[16] Without question, Reverend Mather's pithy assessment constitutes the single greatest cause for America's present demise. When our nation's automobiles sport bumper stickers reading, "Whoever dies with the most toys wins," we can be assured that there are plenty of rough roads ahead.

IMPORTED INTOLERANCE

However, an even greater impediment to sustained blessings at Massachusetts Bay proved to be the Puritans' implacable intolerance of their "fellow" religious dissenters. No sooner had Governor Winthrop's refugees gained a measure of spiritual liberty in the New World than they assumed the very character of their former oppressors by attempting to perfect a *theocratic* form of government that would be based on Old Testament law. With the resultant Congregationalism representing the official state religion of Massachusetts, the right to vote became conditional upon membership in a Congregationalist church (i.e., "if you're not Dutch, you're not much"). If, and when, a "resident" could not conscientiously subscribe to the polity and/or theology of this "Church of the Standing Order," his Puritan taskmasters became his worst nightmare. Benedict summarizes the ugly side of this "anti-American" sentiment:

> What on earth can be more shocking to any being, who has human feelings, than to see a humble and devout christian [sic], who renders to Cesar what is his due, merely for not believing some things which his brethren believe, arrested in his peaceful and pious course, sentenced to be tied to a public whipping post like a malefactor, and there to have his body barbarously scourged, to chastise and cure the conscientious scruples of his mind; and all this by his countrymen, his neighbours; yea, by his fellow christians [sic], who profess to worship the same God, and trust for salvation in the same Redeemer! Who can contemplate such a scene of barbarity without being sickened at the sight, and retiring from it with disgust and horror![17]

Reverend John Cotton attempted to justify his culture of religious intolerance with this inane remark:

> You think, to compel men in matter of worship is to make them sin.... If it do [sic] make men hypocrites, yet better be hypocrites than profane persons. Hypocrites give God part of his due, the outward man, but the profane person giveth God neither outward nor inward man.[18]

Peter Marshall conveniently sidesteps this notorious feature of traditional *Protestant* theology. The answer to his syrupy question, "What went wrong?" is a simple one. With Puritan courts handing down sentences ranging from whippings to hangings for *crimes of conscience*, the Judge of the universe brought His own gavel down on the hypocritical proceedings citing, *"certain king v. wicked servant"* A.D. 33— *"Shouldest not thou also have had compassion on thy fellowservant, even as I had pity on thee?"* (Matthew 18:33) Ignoring the many remonstrances of Jehovah to *"remember that thou wast a bondman in Egypt, and the LORD thy God redeemed thee"* (Deuteronomy 24:18a), Winthrop and company were now the ones prepared to do the "harrowing out of the land"! The Reverend Nathaniel Ward "piously" announced that non-Puritans "shall have free liberty to keep away from us, and such as will come to be gone as fast as they can, the sooner the better."[19]

Ward's "don't-let-the-door-hit-you-on-the-way-out" philosophy represents a classic example of attempting to do a right thing in the wrong way. Although freedom of association is certainly a cardinal precept of true liberty (no longer existing in America, unfortunately), this doctrine can only function when church and state are separate from one another, or, as Armitage put it, when "each is absolute in its own sphere and without mutual interference."[20] What the Puritan couldn't or wouldn't see was that his seventeenth-century theocracy was an unscriptural, dispensational disaster (ditto John Calvin's *Geneva*). The Massachusetts Bay experiment attempted to force the Old Testament order into the present church age, and it just wouldn't fit. As the Saviour told Pontius Pilate, *"My kingdom is **not** of this world."* (John 18:36a) Armitage elaborates on this unscholarly exegesis:

> Membership in the Church was made a test of citizenship, and so they fell into the blunder of making their civil and ecclesiastical polity one, a strange combination of iron and clay, intended to be inexorable after the pattern of the ancient Hebrew Commonwealth, although that exact form of government had perished two thousand years before, and long before the Church of Christ with its spiritual laws existed.[21]

With "the new wine about to break the old bottles," it was, oddly enough, the *Pilgrim* pastor, John Robinson, who possessed enough humility to acknowledge these shortcomings. Prophesying from his deathbed, he declared:

> I bewail the condition of the Reformed churches...the Lutherans cannot be drawn to go beyond what Luther saw. And the Calvinists as you see, stick where Calvin left them...Luther and Calvin were shining lights in their times. Yet God did not reveal His whole will unto them...I am very confident that the Lord hath more truth and light yet to break forth out of His Holy Word.[22]

Unbeknownst to the antiquated advocates of Protestant theocracies, America was about to show the whole world *"what is that good, and acceptable, and perfect, will of God"* (Romans 12:2b) for church-state relationships this side of the millennium—*exclusive churches moving freely within the protective boundaries of an inclusive state.*

ROGER WILLIAMS

The first serious challenge to the Holy Commonwealth of Massachusetts was issued by the impassioned ministry of Reverend Roger Williams. Born of Welsh extraction about the year 1600, Williams embraced the Saviour and took orders in the Church of England during the reign of Archbishop Laud. His strong Puritan views led him to Boston on February 5, 1631, whereupon Governor Winthrop described him as a "godly minister."[23] However, the honeymoon would last less than two months.

Williams was invited to pastor the First Church in Boston but declined because of their ongoing communion with the English churches, writing to John Cotton that he "durst not officiate to an unseparated people."[24] Although frustrated by this semi-separatist compromise, Williams' main bone of contention with his "liberated brethren" was that they were no less intolerant than Archbishop Laud had been. He declared that the magistrates had no business punishing a breach of the first table of the law, comprised of the first four Commandments. Williams' basic argument was that the government should have no authority over the religious convictions of its citizens. His crusade became *the* historic fight for freedom of conscience.

The following April, Williams accepted a call to become co-pastor of the more conservative church in Salem. The Massachusetts Court was not a little disturbed at the Salem church for ignoring their public disapproval of Williams and proceeded to bring much pressure to bear upon them. By summer's end, Williams decided to spare the assembly any further harassment by removing himself to Plymouth, beyond the jurisdiction of the Bay Company. Although disagreeing with Williams on certain points, the humble-minded Bradford wrote of his arrival and ministry:

> He was friendly entertained according to their poor ability, and exercised his gifts amongst them and after some time was admitted a member of the church. And his teaching well approved, for the benefit whereof I still bless God and am thankful to him even for his sharpest admonitions and reproofs so far as they agreed with truth.[25]

After two years of fruitful labor among the Pilgrims, Williams received another invitation from Salem and returned to that grateful congregation. With the death of their senior pastor, Williams became the sole minister of the church. Once again, the officials renewed their hostilities, summoning him to appear before the court in Boston for his teaching that a magistrate ought not to tender an oath to an unregenerate man. Other changes soon followed.

Although his congregation faithfully protested their pastor's innocence throughout, the General Court eventually pronounced upon him the dread sentence of banishment in October of 1635. In the final analysis, his main "crime" consisted of teaching "that the magistrate ought not to punish the breach of the first table [the first four Commandments], otherwise than in such case as did disturb the civil peace."[26] This offense was also brought out in the opening wording of the decree itself: "Whereas, Mr. Roger Williams, one of the elders of the church of Salem, hath broached and divulged new and dangerous opinions against the authority of magistrates."[27]

For his daring resolve, Williams has received the praise of countless historians. Describing him as "a very troublesome man for bigotry to manage," Peck writes:

> When he entered Massachusetts, he was in advance of the general sentiment of the Puritans on the question of religious liberty...Roger Williams was more than a Puritan. He was the great mind ordained of Providence to advance beyond the position of indignant protest against oppression, to the revelation that the highest right must itself be the result of a freedom which might be abused by consenting to the deepest wrong. He was the first true type of the American freeman, conceeding [sic] fully to others the highborn rights which he claimed for himself. This was further than Puritanism could lead the race; and, for the present, it was not ready to follow.[28]

And so, in the dead of winter, Roger Williams, accompanied by a small band of loyal parishioners, entered what he would later describe as a "miserable, cold, howling wilderness,"[29] without either *bed, bread* or *lead.* Fortunately for all, Williams had been a faithful witness to the Indians while sojourning with the Pilgrims.

> While at Plymouth he had gone forth amongst them, had visited their wigwams, learned their language and preached to them the good news of the kingdom; and now his love governed the wild element in their bosoms when he had no power over fierce winter storms. He knew their chiefs or sachems, and on reaching their settlements on Narraganset Bay, his sufferings touched the savage heart. They remembered his former kindness, welcomed him to Indian hospitality, and Massasoit took him to his cabin as he would a brother.[30]

PROVIDENCE

Finally, in the month of June, the Lord led His weary servant to a lovely tract of land near the mouth of the Moshassuck River. With the dense forest, wild beasts and naked savages providing a protective barrier from his "Christian brothers," Williams built an altar there and called the name of the place Providence for he said, "God has been merciful to me in my distress."[31] After paying the local Indians for their land, Williams immediately announced that the site would become "a shelter to persons distressed for conscience."[32] His momentous compact read as follows:

> We whose names are here underwritten, being desirous to inhabit in the town of Providence, do promise to submit ourselves in active and passive obedience, to all such orders or agencies as shall be made for public good of the body in an orderly way, by the major consent of the present inhabitants, masters of families, incorporated together into a township, and such others whom they shall admit into the same, *only in civil things*.[33]

Henry C. Vedder comments on the far-reaching effects of this historic occasion:

> Thus was founded the first government in the world, whose corner-stone was absolute religious liberty. It is true that a few other countries had before this, and for periods more or less brief, tolerated what they regarded as heresy; but **this was the first government organized on the principle of absolute liberty to all, in such matters of belief and practice as did not conflict with the peace and order of society, or with ordinary good morals**... Though he did not originate the idea of soul liberty, it was given to Roger Williams, in the providence of God, to be its standard-bearer in a new world, where it should have full opportunity to work itself out, and afford by its fruits a demonstration that it is of God and not of man.[34]

SOUL LIBERTY

We have now arrived, dear reader, at a pivotal juncture of our study. **The material you are about to read is so vital that it represents the very foundation for the remainder of this work.**

Vedder identified the doctrinal scourge of Williams' "crime" against the magistrates as one of *soul liberty* while his "victims" described it as a *new and dangerous opinion*. Although this concept may have been new to a body of seventeenth-century New England Puritans, it obviously wasn't new to Roger Williams. Therefore, as the assertion by Vedder that soul liberty did not originate with Williams agrees with Ecclesiastes 1:9b (*"There is no new thing under the sun"*), the question arises, just where in England could he have learned this lofty principle?

The answer to this query constitutes a frustrating paradox for lovers of truth, as it simultaneously entails the most important yet least understood ecclesiastical distinction in all of church history. According to Dr. William Cathcart, the person most responsible for influencing Williams in his comprehension of soul liberty was a London pastor by the name of Samuel Howe who specifically taught that "the king was only to be obeyed in civil matters," and that "no prince had power to make laws to bind the consciences of men."[35] In his own work entitled *The Hireling Ministry*, Williams wrote of the "honorable testimony... [of] that eminently Christian witness...that...beloved Samuel Howe," and especially his habit of "searching the Holy Scriptures."[36]

The great lesson of this chapter and that little-known ecclesiastical distinction of church history revolves around the fact that while Roger Williams was, at this time, a Protestant, his spiritual benefactor, Reverend Samuel Howe, was a *Baptist*. Williams did not learn about soul liberty from a fellow Protestant, because soul liberty is not a Protestant doctrine—it is a *Baptist distinctive!* One of the most important teachings from church history, and, sad to say, one of the least understood, is that Baptists are *not* Protestants! While the Protestant Reformation *came out* of corrupted Roman Catholicism in the sixteenth century, Baptist churches were *never* "in" to come "out." While Protestants trace their lineage to Martin Luther ("A Mighty Fortress Is Our God," etc.), and historical reality limits Rome's lineage to somewhere between Constantine (322 A.D.) and Leo I (440 A.D.), Bible-believing Baptists can trace their roots of distinction all the way back to the Lord Jesus Christ (A.D. 33).

Having sustained his Sunday crowds of over 5,000 listeners for nearly 40 years, Charles Hadden Spurgeon has been rightfully acclaimed the "Prince of Preachers." In an 1861 sermon delivered in his famed Metropolitan Tabernacle, this London pastor affirmed:

> We believe that the Baptists are the original Christians. We did not commence our existence at the reformation, we were reformers before

Luther and Calvin were born; we never came from the Church of Rome, for we were never in it, but we have an unbroken line up to the apostles themselves. **We have always existed from the very days of Christ**, and our principles, sometimes veiled and forgotten, like a river which may travel under ground for a little season, have always had honest and holy adherents. Persecuted alike by Romanists and Protestants of almost every sect, yet there has never existed a Government holding Baptist principles which persecuted others; nor, I believe, any body of Baptists ever held it to be right to put the consciences of others under the control of man. We have ever been ready to suffer, as our martyrologies will prove, but we are not ready to accept any help from the State, to prostitute the purity of the Bride of Christ to any alliance with Government, and we will never make the Church, although the Queen, the despot over the consciences of men.[37]

That Protestants and Baptists do not come from the same "mother" can be easily seen by comparing each of the two with Rome. Protestants look and act like their mother. When robed Protestant priests are not sprinkling babies, they will be found chanting around incense pots and candlelit altars exactly like the Catholic "fathers" across the street. Someone said that an Episcopalian is a Catholic who flunked Latin.

Furthermore, not only will a true Baptist church be devoid of such paganistic trappings, but it will also be found to exhibit its own set of doctrinal distinctives. Because these Baptistic distinctions have been taken directly from the book of Acts, they often appear as "new" and "dangerous" to ritualistic Protestants and Catholics alike! J. L. Currey writes:

> A history of the Baptists should be understood in its objects and aims; and cleared, in the beginning, of misapprehension and perversion. It is not the history of a nationality, a race, an organization, but of a people, "traced by their vital principles and gospel practices." The unity to be exhibited and demonstrated was not brought about by force, by coercion of pains and penalties, by repressive and punitive Acts of Conformity; but by the recognition and adoption of a common authoritative and completed divine standard.
>
> The error of many previous attempts has consisted in the assumption that a Church and Christianity were identical. We have had numerous and voluminous histories of Churches and creeds; and untold abuses have resulted from confounding them with Christ's people, with New Testament doctrines and practices. This *petitio principii* has been the source of much evil.[38]

Now the reason why all of this is so critical is that one cannot fully understand America's political foundations without first learning what a *Baptist* is. Although the majority of today's Americans are too busy watching television to care, our Founding Fathers perceived the liberating effects of Baptist distinctives. Dr. D. B. Ray writes:

> The government under which we live was formed and fashioned upon the model of a Baptist church. Thomas Jefferson frequently attended a Baptist church near Monticello, Va., of which the Rev. Andrew Tribble was pastor. Mr. Jefferson, who often witnessed the congregation transacting business, was much impressed with their democratic way of doing things, and concluded that their plan of government would be the best possible one for the American colonies. Mrs. James Madison says: "Mr. Jefferson did gather those views from a Baptist church."[39]

America has been heralded as "the land of the free and the home of the brave." The order of these concepts is an exact one, as a man's courage will always be commensurate with the amount of freedom he stands to gain or lose; i.e., "Give me liberty or give me death." In the benevolent providence of God, America was destined to become a free and a brave republic. When the breakaway colony of Rhode Island petitioned the king for a charter, they wrote with a spirit of pronounced optimism: "We have it much at heart to demonstrate by means of an **efficacious experiment** that there can be a very flourishing civil state, and, indeed, that it can be better maintained, with complete liberty in matters of religion."[40]

With the massive Atlantic doing for America what the Red Sea did for Israel, a new breed of men would now be free to pursue that "efficacious experiment" begun at Providence. Unchecked by papal armies and blessed by Almighty God, the American experiment enabled mankind to shake off the chains of religious intolerance, political tyranny, economic bondage and intellectual dementia, so as to forge the caliber of citizens described by de Tocqueville as both *good* and *great*.

However, as previously stated, none of this could have come about without our political framers receiving an infusion of spiritual thinking; for how can a man be totally free if his soul remains enslaved? Thus it was in a Baptist church that America's third president became acquainted with the essence of legitimate liberty: *"If the Son therefore shall make you free, ye shall be free indeed."* (John 8:36) Through the biblical doctrine of soul liberty, our Founding Fathers discerned that man belongs totally to God and has been endowed with a free will to either accept or reject his Maker, *with the sole responsibility of government being to preserve this freedom by protecting the righteous from the unrighteous.* (Romans 13:1-7) What one human chooses to believe about the God Who made him is no one else's business but his own. *"Who art thou that judgest another man's servant? to his own master he standeth or falleth."* (Romans 14:4a)

BAPTIST DISTINCTIVES

To understand Baptist distinctives, therefore, is to understand America. The Saviour said, *"And ye shall know the truth, and the truth shall make you free."* (John 8:32) Consequently, Baptists begin by basing all their doctrine on the final authority of the Holy Scripture. (II Timothy 3:16,17) On the other hand, Rome's official position has been the "Holy Scripture" (the corrupt Latin Vulgate) *plus* church tradition (the accumulated "papal bull" of a dozen centuries) with "His Holiness" breaking any theological standoffs. And because Protestants came out of the Catholic Church, they also have stopped short of a total submission to Scripture on many occasions. Evangelicals may sing about *"sola Biblia,"* but the Baptists have been the ones practicing it at great peril.

We have already seen how this Baptistic conviction of a "printed authority," though only partially embraced by the Puritans, led them to prefer a philosophy of *limited government*. John Cotton's remark that "the law is not subject to passion" is indicative of a mood that would eventually lead a fledgling nation to entrust its political security to *another* written document.

With the Bible as their authoritative guide, Baptists have also held that a true, New Testament church is a local, autonomous body, and as such, owes no allegiance to any tribunal in the universe, except to that of the Lord Jesus Christ. (Matthew 16:13-18) That the first Christian churches were indeed local assemblies has been corroborated by a number of eminent historians, not the least of which being the liberal, Edward Gibbon, who wrote these words in his *History of the Decline and Fall of the Roman Empire:*

> Such was the mild and equal constitution by which the Christians were governed for more than a hundred years after the death of the apostles. Every society formed within itself a separate and independent republic; and although the most distant of these little states maintained a mutual, as well as friendly, intercourse of letters and deputations, the

Christian world was not yet connected by any supreme or legislative assembly.[41]

Dr. John Christian explains how this satanic "connection" took place under Vatican auspices:

> There was, however, a constant tendency towards centralization. As the pastor assumed rights which were not granted to him by the Scriptures, some of the metropolitan pastors exercised an undue authority over some of the smaller churches. Then the churches in some of the cities sought the patronage and protection of the pastors of the larger cities. Finally Rome, the political center of the world, became the religious center as well. In time the pastor in Rome became the universal pope. All of this was of slow growth and required centuries for its consummation.[42]

With the original state-church arrangement of Constantine in 312 A.D. eventually driving true believers underground, all subsequent religious history has been reduced to the simple motif of the *churches* of Jesus Christ "warring a good warfare" against *the church* of Rome over the Baptist distinctive of *local church autonomy*.

Although the Puritans were unwilling to sacrifice their own New England theocracy on the altar of unmitigated autonomy, they did resist their native church (or, as they had judiciously described her at their port-side farewell, the "dear mother" from whose breasts they had "sucked" the hope of salvation,[43]) by embracing a limited application of the doctrine when constructing their congregationalist polity. The significance of this fact is that the Brownists, who are to be credited with establishing this very Congregationalism through the ministry of John Robinson (a former associate to Brown and the Pilgrims' original pastor), learned the doctrine themselves from a body of nearly 4,000 exiled Dutch Baptists who were in Norwich at the time. Among a number of eminent historians who have corroborated this association (Fuller, Collier, Weingarten, Brandt and others), Scheffer simply affirms: "Brown's new ideas concerning the nature of the Church opened to him in the circle of the Dutch Baptists in Norwich."[44]

Through M. Stanton Evans' assessment of the long-term effects of Brownist Congregationalism on American politics, we are once again reminded of the significant role of Baptist distinctives in our nation's glorious heritage: "And though they are little known to history (except for

Browne, whose name initially was given to the movement), they were largely responsible for the doctrines that shaped our country."[45]

And finally, with reference to their impact on the original New England town meetings, Evans quoting Wertenbaker:

> The town became to the state what the congregation was to the church. Localism in religion, which had become so vital a feature of Puritanism, was to be matched in New England by localism in government.[46]

In addition to biblical authority and local church autonomy, Baptists also believe that the scriptural requirements for membership in a New Testament assembly are *salvation* and *baptism,* in that order. Although the plan of salvation can never be an issue among true believers, there does exist a great amount of disagreement over the doctrines of baptism and church membership. That the crux of this debate has continued to hinge upon the ordinance itself is unfortunate indeed, as the Bible's teaching on this subject could not be any clearer. Whenever a sincere Christian will allow the Bible to settle the issue of baptism, his prayerful study will always lead him to the historic Baptist position. (Whether or not he has the stomach to bear the equally historic *reproach* of this despised "sect" is quite another matter.)

For the record, there are absolutely *no* recorded instances of infant baptism *anywhere* in the New Testament, as the scriptural prerequisite for the ordinance is always a public profession of faith in Jesus Christ as personal Saviour. Secondly, the mode is always immersion. Absolutely no one in the Bible is "baptized" by sprinkling, with the very suggestion being a misnomer, as the Greek word for *baptize* always means *to immerse in water.*

The first Gentile convert in the history of the New Testament church was the Ethiopian eunuch. After his conscious acceptance of the Gospel, he asked Philip, the evangelist, *"What doth hinder me to be baptized?"* (Acts 8:36b) whereupon the man of God replied, *"If thou believest with all thine heart, thou mayest."* (Acts 8:37a) The Ethiopian eunuch then made his public profession, *"I believe that Jesus Christ is the Son of God,"* and then *"they went down both into the water, both Philip and the eunuch; and he baptized him."* (Acts 8:37b, 38b)

The historic Baptist position is so totally unassailable that Catholics and Protestants alike are forced into submission. While Dr. John Dallinger, a former Catholic professor of church history at the University of Munich, conceded, "There is no proof or hint in the New Testament that the apostles baptized infants or ordered them to be baptized,"[47] the Protestant Dr. Dosker, professor of church history at the Presbyterian Theological Seminary in Louisville, likewise concurred, "Every candid historian will admit that the Baptists have, both philologically and historically, the better of the argument, as to the prevailing mode of baptism. The word *baptizo* means immersion, both in classical and Biblical Greek."[48]

PROTESTANT PERSECUTION

Although most Christians have read about martyrs who perished at the hands of Catholic inquisitors, almost nothing is said about the brutalities inflicted upon Baptists by their fellow Christian "brothers"! The Swiss "reformers" were some of the worst, Armitage writing:

> At first, Zwingli and the Council were content with the fine and imprisonment of their victims, but when this failed to cure them they were loaded with chains. On the 7th of March, 1526, the Council of Zurich decreed that those who baptized any person who had been previously christened, should, if condemned, be drowned without mercy. On this ordinance Füsslin makes these remarks: "If any one asks with what kind of justice this was done, the Papists would have an answer. They would say, according to papal law heretics must die. There is no need to enquire further. The maxim is applicable here. What the papacy condemns is condemned. But those who hold to evangelical faith renounce the pope and papal authority, and the question now arises, with what propriety do they compel people to renounce their views or religion, and in case of their refusal inflict upon them capital punishment?"[49]

The decree at the Diet of Speyer three years later in 1529 proclaimed, "in Christian love," of course: "All Anabaptists and rebaptized persons, male or female, of mature age, shall be judged and brought from natural life to death, by fire, or sword or otherwise, as may befit the persons."[50]

For the "crime" of immersing their converts, Baptist preachers were often specifically drowned ("immersed permanently," as their Christian tormenters would say) so as to add insult to injury.

In 1530 (January 20th), Conrad Winkler was drowned at Zurich, as the fourth of its murdered Baptists; and Weesen, who lived at Zurich at the time, says that he was martyred "For having rebaptized, against express command, so many people that he did not know the number. He leaped up, struck his hands together, as if he rejoiced at his death; and immediately before he was thrust under, he sang with a clear voice one or two verses of a hymn."[51]

Incidentally, the Protestants in Zurich were not above executing women either, especially pastors' wives. Three days after the Baptist leader Balthazar Hübmaier was burned at the stake, his beard having been caked with sulphur and gunpowder, his loving wife was thrown from a bridge into the Danube with a stone tied to her neck.

With these bloody scenes in mind, one can better comprehend the spirit of intolerance that was brewing in Massachusetts which threatened to engulf the entire land. In 1638, a law was passed that forced every dissenter who would not voluntarily support the Puritan clergy to be compelled to do so. And, in the same year, the Assembly of Massachusetts passed another incredible law requiring excommunicated persons to seek to be restored to the churches which had booted them out!

Whosoever shall stand excommunicated for the space of six months, without labouring what in him or her lieth to be restored, such person shall be presented to the Court of Assistants, and there proceeded with by fine, imprisonment, banishment, or further for the good behaviour, as their contempt and obstinacy upon full hearing shall deserve.[52]

Two months after Roger Williams arrived in Boston, an outright law against Baptists was even passed, warning, among other things:

If any person or persons, within this jurisdiction, shall either openly condemn or oppose the baptizing of infants, or go about secretly to seduce others from the approbation or use thereof, or shall purposely depart the congregation at the ministration of the ordinance...every such person or persons shall be *sentenced to banishment.*[53]

When Baptists attempted to answer the charges brought against them by appealing to the silence of Scriptures, John Cotton had the audacity to attribute such a defense to the *devil*! Benedict writing:

Mr. Cotton says, Satan, despairing of success by more powerful arguments, "chooseth rather to play small game, as they say, than lose all. He now pleadeth no other argument in these stirring times of reformation, than may be urged from a main principle of purity and reformation, viz. *That no duty of God's worship, nor any ordinance of religion is to be administered in the church, but such as hath just warrant from the word of God.* And in urging this argument against the baptism of children, Satan transformeth himself into an angel of light."[54]

In the year 1659, two Baptist preachers from Rhode Island, Reverend John Clarke and Reverend Obadiah Holmes, were visiting a fellow brother near Lynn on the Lord's Day. While Brother Clarke was preaching from Revelation 3:10, two constables broke into the house and terminated their religious services. Hauled before the court, they were heavily fined, Clarke, £20 and Holmes, £30. (John Cotton had recommended the death penalty.[55]) A friend paid Clarke's fine despite his protest. However, Reverend Holmes was "whipped unmercifully" in the streets of Boston, the victim testifying:

> As the strokes fell upon me, I had such a spiritual manifestation of God's presence, as the like thereof I never had nor felt, nor can with fleshly tongue express, and the outward pain was so removed from me, that indeed I am not able to declare it to you, it was so easy to me, that I could well bear it, yea, and in a manner, felt it not, although it was grievous, as the spectators said, the man striking with all his strength (yea, spitting in his hands three times, as many affirmed) with a three corded [sic] whip, giving me therewith thirty strokes. When he had loosed me from the post, having joyfulness in my heart and cheerfulness in my countenance, as the spectators observed, I told the magistrates, you have struck me as with roses.[56]

In the process of time, this evil spirit began driving others away besides Roger Williams. One of these was the first president of Harvard University, the esteemed Dr. Henry Dunstar, who embraced Baptist principles so fervently that "he not only forbore to present an infant of his own unto baptism, but also thought himself under some obligations to bear his testimony in some sermons, against the administration of baptism to *any infant* whatever."[57] Dr. Dunstar was compelled to resign the presidency of Harvard, and although the magistrates moved in on their prey, his death in 1659 removed him from any further prosecution.

One of the more embarrassing losses involved the departure of Thomas Hooker in 1639, the most popular Puritan minister in Massachusetts at that time. Among other inequities, Hooker took exception to the magistrates holding office for life, declaring: "I must confess, I ever looked at it, as a way which leads directly to tyranny, and so to confusion, and must plainly profess, if it was in my liberty, I should choose neither to live, nor leave my posterity, under such a government."[58]

Hooker went on to found the colony of Connecticut. However, the most significant factor which contributed to the demise of Puritan influence was found to be their recalcitrant bias for pedobaptism. The self-righteous "divines" were apparently too busy flogging Baptist preachers to notice that the perceived heresy of making regeneration a prerequisite for baptism was, in reality, a spiritual safeguard to ensure a regenerate membership.

HALFWAY COVENANT

On June 4, 1657, a historic gathering of Puritan ministers assembled in Boston for a meeting that would signal the beginning of the end for their New England theocracy. The issue under discussion involved a number of second-generation parents who wanted their own children "baptized" (sprinkled) despite the fact that they themselves had yet to be judged regenerate by the official minister of religion. In a drastic move to allow for the superstitious christenings, the decision was made to accept the unconverted parents into the church membership with the stipulation that they refrain from communion. Known as the *Halfway Covenant,* it provided "that all persons of sober life and correct sentiments, without being examined as to a change of heart, might profess religion or become members of the Church, and have their children baptized, though they did not come to the Lord's table."[59]

Within a decade of this momentous compromise, the signs of spiritual depression were everywhere to be seen, Christian writing:

> In 1670 a decay in spirituality was very apparent. Rev. Samuel Danforth, of Roxbury, spoke of "the temper, complexion, and countenance of the churches as being strangely altered" and "a cold, careless, dead frame of spirit" as having "grown steadily" upon them. In 1678 Increase Mather spoke of "conversions" as "rare." "The body of the rising generation is a poor, perishing, unconverted, and, except the Lord pour down his Spirit, an undone generation. Many are profane, drunkards, lascivious, scoffers at the power of godliness." In 1683 Rev. Samuel

Torrey, of Weymouth, spoke: "O the many symptoms of death that are upon our religion! As converting work doth cease, so doth religion die away; though more insensibly, yet more irrevocably. How much is religion dying in the hearts of sincere Christians!" In 1702 Increase Mather said: "Look into our pulpits and see if there is such a glory there as there once was. Look into the civil State. Does Christ reign there as he once did? How many churches, how many towns are there in New England over which we may sigh and say, the glory is gone!"[60]

The Puritans had learned the hard way why their Baptist brethren were insistent upon a regenerated church membership. That the entire Protestant Reformation was destined to share a similar fate is implied in our Lord's description of the Roman Catholic Church in Revelation 17:5 as *"THE MOTHER OF HARLOTS."* For although spiritually productive as "children" (Luther's 95 Theses, etc.), the Protestant denominations would eventually come of age and pursue their mother's career as *religious prostitutes.* Without a built-in safeguard to keep the unregenerate out, decay was inevitable. Only by rejecting infant sprinkling and embracing believer's baptism can a church experience the divine perpetuity promised in Matthew 16:18b, *"And the gates of hell shall not prevail against it."*

While the "Holy Commonwealth" in Massachusetts was dying a natural death, the Baptists were solidifying their sole power base in the colony of Rhode Island. Shortly after the settlement was established, Roger Williams had arrived at the inevitable, historic Baptist position and was immersed by Ezekiel Holliman, a former member of his Salem Church; whereupon Williams baptized Holliman and nine others, founding what some historians believe to be the first Baptist church in America. Regardless of the chronological accuracy of this view, Williams' ever-sensitive conscience eventually got the better of him as he became troubled by the fact that the man who had baptized him (Holliman) had not been baptized himself at the time. Unable to resolve this apparent conflict, Williams resigned his pastorate and another filled his place.

JOHN CLARKE

The long-term leadership among Rhode Island Baptists was provided by Dr. John Clarke, pastor of the First Baptist Church in Newport. Only weeks after his shameful arrest (along with Obadiah Holmes), Clarke traveled to

England to secure a Royal Charter for his colony. This faithful man of God would labor for a dozen years to procure the following document:

> No one in this colony shall henceforth be molested, punished, disturbed, or brought to trial on account of any differences of opinion in the matter of religion... but each one at the same time shall be able freely and lawfully to hold his own judgment and his own conscience in what concerns religious questions... so long as he does not violate peace and quietness, and does not abuse this liberty in a licentious and profane manner.[61]

Although Rhode Island was termed by Mather's orthodox cronies as "the sewer of New England," those who personally visited this smallest of the colonies came away with a totally different perspective: "They are much like their neighbours, only they have one vice less, and one virtue more than they; for they never persecuted any, but have ever maintained a perfect liberty of conscience."[62]

Inspired by Rhode Island's spiritual independence, the Quaker leader, William Penn, in 1681 established the colony that bears his name along a similar goal of religious toleration. Paul Johnson states:

> At its heart was the city of Brotherly Love. The harbor of Philadelphia led to Pittsburgh, at the gateway to the Ohio Valley, and to the west and astride the valleys to the back country of the south, so it was the national crossroads. Hence, it came, simultaneously, to be the center of Quaker influence throughout the world; a stronghold of Presbyterianism; the headquarters in America of the Baptists; an Anglican center; a place where many important German religious sects, the Moravians, the Mennonites, the Lutherans and the German Reformed established their headquarters; and yet, a place where large numbers of Jews and Catholics were tolerated.
>
> It was also the home of the first African Methodist Episcopal Church, the earliest independent black body in America, as well as an area where Deists, the earliest Unitarians, and even humanists could feel safe and at home. Philadelphia was the seat of the American philosophical society. And granted its religious and nonreligious composition, it is no accident that it was a city which gave birth to the libertarian and separatist principles embodied in the Declaration of Independence and the United States Constitution.[63]

When one adds to this Quaker-led confederacy the Lutheran-Presbyterian strongholds in New York and New Jersey and the Episcopal centers in Virginia, Georgia and the Carolinas, all of whom would be digressing spiritually due to their "mixed multitudes," it becomes apparent that something more effective than religious monitors and whipping posts would be needed to reap this growing harvest for Jesus. The divinely appointed means to this end was the eighteenth-century phenomenon known as the Great Awakening, a powerful manifestation of the Holy Ghost that affected saints and sinners on both sides of the Atlantic.

However, this watershed revival was designed to accomplish more than the normal evangelistic campaign. If these widely diversified colonists were to form a united front against the approaching tyranny of King George, something would have to bring them together. Johnson states:

> The Great Awakening, which began in 1719 and continued for the next quarter-century or more, was the formative event in the history of the United States preceeding [sic] the movement for independence and making it possible. The Great Awakening crossed all religious and sectarian boundaries, made light of them indeed and turned what had been a series of European-styled churches into American ones... Certainly it gave a distinctive American flavor to a wide range of denominations.[64]

But before we consider the actual soul-saving particulars of this awakening, together with the greater long-term benefit derived from an enhanced colonial defense against anticipated British aggression, the revival's propitious checking of an even more insidious foe from *within* must first be examined.

VII

Penance or Jesus?

> *"Jesus saith unto him, I am the way, the truth, and the life: no man cometh unto the Father, but by me."* (John 14:6)

I N ORDER TO appreciate the supernatural birth of America, one must realize that the "delivery" was accomplished in spite of several abortive attempts by Satan. These efforts consisted of the Vatican's own "missionary burden" to outflank the Protestant colonies through infiltration, political intrigue and a string of strategic outposts.

Rome's first "missionaries" to America were members of the infamous Society of Jesus, better known as the *Jesuits*. This fanatical order of Catholicism was established by Ignatius de Loyola between 1534 and 1539 for the sole purpose of reintroducing papal authority to the "wayward" nations of Protestantism. Their diabolical deeds are numerous and undeniable. The St. Bartholomew's Day Massacre in 1572 (when more than 10,000 Christians were murdered in Paris), the failed invasion of England by the Spanish Armada in 1588, the foiled attempt to assassinate James I in 1605 (known as the Gunpowder Plot), and the costly Thirty Years War (when millions of believers were slain between 1618 and1648) constitute but a few of their many atrocities.

In light of these historical realities, writers who profess to be born-again persist in exposing their naive Christian readership to a steady diet of non-offensive, God-and-country material that is indirectly pro-Catholic. Peter Marshall's deceptive *The Light and the Glory* is typical:

Next upon the stage of North America were the French, and with them, a new breed of missionaries: the fabled Jesuits. If there was one word to describe the Jesuits, it would be *zeal*—in the very best sense of that maligned word. In 1540, Ignatius of Loyola, a former knight and soldier, founded the Society of Jesus—a band of brilliant young scholars and disciples, who had covenanted together to live in poverty and chastity under absolute obedience to the Pope...these Christian soldiers, superbly trained and strong in the faith yet conditioned to prize humility, looked forward to the tests of the savage wilderness.[1]

If there were one word to describe the Jesuits *according to Webster's dictionary,* it would be *crafty.* The men who founded America were well aware of the Jesuit penchant for treachery and subterfuge. Lamenting a resurgence of Jesuit activity, John Adams wrote to Thomas Jefferson in 1816:

> I am not happy about the rebirth of the Jesuits. Swarms of them will present themselves under more disguises ever taken by even a chief of the Bohemians, as printers, writers, publishers, school teachers, etc. **If ever an association of people deserved eternal damnation, on this earth and in hell, it is this Society of Loyola.**[2]

The first Catholic parish in the continental United States territory, Nombre de Dios, was founded in St. Augustine, Florida, in 1565. Florida also became the first Jesuit mission field in North America.[3] Of course, these "inroads for Christ" could not have been realized had it not been for the slaughter of a Huguenot settlement (French Christians) at Fort Caroline, near the mouth of the St. Johns River, the previous year. Excluding a small strip of land in the lower Mississippi country, the arc of Spanish Catholicism would eventually stretch all the way to California.

Concerning the California missions, even the Jesuit author, James Hennesey, concedes a familiar scenario: "The soldiers treated the Indians badly—a favorite 'sport' was to lasso Indian women—and they also introduced venereal and other diseases which soon reached epidemic proportions."[4]

The first French settlement of Roman Catholics in America was founded on Ste. Croix (De Monts) Island on Maine's Scoodic River in 1604.[5] Jesuit agents arrived seven years later. Aided by Franciscan missionaries, the religion of Rome began an ominous, westward expansion: the Great Lakes in 1679; Minnesota in 1680; the mouth of the Mississippi in 1682; Detroit in 1701 and Kaskaskia in 1703. The Jesuits even ventured into the Dakotas and Montana.[6] The massive Louisiana Territory was worked by French Catholics from 1699 to 1766 and then by the Spanish until 1803.

When ecumenical compromisers like Marshall talk about Jesuit priests being "strong in the faith," one need only consider the testimonies of their benighted converts to conclude that Pete must be talking about *another* gospel (Galatians 1:8, 9). Upon assuming his priestly duties among the people of Vincennes (Indiana), a Canadian missionary by the name of Pierre Gibault described in a letter to his bishop how his hungry parishioners received him after being abandoned by their original Jesuit pastor seven years earlier:

> Some threw themselves on their knees and were quite unable to speak; others spoke only by their sobs; some cried out: Father, save us, we are nearly in hell; others said: **God has not then utterly abandoned us, for it is He who has sent you to make us do penance for our sins;** and others again exclaimed: Ah! Sir, why did you not come a month ago, then my poor wife, my dear father, my loved mother, my poor child would not have died without the **sacraments!**[7]

With plenty of Catholic expansion engulfing the emerging Protestant colonies, the most significant Vatican toehold was established within one of the English settlements itself. In 1632, George Calvert, Lord Baltimore, secured a charter from Charles I to found his own colony for fellow "persecuted" Romanists. Coincidentally, this earliest bastion of American Catholicism would be known as *Mary*land, ostensibly named after the papist wife of Charles I, Henrietta *Maria*. Paul Johnson states:

> Father Andrew White, who kept the first diary of the settlement, adapted the same providential approach as Governor Winthrop. He, too, saw his fellow settlers as chosen people under divine dispensation and Chesapeake Bay as the Promised Land. "This bay," he wrote, "is the most delightful water I ever saw. The land is sweet, firm and fertile. There are plenty of fish, fine woods of walnuts, oaks and cedars, salad herbs and such like, strawberries, raspberries, mulberry vines, rich soil, delicate springs of water, partridge, deer, turkey, geese, ducks and delightful squirrels, eagles and herons. The place abounds not only with profit but pleasure.
>
> "Moreover, Maryland," he said, "being halfway between the extremes of Virginia and New England, has a middle temperature between the two and enjoys the advantages and escapes the evil of each. Thus God," he

concluded, "had been generous to his Catholic Englishmen and had indeed set them up in a land of milk and honey."[8]

This satanic counterfeit (II Corinthians 11:14, 15) of the godly Plymouth Colony may impress the many politically active, pro-Catholic, evangelical charismatics of our day, but America's original patriots were not that *stupid*. A body of 10,000 "citizens" situated between our two most important colonies and only miles from our future national capital, who were, in reality, fanatically committed to another government altogether (the Vatican *State*) was not a light matter. While Samuel Adams declared that "much more is to be dreaded from the growth of Popery in America than from the Stamp Act,"[9] John Jay, a future chief justice of the United States, persuaded his colleagues to withhold naturalization from persons who would not renounce "all allegiance" to "every foreign king, prince, potentate, and state, in all matters, ecclesiastical as well as civil." In the colonies themselves, the adults celebrated November 5th as Pope's Day by ceremonially burning "His Holiness" at the stake while the children played such mild-mannered games as Break the Pope's Neck.[10] And speaking of hate crimes, have you ever read the elementary lessons in the *New England Primer*, specifically, the John Rogers Verses?

> Abhor that arrant whore of Rome
> and all her blasphemies;
> And Drink not of her cursed cup;
> Obey not her decrees.[11]

Although the Catholics were covering a lot of physical territory, their actual numbers within the 13 colonies were negligible, roughly 25,000 out of a total population of 2.5 million. This numerical disparity induced the Marylanders to *appear* as though they favored religious liberty by passing the Toleration Act of 1649 which afforded freedom of conscience to all who accepted the Trinity. However, heavy fines would be leveled against anyone caught using such "offensive" terms as *Papist* or *Jesuit*, etc. Rome's minority status in the New World also led her foreign agents to pursue their standard modus operandi of international political intrigue.

With his nation embroiled in the multi-theater Seven Years War, George III ascended the British throne in 1760 at the age of 22. Three years later, the defeated French relinquished all their territory in North America. The young king's colonial popularity began to decline, however, as he initiated several ill-fated tax schemes to recoup his heavy war debt. When his subjects balked at these measures, he committed an unpardonable offense. On May 20, 1774, Parliament passed the volatile *Quebec Act* which installed Roman Catholicism as the official state religion of Canada, while extending her borders to the Ohio River on the south and the Mississippi on the west. Whereas many Americans had envisioned Canada becoming the fourteenth colony, *they would now have to contend with an influx of 80,000 self-governing French Catholics at their rear!*

In some instances, the Romanists themselves show more candor in acknowledging the historical anti-Catholic sentiment of pre-revolutionary America than professing Christian authors such as Peter Marshall and David Manuel. James Hennesey, a former president of the Jesuit School of Theology in Chicago, confirmed that

> ... the Continental Congress which met at Philadelphia on September 17 took as its own, by unanimous vote, the "Suffolk County Resolves," framed a week earlier in Boston, which denounced the May 20 Quebec Act, "the late Act of Parliament for establishing the Roman Catholic religion in that extensive country now called Canada." This act was "dangerous in an extreme degree to the Protestant religion and to the civil rights and liberties of all Americans." An address to the people of Great Britain, adopted in September 5, spoke of Catholicism as "a religion fraught with sanguinary and impious tenets," which "has deluged your island in blood and dispersed impiety, persecution, murder and rebellion through every part of the world." A "loyal Address" to King George III on October 25 criticized the Quebec Act for establishing "an absolute government and the Roman Catholick [sic] religion throughout those vast regions, that border on the westerly and northerly boundaries of the free protestant English settlements."[12]

For the record, George Washington endorsed the strong language of the September 5th missive by attaching his own signature to the document. The tyrant who invaded the 13 colonies and started the American Revolution was just another dupe of the Vatican. In a letter to the Catholic bishops in England, Pope Pius VI praised George III accordingly:

> He is the best of sovereigns; his authority is full of mildness to Catholics. They do not bear so hard and heavy a yoke; they have been delivered from a part of the severe laws and hard conditions to which they were subjected. They now possess privileges; our brethren may serve in the army, and have obtained Catholic schools for youth. Nor has the beneficent monarch shown his goodness only to Catholics of his kingdom;

he has favored and supported them in the vast Indian realms subject to his authority.[13]

Although these several Catholic inroads were perceived as a viable threat to the emerging American experiment, the Lord of Glory had them positioned according to a sovereign plan. Having strategically distanced His children over 3,000 miles from the papal armies of Europe, America's God thought it wise to leave just enough "Canaanites" in the land to keep His embryonic Republic looking to Him for their sustained well-being. *"Now these are the nations which the LORD left, to prove Israel by them, even as many of Israel as had not known all the wars of Canaan."* (Judges 3:1) As in the identical predicament of both the ancient and modern state of Israel, a fledgling America would grow best when surrounded by enemy forces on three sides and an ocean at her back. (Exodus 14:3, 4)

THE GREAT AWAKENING

In response to this Parliament-sanctioned, three-sided Vatican envelopment and incipient doctrinal polluting of the 13 semi-isolated colonies, the Holy Spirit wrought a timely national bonding of supernatural dimensions. As mentioned in the previous chapter, this unique revival has been called by historians, "The Great Awakening." The American phase of the Great Awakening broke out in 1734 among the parishioners of Reverend Jonathan Edwards, pastor of the First Church of North Hampton, Massachusetts. The years preceding this revival had been viewed by the Congregationalist minister as "a time of extraordinary dullness in religion."[14] All of this changed, however, with the sudden and unexplained deaths of several notable persons. The subsequent conversion of a particular frivolous woman seemed to have a remarkable awakening influence upon the entire community, Edwards writing:

> The minds of the people were wonderfully taken off from the world; it was treated amongst us as a thing of very little consequence; they seemed to follow their worldly business, more as a part of their duty, than any disposition they had to it... There was scarcely a single person in the town, either old or young, that was left unconcerned about the great things of the eternal world.[15]

On July 8, 1741, Jonathan Edwards preached his famous sermon, "Sinners in the Hands of an Angry God," to a congregation in Enfield, Connecticut. Cultured New Englanders cried out for mercy as the powerful Edwards described their perilous predicament:

> The God that holds you over the pit of hell, much as one holds a spider or some loathsome insect over the fire, abhors you and is dreadfully provoked... You hang by a slender thread, with the flames of divine wrath flashing about it, and ready every moment to singe it and burn it asunder.[16]

From Northampton, the revival spread into several New England communities with multiplied conversions occurring. "Sinners" who could no longer be bullied into services by magistrates were being compelled into the kingdom by Spirit-filled preachers. Through the Great Awakening, the Holy Ghost of God miraculously united a religiously diverse people who were also scattered literally "hither, thither and yon" in a manner that is inconceivable to Americans approaching the twenty-first century. When John Adams departed Boston by carriage to attend the historic Continental Congress in Philadelphia, for instance, he was actually making his first trip outside his native colony.[17] The future successor to George Washington was already 39 years of age at the time! Speaking of a trip he made from Richmond to New York in 1790, Thomas Jefferson stated: "The roads through the whole were so bad that we could never go more than three miles an hour, sometimes not more than two, and, in the night but one."[18]

Johnson reiterates how this spiritual coalescence prepared America for her predestined independence:

> We must remember that until the 18th century at least, America was a collection of desperate colonies with little contact with each other; and often, as in all Latin America, then and even today, having more powerful links with cities and economic interests in Europe than with neighboring colonies. Religious evangelism was the first continental force, an all-American phenomena which transcended colonial differences, introduced truly national figures and made colonial boundaries seem unimportant.[19]

GEORGE WHITEFIELD

The first public figure recognized from New Hampshire to Georgia was not a native statesman but rather a British evangelist, the renowned George

Whitefield.[20] Known as the "boy preacher with a golden voice," Whitefield became the international catalyst for the Great Awakening as he fanned the flames of revival in both worlds, logging an incredible 782 days at sea throughout 13 transatlantic crossings for his Master.

At the age of two, George lost his father, a wine merchant, and was reared by his mother, Elizabeth, in and around the Bell Tavern, the family business. After devoting his adolescent years to riotous living, Whitefield decided to clean up his act and enrolled in Oxford University to prepare for the Anglican priesthood. He was converted (through no fault of the "dead" faculty) by his reading of two spiritual books, *The Life of God in the Soul of Man* and Bishop Hall's *Contemplations*, and ultimately through his personal study of the Holy Bible.

Whitefield's radical transformation and immediate preaching on the necessity of the new birth marked him as a renegade Anglican for life. His first sermon reportedly drove 15 people mad. Being shunned by a professional clergy, described by the common man as "dull, duller or dullest," Whitefield boldly declared, "The churches are closed against me. Bless God, the fields are open!"[21] His first attempt at open-air preaching drew an estimated crowd of 20,000 colliers (coal miners) in Kingswood and officially launched the English phase of the Great Awakening. Whitefield's personal diary reads like Ripley's *Believe It or Not*, confirming that truth is certainly stranger than fiction:

> Wednesday, May 2. Preached this evening again to above ten thousand at Kennington Common... Sunday, May 6. Preached this morning in Moorfields to about twenty thousand people, who were very quiet and attentive... and at six preached at Kennington. Such a sight I never saw before. I believe there were no less than fifty thousand people... Thursday, May 10. Preached at Kennington, but it rained most of the day. There were not above ten thousand people, and thirty coaches... Sunday, May 13... Went to public worship twice and preached in the evening to near sixty thousand people... Friday, June 1... gave a short exhortation to a few people in a field, and preached in the evening, at a place called Mayfair, near Hyde Park Corner. The congregation, I believe, consisted of near eighty thousand people.[22]

Whitefield's involvement with the American people centered around the perennial needs of an orphanage that he founded in Savannah, at the invitation of Georgia governor James Oglethorpe. While in this country to deliver supplies and personnel to his beloved Bethesda House, he would pursue his primary call of uniting the colonies through Spirit-filled preaching, continually reminding all that "the heart can never be at unity with itself till it is wholly centred [sic] on God."[23]

Everywhere George Whitefield went, the power of God appeared. On December 2, 1739, Whitefield preached to 10,000 people at Whiteclay Creek, Pennsylvania, for an hour and a half in the rain! And 3,000 of these had arrived by horseback.[24] The following April, Whitefield addressed a throng of 15,000 listeners in Philadelphia when the city's entire population was estimated at only 12,000.[25] The crowd was packed so tightly that a juvenile who had come only to throw stones, found his arms literally pinned to his sides[26] and was, by the sermon's conclusion, smitten himself by *"The stone cut out without hands."* In another service in Philadelphia, he spoke from the gallery of the courthouse on Market Street and it was said that "his voice was distinctly heard on the Jersey shore."[27] On May 14th, the "grand itinerant" spoke to 12,000 people in Nottingham, Delaware, and reported that "thousands cried out, so that they almost drowned my voice."[28] Not only did numerous men and women faint, revive and then faint again under the power of the message, but Whitefield himself swooned during the closing invitation.

As to the long-term effects on Whitefield's listeners, Benjamin Franklin reported:

> The multitudes of all sects and denominations that attended his sermons were enormous, and it was a matter of speculation with me, who was one of the number, to observe the extraordinary influence of his oratory on his hearers, and how much they admired and respected him, notwithstanding his common abuse of them, by assuring them they were naturally *half beasts and half devils.*
>
> It was wonderful to see the change soon made in the manners of our inhabitants. From being thoughtless or indifferent about religion, it seem'd as if all the world were growing religious, so that one could not walk thro' the town in an evening without hearing psalms sung in different families of every street.[29]

The awe of Whitefield's presence and oratory can be gleaned from the following eyewitness account of an open-air meeting in New York City, as published in the *New England Journal* by an anonymous writer:

> I thought it possible that some *enthusiasm* might have mix'd itself with his piety and that his zeal might have exceeded his knowledge. With these prepossessions I went into the fields; when I came there, I saw a

great number of people consisting of Christians of all denominations, some *Jews*, and a few, I believe, that had no religion at all.

When Mr Whitefield came to the place before designed, which was a little eminence on the side of a hill, he stood still and beckoned with his hand, and dispos'd the multitude upon the descent, before and on either side of him. He then *prayed most excellently*... The assembly soon appeared to be divided into two companies... The [one] were collected round the minister, and were very serious and attentive. The other had placed themselves in the skirts of the assembly, and spent most of their time in giggling, scoffing, talking and laughing... Towards the last prayer the whole assembly appeared more united, and all became hush'd and still; a solemn awe and reverence appeared in the faces of most, and a mighty energy attended the Word. I heard and felt something astonishing, but I confess, I was not at that time, fully rid of my scruples.[30]

With the Baptist clergy repressed by ubiquitous magistrates, the providential role played by a renegade, ordained, Anglican evangelist in America's Great Awakening was nothing short of a miracle in itself. Who could better appreciate the need for a Protestant revival than one himself lately raised from the dead, Whitefield declaring, "The Christian world is in a deep sleep! Nothing but a loud voice can awaken them out of it."[31] As everything rises and falls on leadership, the maverick Anglican placed the blame squarely on unregenerate ministers:

I am persuaded the generality of preachers talk of an unknown and unfelt Christ. The reasons why congregations had been so dead is because they had dead men preaching to them. How can dead men beget living children?[32]

One of these "clerical corpses," the Episcopalian, Dr. Cutler, accosted Whitefield on a Boston street with the words, "I am sorry to see you here," to which the undaunted preacher replied, "So is the Devil!"[33] In a letter to a friend, Cutler describes the havoc wrought by Whitefield's powerful sermons:

Whitefield has plagued us with a witness. It would be an endless attempt to describe the scene of confusion and disturbance occasioned by him; the divisions of families, neighborhoods and towns.[34]

What the ignorant Dr. Cutler failed to perceive was that his peaceful parish was being sliced to ribbons by the sword Jesus promised would *"set a man at variance against his father, and the daughter against her mother."* (Matthew 10:35a, b) Could it be that Cutler was also a tad jealous of his clerical nemesis? On the Sunday morning of his final day in Boston, October 12, 1740, Whitefield found the crowds assembled before the Old South Church to be so great that he "was obliged to enter through a window."[35] Of his evening message in Boston Common, he wrote:

> I preached my farewell sermon to near twenty thousand people,—a sight I have not seen since I left Blackheath—and a sight, perhaps, never seen before in America. It being nearly dusk before I had done, the sight was more solemn. Numbers, great numbers, melted into tears when I talked of leaving them...Blessed be God! for what He has done in Boston. **I hope a glorious work is now begun, and that the Lord will stir up some faithful labourers to carry it on.**[36]

CHICKENS BECOME DUCKS

This parting burden was indeed realized but not in a manner that Mr. Whitefield would have desired. Having authored the 1,200-page, two-volume definitive biography on Whitefield's *Life and Times*, the Baptist Arnold Dallimore surmised, "There can be little doubt that far more than half of the total population of the Colonies had heard him preach."[37] This would have amounted to well over one million listeners! Of the numerous conversions and schisms that ensued, Whitefield's "sword" divided the Congregationalists into New Lights (proponents of the Great Awakening) and Old Lights (opponents) while the Presbyterian Church was similarly split between New Sides and Old Sides. *With the future freedom of America in view, the Holy Spirit providentially led the majority of these Separatist assemblies to become Baptist churches.* Leonard Bacon explains how the "faithful labourers" longed for by Whitefield turned out to be the historic guardians of individual soul liberty:

> An even more important result of the Awakening was the swift and wide extension of Baptist principles and churches. This was altogether logical. The revival had come, not so much in the spirit and power of Elijah, turning to each other the hearts of the fathers and of children, as in the spirit of Ezekiel, the preacher of individual responsibility and duty. The temper of the revival was wholly congenial with the strong individualism of the Baptist churches. **The Separatist churches formed**

in New England by the withdrawal of revival enthusiasts from the parish churches in many instances became Baptists. Cases of individual conversion to Baptist views were frequent, and the earnestness with which the new opinion was held approved itself not only by debating and proselyting, but by strenuous and useful evangelizing. Especially in the South, from Virginia to Georgia, the new preachers, entering into the labors of the annoyed and persecuted pioneers of their communion, won multitudes of converts to the Christian faith, from the neglected populations, both black and white, and gave to the Baptist churches a lasting prominence in numbers among the churches of the South.[38]

As Samson's parents *"knew not that it was of the LORD, that he sought an occasion against the Philistines"* (Judges 14:4a), likewise, Whitefield little perceived that God would ultimately use him to disenfranchise the powerful state churches of American Protestantism. Baron Stow further illuminates this amazing twist of fate:

At this period, the Baptist denomination on this continent was exceedingly limited, numbering only thirty-seven churches, and probably less than three thousand members. The preaching of Mr. Whitefield and others who caught from heaven the same hallowed fire, and the great awakening consequent upon their sanctified labors, gave currency to the principles which wrought undesired changes, and conducted to results which were neither anticipated nor desired. Little did those men of God who were such efficient agents in the "New Light Stir," as it was opprobriously called, and who pushed their measures with almost superhuman vigor, amidst a tempest of opposition and obloquy, imagine that they were breaking up the fallow ground of their own ecclesiastical system, and sowing seed from which a sect that was everywhere spoken against, would reap a bountiful harvest.

The converts who received the name of "Separatists," were taught to throw aside tradition, and take the Word of God only as their guide in all matters of religious faith and practice. This was in perfect coincidence with all Baptist teaching, and, as was predicted by the most sagacious among the opposers of the revival, ultimately led thousands, among whom were many ministers, to embrace our views and enter our churches.[39]

As we expected, Armitage confirms that it was the unscriptural practice of sprinkling infants (pedobaptism) that most repulsed the "New Lights":

It was not strange that these converts, finding such opposition or cold welcome in the Congregational Churches, should seek homes elsewhere.

In many cases they formed Churches of their own and were known as Separatists... **These new converts were insensibly and inevitably led nearer to the Baptist position than to that taken by the great body of the Congregational State Churches.** The Churches of the Standing Order were filled with unconverted persons, with many who had grown up in them from infancy, being introduced at that time by christening; and but a small proportion of their members made any claim to a spiritual regeneration. The intuitions of a converted soul recoil from Church associations with those whose only claim to membership in Christ's mystical body is a ceremony performed over an unconscious infant, for the renewed man seeks fellowship with those who, like himself, have exercised faith in Christ's saving merits, and he is likely to take the Scriptures for his guide in seeking his Church home.[40]

Looking back on his converts' deciding to be immersed, a candid George Whitefield acquiesced, **"All my chickens have turned into ducks."**[41]

A PERSONAL INVITATION

As a fitting conclusion to this survey of America's Great Awakening, I believe the Lord would have me extend an invitation to my readers to consider the possibility of a *personal* application of this spiritual subject matter.

The major theme of the revival era centered on our Lord's mandate to Nicodemus, *"Except a man be born again, he cannot see the kingdom of God."* (John 3:3b) At a time when Benjamin Franklin's experiments with electricity were first becoming widely known, Whitefield challenged his friend to investigate this doctrine of the second birth as comprising the *key* to an even greater source of energy. In a letter dated August 17, 1752, he wrote:

> I find that you grow more and more famous in the learned world. As you have made a pretty considerable progress in the mysteries of electricity, I would now humbly recommend to your diligent unprejudiced pursuit and study the mystery of the new-birth. It is a most important, interesting study, and when mastered, will richly answer and repay you for all your pains. One at whose bar we are shortly to appear, hath solemnly declared, that without it, *"we cannot enter the kingdom of heaven."*...My

respects await your whole self, and all enquiring friends, and hoping to see
you yet once more in this land of the dying, I subscribe myself, dear Sir,
  Your very affectionate friend, and obliged servant,
  G.W.[42]

Dear reader, have *you* ever experienced this marvelous new birth? Have
you been born again? Are you saved? If you died today, do you *know* for
sure that you would go to Heaven? If these questions appear confusing, you
are probably a sincere, God-fearing patriot who has yet to hear the Bible's
teaching on how a person gets to Heaven when he dies. This was my own
experience as a young man growing up in the Catholic Church. Like the
benighted inhabitants of that Jesuit settlement in Vincennes, I, too, had been
taught to do *penance* for my own sins. When I was eventually liberated from
Rome by the Gospel preaching of Dr. Randy Carroll, a faithful Baptist
pastor, I gained the same immediate appreciation for the presence of a *real*
man of God as did Mr. Whitefield's converts in Catholic Ireland, of whom
he wrote, "Many of the papists said 'if I would stay, they would leave their
priests.' "[43]

The most important thing you have to learn is that one cannot *earn* his
own way into Heaven by doing more good deeds than bad ones. *"Knowing
that a man is not justified by the works of the law."* (Galatians 2:16a)
Because the true God of the Bible is holy, just and righteous, He demands
complete adherence to His commandments. *"For whosoever shall keep the
whole law, and yet offend in one point, he is guilty of all."* (James 2:10) This
is precisely why Adam and Eve were evicted from the Garden of Eden—for
only *one* offense!

Therefore, the Bible not only declares in Romans 3:23 that, *"all have
sinned and come short of the glory of God,"* but it pronounces the divine
penalty of everlasting judgment on the sinner as well: *"For the wages of sin
is death."* (Romans 6:23a) Because we have a body as well as a soul, the
Bible differentiates between the first death (physical) and the second death
(spiritual): *"All liars, shall have their part in the lake which burneth with
fire and brimstone: which is the second death."* (Revelation 21:8b) When
preaching on the fires of Hell, Whitefield would often break out in sobs:

> You blame me for weeping... but how can I help it when you will not
> weep for yourselves although your immortal souls are on the verge of
> destruction, and for aught I know, you are hearing your last sermon and
> may never more have another opportunity to have Christ offered to you?[44]

The Bible further declares that because God loves us He sent His own Son, Jesus, to die on the cross in our place for the sins that we have committed: *"While we were yet sinners, Christ died for us."* (Romans 5:8b) And after He arose victoriously from the grave, and just before His glorious ascension back into Heaven, He commissioned his first preachers to proclaim to a dying world that anyone could now be saved if he would place his trust in His substitutionary death for him, and not in his own delusion of self-righteousness. *"For whosoever shall call upon the name of the Lord shall be saved."* (Romans 10:13)

This same Gospel message that Mr. Whitefield preached to colonial America has an enduring appeal in the closing days of the twentieth century, as well. Had you attended one of Mr. Whitefield's indoor services in Boston, this is what you would have observed and heard:

> After he had finished his prayer, he knelt for a long time in profound silence; and so powerfully had it affected the most heartless of his audience, that a stillness like that of the tomb pervaded the whole house.
>
> Before he commenced his sermon, long, darkening columns crowded the bright sunny sky of the morning, and swept their dull shadows over the building, in fearful augury of the storm that was approaching. "See that emblem of human life," said he, as he pointed to a flitting shadow. "It passed for a moment, and concealed the brightness of heaven from our view; but it is gone. And where will you be, my hearers, when your lives have passed away like that dark cloud?...Every eye will behold the Judge. With a voice whose call you must abide and answer, He will enquire, whether on earth you strove to enter in at the strait gate; whether you were supremely devoted to God; whether your hearts were absorbed in Him. My blood runs cold when I think how many of you will then seek to enter in, and shall not be able. O, what plea can you make before the Judge of the whole earth?...you must answer, I made myself easy in the world, by flattering myself that all would end well; but I have deceived my own soul, and am lost!
>
> "O false and hollow Christians, of what avail will it be that you have done many things? that you have read much in the sacred Word? that you have made long prayers? that you have attended religious duties, and appeared holy in the eyes of men? What will all this be, if, instead of loving God supremely, you have been supposing you should exalt yourself in heaven by acts really polluted and unholy?
>
> "O sinner! by all your hopes of happiness, I beseech you to repent. Let not the wrath of God be awakened! Let not the fires of eternity be kindled against you! See there!" cried the impassioned preacher, pointing to a flash of lightning, "It is a glance from the angry eye of Jehovah! Hark!" he

continued, raising his finger in a listening attitude, as the thunder broke in a tremendous crash, "it was the voice of the Almighty as He passed by in His anger!"

As the sound died away, Whitefield covered his face with his hands, and fell on his knees, apparently lost in prayer. The storm passed rapidly by, and the sun, bursting forth, threw across the heavens the magnificent arch of peace. Rising and pointing to it, the young preacher cried, "Look upon the rainbow, and praise Him who made it. Very beautiful it is in the brightness thereof. It compasseth the heavens about with glory, and the hands of the Most High have bended it."[45]

Appropriately enough, on the day before he died in Newberryport, Massachusetts, an exhausted Mr. Whitefield entered the fields one more time and conducted his last open-air meeting from the text, *"Examine yourselves, whether ye be in the faith."* (II Corinthians 13:5a) Pollock writes:

> He spoke of men's attempt to win the favour of God by good works and not by faith. George contemplated, as if thinking out loud, the enormity of such effrontery. His mind suddenly kindled and his voice rose and he thundered in tones that reached the edge of the immense crowd: "Works? Works? A man get to heaven by *works*? I would as soon think of climbing to the moon on a rope of sand." After that any weakness seemed engulfed in a mighty power that swept him into an unforgettable sermon in which he proclaimed, once again, the glories of Christ.[46]

My friend, if you are not 100% sure that you would go to Heaven if you died today, you can obtain this assurance if you choose to put your faith in Christ as your personal Saviour. Whitefield knew where he was going when he died, his sermon concluding,

> I have outlived many on earth but they cannot outlive me in heaven. O thought divine! I shall soon be in a world where time, age, pain and sorrow are unknown. My body fails, my spirit expands. How willingly would I live for ever to preach Christ! But I die to be *with him!*[47]

Although Benjamin Franklin heard many of Whitefield's sermons, the man credited with organizing America's first fire department was apparently less concerned with the burning fires of eternity. The Christ-rejecting patriot confessed a decade after Whitefield's departure from "the land of the dying":

> Mr. Whitefield used, indeed, to pray for my conversion, but he never had the satisfaction of believing that his prayers were heard. Ours was a mere civil friendship, sincere on both sides, and lasted to his death.[48]

While super-patriot Samuel Adams not only became a Christian, but nearly entered the ministry after hearing Whitefield preach at Harvard,[49] the theist Franklin chose to illustrate the words of Job, *"Great men are not always wise."* (Job 32:9a)

As this chapter draws to its conclusion, what is **your** response to Mr. Whitefield's scriptural entreaty to *"Examine yourself, whether ye be in the faith"*? If you cannot honestly answer in the affirmative, I would then ask you the following question: would you like to become a **Christian** patriot? You can *"know that ye have eternal life"* (I John 5:13b) by simply calling on Christ to save you. *"For whosoever shall call upon the name of the Lord shall be saved."* (Romans 10:13) On August 25, 1974, I prayed a simple prayer to the Lord along the lines of the written prayer which follows. If you would like to be saved, won't you pray a prayer like this right now?

> Dear Lord, I know that I'm a sinner, and if I died right now I would go to Hell. But I believe that You died for me and were buried and rose again from the grave. Right now, I want You to come into my heart, save me and take me to Heaven when I die. In Jesus' name, Amen.

For this let men revile my name,
No cross I shun, I fear no shame:
All hail reproach, and welcome pain,
Only thy terrors, Lord, restrain.

The love of Christ doth him constrain,
To seek the wand'ring souls of men:
With cries, entreaties, tears, to save,
And snatch them from the gaping grave.

–George Whitefield
December 23, 1742

VIII

Gaols and Grates

> *"Whether it be right in the sight of God to hearken unto you more than unto God, judge ye. For we cannot but speak the things which we have seen and heard."* (Acts 4:19b, 20)

WHENEVER CATHOLICS CEASED to be persecuted in the mother country, discerning colonial leaders would suspicion a potential merger between the Anglican and Roman communions. As early as April, 1764, George Whitefield warned his American friends that the king was up to no good and was, in fact, planning to slip an Anglican bishop into the colonies as a constructive, half-step back to the Vatican. His words to a couple of Portsmouth ministers had an ominous ring to them:

> I cannot in conscience leave the town without acquainting you with a secret. My heart bleeds for America. O poor New England! There is a deep laid plot against both your civil and religious liberties, and they will be lost. Your golden days are at an end. You have nothing but trouble before you. My information comes from the best authority in Great Britain.[1]

Whitefield's concern over Anglican encroachments touches on a second manner in which the devil was attempting to thwart the providential emergence of American sovereignty. While a Catholic presence in and around the colonies posed only an embryonic threat at this time, the intolerant rule of the Episcopalian Church throughout Virginia, Georgia and the Carolinas constituted a hostile impediment to the advancement of New Testament soul liberty. The most striking manifestation of this religious tyranny involved the documented cases of numerous Baptist preachers being arrested and imprisoned for the crime of preaching the Gospel of our Lord Jesus Christ! Yet, a tragedy nearly as sad as the persecution itself is the almost total ignorance of the fact that these events ever occurred in the first place. While it is one thing for the standard, fluff-filled "God and Country" books (*The Light and the Glory*, etc.) to avoid these convicting accounts, it is quite another for the average Baptist to be unaware of his own enriching legacy.

During the early years of Virginia's history, no minister was permitted to preach unless he had received ordination from an Anglican bishop across the sea. Attendance at the Episcopalian church was mandatory with absentees being fined 50 pounds of tobacco. With the ascension of William and Mary following England's Glorious Revolution, this ecclesiastical monopoly was technically dissolved by the Toleration Act of 1689. Dissenting clergy could now apply for a license provided they would ascribe to the Anglican Articles of Religion (excluding articles 34, 35 and 36, with a rewording of 20), denounce the Romish doctrines of transubstantiation and Mariolatry, affirm as abhorrent the Jesuit doctrine of political assassination and swear allegiance to their Majesties, William and Mary.[2]

Under these less-than-ideal conditions, nearly a century of exclusion was ended with the founding of several Baptist churches in Virginia. Some of the earliest on record were the assemblies in Prince George, Surry and Isle of Wight counties established in 1714. Among the others that followed were those in Berkeley County (Mill-creek, 1743); Loudon County (Ketocton, 1751); and Rockingham County (Smith's and Linville's Creek, 1756).[3]

However, it was from a church in another state that a host of preachers came pouring into Virginia proclaiming Baptist doctrines. Shubal Stearns, a native of Boston, was converted under the preaching of George Whitefield and thereafter united with the pro-revival New Light Movement. However, after pastoring a Separatist church for six years, he became convinced from a study of the Scripture that infant baptism was a human institution. Accordingly, he was immersed by Elder Wait Palmer at Tolland, Connecticut, on May 20, 1751, and ordained into the Baptist ministry. Three years later, the Holy Spirit led him southward to the Mill-creek Church where he rendezvoused with his layman brother-in-law, Daniel Marshall, learning to his delight that he, too, had become one of Whitefield's Baptist "ducks." The following year, Stearns led a small company of eight families some two hundred miles to Sandy Creek, in Guilford County, North Carolina. Soon after their arrival on November 22, 1755, the Sandy Creek Baptist Church was constituted with 16 members. Under the anointed leadership of Pastor Stearns, the church quickly grew to a membership of over 600.

From this holy mission station in North Carolina, numerous churches were planted back in the fertile fields of Virginia: Deep River, Abbot's Creek, Little River, Neus River, Black River, Dan River and Lunenburg City, to name but a few. With multitudes of the resultant converts deserting their dead Episcopalian churches, the inevitable backlash of historic persecution brought about the most ignominious chapter in Old Dominion history. Throughout this period, Satan tested both the preachers' resolve and the people's reaction by initiating his opposition through an unrestrained rabble of the baser sort. While a preacher's sermon could be interrupted by the unexpected arrival of a snake or hornets' nest being tossed in through an open window,[4] or the outright smashing to bits of his pulpit and communion table,[5] his baptismal candidates might be scattered in the local creek by a mob of mounted drunks.[6] When one gang violently submerged Reverend David Barrow and a fellow pastor seven times, and then asked him if they "believed," the exasperated but colorful preacher replied, "*I believe* you mean to drown me."[7]

David Thomas, pastor of the church at Broad-run, Fauquier County, was an early target of such irreverent harassment:

> Outrageous mobs and individuals frequently assaulted and disturbed him. Once he was pulled down as he was preaching, and dragged out of doors in a barbarous manner. At another time a malevolent fellow attempted to shoot him, but a bystander wrenched the gun from him, and thereby prevented the execution of his wicked purpose. "The slanders and revilings," says Mr. Edwards, "which he met with, are innumerable; and if we may judge of a man's prevalency against the devil, by the rage of the devil's children, Thomas prevailed like a prince."[8]

A notable trophy of this period was Samuel Harris, a colonel in the Virginia militia and one-time commander of Fort Mayo. Taylor recounts the thrilling roadside encounter of this eighteenth-century Cornelius with the preaching team of siblings Joseph and William Murphy:

> As the people were collecting, Colonel Harris rode up, splendidly attired in his military habit. "What is to be done here, gentlemen?" said

Harris. "Preaching, colonel." "Who is to preach?" "The Murphy boys, sir." "I believe I will stop and hear them." He dismounted. The house was small, and in the corner stood a loom, behind which the colonel seated himself. The Lord's eye was upon him, and the truth became effectual in deepening his convictions. Such was his agony of mind, that at the close of the meeting his sword and other parts of his regimentals were found scattered around him.[9]

Baptized in 1758 by Daniel Marshall, the colonel himself took to preaching the following year. Little writes, "Rough was the treatment which Mr. Harris met with amongst his rude countrymen."[10] On one occasion while he was preaching in a house, an enraged mob smashed down the front door and a violent altercation ensued.[11] Although Colonel Harris would eventually be jailed in Hillsborough, Loudon County, "and kept for some time,"[12] the distinction of being the first Baptist minister to be imprisoned in the state of Virginia for preaching the Gospel fell upon one of his personal converts.

GAOLS

Lewis Craig, a notorious sinner, was awakened under the ministry of Colonel Harris sometime around the year 1765. Having begun his own preaching immediately thereafter, a new church was soon established in Spotsylvania. However, his zeal for Christ drew the unwanted attention of several magistrates who promptly arrested him in 1766, for "keeping unlawful conventicles (meetings) and worshipping God contrary to the law of the land."[13] Although indicted, this first clash with the authorities did not result in his notable incarceration. While the jury for his trial was in recess at a nearby tavern, the defendant showed up and made them all wish they were in another place!

> "Gentlemen I thank you, for your attention to me, when I was about this court yard, in all kind of vanity, folly and vice, you took no notice of me; but when I have forsaken all these vices, and warn men to forsake and repent of their sins, you bring me to the bar as a transgressor,... how is all this!"... The great solemnity of this address filled the hearers with dismay, and Mr. John Waller, one of the jurors, a very wicked man, became so struck, that he never got rest, till he found it in the Lord, and became one of the most successful preachers that was ever in Virginia, and was often times honoured with a prison for his preaching.[14]

His subsequent acquittal and release was short-lived. On June 4, 1768, Pastor Craig and four fellow laborers, one of whom being John Waller (the converted juror from the last trial), were arrested on charges of disturbing the peace. Although it is doubtful that a law ever existed in Virginia that authorized imprisonment for preaching *per se*, the statutes for preserving peace and order were so constructed that men of God were routinely arrested and jailed through means of a peace warrant. The prosecuting attorney addressed the court accordingly: "May it please your worships, these men are great disturbers of the peace, they cannot meet a man upon the road, but they must ram a text of scripture down his throat."[15]

This time the preachers were found guilty on all counts. As the condemned prisoners passed through the streets of Fredericksburg on their way to the Spotsylvania County Jail, their voices suddenly united in song, causing what Dr. Semple said was "an awful appearance" on all who did hear. (Spotsylvania County never jailed another preacher.)

> *Broad is the road that leads to death,*
> *And thousands walk together there;*
> *But wisdom shows a narrow path,*
> *With here and there a traveler.*
>
> *"Deny thyself and take thy cross, "*
> *Is the Redeemer's great command;*
> *Nature must count her gold but dross,*
> *If she would gain this heav'nly land.*
>
> *The fearful soul that tires and faints,*
> *And walks the ways of God no more,*
> *Is but esteemed almost a saint,*
> *And makes his own destruction sure.*
>
> *Lord, let not all my hopes be vain,*
> *Create my heart entirely new,—*
> *Which hypocrites could ne'er attain*
> *Which false apostates never knew.*[16]

Furthermore, these men of God were imprisoned despite an impassioned defense by the famed patriot-lawyer, Patrick Henry. Although the traditional *wording* of Henry's speech is often disputed by historians, the fact of his *presence* at the trial is conceded by many authorities, including W. W. Henry in his *Life of Patrick Henry* (Volume I, page 119). At any rate, not only did Henry make it a point to defend as many Baptist preachers as he could, but He did so at his own expense, often paying whatever fines which may have ensued out of his own pocket.[17] In Semple's *History of the Virginia Baptists*, he gives us the following tribute:

> It was in making these attempts that they were so fortunate as to interest in their behalf, the celebrated Patrick Henry; being always the friend of liberty, he only needed to be informed of their oppression; without hesitation, he stepped forward to their relief. From that time, until their complete emancipation, from the shackles of tyranny, the Baptists found in Patrick Henry, an unwavering friend. May his name descend to posterity with unsullied honor![18]

The patriot who said, "Give me liberty or give me death," and was subsequently elected to *five* terms as Governor of Virginia, was perhaps the most outspoken of his political peers with respect to the *specific* spiritual foundations of these United States:

> It cannot be emphasized too strongly or too often that this great nation was founded, not by religionists, but by Christians; not on religions, but on the Gospel of Jesus Christ. For this very reason peoples of other faiths have been afforded asylum, prosperity, and freedom of worship here.[19]

There are many today who would add insult to injury by their disregard, playing down or outright denying that these events ever occurred. Despite the natural deterioration of many court records, a number of surviving documents bear testimony to this deplorable persecution.

For missing church:

> We present Gawin Corbin, Esquire for willfully absenting himself from Divine Service at his Parish church or chapel for the space of one month. (County Court for Middlesex, Monday, May 27, 1771)[20]

For preaching without a license:

> Augustine Easten appearing according to his Recognizance and it appearing That he had practised [sic] preaching in this County as a Baptist not having a license wch [sic] the Court adjudging to be a breach of good behavior & contrary to law Whereupon it is ordered that he enter into

recognizance for being of good behavior for the space of one year next ensuing himself in the penalty of Fifty Pounds & two Sureties in penalty of Twenty-five pounds each and that he be committed til he do so. (County Court for Chesterfield County, June term, 1772)[21]

For assembling the people:

> David Tinsley being committed charged with having assembled & preached to the people at sundry times & places in this County as a Baptist preacher and the said David acknowledging in Court that he had done so On consideration thereof the Court being of opinion that the same is a breach of the peace & good behavior It is ordered that he give Surety for keeping the peace & being of good behavior for one year next ensuing himself in the penalty of £50 & two Sureties in the penalty of £25 each. (County Court for Chesterfield County, February 4, 1774)[22]

In their camaraderie of affliction, these Virginia Baptists were strengthened by a vicarious appreciation of their first-century forefathers who rejoiced on a daily basis *"that they were counted worthy to suffer shame for his name."* (Acts 5:41b)

When Pastor Joseph Craig of Spotsylvania County climbed a tree in the local swamp to evade a pack of yelping hounds, the pursuing magistrates shook him to the ground as if he were a wild beast.[23] Pastor John Waller was given "not much less than twenty lashes" with a "horse whip" by the sheriff in Caroline County. An eyewitness to the attack testified that "poor Waller was presently in a gore of blood and will carry the scars to his grave."[24]

These holy men were likewise abused in the courtroom as well. After his third arrest for preaching the Gospel, Pastor Jeremiah Moore was flatly told by the judge, "You shall lie in jail till you rot, or obey the law."[25] As our Saviour was compelled to carry His own cross to Calvary, likewise, His servants in colonial Virginia had to suffer the humiliation of renting the very beds in which they were consigned to rot! The Culpeper jail offered "bed and furniture, at five dollars a month."[26] Their cells were often infested with spiders and mice and their meals were seldom much better. Concerning his *month*-long imprisonment with several fellow preachers in the Culpeper jail, Pastor Elijah Craig (not to be confused with Joseph or Lewis Craig) testified that they "were fed on rye bread and water, to the injury of [their] health."[27] (For the record, the word *gaol* as used in the original documents and court records of that day was the designated place of confinement for criminals.

Frequently misspelled *goal*, it was anything *but* the objective point or terminus that men were striving to reach.[28])

The magistrates tried to further unnerve the preachers by assigning them depraved cell mates. This ploy would often backfire, however, with the conversion of many an eighteenth-century Onesimus.[29] In fact, the entire persecution blew up in Satan's face as *"the word of God increased; and the number of the disciples multiplied."* (Acts 6:7a) Between the years 1769 and 1774, the number of Baptist churches in Virginia grew from seven to *fifty-four!*[30] Much of their growth was attributed to the glowing testimonies of the afflicted. Dr. Semple, describing the spirit of four jailed preachers in Middlesex, writes:

> The prison swarmed with fleas; they borrowed a candle of the jailer; and, having sung the praises of that Redeemer, whose cross they bore, and from whose hands they expected a crown in the end; **having returned thanks that it was a prison, and not hell that they were in;** praying for themselves, their friends, their enemies and persecutors, they laid down to sleep.[31]

Six days after his arrival in the Culpeper County Jail, Pastor Nathaniel Saunders received the following letter of encouragement from the previously mentioned David Thomas:

> Dear Brother,—I hear you are put in prison for preaching the Gospel of Jesus Christ. Perhaps you think it hard. But O, what honor the Lord put upon you! I think you may be willing to suffer death now, seeing you are counted worthy to enter a dungeon for your Master's sake. Hold out, my dear brother! Remember your Master—your royal, heavenly, divine Master—was nailed to a cursed tree for us. O, to suffer for Him is glory in the bud! O, let it never be said that a Baptist minister of Virginia ever wronged his conscience to get liberty, not to please God, but himself! O, your imprisonment (which I am satisfied is not from any rash proceedings of your own) is not a punishment, but a glory! "If you suffer with Him you shall also reign with him."
>
> Dear Brother, the bearer is waiting or I should have enlarged. This is only to let you know that I can pray for you with great freedom. Give my kind love to your fellow-prisoner, though I know him not. I hope he is a dear child of God. Pray for me, for I need it. I remain, your brother,
>
> Yours in our dear Lord Jesus,
David Thomas[32]

GRATES

However, the most convicting and sensational facet of this entire period occurred just outside the prison bars themselves! When the preachers could no longer go to the people, *the congregations boldly came to the jails*! The "grates" were the sturdy iron bars that ran perpendicularly or horizontally (or sometimes both ways) across the small windows or openings in the wall of a cell in which the prisoner was being held. Some of the most powerful sermons in the history of the New Testament church were preached through these very grates. As the poet William Cowper wrote, "God moves in a mysterious way His wonders to perform." Dr. Little expounds:

> Who would have thought that stopping these men from preaching from house to house, and shutting them up in a loathsome prison, would be the means of their reaching more people with the Gospel and accomplishing more good than they could possibly have done if they had been at liberty? But it was so ordered of God. "They collected larger congregations, and accomplished more in spreading their views and in winning souls to Christ, than they probably could have done had they been let alone. Their enemies were helping them more than they were hindering them, in promulgating the truth and advancing the kingdom of Christ."[33]

As we darken the cages of our birds when we desire them to sing, these anointed men of God ("jailbirds" in the eyes of some) possessed their own *"songs in the night."* (Job 35:10b) However, not everybody was in a listening mood:

> Their persecutors ordered a drum to be beat under the windows, in order to drown their voices; but no jangle of drums could equal the force and volume of their utterances, as they eloquently proclaimed the gospel of the Son of God. Sanctified lungs overpowered the rattle of dried sheep skin. Above all the hubbub swelled the clear tones of these fearless orators of freedom and truth. The people heard them, and the faithful were strengthened, and scoffers were confounded, convinced and converted.[34]

And as the number of incarcerated pastors at any one jail increased, so did the unwanted pandemonium and publicity at "preaching time." A woman recalls her childhood visits to the Caroline County Jail where her grandfather, Pastor John Young, and a number of other preachers were confined:

> Each preacher was in a room to himself. Each room had one small window, placed so high up in the wall that only a patch of the sky could be seen, nothing on the earth. The congregations of the different ministers learned, each, which was his pastor's window. Once a week John Young's congregation (and I suppose the others, too), would assemble under his window, and run up a flag, to let him know they were there [and] he would preach to them. In this way a great many people were converted. The authorities said, "These heretics make more converts in jail than they do out."[35]

The incensed officials in Chesterfield County were determined to hinder the powerful preaching of Pastor John Weatherford. After failing to discourage their victim by slashing his outstretched hands with a sword, they constructed a massive brick wall nearly 12 feet in height directly outside his cell grate. They even went to the trouble of lining the top of this wall with glass bottles, set in mortar, so as to prevent the more daring listeners from employing the strategic perch. However, the resourceful Weatherford devised a plan to overcome their foolish designs. As in the case at Caroline County,

> A handkerchief was to be raised by the congregation on a pole above the wall, as a signal that the people were ready to hear. His voice being very strong, he could throw it beyond the impediments and convey the words of life and salvation to the listening crowd. Souls were blessed and converted by his preaching. Of those who felt they had experienced the renovating influence of Divine grace, nine wished to follow their Master by being buried in baptism. Elder Christian (Chastain), of Buckingham, came and in the night or perhaps about twilight these persons were buried in baptism.[36]

The six-month stay of Pastor James Ireland in the Culpeper County Jail is the most widely publicized case of ministerial imprisonment in the colonies' history. This may be due to the fact that Ireland is the only one in that long list of persecuted Baptists who left an autobiography. Whereas the conversion of Lewis Craig, Virginia's first imprisoned preacher, has been previously traced to the ministry of Samuel Harris, it is worthy to note that the Colonel's first baptismal candidate was the distinguished James Ireland.[37]

In the fall of that same year (1769), Ireland was arrested at a preaching service during his own closing prayer by two officials who seized him by the collar before he could even open his eyes. When he appeared in court to answer their charge of "preaching without proper credentials," the quorum of 11 magistrates declared that they would have no more of his "vile, pernicious, abhorrible [sic], detestable, abominable, diabolical doctrines" as they "were naucious [sic] to the whole court."[38] The convicted pastor spent his first night of confinement in a cell full of drunks. In the morning, he was informed by the avaricious jailer, a certain Mr. Steward (who was also the local tavern keeper), that any visitors he might receive would have to pay a "fee" of four shillings and eight pence.[39] Apparently, it was going to be a *long* six months.

Because of the immense crowds that were assembling to hear Ireland preach through the grates, a number of plots were set in motion against him. A bomb was planted in his cell which "went off with a considerable noise," but the preacher was miraculously spared, testifying, "I was singing a hymn at the time the explosion went off, and continued singing until I finished it."[40] On another occasion, his captors attempted to smother him by burning pods of Indian peppers filled with brimstone near the bottom of his cell door. Stating that the "whole jail would be filled with the killing smoke," Ireland recounted that the threatening situation would "oblige me to go to cracks, and put my mouth to them in order to prevent suffocation."[41] A scheme between the jailer and a certain doctor to poison the preacher also met with failure.[42] (Three years later, another attempt to poison Ireland at his home left one of his children dead.[43]) Despite these many hardships, the man of God testified:

> My prison then was a place in which I enjoyed much of the divine presence; a day seldom passed without some signal token and manifestation of the divine goodness towards me, which generally led me to subscribe my letters, to whom I wrote them, in these words, "From my Palace in Culpeper."[44]

At times, this divine presence was manifested through an unmistakable act of vengeance upon Ireland's tormentors. With reference to the miscreant who traveled 12 miles to retrieve the gunpowder for the failed bombing attempt, he wrote:

> He with other two young men, went to the back woods to spend some time in hunting. As the three lay by the fire, with their feet towards it, there came up a mad wolfe [sic], and although my persecutor lay in the middle, singled him out from the other two, bit him in the nose, of which bite he

died in the most wretched situation of the hydrophobia, or canine madness.[45]

While some of his enemies were laid low, others were brought under deep conviction. After doing everything to disrupt Ireland's services, from having horses ridden at a gallop over those in attendance,[46] to the securing of vile persons who "made their water in his face"[47] while he was preaching, the exasperated jailor succumbed to the kindness of his captive. Ireland writing:

> He, with a number of his accomplices, were at the jail window going on with their abusive language, when he applied to one of his companions for ten shillings, as he wanted some more necessaries against court for the tavern. He could not obtain that small sum from any of them, although they were generally applied to. I stepped to the window with the money in my hand, and addressed him thus, "Mr. Steward, I have heard you applying to your friends for ten shillings, and although unapplied to, I rest in your honesty, here it is, if you will accept of it, and at any time hereafter when it suits you to return it, you may do so." He accepted of it immediately, and struck with apparent astonishment and confusion, he made a kind of bow and retired.
>
> I perfectly gained him over to be my friend that instant, neither would he suffer any person to throw out a word of insult against me from that time, without his resenting it. He and his companion would repeatedly... come in and visit me, at which times we often spent many hours together in friendly conversation.[48]

However, the greatest "manifestation of the divine goodness" toward Ireland developed into a classic case of poetic justice at its best. V. M. Fleming relates "the rest of the story":

> Near Culpeper, there lived a man named Arnold who was the head of this persecution. He had a daughter named Amy, an attractive child of 12 or 14 years. The time we refer to was the time Mr. Ireland, a Baptist preacher, was confined in the Culpeper jail, put there by Arnold. In spite of all commands to the contrary he spoke through the gratings of the jail windows. One morning Amy Arnold asked her father to permit her to go to Culpeper two miles off to hear this wonderful man of God and an orator as well. Her father denounced her desire to go and forbade it, but the intercession of her mother prevailed. She started off with some other neighbors, who lived about her, all these girls going bare-footed, until they had crossed the creek just beyond Culpeper, where they stopped to put on

their shoes and stockings. When they neared the jail they heard the singing. Boys and girls in evidence everywhere, in the trees and on house-tops. As they approached the jail, they were singing that old time hymn, "As we journey, let us sing, Praises to our Heavenly King."

When the preaching began some word of the Spirit sped its way to Amy Arnold's heart and she was converted. It is useless to go into the scene which transpired on her return home, they were severe indeed, as one can imagine. Her faith, however, stood firm, and she was baptized in the Baptist faith. After growing to womanhood, she moved with some of her friends to Charleston, S.C., where she married a man named Hamilton. By this marriage there were many descendents, all Baptists and men of distinction through whom to a large extent was the Baptist influence in the South spread. One of whom was Judge Haralson, who ten or fifteen years ago was President of the Southern Baptist Convention, than whom there was no man distinguished more in the South, and through whose influence the growth of the Baptist church was greatly enlarged.[49]

No doubt there are numerous Monday-morning quarterbacks from the ranks of today's cream-puff brand of professing born-again Christians who would say, "So what was (or is) the big deal about a license anyhow?" Dr. George W. Beale explains why these men were willing to be singled out from their clerical contemporaries as "deserving the pain and ignominy of arrests, bonds, imprisonments, and stripes":

> The right to preach the Gospel was inalienable and divine, quite beyond the pale of the court's jurisdiction or government control. Therefore, whilst others took the prescribed oaths, subscribed to the necessary articles, and secured licenses from the court for certain preaching-places, many Baptist preachers proceeded to preach, as opportunities offered, without consulting the general court and regardless of legal sanction. It was this bold and intrepid action that aroused against them the resentment of the clergymen, the rage of the magistrates, and the terror of the courts. It was this that led the fathers of our faith to suffer the stings of the cruel lash, and to preach to their fellow-men through the grated windows of our county jails.[50]

As these faithful men of God continued to choose "Caesar's jail" over a violated conscience (Matthew 22:21), Satan had to contend with a growing number of disturbed onlookers. With his options limited to scorn and ridicule, the following notice, which appeared in the *Virginia Gazette* of October 31, 1771, was a typical attempt to discredit their convicting testimony:

A RECIPE TO MAKE AN ANABAPTIST
PREACHER IN TWO DAYS TIME

Take the Herbs of Hypocrisy and Ambition, of each an Handful, of the Spirit of Pride two Drams, of the Seed of Dissention and Discord one Ounce, of the Flower of Formality three Scruples, of the Roots of Stubbornness and Obstinacy four Pounds; and bruise them altogether in the Mortar of Vain-Glory, with the Pestle of Contradiction, putting amongst them one Pint of the Spirit of Self-conceitedness. When it is luke-warm let the Dissenting Brother take two or three Spoonfuls of it, Morning and Evening before Exercise; and whilst his Mouth is full of the Elestuary he will make a wry Face, wink with his Eyes, and squeeze out some Tears of Dissimulation. Then let him speak as the Spirit of Giddiness gives him Utterance. This will make the Schismatick endeavor to maintain his Doctrine, wound the Church, delude the People, justify their Proceedings of Illusions, forment Rebellion, and call it by the Name of Liberty of Conscience.[51]

Although such lampoonery was enjoyed by some, those to whom the future liberties of an emerging nation were entrusted grew more than a little disturbed at the deplorable proceedings. In Rives' *Life and Times of James Madison*, 1866, Second Edition, Volume I, page 43, the following excerpt from a letter dated January 24, 1774, written by the future two-term president of the United States to a friend, William Bradford, Jr., in Philadelphia, reveals his disgust with religious persecution, in general, and the jailing of five or six Baptist preachers in the adjacent county of Culpeper, in particular:

I want again to breathe your free air. I expect it will mend my constitution and confirm my principles. I have, indeed, as good an atmosphere at home as the climate will allow, but have nothing to brag of as to the state and liberty of my country. Poverty and luxury prevail among all sorts; pride, ignorance, and knavery among the priesthood; and, vice and wickedness among the laity. This is bad enough; but it is not the worst I have to tell you. **That diabolical, hell-conceived principle of persecution rages among some;** and, to their eternal infamy, the clergy can furnish their quota of imps for such purposes. There are, at present in the adjacent county not less than five or six well-meaning men in close jail for publishing their religious sentiments, which, in the main, are very orthodox. I have neither patience to hear, talk, or think of anything relative to this matter; for I have squabbled and scolded, abused and ridiculed so long about it, to little purpose, that I am without common patience. So I must beg you to pity me, and pray for liberty of conscience to all.[52]

Not only did James Madison side with the Baptists in his private correspondence but, like his colleague, Patrick Henry, publicly defended them in courts throughout Virginia. In Johnson's *New Universal Encyclopedia* (1876), Volume III, page 201, we read that after Madison graduated from the College of New Jersey (Princeton University) in 1771, he returned to his home in Orange County, Virginia, where

> His attention was then absorbed by the impending struggle for independence, with which was closely connected in Virginia a local controversy on the subject of religious toleration. The Church of England was the established state religion in the Old Dominion, and other denominations labored under serious disabilities, the enforcement of which was rightly or wrongly characterized by them as persecution. Madison took a prominent stand in behalf of the removal of all disabilities, *repeatedly appearing in the court of his own county to defend the Baptist nonconformists.*[53]

As stated in an earlier chapter, Thomas Jefferson was also a careful student of Baptist church polity. Although Jefferson's own religious sentiments fluctuated between deism and theism, his sister[54] and his favorite aunt[55] were Baptists. Like Madison and Henry, he was deeply moved by the degree of suffering endured by these Baptist preachers. Observing such men as Pastor John Weatherford, who willingly entered the gaol despite a dependent family of 15 children, 12 of whom were girls,[56] made Jefferson even more willing to "check out" the Baptist church. Armitage, citing Curtis:

> There was a small Baptist Church which held its monthly meetings for business at a short distance from Mr. Jefferson's house, eight or ten years before the American Revolution. Mr. Jefferson attended these meetings for several months in succession. The pastor on one occasion asked him how he was pleased with their Church government. Mr. Jefferson replied, that it struck him with great force and had interested him much, **that he considered it the only form of true democracy then existing in the world, and had concluded that it would be the best plan of government for the American colonies.** This was several years before the Declaration of Independence.[57]

That so many Baptists were known to be suffering over matters of conscience was beginning to have a telling effect upon the conscience of the colony itself. (The Culpeper gaol itself would eventually be converted into a Baptist church.) Before the era of ministerial imprisonment, Old Dominion was the outstanding Loyalist settlement. The Puritans in Massachusetts would have no dealings with their pro-Stuart cousins to the south. For these reasons, humanistic historians are at a loss to explain how Virginia came to be *first* in rank among the revolting colonies. In his *Notes on Virginia,* Thomas Jefferson shares a statistic that is quite familiar to the *Christian* historian. As a backlash to Virginia's religious intolerance, two-thirds of her population had become dissenters (Baptists, Quakers and Presbyterians) by the time of the Revolution.[58] Armitage expands on the cause and significance of this political paradox:

> By the intolerable sufferings and indefatigable labors of the Baptist preachers, they had cherished and diffused their own love of liberty throughout the whole colony for half a century. Their memorial to the Convention had deeper root than the feeling of the hour; it was grounded in those evangelical convictions which were shared by a majority of the people of Virginia. **That Virginia cast her Royalist antecedents aside and loyally espoused the cause of the revolution was largely due to the fact that Baptist suffering, preaching and democratic practice had educated her people for the issue.** Thomas Jefferson, possibly an advanced Unitarian; Patrick Henry, a devout Presbyterian; and James Madison, thought to be a liberal Episcopalian, felt the throb of the public heart, saw that its patriotism was founded upon religious conviction, and, like wise men, instead of stemming the strong tide they gave it their leadership, under which it swept on, notwithstanding the opposition of English rectors and the entangling traditions of a grinding hierarchy.[59]

Thus we are confronted, once again, with the rarely discussed and little-known historical reality of America's *Baptistic* foundations. However, the full force of this premise will be felt in the following chapter.

"And when they had laid many stripes upon them, they cast them into prison, charging the jailor to keep them safely: Who, having received such a charge, thrust them into the inner prison, and made their feet fast in the stocks. And at midnight Paul and Silas prayed, and sang praises unto God: and the prisoners heard them." (Acts 16:23-25)

IX

Free Indeed!

> *"If the Son therefore shall make you free, ye shall be free indeed."* (John 8:36)

W HILE GATHERING VARIOUS reference materials for this book, I happened upon a political catalog espousing a strongly conservative agenda. The April, 1995, edition of *Laissez Faire Books* sported an impressive heading across the top of its front cover: "The World's Largest Selection of Books on Liberty—Readers in 90 Countries." The cover's feature promotion stated: "Historian George Smith—Great champions, enemies and issues of American liberty—page 5." A sober scene depicting several of the Founding Fathers accentuated this advertisement for Smith's lectures on audiotape.

There were many patriotic, right-wing selections contained in this publication: *Liberty vs. the Welfare State; What Has the Government Done to Our Money?, Challenging the Civil Rights Establishment, Capitalism and the Individual, Environmentalist: Threat to Freedom, The Real Anita Hill,* etc. The authors read like a "Who's Who" of traditional capitalists: Adam Smith, Milton Friedman, Ludwig von Mises, F. A. Hayek, Henry Hazlitt and others.

However, it wasn't until I reviewed the August issue of *Laissez Faire* that the true condition of America became sadly apparent. On page 30 of this openly anti-left periodical, the following review was given for a book entitled *Atheism: The Case Against God*:

A comprehensive analysis and refutation of the arguments made over the centuries to prove the existence of a god. Insists that reason, not faith, should be man's guide in all matters.[1]

After noting that the author was none other than George Smith, the so-called authority on American liberty (recommended in the April issue), I called the vice president of *Laissez Faire Books* for an explanation. When I pointed out the historical inconsistency between atheism and America's supernatural origins, I was politely informed that a significant number of their readers would disagree with my "opinion."

Interestingly, another historian recommended by *Laissez Faire Books* (and a Frenchman, at that) left us his own eyewitness assessment of the period in question. Less than a decade after Thomas Jefferson's death, Alex de Tocqueville confirmed in his classic, *Democracy in America*:

> Upon my arrival in the United States the religious aspect of the country was the first thing that struck my attention; and the longer I stayed there, the more I perceived the great political consequences resulting from this new state of things. In France I had almost always seen the spirit of religion and the spirit of freedom marching in opposite directions. But in America I found they were intimately united and that they reigned in common over the same country.
>
> **Religion in America...must be regarded as the foremost of the political institutions of that country;** for it does not impart a taste for freedom, it facilitates the use of it. Indeed, it is in this same point of view that the inhabitants of the United States themselves look upon religious belief....**In the United States the sovereign authority is religious...there is no country in the world where the Christian religion retains a greater influence over the souls of men than in America,** and there can be no greater proof of its utility and of its conformity to human nature than that its influence is powerfully felt over the most enlightened and free nation of the earth.[2]

The *Laissez Faire* vice president further informed me that in the spirit of true libertarian thinking, they were also willing to promote the rights of pornographers through such books as *Defending Pornography* by Nadine Strossen.[3] And then there is the suggestive *Ain't Nobody's Business if You Do* by Peter McWilliams, subtitled *The Absurdity of Consensual Crimes in a Free Society*. The "Father of Our Country" would have strongly disagreed with this distorted view of freedom. Believing in that old maxim, "Your right to swing your fist ends where my nose begins," Washington's first official directive as Commander in Chief of the Continental Army, dated July 4, 1775, prohibited his men, among other things, from "profane cursing, swearing, and drunkenness."[4]

America is surely in a mess when a growing number of her political conservatives are apparently unashamed to promote the views of atheists and perverts. (For the record, *Laissez Faire Books* just happens to be located in *San Francisco*.) Notwithstanding the "religious" trappings of charismatics like Pat Robertson and Chuck Colson, the average conservative ("ditto head") is now more concerned with recouping lost revenues from Big Brother than in regaining the forfeited blessings of a Heavenly Father! No longer in tune with the Holy Bible, today's money-hungry Americans would rather read *The Citizen's Guide to Fighting Government* by Symms and Grupp or *Our Enemy, the State* by Grunder.

However, when attempting to answer the question, "What's really wrong with America?" a spiritual problem more subtle than materialistic citizens forgetting their divine benefactor is often overlooked by the so-called Religious Right. Whereas the typical humanist is woefully ignorant of America's *Christian* foundation, the typical Christian is himself oblivious of the more significant role played by his *Baptist* brethren in the actual securing of our precious freedoms. The purpose of our present chapter is to review the patriotic contributions of revived Protestants (New Lights) but also, more particularly, those made by "the sect that is everywhere spoken against."

The fact that America's brief but extraordinary history has occurred within the last 200 years of man's 6,000-year earthly pilgrimage can be explained only by the truth that *"one day is with the Lord as a thousand years, and a thousand years as one day."* (II Peter 3:8b) Forty centuries after our first parents were promised a Redeemer, the lovely Lord Jesus was born in Bethlehem's manger (not to be confused with Julia Ward Howe's "beauty of the lilies"). With His death, burial and resurrection for man's sin accomplished, the ascending Saviour commissioned that the glad tidings be proclaimed throughout the whole earth. However, as the convicted Gadarenes had *"besought him that he would depart out of their coasts"* (Matthew 8:34b), the entire Roman empire eventually did the same to the early Christians through the corrupted merger of church and state by Constantine in 312 A.D.

Following a leadership vacuum created by the relocation of the imperial residence to Constantinople, Leo I became the world's first authentic "pope" in 440 A.D. by having forcefully secured universal submission to his personal authority. By the reign of Pope Gregory in 590 A.D., the stage was set for rebellious mankind to enter into the "blessings" of *Satan's* Millennial Kingdom. Throughout the ensuing ten centuries (appropriately called the "Dark Ages"), Europe's laity wallowed in filth, ignorance, famine, despair, pestilence and barbarism for having preferred a "papal toe" to a "nail-scarred foot."

Finally, within a century and a half of the dramatic, west-bound enlargement of Japheth, the Lord was ready to show a sin-sick world what the Psalmist meant by, *"Blessed is the nation whose God is the LORD."* (Psalm 33:12a) After 5,780 years of stagnant, dreary subsistence (Job 14:1), two solitary acts occurred within the brief period of 14 years that would dramatically alter the remaining two centuries of human existence on planet Earth. A mere 180 years after Thomas Jefferson's remark about traveling only 3 mph between Richmond and New York, commercial airliners were crossing the 3,600-mile-wide Atlantic in 3 hours flat! With Daniel's end-day prophecy of men running *"to and fro"* (Daniel 12:4b) lying dormant for multiplied hundreds of years, Israeli pilots can now fly American-made fighters the entire length of the prophet's ancient homeland in an incredible 90 seconds!

The 14-year watershed to which I refer was the period of 1776–1790, and the two noteworthy events were the winning of our physical freedom via the American Revolution and the more significant securing of "soul liberty" through the First Amendment of the Bill of Rights. With the Pope as their common enemy, a predominantly *Protestant* body of Founding Fathers supplied the political leadership for the former while a "chain gang" of *Baptist* preachers successfully lobbied for the latter.

From the vantage point of hindsight, one can see that America had been destined to become the world's first truly *Christian* nation, not in an eventual *preponderance of numbers* (for the Saviour had warned in Matthew 7:14d, *"few there be that find it"*), but rather in a *permeation of righteousness.* With the combined spirituality of persecuted Baptists and revived Protestants (New Light Congregationalists and New Side Presbyterians) resting upon a foundation of several generations composed of unprecedented percentages of saved people (and all having issued from Plymouth Colony), **a political climate was created that would afford the local, New Testament church its first official haven of unmolested opportunity.**

This high concentration of salt ensured that America's earliest leaders would exhibit a great reverence for God, the Bible and organized religion in general, regardless of their own theological positions. The few who did hold unorthodox views have often been claimed and exploited by the modern, God-hating humanist who would seek to undermine America's Christian heritage. Thomas Jefferson is a classic case in point. Yet, whatever personal hang-ups these men may have had because of intellectual pride, monetary pursuits, moral impurities, etc., they were not ashamed to publicly acknowledge a need for and fear of their Almighty Creator. For instance, on the Jefferson Memorial in Washington, D.C., are the following remarks of the third president taken from his *Notes on the State of Virginia:*

> God who gave us life gave us liberty. And can the liberties of a nation be thought secure when we have removed their only firm basis, a conviction in the minds of the people that these liberties are of the Gift of God? That they are not to be violated but with His wrath? **Indeed, I tremble for my country when I reflect that God is just;** that His justice cannot sleep forever.[5]

If men such as Thomas Jefferson died without Christ, they went to Hell, *period!* On the other hand, as agents of Providence, they were at worst no different than the Gentile centurion who was acclaimed by his Jewish beneficiaries in Capernaum as being worthy, *"For he loveth our nation, and he hath built us a synagogue."* (Luke 7:5)

Furthermore, although possessing a sinful nature like all men, our Founding Fathers exhibited a work ethic and personal integrity unparalleled by the professional politicians of our day. When John Quincy Adams was only *14* years old, Congress appointed him secretary to the ambassador at the Russian court of Catherine the Great.[6] When John Jay was the same age, one of the many entrance requirements he had to fulfill when applying for admission to King's College in New York was to translate the first ten chapters of the Gospel of John from Greek into Latin.[7] God in His mercy had surrounded His exhausted church with an army of disciplined defenders. Rising at dawn to study 15 hours a day, Thomas Jefferson exemplified the spirit of a self-controlled generation which would later be called upon to hold their fire 'til they could see the whites of their enemies' eyes. On the definition of a true manly attitude he said, "Few things will disturb him at all; nothing will disturb him much."[8]

BOSTON MASSACRE

One of the more striking examples of American character was occasioned by the infamous *Boston Massacre* of March 5, 1770. On that snowy evening, Captain Thomas Preston and a squad of British redcoats were confronted by an angry mob of patriots who were fed up with the growing English presence in their city. After chunks of ice were thrown and insults exchanged, a soldier was knocked to the ground. In the ensuing melee, five Americans were killed. Amid inflammatory cries for vengeance, Preston and his men were arraigned before a Massachusetts court. Claiming that they had acted in self-defense, the accused entered a plea of not guilty. While Sam Adams kept the city stirred to a frenzy, the lead attorney for the unfortunate defendants turned out to be none other than Sam's cousin, John Adams. With the assistance of Josiah Quincy, Jr., another patriot spokesman, Preston was acquitted, as were most of his men. (Six were declared not guilty, while two were convicted of manslaughter but let off with light sentences.) The liberal historian who would lump the French and American "revolutions" together cannot reconcile these "not guiltys" with, "off with his head!" Evans comments on this exceptional display of moral integrity:

> That incident tells us much about the American Revolution, the leaders who nursed it into being, and the people who would thereby gain their independence. It is noteworthy that Adams and Quincy would defend the soldiers at the height of an emotional outcry against the British—an outcry to which they were intensely sympathetic. Even more so is that a Massachusetts jury could see its way to an acquittal, however sharp the lawyers. That says something about the average American of the day, and prevailing notions of law and justice. (So does the fact that Adams, weeks after having accepted the soldiers as his clients, was elected to the colonial assembly, receiving almost 80 percent of the ballots cast.)[9]

Six months after this historic riot, Evangelist George Whitefield rode into Boston to spread encouragement and cheer for the last time. In what would become the final letter of his ministry, Whitefield later wrote to an English associate, Robert Keen, from Portsmouth, New Hampshire, on September 23:

> Poor *New England* is much to be pitied. *Boston* people most of all. How falsely misrepresented! What a mercy that our *Christian charter* cannot be dissolved.[10]

Exactly one week after expressing these pro-American sentiments, Whitefield was called to his Heavenly reward from the parsonage of the Presbyterian church of Newburyport, Massachusetts. Appropriately, the Englishman who had singlehandedly united practically the entire Eastern seaboard was laid to rest in his beloved America, being entombed (by personal request) under the pulpit of the Newburyport church. His passing was reported in the entire colonial press.

A PATRIOTIC CLERGY

As Whitefield's body was about to be lowered into the burial vault, Reverend Jedediah Jewet charged the attending ministers that they should "endeavour to follow his blessed example."[11] A revived American clergy would take this challenge to heart by providing the leadership requisite throughout the ensuing years of emotional and ideological turbulence.

Not only did these ministers help the colonists through their initial identity crisis, but they also inspired the beleaguered Continental Army to their ultimate victory at Yorktown. While America's debt-ridden "mother" continued her inflammatory maneuvers, the pulpits of the land were kindling a flame of their own with an even greater intensity. J. T. Headley enlightens us accordingly:

> It must be remembered that newspapers at that day were a novelty, and ideas were not so easily disseminated as now. The pulpit, therefore, was the most direct and effectual way of reaching the masses.[12]

With consummate idiots like Benny Hinn and Paul Crouch making a mockery of the highest calling, the average American doesn't have the foggiest idea of the respect once afforded the preachers of our nation. Noting that "Clergymen were treated with the kind of reverential regard that Americans refused to give kings and Anglican bishops," James Adams cites nineteenth-century historian William Sprague's description of the "almost electrifying effect the entrance of the minister and his family into the meetinghouse had on the congregation"[13] as follows:

> The whole space before the meeting-house was filled with a waiting, respectful, and expecting multitude. At the moment of the service, the pastor issued from his mansion with Bible and manuscript sermon under his arm, with his wife leaning on one arm, flanked by a negro man on his

side, as his wife was by her negro woman, the little negroes being distributed, according to their sex, by the side of their respective parents. Then followed every other member of the family, according to age and rank, making often, with family visitants, somewhat of a formidable procession.

As soon as it appeared, the congregation, as if moved by one spirit, began to move towards the door of the church; and, before the procession reached it, all were in their places. As soon as the pastor entered the church the whole congregation rose, and stood until the pastor was in the pulpit and his family were seated—until which was done, the whole assembly continued standing. At the close of the service, the congregation stood until he and his family had left the church, before any one moved toward the door. Forenoon and afternoon the same course of proceeding was had, expressive of the reverential relation in which the people acknowledged that they stood toward their clergyman.[14]

Although commanding the respect of his office (Romans 11:13), this man did not expect anyone to kiss his big toe. The reader will also note the presence of two other non-Catholic clerical distinctions—a *Bible* under one arm and a *wife* on the other!

Headley further states that in addition to these hundreds of weekly Sunday messages, an extremely influential "State of the Union" sermon was delivered in most colonies on an annual basis:

There was one way in which the clergy of New England acted directly and systematically on the popular judgment and heart, in producing and sustaining the revolution which, it seems a little strange, should have escaped the attention of those historians, who have investigated so carefully the means by which it was brought about. I refer to the annual "election sermon," as it was called, that was preached before the Governor and House of Representatives, especially in Massachusetts, at the election of His Majesty's Council.

These sermons were as much a part of the stately and imposing ceremonies as the election itself. The ablest divines in the Colony were invited to deliver them—not as a mere compliment to religion, nor were they listened to simply with that quiet decorum and respectful attention, which is accorded in ordinary worship, but with the deep interest of those seeking light and instruction. The preachers did not confine themselves to a dissertation on doctrinal truths nor mere exhortation to godly behavior. They grappled with the great question of the rights of man, and especially the rights of the colonists in their controversy with the mother country.[15]

Headley also points out that their messages were not the kind of "sermonettes for Christianettes" that Billy Graham would preach to Bill and Hillary Clinton, but rather a "no-holds-barred, in-your-face ultimatum" that formulated colonial thought in the main:

> The profound thought and unanswerable arguments, found in these sermons, show that the clergy were not a whit behind the ablest statesmen of the day in their knowledge of the great science of human government. In reading them one gets at the true pulse of the people, and can trace the steady progress of the public sentiment. They are like the hands of a clock that, at regular intervals, tell the time of day. The publication of these sermons in a pamphlet form was a part of the regular proceedings of the assembly, and being scattered abroad over the land, clothed with the double sanction of their high authors and the endorsement of the legislature, became the text books of human rights in every parish. They were regarded as the political pamphlets of the day. Thus the thorough indoctrination of the people into the duties and powers of government, the reciprocal obligations resting on them and the mother country were reduced to a system.[16]

One can appreciate Headley's likening of these election-year sermons with the hands on a clock by comparing the texts for 1770 and 1774 respectively. In the first instance, Reverend Samuel Cook[17] of the Second Church of Cambridge chose II Samuel 23:3 and 4 as his text: *"He that ruleth over men must be just, ruling in the fear of God. And he shall be as the light of the morning, when the sun riseth, even a morning without clouds; as the tender grass springing out of the earth by clear shining after rain."*

Things were obviously heating up a bit by the time Reverend Gad Hitchcock of Pembroke[18] preached on May 25, 1774, from Proverbs 29:2: *"When the righteous are in authority, the people rejoice: but when the wicked beareth rule, the people mourn."*

With the Boston Tea Party of the previous autumn and the expected British reprisals on everyone's mind, Reverend Hitchcock blasted His Majesty's Council, Governor Hutchinson and all. His concluding remarks were as follows:

> Our danger is not visionary but real; our contention is not about trifles, but about liberty and property, and not ours only, but those of posterity to the latest generation.
>
> If I am mistaken in supposing plans are formed and executing, subversive of our natural and chartered rights and privileges, and

incompatible with every idea of liberty, *all America is mistaken with me.*
Our continued complaints, our repeated humble, but fruitless, unregarded
petitions and remonstrances, and, if I may be allowed the sacred allusion,
our groanings that can not be uttered, are at once indications of our
sufferings, and the feeling sense we have of them.

Let the Governor in his chair of state hear it, we not only mourn, but
with groanings that can not be uttered, and all because *the wicked rule.*
The castle can not shelter him from that scorching thunderbolt. Families
are divided, brother is arrayed against brother, friend against friend.
Society is cut from its mooring, and hate and consternation reign on every
side, and all because *the wicked bear rule.* King George may say the evils
that produce this state of things are imaginary, but I tell you and I tell the
tyrant to his face, it is because *the wicked bear rule.*[19]

This was the last sermon Thomas Hutchinson ever heard in America.
Having been formally recalled by Parliament, he boarded the *Minerva* on
June 1, for his ignoble return to England. As the ex-governor sailed out of
Boston, the harbor closed ominously behind him with the implementation of
the notorious Port Act that same day, diverting all commercial shipping to
the "new" customs office at Portsmouth. Lieutenant General Thomas Gage
was now in charge and by mid-June, an additional 4,000 British redcoats
were on hand to assist him. The handwriting was now on the wall.

Consequently, the First Continental Congress met in Philadelphia from
September 5 through October 26, 1774, and was appropriately opened with
a Scripture reading from Psalm 35: *"Plead my cause, O LORD, with them
that strive with me: fight against them that fight against me. Take hold of
shield and buckler, and stand up for mine help. Draw out also the spear,
and stop the way against them that persecute me: say unto my soul, I am thy
salvation."* (Psalm 35:1-3) With the reading concluded, the honorable
members of Congress knelt with the presiding minister who then led the
august assembly in prayer. Having gotten down to business, it was
determined after seven exhausting weeks that a petition of colonial
grievances, backed by a threat of embargo, should be sent to George III with
dispatch. The petition would be all but ignored.

Virginia's Revolutionary Convention met at St. John's Church in
Richmond on March 20, 1775, to ratify the recommendations of the
Philadelphia assemblage. While the majority was complacent with these
latest attempts at appeasement, Patrick Henry changed all of this by
prevailing upon their very souls. With men like George Washington and

Thomas Jefferson sitting on the edges of their pews, Henry moved that the Virginia militia be prepared to defend the colony in case of war. Unknown to most of his listeners, Henry had been given his own unique burden to bear—one which provided him with a deeper insight into the approaching British tyranny. While this noble Christian patriot warned that the redcoats had been "sent over to find and rivet upon us those **chains** which the British Ministry has been so long forging,"[20] his own beloved wife Sarah, the mother of his six children, was herself bound at that very moment in a straitjacket, having threatened suicide repeatedly due to mental insanity. Sarah Henry would be dead in less than a year. Langguth transports us to a pew of our own to catch the dramatic conclusion:

> Henry had begun calmly, but as his voice rose, tendons in his neck were standing out white and rigid. He said that if the colonists wished to be free, they must fight. "I repeat, sir, we must fight! An appeal to arms and to the God of Hosts is all that is left to us. They tell us, sir, that we are weak—unable to cope with so formidable an adversary. But when shall we be stronger? Will it be next week, or next year? Will it be when we are totally disarmed, and when a British guard shall be stationed in every house?" They were not weak, Henry said. "Three millions of people, armed in the holy cause of liberty, and in such a country as that which we possess, are invincible to any force which our enemy can send against us." Besides that, they had no choice. "The war is inevitable. And let it come! I repeat, sir: Let it come!"
>
> As Patrick Henry turned his eyes around the church, men leaned forward in their seats. "Gentlemen may cry peace, peace—but there is no peace. The war is actually begun! The next gale that sweeps from the north will bring to our ears the clash of resounding arms! Our brethren are already in the field! Why should we idle here? What is it that gentlemen wish? What would they have?"
>
> Patrick Henry's shoulders sank. He crossed his wrists as though he were the one in a straitjacket. "Is life so dear," he asked, "or peace so sweet, as to be purchased at the price of chains and slavery?" He paused, raised his eyes and lifted up his hands, still held together. "Forbid it, Almighty God!" Henry turned to stare at the men who opposed him. Slowly, he bowed his body down. "I know not what course others may take." He rose and straightened to his full height, and his next words came from between clenched teeth: "But as for me, give me liberty—" He paused to let the word die away. His left hand fell to his side. His right hand formed a fist as though he held a dagger, and he struck that fist to his heart. "—or give me death."
>
> There was no applause, only silence.[21]

LEXINGTON & CONCORD

It took only 30 days for Henry's spiritual premonition to be confirmed. At approximately 1:00 a.m. on the nineteenth of April, a loud knock was heard on the door of a country parsonage. As the door swung open, Paul Revere strode into the presence of Sam Adams, John Hancock and Reverend Jonas Clark, pastor of the Congregational Church at Lexington, Massachusetts. His report of 700 approaching redcoats was met with excited ambivalence. After Revere rode off into the history books (as well as into the arms of his British captors), a council of war was hurriedly convened. The responsibility for calling out the militia lay with Hancock, who was the chairman of the Committee of Safety. The question of the hour was whether or not the people would fight. Would these humble farmers and mill hands dare resist the greatest army of professional soldiers in the world?

Reverend Clark assured his guests that he was well acquainted with the state of his flock. They would not only fight, but they would also be willing to lay down their lives for the cause of liberty. This confidence stemmed from his faithful pulpit ministry. In a recounting of Clark's pastoral patriotism, Headley states: "Earnestly, yet without passion, he discussed from the pulpit the great questions at issue, and that powerful voice thundered forth the principles of personal, civil, and religious liberty, and the right of resistance, in tones as earnest and effective as it had the doctrine of salvation by the cross."[22]

Hancock was convinced. At approximately 2:00 a.m., the church bells started ringing. As the sleepy-eyed Minutemen began assembling on the church green, two 16-year-old lads played an accompaniment on the fife and drum. However, after waiting over an hour, the 45-year-old militia commander, Captain John Parker, ordered his men to disband, but to remain on alert. Suddenly, at about 4:30 a.m., the bells began to clang again; this time, the enemies' presence was certain. As the approaching columns of seasoned marines advanced ever nearer, Captain Parker assembled his meager force of only 77 men in two anemic ranks. A palsied Sam Adams prevailed upon Hancock to retire with him as their cabinet positions necessitated that they avoid being captured at all cost. However, Pastor Clark would fight alongside his sheep. Bancroft states:

> Among the most alert was...the minister with gun in hand, his powder-horn and pouch of balls slung over his shoulder. By his sermons

and his prayers, he had so hallowed the enthusiasm of his flock that they held the defense of their liberties a part of their covenant with God; his presence with arms strengthened their sense of duty. Under the eye of the minister...Lexington common was alive with the minutemen.[23]

Outnumbered 10 to 1, Captain Parker had ordered his men to allow the redcoats to pass by unmolested, yet with the manly stipulation, "Stand your ground. Don't fire unless fired upon, but if they mean to have a war let it begin here."[24] When the lead British commander, Major John Pitcairn, shouted at the patriots from his steed, "Disperse, you [expletive] rebels! lay down your arms," they indignantly complied with the first order only. In the ensuing confusion, the nervous trigger finger of an unidentified participant set off the bloody encounter that would last only minutes.

From a mile or so down the road, the din of musket fire inspired Adams to remark to Hancock (and rightfully so), "Oh, what a glorious morning is this!"[25] However, Pastor Clark's firsthand view of his mangled parishioners was anything but a glorious spectacle. When the smoke had cleared, eight Americans lay dead or dying in and around the church property with another nine being wounded. The British losses were given as only two slightly injured, one of which was Pitcairn's horse. While the Major's exuberant troops were firing volleys into the air along with a hearty "three cheers" for victory, Christian patriots like Jonathan Harrington, Jr., were writhing in agony. As Mrs. Harrington observed the fight from her window, she witnessed her own husband get shot down and then arise to his feet only to fall again. While he crawled through his own blood on hands and knees toward his home, Mrs. Harrington rushed to meet him only to have him die at her feet.[26]

With all due respect to Ralph Waldo Emerson, the *real* shot heard around the world was fired *first* on a *church green* in Lexington. (Note the number of letters in the name LEXINGTON.) Headley gives us Pastor Clark's prophetic declarations:

> The bright spring morning broke tranquilly over this sad scene—the dew-drops glittered beside the red stains that sprinkled the starting grass—the birds came out and sang upon the budding trees, and nature gave no token of the bloody murder that had just been committed. Clark gazed long and earnestly on this tragic spectacle, but no tear of regret mingled with those of sympathy which he shed. Those lifeless forms before him were holy martyrs in his sight, the first precious sacrifices laid upon the altar of his country, which was yet to groan under its load of

victims. He had no misgivings, for *"from this day,"* said he, *"will be dated the liberty of the world."* No sound broke the stillness of the scene, but *he* heard far up in the dome of the universe a bell tolling the knell of tyranny.[27]

The expedition commander, Colonel Francis Smith, resumed his march toward Concord to achieve the mission's initial objective of destroying the town's munitions reserves. As the British neared the end of their five-mile march, the vastly outnumbered Concord militia withdrew to the surrounding heights to await reinforcements. Once again, it was the local parson who steadied their resolve for a righteous scrap, Reverend William Emerson exhorting: "Let us stand our ground. If we die, let us die here."[28]

By approximately 8:00 a.m., Smith and Pitcairn were "under the impression" that they were occupying the rebel town of 1,500. While the privates searched unsuccessfully for hidden weapons and powder, their officers reclined in chairs on the lawn. Still smarting over the audacious resistance of those "country bumpkins" at Lexington, Pitcairn uttered a casual vow over his breakfast of meat and potatoes. Stirring a brandy-and-water with his finger, he said he hoped he "would be stirring [expletive] Yankee blood before nightfall."[29] Unbeknownst to the major, there would be plenty of blood stirred by day's end, but most would not belong to Yankees.

Before the breakfast dishes could be washed, over 400 grim-faced, musket-toting farmers were on the move "fixin' " to cross the Old North Bridge, despite the presence of three companies of marine defenders. When 20 British guns suddenly discharged an opening volley of lead that killed two militia officers, Major Buttrick gave the command for which the Minutemen had been waiting: **"Fire, fellow soldiers! For God's sake, fire!"**[30] In addition to three direct kills, a patriot eyewitness reported, "Eight or ten were wounded and a-running and hobbling about, and looking back to see if we were after them."[31] The battle had lasted all of two minutes.

For some strange reason, Colonel Smith and company did not hang around for lunch. With the swelling numbers of Minutemen in doubt, not to mention the whereabouts of their own expected reinforcements, the rattled redcoats beat a hasty retreat for Boston on the very road they had so haughtily trod that same morning. A five-mile, two-and-one-half-hour turkey shoot ensued with telling fire pouring in from behind rocks, trees and stone walls upon the hapless invaders. When the bandaged survivors of the Lexington militia opened fire, Colonel Smith was shot off his horse (wounded in the leg) while Major Pitcairn was thrown from his.[32] Smith's timely rendezvous with Lord Percy's 900 reinforcements at Lexington saved his force from total annihilation. Major Charles Stedman, a contemporary British officer and celebrated military historian, described the scene on the very ground of their earlier short-lived celebration accordingly: "Percy now formed his detachment into a square, in which enclosed Smith's party, who were so exhausted with fatigue, that they were obliged to lie down for a rest on the ground, their tongues hanging out of their mouths, like those of dogs after a chase."[33]

As the combined British forces limped back to Boston (via a detour through Charleston), American marksmen continued to decimate their ranks, "running from front to flank, and from flank to rear, loading their pieces at one place, and discharging them at another."[34] An expanding network of pealing church bells ensured a steady influx of fresh shooters along the highway of death. When His Majesty's troops finally staggered into Charleston at sunset, the official figures were received with great alarm. While the inexperienced colonial volunteers had suffered 49 killed, 39 wounded and 5 missing in action, the seasoned British grenadiers, fusiliers, and marines had sustained numbers three times as high—73 killed, 174 wounded and 26 missing, for an incredible overall casualty factor of *20%!*[35]

On the heels of these two historic battles, the Second Continental Congress convened in the Pennsylvania State House on May 30, 1775. The great topic of discussion was the formation of a Continental Army. The session was barely under way when the encouraging news of Fort Ticonderoga's surrender was received. The capture of her 59 cannons would prove invaluable in the days ahead.

BUNKER HILL

While these events were transpiring, the siege of Boston was underway with General Gage and his entire army hemmed in by several thousand angry patriots. When word leaked out that Gage intended to gain an artillery advantage by securing the adjacent Dorchester Heights, the Americans decided to beat him to the punch by claiming some high ground of their own. Bunker Hill was thought to afford a more tactical advantage, as it overlooked both the city and harbor.

On the evening of June 16, approximately 900 colonial troops under the command of Colonel William Prescott assembled at Cambridge and were led in solemn prayer by Dr. Samuel Langdon, president of Harvard University. Afterwards, the soldiers marched by lantern lights to the base of Bunker Hill, only to pass it by for the lower rise, Breed's Hill. (There remains some debate among historians whether this was accidental or intentional.) Digging by moonlight, Prescott directed his men in the hasty construction of a primitive fort of earth and timber. By 3:30 a.m., the angled redoubt sporting 136-foot sides with ramparts five and six feet in height was still only partially completed.

At first light, Gage and his fellow generals (the newly arrived William Howe, Henry Clinton and John Burgoyne) were astounded at what they saw. Artillery shells from the *Lively* and other British ships began careening into the patriot fortress. The defenders became particularly rattled when a cannonball tore off the head of Asa Pollard, a stocky farm boy and the battle's first casualty.[36] Soon the more timid at heart began disappearing down the slope. Crouched behind inadequate breastworks, a mood of gloom descended on Prescott's men as they anticipated the imminent assault of the redcoats. If they only had more time. However, as the hours began to pass, the attack did not commence. Fortunately for America, the spot where Howe chose to ferry his troops was too shallow at that time due to an unfavorable tide. The resulting six-hour delay before the crossing gave Colonel Prescott a providential opportunity to shore up his defenses, encourage the spirits of his apprehensive volunteers, and receive some last-minute reinforcements.

The source for this initial blessing, as well as for the battle's supernatural unfolding, is one that is totally incomprehensible to the mind of a secular historian. Yet, it solves the mystery as to why a battle that was clearly fought on one location, *Breed's Hill,* has been (and will continue to be) identified with another site altogether, the celebrated *Bunker Hill—no matter how many history books attempt to clarify this mistake*! Because this battle, and the entire war, were being fought to establish a nation built on Christian principles, the answer to our riddle must begin with the entrance of a man of God.

David Avery of Norwich, Connecticut, was one of those many thousands of impressionable youths who went to hear George Whitefield out of curiosity, only to return a born-again believer. Having surrendered to the ministry, Avery graduated from Yale College and was subsequently ordained in 1773. He later moved to Gaysboro, Vermont, and assumed the pastorate of the local Congregational church. When news of Lexington and Concord reached his sleepy community, Pastor Avery shocked his flock by resigning his position to join the army as a chaplain. As he marched out of town for Boston, 20 of his former parishioners, having chosen him as their captain, followed closely behind with muskets to their shoulders. When the little band arrived in Cambridge on April 29, the "troops assembled to receive the 'reverend captain and his men' as they were called, for the spirited example encouraged the hearts of all."[37] On the morning of the battle, Chaplain David Avery performed a most unusual service for his country. Headley describes the holy scene:

> In the battle of Bunker Hill, as it is called, but which it is well known took place on Breed's Hill, this brave, godly man stood on Bunker Hill in full sight of the conflict, and as Moses, who stood on the hill, and held up his hands that Joshua might smite the Amalekites, so he, while the adjacent heights and shores were shaking to the thunder of cannon, and the flames of burning Charlestown were rolling heavenward, lifted up his hands and prayed that God would give victory to the Americans. Breed's Hill, dimly seen through the rolling smoke of battle, amid which flashed the deadly vollies, and gleamed the glittering lines, and in the back-ground this patriotic divine, with upraised hands beseeching Heaven for victory, would make an appropriate picture of that bloody prelude to the revolution.[38]

Headley has preserved the exhilarating account as recorded in Reverend Avery's personal diary for June 18th:

> I stood on a neighboring hill (Bunker) with hands uplifted, supplicating the blessing of Heaven to crown our unworthy arms with success. To us infantile Americans, unused to the thunder and carnage of battle, the flames of Charlestown before our eyes—the incessant play of cannon from their shipping—from Boston, and their wings in various cross directions, together with the fire of musketry from more than four times our number, all heightened the majestic terrors of the field, exhibiting a scene most awful and tremendous, but amid the perils of the dread encounter the Lord was our rock and fortress.[39]

By 3:00 p.m., the British were in place and the main frontal assault began. Howe's men were permitted to march within a hundred feet of Prescott's fortress. The only sound from behind the breastworks was the click of musket hammers for, as that solitary figure atop the higher hill continued his supplication, a surge of reassurance pervaded the ranks below. While taking careful aim at the enemy, an 80-year-old, white-haired patriot was heard to pray, "I thank Thee, O God, for having permitted me to have lived to see this day to fight for my country."[40] With the "whites of their eyes" finally in focus, a hundred flintlocks made their deadly appearance.

Ellis (cited by Collins) describes the immediate aftermath of Prescott's order to "Fire!":

> As the wind rolled away... the... smoke, and the blasts of artillery and musketry for a few minutes ceased, the awful spectacle, the agonizing yells and shrieks of the sufferers, were distracting... some of the wounded were seen crawling with the last eneries [sic] of life from the gory heap of the dying and dead... The insanity of war never had a more full demonstration than in that scene.[41]

The men were so terrified that as they broke ranks, literally running for their lives, many even dove headlong into the boats for cover. After 15 minutes, the recomposed columns started up for a second dose, sidestepping what was left of their fallen comrades. Once again, a savage hail of fire tore through their ranks without mercy. Between 70 and 90% of each company fell to the earth, causing a second panic-stricken retreat.

Henry Clinton's arrival with reinforcements from Boston helped rally the morale of the bewildered survivors for a third attempt at dislodging their foes. This time, the Americans' powder was all but gone. After inflicting a final round of destruction, the Minutemen were forced to fall back to fight another day. Major Pitcairn entered the fort in the closing moments declaring excitedly, "The day is ours!"[42] As he did, he was shot through the head by a black American named Salem Prince. The mortally wounded major collapsed into the arms of his own son, who carried him to a boat, kissed him farewell, and promptly returned to the fight.[43] Although Major Pitcairn was the "bad guy," I wept when I read this account. *"As I live, saith the Lord God, I have no pleasure in the death of the wicked; but that the wicked turn from his way and live."* (Ezekiel 33:11a)

As the sweat-drenched Reverend Avery descended Bunker Hill at the conclusion of his prayer meeting for America, the extent to which the Lord answered would not be fully appreciated for many years to come. Not only did the colonial soldiers receive an infusion of confidence for the struggles that lay ahead, but the British gained a healthy respect for their unpolished American cousins as well. Although the enemy occupied their opponent's fortress at day's end, the triumph was a Pyrrhic victory at best. With 1,054 dead and wounded to be cared for (compared to only 449 American casualties), there was no time for the shouts and cheers of Lexington. The personal observations of General Gage were as follows:

The success, which was very necessary in our present condition, cost dear. The number in killed and wounded is greater than our forces can afford to lose. We have lost some extremely good officers. The trials we have had show the rebels are not the despicable rabble too many had supposed them to be, and I find it owning to a military encouraged among them for a few years past, joined with uncommon zeal and enthusiasm... The conquest of this country is not easy; you have to cope with vast numbers. In all their wars against the French, they never showed so much conduct, attention, and perseverance, as they do now.[44]

The British never forgot their "stinging" achievement and fought thereafter with a pronounced reluctancy that would eventually cost them the war. Dr. Wendell Evans writes:

Many historians have felt that Howe's bitter experience at Bunker Hill crippled him psychologically for completely effective military action against Americans. Whether this is true or not, there is no doubt about the fact that Howe showed a healthy respect for American forces after that bloody battle. He became especially skeptical of using a *frontal assault on a defended position.*[45]

Therefore, the *spiritual* explanation for the persistent confusing of Breed's Hill with Bunker Hill is that the *real* victory was fought and won on the *higher* elevation, for it was there that a man of God *"went up to the top of the hill."* (Exodus 17:10b) *"Not by might, nor by power, but by my spirit, saith the LORD of hosts."* (Zechariah 4:6b)

GEORGE WASHINGTON

Unbeknownst to the fighting men at "Bunker Hill," Congress had established the "Grand American Army" on the 15th of April and appointed Colonel George Washington as its first commander in chief. It was Robert Ellis Thompson who wrote, "Washington was God's unique gift to America."[46] As anyone who has made an unbiased study of the American Revolution will admit, there was no human way that an unorganized collection of humble farmers could have defeated the most powerful army on the face of the earth. A colonial victory would have to be achieved through supernatural means, *"That no flesh should glory in his presence."*

(I Corinthians 1:29) And such a deliverance could only be orchestrated by one who was already well acquainted with the power of Providence.

In 1751 when George Washington was only 19, Governor Dinwiddie made him a major in the Virginia militia. Four years later, Colonel Washington was invited to become an aide to the British general, Edward Braddock, at the outset of the French and Indian War (known internationally as the Seven Years War). Braddock's initial goal was to drive the French out of the Ohio Valley with the capture of Fort Duquesne (the site of present-day Pittsburgh, Pennsylvania). On the morning of July 9, 1755, Braddock's army of 2,000, which included three companies of Virginia militia under Washington's command, was ambushed by a smaller but well-entrenched force of 800 French and Indians near the Monongahela River, just ten miles from their mission's objective.

Because the egotistical general had refused to discard the conventional, European style of open-air fighting, his redcoats were picked off like sitting ducks by an enemy they couldn't even see. With the ease and number of direct kills causing the Indians to laugh out loud as they fired, Braddock suddenly ordered that none of his troops could take cover behind trees. In the ensuing carnage, 714 soldiers and 63 of the 86 officers were either killed or wounded, while the enemy lost less than a tithe of these. Braddock himself was killed with a musket ball through the lung. Only *one* mounted officer out of the entire army remained unscathed by battle's end. The fever-ridden Washington carried Braddock's orders throughout the storm of lead; an eyewitness later remarked, "I expected every moment to see him fall. Nothing but the superintending care of Providence could have saved him."[47] In a letter to his brother, John A. Washington, the colonel soberly concurred:

> As I have heard, since my arrival at this place [Fort Cumberland], a circumstantial account of my death and dying speech, I take this early opportunity of contradicting the first, and of assuring you, that I have not as yet composed the latter. But, by the all-powerful dispensations of Providence, I have been protected beyond all human probability or expectation; for I had four bullets through my coat, and two horses shot under me, yet escaped unhurt, although death was leveling my companions on every side of me![48]

However, as "truth is stranger than fiction," consider the "rest of the story." Fifteen years after the battle (1770), Washington and a close friend, Dr. Craik, were traveling near the junction of the Great Kanawha and Ohio River when a company of Indians approached with great reverence.

Speaking through an interpreter, their aged chieftain related a spine-tingling epilogue:

> I am a chief and ruler over my tribes. My influence extends to the waters of the great lakes and to the far blue mountains. I have traveled a long and weary path that I might see the young warrior of the great battle. It was on the day when the white man's blood mixed with the streams of our forest that I first beheld this chief [Washington]. I called to my young men and said... Quick, let your aim be certain, and he dies. Our rifles were leveled, rifles which, but for you, knew not how to miss—'twas all in vain, a power mightier far than we, shielded you. **Seeing you were under the special guardianship of the Great Spirit, we immediately ceased to fire at you.** I am old and soon shall be gathered to the great council fire of my fathers in the land of shades, but ere I go, there is something bids me speak in the voice of prophecy. Listen! The Great Spirit protects that man [pointing at Washington], and guides his destinies—he will become the chief of nations, and a people yet unborn will hail him as the founder of a mighty empire. **I am come to pay homage to the man who is the particular favorite of Heaven, and who can never die in battle.**[49]

Arriving in Cambridge late on July 2, Washington took official command of the army on the following day. While President Clinton endorsed a "Don't ask, don't tell" policy for queers, Washington's first official order, issued on July 4, 1775, read:

> The General most earnestly requires and expects a due observance of those articles of war established for the government of the army, which forbid profane cursing, swearing, and drunkenness. And in like manner he requires and expects of all officers and soldiers, not engaged in actual duty, a punctual attendance on Divine service, to implore the blessing of Heaven upon the means used for our safety and defense.[50]

Five days later, the Commander in Chief fired off another "religious" directive:

> The honorable Continental Congress having been pleased to allow a chaplain to each regiment, with the pay of thirty-three and one-third dollars per month, the colonels or commanding officers of each regiment are directed to procure chaplains— accordingly persons of good character and exemplary lives—to see that all inferior officers and soldiers pay them a suitable respect, and attend carefully upon religious exercises. *The blessing and protection of Heaven are at all times* necessary, but

especially is it in times of public distress and danger. The General hopes and trusts that every officer and man will endeavor so to live and act as becomes a Christian soldier, defending the dearest rights and liberties of his country.[51]

The pivotal role played by Washington's chaplains would become increasingly significant as the war proceeded. That such a *spiritual* standard was being established by America's political and military leaders is highly reflective of the sustained influence of her dedicated clergy. Within a week of Washington's arrival, President Langdon of Harvard College was appointed to preach the election sermon for 1775 despite the absence of His Majesty's Council. With the state capitol in the hands of brutal soldiery, Dr. Langdon took for his text Isaiah 1:26 which says, *"And I will restore thy judges as at the first, and thy counsellors as at the beginning: afterward thou shalt be called, The city of righteousness, the faithful city."* After recounting the many disasters that had befallen them, he reaffirmed that the *real* battle was over the legitimacy of biblical Christianity:

> If God be for us, who can be against us? The enemy has reproached us for calling on his name, and professing our trust in him. They have made a mock of our solemn fasts and every appearance of Christianity in the land. On this account, by way of contempt, they call us saints, while their mouths are full of cursing and bitterness. And may we not be confident that the Most High who regards these things will vindicate his own honor, and plead our righteous cause against such enemies to his government as well as to our liberties. O may our camp be free from every accursed thing. May we be truly a holy people, and all our towns and cities of righteousness. Then the Lord will be our refuge and strength, a very present help in time of trouble, and we shall have no reason to be afraid, though thousands of our enemies set themselves against us round about, though all nature should be thrown into tumults and convulsions. He can command the stars in their courses to fight his battles, and all the elements to wage war with his enemies. He can destroy them with innumerable plagues, and send faintness into their hearts, so that the men of might shall not find their hands. May the Lord hear us in the day of trouble, and the name of the God of Jacob defend us, send us help from his sanctuary, and strengthen us out of Zion.[52]

President Langdon knew what he was talking about. At that very moment, the British troops were using the auditorium of the Old South Church as a horse stable, much to the disgust of Boston's God-fearing citizenry. A deacon's pew had even been chopped up to provide wood for a pigsty.[53] A severe shortage of supplies, especially gunpowder (only 38 barrels on hand, or 9 rounds per man) precluded any serious attempt at dislodging the enemy. Losing one-third of his army (5,000 men) to enlistment expirations on December 31 did not help matters either. By winter's end, however, things began to change. Eighty yoke of oxen pulling 42 sleds hauled the captured Ticonderoga cannons through the snow to Cambridge. On the night of March 4, 1776, Washington positioned them on Dorchester Heights overlooking Boston. The entire British army and 1,200 Loyalists sailed out of the harbor for Halifax on the 17th of March. General Washington entered Boston on the following day and hoisted a new flag—13 red and white stripes with the Union Jack in the center.

Although Howe's men were gone, everyone knew they would be back. (Sir William Howe had replaced Thomas Gage.) In the aftermath of their inglorious retreat, a number of Americans began to second-guess the "revolution." Defection and disloyalty began to rear its ugly head. One of the traitors, Thomas Hickey, sold out for half a dollar.[54] Rumors were growing that a massive armada was sailing toward New York. In the midst of this national anxiety, the Baptists came to the forefront, Christian writing:

> They [American leadership] were surrounded with enemies from without; and Tories and traitors within. The most careful watchfulness was demanded. Only patriots could be trusted; and true men with the American spirit and liberty were imperatively demanded. **The Baptists were such men.** They were accustomed to a hardy life; had long been trained in the rugged school of experience; were loyal and trusted citizens; and above all were endued with the spirit of wisdom and liberty. **Not a man of them proved a traitor. They cast their united strength into the American cause.**[55]

The Baptists had been among the first Christian communities to recognize the legitimacy of the fledgling government. Eight days after the First Continental Congress convened, the Suffolk County representatives of the Warren Association of Baptist Churches in Massachusetts affirmed:

> This county, confiding in the wisdom and integrity of the Continental Congress, now sitting in Philadelphia, will pay all due respect and submission to such measures as may be recommended by them to the

colonies, for the restoration and establishment of our just rights, civil and religious.[56]

Within weeks of the aggression at Lexington and Concord, the Rhode Island legislature voted to send 1,500 men to the aid of their oppressed neighbors. And while the other, larger colonies were hesitating, this predominantly Baptist settlement became the first provincial government to sever formal ties with Britain, doing so on May 4, 1776, two full months before the Declaration of Independence and 33 days ahead of Virginia. Even the Baptists in England were supportive of the colonists, Dr. Rippon of London writing, "I believe all of our Baptist ministers in town, except two, and most of our brethren in the country were on the side of the Americans."[57]

As the Lord would have it, the zeal of these Baptist patriots was especially convicting in light of their own persistent suffering for the sake of matters of conscience. An excerpt from the formal resolution of the Warren Association to Congress reads:

> [We] are most heartily concerned for the preservation and defense of the rights and privileges of the country... and are willing to unite with our dear countrymen, vigorously to pursue every prudent measure for relief... and yet have long been denied the free and full enjoyment of those rights, as to the support of religious worship.[58]

In addition to the guilt occasioned by this "double standard," a British armada of some 42,000 men was due to arrive in New York at any time. Washington had already marched his new army of 25,000 men to the vicinity (thanks to numerous Baptist recruits), splitting them between Manhattan and Brooklyn Heights (across the East River on Long Island). With no time to lose, and a righteous God in Heaven to appease, the momentous Virginia Declaration of Independence was passed on June 12, 1776, with the inclusion by James Madison and Thomas Jefferson of the all-important Article XVI which set forth the Baptist distinctive of soul liberty as the cornerstone of Virginia's government:

> That religion, or the duty which we owe to our Creator, and the manner of discharging it, can be directed only by reason and conviction, not by force or violence; and, therefore, that all men are equally entitled to the **free exercise** of religion according to the dictates of conscience; and that it is the mutual duty of all to practise Christian forbearance, love and charity toward each other.[59]

It is highly significant that the phrase "free exercise" represents an amendment made by the bill's author, George Mason, at the insistence of James Madison, from the original wording "that all men should enjoy the fullest **toleration** in the exercise of religion."[60] On October 6, 1776, a petition requesting that "sects" be exempted from legal taxation for the support of any one church resulted in the salaries of the Episcopal clergy being suspended.

With the ink barely dried in Virginia, an alert lookout scanning the New York harbor at dawn saw what appeared to be "a forest of trimmed pine trees floating across the water."[61] America held her breath at the return of General Howe accompanied by the powerful fleet of his brother, Admiral Sir Richard Howe.

DECLARATION OF INDEPENDENCE

About this same time (mid-June) in yet a third location, Thomas Jefferson, at the insistence of John Adams (eight years his senior), began his writing of the famed Declaration of Independence. Having dutifully acknowledged, "I did not consider it as any part of my charge to invent new ideas,"[62] he was able to complete his summary of prevailing patriot sentiment in less than two weeks despite suffering from severe migraine headaches. It is noteworthy that the opening line of the document's lofty preamble contains a veiled appeal, not only to the authority of natural law, but to the God of nature Himself.

> When, in the course of human events, it becomes necessary for one people to dissolve the political bands which have connected them with another, and to assume among the powers of the earth, the separate and equal station to which the laws of Nature and of Nature's God entitles them, a decent respect to the opinions of mankind requires that they should declare the causes which impel them to the separation.

As Congress began formal deliberation over the paramount theme of separation from Great Britain, the Scottish preacher, Dr. John Witherspoon, president of the College of New Jersey (Princeton University), set the tone by declaring that "the country was not only ripe for independence but in danger of becoming rotten for lack of it."[63] The justification for Dr. Witherspoon's intensity (and that of many others) became apparent as Jefferson's noble words continued:

> We hold these truths to be self-evident, that all men are created equal, that they are endowed by their Creator with certain unalienable Rights, that among these are Life, Liberty, and the pursuit of Happiness. That to secure these rights, Governments are instituted among Men, deriving their just powers from the consent of the governed. That whenever any Form of Government becomes destructive of these ends, it is the Right of the People to alter or to abolish it, and to institute new Government, laying its foundation on such principles and organizing its powers in such form, as to them shall seem most likely to effect their Safety and Happiness.

This courageous placing of the blame where it belonged was precisely what Patrick Henry meant when he wrote that "Government is a conditional compact between king and people...violation of the covenant by either party discharges the other from obligation."[64] In the remaining three-quarters of Jefferson's *legal* masterpieces (rarely studied by those who would challenge the moral legitimacy of our nation's dramatic formation), the author proves that the so-called "American Revolution" was, in reality, a righteous reaction to a British repudiation of their own political system! For while the King and Parliament were the ones revolting against their "Saxon heritage" (Jefferson's reference to the Saxon chiefs Hengist and Horsa, "from whom we claim the honor of being descended, and whose political principles and form of government we have assumed"[65]), the *Americans* simply desired to go right on living as *Englishmen* under the blessings of *British* common law as prescribed by the *British* Constitution. Referring to the American Revolution as "a kind of affirmation of faith in ancient British institutions,"[66] Boorstin points out some of the more notable Saxon contributions as being: "trial by jury, due process of law, representation before taxation, habeas corpus, freedom from attainder, independence of the judiciary, and the rights of free speech, free petition, and free assembly, as well as our narrow definition of treason and our antipathy to standing armies in peacetime."[67]

Jefferson wrote, "The history of the present King of Great Britain is a history of repeated injuries and usurpations, all having in direct object the establishment of an absolute Tyranny over these States."[68] He then proceeded to lay before the world 27 specific grievances, including the charge that King George "abdicated Government here, by declaring us out of his Protection, and waging War against us."[69] With an appeal to the "Supreme Judge of the world," he winds down his indictment with the climactic pronouncement that "these United Colonies, are and of Right ought to be free and independent States; that they are Absolved from all

Allegiance to the British Crown."[70] And his final line was no less awe-inspiring than the first:

> And for the support of this Declaration, with a firm reliance on the protection of Divine Providence, we mutually pledge to each other our Lives, our Fortunes, and our sacred Honor.

An accurate understanding of the interconnecting events that followed will yield an enhanced appreciation for the dramatic delivery of the world's newest arrival. On the first of July, Congress began its formal debate over Richard Henry Lee's resolution that the American states should declare their independence. Nine of the thirteen colonies endorsed the resolution at the initial vote. Understanding that the final vote would be taken the next day, the session ended with the arrival of a dispatch from Washington that a British invasion was imminent. On the following day, New York, Pennsylvania, Delaware and South Carolina made the break with Britain official. Nine thousand British soldiers came ashore on New York's Staten Island on July 3. And on the glorious 4th of July, the Declaration of Independence was formally adopted by Congress. That evening the handwritten scribblings of Jefferson, defaced with several corrections and excisions, were transported to the printer, John Dunlap, for the document's first printing, known as the Dunlap Broadside.

Congress ordered that a handsome engrossed parchment be prepared for the delegates to sign. (The work was done by one Timothy Matlack.) On the 8th of July, the Declaration was read by Colonel John North in the courtyard of Philadelphia's State House. It is significant that Samuel Adams observed, **"The people seem to recognize this resolution as though it were a decree promulgated from heaven."**[71] With a returned enemy fleet of 430 ships (ten times the size of the one that had retreated earlier) only 115 miles away, the prospect of Heaven's endorsement was a more-than-welcome consideration.

As far as that esteemed body of 50-plus patriots was concerned, "the times that try men's souls" would commence with the moment their personal signatures became attached to that precious parchment. When the congressional president, John Hancock, affixed his famous autograph (the first to do so), he was heard to say, "We must be unanimous. There must be no pulling different ways. We must all hang together." Benjamin Franklin was reported to have replied, "Yes, we must indeed all hang together, or most assuredly we shall all hang separately."[72]

Hancock, reputed to be the richest man in all of America, had already proven his commitment by ordering a cannonade on occupied Boston, realizing that much of his own commercial property would be destroyed. In the painful years ahead, most of the signers would pay dearly for their convictions:

> Five were captured by the British and tortured before they died. Twelve had their homes ransacked and burned. Two lost their sons in the war, another had two sons captured. Nine either died from war wounds or from hardships suffered in the war. Carter Braxton of Virginia, a wealthy planter and trader, watched his ships being destroyed by the British navy. He died impoverished. Thomas McKean had to keep himself and his family in hiding, and lost all his possessions. The British destroyed the property of Francis Lewis and jailed his wife; she died a few months later.[73]

One of the signers paid a particularly high price for his fidelity. John Hart was a farmer and congressional delegate from New Jersey. Known as "Honest John" Hart, he was also sympathetic to the plight of the Baptists, having donated a portion of his own land for the Baptist church in Hopewell. As such, Hart was prepared to go the second mile for the cause of liberty. With his farm situated on the enemy's highway, the document before him loomed as a personal death warrant. Despite his age of nearly 60 years, he signed the Declaration of Independence only to become an immediate exile for his fellow countrymen. The approaching enemy compelled him to leave the bedside of his dying wife and 13 loving children so as to flee into the forest for safety. He would never see any of them again. His home, mill and crops were all destroyed. His children fled into the mountains themselves. His wife died from the stress. For more than a year, the Baptist patriot lived in swamps and caves with his most civilized shelter being an outhouse which he shared with a dog.[74] Learning of his wife's Homegoing and the destruction of his property, he died from exhaustion and a broken heart.

Meanwhile, back in New York, on the 12th of July, two British officers approached the American camp under a flag of truce. Being received by the American adjutant general, Joseph Reed, a certain Lieutenant Brown tipped his hat, bowed and said with all gravity, "I have a letter, sir, from Lord Howe to *Mr.* Washington." Colonel Reed replied, "Sir, we have no person here in our Army with that address."[75]

Esteeming the honor of his commander in chief, Reed had refused to accept the dispatch addressed simply to "George Washington, *Esq.*" Brown departed in a daze and returned four days later with a new letter addressed to "George Washington, Esq., *etc.*" This time, Washington himself sent the messenger boy home. The following day, Admiral Howe sent a verbal request asking if Washington would be willing to receive his own adjutant general. The Commander agreed, and the July 20 meeting lasted 30 minutes, with Lieutenant Colonel James Patterson repeatedly addressing Washington by the title of "Excellency." The jist of Howe's message was that if the colonists repented, he would "let bygones be bygones" and extend a royal pardon. Although cordial to Patterson, the jist of "His Excellency's" reply to Lord Howe was to— "hit the road."

This story by Langguth is not only humorous and refreshing but insightful as to the spirit of Washington and his cause. What the American army lacked in just about everything else, they would make up for with *guts and God.* Washington's curt reply had shaken Howe good. Over a month had passed by and still no attack was launched. Washington confided to a cousin, "There is something exceedingly mysterious in the conduct of the enemy."[76]

LONG ISLAND

The assault finally came on the 27th of August. Howe's generals outflanked Washington's outnumbered troops and a terrible slaughter took place, with America's losses put at over 1,000. It was at this battle of Long Island that Howe unleashed a new secret weapon, German mercenaries (hired at $36 each) known as Hessians. Although George III was born in London, both his father and grandfather had been reared in the heavily Catholic area of Hanover, Germany. The pro-Vatican George III found the Roman Catholic Frederick II, Landgrave of Hesse-Cassel, only too happy to send his murderous Hessians into the fight against the American Protestants. A letter from a British officer describes the butchery of these foreign agents: "The Hessians and our brave Highlanders gave no quarter; and it was a fine sight to see with what alacrity they dispatched the rebels with their bayonets, after we had surrounded them so that they could not resist."[77]

While watching the carnage from a higher elevation, Washington sorrowfully eulogized his men, "Good God! What brave fellows I must lose this day!"[78]

Washington was now in trouble. Having fallen back to the makeshift fort at Brooklyn Heights, the Americans were in danger of being totally surrounded should Admiral Howe bring his fleet up the Hudson and position it behind them. (Also, many of the Irish-Americans had deserted under pressure from their Catholic priests.[79]) Fortunately for the colonials, Howe was still thinking of "Bunker Hill" and called his men off with the words, "Enough has been done for one day."[80]

Most military historians are convinced that Howe could have annihilated the entire American army had he chosen to press his advantage at this point in time! Washington rallied his officers together for prayer and "Nature's God" did the rest. An immediate retreat was ordered despite the inclement weather. While the paranoid Howe twiddled his thumbs throughout two rainy days, the Lord's people prepared for a Red Sea miracle, Collins writing:

> The weather made it impossible to transport the army by boats from Long Island; a high northeast wind had been raging for three days, but, nevertheless, Washington and his officers resolved to try during the night of August 29. When the main army got ready to start embarking, suddenly, about 11 p.m., the wind died down and the water became very smooth. A gentle breeze sprung up from the south and southwest which aided the boats in crossing the East River to Manhattan. The moonlight was fairly bright and the ships of the enemy were very close by, but, strange as it may seem, the patriot army was not discovered as they made their evacuation. It was a momentous task to get nine thousand men across the river and it was obvious that the mission could not be completed before daylight came. As daylight approached, a thick sea fog came rolling in and shrouded the British camp. Who would question that the hand of God intervened to save the American cause?[81]

As the war continued to drag on, the vastly outnumbered Continental Army would see the "God of Nature" deliver them over and over again.

Finally, after being chased out of New York on September 15, Harlem Heights on October 18, and even Fort Washington (on the east bank of the Hudson) on November 16, the Lord *"turned again the captivity of Zion."* (Psalm 126:1) Congress had decreed a solemn day of prayer, fasting and humiliation to implore divine intervention. Although Washington's army was down to a measly 3,000 men (less than 10% of the enemy's troop strength), he knew from experience that "man's extremities are God's opportunities."

TRENTON

Washington crossed the Hudson into New Jersey and then crossed the Delaware into Pennsylvania. The trail of his troops could be easily traced by the blood on the snow, the desperate men slaughtering cattle along the way so they could wrap their feet in the hides. The British were so sure that the war was over that General Cornwallis put his baggage on a ship for England![82] What the arrogant general didn't know was that Washington was heading for some boats himself. At 9:00 p.m. on Christmas night, Washington made his immortal crossing of the Delaware to attack the Hessian garrison at Trenton. Once again, the Lord came through despite the horrendous weather conditions described by one of the soldiers as "fearfully cold and raw." A Loyalist farmer spotted the approaching Americans and rushed to inform the Hessian colonel, Johann Gottlieb Rall. However, the commandant was too busy drinking and playing cards to be disturbed. The frustrated Tory left a scribbled note of warning with Rall's host, Abraham Hunt, who eventually passed it on to the inebriated Hessian who *stuck it in his vest pocket without reading it!*[83]

While the party animal was snoring away with the unread report on his person, shouts of "Der Feind! Heraus! Heraus!" ("The enemy! Turn out! Turn out!") began to be heard. It was 7:45 a.m. and George Washington was about to give George III a wake-up call. As everything rises and falls on leadership, most of Johann's boys were staggering around with hangovers as well. The battle lasted 90 minutes. Washington's men killed 23 of the enemy and captured over 1,000 prisoners while suffering only 4 wounded. (Two other patriots had frozen to death on the march.) As Rall himself lay dying, his attendants found the farmer's note while attempting to dress his wounds. After reviewing its contents, he sighed, "Hätte ich dies zu Herrn Hunt gelesen, so wäre ich jezt nicht hier." ("If I had read this at Mr. Hunt's, I would not be here.")

SPIRITUAL CHAPLAINS

If Washington were alive today, he would be appalled to see the cowardly way in which the modern historian refuses to report the many factual occurrences of supernatural intervention throughout the War of Independence. The great Commander in Chief could never say enough about that "Unseen Hand" which guided him to victory. In a letter in 1778 to his Virginia friend, Thomas Nelson, he wrote:

> The hand of Providence has been so conspicuous in all this (the course of the war) that he must be worse than an infidel that lacks faith, and more wicked that has not gratitude to acknowledge his obligations; but it will be time enough for me to turn Preacher when my present appointment ceases.[84]

Beyond any doubt, it was the presence of Washington's Spirit-filled chaplains that kept his men from throwing in the towel. His official order procuring their services paid America's war effort untold spiritual dividends. These faithful men of God could not only preach and pray, but many of them displayed heroic leadership under fire. Although not a chaplain at the time, Reverend Naphtali Dagget, professor of divinity at Yale College, represents this special class of men sardonically referred to by the British as the "Rebel Parsons." As an army of redcoats under General Tyron marched on New Haven, Connecticut, on July 5, 1779, the aged preacher climbed to the top of a hill with fowling piece in hand to personally reconnoiter the enemy. Suddenly, Dr. Dagget began firing at the whole regiment! Headley writes:

> As the British pressed after the fugitives, they were surprised at the solitary report of a gun every few minutes from the grove of trees on that hill. At first they paid but little attention to it, but the bullets finding their way steadily into the ranks, they were compelled to notice it, and an officer sent a detachment up to see what it meant. The professor saw them coming, but never moved from his position. His black mare stood near him, and he could any moment have mounted and fled, but this seemed never to have entered his head. He was thinking only of the enemy, and loaded and fired as fast as he could.
>
> When the detachment reached the spot where he stood, the commanding officer, to his surprise, saw only a venerable man in black before him, quietly loading his gun to have another shot. Pausing a moment at the extraordinary spectacle of a single man thus coolly fighting a whole army, he exclaimed, "What are you doing there, you old fool, firing on His Majesty's troops?" The staunch old patriot looked up in the most unconcerned manner, and replied, *"Exercising the rights of war."* The whole affair seemed to strike the officer comically; and, rather amused than offended at the audacity of the proceeding, he said, "If I let you go this time, you old rascal, will you ever fire again on the troops of His Majesty?" *"Nothing more likely,"* was the imperturbable reply. This was too much for the good temper of the Briton, and he ordered his men

to seize him. They did so; and dragged him roughly down the hill to the head of the column.[85]

Dr. Dagget died 16 months later as a result of the rough treatment he received while confined. However, numbers of these "rebel parsons" fared much worse. Few were taken prisoner. Many had literal bounties on their heads. In a skirmish near Trenton, Reverend John Rossburgh got separated from his horse and was captured. With his request for mercy refused, Headley informs us that he "knelt down and committed his soul in prayer to his Maker—and while in this attitude was thrust through with the bayonet, and left weltering in his blood."[86]

Reverend James Caldwell, a Presbyterian pastor in Elizabethtown, New Jersey, was hated so much that the British troops burned his church, burned his parsonage and shot his wife through the breast in cold blood in front of their nine children! Headley describes the fate of this exceptional first lady:

> Arising from her devotions she sat down upon the bed, and was pondering on her desolate condition when the maid, who had accompanied her with the other children, stepped to the window to look out. As she did she saw a "red coat" jump over the fence into the yard. Alarmed, she turned quickly and told Mrs. Caldwell. The latter knew at once that evil was intended her, and arose from the bed either to watch the man's actions or to pass out of the room, when the villain caught a glimpse of her through the window. He knew her at a glance, and having come on purpose to kill her, he raised his musket, and fired at her through the window, when she fell amid her terrified children, pierced by two balls.[87]

Another writer adds:

> Not content with depriving her of her life, the inhuman monsters wreaked their cruelty on her senseless body. Her clothes were nearly torn off, and her body removed to the roadside, where it was subjected to every indignity, while the torch was applied to the dwelling.[88]

After burying his wife and placing the children with various parishioners, Reverend Caldwell reentered the conflict. When the American troops engaged in battle near Springfield began to falter for lack of wadding, Caldwell galloped to a nearby church and returned with an armful of hymnbooks. As he tossed them to the astounded men he cried, "Now put Watts into them, boys!"[89]

Of the 100-plus chaplains employed in the Continental Army, over a third were Baptists. Because of their reproachful tag as "dissenters," the Baptist clergymen were compelled to seek written permission that they "might be allowed to preach to the troops during the campaign with the same freedom as chaplains of the established Church."[90] As we should understand by now, these freedom-loving ministers were perceived as being a cut above the rest. Reverend David Jones was considered so dangerous that the British offered a reward for his capture.[91] Not only did Washington concur in this analysis, declaring, "Baptist chaplains were among the most prominent and useful in the army," but even the British general, Howe, was forced to concede, "The Baptists were among the most strenuous supporters of liberty."[92] With reference to Richard Furman, a Baptist pastor from South Carolina, Lord Cornwallis is said to have remarked that "he feared the prayers of that godly youth more than the armies of Sumter and Marion."[93]

Reverend John Gano, pastor of the First Baptist Church in New York City, became one of the most influential chaplains of the entire war, especially with Washington. Christian states, "As a minister of Christ he shone like a star of the first magnitude in the American churches, and moved in a widely extended field of action."[94] His courage under fire was legendary, making him "a great favorite with the troops and indeed an object of admiration as a man to the officers."[95] When gently reproved for getting too near harm's way, he was known to reply (on more than one occasion), "I somehow got in front of the regiment." The soldiers and officers alike loved to hear him preach, as his "plain, familiar way of talking...never failed to give him an attentive audience."[96] (Even the great Whitefield was once blessed by a sermon Gano preached years earlier in Charleston, South Carolina.[97]) He was with the men at Long Island. He crossed the icy Delaware with Washington and helped to pray down the amazing victory at Trenton. He is also thought to have ministered to the suffering men at Valley Forge where over 3,000 would die from exposure and disease.

VALLEY FORGE

While Catholic and Episcopal priests were under constant suspicion for their Loyalist sentiments, Baptist preachers like Gano were having a profound influence on Washington. In his famous biography, *The Life of George Washington*, M. L. Weems shares the unforgettable encounter that a friend of the General's named Potts experienced while walking through the snow at Valley Forge during the awful winter of '77.

> Treading his way along the venerable grove, suddenly he heard the sound of a human voice, which as he advanced increased on his ear, and at length became like the voice of one speaking much in earnest. As he approached the spot with a cautious step, whom should he behold, in a dark natural bower of ancient oaks, but the commander in chief of the American armies on his knees at prayer! Motionless with surprise, friend Potts continued on the place till the general, having ended his devotions, arose, and with a countenance of angel serenity, retired to headquarters: friend Potts then went home, and on entering his parlour called out to his wife, "Sarah, my dear! Sarah! All's well! All's well! George Washington will yet prevail."[98]

And prevail he did! Soon a number of rather unusual reinforcements began "showing up." A red-haired, 19-year-old French lad by the name of Gilbert du Motier volunteered his services free of charge. Better known as the *Marquis de Lafayette*, his propitious contributions were a "Godsend." His personal relationship with Washington induced him to predict, "His name will be revered throughout the centuries by all who love liberty and humanity."[99] Then there was the Prussian military veteran, Baron Friedrich Wilhelm Ludolf Gerhard Augustin von Steuben, who turned out to be a parson's son with no higher rank in the old country than that of a major. However, the "Baron" likewise proved his mettle, especially when training raw recruits. (Washington would later raise his rank to major general.) Once, while particularly frustrated, the colorful Prussian called to a translator, "These fellows won't do what I tell them! Come swear for me!"[100]

Angels seemed to be directing the musket balls fired from American rifles. Testifying of the intense rain of death pouring down upon his men from nearby treetops, Burgoyne exclaimed, "There was seldom a minute's interval of smoke, in any part of our line without officers being taken off by single shots."[101] Pointing to a particular British general, the American commander, Dan Morgan, said to one of his best shots, "That gallant officer is General Fraser. I admire him, but it is necessary that he should die. Do your duty." Within moments, the general lay mortally wounded.[102]

In addition to these sharp-shooting Virginia Rangers, Washington was blessed with hundreds of backwoods recruits from Pennsylvania (many exceeding six feet in height) who could fire "their balls into objects of seven inches diameter, at the distance of two hundred and fifty yards."[103] A captured rifleman from the Quebec campaign was actually sent to England to display his marksmanship to the British people as a demonstration of what their troops were enduring.[104]

General "Gentleman Johnny" Burgoyne surrendered his entire army of 5,000 men (and 300 "auxiliary" prostitutes[105]) to Washington at Saratoga on October 9, 1777. Most historians date this American victory as the turning point of the war.

YORKTOWN

In the year 1780, Cornwallis invaded the South with untold brutality, sparing neither age, sex, or infancy. When a force of volunteers from Virginia, Tennessee and both Carolinas came to the rescue on October 7, they learned that the British major, Patrick Ferguson, was entrenched atop South Carolina's King's Mountain with an army of 1,100 regulars. Ferguson boasted, "God Almighty Himself could not drive me from this hill."[106] What a fool! While his entire force was being wiped out (225 killed, 163 wounded and 716 captured), the major tried to escape on horseback but was riddled with lead. American casualties consisted of 28 killed and 62 wounded. The end was drawing near.

With the additional disasters at Cowpens on January 17 and the Guilford Courthouse on March 15, "Lord" Cornwallis was found licking his wounds at the seaport of Yorktown. Returning to his native Old Dominion with 2,000 Continentals, Washington assumed command of the siege force which now included, in addition to Lafayette's 5,000 men, the recently committed support of the French—an army of 4,000 under General Rochambeau and another 3,000 who came ashore from the fleet of Admiral Comte de Grasse, who proceeded to block an escape route by sea. If, as it has been said, Valley Forge was America's Gethsemane, Yorktown was destined to be Britain's Waterloo.

Once again, "Nature's God" would have the preeminence. In the midst of Virginia's mid-autumn Indian summer, Washington's prayer for a few nights of darkness was answered with an unseasonal rain, enabling him to position artillery close to the enemy's redoubts undetected. At approximately 5:00 p.m. on October 9, American soldiers ran up their flag which they called the star-spangled banner, and His Excellency, General Washington, personally fired the first cannon. Over 3,600 shells hit their mark in the next 24 hours. Dr. James Thacher, an American surgeon, testified:

All around was thunder and lightning from our numerous cannon and mortars, and in the darkness of night, presented one of the most sublime and magnificent spectacles which can be imagined...I have more than once witnessed fragments of the mangled bodies and limbs of the British soldiers thrown into the air by the bursting of our shells.[107]

On October 16, a desperate Cornwallis attempted to escape by night across the York River to Gloucester Point. However, Washington's God had other plans. Henry Johnson, an acclaimed authority on the Yorktown campaign, says:

It is possible that he could have succeeded; **but the elements interposed to stop him.** At midnight a storm arose, preventing the crossing of all the troops, and at dawn those who had already crossed returned to their old stations at the works, which were now crumbling away under the pointblank fire of the new batteries opened on the second parallel.[108]

By 10:00 a.m. on the 17th, Lord Cornwallis could be described as shell-shocked. His request for a 24-hour truce to discuss terms of capitulation was denied, Washington giving him only two. It was then agreed that a formal surrender would take place at 11:00 a.m. on the following day. However, when the appointed hour arrived, the big wimp was nowhere to be seen. Claiming he was "indisposed," Cornwallis sent an aide, General Charles O'Hare, in his place. Even Charlie tried to pull a fast one by attempting to surrender his sword to Rochambeau as a final snub to the American commander. The French general wisely deferred to Washington, who then deferred to his own aide, General Benjamin Lincoln.

Six and one-half years after Percy's troops played a mocking rendition of "Yankee Doodle" as they swaggered out of Boston toward Lexington, 7,247 bedraggled redcoats followed O'Hare with "a disorderly and unsoldierly conduct, their step was irregular, and their ranks frequently broken"[109] as their own band played, "The World Turned Upside Down." When they were ordered to stack arms, some threw down their weapons to damage them while others hugged them farewell; many were weeping as the band played on:

If ponies rode men and if grass ate cows,
And cats should be chased into holes by the mouse...

If summer were spring and the other way round,
Then all the world would be upside down.[110]

The news of this American victory caused veritable shock waves on both sides of the Atlantic. While Collins informs us that "the doorkeeper of the Continental Congress dropped dead with joy when he heard of the surrender of Cornwallis,"[111] the first words uttered by Lord North in London upon being informed of the British defeat were: "Oh, God, it is all over."[112] The British military historian, Major C. Stedman, concedes in his *History of the American War*:

> If we take a view of the strength and resources of Great Britain at the commencement of the hostilities, and contrast with the weakness and almost total inability of the revolting colonies, we shall have reason to conclude that the termination of the war in favor of the latter, with their final separation from the British empire, was one of those extraordinary and unexpected events, which in the course of human affairs rarely occur, and which bid defiance to all human foresight and calculation.[113]

America's Commander in Chief certainly knew *who* deserved the credit for the "extraordinary event." Thacher informs us that after Washington formally thanked his own men, as well as the French troops, he turned everyone's attention Heavenward. Having begun his war effort with an official directive to attend "divine services,"

> He closed by ordering that divine service shall be performed in the several brigades to-morrow, and recommends that the troops attend with a serious deportment, and with that sensibility of heart which the recollection of the surprising and particular interposition of Providence in our favor claims.[114]

GANO AND WASHINGTON

The Baptist pastor, John Gano, continued to be an obvious favorite of the General who normally maintained a reticence in religious matters throughout his long political career. When the eighth anniversary of the battle of Lexington was commemorated at New Windsor, New York, with the official proclamation by Congress of a formal cessation of hostilities, it was Washington's personal request that "prayer was offered to the Almighty

Ruler of the world by Rev. John Gano."[115] However, the apex of Washington's confidence in Gano just may be the best-kept secret in "religious" history. Despite the lack of official documentation, three of the pastor's own children personally testified that their father baptized Washington in the Hudson River at the close of the war.[116] Citing *The Baptism of George Washington* as recorded in the archives of the First Baptist Church of New York, New York, E. Wayne Thomson writes that Washington declared to Gano:

> I have been investigating the Scripture, and I believe immersion to be the baptism taught in the Word of God, and I demand it at your hands. I do not wish any parade made or the army called out, but simply a quiet demonstration of the ordinance.[117]

Dr. James Norwood, a former associate pastor of Dr. J. Frank Norris, cites from *A History of the First Baptist Church in the City of New York* by I. M. Haldemann, D.D.:

> While in camp at Newburgh, General Washington requested Pastor Gano to baptize him according to the Scriptures. He did so immersing him in believer's baptism, in the name of the Father, Son and Holy Ghost.[118]

Thompson further writes:

> Daniel Gano, one of Gano's sons and a captain of the artillery, was present and said that he, with about forty officers and men, accompanied the chaplain down to the Hudson River where the Reverend John Gano baptized George Washington.
>
> In 1908, E. T. Sanford of Manhattan's North Church commissioned a painting of Gano baptizing Washington. The painting was taken to the Baptist Church at Asbury, New Jersey, where it hung until Mrs. Elizabeth Johnston, John Gano's great-granddaughter, presented it to William Jewell College, Liberty, Missouri, in 1926.[119]

Those who would be quick to discredit this account on the basis that Washington maintained his membership in the Episcopalian church betray their ignorance of Scripture—John 3:1-2; 12:42-43; 18:17, 25, 27 to list but a few relevant passages. (The same would apply to aspersions they would cast on any other momentary weakness of character.) Furthermore, it was not an uncommon practice at that time for certain, more enlightened Episcopalians to request and receive scriptural baptism without leaving the visible security of the established church. If the Masonic Lodge can exploit our first president as some kind of "grand Pooh Bah" despite his written testimony that *"he had not attended lodge meetings more than once or twice in thirty years,"*[120] why should the word of three "p.k.'s" be dismissed so lightly?

VIRGINIA STATUTE OF RELIGIOUS LIBERTY

Although the colonists had won their political independence from England, they were still at odds with one another. The previously ratified Articles of Confederation would prove to be unsatisfactory—but why did America have to take the same amount of time (6½ years) to advance to the Constitution as she did to arrive at Yorktown? Who but a preacher of the Gospel would discern a *spiritual* "fly in the ointment"?

A full two years after the signing of the Declaration of Independence, Baptist ministers were *still* being sent to the gaols for crimes of conscience. With reference to the imprisonment of Reverend Elijah Baker in the Accomac County jail from July 1 to August 25, 1778, the underlying hypocrisy was sending forth more and more of a "stinking savour" in Old Dominion. Little writes:

> And this took place during the Revolution, when our forefathers were nobly battling for freedom. Strange anomaly that men who thought it to be their right and duty to sacrifice life and property for political and civil liberty, should deny their fellows liberty of conscience.[121]

Furthermore, Reverend Baker's case was about as harsh as you can find. This man of God was literally thrust into the hold of a ship with the captain being instructed to "land him on any coast out of America."[122]

By now, Jefferson and Madison were aware that their celebrated Article XVI was insufficient in itself to ensure religious liberty in Virginia, especially for the Baptists. As early as October 17, 1777, Jefferson had led a committee of five in producing the first draft of a radical new piece of legislation known as the *Virginia Statute of Religious Liberty* that would be strong enough to guarantee freedom of conscience for all. Ironically enough, the five reformers—Jefferson, George Mason, Edmund Pendleton, George Wythe and Thomas Ludwell Lee collaborated in Fredericksburg, the same town where the first imprisonment of Baptist preachers occurred in June,

1768. And was it a double coincidence that the protomartyrs involved totaled five in number—Lewis Craig, John Waller, James Chiles, James Reed and William Mash?

Jefferson's reforms got off to a constructive start in 1779 with a vote on December 13 repealing the old law that empowered the established church. However, with the pressure of the British invasion behind them, the bill's progress slowed considerably in post-war years. The old complacency soon began settling in again, characterized by the statement of John Adams in 1774 that, "they might as well expect a change in the Solar system, as to expect that we would give up our ecclesiastical establishment,"[123] (referring to the support of the Congregational churches through taxation). With supernatural interruptions in the heavens having already occurred from Long Island to Yorktown, the time had arrived for the Founding Fathers and the Heavenly Father to have a meeting of the minds. If they intended to put the more important "religious revolution" on the back burner, they could rest assured that the country would continue to spin its wheels under the ineffectual Articles of Confederation.

After three further years of "kicking against the pricks," America's most influential colony finally began to see the light. But as Cornwallis had attempted a last-minute escape on the eve of his surrender, the devil threw an incredibly subtle monkey wrench into the proceedings known as the General Assessment Bill. Without an understanding of New Testament soul liberty, a number of otherwise conservative Fathers, such as Henry and Washington, had arrived at the erroneous conclusion that a religious tax which left the church of designation up to the individual citizen was an even better idea than dismantling the entire system. While almost every denomination supported the proposal, three Baptist preachers, Jeremiah Moore, Jeremiah Walker and John Young, arrived at the Virginia legislature (meeting in a warehouse in Richmond) pushing a wheelbarrow that contained a petition opposing the general assessment, *signed by 10,000 Virginians!*[124] Predictably, it was the Baptists, whose grasp of Scripture enabled them to exercise a superior discernment, warning, "Who does not see that the same authority which can establish Christianity in exclusion of all other religions may establish, with the same ease, any particular sect of Christians, in exclusion of all other sects?"[125]

As Jefferson was abroad, James Madison represented the Baptists with his remarkable treatise entitled *Memorial and Remonstrance,* arguing from history that Christianity would flourish best without the support of the government:

> The establishment proposed by this Bill is not requisite for the support of the Christian Religion. To say that it is, is a contradiction to the Christian Religion itself...for it is known that this Religion both existed and flourished, not only without the support of human laws, but in spite of every opposition from them.[126]

Logic such as this rendered the bill untenable, and it died of natural causes on October 17, 1785. Madison subsequently reentered Jefferson's bill on December 17, 1785, and, this time it was gloriously passed and signed by the Speaker on January 19, 1786. The revolutionary legislation read as follows:

> Be it enacted by the General Assembly, That no man shall be compelled to frequent or support any religious worship, place or ministry whatsoever; nor shall be enforced, restrained, molested or burthened in his body or goods, nor shall otherwise suffer on account of his religious opinions or belief; but that all men shall be free to profess and by argument to maintain their opinions in matters of religion, and that the same shall in no wise diminish, enlarge or affect the civil capacities.[127]

Lest anyone doubt the historical link between Thomas Jefferson and Baptist polity molding his reported conclusion "that it would be the best plan of government for the American colonies,"[128] one need only refer to the words on his tombstone: "Thomas Jefferson, Author of the Declaration of Independence, of the Statute of Virginia for Religious Freedom, and Father of the University of Virginia."[129]

THE FIRST AMENDMENT

Now that the Lord was pleased, the creation of the United States Constitution would be right around the corner. However, when that venerable document, penned by James Madison, was submitted to the states for ratification, the Baptists showed an immediate alarm over the absence of any *specific* guarantees of religious liberty. The man of the hour for this climactic period of America's destiny was yet another Baptist pastor, Reverend John Leland. Thomas Armitage, citing Dr. Semple's *History*, says of Leland, "He was probably the most popular preacher who ever resided in Virginia."[130]

John Leland, a neighbor of both Thomas Jefferson and James Madison, was nominated to be the Orange County delegate to the Virginia convention for ratification. Knowing that Reverend Leland's concerns were not so much with what the Constitution said, but rather with what it specifically did *not* say, Madison embarked upon an historic private conference with the influential Baptist. When Madison assured the man of God and that he would lobby for a favorable amendment as a forthcoming member of the Virginia House of Representatives, his would-be rival not only pledged his personal support but graciously stepped aside, allowing the more persuasive and articulate Madison to attend the convention in his place.

After a long and hot debate, the Virginia convention ratified the Constitution on July 28, 1788, by a vote of 89-79, five days after New Hampshire's endorsement had settled the nine-state minimum. The following year, Madison defeated James Monroe for Congress and set out to fulfill his part of the bargain.

In the meantime, George Washington was elected America's first president on April 6 and established a wonderful tradition by adding to the proposed inaugural oath "so help me, God." When the General Committee of the United Baptist Churches of Virginia sent Washington their formal congratulations, as well as their concerns over Madison's pending amendment, the Father of our country sent back his warmest personal assurances:

> If I could have entertained the slightest apprehension that the Constitution framed in the convention where I had the honor to preside might possibly endanger the religious rights of any ecclesiastical society, certainly I would never have placed my signature to it; and if I could now conceive that the General Government might ever be administered as to render the liberty of conscience insecure, I beg you will be persuaded that no one would be more zealous than myself to establish effectual barriers against the horrors of spiritual tyranny and every species of religious persecution.[131]

In his closing remarks, the first president of the United States praised the Baptists for the exceptional patriotism they displayed throughout the revolution:

> While I recollect with satisfaction that the religious society of which you are members have been throughout America, uniformly and almost

unanimously, the firm friends to civil liberty, and the persevering promoters of our glorious revolution, I cannot hesitate to believe that they will be faithful supporters of a free yet efficient General Government. Under this pleasing expectation I rejoice to assure them that they may rely upon my best wishes and endeavors to advance their prosperity.[132]

We can all be grateful that these promises of Washington and Madison were made in a time when a man's word was his bond. James Madison faithfully championed the historic Baptist distinctive of soul liberty, and there was no way to refute the argument. As Eidsmoe summarized: "Society is unable to give government authority over religion because society has no authority over religion—religion is a matter between God and each individual."[133]

When Madison introduced his initial proposal of the First Amendment on the floor of the House of Representatives on June 7, 1789, the wording stated: "The Civil Rights of none shall be abridged on account of religious belief or worship, nor shall any national religion be established, nor shall the full and equal rights of conscience be in any manner, nor on any pretext infringed."[134]

Because the First Amendment was such a political hot potato, Madison's original draft was altered several times in committee. However, the cardinal point regarding his first proposal confirms the author's clarity of intent. From the phrase, "nor shall any national religion be established," we understand that the primary objective of the First Amendment was to check the possibility of another state church ever rearing its ugly head in America again.

Finally, 1,757 long years after God's first preachers were confronted by local authorities who *"laid hands on them, and put them in hold unto the next day"* (Acts 4:3a), the dawn of a new era had most definitely arrived. Collectively ratified on December 15, 1791, the First Amendment of the Bill of Rights reads as follows:

> Congress shall make no law respecting an establishment of religion, or prohibiting the free exercise thereof; or abridging the freedom of speech, or of the press; or the right of the people peaceably to assemble, and to petition the Government for a redress of grievances.

Is it any wonder that the renowned John Locke wrote: "The Baptists were the first and only propounders of absolute liberty."[135]

Thanks to the doggedness of a patriotic Baptist preacher, America could now be *"free indeed."* (John 8:36b) The pastor's memorial can be seen alongside a lone highway in Orange County, Virginia:

1754–1841
ELDER JOHN LELAND
COURAGEOUS LEADER OF
THE BAPTIST DOCTRINE
ARDENT ADVOCATE OF THE PRINCIPLES
OF DEMOCRACY
VINDICATOR OF SEPARATION
OF CHURCH AND STATE

NEAR THIS SPOT IN 1788 ELDER JOHN LELAND AND
JAMES MADISON, THE FATHER OF THE AMERICAN
CONSTITUTION, HELD A SIGNIFICANT INTERVIEW
WHICH RESULTED IN THE ADOPTION OF THE
CONSTITUTION BY VIRGINIA. THEN MADISON
A MEMBER OF CONGRESS FROM ORANGE PRESENTED
THE FIRST AMENDMENT TO THE CONSTITUTION
GUARANTEEING RELIGIOUS LIBERTY, FREE SPEECH AND
A FREE PRESS. THIS SATISFIED LELAND AND HIS
BAPTIST FOLLOWERS.
PRESENTED BY EUGENE BUCKLIN BOWEN PRESIDENT
BERKSHIRE COUNTY MASSACHUSETTS CHAPTER
SONS OF THE AMERICAN REVOLUTION

X

A Turnpike to the Pacific

> *"I know thy works: behold, I have set thee an open door, and no man can shut it: for thou hast a little strength, and hast kept my word, and hast not denied my name."*
> (Revelation 3:8)

WHENEVER MEN DEBATE the character of America, their opposing points of view often tend toward a natural polarization. While one side yells, "Down with America!" the other answers, "My Country—right or wrong!" Unfortunately, Christians also gravitate to these ideological extremes. Whereas one group of believers can be so "hyper-conspiracy minded" that they will depict the Founding Fathers as borderline agents of Satan (through any number of suggested relationships with the Illuminati, Masonic Order, etc.), the others are so "God-and-country" oriented that they will unite with the Catholic Church, *the historical enemy of Christianity*, in order to salvage what is left of America, despite the clear injunctions of Scripture such as II Corinthians 6:14-17 and Ephesians 5:11. The first faction has been terribly spoiled while the other chooses to remain in willful ignorance.

What kind of fool would expect America to be perfect? Is it fair to require a higher level of consistency from the United States than was ever attained by God's covenant nation of Israel? America has always been a land consisting of flawed human beings commonly known as sinners. As noted in the previous chapter, her early rise to greatness was occasioned by an unparalleled concentration of salt in her Christian foundation. With Clinton initiating his presidency by advancing the rights of queers, who could fail to note the appreciable difference in Washington's inauguration prayer?

> Almighty God, we make our earnest prayer that thou wilt keep the United States in thy holy protection; that thou wilt incline the hearts of the citizens to cultivate a spirit of subordination and obedience to government; to entertain a brotherly affection and love for one another and for their fellow citizens of the United States at large. And finally that thou will most graciously be pleased to dispose us all to do justice, to love mercy and to demean ourselves with that charity, humility, and pacific temper of mind which were the characteristics of the divine Author of our blessed religion, and without a humble imitation of whose example in these things we can never hope to be a happy nation. Grant our supplication, we beseech thee, through Jesus Christ our Lord. AMEN.[1]

And in his opening address to Congress:

> It would be peculiarly improper to omit, in this first official act, my fervent supplication to that Almighty Being who presides in the councils of nations, that his benediction may consecrate to the liberties and happiness of the people of the United States a government instituted by themselves. Every step by which they have advanced to the character of an independent nation seems to have been distinguished by some token of providential agency...Heaven can never smile on a nation that disregards the eternal rules of order and right.[2]

It would take less than five years (1794) for the shocking suppression of Pennsylvania's Whiskey Rebellion by 15,000 troops to reveal the new government's potential for inciting charges of malfeasance in the future (not to mention the moral implications of the taxed "product" itself). However, America's current record status as the world's longest-surviving republic-democracy confirms that "some token of providential agency" has indeed sustained her less-than-utopian measures.

Therefore, it would behoove us all to discern America's true purpose of existence in the light of an eternal blueprint. *With the securing of the First Amendment in 1789, the church of Jesus Christ was given its first haven of rest in over 15 centuries of political-religious suppression!*

DOCTRINE OF ORIGINAL INTENT

Against the historic context that the First Amendment was originally secured by Baptists for the sole purpose of ensuring that no one religious denomination (i.e., the Episcopalian in the South or the Congregational in the North) would gain a politically induced ascendancy over the other faiths, the absurdity of the Supreme Court's present-day interpretation becomes apparent. How could an *honest* man (Supreme Court justice or not) misread such a clearly worded statement: "Congress shall make no law respecting the establishment of religion, or prohibiting the free exercise thereof." Isn't it strange how the term *separation of church and state* is not contained in either the Constitution or the Bill of Rights? And the setting in which this statement was actually issued, *13 years after the First Amendment was adopted*, is a further indication of the insidious mind-set of today's humanistic judiciary.

Upon receipt of a letter from the Danbury Baptist Association of Danbury, Connecticut, expressing concern over rumors that a certain church was being considered as a national denomination, President Thomas Jefferson issued a written reassurance on June 1, 1802, that the "*wall* of the First Amendment" would keep the government from interfering in religious matters: "I contemplate with solemn reverence that act of the whole American people which declared that their legislature should 'make no law respecting an establishment of religion, or prohibiting the free exercise thereof,' thus building a wall of separation between Church and State."[3]

When one becomes further acquainted with the source of Jefferson's metaphor, the "original intent" of his phrase (which, in itself, is not even a part of any authoritative legislation) becomes absolutely unmistakable. As the President was addressing an association of Baptists, he chose a meaty and illuminative statement from the pen of Roger Williams who wrote:

> When they have opened a gap in the hedge or **wall of separation between the garden of the church and the wilderness of the world**, God hath ever broke down the wall itself, removed the candlestick, and made his garden a wilderness, as at this day. And that there fore if He will eer [sic] please to restore His garden and paradise again, **it must of necessity be walled in peculiarly unto Himself from the world**.[4]

According to Roger Williams, the "wall of separation" was intended to protect the "garden of the church" from the "wilderness of the world." Jefferson made this interpretation clear on many other occasions. In his second inaugural address he stated, "In matters of religion I have considered that its free exercise is placed by the Constitution independent of the powers of the General Government."[5] And in a letter to Reverend Samuel Miller in 1808 he wrote, "I consider the government of the United States as interdicted by the Constitution from intermeddling with religious institutions, their doctrines, discipline, or exercises."[6] To insist that this sacrosanct "wall" was erected to debar the slightest allusion to Almighty God within the halls of American government is ludicrous in the extreme! How could anyone with even the slightest understanding of the facts promote such a lie? My dear friend, our Founding Fathers were so sensitive to their need of God that when the shortages of a war-strained economy began including Bibles, an appeal to Congress in 1777 requesting an emergency supply of Scriptures was forwarded to the appropriate committee and resulted in the following recommendation:

> **That the use of the Bible is so universal, and its importance so great**...your Committee recommend[s] that Congress will order the Committee of Commerce to import 20,000 Bibles from Holland, Scotland, or elsewhere, into the different parts of the States of the Union. Whereupon, the Congress was moved, to order the Committee of Commerce to import twenty-thousand copies of the Bible.[7]

Having graduated from a Roman Catholic high school in Wilmington, Delaware, I was amazed to discover the requirements for a delegate to the Constitutional convention from the state that would later hold the distinction of being the first to ratify the Constitution itself:

> Article 22. Every person, who shall be chosen a member of either house, or appointed to any office or place of trust... shall...make and subscribe the following declaration, to wit: "I, _____, do profess faith in God the Father, and in Jesus Christ, His only Son, and in the Holy Ghost, one God, blessed for evermore; and I do acknowledge the holy scriptures of the Old and New Testament to be given by divine inspiration."[8]

A FAIR FIGHT WITH ROME

Along with the unprecedented protection of the First Amendment came an equally unprecedented opportunity and responsibility. The local New Testament churches in America were now free to do what their colonial and European predecessors could never have dreamed of accomplishing for Christ. What had been addressed to a single church, 17 centuries earlier, was now coming to pass for an entire nation of churches. Is it any wonder that this uniquely privileged church of the first century just happened to be located in the city of **Philadelphia**? *"I know thy works: behold, I have set before thee an open door, and no man can shut it: for thou hast a little strength, and hast kept my word, and hast not denied my name."* (Revelation 3:8)

For their refusal to deny His name, scores of Baptist pastors had been confined to "the gaols" where they exchanged physical strength for spiritual power and, from hearts of *brotherly love*, proclaimed His Word through iron grates to the masses assembled without. Their *"works"* did not go unnoticed by *"he that hath the key of David."* Not only did God use the First Amendment to reward His servants with an open door of evangelistic opportunity, but He also promised that no *human* would ever close the same. And herein lies the great secret to a proper interpretation of American history. The same Bill of Rights that would now afford the Baptists their long-awaited asylum would give the Bloody Whore proselyting privileges as well. The same would also be true for an array of lesser cults, atheists and miscellaneous reprobates poised on the horizon. It is no coincidence that in 1789, the very year that the federal government was established, the Vatican's American hierarchy was also initiated with the consecration of former Jesuit John Carroll in England. In the providence of God, John Leland and James Madison had merely ensured that the historic conflict between Christianity and Catholicism would henceforth be a "fair fight." Not only would the United States have a free market in economics (yet another application of soul liberty), but she would also have one in religious matters as well. Speaking on behalf of his Catholic minority, Bishop Carroll hypocritically proclaimed:

> Thanks to the genuine spirit of christianity [sic]! The United States have banished intolerance from their systems of government, and many of them have done the justice to every denomination of christians [sic], which ought to be done to them in all, of placing them on the same footing of citizenship, and conferring an equal right of participation in national privileges.[9]

The church of Jesus Christ would now have to win more converts than the Vatican or her newfound haven would revert back to papal tyranny. Also, the size of the playing field was destined to expand considerably, as Dr. John Witherspoon once remarked to his friend, Ashbel Green: "Don't be surprised if you see a **turnpike all the way to the Pacific Ocean** in your lifetime."[10] In a deeper, spiritual application of Wendell Phillips' admonition that "Eternal vigilance is the price of liberty," whatever blessings America would enjoy would be henceforth determined by the *salt* in her soil and the *light* on her hills, for *"Righteousness exalteth a nation; but sin is a reproach to any people."* (Proverbs 14:34) The Baptists and a periodic confederation of revived Protestants would have to outwork the subversive agents of His Holiness.

Though not a Baptist, John Adams was one of the more important Founding Fathers because of his perception of the enslaving tenets of Romanism and his willingness to be outspoken on the matter. In his 1765 "Dissertation on Canon and Feudal Law," Adams exposed the Vatican's track record by declaring that her clergy had

> found Ways to make the World believe that God had entrusted them with Keys of Heaven whose Gates they might open and shut at Pleasure, with the Power of Dispensation over all the Rules and Types of Morality, the Power of Licensing all sorts both of sins and Crimes, with the Power of Deposing Princes, and absolving all their subjects from their Allegiance, with the Power of Procuring or withholding the Rain of Heaven, and the Beams of the Sun, with the Power of Earthquakes, (Plagues,) Pestilence, Famine; nay with the Power of creating Blood Nay the Blood of God out of Wine, and Flesh the Flesh of God out of Bread. Thus was human Nature held for Ages, fast Bound in servitude, in a cruel, shameful, deplorable Bondage to him and his subordinate Tyrants who it was foretold in the Apocalypse, would exalt himself above all that is called God and that is worshiped.[11]

As America's crisis hour drew near, Adams sent the following warning to the president of Congress:

> The Court of Rome, attached to ancient customs, would be one of the last to acknowledge our independence, if we were to solicit it. But Congress will probably send a Minister to his Holiness, who can do them no service, upon condition of receiving a Catholic legate in return; or, in other words, an ecclesiastical tyrant, which, it is to be hoped, the United States will be too wise ever to admit into their territories.[12]

On a Sunday afternoon, October 9, 1774, the ever-wary Adams was in Philadelphia with George Washington, when, "led by curiosity and good company," they opted for an impromptu visit at the local Catholic church to observe their ritualistic vespers. Adams' eyewitness account as preserved in a letter to his wife Abigail (described by the Jesuit Hennesey as coming from a "jaundiced pen,"[13]) depicts the religious mumbo-jumbo which only reinforced his suspicions:

> This Afternoon's Entertainment was to me most awfull and affecting; the poor Wretches fingering their beads, chanting Latin, not a Word of which they understood; their Pater Nosters and Ave Marias, their holy Water, their Crossing themselves perpetually; their Bowing to the Name of Jesus, whenever they hear it, their Bowings, Kneelings and genuflections before the Altar.... The Altar-Piece was very rich, little Images and Crucifixes about; Wax Candles all lighted up. But how shall I describe the Picture of our Saviour in a Frame of Marble over the Altar, at full Length, upon the Cross in the Agonies, and the Blood dropping and streaming from his Wounds! The Music, consisting of an Organ and a Choir of Singers, went all the Afternoon except Sermon Time, and the Assembly chanted most sweetly and exquisitely. Here is everything which can lay hold of the eye, ear and imagination—everything which can charm and bewitch the simple and the ignorant. I wonder how Luther ever broke the spell.[14]

However, as "the best of men are but men at best," Washington and the Congress began to earnestly solicit an alliance with Catholic France as the war with their Protestant mother country continued to escalate. Having never started a country before, the novice legislators (with the exception of Adams and a few others) were in for some humbling lessons. They soon discovered (as did King Jehoshaphat from his unholy alliance with Ahab) that these political "deals" would have a religious price tag attached. The Jesuit historian, James Hennesey, smugly relates the pitiful spectacle of America's Bible-believing legislators having to "toe the line" by visiting Catholic churches on several occasions in order to secure the eventual participation of a token French force at the final battle of the war:

> Congress came four times in a body to St. Mary's, twice for requiem masses and twice for thanksgiving services arranged by the French Minister. James Rivington's New York *Royal Gazette* could not let slip the chance to mock President Samuel Huntington of the Continental Congress, who "besprinkled and sanctified himself" with the holy water offered him at the church door, and the members of "this egregious Congress" who, "now reconciled to the Papish Communion," carried lighted tapers in their hands at a mass for Spanish agent Don Juan de Miralles, who had died while visiting the army at Morristown. Dr. Benjamin Rush sent regrets and wrote on the back of his invitation:

"Declined attending as not compatible with the principles of a Protestant."[15]

VATICAN DUPLICITY

Unfortunately, few of the esteemed members of Congress dared exhibit the conviction of Dr. Rush for fear of alienating France. As it turned out, the French "support" showed itself to be consistent with the political track record of their church; casuistic in thought, equivocal in speech, amphibological in print, and "crawdadish" in sticky wicket predicaments. Both General Rochambeau and Admiral de Grasse gave Washington fits as they undermined his stratagems behind the scenes. Although Rochambeau had nominally submitted to the authority of the American commander-in-chief (seven years his junior), Langguth exposed the Frenchman's true convictions by affirming, "When he thought Washington was mistaken, he felt no obligation to abet him."[16]

After Washington had planned for months to use his new allies in a major assault on the British defenses in New York, Rochambeau pulled a last minute fast one on his American superior by secretly redirecting Admiral de Grasse to sail for the Chesapeake Bay instead. In a rare response to this first of many surprises by the French (which providentially opened the southern campaign that culminated at Yorktown), Washington got out of character and literally pitched a holy fit!

> When he realized that Rochambeau had forced the change on him, Washington had gone into a rage. Oblivious to the others in his headquarters room, he strode back and forth, crying out that his hopes were blasted and his country lost. That went on for half an hour, until Washington regained himself and apologized to a group of civilian visitors who had witnessed the scene. But then Washington burst out again: If only the French would either fulfil his expectations or not raise them at all. Washington had wanted desperately to retake New York. Now that would have to wait still another year.[17]

The real attitude of the average Frenchman back in the old country (excluding antsy military officers in search of adventure) can be detected from an earlier letter the Marquis de Lafayette sent his wife Adrienne following Howe's capture of Philadelphia, which informed her how to respond when assailed by their own anti-American countrymen:

> You will reply politely, "You are all absolute idiots. Philadelphia is an uninteresting little town, open on all sides; its port was already blockaded; it was made famous, God knows why, because Congress resided there; that's what this famous city really is; and, by the way, we'll undoubtedly take it back sooner or later."[18]

The average secular historian would like you to think that America could have never won the war without the intervention of Catholic France. In his classic work, *A History of Warfare*, author John Keegan, described by Tom Clancy as "the best military historian of our generation," gives the *above-average* assessment: "Yet, despite foreign assistance, the victory was unquestionably the Americans' own and the example they gave was a major stimulus to the demands laid by the French constitutionalists against Louis XVI."[19]

Due to the unbiblical constraints of diplomatic courtesy, America's victorious leadership would now be expected to express their humble appreciation to the "Johnny-come-lately" French by making yet another political pilgrimage, back to the St. Mary's Catholic Church in Philadelphia. Thacher's eyewitness account begins: "The Congress of the United States, the assembly and council of the state of Pennsylvania, and a number of principal gentlemen of various orders, having been invited by the minister of France to be present at the praises offered to Heaven in the Catholic Church..."[20]

Now since when would the Glory World be interested in the pagan praises of a Roman Catholic temple in the city of Philadelphia? Note the ecumenical double-talk that flowed from the lips of this eminent muckety-muck, the Abbe Bandole, Almoner to the Embassy of His Most Christian Majesty:

> Who but he, in whose hands are the hearts of men, could inspire the allied troops with the friendship, the confidence, the tenderness of brothers? How is it that two nations, once divided, jealous, inimical, and nursed in reciprocal prejudices, are now become so closely united as to form but one?... **Let us prostrate ourselves at the altar**... Let us beseech him to continue to shed on the councils of the king, your ally, that spirit of wisdom, of justice, and of courage, which has rendered his reign so glorious... let us, with one will and one voice, pour forth to the Lord that hymn of praise, by which Christians celebrate their gratitude and his glory.[21]

For the record, by the time this little propaganda speech was given asking for continued "wisdom, justice and courage" upon the "glorious reign" of Louis XVI and Marie "Let-them-eat-cake" Antoinette, the passive puppet king had already allowed the Catholic Church to accumulate 20% of his nation's real estate[22] (generating an annual income of 120 million livres), rake in an additional 123 million in peasant tithes levied on the produce and livestock of the soil,[23] and maintain a strong anti-Christian climate that prohibited Protestant meetings, marriages, education and the holding of public office by Protestants. (Louis' clamping down on the church through his treasury-replenishing reforms of 1787 were basically too little and too late, as the guillotine would shortly confirm.)

By the end of his second term in office, Washington had grown wise to the danger of foreign entanglements, especially with the satellite governments of the Vatican. In his famous Farewell Address of September 17, 1796, he warned:

> Europe has a set of primary interests, which to us have none, or a very remote relation.—Hence she must be engaged in frequent controversies, the causes of which are essentially foreign to our concerns... Our detached and distant situation invites us to pursue a different course... 'Tis our true policy to steer clear of permanent alliances, with any portion of the foreign world.[24]

Furthermore, contrary to the self-defeating, anti-historical and un-American efforts of such generic libertarians as Laissez Faire Books, who would publish trash like *Atheism, the Case Against God*, the Father of our country left his young republic with a pretty narrow message:

> **Of all the dispositions and habits which lead to political prosperity, Religion and Morality are indispensable supports.** In vain would that man claim the tribute of Patriotism, who should labor to subvert these great pillars of human happiness, these firmest props of the duties of Men and Citizens. The mere Politician, equally with the pious man ought to respect and cherish them....
> **It is substantially true that virtue or morality is a necessary spring of popular government.** The rule, indeed, extends with more or less force to every species of free government. Who, that is a sincere friend to it, can look with indifference upon attempts to shake the foundation of the fabric?[25]

When Washington declined to run for a third term in 1796, his vice president, John Adams, narrowly defeated the Republican challenger, Thomas Jefferson, by only three electoral votes. President Adams was another early leader who often spoke on the vital role of the Christian faith in our nation. With reference to the greater heavenly purpose for America's existence, he wrote: "I always consider the settlement of America with reverence and wonder, as the opening of a grand scene and design in Providence for the illumination of the ignorant, and the emancipation of the slavish part of mankind all over the earth."[26]

JEFFERSON & THE LOUISIANA PURCHASE

The 12-year reign of the Federalist party ended in 1800 with the election of Adams' long-time friend and sometimes political rival, Thomas Jefferson. Although the expression *Manifest Destiny* was not in vogue as yet, the seeds of expansion began to germinate during the Jefferson administration. In his inaugural address of March 4, 1801, he proclaimed:

> Kindly separated by nature and a wide ocean from the exterminating havoc of one quarter of the globe;...possessing a chosen country, with room enough for our descendants to the hundredth and thousandth generation; entertaining a due sense of our equal right to the use of our own faculties, to the acquisitions of our industry... acknowledging and adoring an overruling Providence, which by all its dispensations proves that it delights in the happiness of man here and his greater happiness hereafter; with all these blessings, what more is necessary to make us a happy and prosperous people? Still one thing more, fellow citizens—a wise and frugal government, which shall restrain men from injuring one another, which shall leave them otherwise free to regulate their own pursuits of industry and improvement, and shall not take from the mouth of labor the bread it has earned. This is the sum of good government, and this is necessary to close the circle of our felicities.[27]

Jefferson's noble words were soon crowned with the real estate deal of the century. In April of 1803, James Madison and Robert Livingston orchestrated the now-famous Louisiana Purchase in which the United States government paid Napoleon $15 million for all his American holdings totaling over 827,987 square miles. For the unbelievable price of three cents an acre, the desperate Catholic dictator had enabled America to literally double in size. Thirteen states would eventually be created in whole or part from this amazing stroke of Providence. (The constitutionality of the Louisiana Purchase has been the source of much debate.)

With the Louisiana Purchase being added to the vast territory acquired by the treaty with Great Britain in 1783, America's "turnpike to the Pacific" was already stretching to the base of the Rocky Mountains. From 1790 to 1820, the following new states were admitted to the Union: Vermont (1791), Kentucky (1792), Tennessee (1796), Ohio (1803), Louisiana (1812), Indiana (1816), Mississippi (1817), Illinois (1818), Alabama (1819) and Maine (1820). Their combined population totaled 2,662,000.

Of course, all of this activity was not making the devil happy. As a million Easterners had already *"gone* west," before Horace Greeley was even born ("Go West, young man and grow up with the country," 1851), the churches were beginning to experience a serious depletion in their ranks. James Freeman (1759-1835) planted the Unitarian banner in New England, with the American Unitarian Association being formed in 1825. Many of the colleges were in serious trouble. Writing of Yale, Hardman states, "Christianity was dead at what had once been its proudest Connecticut fortress; infidelity reigned."[28] Dr. Ashbel Green, who enrolled in Princeton in 1782, wrote, "While I was a member of the college, there were but two professors of religion among the students, and not more than five or six who scrupled the use of profane language in common conversation."[29]

Much of this spiritual deterioration was attributable to the theistic writings of Thomas Paine; particularly his blasphemous booklet entitled *The Age of Reason*, which was printed in France and imported to America in great quantities. Tom should have quit while he was ahead with "the times that try men's souls." Ridiculing the fundamental doctrines of the Bible, he wrote: "Putting aside everything that might excite laughter by its absurdity, or detestion by its profaneness, and confining ourselves merely to an examination of the parts, it is impossible to conceive a story more derogatory to the Almighty, more inconsistent with his wisdom, more contradictory to his power than this story is."[30]

Ethan Allan's 477-page book attacking divine revelation entitled *Reason, the Only Oracle of Man*, didn't help matters either. The revolutionary hero who had once demanded the surrender of Fort Ticonderoga "in the name of the Great Jehovah and the Continental Congress" was now rationalizing that "there could be no justice or goodness in one being's suffering for another, nor is it at all compatible with reason to suppose, that God was the contriver of such a propitiation."[31]

Other key personages were also challenging the Christian faith. Henry Dearborn, Jefferson's secretary of war, and an avowed atheist, said of America's churches, "So long as these temples stand we cannot hope for good government."[32] General Charles Lee was so violently opposed to the faith that in his will he stipulated he not be buried "in any church or church yard, or within a mile of any Presbyterian or Anabaptist meeting-house."[33] The disloyal wretch who had caused Washington so much grief kicked the bucket in a squalid Pennsylvania tavern. And all these problems were just the ones that affected the churches in the East.

When we come to America's new frontier (west of the Allegheny Mountains), a whole new set of satanic challenges had to be met. In addition to the thousands of Catholic settlers left over from the Quebec Act, a heathen "Injun" population was being augmented by a migration of land-crazed palefaces with little time or patience for religion. Hardman describes this rugged mission field:

> Because the awakening had not begun as yet, Sunday was used for hunting, fishing, horse racing, dancing, and anything else... On the whole, frontiersmen were a hardworking group. They were rough and ready in speech, impatient with hypocrisy and ceremony, and conditioned to severe situations and toughness. Their entire lives were simple and direct... Hunters might be seen with their long rifles over their shoulders, perhaps some small game hung from their belts, and a pack of bear-dogs yelping after them. The days would be spent hunting or at work on a farm, and the evenings given to storytelling interspersed with the consumption of hard liquor....For the most part the frontiersmen were not determined against Christianity, but they had been in something of a moral and spiritual vacuum since their moving to the frontier and leaving the churches behind. Many of the pioneers had some knowledge, however inadequate, of Christian teachings. But on the frontier to that time the spiritual life was not cultivated, Bibles and other literature in the rude homes were few, and worship services fewer yet.[34]

Some parts of the West were more wicked than others. The early settlers in Kentucky named a number of their towns after prominent atheists such as Altamont, Bourbon, LaRue and Rousseau. In 1743 the Kentucky legislature voted to dispense the office of chaplain as being no longer necessary. Entire towns of desperadoes were formed such as the infamous "Rogues Harbor" of Logan County, Kentucky. The evils of drunkenness, profanity, gambling, horse racing, cockfighting, dueling, fornication and adultery were claiming multitudes of debilitated disciples. Numbers of cults began moving in for the kill; Campbellism (1810), Mormonism (1831), Seventh Day Adventism (1844) and Russellism—better known as the "J.W.'s"— (1872) all added to the confusion of the times. In the absence of a strong Gospel witness, half of America was dangling "hair-hung and breeze-shaken over the very pit of Hell," as the saying was wont to be made.

The declining state of America's spirituality was also cause for alarm among believers in possession of a vision for worldwide evangelism. Hardman explains:

> But in another sense, there was a new meaning and urgency in the conviction of an increasing number that America was meant to be God's light to the world. In Puritan days the concept of missions was still embryonic, and the sending of missionaries was an occasional thing. By 1800, however, a new dynamic had arrived, and ambassadors of the cross were going to distant lands. That was undoubtedly an extension of God's original purpose in colonizing the New World. It was hoped that in time, as America matured, it might send missionaries back to Europe and throughout the world to spread the good news of Christ. Therefore, as Charles Hodge proclaimed, the character of America was of "unutterable importance to the world." If God's purpose was to use America as a major base for the evangelization of all men, Hodge asked, "whether a generation ever lived on whose fidelity so much depended?"[35]

In the midst of this growing national despair, the Lord of Glory was at work behind the scenes. Hardman relates the insights of Reverend Silas Mercer, a notable Baptist pastor from Georgia who, in 1795, "in one of the more profound interpretations of the time endeavored to trace the finger of God":

> But why are these things so? To which we answer. The great Governor of the Universe does not always work by miracles, neither offers violence to the human will. It cannot be thought, but that he could have made his people perfect in soul, body, and spirit, at the same time when he converted their souls. But it appears to us, that Jehovah, in his wise providence, saw proper to continue them in connection with an old corrupt nature, in order to properly discipline them, that by the various combats between flesh and spirit, they may be weaned from sensual delight, and learn to trust their all in him. But again: in a lively time of religion, hypocrites and formalists are apt to creep into the Church, therefore, a

time of trial is necessary to purge these, as dross from the pure gold or real Christians. And further: the Lord intends, it may be, by this way to prove that salvation is by grace alone; for in a time of declension no man or set of men, no, not all the people in the world, can make a stir of religion. So this proves that religion is of the Lord.[36]

True to his Baptist heritage of individual soul liberty, Reverend Mercer was careful to point out that the Lord never "offers violence to the human will"; which brings us to another important lesson of this book. The Wild West was not about to be won by possibility thinkers, Christian dramatists, lifestyle evangelists or "promise keepers," but rather through a prayerful army of Spirit-filled, soul-winning pastors, deacons and church members who would use their King James Bibles to boldly confront sinners with the Gospel of Jesus Christ. Stating rather frankly, with respect to Baptist expansion, historian Henry Vedder adds:

> The secret of this growth was incessant evangelization...But for the most part this evangelization was the work of men who were not sent forth, but went forth to preach in obedience to a divine call. Many Baptist preachers spent at least a part of their lives, if not the whole of them, as itinerant preachers; and to their labors was due the growth of Baptist churches in the closing quarter of the eighteenth century.[37]

HYPERCALVINISM

It is when we discuss the doctrinal implications of the Great Commission (Matthew 28:19, 20) that the ultimate expression of soul liberty is acknowledged. Although at times possessing a wide latitude of doctrinal views (due to the very nature of their non-restrictive soul liberty), the great majority of evangelistic Baptists have traditionally opposed the *Protestant* heresy known as Calvinism. For the benefit of my uninformed readers, Calvinism basically teaches that God decided in eternity past whom He would save and whom He would leave behind for the fires of Hell. The focus of debate has centered around the historical attempt to reconcile the "Sovereignty of God" with the "Responsibility of Man."

Calvinists contend that were a mere sinful creature to be given a free will to accept or reject God's gift of salvation, he might have the audacity to refuse His gracious offer and thereby "frustrate the pleasure of a sovereign and holy God, blah, blah, blah, etc." So, to avoid getting "burned," the Lord simply fixed things so that *no one* could decline His invitation, *even if he wanted to!* For some reason, it has never dawned on the spooky Calvinists that God's children knowingly and regularly frustrate His will for *their* lives. This is known in the Bible as *backsliding.* By the way, do you suppose that God allowed Adam and Eve to frustrate His will for *their* lives?

The basic tenets of Calvinism have been enshrined in the acrostic "**TULIP**," which stands for **T**otal depravity, **U**nconditional election, **L**imited atonement, **I**rresistible grace and **P**reservation of the saints. First of all, the *theological* term *total depravity*, stressing that the depravity of a man's sinful nature extends to his volition, thus preventing him from voluntarily coming to Jesus Christ for salvation, is found nowhere in Scripture, while the *biblical* term *free will* is used in various passages such as Ezra 7:13 and 16. (See also Exodus 35:5, 21 and 29.)

The term *unconditional election,* stressing that God arbitrarily elected certain individuals to salvation without any relevant conditions, is also a scriptural misnomer according to I Peter 1:2, which plainly says that Christians are *"elect according to the foreknowledge of God the Father."* (See also Romans 8:29, 30.) When asked if he believed in election, the witty D. L. Moody said that he did with the clarification that "the whosoever wills are elected to salvation while the whosoever won'ts are elected to damnation." The first chapter of Romans shows that God only rejects man after man rejects divine revelation. (Romans 1:21, 24) There has never been a Calvinist who could explain how a man cannot be responsible for receiving Christ yet *is* responsible for rejecting Christ.

As to the heresy of a "limited atonement" teaching that Christ died only for the elect, the Bible clearly states that Christ died for *all* men: *"Who will have all men to be saved"* (I Timothy 2:4a); *"Who gave himself a ransom for all"* (I Timothy 2:6a); *"Not willing that any should perish, but that all should come to repentance."* (II Peter 3:9b) The teaching in II Peter 2:1 is that Christ shed His blood even for the souls of false prophets. Hebrews 10:29 says that a man can go to Hell *after* being sanctified by the blood of the covenant. II Corinthians 5:14b clearly states *"that if one died for all, then were all dead."* I Timothy 4:10b states that *"we trust in the living God, who is the Saviour of all men, specially of those that believe."* Hebrews 2:9b says *"that he by the grace of God should taste death for every man."* Romans 5:6b states that *"in due time Christ died for the ungodly."* I John 2:2 really says it all—*"And he is the propitiation for our sins: and not for our's only, but also for the sins of the whole world."*

The teaching that *irresistible grace* falls upon the elect when "it's their time to go" is really funny. Stephen didn't buy it. *"Ye stiffnecked and uncircumcised in heart and ears, ye do always resist the Holy Ghost: as your fathers did, so do ye."* (Acts 7:51) When a man refuses to come to Christ, the Bible clearly shows that this action is a result of his own free will; he could have believed had he wanted to. In Matthew 23:37b, the Lord cries out to Jerusalem, *"How often would I have gathered thy children together, even as a hen gathereth her chickens under her wings, and ye would not!"* In John 5:40 He simply states, *"And ye will not come to me, that ye might have life."* Paul warns the believers in II Corinthians 6:1, *"We then as workers together with him, beseech you also that ye receive not the grace of God in vain."* Centuries earlier, Isaiah the prophet recorded the Word of the Lord: *"I said not unto the seed of Jacob, Seek ye me in vain: I the LORD speak righteousness, I declare things that are right."* (Isaiah 45:19b) And finally, the heart of our Heavenly Father is beautifully revealed in Ezekiel 18:32, which states: *"For I have no pleasure in the death of him that dieth, saith the Lord GOD: wherefore turn yourselves, and live ye."*

That an evangelical should pursue the theological fantasies of a fellow Protestant is understandable, but for a Baptist to embrace John Calvin is a repudiation of Scripture, logic and heredity. Why in the world would a freedom-loving Baptist want to be identified with some coldhearted tyrant who would burn a fellow minister at the stake over a doctrinal dispute (Servetus),[38] or behead a 15-year-old girl for slapping her parents? This makes about as much sense as a Baptist (or any born-again believer, for that matter) "preferring" a modern English translation of the Bible, predicated on *Codex Vaticanus*—a Greek manuscript that was literally named after the *Vatican*, the site of its discovery and the place where it presently resides! (Ditto for the ignorant Baptist *dummkopfs* who like to brag about being Notre Dame football fans!) In his polemical classic, *The Other Side of Calvinism*, Dr. Laurence Vance writes:

> Baptists are not Protestants… The Baptists were not a product of the Reformation and hence may be termed the original Protestants, since they protested the errors of the Roman Catholic Church hundreds of years before the Reformation, although from without instead of as a dissenter or descendant. Calvinism is therefore distinctly a Reformed doctrine, the Baptists notwithstanding.[39]

The Baptists who rejected Calvinism were usually known as *General* or *Separate* Baptists, while those advocating the heresy were referred to as

Particular, Regular or *Two-seed-in-the-Spirit Predestinarian* Baptists, with their later adherents being called *Hardshell, Primitive* or *Sovereign Grace* Baptists. This isn't to say that there were not some sincere men who were deceived by these errors, or even still, ones who pursued an aggressive evangelistic thrust in spite of the fatalistic doctrine. The simple fact of the matter is that a man's ability to make a personal decision to either accept or reject Christ as Saviour is the ultimate application of the glorious, New Testament doctrine of "soul liberty."

In the great majority of cases, whenever Calvinism would rear its ugly head in a New Testament, soul-winning church, the fire would inevitably go out. Dr. Vance points out that although the "Calvinistic Baptists" (What a misnomer!) of our day frequently quote the "renowned" pastor, Dr. John Gill, Calvin's greatest *postobitum* convert from the ranks of the eighteenth-century Baptists, "it is never mentioned that during the time he ministered in London (1719–1771) the church dwindled down to 153 people by 1753 in a place where seating was 2,000."[40] Reverend Andrew Fuller, another Baptist pastor in eighteenth-century London, but of a different stripe, bluntly declared about those Calvinistic Baptists, "Had matters gone on but a few years the Baptists would have become a perfect dunghill in society."[41] (Talk about a subliminal message!) Vedder elaborates on the fact that a "*hyper-*Calvinist" is, in reality, anything *but* hyper!

> Hyper-Calvinism was developed… and everywhere proved a blighting doctrine… This is practically to nullify the Great Commission; and, in consequence of this belief, Calvinistic Baptist preachers largely ceased to warn, exhort, and invite sinners; holding that, as God will have mercy on whom he will have mercy, when he willed he would effectually call an elect person, and that for anybody else to invite people to believe was useless, if not an impertinent interference with the prerogatives of God. What wonder that a spiritual dry-rot spread among the English churches where such doctrines obtained![42]

Believe it or not, a number of these theological deadbeats actually got together and formed a denomination called, "Anti-Missionary Baptists." Writing of Baptists and missionary outreach, Dr. B. A. Ray states:

> The fields are white unto the harvest, and God demands of us that we send laborers into the harvest. **When a Baptist ceases to be a missionary, he ceases to be a Baptist, and is, therefore, sailing under false colors.** All of the wonderful efforts to evangelize the world are solely due to Baptist initiative.[43]

The famous exchange between Dr. John Ryland and the missionary statesman, William Carey, is a classic illustration of fatalistic Calvinism at its best. When the youthful Carey spoke up for the prospect of foreign missions at a certain Baptist gathering, the Calvinist Ryland exclaimed, "Sit down, young man; when the Lord gets ready to convert the heathen he will do it without your help or mine!"[44] Literally hundreds of thousands of Indian converts will be eternally grateful that William Carey refused to sit down in his heart. (Carey taught himself 5 languages and stayed on the field in India for 42 years without a furlough to translate the Scripture into 44 languages and dialects.)

BAPTIST SOUL WINNERS

Having claimed the ancient promise to Joshua, *"Every place that the sole of your foot shall tread upon, that have I given unto you,"* (Joshua 1:3a) an army of Baptist soul winners decided to "pluck tulips" and "raise lilies" (as in the "Lily of the Valley") throughout the sin-cursed West. Vedder writes of their initial gains:

> Many Baptists from North Carolina and Virginia were among the **first** settlers of Kentucky and Tennessee...Baptists were among the **first** to enter Ohio as settlers and religious workers...In Illinois, Baptists from Virginia were the **first**...to enter and possess the land...The **first** sermon on the site of what is now the great city of Chicago was preached October 5, 1825, by the Rev. Isaac McCoy, then a Baptist missionary to the Indians of Michigan.[45]

Appropriately enough, it was a Baptist preacher by the name of Charles C. Luther who penned these convicting words:

Must I go, and empty-handed, Thus my dear Redeemer meet?
Not one day of service give Him, Lay no trophy at His feet?
Must I go, and empty-handed? Must I meet my Savior so?
Not one soul with which to greet Him; Must I empty-handed go?

And should some non-soul-winning, deeper-life critic question the capacity of "wildfire" Baptists to engage in quality worship, it should be noted that it was another Baptist preacher by the name of Samuel Stennett who composed this inspiring verse:

Majestic sweetness sits enthroned Upon the Saviour's brow;
His head with radiant glories crowned, His lips with grace o'erflow
His lips with grace o'erflow.

The truth of the matter is that any Christian who truly perceives the majestic sweetness of Jesus would not even *think* of coming in empty-handed! And while we are on the subject of spiritual music, should we really be surprised that still *another* Baptist by the name of Samuel Smith possessed the insight to compose a third song commemorating the final product of the first two themes?

My country, 'tis of thee, Sweet land of liberty,
Of thee I sing: Land where my fathers died,
Land of the pilgrims' pride, From ev'ry mountainside
Let freedom ring!

The early frontier was no place for "sissy-britches" reverends who wanted to share some devotional ditty about coping, hoping or *whatever*. The preachers who were effective in the West did not read polished essays from a manuscript, as the rough backwoodsman had no use, as he phrased it, "for a preacher who couldn't shoot without a rest." Vedder acquaints us with the caliber of Baptist circuit riders who made America great:

> Many men of God went forth into this wilderness not knowing where they should find a night's lodging or their next meal, willing to suffer untold privations if they might only point some to the Lamb of God. It is impossible to estimate too highly or to praise too warmly the services of these men of strong faith and good works. Their hardships were such as we of the present day can hardly imagine. They traveled from little settlement to settlement on horseback, with no road save an Indian trail or blazed trees, fording streams over which no bridges had been built, exposed to storms, frequently sleeping where night found them, often prostrated by fevers or wasted by malaria, but indomitable still. If they did not wander "in sheepskins and goatskins," like ancient heroes of faith, they wore deerskins; and homespun took the place of sackcloth. Their dwelling was "all out o' doors." Living in the plainest manner, sharing all the hardships of a pioneer people, the circuit preacher labored in a parish that, as one of them said, "took in one-half of creation, for it had no boundary on the west." One of them writes in 1805: "Every day I travel I have to swim through creeks or swamps, and I am wet from head to feet, and some days from morning to night I am dripping with water...I have rheumatism

in all my joints... What I have suffered in body and mind my pen is not able to communicate to you. But this I can say: While my body is wet with water and chilled with cold my soul is filled with heavenly fire, and I can say with St. Paul: 'But none of those things move me, neither count I my life dear unto myself, so that I might finish my course with joy.' "[46]

THE METHODISTS

About this time, the work of evangelizing the West was greatly enhanced by the indefatigable labors of the Methodist circuit riders led by their godly American bishop, Francis Asbury. Although the Baptists were strong in their convictions, especially concerning baptism and the local church, they were, nonetheless, always willing to rejoice in the legitimate, soul-saving efforts of the various revived sects of Protestantism. And it did not matter whether this respect was mutually enjoyed, though much of the time it was. In the spirit of their master Who had defended the sincere but less-enlighted exorcists with the words, *"he that is not against us is for us,"* (Luke 9:50b) the Baptists continued to practice their historic toleration of their weaker, thirtyfold and sixtyfold brethren, but not to doubtful disputations. (Romans 14:1) Like the Apostle Paul, they rejoiced that Christ was being preached. (Philippians 1:18)

Holding exclusively to Armenian doctrine (the opposite of Calvinism), the Methodist preachers were exceptionally aggressive in their reaching out to all sinners, "elect" or not. Also, because of the unbelievable violence they endured at the hands of the English mobs, the movement as a whole was conditioned for the hardships and privations of the frontier. With regard to their tumultuous tradition of persecution under the able leadership of John and Charles Wesley (and, to a large extent, George Whitefield), Simon writes:

> If Methodism had not come into contact with the mob it would never have reached the section of the English people which most needed salvation. The "Religious Societies" shut up in their rooms, would never have reformed the country.
>
> It was necessary that a race of heroic men should arise, who would dare to confront the wildest and most brutal men, and tell them the meaning of sin, and show them the Christ of the Cross and of the Judgment Throne.

The incessant assaults of the mob on the Methodist preachers showed they had reached the masses. With a superb courage, rarely, if ever, equaled on the battlefield, the Methodist preachers went again and again, to the places from which they had been driven by violence, until their persistence wore down the antagonism of their assailants. Then, out of the once furious crowd, men and women were gathered whose hearts the Lord had touched.[47]

Although the Baptists differed from their Methodist and Presbyterian brethren in several important doctrinal issues, they did share a surprising amount of common ground, especially in the crucial area of winning lost souls to Christ. For one thing, everyone used the same English Bible, the 1611 Authorized Version, commonly known as the King James Bible. This was the age where the folk were still "simpleminded" enough to comprehend the concept of a singular or final authority. While the minister was often referred to as the *parson*, meaning *person,* thus, *the* person, the Bible, meaning *book,* was likewise understood to be *the* Book! The modern perversions would not begin showing up for another century.

Not only did these frontier parsons have the right Bibles on their pulpits, but they also knew just how to use them, especially when preaching on the fires of Hell. Although a convicted sinner in today's America can find refuge in any number of compromising, Hell-denying "churches," such was not the case in our nation's earlier days. When an unsaved person visited the Baptist church in town, he was certain to hear, "If you don't get 'borned ag'in,' you'll split Hell wide open!" Petrified, he would run out of the building and flee into the First Presbyterian Church next door. Because the minister appeared more reserved, the sinner was prone to lower his guard. This time, the shocking message was, "*If you're not one of the elect,* you'll split Hell wide open, and there's nothing you can do about it either!!" Having staggered out the back door and across the street into the last church in town, the poor wretch is last seen jumping out the window with the Methodist preacher screaming at the top of his lungs, "Even if you *are* born again, you can still lose it and split Hell wide open anyway!!!"

Preaching like this kept a nation on the edge of her pew. Recalling his first impression of the fiery Presbyterian pastor, James McGready, Reverend Barton Stone writes:

Such earnestness, such zeal, such powerful persuasion, enforced by the joys of heaven and the miseries of hell, I had never witnessed before. My mind was chained by him, and followed him closely in his rounds of heaven, earth, and hell with feelings indescribable. His concluding remarks were addressed to the sinner to flee the wrath to come without delay. Never before had I comparatively felt the force of truth. Such was my excitement that, had I been standing, I should have probably sunk to the floor under the impression.[48]

THE REVIVAL OF 1800

In answer to the faithful prayers of many burdened saints, the Lord sent a glorious revival to the West in the summer of 1800. Following an initial movement of the Holy Spirit in June at an outdoor communion service conducted by Reverend McGready in Logan County, Kentucky, the elated preacher planned for another, more protracted meeting to be held in late July at Gasper River.

Convinced that the Lord was moving, the Christians who attended (some from distances of 100 miles), were determined to stay "till they were touched from on high." Tents went up everywhere in what would later come to be recognized as America's first legitimate *camp meeting*. On the fourth evening of the meeting, while Reverend William McGee was preaching by torchlight about a doubting Peter sinking beneath the waves, the fire of Heaven came down in unmistakable fashion. McGready describes the holy event:

> The power of God seemed to shake the whole assembly. Towards the close of the sermon, the cries of the distressed arose almost as loud as his voice. After the congregation was dismissed the solemnity increased, till the greater part of the multitude seemed engaged in the most solemn manner. No person seemed to wish to go home—hunger and sleep seemed to affect nobody—eternal things were the vast concern. Here awakening and converting work was to be found in every part of the multitude; and even some things strangely and wonderfully new to me.[49]

Reverend Barton Stone, a Presbyterian pastor from Bourbon County (northeast of Lexington), had traveled across the state to view the revival firsthand. He testified that, "The scene was new to me and passing strange. It baffled description."[50] Rather than criticize, Stone became burdened for his own area and decided to conduct a similar meeting at Cane Ridge in August of the following year. With more time for prayer, preparation and promotion, the results were astronomical. At a time when the population of

Lexington, the largest town in Kentucky, was only 1,800 inhabitants, as many as 25,000 human beings began descending on Cane Ridge from as far away as Tennessee and Ohio. Stone remarked that "the roads were crowded with wagons, carriages, horses, and footmen moving to the solemn camp."[51] The preacher's labor was not in vain. In a letter from John Finley to his uncle, dated September 20, 1801, we have the following eyewitness account:

> Great numbers were on the ground from Friday until the Thursday following, night and day without intermission engaged in some religious act of worship. They are commonly collected in small circles of ten or twelve, close adjoining another circle, and all engaged in singing Watts' and Hart's hymns; and then a minister steps upon a stump or log and begins an exhortation or sermon, when as many as can hear, collect around him. On Sabbath night I saw above one hundred candles burning at once—and...I suppose one hundred persons at once on the ground crying for mercy of all ages from eight to sixty years. When a person is struck down he is carried by others out of the congregation, where some minister converses with and prays for him; afterwards a few gather around and sing a hymn suitable to his case...The sensible, the weak, learned and unlearned, the rich and the poor are the subjects of it.[52]

The fact that so many people were getting saved was certain to arouse "old smutty face." Accordingly, some of the "converts" began to display a number of weird antics such as barking, jerking or excessive laughter. Although the Holy Ghost has been known to put tongues of fire on people's heads (Acts 2:3), shake buildings (Acts 4:31), knock a man off his horse (Acts 9:4), raise the dead (Acts 9:40), and cause earthquakes (Acts 16:26), most of the excessive camp meeting hysteria was attributed to Satan by the leaders themselves. Stone writes:

> Much did I see then, that I considered to be fanaticism; but this should not condemn the work. The devil always tries to ape the works of God, to bring them into disrepute; but that cannot be a satanic work which brings men to humble confession, to forsaking sin, to prayer, fervent praise and thanksgiving, and a sincere and affectionate exhortation to sinners to repent and come to Jesus the Saviour.[53]

From Gasper River and Cane Ridge, the spirit of revival spread almost everywhere. Camp meetings became the order of the day, Christian writing:

The woods and paths seemed alive with people, and the number reported attending is almost incredible. The laborer quit his task; age snatched his crutch; youth forgot his pastime; the plow was left in the furrow; the deer enjoyed a respite in the mountains; business of all kinds was suspended; dwelling houses were deserted; whole neighborhoods were emptied; bold hunters and noble matrons, young women, maidens and little children, flocked to the common center of attraction; every difficulty was surmounted, every risk ventured, to be present at the Camp Meeting.[54]

Many of the Baptists cooperated with their Presbyterian and Methodist brethren in the camp meeting era, "so far as they could consistently with their principles,"[55] (i.e., they would not sit down with the Protestants at communion.) Of course, they also held meetings of a similar nature among themselves. Furthermore, their gatherings were rarely beset with the eccentricities previously discussed. In a letter written by Reverend David Lilly to the editor of the Georgia Analytical Repository, dated August 23, 1802, the heavenly atmosphere enjoyed by the Baptists of South Carolina has been preserved:

A great work of God is going on in the upper parts of this State. Multitudes are made to cry out, "What shall we do to be saved?"...A vast concourse of people assembled on Saturday, and considerable appearances of solemnity soon took place; but no uncommon effect till Sunday late in the evening. Then the Lord was pleased to manifest His power to many hearts. Numbers were powerfully exercised through the whole night, and some were thrown to the ground.

On Monday the work increased. The hearts of many were made to melt; and several men, noted for their impiety, were stricken and lay among the prostrate. I must acknowledge it was a memorable time with my soul; the like I had not felt for many years before. In general, the people were much engaged through the greater part of Monday night.

Before sun-rise, on Tuesday morning, the sacred flame began to burn afresh; several, who had been before unaffected, came to the earth...some of the ministers continued with them, in constant exercise, till midnight...

Be assured, my brother, the Lord is doing great things for his people in this country. The hearts of sinners melt before the word of truth, like wax before the sun. Infidelity is almost ashamed to show its head. Several deists have been constrained, under a sense of their lost condition, to cry out aloud for mercy. A few, even of those who attributed the effects produced among us to infernal agency, have been reached, and overcome by an influence, which they now acknowledge to be divine.[56]

Throughout the ensuing months, the Holy Ghost of God literally cleaned house. George A. Baxter, president of Washington College, Virginia, personally toured Kentucky in 1801 and declared:

> On my way I was informed by settlers on the road that the character of Kentucky travelers was entirely changed, and that they are as remarkable for sobriety as they had formerly been for dissoluteness and immorality. And indeed I found Kentucky...the most moral place I have ever seen. A profane expression was hardly ever heard. A religious awe seemed to pervade the country. Upon the whole, I think the revival in Kentucky the most extraordinary that has ever visited the church of Christ; and all things considered, it was peculiarly adapted to the circumstances to the country into which it came. Infidelity was triumphant and religion was on the point of expiring. Something extraordinary seemed necessary to arrest the attention of a giddy people who were ready to conclude that Christianity was a fable and futurity a delusion. The revival had done it. It has confounded infidelity, awed vice into silence, and brought numbers beyond calculation under serious impressions.[57]

IVY LEAGUE AWAKENING

Not only did the fire of revival sweep through the West, but it also worked its way back East. In 1802, Reverend Timothy Dwight, president of Yale College and a former army chaplain to George Washington, witnessed the formal conversion of 80 men out of the school's total enrollment of 160 students. Benjamin Silliman, a faculty member who came to Christ at this time, wrote his mother excitedly, "Yale College is a little temple, prayer and praise seem to be the delight of the greater part of the students,while those who are still unfeeling are awed into respectful silence."[58] Under Dwight's able leadership, additional awakenings occurred in 1808, 1813 and 1815. Soon, other Ivy League schools, such as Princeton and Dartmouth, were similarly blessed. It is significant that Dwight was very much a revivalist innovator who parted company with the Calvinism of his grandfather, Jonathan Edwards, and great-great grandfather, Solomon Stoddard. Whereas they had been "genuinely surprised when the revival began," Dwight "deliberately set out to start a revival in the college and among the eminent men of the state."[59]

PETER CARTWRIGHT

One of the more fruitful converts from the great revival of 1800 was a Kentucky lad of 16 by the name of Peter Cartwright, who would go on to preach 18,000 sermons himself during a ministry spanning seven decades. Considered by many the outstanding circuit rider of American Methodism at that time, Cartwright was in every respect a man's man and perfectly embodied that caliber of hardy backwoods preachers who won the West for Christ. The stories of his life are legendary.

Upon visiting a certain town in Ohio, Cartwright discovered that the owner of the local tavern was a notorious bully who delighted in threatening Methodist ministers, whereupon the indignant preacher made a beeline for the beer joint. As the story is told, no one knows for sure who threw the first punch, but "Reverend" Cartwright was able to straddle the bewildered bartender in short order and proceeded to beat the nasal mucous out of him, while singing, "All hail the power of Jesus' name" in the process. Cartwright later added that he had to sing all four stanzas before the bully would promise not to pick on any more Methodists. (Kind of reminds you of Benny Hinn and James Dobson..., doesn't it?)

In his classic biography on the life of Abraham Lincoln, author Carl Sandburg makes a reference to Cartwright as "a famous and rugged old-fashioned circuit rider, a storming evangelist...who...carried his Bible and rifle over wilderness...and who...had more than once personally thrown out of church a drunk interrupting his sermon."[60] Sandburg also related that in response to a particular deacon's cold and precise prayer, Cartwright was reported to have said, "Brother, three prayers like that would freeze Hell over."[61]

In a rather humorous story from the preacher's autobiography, Cartwright tells of the time when he and a fellow preacher almost became accidentally inebriated at a roadside guest house after innocently drinking what they had *thought* to be new cider. By the time Cartwright had perceived, "there is surely something more than cider here," it was, alas, too late. Declaring that he "began to feel light-headed," he and Brother Walker attempted to resume their travel, "fearing we were snapped for once." Cartwright continues:

> We mounted, and started on our journey. When we had rode about a mile, being in the rear, I saw Brother Walker was nodding at a mighty rate. After riding on some distance in this way, I suddenly rode up to brother

[sic] Walker and cried out, "Wake up! wake up!" He roused up, his eyes watering freely. "I believe," said I, "we are both drunk. Let us turn out of the road, and lie down and take a nap till we get sober."[62]

Cartwright added that they were fortunately able to push on to their desired haven without having to "sleep it off" and stated that he had decided to relate the incident "with a view to put others on their guard."[63] Shortly after this incident, Cartwright found himself in another potentially compromising situation. Having settled for a late evening's lodging at a certain guest house in the Cumberland Mountains, the weary preacher was informed that a dance was scheduled to be held that very evening. Although Cartwright had intentionally positioned himself outside of harm's way by sitting in a "corner of the house," a "beautiful, ruddy young lady" sought him out for a dance! In the understatement of the century, he testified, "I can hardly describe my thoughts or feelings on that occasion." Finally, he relates, "I resolved on a desperate experiment." The rest of the account made Cartwright a legend in his own time:

> I grasped her right hand with my right hand, while she leaned her left arm on mine. In this position we walked on the floor... The colored man, who was the fiddler, began to put his fiddle in the best order. I then spoke to the fiddler to hold a moment, and added that for several years I had not undertaken any matter of importance without first asking the blessing of God upon it... Here I grasped the young lady's hand tightly, and said, "Let us all kneel down and pray," and then instantly dropped on my knees, and commenced praying with all the power of soul and body that I could command. The young lady tried to get loose from me, but I held her tight. Presently she fell on her knees. Some of the company kneeled, some stood, some fled, some sat still, all looked curious. The fiddler ran off into the kitchen, saying, "Lord a marcy, what de matter? what is dat mean?"
>
> While I prayed some wept, and wept out loud, and some cried for mercy. I rose from my knees and commenced an exhortation, after which I sang a hymn. The young lady who invited me on the floor lay prostrate, crying earnestly for mercy. I exhorted again, I sang and prayed nearly all night. About fifteen of that company professed religion, and our meeting lasted next day and next night, and as many more were powerfully converted. I organized a society, took thirty-two into the Church, and sent them a preacher... This was the commencement of a great and glorious revival of religion in that region of country, and several of the young men converted at this Methodist preacher dance became useful ministers of Jesus Christ.[64]

JAMES MADISON & THE WAR OF 1812

As these various Baptist, Methodist and Presbyterian circuit riders continued salting down America's growing turnpike to the Pacific, Thomas Jefferson was succeeded at the end of his second administration by James Madison, who easily defeated the Federalist Charles Cotesworth Pinckney in the election of 1808. Jefferson's handpicked successor would also serve two terms as our nation's fourth chief executive. As noted previously, Madison's credentials were impressive indeed; chief architect of the Constitution, original author and promoter of the Bill of Rights, secretary of state under Jefferson, etc. Trained at the feet of Reverend John Witherspoon at Princeton, Madison's personal exposure to an orthodox view of justification by faith would have been more than adequate.

James Madison was another one of the many gracious bestowments of providence upon our young nation, the collective testimony of which exposes the degeneracy of our present-day Laissez Faire conservatism. Would some joke book like *Atheism, the Case Against God* have impressed a man like Madison who wrote, "The belief in a God All Powerful wise and good, is so essential to the moral order of the World and to the happiness of man, that arguments which enforce it cannot be drawn from too many sources."[65] Attitudes such as these resulted in a natural circumspection, Madison declaring, "A watchful eye must be kept on ourselves lest while we are building ideal monuments of Renown and Bliss here we neglect to have our names enrolled in the Annals of Heaven."[66] But first and foremost, Madison was guided by that pervasive conviction that America was special:

> We have staked the whole future of American civilization, not upon the power of government, far from it. We have staked the future of all of our political institutions upon the capacity of mankind for self-government; upon the capacity of each and all of us to govern ourselves, to control ourselves, to sustain ourselves according to the Ten Commandments of God.[67]

It was during Madison's second term as president that hostilities were resumed between England and the United States in the War of 1812. Like the parent who is unwilling to recognize when a child has come of age, Britain's navy began a campaign of harassment against American commercial vessels to enforce her wartime embargo against France, and to capture a growing number of deserting sailors (known as impressment). A number of Indian uprisings led by Tecumseh were also thought to have been instigated by British agents in Canada. Peter Cartwright noted in his journal:

> We felt the sad effects of war throughout the west, perhaps as sensibly as in any part of the Union. A braver set of men never lived than was found in this western world, and many of them volunteered and helped to achieve another glorious victory over the legions of England, and her savage allied thousands. Of course there were many of our members went into the war, and deemed it their duty.[68]

Although most of the war's decisive action resulted from a number of "sea" battles that were fought, ironically enough, on fresh water (Lake Erie, Lake Champlain, etc.), a significant British expeditionary force came ashore and captured Washington on June 24, 1814, literally forcing Madison and the First Lady to flee the presidential dining room. Upon entering the capitol building itself, an admiral seated himself in the Speaker's chair and announced sarcastically, "All in favor of burning, say aye." Following a unanimous vote, every public building in the city, including the White House, was put to the torch.

Three months later, on September 14, the British fleet subjected Baltimore's Fort McHenry to a spectacular, all-night, aerial bombardment that failed to effect an American capitulation. A young Washington attorney who happened to be aboard the enemy's flagship on that fateful night, pursuing a diplomatic mission to free a popular physician, made an enduring contribution to his nation's culture that more than compensated for the momentary destruction. As the thick smoke of that long evening gave way to the first strains of morning light, the sight of Old Glory still fluttering in the wind inspired Francis Scott Key to pen the words to our glorious "Star-Spangled Banner." For the record, Key was a Bible-believing Christian who would later declare:

> The patriot who feels himself in the service of God, who acknowledges Him in all his ways, has the promise of Almighty direction, and will find His Word in his greatest darkness, "a lantern to his feet and a lamp unto his paths." He will therefore seek to establish for his country in the eyes of the world, such a character as shall make her not unworthy of the name of a Christian nation.[69]

A number of embarrassing naval defeats in the Great Lakes had convinced the British that a protracted campaign of aggression was untenable. The Treaty of Ghent (present-day Belgium) was signed on Christmas Eve, 1814, and brought the war to an official end. However, it appears as though God felt the British needed a parting object lesson to discourage any thoughts of a third invasion in the future.

ANDREW JACKSON

Fourteen days *after* the peace treaty was signed in Europe on the 8th of January, 1815, the bloodiest battle of the war was fought. By a stroke of fate, neither army was aware that the war was technically over. As heavy morning fog descended on the field, Sir Edward Pakenham, 38-year-old brother-in-law of the famed Duke of Wellington, gave the fateful order to advance and a disciplined mass of 8,000 veteran British redcoats somberly moved forward. The immortal Battle of New Orleans had begun.

Sir Edward had desired to meet the American "dogs" in the open and fight on his appointed terms of European combat pageantry. General "Andy" Jackson, the American commander, refused, for he had a 34-year-old score to settle with these foreigners, and he wasn't about to jeopardize things by succumbing to deceitful intimidation. When but a youth of 14, Andy had been captured by the British in the closing months of 1781. "You, there, clean my boots," barked the taunting officer in charge. "I may be your prisoner, sir, but I am not your bootlick," replied the defiant young Jackson. "I claim treatment due to a prison of war," he added. In a flash, an explosion of wrath brought the officer's sword within an inch of Andy's stiffened neck. The quick reflex of a left arm and the tender mercies of divine providence joined forces to ensure that the "young sapling" would survive to become America's beloved "Old Hickory," forever bearing on his scarred forehead the evidence of youthful heroics and patriotism.

Suddenly, this momentary reminiscing was interrupted by the deafening cheers of 8,000 sets of over-confident lips emanating from somewhere within the foreboding fog. How prophetically had Jackson written his beloved Rachel but a few days previously that, figuratively, "dark and heavy clouds hang over us." Did not the British have justified optimism? Had not several American deserters assured them of panic, depleted manpower and a non-existent will to exist? All that stood between them and the splendor of New Orleans booty was but a few hundred yards of turf, ripe for the picking.

Yet the most convincing evidence of all was supplied by Pakenham's own spyglass. What he had viewed of Jackson's defenders absolutely defied every rule in the book of military protocol and combat stratagem. Jackson's line of defense ran for 1,000 yards along the Rodriguez Canal, a dried-up drainage ditch connecting his two natural flanks, the Mississippi on his right and a cluster of cypress swamps on his left. It was a thousand yards of defiance.

However, it was the state of Jackson's defenses that most deceived Pakenham and caused him to chuckle. Behind those crude breastworks of earth, trees and scattered cotton bales were positioned what appeared to be the mottliest assemblage of ragamuffins and miscellaneous misfits ever united in the history of military campaigns. Three thousand strong and more or less inclusive of every male capable of shooting a gun, they included, in addition to the nucleus of the smaller regular army and artillery units: Tennessee and Kentucky sharpshooter volunteers, toting their deadly Kentucky long rifles; various sailor escapees from the *Carolina* and other recently captured United States vessels; a battalion of free blacks; numerous slaves; a contingent of French Santo Domingo refugees; the New Orleans militia of sharpshooters and ordinary citizens; Louisiana Creoles in their gaudy red and blue uniforms; a few Choctaw Indians; some old French veterans with scores to settle; a number of prisoners under temporary release from the local jails; and even several hundred pirates under the leadership of the famous Jean Lafitte. A couple of weeks before the battle, the Governor of Louisiana put a $500 bounty on Lafitte's head whereupon the pirate captain returned the favor by placing a *$30,000* bounty on the Governor's head.

All were united, however, by the site of Old Glory waving high in the sky above the center of Jackson's thousand yards of defiance. A New Orleans band struck up continued strains of encouragement. It would all be over in less than 20 minutes.

Pakenham's fog completely dissipated at the strangest of providential moments, suddenly exposing some 8,000 red bull's-eyes to the dispatchful aim of 3,000 redneck marksmen. The ranks were decimated! When the smoke cleared, 700 British dead could be seen in the field (including Pakenham, 3 fellow generals, 11 colonels, and 75 lower officers) and over 2,000 enemy soldiers were wounded. The American casualties were put at 13 killed and 58 wounded!

The Battle of New Orleans had made Andrew Jackson a national hero overnight. But mere earthly accomplishments can never fill the void that exists in a lost man's soul. Besides, the humble general had more sense than the editors of *Laissez Faire Books* concerning the ultimate cause for his victory, acknowledging to a friend, "It appears that the unerring hand of Providence shielded my men from the shower of balls, bombs, and rockets, when every ball and bomb from our guns carried with them a mission of death."[70]

Andrew Jackson was better known for his attendance at duels than at church, but on a particular Monday in October of 1818, he decided to visit a revival service in Nashville where the controversial Peter Cartwright was scheduled to speak. As it happened, the General entered as the preacher was reading his text, *"For what shall it profit a man, if he shall gain the whole world, and lose his own soul?"* (Mark 8:36) With all the seats already occupied, the famous Indian fighter and war hero was content to stand, gracefully leaning on the middle post. At the sight of his stately appearance, the host pastor, a certain "Brother Mac," became nervous in the extreme. Seated on the platform directly behind the pulpit, he tugged on Cartwright's jacket, whispering, "General Jackson has come in; General Jackson has come in." Cartwright was aghast at the pastor's double standard:

> I felt a flash of indignation run all over me like an electric shock, and facing about to my congregation, and purposely speaking out audibly, I said, "Who is General Jackson? If he don't get his soul converted, God will damn him as quick as he would a Guinea negro."[71] The preacher tucked his head down, and squatted low, and would, no doubt, have been thankful for leave of absence. The congregation, General Jackson and all, smiled or laughed right out, all at the preacher's expense.
>
> When the congregation was dismissed, my city-stationed preacher stepped up to me, and very sternly said to me: "You are the strangest man I ever saw, and General Jackson will chastise you for your insolence before you leave the city." "Very clear of it," said I, "for General Jackson, I have no doubt, will applaud my course; and if he should undertake to chastise me…there is two as can play that game."
>
> Next morning, very early, my city preacher went down to the hotel to make an apology to General Jackson for my conduct in the pulpit the night before. Shortly after he had left I passed by the hotel, and I met the General on the pavement; and before I approached him by several steps he smiled, and reached out his hand and said: "Mr. Cartwright, you are a man after my own heart. I am very surprised at Mr. Mac, to think that I would be offended at you. No, sir; I told him that I highly approved of your independence; that a minister of Jesus Christ ought to love every body and fear no mortal man. I told Mr. Mac that if I had a few thousand such independent, fearless officers as you were, and a well drilled army, I could take Old England."[72]

Acknowledging that Jackson was "no doubt in his prime of life, a very wicked man," Cartwright relates the following story to illustrate the General's "great respect for the Christian religion, and the feelings of religious people, especially ministers of the Gospel":

> I had preached one Sabbath near the Hermitage, and, in company with several gentlemen and ladies, went, by special invitation, to dine with the General. Among this company there was a young sprig of a lawyer from Nashville, of very ordinary intellect, and he was trying hard to make an infidel of himself. As I was the only preacher present, this young lawyer kept pushing his conversation on me, in order to get into an argument. I tried to evade an argument, in the first place considering it a breach of good manners to interrupt the social conversation of the company. In the second place I plainly saw that his head was much softer than his heart, and that there were no laurels to be won by vanquishing or demolishing such a combatant, and I persisted in evading an argument.
>
> This seemed to inspire the young man with more confidence in himself; for my evasiveness he construed into fear. I saw General Jackson's eye strike fire, as he sat by and heard the thrusts he made at the Christian religion. At length the young lawyer asked me this question: "Mr. Cartwright, do you really believe there is any such place as hell, as a place of torment?" I answered promptly, "Yes, I do." To which he responded, "Well, I thank God I have too much good sense to believe any such thing."
>
> I was pondering in my mind whether I would answer him or not, when General Jackson for the first time broke into the conversation, and directing his words to the young man, said with great earnestness: "Well, sir, I thank God that there is such a place of torment as hell." This sudden answer, made with great earnestness, seemed to astonish the youngster, and he exclaimed: "Why, General Jackson, what do you want with such a place of torment as hell?" To which the General replied, as quick as lightning, "To put such [expletive] rascals as you are in, that oppose and vilify the Christian religion."[73]

It was about this same time (1818) that Jackson invaded the Spanish-held territory of eastern Florida in order to stop frontier attacks by the Seminole Indians. He eventually defeated the Seminoles, drove out the Spanish and seized control of Florida. By the year 1828, Andrew Jackson was the undisputed people's choice for president. A contemporary of the new chief executive wrote, "History is sure to preserve the name of any man who has had the strength and genius to stamp his own character on the people over whose destinies he presided."[74]

However, Jackson's greatest triumph came on the eve of his greatest personal tragedy. Before the new president could be sworn into office, his beloved wife succumbed to a massive heart attack. On Christmas Eve, 1828, Rachel Jackson was laid to rest in her garden. A friend of the widower related, "I never pitied any person more in my life...I shall never forget his look of grief."[75]

Jackson had many enemies in the banking industry because of his incessant attacks on the nation's third central bank, called the Second Bank of the United States (a battle he would eventually win). In January of 1835, a bearded man attempted to assassinate the President, firing two pistols at him at point-blank range. For some reason, both guns failed to discharge. Having received a letter of concern from the King of England, Jackson wrote back exclaiming, "A kind of Providence had been pleased to shield me against the recent attempt upon my life, and irresistibly carried many minds to the belief in a superintending Providence."[76]

On March 4, 1837, President Jackson delivered his Farewell Address and reiterated the theme of America's unique destiny in world history:

> You have the highest of human trusts committed to your care. Providence has showered on this favored land blessings without number, and has chosen you as the guardians of freedom, to preserve it for the benefit of the human race. May He who holds in His hands the destinies of nations, make you worthy of the favors He has bestowed, and enable you, with pure hearts and hands and sleepless vigilance, to guard and defend to the end of time, the great charge He has committed to your keeping.[77]

Retirement years brought on seasons of serious reflection. The seed sown by Peter Cartwright was finally ready to bear fruit as God's Word was not about to return void. Chamberlain writes:

> The evening of his stormy life had come. The remains of his much-loved wife were resting in the humble graveyard near the house. At last thoughts of eternity were forced upon him. After attending a series of religious meetings Jackson became greatly convicted of his sin. He passed the night walking in his chamber in anguish and prayer. In the morning he announced to his family his full conviction that he had repented of his sins, and, through faith in Jesus Christ, had obtained forgiveness. Family prayer was immediately established...he was privileged to read through the Bible twice.[78]

On May 29, 1845, only a few weeks before his death, Jackson declared:

> Sir, I am in the hands of a merciful God. I have full confidence in his goodness and mercy.... The Bible is true... Upon that sacred volume I rest my hope for eternal salvation, through the merits and **blood** of our blessed Lord and Saviour, Jesus Christ.[79]

Finally, on June 8, 1845, just moments before he sailed into eternity, Jackson reassured everyone with these words:

> My dear children, do not grieve for me; it is true, I am going to leave you; I am well aware of my situation. I have suffered much bodily pain, but my sufferings are as nothing compared with that which our blessed Redeemer endured upon the accursed Cross, that all might be saved who put their trust in Him... God will take care of you for me. I am my God's. I belong to Him. I go but a short time before you, and... I hope and trust to meet you all in Heaven, both white and black.[80]

Before expiring, Andrew Jackson made a last appeal for America to build her future on the blessed Word of God. **"That book, Sir, is the Rock upon which our republic rests."**[81] *Hallelujah* for the old-time religion!

XI

What Hath God Wrought!

> *"Righteousness exalteth a nation: but sin is a reproach to any people. "*(Proverbs 14:34)

ON THE DAY after Jackson's death, a certain man and his young son had arrived at the Hermitage hoping to see the General one last time. Startled at the news of his passing, the grief-stricken visitor rushed into the room containing the open casket and fell to his knees before the corpse, burying his tear-stained face on his mentor's cold breast. Embracing his boy after several moments had passed, a composed Sam Houston implored, "My son, try to remember that you have looked upon the face of Andrew Jackson."[1]

Sam Houston had already made his own contribution toward America's "Turnpike to the Pacific" nine years earlier by having led his fellow Texans to victory in their war of independence with Mexico. Although outnumbered 1,600 to 740, Houston was able to rout Santa Anna's forces in the decisive battle of the San Jacinto River, April 21, 1836, after only 20 minutes of fighting, by having purposely delayed the attack till his Mexican foes were indulging in their daily 4:00 p.m. siesta. With the cry, "Remember the Alamo," still ringing in his ears, the illustrious, opium-smoking *El Presidente* of Mexico was led away under tight security along with the other dumbfounded captives. Houston was subsequently inaugurated president of the Lone Star Republic in the fall of 1836. Having previously stated that, "Texas [is] the key to our future safety,"[2] Jackson rejoiced with Houston at the formal entrance of Texas into the Union early in March of 1845.

As Houston reached his senior years, he passed through a period of spiritual reflection similar to that experienced by his hero, Andy Jackson. Perhaps he reasoned that if Christ would accept a crusty old Indian fighter with dueling slugs still in his body, there might be hope for him as well. Cummins citing Elliott:

> Houston's...conversion...was doubtless due primarily to the remarkable influence of his devout wife, who was Maggie Lea, prior to their marriage in 1840...He did not make a public profession of faith until 1854, when he united with the Baptist church at Independence and was baptized by Dr. R. C. Burleson November 19 of that year....He then became a regular attendant upon preaching and prayer meeting service....He led in public prayer, and when he lay dying at his home in Huntsville, he expressed to his family and friends his implicit faith in the Savior.[3]

As Texas became the Union's twenty-eighth state, the term *Manifest Destiny* made its debut in the March edition of the *United States Magazine and Democratic Review*. The prospect that it was God's will for Americans to possess the entire continent gained a timely notoriety on the eve of our war with Mexico. The principal grievances that were being voiced by transplanted Americans residing under Mexican rule in California were a lack of courts, police, schools and postal facilities. Rare and unpredictable communication links between Mexico City and the various California settlements only strained relations further. However, as matters proved, it was a boundary dispute involving the land between the Rio Grande and the Nueces River that eventually led General Zachary Taylor and an army of 3,500 men into the volatile region.

Upon the recommendation of President James Polk, Congress declared war on Santa Anna's *Catholic* government on May 13, 1846. Assisted by Captain John Charles Frémont of the United States Army, American residents in California defiantly hoisted a white flag with a bear and a star painted on it, proclaiming the "Bear Flag Republic" on June 14, 1846. While General Taylor went on to capture Monterrey and defeat a formidable foe at the battle of Buena Vista, another army led by Winfield Scott took Mexico City and raised the stars and stripes in "the halls of Montezuma." When a formal peace was secured in February of 1848, the United States had acquired, in addition to California, the present territory of New Mexico, Utah and Nevada for a total of roughly 918,000 square miles. And finally, the creation of the Oregon Territory later that same year fulfilled Dr.

Witherspoon's vision of a "Turnpike to the Pacific," inspiring Katherine Bates to pen, "From sea to shining sea."

At this juncture, the reader will note that we have now covered over two-and-a-quarter centuries of American history since the Pilgrim fathers landed at Plymouth. Before proceeding, a number of paramount themes must be reviewed, especially as they relate to the central thesis of this work.

Forty-two centuries before John O. Sullivan coined the phrase *Manifest Destiny*, the God Who created Sullivan prophesied through Noah, *"a preacher of righteousness,"* that the physical descendants of Japheth would one day experience a substantial geographical enlargement. Would a sane person question the Japhetic   (or, *Caucasian*)   roots of such famous explorers as Vasco da Gama, Cabot, Columbus, Magellan, Ponce de Leon, Cabral, Raleigh or La Salle? And as Japheth completed his westward expansion across the frontier of the emerging United States, should we be surprised that the so-called "native Americans" were displaced in the process, when Noah had also predicted that Japheth would *"dwell in the tents of Shem"*? (Genesis 9:27a) And regardless of pertinent ethical considerations, should the *fact* that the "moral and political evil"[4] of slavery (Robert E. Lee's words) was a part of early American culture surprise anyone who could read English, given that the Bible pronounced of Ham's posterity, *"a servant of servants shall he be unto his brethren"*? (Genesis 9:25b) The issue I wish to press is not whether this trilogy of ethnic prognostication meets anyone's personal standard of right or wrong, but rather—*did the historical drama unfold precisely as God Almighty declared that it would? Should we not stand in awe at the incredible accuracy of Holy Scripture?*

This is not to say that the Bible would endorse the perpetuation of individual atrocities. At the same time, however, as Sovereign Potentate of the Universe, God hardly checks with puny mortals when determining the course of human events, for *"the most High ruleth in the kingdom of men, and giveth it to whomsoever he will."* (Daniel 4:17b) To reiterate, although Christians concur that America's present borders were conceived in the "determinate counsel and foreknowledge of God," they would not condone whatever part may have been played by *"wicked hands"* in the process. (Acts 2:23) Our Lord reconciled these lofty themes of divine decrees and human accountability by declaring, *"It is impossible but that offences will come: but woe unto him, through whom they come!"* (Luke 17:1b, c)

As stated in a previous chapter, only a fool would expect a nation of flawed humans to evolve into a utopian society this side of the New Jerusalem. Even King Jesus will have to put down a massive revolt at the end of His glorious millennial reign (Revelation 20:9). How consistent can we expect our *human* leaders to be? The most spiritual king in Israel's history committed adultery and murder during a season of backsliding. Someone has rightly said that "the best of men are but men at best" and "great men have great weaknesses." Should one judge Abraham Lincoln harshly due to any number of perceived ideological shortcomings, how would Bill Clinton fare in comparison? (Ditto for their First Ladies, too.)

However, returning to the aforementioned injustices occasioned by *Manifest Destiny*, the Bible also assures that, *"where sin abounded, grace did much more abound."* (Romans 5:20b) Although initially subjected to many oppressive policies by the "white man's government," thousands of redeemed Indians, including the celebrated Geronimo himself, eventually made it to the *real* "Happy Hunting Grounds" because a dedicated band of Gospel-preaching missionaries was able to break the spell of their satanic medicine men. And for all their purported tales of a ubiquitous mistreatment of slaves throughout the antebellum South, the pious civil rights advocates of today are at an embarrassing loss to explain why these same slaves went on to embrace the religion of their "ungodly masters." By contrast, only 100,000 Negroes out of a total slave population of 4,000,000 converted to Catholicism.[5] With regard to the unfathomable councils of Heaven, would Uncle Tom have had a better chance of escaping the fires of Hell under the rantings of some demon-possessed witch doctor back in Africa? Of a truth did the Psalmist exclaim, *"Surely the wrath of man shall praise thee."* (Psalm 76:10a)

But then, how could a mere secular historian begin to comprehend that the personal salvation of a poor child on some reservation or plantation could possibly be of greater consequence than the so-called newsworthy items of that time? By now it should be obvious that you are reading a *spiritual* history of the United States. Make no mistake about it, *"that which is highly esteemed among men is abomination in the sight of God."* (Luke 16:15b) As far as nineteenth-century America was concerned, the Lord couldn't care less about Astor's millions, Hawthorne's novels, Audubon's birds, Wright's architecture, Whitman's paintings, Holmes' philosophy, Mann's educational fantasies, Doubleday's creation of baseball, Mrs. Vanderbilt's tea parties or Susan B. Anthony's sour puss! The salvation of lost mankind has been and will continue to be the great concern of our loving Heavenly Father, and to whatever degree His children have shown their willingness to participate in that burden, He has faithfully made His presence known. Was it mere coincidence that Thomas Jefferson and John Adams both died on the same day, July 4, 1826—the *fiftieth anniversary* of the Declaration of Independence?

BAPTIST EXPANSION

Accordingly, the local New Testament church continued her own westward expansion. Virgil Bopp writes:

> Up until about 1840, the Baptist movement in America was highly evangelistic, strong in home and foreign mission development, preferring denominational work but willing to cooperate interdenominationally if needed, concerned for education and desiring to keep the West from Catholicism. Such was the Baptist growth by 1844 that Torbet reports a total membership of 720,046 in 9,385 churches, with 6,364 ministers. That computes out to be an increase of 360 percent from 1814–1844, during which time the population growth of the United States was at 140 percent.[6]

The great majority of these assemblies were committed to high standards of holiness and would not put up with incorrigible members who might bring reproach upon the rest. The Bethel Baptist Church of Girardeau County, Missouri, was just such a body. Organized on July 19, 1806, with the distinction of being the first permanent non-Catholic church west of the Mississippi, the membership intended to guard their strategic testimony. Collins cites from official church records:

> 1808 - June 11—The church met in conference and Brother Spears for profane swearing and refusing to hear the church was excommunicated.
> 1810 - April 7—The church met in conference. Mr. Shields excommunicated for...telling untruths.
> 1816 - July 13—Rebecca Hubble excommunicated for leaving her husband and going off with another man, Jemima Hall excluded for the same crime.
> 1816 - August 8—Green B. League excluded for absenting himself from the country without settling with his creditors.
> 1819 - April—An accusation laid in against Bro. Richard Willard for having drank to an excess, and for stripping to fight.

1822 - June 8—Bro. Ezekiel Hill laid in a complaint against himself for killing a deer on Sunday, and after acknowledgment of his fault, was forgiven.[7]

The Baptists were also concerned with spiritual education. The first Sunday school in America was founded by Samuel Slater, a Baptist layman, on September 15, 1799, in Pawtucket, Rhode Island. By 1850 there were five Baptist institutions of higher learning in the East: Brown University (1764), Waterville College, now Colby (1818), Madison University, now Colgate (1819), Columbian University (1821) and Lewisburg University, now Bucknell (1846). As the century progressed, numbers of other Baptist schools were founded such as Baylor University, Furman University, Crozer Theological Seminary and the University of Chicago.

A great emphasis on foreign missions was also being stimulated by Dr. Carey's fruitful labors in India. The Baptist Missionary Society of Massachusetts was formed in 1802. In the year 1812, the Salem Bible Translation and Foreign Mission Society was organized, followed by the Baptist General Convention for Foreign Missions in 1814. And in 1824, the Baptist General Tract Society was started in Washington, D.C.

As was frequently the case, Baptist missionary zeal was found to be contagious. On a hot Wednesday afternoon in August of 1806, five ministerial students at Williams College (Congregational) in western Massachusetts were on their way to a prayer meeting when they found themselves caught by a sudden thunderstorm. The five fellows dove into a nearby haystack for shelter. While the lightning flashed and thunder caromed across the hills, Samuel J. Mills, Harvey Loomis, Byram Green, James Richards and Francis L. Robbins were soon engrossed in a serious discussion about the prospect of missionary activity to India. After several moments, they were struck with the obvious, Hardman relating:

> Samuel J. Mills, leader of the group, saw that the discussion presented an opportunity: "Why should *we* not be the ones to take the gospel to these who are so oppressed and benighted under the weight of sin?" Mills grew more earnest, *"We can do it if we will!"*... "Fellows," he said, "we came here to talk with God. I have great faith in prayer. Come, let us make India and foreign missions the subject of prayer under this haystack, while the dark clouds are leaving and a clear sky is coming."... When they concluded their devotions, they closed by singing a stanza of an Isaac Watts hymn.

Let all the heathen writers join
To form one perfect book;

Great God, if once compared with thine,
How mean their writings look!

As the skies cleared, anyone who chanced to walk across that meadow and hear loud singing coming from a haystack would have been astonished, until he realized that he was near a college and those must be students at one idiocy or another. The actions could be dismissed with a tolerant smile, as all college antics could be. But if our walker were then told that he had just overheard one of the most important prayer meetings in all history, the smile might be replaced by bewilderment. Unnumbered thousands of prayers have pled to God on behalf of missions and the unsaved, but a world shaking movement begun and vast numbers saved in foreign places because of prayers in a haystack during a thunderstorm? Most unlikely.[8]

In four short years, Mills followed through with his burden and led in the formation of the American Board of Commissioners for Foreign Missions. Although the ABCFM was a Protestant society, the story is significant because two out of the first five missionaries sent overseas by that body converted to Baptist views before reaching land. Convinced of their need for the ordinance after studying the Bible while en route to India, Adoniram and Ann Judson were subsequently immersed in a Baptist church at Calcutta on September 6, 1813. Shortly after, Luther Rice arrived and was also baptized having passed through a similar period of reflection. The Judsons would labor in Rangoon for six long years before seeing their first convert, Moung Nan, baptized on June 27, 1819. Before expiring in 1850, Judson translated the Bible into several languages and dialects and left a work consisting of 98 missionaries, 118 ordained native preachers and 25,371 members.[9]

CHARLES G. FINNEY

A notable personality about this time was the fiery Presbyterian evangelist, Charles Grandison Finney (1792–1875). Converted in October of 1821 through the influence of the Adams County Presbyterian Church in Adams, New York, the accomplished attorney made an immediate and full surrender to the Gospel ministry. Having no use for Calvinism, Finney stressed the sinner's personal accountability and publicly invited his listeners to use the "anxious seat." The fires of revival seemed to break out wherever he would minister. After having preached for Reverend Moses Gillet at his Congregational church in Rome, New York, the pastor reported, "Religion was the principle [sic] subject of conversation in our streets, stores, and even taverns."[10]

His preaching exploits read like the book of Acts. Having married Lydia Andrews in October of 1824, their honeymoon had to be delayed six months because a revival broke out where the groom happened to be preaching. On another occasion, a factory owner got so burdened that he shut down his plant so that the visiting evangelist could proclaim the Gospel to his needy employees. Hardman writes:

> Finney's personal and extemporaneous pulpit style had a rapid-fire impact on the packed congregation, but perhaps it was his uncannily penetrating and hypnotic eyes that most riveted his audience. Set under firm brows in a handsome face, those eyes were "large and blue, at times mild as an April sky, and at others, cold and penetrating as polished steel." In addition to those unforgettable eyes, observers were always impressed with Finney's grace in the pulpit, his fitting illustrations, his appropriate but not exaggerated gestures that dramatized his delivery, and his majestic voice, which was a fitting companion to the eyes.[11]

It is estimated that Finney put 100,000 members into the Northern Presbyterian churches and influenced another 500,000 decisions through the related influence of his numerous revivals. Lawson states that 85% of Finney's converts remained true to their professions of faith.[12]

It was against this backdrop of prevailing evangelistic activity that Alexis de Tocqueville wrote, "Upon my arrival in the United States the religious aspect of the country was the first thing that struck my attention."[13] He also made the astute observation that legitimate Christianity liberates the intellect, stating, "In the United States the influence of religion is not confined to the manners, but it extends to the intelligence of the people."[14] As he traveled through a nation of Bible-literate citizens, de Tocqueville was simply witnessing the marvelous fulfillment of John 8:32 which says, *"And ye shall know the truth, and the truth shall make you free."*

This lofty correlation between biblical truth and intellectual freedom has never existed within the benighted nations of Roman Catholicism. On the 22nd of June, 1663, Galileo had to fall on his knees to avoid a papal death sentence, signing with his own hand the retraction, "I abjure, curse, and detest the error and heresy of the motion of the earth."[15] The "infallible" decree of Pope Urban VIII *against* the motion of the earth was signed by

Cardinals Felia, Guido, Desiderio, Antonio, Bellingero and Fabriccio: "In the name and by the authority of Jesus Christ, the plenitude of which resides in His Vicar, the pope, that the proposition that the earth is not the center of the world, and that it moves with a diurnal motion is absurd, philosophically false, and erroneous in faith."[16]

A true Roman Catholic is not allowed to think for himself. While Bible-believing Americans were being challenged to expand their horizons by such Scriptures as, *"Wise men lay up knowledge"* (Proverbs 10:14a), and *"a man of knowledge increaseth strength"* (Proverbs 24:5b), Pope Gregory XVI was admonishing the faithful on August 15, 1832: "If the holy Church so requires, let us sacrifice our own opinions, our knowledge, our intelligence, the splendid dreams of our imagination, and the most sublime attainments of the human understanding."[17]

AMERICA PROSPERS

As a total repudiation of such nonsense, it is the central thesis of this book that America's unique religious liberties were designed to afford the New Testament church an unprecedented opportunity of displaying the liberating power of the Gospel. In light of the biblical incentive that, *"Righteousness exalteth a nation"* (Proverbs 14:34a), the Lord was obligated by His own Word to reward the soul-winning efforts of His churches. And yet the modus operandi by which this exaltation would occur was already set in place, like the fruit trees in Genesis 1:12d, *"whose seed was in itself."* For, the applying of our familiar Baptist distinctive of *soul liberty* to an economic system beyond the reach of Vatican interference would be guaranteed to exalt *any* nation on the face of God's earth. A free enterprise system controlled only by the natural laws of supply and demand constitutes the greatest blessing that God can bestow upon a Bible-honoring society this side of Heaven itself.

No greater evidence can be found to confirm the superiority of Christian America over Catholic Europe than the obvious disparity between the two in the number of life-enhancing inventions and medical advances. And remember, we are not comparing Japheth with either Ham or Shem, but rather two antithetical branches of Japheth with each other.

During the colonial era, manufacturing was dwarfed by English Mercantile Theory which forbade the first Americans from engaging in arts and crafts based on natural phenomenon. Wilson writes, "The stated policy of the British government demanded that its colonies be *only* sources of raw materials to be shipped home to England in English ships."[18] The renowned eighteenth-century economist, Adam Smith, protested this early intrusion on soul liberty. "To prohibit a great people from making all that they can of every part of their own produce, or from employing their stock and industry in a way that they judge most advantageous to themselves, is a manifest violation of the most sacred rights of mankind."[19]

With so much required to make life liveable and so few to do it, the average American developed into a "jack of all trades" where the phrase, "half finished is all finished" became the order of the day. The successful completion of the American Revolution changed all of that, however, by forcing the severed colonies to fend for themselves, Wilson stating:

> The years following the war were a time of confusion, despair, and rebellion. Whatever commerce had existed before was now in a state of ruin. Independence was what the colonies had sought; and now the deserted mother country gave it in full measure. The British mercantile theory had stated that the Empire was composed of the heart and stomach—The British Isles, to be fed by the limbs, the colonies. The limbs in turn were to be nourished by the blood and wealth pumped to them from the heart. One limb had severed itself. Now, said the British, let it shift for itself.[20]

As mentioned in a previous chapter, although 13 in number, and possessing a population of 2.5 million, the new states were still existing in a stagnant, geographic isolation. The untamed wilderness appeared as terrible then as it had to Dorothy Bradford 150 years earlier:

> The "American Colonies" were still nothing but the sparsest fringe of seacoast settlements separated by swamps, desolation, empty beaches, and primeval forests of terrifying silence, stretched out in a thin line for a thousand miles from Maine to Georgia. The innermost penetrations were rarely more than one hundred miles from where the Atlantic surf seethed up on the sand. Deeper than one hundred miles was a forested land of silence in which only stealthy shadows moved; a region as remote as the moon, as terrifying as the blackest nightmare. It was called simply, the Wilderness.
>
> The awareness of the Wilderness colored every strand of American life. The immensity of the Wilderness was an ever-present nightmare reducing human beings to insignificance. The war against this terror determined the national character. Americans became more pragmatic than

any other people since the Romans; yet the purpose of their science and invention was to safeguard and exalt the rights of the individual. Science became a strategy for exploring and settling the unknown world; invention became the way to give twelve hands to a man beleaguered in his struggle to clear the continent.[21]

As a young nation of rugged individualists began to harness the doctrine of soul liberty in relation to their goods and services, the "Old World" soon took notice of a new and emerging dynamo known as "Yankee ingenuity." From Franklin's kite in the sky to Armstrong's walk on the moon, America's track record of science and invention bears indisputable testimony that *"Righteousness exalteth a nation."* (Proverbs 14:34a) In the few cases where the discovery itself was not made by an American, Yankee know-how either perfected the find or successfully mass produced it, or both.

We have Ben Franklin to thank for giving us a vocabulary of electrical terms such as *battery, condenser, conductor, charge, discharge, armature, electric shock, electrician, positive and negative electricity* and concepts of *plus* and *minus* charge. Wilson writes:

> The true story of Franklin's work on lightning is further proof of his superiority to all other eighteenth-century electricians. For almost half a century before him, men had been suggesting the identity of lightning and the electric spark. However, no one had ever worked out a means of proving it. Franklin not only suggested an actual experiment, but he was able to explain lightning in rational terms and not as an awesome supernatural manifestation.[22]

Even at the age of 83, following a lifetime of scientific contributions, the senior inventor got tired of having to change his own eyeglasses and created the bifocal lens in 1784. Three years later John Fitch gave us the steamboat, while Robert Fulton's *Clermont* improved the same in 1807. Eli Whitney invented the cotton gin in 1793, and the world's first factory to convert raw cotton into cloth by powered machinery within the walls of a single building was begun in Waltham, Massachusetts, in 1814 by the Boston Manufacturing Company. Joseph Henry was credited in 1831 for his discovery of electrical induction and the principle of induced current.

An accomplished American artist by the name of Samuel F. B. Morse perfected the "Morse Code" in 1838 and, in 1844, strung a test line of 40 miles between Washington and Baltimore for the nation's first telegraph service with the initial message being taken from the Word of God. Dr. Tan's encyclopedia states:

> In conversation with Professor S. F. B. Morse, the inventor of the telegraph, the Rev. George W. Hervey asked this question: "Professor Morse, when you were making your experiments yonder in your room in the university, did you ever come to a stand, not knowing what to do next?" "Oh, yes, more than once." "And at such times what did you do next?" "I may answer you in confidence, sir," said the professor, "but it is a matter of which the public knows nothing. I prayed for more light." "And the light generally came?" "Yes, and may I tell you that when flattering honors came to me from America and Europe on account of the invention which bears my name, I never felt I deserved them. I had made a valuable application of electricity, not because I was superior to other men, but solely because God, who meant it for mankind, must reveal it to someone, and was pleased to reveal it to me."
>
> In view of these facts, it is not surprising that the inventor's first message was, *"What hath God wrought!"*[23]

America's original steam locomotive was built by John Stevens in 1825, while Peter Cooper produced a more practical engine in 1830, known as *Tom Thumb*. For the first time since the Garden of Eden, man could now travel faster than 18 to 22 miles per day. The age of *"running to and fro"* (Daniel 12:4) was inaugurated in America a mere 50 years after the Constitution was signed.

John Deere invented the steel plow in 1833 and Silas McCormick the reaper in 1847. Charles Goodyear gave us vulcanized rubber in 1839. An American physician, Dr. Crawford Long, introduced anesthesia to the medical community in 1846, while Elias Howe invented the world's first sewing machine the same year.

This marvelous forward motion continued through the second half of the century as well: Hammond and Davis' refrigerated boxcar in 1867; Glidden's barbed wire in 1874; the first typewriter in 1873 by Sholes, Glidden and Soule; the 1872 air brake by Westinghouse; Bell's telephone in 1876; and the amazing contributions of Thomas Edison who was sent home by his teacher at the age of six with a note stating that he was "too stupid to learn"—the phonograph in 1877, the incandescent lamp in 1879, and the motion picture in 1889, to name but a few. Edison, whose family attended a Baptist church in Llewellyn, New Jersey,[24] was able to see the "bigger picture," stating: "No one can study chemistry and see the wonderful way in which certain elements combine with the nicety of the most delicate machine ever invented, and not come to the inevitable conclusion that there is a Big Engineer who is running this universe."[25]

The Yankee version of the "horseless carriage" in 1895 closed out the nineteenth century, while that incredible "flying machine" of Kitty Hawk in 1903 inaugurated the twentieth. However, when considering the many blessings on our nation, one of the most important ones is often overlooked. As human beings approach the turn of the present millennium, the ingestion of a common drink of water can still be a harrowing experience, unless, of course, you get it in America. Dr. Tan reports:

> At present, impure water—not scarcity of water—is the world's major hazard. Each year, 10 million deaths result from waterborne intestinal diseases. And over one-third of humanity are debilitated as a result of impure water. A pure water supply could slash the incidence of cholera, diarrhea, dysentery and typhoid up to 75%.
> About $21 billion were pledged by the "family of nations" between 1977 and 1980 to provide safe water. But the World Bank estimates that it would take about twice that sum to eliminate most of earth's water problems.[26]

As was the experience with Old Testament Israel, the very water we drink may be the most significant blessing of all.

> *"And it shall come to pass, if ye shall hearken diligently unto my commandments which I command you this day, to love the LORD your God, and to serve him with all your heart and with all your soul, That I will give you the rain of your land in his due season, the first rain and the latter rain, that thou mayest gather in thy corn, and thy wine, and thine oil."* (Deuteronomy 11:13, 14)

SATANIC RESISTANCE

As we have noted repeatedly, the devil was not about to sit back and watch America continue to prosper before the eyes of the world. In the very year of our nation's birth, Adam Weishaupt, professor of canon law at Ingolstadt and a former Jesuit, founded a secret society which he called *Perfektibilisten* which came to be known as the *Illuminati*. Divided into grades of initiation, the members pledged to obey their leaders in a campaign to "unite all men capable of independent thought," and to make man "a masterpiece of reason, and thus attain the highest perfection of the art of government."[27] Although the order was outlawed in 1784 by Karl Theodor, elector of Bavaria, a number of prominent Americans, particularly in New England, suspicioned that the Illuminati had contributed to the French Revolution and desired to penetrate the United States as well. Some believe that the *Rosicrucians* are the present-day embodiment of Weishaupt's original society.

The Northeast also became a breeding ground for the Christ-denying Unitarian movement. Spearheaded by apostate Presbyterian intellectuals, Unitarianism became the religion of elitist humanitarians. The views of this cult were propagated through such literary publications as the *North American Review* founded in 1815 and the *Christian Examiner* of 1824. These were journals whose editors included Henry Adams, Edward Everett, William Emerson, Jared Sparks, Richard Henry Dana, George Ticknor, James Russell Lowell and Edward Everett Hale. Having turned an indifferent ear to the earlier Ivy League revivals, Harvard University now chose to glory in such Unitarian faculty as Longfellow, Lowell and Oliver Wendell Holmes. Critics lampooned these highbrow religionists by saying that their creed was confined to "the Fatherhood of God, the brotherhood of man and the neighborhood of Boston."[28]

Of far greater concern to Baptists during the early 1800's was a major schism involving baptismal regeneration initiated by "Reverend" Alexander Campbell. Although reared as a Presbyterian, Campbell was immersed by a Baptist minister in 1812 but continued to maintain a number of questionable views. After gaining a considerable following in West Virginia, Kentucky and the southern portions of Ohio, Indiana and Illinois, Campbell began advocating a "reformation" or return to a primitive form of New Testament Christianity. His impressive-sounding motto was, "When the Scriptures speak, we speak; where they are silent, we are silent." In time he was discovered to be preaching a baptism "unto remission of sins" and caused his greatest amount of dissension in Kentucky. The orthodox Baptist assemblies separated themselves from this dangerous heresy but lost a considerable number of members in the process. Campbell's movement came to be known as the "Church of Christ" or "Campbellites" and continues to deceive people today.

Another deceptive cult that appeared at this time was the so-called Church of Jesus Christ of Latter Day Saints, known as the Mormons (or *Morons*). Their leader, Joseph Smith, claimed he had a heavenly vision in Palmyra, New York, in the year 1820. Of course, Joe wasn't about to hang around "Finney country," so he took his freshly translated *Book of Mormon* and led his deluded disciples to Kirtland, Ohio, and then on to Nauvoo, Illinois. Joe's polygamy and other assorted crimes did not go over with the normal townspeople, so they "eliminated" him in 1846. Brigham Young assumed the mantle (not to mention 5 of the fallen leader's 27 widows) and two years of further bloodshed ensued. Finally, Brigham saw the handwriting on the wall and led his clan of 5,000 members to the Great Salt Lake in Utah where he established one of the biggest religious con games in history. To this day, the Mormon Tabernacle Choir is respected as one of the top performing chorales in the nation.

Yet another "monkey wrench" that Satan pitched at nineteenth-century religious America was the heretical eschatology of Deacon William Miller, founder of the Seventh Day Adventist cult. Residing near Poultney, Vermont, Miller began to proclaim that Christ would return "on or about" the 15th of February, 1843. As the big day drew near, immense crowds came to hear him. Armitage writes:

> The craze went so far that many made white ascension robes and stood shivering in the snow on the nights of February 14th and 15th, expecting to be caught up into the air, and meetings were held in hundreds of places of worship during those nights, while many sold all that they had and proved their sincerity by giving the money to the sick and suffering.[29]

When a second date of October 22, 1844, was set and passed, Bill's crowds began to diminish accordingly. Of course, the heathen had a golden opportunity to mock legitimate Christianity in the process. Many churches, especially among the Baptists, Methodists and Congregationalists, were disturbed over the controversy and some were split as a result.

Although these various heretics were spreading their doctrinal poison across the land, a far more insidious movement was stealthily afoot. In fact, this satanic stratagem would eventually surpass the combined evil of every cult in America. And had it not been for the patriotic vigilance of a previously mentioned inventor, the eventual toll would have surely been higher. What you are about to read in the ensuing chapter constitutes one of the least-known eras in all of United States history. The reason for this reprehensible blackout will also be apparent in short order.

XII

The Devil's D-Day

> *"Seducing spirits and doctrines of devils."*
> (I Timothy 4:1b)

I N HIS MASSIVE biography on the life of Samuel F. B. Morse, the learned Dr. S. Ireneus Prime writes:

> Professor Morse was a Christian in his faith and practice. In his long life, there was probably not an hour when his inquiring and inventive mind was perplexed with doubts or fears in regard to religious truth...He first made a public profession of religion in Charlestown, Massachusetts, in the church of which his father was pastor. He was the superintendent of its Sabbath-school, one of the first established in this country. When the family removed to New Haven, he became a member of the First Congregational Church of that city...Those who knew him most intimately, and held communion with him in hours of retirement from the conflicts of the world, knew that he was governed in all his actions by the fear of God and love of his fellow-men. He had a sense of being surrounded at all times by the Infinite and Eternal, in whom he lived and moved and had his being. He received the Word of God, the sacred Scriptures, as the guide and rule of his life; believing in their inspiration, and never questioning their authority.[1]

My readers may be surprised to learn that Dr. Morse was already an accomplished artist and world traveler by the time he invented the telegraph. However, long before designing the transmission code that would eventually bear his name, Morse was providentially led to uncover a clandestine plot against the American government which moved him to send his endangered countrymen an emphatic warning in the form of two books, *Foreign Conspiracies Against the Liberties of the United States* and *Imminent Dangers to the Free Institutions of the United States Through Foreign Immigration*. Dr. Prime relates:

> While Mr. Morse was in Italy in the years 1830 and 1831, he became acquainted with several ecclesiastics of the Church of Rome, one of whom, a cardinal, made a vigorous attack upon the faith of the young artist. A correspondence between them ensued, and frequent interviews. Mr. Morse was led to believe, from what he learned in Rome, that a political conspiracy, under the cloak of a religious mission, was formed against the United States of America. When he came to Paris in 1832 and enjoyed the confidence and friendship of Lafayette, he stated his convictions to the General, who fully concurred with him in the reality of such a conspiracy. Returning to this country in the autumn of 1832, inventing the Telegraph on his homeward voyage, he never became so absorbed in his invention as to forget the impressions made in Italy respecting the danger to which his country was exposed. The conviction was so strong that he gave much time in subsequent years to the publication in periodicals, in pamphlets, and in volumes, of the facts and arguments which, in his judgment, were important to a fair understanding of the subject.[2]

HISTORICAL BACKGROUND

In order to comprehend the substance of this foreign conspiracy, one must first review a bit of early nineteenth-century European history. Following the collapse of the Napoleonic era, the Congress of Vienna (1814–1815) was convened to redefine Europe's post-war boundaries. The three leading personalities in attendance were Emperor Francis I of Austria, Czar Alexander I of Russia and Friedrich William IV, King of Prussia. The principal negotiator was Austria's minister of foreign affairs, Klemens Wenzel Lothar von Metternich. The bottom line of this august congress was that Europe would now be lorded over by a trilogy of tyrants piously calling themselves the "Holy Alliance." With Catholic Austria as their power base, the period of time between 1815 and 1848 has been called the *Age of Metternich*. Espionage, censorship and armed repression of democratic movements were the essential features of Metternich's policy. Noting that the German word *mitternacht* means *midnight*, the Saxons reacted to his diabolical efforts to cover Europe with political darkness by dubbing him Prince Midnight! Dwight simply states that Metternich was "regarded as the greatest enemy of the human race who has lived for ages."[3]

Despite official assurances from the "Holy Alliance" that Europe's newest political status was divinely inspired, most of their subjects were not very impressed. (Alexander I "learned" of this divine inspiration at a séance conducted by the German mystic, Baroness Barbara von Krudener.[4]) Naples and Piedmont revolted in 1820 with the Greek War of Independence raging from 1821–1830. Belgian liberty was declared in 1830 and revolutions broke out simultaneously in Warsaw and central Italy in 1831. As the years dragged on, it became all too clear that the rising American republic was providing Europe with her will to revolt. Morse asked rhetorically, "Can the example of Democratic liberty which this country shows, produce no uneasiness to monarchs?...And is there no danger of a *re*-action from Europe?"[5]

He continues:

> Is it asked, Why should the Holy Alliance feel interested in the destruction of transatlantic liberty? I answer, the silent but powerful and increasing influence of our institutions on Europe, is reason enough. The example alone of prosperity which we exhibit in such strong contrast to the enslaved, priest-ridden, tax-burdened despotisms of the old world, is sufficient to keep those countries in perpetual agitation. How can it be otherwise? Will a sick man, long despairing of cure, learn that there is a remedy for him, and not desire to procure it? Will one born to think a dungeon his natural home, learn through his grated bars, that man may be free; and not struggle to obtain his liberty?
>
> And what do the people of Europe behold in this country? They witness the successful experiment of a free government; a government of the *people*; without rulers *de jure divino*, (by divine right:) having no hereditary privileged classes; a government exhibiting good order and obedience to law, without an armed police and secret tribunals; a government out of debt; a people industrious, enterprising, thriving in all their interests; without monopolies; a people religious without an establishment; moral and honest without the terrors of the confessional or the inquisition; a people not harmed by the uncontrolled liberty of the press, and freedom of opinion; a people that read what they please, and think, and judge, and act for themselves; a people enjoying the most unbounded security of person and prosperity; among whom domestic conspiracies are unknown; where the poor and rich have equal justice; a

people social and hospitable; exerting all their energies in schemes of public and private benefit without other control than mutual forbearance.

A government so contrasted in all points with absolute governments, must, and does engage the intense solicitude, both of the rulers and people of the old world. Every revolution that has occurred in Europe for the last half century, has been in a greater or lesser degree the consequence of our own glorious revolution.[6]

That such a scenario was indeed a bona fide concern on the Continent was confirmed in 1828 by the German scholar and devout Roman Catholic, Karl Wilhelm Friedrich von Schlegel, who was at that time Counselor of Legation in the Austrian cabinet. In a series of lectures given in Vienna for the purpose of strengthening the cause of absolute power, Schlegel

> ...clearly and unanswerably proved, that the *political revolutions to which European governments have been so long subjected, from the popular desires for liberty, are the natural effects of the Protestant Reformation.* That *Protestantism* favors *Republicanism,* while *Popery* as naturally supports *Monarchical* power.[7]

In no uncertain terms Dr. Schlegel, the confidential friend of Prince Metternich, declared, "THE GREAT NURSERY *of these destructive principles,* (the principles of Democracy,) *the* GREAT REVOLUTIONARY SCHOOL for FRANCE *and* THE REST OF EUROPE, *is* NORTH AMERICA!"[8]

Dr. Morse writes:

> Yes, Austria has turned her eyes towards us, and she loves us as the owl loves the sun. Can any one doubt that she would extinguish every spark of liberty in this country, if she had the power? Can any one believe that she would make no attempt to abate an evil which daily threatens more and more the very existence of her throne?[9]

ST. LEOPOLD FOUNDATION

The prospect of a *military* invasion was, of course, out of the question. Something far more subtle was required if the stream of liberty would be dammed at its source. As previously noted, it was while Dr. Morse was traveling in Italy that he was led of the Lord to discover the framework of this intended Austrian subversion. The godly inventor felt it more than coincidental that within a year of Schlegel's weighty pronouncement, a powerful society named the *St. Leopold Foundation* was established in the Austrian capital for the avowed purpose *"of promoting the greater activity of Catholic missions in America."*[10] Dr. Morse elaborates:

> But how shall she attack us? She cannot send her armies, they would be useless. She has told us by the mouth of her Counsellor of Legation, that Popery, while it is the natural antagonist to Protestantism, is opposed in its whole character to Republican liberty, and is the promoter and supporter of arbitrary power. How fitted then is Popery for her purpose! This she can send without alarming our fears, or, at least, only the fears of those *"miserable,"* *"intolerant fanatics,"* and *"pious bigots,"* who affect to see danger to the liberties of the country in the mere introduction of a *religious system* opposed to their own, and whose cry of danger, be it ever so loud, will only be regarded as the result of *"sectarian fear,"* and the plot ridiculed as a *"quixotic dream."* But is there any thing so irrational in such a scheme? Is it not the most natural and obvious act for Austria to do, with her views of the influence of Popery upon the form of government, its influence to pull down Republicanism, and build up monarchy; I say, is it not her most obvious act *to send Popery to this country if it is not here, or give it a fresh and vigorous impulse if it is already here?*[11]

Does such a plot stagger the imagination as being too fantastic to be taken seriously? Should a reader be suspicious that he has never heard of such "goings on," I would suggest that in present-day America which idolizes Mike Jackson, Oprah, O. J. Simpson and the Psychic Friends Network, there are probably a lot of other things that have been squeezed out of our nation's history books to make room for Susan B. Anthony and Harriet Tubman. For instance, if you had not read this book, would you have ever known that, at one time, America was so hostile to the destructive inroads of popery that at least 45 fanatically anti-Catholic newspapers and periodicals could be purchased in the good old U. S. of A. (three in New York City alone)?

There were also well over 500 books and pamphlets written on this anti-popery theme as well. One of these, a 750-page tome entitled *The Papacy and the Civil Power* (Harper and Brothers, New York, 1876) was authored by Richard Wigginton Thompson. Like Professor Morse, Mr. Thompson's credentials are quite impressive. After being admitted to the Indiana Bar in 1834, Thompson entered into a distinguished career of public service which spanned four decades and included stints as acting Indiana lieutenant-governor, two terms in Congress, two years as circuit judge in the eighteenth district and four years as secretary of the navy under President Rutherford Hayes. It is also rather ironic that the patriotic Thompson just happened to be reared in *Culpeper County, Virginia*. Concerning Vatican designs on American liberties, he affirmed: "The Papacy is now endeavoring, by the most active and persistent efforts, to substitute an ecclesiastical government of the people—a grand 'Holy Empire' for this free and popular republic which it has cost so much blood and treasure to establish and maintain."[12]

As the prophet wrote in Hosea 4:6a, *"My people are destroyed for lack of knowledge,"* the Vatican has been able to infiltrate America primarily because the average citizen, Christian or not, has never analyzed the organizational and operational structure of the Roman Catholic Church. Whenever this is done, the shocking discovery is made that *pure* Catholicism—*not the fake type that knows how to lay low when in the minority*—functions in the precise manner as do the despotic monarchies in Europe. The trick is not to let the "religious front" throw you! It was Milton who wrote, "Popery is a double thing to deal with, and claims a twofold power, ecclesiastical and political, both usurped, and the one supporting the other."[13] Along this line, Dr. Morse adds:

> We cannot be too often reminded of the *double* character of the enemy who has gained foothold upon our shores, for although Popery is a religious sect, and on this ground claims toleration side by side with other religious sects, yet Popery is also a *political, a despotic system,* which we must repel as altogether incompatible with the existence of freedom. I repeat it, Popery is a *political, a despotic system,* which must be resisted by all true patriots.[14]

What Professor Morse and Secretary Thompson were attempting to explain is that to whatever degree a citizen of the United States embraces the orthodox tenets of Roman Catholicism, he must, of necessity, become dysfunctional with regard to the American way of life and particularly so in the democratic process. To begin with the fundamental principle of government, Dr. Morse writes:

> *From whom is authority to govern derived?* Austria and the United States will agree in answering,—*from God.* The opposition of opinion occurs in the answers to the next question. *To whom on earth is this authority delegated?* Austria answers, *To the* EMPEROR, *who is the source of all authority,—"I the Emperor do ordain,..."* The United States answers, *To the* PEOPLE, *in whom resides the Sovereign power,—"We the*

People do ordain, establish, grant,"... In one principle is recognized the necessity of the *servitude of the people,* the absolute dependence of the subject, unqualified submission to the commands of the rulers without question or examination. The *Ruler* is *Master,* the *People* are *Slaves.* In the other is recognized the *supremacy of the people,* the equality of rights and powers of the citizen, submission alone to laws emanating from themselves; the Ruler is a public servant, receiving wages from the people to perform services agreeable to their pleasure; amenable in all things to them; and holding office at their will. The *Ruler* is *Servant;* the *People* are *Master.*

The fact and important nature of the difference in these antagonistic doctrines, leading, as is perceived, to diametrically opposite results, are all that is needful to state in order to proceed at once to the inquiry, which position does the Catholic sect and the Protestant sects severally favor? The *Pope,* the supreme Head of the Catholic church, claims to be the *"Vicegerent of God,"* "supreme over all mortals;" "over all Emperors, Kings, Princes, Potentates and People;" "King of kings and Lord of lords." He styles himself, "the divinely appointed dispenser of *spiritual* and *temporal* punishments;" "armed with power to depose Emperors and Kings, and absolve subjects from their oath of allegiance:" "from him lies no appeal;" "he is responsible to no one on earth;" "he is judged of no one but God."[15]

Does the political philosophy of Roman Catholicism appear the least bit compatible with American democracy? Take the matter of a free press. Have you ever heard of a Catholic nation that has enjoyed such a privilege? Although the typical, indifferent Catholic of today is too busy watching Notre Dame football or going into debt at the mall to be intimidated by a "forbidden book list," such an index was absolutely one of the key methods used by the Vatican to become the largest and most powerful religious denomination in this country. Secretary Thompson wrote:

There is at Rome, as an essential department of the papal court, what is called the "Congregation of the Index." To this tribunal are submitted all publications that are, in any degree, under the suspicion of heresy; and if, upon examination, they are found to teach what the pope does not desire to be taught, they are condemned and placed upon the "Index expurgatorius;" so that thereafter it shall be regarded as an offense against the Church and against God for any person to read them.[16]

Do you really believe that *traditional* Catholic Americans have felt the liberty to think for themselves or to form opinions about the Bible—

according to the official teachings of their infallible Church? Whereas article nine of the Pontifical Law states, "The Pope has the power to interpret Scripture and to teach as he pleases, and *no person is allowed to teach in a different way,"*[17] the Council of Latearn in 1215 decreed "that all heretics [that is, all who have an opinion of their own], shall be delivered over to the civil magistrate *to be burned.*"[18] In his encyclical letter of September, 1832, Gregory XVI, the reigning pontiff who implemented the infamous St. Leopold Foundation, had this to say about "liberty of conscience":

> From this polluted fountain of "indifference," flows that absurd and erroneous doctrine, or rather raving, in favor and defence of "liberty of conscience," for which most pestilential error, the course is opened to that entire and wild liberty of opinion, which is every where attempting the overthrow of religious and civil institutions; and which the unblushing impudence of some has held forth as an advantage to religion. Hence *that pest, of all others most to be dreaded in a state, unbridled liberty of opinion,* licentiousness of speech, and a lust of novelty, which, according to the experience of all ages, portend the downfall of the most powerful and flourishing empires. Hither tends that worst and never sufficiently to be execrated and detested LIBERTY OF THE PRESS, for the diffusion of all manner of writings, which some so loudly contend for, and so actively promote.[19]

Remember that this was the statement of Gregory XVI in 1832! To see how this translated to Catholics living in the United States, consider the following "admonition" that was attached to the American edition of the Douay Bible (the official Catholic translation of the Bible in English), published in 1837 under the auspices of the Provincial Council of Baltimore: "To prevent and remedy this *abuse,* and to guard against *error*, it was judged necessary to *forbid the reading of the Scriptures* in the vulgar language *without the advice and permission of the pastors and spiritual guides whom God has appointed to govern his Church."*[20]

For a Catholic to defy any of these papal restrictions of his God-given freedoms is to make the worst mistake of his religious experience. The August, 1868 edition of the *Catholic World* stated, "["His Holiness,"] as the head and mouthpiece of the Catholic Church, administers its discipline and issues orders to which every Catholic, *under pain of sin,* must yield obedience."[21]

Such was the kind of mindless religion that the Austrian-Vatican alliance was determined to spread throughout America via the St. Leopold

Foundation. The threat posed was real, and patriots like Secretary Thompson were willing to be outspoken on the matter:

> Nothing is plainer than that, if the principles of the Church of Rome prevail here, our Constitution would necessarily fall. The two cannot exist together. They are in open and direct antagonism with the fundamental theory of our government and of all popular government everywhere.[22]

FOREIGN IMMIGRATION

Added to these many sober warnings was the statement by the Marquis de Lafayette, friend to both George Washington and Samuel Morse, that "American liberty can be destroyed only by the popish clergy."[23] Through discussions with Lafayette and others, Morse learned that the Vatican's plan for a Romanized America was to be expedited through abnormal waves of Catholic immigration. Secretary of State John Quincy Adams recommended in 1817, "It may be observed that for the repose of Europe, as well as of America, the European and American political systems should be kept as separate and distinct from each other as possible."[24] This threatening scenario was also foreseen by Thomas Jefferson who warned his nation accordingly:

> "The present desire of America, (in 1781,) is to produce rapid population by as great *importations of foreigners* as possible. *But is this founded in policy?* Are there no *inconveniences* to be thrown into the scale against the advantage expected from a multiplication of numbers by the importation of foreigners? It is for the happiness of those united in society to harmonize as much as possible in matters which they must of necessity transact together.
>
> "Civil government being the sole object of forming societies, its administration must be conducted by common consent. Every species of government has its specific principles. Ours, perhaps, are more peculiar than those of any other in the universe. It is a composition of the freest principles of the English constitution, with others derived from natural right, and natural reason. To these nothing can be more opposed than the maxims of absolute monarchies. Yet, from such, we are to expect the greatest number of emigrants. *They will bring with them the principles of the governments they leave, imbibed in their early youth; or, if able to throw them off, it will be in exchange for an unbounded licentiousness,* passing, as is usual, from one extreme to another. It would be a miracle

were they to stop precisely at the point of temperate liberty. These principles, with their language, they will transmit to their children. *In proportion to their numbers, they will share with us the legislation. They will infuse into it their spirit, warp and bias its directions, and render it a heterogeneous, incoherent, distracted mass.*

"I may appeal to experience, for a verification of these conjectures. But if they be not *certain in event,* are they not *possible, are they not probable?* Is it not safer to wait with patience—for the attainment of any degree of population desired or expected? May not our government be more homogeneous, more peaceable, more durable?" He asks what would be the condition of France if 20 millions of Americans were suddenly imported into that kingdom? and adds—"If it would be *more turbulent,* less happy, less strong, we may believe that the addition of *half a million of foreigners* would produce a *similar effect here.* "[25]

As to the actual strategy of this immigration invasion, the St. Leopold Foundation would help to finance a twofold resettlement area. First, the Irish would fill up the influential cities of the Northeast, then the Germans would overrun the fertile Mississippi Valley. With regard to the former stage, yet another venerable witness deserves a hearing. Having received a world-famous inventor, a secretary of the navy, the distinguished Lafayette and the author of the Declaration of Independence, we now entertain the testimony of a former Catholic priest who became a Presbyterian minister after trusting the Lord Jesus Christ as his personal Saviour. In his autobiography, *50 Years in the "Church" of Rome,* Reverend Charles Chiniquy describes a meeting of Catholic priests which he attended in Buffalo, New York, in the spring of 1852, where the subject of infiltrating the major Northern cities was being discussed. Reverend Chiniquy relates the insidious justification that was voiced for this approach:

> We are also determined to take possession of the United States; but we must proceed with the utmost secrecy and wisdom. What does a skillful general do when he wants to conquer a country? Does he scatter his soldiers over the farm lands, and spend their energy in plowing the fields? No! he keeps them close to his flanks and marching toward the strongholds: the rich and powerful cities. The farming countries then submit and become the price of this victory without moving a finger to subdue them.
>
> So it is with us. Silently and patiently, we must mass our Roman Catholics in the great cities of the United States, remembering that the vote of a poor journeyman, though he be covered with rags, has as much weight in the scale of power as the millionaire Astor, and that if we have

two votes against his one, he will become as powerless as an oyster. Let us then multiply our votes; let us call our poor but faithful Irish Catholics from every corner of the world, and gather them into the very hearts of the cities of Washington, New York, Boston, Chicago, Buffalo, Albany, Troy, Cincinnati, etc.

Under the shadows of those great cities, the Americans consider themselves a giant unconquerable race. They look upon the poor Irish Catholics with supreme contempt, as only fit to dig their canals, sweep their streets and work in their kitchens. Let no one awake those sleeping lions, today. Let us pray God that they continue to sleep a few years longer, waking only to find their votes outnumbered as we will turn them forever, out of every position of honor, power and profit! When not a single judge or policeman, will be elected if he be not a devoted Irish Catholic! What will those so-called giants think when not a single senator or member of Congress will be chosen, unless he has submitted to our holy father the pope!

We will not only elect the president, but fill and command the armies, man the navies and hold the keys of the public treasury. It will then be time for our faithful Irish people to give up their grog shops, in order to become the judges and governors of the land.

Then, yes! then, we will rule the United States, and lay them at the feet of the Vicar of Jesus Christ, that he may put an end to their godless system of education, and impious laws of liberty of conscience which are an insult to God and man![26]

Having reviewed the particulars of Dr. Morse's "theory"—*an alarm that was sounded as early as 1835*—the reader is invited to examine the subsequent historical developments. Was S. F. B. Morse a *patriotic prophet* or just a *prejudiced Protestant*? Before the evidence is considered, allow me to expose the ludicrous "theory" that is frequently advanced by Catholics and humanists alike to account for the "bigoted behavior" of the otherwise politically correct inventor. Unable to deal with the *facts* of his vindication, Catholic apologists would divert the attention of thinking people to an incident in Rome where the American had his hat knocked off his head by an indignant Italian soldier as the "host" (Jesus, to the Catholics) was being borne along in a sacred procession. The Jesuit professor, James Hennesey, wrote, "His own feelings seem to have been largely shaped by an unfortunate confrontation with a papal soldier in Rome which he saw as symbolic of Catholic despotism."[27]

British historian Paul Johnson simply states that Morse "harbored anti-Catholic feelings ever since, during a visit to Rome, he had failed to doff his hat to a papal procession and one of the papal guards knocked it off."[28]

Harvard graduate Ray Billington wrote in his volume, *The Protestant Crusade*, "While Morse was watching a papal procession pass, an event occurred which accounted for much of his later bigotry." After relating the encounter, Billington smugly concludes, "This episode changed Morse's whole point of view...His trampled hat was to make him a life-long opponent of Rome."[29]

Now what these amateur psychologists "forgot" to tell you concerns *another* incident in Dr. Morse's book which also involves the Roman wafer god. In fact, I am rather surprised that our dedicated scholars "missed" it, since the account can be found on the very page before the "trampled hat" story. To be candid, the reason why they never dreamed of acknowledging *this* event is because it so perfectly symbolizes the true anti-American sentiment harbored by Catholic prelates in this nation. What you are about to read is the actual account taken from the *Catholic Telegraph*, as cited by Dr. Morse, which describes the elaborate dedication service of the 8,000-seat Cathedral of St. Louis, on Sunday, October 26, 1834:

> At an early hour, 7, A.M. on the day of consecration, four Bishops, twenty-eight Priests, twelve of whom were from TWELVE different nations—and a considerable number of young aspirants to the holy ministry, making the entire ecclesiastical corps amount to fifty or sixty, were habited in their appropriate dresses. As *soon as the procession was organized,* the pealing of three large and clear-sounding bells, *the thunder of two pieces of artillery* raised all hearts, as well as our own to the Great Almighty Being.
>
> When the HOLY RELICS were moved towards their new habitation, where they shall enjoy an anticipated resurrection—the presence of their God in His holy tabernacle, *the guns fired a second salute.* We felt as if the SOUL OF ST. LOUIS, Christian, Lawgiver and Hero, was in the sound, and that he again led on *his victorious armies* in the service of the God of Hosts, for the defence of his religion, his sepulchre, and his people.
>
> When the solemn moment of the consecration approached, and the *Son* of the *living God* was going to descend for the *first time,* into the new residence of his glory on earth, the *drums* beat the *reville,* **three of the star-spangled banners were lowered over the balustrade of the sanctuary,** the *artillery* gave a deafening discharge...
>
> Well and eloquently did the Rev. Mr. Abell, pastor of Louisville, observe in the evening discourse, alluding to his own and the impressions of the clergy and laity, who were witnesses to the scene; "Fellow-Christians and Fellow-Citizens! **I have seen the flag of my country proudly floating at the mast-head of our richly freighted**

merchantmen; I have seen it fluttering in the breeze at the head of our armies, but never, *never* did my heart *exult*, as when I this day behold it, for the *first time, bow* before its *God!*"[30]

Can you believe what you have just read? *The flag of the United States of America having to be lowered in the presence of a Roman Catholic wafer!* I can assure you that patriots such as Dr. Morse placed a much higher priority on the *flag* than upon some stupid *hat*. Oh, and by the way, it is now within the protection of the law for anyone to *burn* an American flag thanks to the surprise crossover votes of two *normally* conservative Supreme Court justices in *U.S. v. Eichman,* May of 1990. And would you like to venture a guess as to the religious affiliation of Justices *Antonin* Scalia and *Anthony* Kennedy? (Hint: Judge Scalia's father was an Italian *immigrant*, and his son, Paul, is a Catholic priest.)

MORSE VINDICATED

Now, when the record is examined, one discovers that events transpired exactly as Dr. Morse and his compatriots had predicted they would. Within four years of Jefferson's death in 1826, his nation showed a disastrous disregard for his sagacious warnings on immigration. For the two decades of 1810 to 1830, a mere 131,000 foreigners were absorbed into America. The total Catholic population was only 318,000 by 1830, compared to a total population of 12,866,020 nationwide. But then the St. Leopold Foundation began its diabolical work. Just 15 years later, over 100,000 immigrants were arriving *annually*! Two years later, that figure was doubled!! By 1850 the number of foreigners entering this country was up to 300,000 per year and pressing half a million per annum four years after that. Many believe those figures are woefully low. In just the three decades between 1830 and 1860, it was estimated that over 2 million immigrants entered the United States of America. Whereas the Catholic population had been only 30,000 at the time of the American Revolution, her numbers were ballooning at 3,103,000 by the eve of the Civil War, or roughly 10% of the entire nation's population. In eight more years, the figure would exceed 5 million! (What do all these figures have to do with Dr. Morse's "trampled hat"?)

Furthermore, the Irish were infiltrating the Northeast precisely as Reverend Chiniquy had reported. Rhode Island claimed a 20% immigrant population by 1850 while Boston was at 50%. Five years later, native

Bostonians found themselves outnumbered by 10,000 more immigrants than their own population. Concurrently, the Germans were migrating westward, with over 270,000 by 1850. A decade later saw the figure climb to over 1 million. Wisconsin had an incredible 50% foreign-born population. St. Louis, Chicago and Cincinnati had unusually high percentages as well. Of course, this was all one big coincidence, and it was certainly nothing to get alarmed about, right? *Wrong!!*

Overnight the character of America began to change. Whereas Jefferson had cautioned that even *half a million* foreigners could cause our nation problems, over *four times* that number constituted but the vanguard of what was yet to follow. Dr. Morse asked the question, "Can one throw mud into pure water and not disturb its clearness?"[31] Unfortunately, there were many muddy categories to consider. To begin with, most of the immigrants arrived penniless and became immediate wards of the state. New York was paying $280,000 a year (1837) to care for the poor, three-fifths of whom were foreign born. Approximately $4 million was being spent nationwide on 105,000 paupers, half of whom were immigrants.[32] In Philadelphia, more than three-fourths of the inmates at the Almshouse were foreigners and in the Boston Dispensary in 1834, 441 of 477 patients from two districts alone were European castaways![33] By 1850, there was 1 pauper for every 317 natives, but 1 for every 32 foreigners.[34]

Not only were these immigrants poor, but many were of the baser sort as well, especially in respect to alcohol abuse; it was whiskey with the Irish, beer for the Germans. Furthermore, much of this drinking went on during the "Christian Sabbath," which became an increasing source of irritation to God-fearing native Americans. One temperance society stated that this "refuse of European population, has been one of the most formidable obstructions to this cause."[35] And, of course, drinking led to crime. By 1850 the immigrants constituted 11% of the total population, but *50%* of the 27,000 criminals![36] One angry patriot declared, "America has become the sewer into which the pollutions of European jails are emptied."[37] As time went on the conviction grew that the foreign governments were simply draining off their undesirable population on America and gaining the added bonus of weakening this country in the process. (Remember Castro's boat people?)

Another area of abuse was the general "lawlessness of the otherwise law-abiding immigrants." By this I mean that many of the Irish were at constant war with one another. Mob violence was becoming a new part of American culture. Billington wrote:

In New York and Philadelphia each election after 1834 was the occasion for violent street fighting between rival Irish factions or between natives and foreigners. Bloodshed was common and deaths were not infrequent. In 1834 in New York Irishmen armed with stones and cudgels put the mayor, sheriff, and a posse to flight and terrorized the city.[38]

Many of these riots were "job-related" as the Irish killed each other while digging canals or laying railroad track. Sometimes the battles were fought between the Irish and the Germans. Ten rioters were killed by troops in 1839 at a battle on the Chesapeake and Ohio Canal. But, to be honest, any old occasion would do for "Paddy." On the 4th of July in 1835, drunken mobs attacked defenseless citizens in Detroit. In Pennsylvania, another mob of Irish drunks stormed and damaged a Lutheran church. Then there were the Bread Riots in New York City in 1837.[39] And the Germans out west were not much better. St. Louis was ravaged in 1840, Cincinnati in 1842, and Louisville in 1844. Even Billington was forced to concede:

> This rioting and disorder naturally alarmed many Americans. Their country, long quiet and peaceful, now seemed teeming with violence. Mob rule was displacing the ordinary forces of law wherever the foreigners were centered.[40]

JESUIT LEADERSHIP

Unbeknownst to many, the principal source of agitation behind this immigrant disorder was the infamous Society of Jesus. It was the Jesuits who were coming and going through the St. Leopold Foundation. Morse confirms: "These are the soldiers that the Leopold Society has sent to this country, and they are agents of this society, to execute its designs, whatever these designs may be."[41] Who could possibly say enough *bad* things about these diabolical Jesuits? Their deeds have been so evil that they have even been expelled from numerous *Catholic* nations; Spain, Portugal, France and Sicily, to name but a few. By 1775 their exploits were so abominable that Pope Clement XIV had to disband the entire order. Less than two years later, the pontiff suddenly died under "unusual" circumstances. As his corpse turned black, many Italians suspicioned that he had been poisoned by Jesuits.

However, with countless liberal factions threatening the "Holy Alliance," Pius VII reversed Clement's ban and reinstated the religious terrorists in 1814, calling them the "Sacred Militia of the Church." When Gregory XVI inherited this militia in 1831, he immediately set them loose on an unsuspecting America. Secretary Thompson writes: "His attention was directed toward the United States, and the hope was excited in his mind that the tolerance of our institutions would enable him, through the agency of his Jesuit allies, to build up a papal party here, sufficiently strong and powerful."[42]

In his book, *Protestantism and Infidelity*, Jesuit author F. X. Weninger wrote in 1862, "One of the most glorious enterprises for the Catholic Church to engage in at this day is *the conversion of the United States to the Catholic faith*."[43] And what do the Jesuits think of democracy? Vallestigny, a Jesuit priest and deputy of Alva, stated in his address to His Majesty:

> *The mass of the human family are born, not to govern, but to be governed.* This sublime employment of government *has been confided* by Providence *to the privileged class,* whom he has placed upon an eminence *to which the multitude cannot rise* without being lost in the labyrinth and snares which are therein found.[44]

What this basically means is that Jesuits don't get really excited about expressions like, "We, the people of the United States, in order to form a...." According to Jesuit law, members of the order believe the identical doctrines no matter where they are "ministering." Morse cites one of their official sources, [Imago. Soc. Jes. Proleg. p. 33]:

> The members of the Society of Jesuits are dispersed through all nations of the world, and *divided only by distance of place,* NOT IN SENTIMENT; by difference in language, not in affection; by variety in colour, not in manner. In this fraternity, the Latin, Greek, Portuguese, Brazilian, Irish, Sumatran, Spanish, French, English and Belgic Jesuits, ALL THINK, FEEL, SPEAK, AND ACT ALIKE; for among them there is neither debate nor contention.[45]

This means that Jesuits in America will be just as sneaky and disruptive as their brethren who are without. The editor of the *American Protestant Vindicator* wrote on Christmas Day, 1834:

> It is an ascertained fact that Jesuits are prowling about all parts of the United States in every possible disguise, expressly to ascertain the advantageous situations and modes to disseminate Popery. A minister of

the Gospel from Ohio has informed us that he discovered one carrying on his devices in his congregation; and he says the western country swarms with them under the names of puppet show men, dancing masters, music teachers, peddlers of images and ornaments, barrel organ players, and similar practitioners.[46]

Of course, not all Jesuits operate incognito. The most visible arm of the Society is their influential educational outreach. A Missouri patriot reported in the *Home Missionary* for April, 1830:

It is by no means certain that the Jesuits are not to prevail to a great extent in this western country. Their priests are coming in upon us, and with a zeal that ought to make the Protestant Christian blush, —they are establishing their schools and their nunneries throughout the land.[47]

Although Dr. Morse had alerted his countrymen about the St. Leopold Foundation and the approaching waves of Catholic immigration, an anti-popery movement was already active in America at this time. In fact, the first newspaper of this type to appear in New York, the *Observer*, was established in 1823, ironically, *by two brothers of S. F. B. Morse!* Once again, we are reminded of Billington's own bigoted fantasy about Morse and his "trampled hat." Despite his strong Christian upbringing, which included a fire-breathing preacher for a father and two discerning, anti-popery brothers, we are still to believe of the brightest Morse of all that, "Heretofore his artistic nature had led him to admire the beauty of Catholic ceremony; now he saw only the harshness of a despotic religious system."[48]

Billington did acknowledge that the *Observer* became the leading American church publication of the day. This was significant as there were already *30* anti-popery newspapers in America as early as 1827. The Morse brothers made their intentions clear at the outset, writing in an early edition:

Many Protestants begin to think that Popery has of late assumed a more mild form. It is no doubt true that the Papal church has lost her power, and therefore *cannot* play the tyrant as heretofore....But Protestants ought to remember that it is Papal policy to be mild until they have power to be severe.[49]

This is an important observation because Jesuit apologists often employ the public or written commendations which various political leaders have bestowed upon Catholic Americans for "patriotism," "civic responsibility" or "love of freedom," etc. However, you can bet these platitudes were issued *before* "Paddy's" bricks started flying around! In a veiled concession of this papal ploy, Catholic author John Ellis stated, "The policy of clerical aloofness from politics was in part induced by the shyness of an unpopular minority."[50] *(Give me a break!)* Even de Tocqueville made the naive observation that Catholics *appeared* to be well-fitted for democracy as there were no caste systems *within the laity* (i.e., everyone was in equal bondage to the priests).[51] Again, this evaluation was also formed prior to the arrival of heavy immigration. It must never be forgotten that the Roman Catholic Church has operated as the consummate *chameleon* throughout her turbulent, 15-century existence. For the record, Pope John Paul II, "your friend and mine," was a professional *actor* before entering the priesthood! Dr. Morse reiterates this theme of Vatican duplicity:

> Let me not be charged with accusing the Catholics of the United States with intolerance. They are too small a body as yet fully to act out their principles, and their present conduct does not affect the general question in any way, unless it may be to prove that *they are not genuine and consistent Catholics.* The conduct of a small insulated body, under the restraints of the society around it, is of no weight in deciding the character of the sect, while there are nations of the same infallible faith acting out its legitimate principles uncontrolled, and producing fruits by which all may discern, without danger of mistake, the true nature of the tree. If Popery is tolerant, let us see Italy, and Austria, and Spain, and Portugal, open their doors to the teachers of the Protestant faith; let these countries grant to *Protestant* missionaries, as freely as we grant to Catholics, leave to disseminate their doctrine through all classes in their dominions.[52]

As we have already seen, however, the domestic trauma caused by unprecedented Catholic immigration had begun to arrest the attention of many native American patriots. On January 2, 1830, Reverend George Bourne established a new anti-popery newspaper in New York City entitled *The Protestant.* It was Bourne's contention that a reconciliation with Rome was impossible, thereby necessitating an exposure and denunciation of her errors. The first edition declared:

> The sole objects of this publication are, to inculcate Gospel doctrines against Romish corruptions—to maintain the purity and sufficiency of the Holy Scriptures against Monkish traditions—to exemplify the watchful care of Immanuel over the "Church of God which he hath purchased with his own blood."[53]

A survey of subsequent articles would include, "Code of the Jesuits," "A Canadian Papist Converted," "Roman Excommunication," "Bigotry and Persecution," "Monkish Legends" and "Popery Characterized."[54]

By now, the momentum being caused by America's *40-plus anti-popery newspapers* (including the Baptist *Christian Watchman*, the nation's second oldest, established in 1819) gave rise, in 1831, to the country's first *nativist* society, *The New York Protestant Association*. The original charter declared that the body had been formed "for the express purpose of eliciting knowledge respecting the state of Popery, particularly on the Western Continent."[55] The society was reorganized the following year "to promote the principles of the Reformation by public discussions which shall illustrate the history and character of Popery."[56] Billington writes:

> The founders believed that if they could be successful in this, they would drive Romanism from America. "Popery," they declared, "to be hated needs but to be seen in its true character, and if the American people can be induced to look the monster in the face, and observe his hideous features, they would turn from it with horror and disgust."[57]

With the Catholic Church already reeling from the direct hits of a *free press* (unheard of back in the "Holy Alliance"), she would now have to suffer an ignominious scrutiny by patriotic Americans expressing their *freedom of speech* (another novel Yankee invention). The first meeting of the society drew a crowd of 300 to hear a "lecture" entitled "Is Popery that Babylon the Great, which John the Evangelist has Described in the Apocalypse?" By the beginning of May, the attendance had swelled to 1,500.[58] The meetings began spreading to other New York locations as well.

CATHOLIC DOCTRINES

As time went on, ordinary Americans became shocked, horrified and outraged at the discovery of the orthodox tenets of Roman Catholicism. No matter how much these wacky doctrines may be played down by the Bloody Whore in America's last days, what these dumbfounded citizens heard in 1831 is exactly what I heard while attending St. Stephen of Hungary Catholic Grade School in New York City between 1958 and 1966! The first thing that was rammed down my throat by Sister Beatrice in the *first* grade was that Mary was the one to pray to if I *really* wanted an answer. In his definitive work on official Catholic teaching entitled *The Faith of Our Fathers* (49 editions), James Cardinal Gibbons, archbishop of Baltimore, wrote in 1876:

> In speaking of the patronage of the Blessed Virgin, we must never lose sight of her title of Mother of our Redeemer, nor of the great privileges which that prerogative implies. Mary was the Mother of Jesus. She exercised toward Him all the influence that a prudent mother has over an affectionate child. "Jesus," says the Gospel, "was subject to them," that is, to Mary and Joseph. We find this obedience of our Lord toward His Mother forcibly exemplified at the marriage feast of Cana. Her wishes are delicately expressed in these words: "They have no wine." He instantly obeys her by changing water into wine, though the time for exercising His public ministry and for working wonders had not yet arrived.
>
> Now, Mary has never forfeited in heaven the title of Mother of Jesus. She is still His Mother, and while adoring Him as her God, she still retains her maternal relations, and He exercises toward her that loving willingness to grant her request which the best of sons entertains for the best of mothers...Never will our prayers find a readier acceptance than when offered through her.[59]

For the Catholic, human reasoning simply cancels out the clear teaching of Scripture, *"For there is one God, and one mediator between God and men, the man Christ Jesus."* (I Timothy 2:5) Reverend Chiniquy describes the very experience of *my* Catholic childhood:

> It is during this religious instruction that Jesus is removed from the hearts for which He paid so great a price, and Mary is put in His place. This great iniquity is so skillfully executed that it is almost impossible for a poor child to escape.[60]

With my prayer time diverted to Mary, the next thing I learned was that I needed to confess my sins to the priest. Cardinal Gibbons writes:

> It follows...that the power of forgiving sins, on the part of God's minister, involves the obligation of confessing them on the part of the sinner. The priest is not empowered to give absolution to every one indiscriminately. He must exercise the power with judgment and discretion. He must reject the impenitent, and absolve the penitent. But how will he judge of the disposition of the sinner, unless he knows his sins? and how will the priest know his sins, unless they are confessed?[61]

When only seven years of age, I opened the door to a closet-sized room and entered into the first confessional box of my 22-year career as a Catholic. As the door closed behind me, I literally shook in the darkness. After a few moments (which seemed like an eternity), a priest, who was seated in an adjacent booth, slid back a small panel to hear what I had to confess. Having been a pretty good kid, I sputtered along and probably made up a few sins by the end of the confession. After handing down his sentence to me, three "Our Fathers" and two "Hail, Marys" (or was it the other way around?), he pronounced his mumbo-jumbo over my soul, and I took off for the nearest pew to do my penance (say those five prayers) just as fast as I could. Then I was *out of there*...till the next Saturday.

However, the confessional was never a laughing matter to the chaste Catholic female. Reverend Chiniquy writes:

> For I do not exaggerate when I say, that for many noblehearted, well-educated, high-minded women, to be forced to unveil their hearts before the eyes of a man, to open to him all the most secret recesses of their souls, all the most sacred mysteries of their single or married life, to allow him to put to them questions which the most depraved woman would never consent to hear from her vilest seducer, is often more horrible and intolerable than to be tied on burning coals.
>
> More than once, I have seen women fainting in the confessional-box, who told me afterwards, that the necessity of speaking to an unmarried man on certain things, on which the most common laws of decency ought to have for ever sealed their lips, had almost killed them![62]

When one remembers that the crazy "father" has taken a vow of celibacy, his perverted antics are better understood. Chiniquy adds: "It takes many years of the most ingenious (I do not hesitate to call it diabolical) efforts on the part of the priests to persuade the majority of their female penitents to speak on questions, which even pagan savages would blush to mention among themselves."[63] (There are so many documented cases of promiscuity involving auricular confession, whether limited to "mere" seduction or the channeling of the victimized confessor into prostitution, that Reverend Chiniquy authored an entire book on the subject!)

Well, with my own slate wiped clean, I was then judged worthy to commit *cannibalism*—only I was not about to eat another human, but the very Son of God Himself! It was called the Holy Eucharist. As a second grader, I was told that the priest could turn the little wafer into Jesus' literal body, and then I could eat Him! According to my own souvenir booklet entitled *Remembrance of My First Holy Communion*, the first time I "chewed up and swallowed Jesus" was on Sunday, April 30, 1960. The little certificate reassured me that, "Jesus, because He loves me and wishes to come to me, hides Himself under the appearance of a little bread." Now if anyone thinks I am nuts, I would say without hesitation that I am more sane today than I was on April 30, 1960! The official *New York Catechism* reads:

> Jesus Christ gave us the sacrifice of the Mass to leave to His Church a visible sacrifice which continues His sacrifice on the cross until the end of time. The Mass is the same sacrifice as the sacrifice of the cross. Holy Communion is the receiving of the body and blood of Jesus Christ under the appearance of bread and wine.[64]

Reverend Chiniquy shares some "precious memories" from *his* first holy communion:

> Two feelings were at war in my mind. I rejoiced that I would soon have full possession of Jesus Christ. At the same time I was humbled by the absurdity of it. Though scarcely twelve I had been in the habit of trusting my eyes. I thought that I could easily distinguish between a small piece of bread and a full grown man!
> Besides, I extremely abhorred the idea of eating human flesh and drinking human blood, even when assured that they were the flesh and blood of Jesus Christ Himself. But what troubled me most was the idea that God, so great, so glorious, so holy, could be eaten by me like common bread! Terrible then was the struggle in my young heart, where joy and dread, trust and fear, faith and unbelief by turns had the upper hand.[65]

Chiniquy then renders the sad application of the defenseless Catholic child who defiles his own conscience by "believing" a lie (Dr. William P. Grady's experience at the tender age of *eight*):

> He opens his mouth, and the priest puts upon his tongue a flat, thin cake of unleavened bread, which either firmly sticks to his palate or melts in his mouth, soon to go down into his stomach just like the food he takes three times a day!
> The first feeling of the child, then, is surprise at the thought that the Creator of heaven and earth, the upholder of the universe, the Saviour of the world, could so easily pass down his throat!...
> The first communion has made of him, for the rest of his life, a real machine in the hands of the pope. It is the first most powerful link of that long chain of slavery which the priest and the Church pass around his

neck. The pope holds the end of that chain, and with it will make his victim go right or left at his pleasure, just as we govern the lower animals. As Loyola said, "If those children have made a good first communion they will be submissive to the pope. Like the stick in the hands of the traveler, they will have no will, no thought of their own!"[66]

NATIVISM V. ROMANISM

As the New York Protestant Association continued to acquaint the common man with these detestable doctrines of Romanism, an anticipated Jesuit resistance began manifesting itself through a number of coordinated disruptions. Hecklers were joined by other papists demanding "equal time" for Holy Mother Church. The first riot occurred on May 2, 1832, with the assembly hall being evacuated before the speakers could finish. More meetings were scheduled and priests were challenged to attend. Once again, the Romanists showed their contempt for constitutional liberties. While Samuel Smith was addressing a Baptist gathering in Baltimore in March, 1834, he was assaulted by a Catholic mob and had to literally flee for his life. During a debate in New York City a year later on the theme, "Is Popery Compatible with Civil Liberty?" another Catholic gang provided the answer by breaking down the door, chasing out the speaker and destroying the hall's furniture and fixtures [67] (in "Jesus' name," of course)!

These public disturbances led to an extended series of printed debates between the Reverend John Breckenridge, a Presbyterian pastor in Philadelphia, and the Catholic "Father," John Hughes, of the same city (later to become the influential archbishop of New York). When the papist tried to intimidate Reverend Breckenridge in a particular correspondence, the latter replied, "I thank God that the time is not yet come when the *threat* of a Roman priest can make me tremble for my reputation, my liberty, or my hopes of heaven."[68] The two men later engaged in a dozen public debates which, in turn, inspired a host of similar exchanges elsewhere as interest in the nativist movement continued to grow.

In the year 1835, yet another imported vice began to draw the ire of traditional American morality. Still appalled at the licentiousness of the confessional box, God-fearing patriots were now introduced to the Roman Catholic *convent* through such shocking works as Scippio de Ricci's *Female Convents: Secrets of the Nunneries Exposed*. Although some writers attempted to cash in on the opportunity with unfounded sensationalism, this new wave of literature merely informed American readers what the Europeans had known about convents for centuries, Billington writing:

> All of which depicted Catholicism as a highly immoral system in which lecherous priests employed convents to evade the vows of celibacy to which they bound themselves. In these books appeared tales of secret passageways connecting nunneries with the homes of the clergy, of babies' bodies found beneath abandoned convents, and of confessors who abused both their trust and the young ladies whom they confessed.[69]

Decent people became incensed at the thought that these "papal brothels" of Europe would now become a permanent fixture of America's "religious diversity." Dr. Morse rightly surmised that "we are the dupes of our own hospitality."[70] The fact that these convents frequently operated schools for girls only exacerbated community contempt. Furthermore, a number of the students were being recruited from Protestant families.

The Ursuline Convent and School in Charlestown, Massachusetts, became the center of controversy in 1834 when a former nun, Rebecca Theresa Reed, claimed to have escaped from that deplorable institution. The Mother Superior of the Ursulines denied Reed's account, contending instead that she had merely been "dismissed" from the order. However, a short time later, another escapee had to be accounted for. This time, the exodus of Sister Elizabeth (Harrison) was acknowledged but explained away as only a case of temporary insanity. After "counseling" with Bishop Fenwick, the repentant nun was permitted back within the "protective" walls of the convent. The citizens of Boston became outraged as they read of Sister Elizabeth's ordeal in the local press. Reverend Lyman Beecher, pastor of the Park Street Church in Boston, condemned the ungodly affair in three blistering sermons. Many other ministers followed Beecher's example.

When the Charlestown selectmen requested an inspection of the Mount Benedict institution, they were promptly denied access. On the following day, they were allowed to interview Sister Elizabeth, who reassured them that it had all been a terrible mistake, etc. But by then, the community had all they could stomach. That same evening, an angry crowd began assembling at the convent carrying banners and shouting, "No Popery." This may well have been the extent of public protest had the Mother Superior used a little discretion.

With *Bunker Hill* in plain sight of all, she had the audacity to threaten the Protestant assembly with, "The Bishop has twenty thousand Irishmen at his command in Boston."[71] Well, that certainly did it! At a little past midnight, the convent was *torched* and completely consumed. Morse wrote:

> I know of no one who justifies the illegal violence in burning the Convent, but I unhesitatingly say, that the feeling of indignation which animated the populace, was a just and proper feeling. It was roused by the belief, that a young and helpless female had been illegally and cruelly abducted from her friends, and subjected to a secret tyrannical punishment. The feeling, I say under this belief, was not only honorable to the Charlestownians, but had they viewed such an outrage with indifference, they would have shown themselves unworthy of American citizens. Their error, (and it cannot be defended, however it may be *palliated* by the gross insult which they received,) consisted in suffering their just indignation to flow in an illegal channel, and instead of rallying round the laws, and strengthening them by a strong expression of public opinion at a special meeting of citizens, they leaped the bounds of law and committed a crime which the Papists are trying every possible means to cause to react in their favor.[72]

Although Dr. Morse was *philosophically* correct in his recommended appeal to "due process," the sad reality was that the heavy immigrant vote was giving rise to a commensurate increase in political corruption. Current naturalization laws gave immigrants full suffrage after only *five* residence years (compared to the required 21 years for native-born Americans)! During that brief time, it was the task of the Jesuits to keep the new arrivals herded together in the same ignorant stupor in which they had subsisted in the "Old Country." Morse comments on this sad "*pray, pay* and *obey*" mentality:

> They live surrounded by freedom, yet liberty of conscience, right of private judgment, whether in religion or politics, are as effectually excluded by the priests, as if the code of Austria already ruled the land. They form a body of men whose habits of *action*, (for I cannot say *thought,*) are opposed to the principles of our free institutions, for they are not accessible to the reasonings of the press, they cannot and do not think for themselves.[73]

Lest one should think that Dr. Morse was guilty of exaggeration, consider the official pledge required as a condition for church membership as stated in *The Grounds of the Catholic Doctrine, Contained in the Profession of Faith* published by Pope Pius IX, 1855, p. 6, as cited by Secretary Thomas: "I acknowledge the Holy Catholic Apostolic *Roman*

Church for the mother and mistress of all churches, and *I promise true obedience to the Bishop of Rome,* successor to St. Peter, Prince of the Apostles, and Vicar of Jesus Christ."[74]

Dr. Morse relates how the Roman shepherds would barter the votes of their flocks to unscrupulous politicians:

> The *recklessness* and *unprincipled* character of too many of our politicians give a great advantage to these conspirators. There is a set of men in the country who will have power and office, cost what they may; men who, without a particle of true patriotism, will yet ring the changes on the glory and honor of their country, talk loud of liberty, flatter the lowest prejudices, and fawn upon the powerful and the influential; men who study politics only, that they may balance the chances of their own success in falling in with, or opposing, this or that fluctuating interest, without caring whether that interest tends to the security or the downfall or their country's institutions. To such politicians a body of men thus drilled by priests, presents a well fitted tool. The bargain with the priest will be easily struck. "Give me *office,* and I will take care of the interests of your church." The effect of the bargain upon the great moral or political interests of the country, will not for a moment influence the calculation. Thus we have among us a body of men, a *religious sect,* who can exercise a direct controlling influence in the politics of the country, and can be moved together in a solid phalanx; we have a *church interfering directly and most powerfully in the affairs of state.* There is not in the whole country a parallel to this among the other sects. What clergymen of the Methodists, or Baptists, or Episcopalians, or of any other denomination, could command the votes of the members of their several congregations in the election of an individual to political office? The very idea of such power is preposterous to a Protestant. No freeman, no man accustomed to judge for himself, would submit even to be advised, unasked, by his minister in a matter of this kind, much less *dictated to.*[75]

This unethical relationship between priest and politician became a vicious cycle in that the number of foreign-born voters was constantly increasing. Even Billington concedes this point when referring to the avoidance by legislatures of naturalization reforms in 1836, stating, "Obviously politicians believed that the nativistic support that they would gain by furthering these proposals did not balance the alien vote which they would lose by such a step."[76]

Things were not much better on the international scene. On August 2, 1848, President Polk appointed Jacob L. Martin as America's official ambassador to the Vatican.

ATTACK ON THE KJV

A classic illustration of political concessions to Roman Catholics concerns the major battle that was fought over the reading of the King James Bible in America's public schools. (And we thought Madalyn Murray O'Hair caused all the problems.) As early as 1829, the first Provincial Council of Catholicity, meeting in Baltimore, issued *38* decrees warning Catholics against "corrupt translations of the Bible"[77]—i.e., the "corrupt" AV 1611 that had built the very nation in which these reprobates desired to reside! The source of Catholic frustration was aimed at the American Bible Society for limiting their distribution of "Bibles" to the King James Version, Billington writing:

> Its constitution declared that its "sole object shall be to encourage a wider circulation of the Holy Scriptures without note or comment. The only copies in the English language to be circulated by the Society shall be the version now in common use." **The Catholic church, believing itself the "divinely appointed custodian and interpreter of the Holy Writ" insisted that only versions of the Bible which had been properly approved could be read by Catholics.** A clash developed as soon as the American Bible Society attempted to spread the Protestant version of the Bible among Catholics. The indignation of the Catholic hierarchy, the refusal of poverty-stricken Catholics to accept free Bibles and papal letters denouncing the society all were interpreted by Protestants as an attack on the Bible rather than on one version of the Bible.[78]

This last statement by Billington is misleading in the extreme as it implies that Roman Catholics were in the habit of reading their own English version of the Scriptures, the Douay-Rheims, as Protestants were in reading the King James Version. *Nothing could be further from the truth!* We have already seen that the Douay Bible was even published with a printed prohibition against the "reading of the Scriptures in the vulgar language without the advice and permission of the pastors, etc." Catholics have never been encouraged to read *any* translation of the Bible, *"lest the light of the glorious gospel of Christ, who is the image of God, should shine unto them."* (II Corinthians 4:4) In Cardinal Gibbons' lengthy chapter entitled "The Church and the Bible," we find the following "nuggets of truth":

> The Church, as we have just seen, is the only divinely constituted teacher of Revelation. Now, the Scripture is the great depository of the Word of God. Therefore, the Church is the divinely appointed Custodian and Interpreter of the Bible...God never intended the Bible to be the Christian's rule of faith, independently of the living authority of the Church...Jesus Himself never wrote a line of Scripture...Do not tell me that the Bible is all-sufficient...I will address myself now in a friendly spirit to a non-Catholic, and will proceed to show him that he cannot consistently accept the silent Book of Scripture as his sufficient guide.[79]

Another reason why Catholics have never been students of *any* Bible is because they are not allowed to believe what their own two eyes may tell them. For instance, should the Catholic who has been taught that Mary was "ever-virgin" read Mark 6:3 which says, *"Is not this the carpenter, the son of Mary, the brother of James, and Joses, and of Juda, and Simon? and are not his sisters here with us?"* his priest would simply tell him that these individuals were Jesus' *cousins.* Secretary Thompson cites the Catholic author Monsigneur Ségur accordingly:

> *WE HAVE TO BELIEVE* ONLY *what the pope and the bishops teach. We have to reject only that which the pope and the bishops condemn and reject.* Should a point of doctrine appear doubtful, we have only to address ourselves to the *pope* and to the *bishops* in order to know what to believe. *Only* from that tribunal, forever living and forever assisted by God, emanates the judgment on religious belief, and particularly on the true sense of the Scriptures.[80]

In 1840, Bishop Hughes declared war on the King James Bible in the public schools by *coming in the back door* with the complaint that Catholic children should not be forced to read the Protestant Bible or be exposed to a Protestant interpretation of religious history (i.e., the pope is "the man of sin," etc.). At the time, New York schools were under the jurisdiction of the Public School Society, a benevolent association formed in 1805 to "inculcate the sublime truths of religion and morality contained in the Holy Scriptures."[81] Bishop Hughes wanted legislators to disband the Society and place the citiy's public schools under state control which would permit individual commissioners to be elected in each ward. These local officials could then be free to select (or ban) whatever curriculum their particular constituents preferred.

When the Democratic party (normally sensitive to the "plight of the immigrants") began to vacillate on this political time bomb, Bishop Hughes decided to flex his muscles by organizing his own *Catholic* party only four days before the fall elections of 1841. Hughes had no illusions of winning, but he was determined to make his presence felt. As the Whigs were swept into office by only 290 votes, the 2,200 Catholics who had "voted their conscience" *the way Hughes had directed*, made the Bishop a force to be reckoned with for the future. When the proposed legislation came up again the following year as the Maclay Bill, Billington informs us that the Democratic party "was anxious to regain Catholic support and recognized in this measure an admirable opportunity for doing so. Consequently the bill was passed by the Assembly immediately."[82]

Despite some last-minute maneuvering by nativist candidates, the worst was realized as Billington relates:

> The elective commissioners in charge of education in each ward had the right to select books to be used in the schools under their supervision, and in wards where Catholics were concentrated they did not hesitate to use this power to exclude Bible reading so that by 1844 the practice had been abandoned in thirty-one of the city schools.[83]

Thus we see that the first Bibles to be kicked out of America's public schools were *kicked out by the Roman Catholic Church,* not by Madalyn Murray O'Hair! That the Catholic Church was never the least bit concerned about their precious children being deprived of *Catholic* Bibles can be confirmed by observing how much Catholic Bible was later taught when the Church went on to establish its own parochial schools! The reason Billington's opinions don't move me a great deal is because *I personally attended eight years of Catholic grade school in New York City and never even saw a Catholic Bible in the classroom one time!* After 22 years as a faithful Roman Catholic, the first Bible I ever owned of any kind was a giant print, King James Bible that my wife gave me as a wedding gift, the same day we were married in a Catholic church!

When word started spreading that the politicians had finally "seen the light," attacks on the AV 1611 became more frequent and brazen. School districts in other cities, such as Cleveland and Newark, also bowed to Catholic pressures and banished the Word of God. Only five months after Governor Seward had affixed his signature to the Maclay Bill, a Catholic priest in Carbeau, New York, shocked the nation by **publicly burning 42 King James Bibles!**[84] Almost equally as deplorable was the bold declaration in Bishop Hughes' own paper, the *Freeman's Journal*: "To burn or otherwise destroy a spurious or corrupt copy of the Bible, whose circulators would tend to disseminate erroneous principles of faith or morals, we hold to be an act not only justifiable but praiseworthy."[85]

Outrage at the "Champlain Bible burning," as it was promptly labeled, began to race across the nation. The New York *Observer* for January 21, 1843, declared that "the embers of the late Bible conflagration in Carbeau may kindle a flame that shall consume the last vestige of Popery in the land."[86] New reports of Catholic attempts to burn Bibles in other states were received including the burning of an anti-Catholic publishing concern in Baltimore.[87]

In the meantime, the *American Protestant Union* had been established in May, 1841. Headed by Professor S. F. B. Morse, the union declared itself opposed to the "subjugation of our country to the control of the Pope of Rome, and his adherents and for the preservation of our civil and religious institutions"[88] and proposed to function as a "national defense society" in the interest of Protestants.[89] Smaller, local societies sprang up spontaneously in many other cities and towns. The first nativist political organization, the *American Republican Party* was also founded in June, 1843, with the *American Citizen* becoming the party's official paper in October. Slowly, but surely, the nation's Protestant population was becoming an informed people, Billington reporting: "By 1838 an observer complained that books on the subject had become so numerous that it was impossible to read them all, and bookstores were established in the larger cities to deal solely in anti-Catholic works."[90]

Billington summarizes the threefold objectives of this mass of anti-popery literature:

> First, to show that Catholicism was not Christianity, but an idolatrous religion, the ascendency of which would plunge the world into infidelity; secondly, that Popery was by nature irreconcilable with the democratic institutions of the United States and was determined to insure its own existence by driving them out; and thirdly, that the acceptance of the moral standards of the Catholic church would be suicidal to the best interests both of Protestantism and the nation.[91]

The apex of Catholic-Protestant antagonism occurred in the City of Brotherly Love during the summer of 1844. Francis Patrick Kenrick, bishop of Philadelphia, had successfully petitioned the school board to allow Catholic students to read their own version of the Bible. When a board member attempted to stop the reading of the King James Bible in a school in Kensington, a rally was held to demand his resignation. A similar meeting was held in Independence Square on March 11, where it was resolved: "That the present crisis demands that without distinction of party, sect, or profession, every man who loves his country, his Bible, and his God, is bound by all lawful and honorable means to resist every attempt to banish the Bible from our public institutions."[92]

Despite the Bishop's double-talk that he "did not object to the use of the Bible, providing Catholic children be allowed to use their own version,"[93] these patriots were well aware of those *31 schools in New York with no Bible reading.* Besides, was not the church in Philadelphia commended for having *"kept the word"*? (Revelation 3:8)

The American Republicans called for a public rally in the third ward of Kensington. As matters proved, this utilization of yet the third guarantee of the First Amendment, "the right of the people peacefully to assemble," became the straw that broke the Roman camel's back. When the citizens assembled for their rally on the night of May 3, a violent mob of Irish scattered them accordingly. A second meeting was called for Monday, May 6, at 4:00 p.m. On the morning of the scheduled rally, the following proclamation was printed in the *Native American*:

> The American Republicans of the city and county of Philadelphia, who are determined to support the NATIVE AMERICANS in their Constitutional Rights of peaceably assembling to express their opinions on any question of Public Policy and to *Sustain them against the assaults of Aliens and Foreigners* are requested to assemble on *THIS AFTERNOON,* May 6th, 1844, at 4 o'clock, at the corner of Master and Second streets, Kensington, to express their indignation at the outrage on Friday evening last, and to take the necessary steps to prevent a repetition of it. *Natives be punctual and resolved to sustain your rights as Americans, firmly but moderately.*[94]

That evening, as the patriots attempted to enter Market House, shots rang out from the Irish rabble (later corroborated by 18 different newspapers, sacred and secular) and a number of civilians were slain, George Shiffler being the first. The Irish mob then dispersed the bloodied and bewildered marchers.

On the following day, the citizens rallied around a flag that had been trampled under foot by the Irish and bravely marched into Kensington once again. In the fighting which ensued, at least 30 houses were burned to the ground.

The fighting resumed on Wednesday, May 8. On confirmed reports that the Irish were storing guns and ammunition in their churches, the natives promptly torched St. Michael's and St. Augustine's. The next day brought a wave of national criticism as word of the burned churches was spread abroad. Dr. Morse had warned about the Jesuit penchant for provoking attacks so as to reap the resulting public sympathy. As the German ambassador, Baron Cuvier, had put it, "They will be hammer or nails, Sir, they will persecute, or be persecuted."[95] With the arrival of the military, things calmed down for a season.

On the 4th of July, *a procession of 70,000 citizens* escorted carriages containing the widows and orphans of the slain patriots. With reports of another cache of arms at the church of St. Philip de Neri in Southwark, hostilities resumed on July 5. When authorities were pressured into inspecting the "church," 87 muskets and a horde of ammunition was discovered. The arrival of an Irish militia dispersed the crowd but they reassembled the next morning. One of their own had been kidnapped in the meantime and was being held in the church. Everything broke loose on Sunday, July 7.

The frustrated citizens were able to break into the church and rescue Charles Naylor. Fresh troops who arrived on the scene "accidentally" opened fire on the patriots and seven were killed with a score wounded. **The outraged citizens returned with a cannon of their own and fired at the church doors at point-blank range!** A shooting battle ensued for several hours before the citizens were forced to retire. With the arrival of the governor and his personal pleas for peace, an extended lull in the fighting occurred. This time the patriots were determined not to get a "bum rap" in the public opinion polls. Expressing the feelings of most, the New York *Republican* declared: "We love not riots, we abhor bloodshed; but it is idle to suppose that Americans can be shot down on their own soil, under their own flag, while in the quiet exercise of their constitutional privileges, without a fearful retribution being exacted."[96]

It seemed that the general public agreed. Two separate grand juries placed the blame for the rioting squarely on the Catholics. More and more Americans were beginning to note an ominous rise in Catholic assertiveness keeping pace with an unchecked immigration policy that was processing over a thousand foreigners per day!

HUGHES ACKNOWLEDGES CONSPIRACY

Any doubts that a foreign conspiracy existed against the United States were ironically put to rest by the Catholic Church itself. Although Billington could subliminally assail the nativist movement by using the words *propaganda* and *propagandist* at least 110 times in 322 pages of text (for an average of once every 2.92 pages) and still be acclaimed as "devastatingly impartial" by Catholic author Theodore Manyard,[97] the "Harvard Man" was eventually forced to eat his own words when the outspoken John Hughes decided to finally take off his mask! No sooner had "Bishop" Hughes become the first archbishop of New York in 1850 than he absolutely lowered the boom on freedom-loving Americans! In his chapter entitled "The Catholic Church Blunders," Billington gives the following excerpt from a message delivered by Hughes in his own cathedral that November entitled "The Decline of Protestantism and Its Causes." Fasten your seat belt!

> There is [he said] no secret about this. The object we hope to accomplish in time, is to convert all Pagan nations, and all Protestant nations, even England with her proud Parliament and imperial sovereign. **There is no secrecy in all this.** It is the commission of God to his church, and not a human project...Protestantism pretends to have discovered a great secret. Protestantism startles our eastern borders occasionally on the intention of the Pope with regard to the Valley of the Mississippi and dreams that it has made a wonderful discovery. Not at all. Everybody should know it. **Everybody should know that we have for our mission to convert the world—including the inhabitants of the United States,**—the people of the cities, and the people of the country, the officers of the navy and the marines, commanders of the army, the Legislatures, the Senate, the Cabinet, the President, and all![98]

Even Billington was at a loss to explain away this brazen declaration and simply resigned himself to the obvious:

> Protestants who had for years disregarded the warnings of Morse and his followers as the ravings of fanatical alarmists now heard an acknowledged church leader freely admitting that a Romish plot did exist.

The Pope did intend to move to the Mississippi valley; he did seek to subjugate free America![99]

Other prelates and Catholic editors took their cue accordingly. *Brownson's Review* for June, 1851, stated:

> The power of the Church exercised over sovereigns in the Middle Ages was not a usurpation, was not derived from the concessions of princes or the consent of the people, but was and is held by divine right, and whoso resists it, rebels against the King of kings and Lord of lords.[100]

The *Shepherd of the Valley*, the official journal of the Bishop of St. Louis (the church where the flag was lowered in front of the host), declared five months later:

> The Church is of necessity intolerant. Heresy she endures when and where she must, but she hates it and directs all her energies to destroy it... **If Catholics ever gain a sufficient numerical majority in this country, religious freedom is at an end.** So our enemies say, so we believe.[101]

On January 26, 1852, Hughes' own paper, the *New York Freeman*, pretty well summarized what Dr. Morse and others had been trying to say all along. **"No man has a right to choose his religion."**[102]

Shocking disclosures such as these set off a whole new storm of public outcry. A Catholic priest in Ellsworth, Maine, was tarred and feathered and run out of town on a rail for opposing the reading of the King James Bible in the local school.[103] While disgruntled voters in Connecticut were able to preserve Bible reading in their districts, 10,000 protesters in Baltimore staged a related rally in front of city hall. A street preacher in Pittsburgh by the name of Joseph Baker was arrested for blasting the Pope and sentenced to a year in jail. However, in the next mayoral campaign, Baker's supporters announced that they were placing his name on the ballot! While languishing in the local lockup, Reverend Baker became Mayor Baker by an uncontested majority. Billington adds, "His term as mayor was a sad one for Pittsburgh Catholics."[104]

The itinerant lay preacher James S. Orr became known as the "Angel Gabriel" because he spoke while clothed in a long white gown and summoned his listeners by the thousands with blasts from a brass horn.[105] Another street preacher, Reverend Daniel Parsons, was addressing a throng of 10,000 hearers in an open-air meeting in New York's Central Park in

December, 1853, when he was abruptly arrested in the middle of his sermon. Parsons' infuriated congregation promptly laid siege to the mayor's residence who suddenly felt "led" to release the popular preacher. On the following Sunday, over *20,000* listeners gathered in the park to hear Reverend Parsons denounce Hughes and popery in general.[106]

THE KNOW-NOTHINGS

Determined to make a last stand in the political arena, concerned nativists organized the *American Party* in 1852. Because of their affiliation with a supportive, secret society, the *Order of the Star Spangled Banner*, members of the American party were called "Know-Nothings." In the fall elections of 1854, *75* Know-Nothings were sent to Congress in an initial show of strength. However, the ever-growing clout of the immigrant vote combined with the increasing distraction of the slavery controversy eventually led to the demise of the American party as a viable political force.

A final symbolic gesture of nativist defiance centered around a slick propaganda ploy by the Vatican. In 1852, a special block of marble arrived in Washington, D.C., as a designated gift from Pope Pius IX for the Washington Monument, then under construction. After seeing their legitimate protests ignored for two years, an indignant band of anti-popery citizens forced their way into the shed where the so-called gift was in storage, secured the marble block, and **promptly threw it into the Potomac River!**[107]

With their cause disregarded by politicians and distracted by abolitionists, America's Bible-believing citizens were in dire need of a supernatural deliverance. Yes, the future looked bleak, but man's extremities are always God's opportunities. Although "His Holiness" didn't know it at the time, the God Who had promised to "keep the door open" was about to *really* knock his block off at a place called **Fulton Street!**

XIII

A Spiritual Interlude

> *"These all continued with one accord in prayer and supplication."* (Acts 1:14a)

AS CORRUPT POLITICIANS continued to encourage unprecedented waves of Catholic immigration, the decline of the *American party (Know-Nothings)* in 1856 was a source of consternation to Baptists and Protestants alike. Convinced that the political process had faltered, a society of law-abiding citizens concluded, *"All hope that we should be saved was then taken away."* (Acts 27:20c) This is not to imply that the Christians had been negligent in attempting to win the new arrivals to Christ. The problem, as previously noted, was that the priests kept their immigrant parishioners abnormally insulated from "Protestant heresies." "Bible-thumping" soul winners were more than discouraged from entering Irish neighborhoods, etc.

Another obstacle had to do with the actual *size* of the foreign-born population itself. For every immigrant who was reached with the Gospel, a hundred more would "get off the boat" wearing scapulars around their necks. Also, lest we overlook the obvious, allow me to say that such massive immigration was necessitated in the first place because the Catholic Church in America could not begin to compete with the local New Testament church in the arena of *personal soul winning*. I mean, really, how many Catholic evangelists have you ever heard of anyway? In his massive work, *History of the Christian Church*, Dr. George Fisher relates what Bible believers have known all along—the Catholic cult is completely powerless to reproduce itself from without:

The progress of the Roman Catholic Church in the United States is owing to the vast immigration of members of that body from foreign countries. The American converts from Protestantism have not been very numerous.[1]

Furthermore, this spiritual impotency explains why the Vatican took an early stand against birth control so as to bolster the local parish with those traditionally large Catholic families (i.e., the "McGillicuddys," the "O'Hoolihans," etc.). Yet some Christian pro-life activists are so naive, they believe that the Catholic Church is opposed to abortion on *moral* grounds.

By 1857, therefore, the largest cities in America had become an entrenched network of strategic Vatican strongholds. Strange as it may sound, "His Holiness" was actually enjoying more freedom under the First Amendment than he did back in the old country where the church-state relationship obligated him to share power with the emperor. Gregory XVI once remarked, "Out of the Roman States, there is no country where I am pope, *except in the United States.*"[2]

However, when the worst fears of Professor Morse and other nativist patriots were about to be realized, the Lord of Hosts decided to drop a spiritual bomb. The decade following the Mexican War had proved a substantial boom to the American economy. Loosely regulated banking, speculation in railroads, land and manufacturing, an expansion of the wheat belt and the opening of California's gold fields had created the inevitable spirit of financial invincibility. All of this suddenly changed in August, 1857, when the Ohio Life Insurance Co. of Cincinnati failed, causing a number of area banks to go under as well. While banks in New York closed their doors to prevent runs, other lending institutions throughout the East suspended specie payments. Railroads went bankrupt. Mercantile houses withdrew their credit from retailers causing a colossal chain reaction, culminating in unemployment and bread lines. (The South's economy would remain unaffected.)

With the *Panic of 1857* well underway, a tall, forty-eight-year-old Christian businessman by the name of Jeremiah C. Lanphier was hired as an urban missionary by the Fulton Street Dutch Reformed Church in New York City. Mr. Lanphier, a personal convert of Charles G. Finney, promptly announced that on Wednesday, September 23, the upper room of the church's Consistory Building would be open for a special noon-hour prayer meeting. Although the event was widely promoted, only six people chose to attend out of a population of over a million. Of the six, one was a Baptist, one a Congregationalist, one a member of the Dutch Reformed Church and one a Presbyterian. Undaunted, the quiet layman scheduled a second meeting for the following Wednesday and was encouraged by a larger turnout of 20. When twice that number showed up on October 7, it was agreed to begin meeting on a daily basis.

The timely crash that same week of the New York Stock Exchange helped drive the attendance figures higher. Within six months, *10,000* New Yorkers were assembling for daily prayer at 20 different locations. Facilities employed included firehouses, theaters and even a few saloons.

As to the format that was followed, anyone could pray or share a word of testimony but had to limit his time to five minutes or less, "in order to give all an opportunity." Although well-known preachers frequented the services, the Fulton Street Prayer Revival was unique in that the primary leadership was provided by Spirit-filled laymen. There was no hysteria nor were there any unusual disturbances, just prayer. Charles G. Finney said,

> There is such a general confidence in the prevalence of prayer, that the people very extensively seemed to prefer meeting for prayer to meeting for preaching. The general impression seemed to be, "We have had instruction until we are hardened; it is time for us to pray."[3]

By meeting's end, multitudes of the convicted would receive Christ as personal Saviour. The Catholic priests were no match for the Holy Ghost. *Over 10,000 people of differing nationalities were getting saved in New York City every week!* The individual testimonies were astounding:

> One time a man wandered into the Fulton Street meeting who intended to murder a woman and then commit suicide. He listened as someone was delivering a fervent exhortation and urging the duty of repentance. Suddenly the would-be murderer startled everyone by crying out, "Oh! What shall I do to be saved!" Just then another man arose, and with tears streaming down his cheeks asked the meeting to sing the hymn, "Rock of Ages, Cleft for Me." At the conclusion of the service both men were converted.
>
> Another time an aged pastor got up to pray for the son of another clergyman. Unknown to him, his own son was sitting some distance behind him. The young man, knowing himself to be a sinner, was so impressed at hearing his father pray for another man's son that he made himself known to the meeting and said he wanted to submit to God. He became a regular attender at the prayer meeting.

A prize fighter named "Awful Gardiner" was a prayer-meeting convert. He visited his old friends at Sing Sing Penitentiary and gave his testimony. Among those who were convicted was a noted river thief, Jerry McAuley, who later founded the Water Street Mission. It was one of the first missions for down-and-outs.[4]

The following rare eyewitness account of a typcial noon-hour prayer meeting is found in *America's Great Revivals*:

We take our seat in the middle room, ten minutes before 12 o'clock M.... A few ladies are seated in one corner, and a few businessmen are scattered here and there through the room. Five minutes to 12, the room begins to fill up rapidly. Two minutes to 12, the leader passes in, and takes his seat in the desk or pulpit. At 12 M., punctual to the moment, at the first stroke of the clock the leader arises and commences the meeting by reading two or three verses of the hymn,

> Salvation, oh the joyful sound,
> 'Tis pleasure to our ears;
> A sovereign balm for every wound,
> A cordial for our fears.

Each person finds a hymnbook in his seat; all sing with heart and voice. The leader offers a prayer—short, pointed, to the purpose. Then reads a brief portion of Scripture. Ten minutes are now gone. Meantime, requests in sealed envelopes have been going up to the desk for prayer.

A deep, solemn silence settles down upon our meeting. It is holy ground. The leader stands with slips of paper in his hand.

He says: "This meeting is now open for prayer. Brethren from a distance are specially invited to take part. All will observe the rules."

All is now breathless attention. A tender solicitude spreads over all those upturned faces.

The chairman reads: "A son in North Carolina desires the fervent, effectual prayers of the righteous of this congregation for the immediate conversion of his mother in Connecticut."

In an instant a father rises: "I wish to ask the prayers of this meeting for two sons and a daughter." And he sits down and bursts into tears, and lays his head down on the railing of the seat before him, and sobs like a broken-hearted child.

A few remarks follow—very brief. The chairman rises with slips of paper in his hand, and reads: "A praying sister requests prayers for two un-converted brothers in the city of Detroit; that they be converted, and become the true followers of the Lord Jesus Christ."

Another, "Prayers are requested of the people of God for a young man, once a professor of religion, but now a wanderer, and going astray..."

Two prayers in succesion followed these requests—very fervent, very earnest. And others who rose to pray at the same time, sat down again when they found themselves preceded by the voices already engaged in prayer. Then arose from all hearts that beautiful hymn, sung with touching pathos, so appropriate too, just in this stage of this meeting with all these cases full before us,

> There is a fountain filled with blood
> Drawn from Immanuel's veins,
> And sinners plunged beneath that flood
> Lose all their guilty stains.

Then followed prayer by one who prays earnestly for all who have been prayed for, for all sinners present, for the perishing thousands in this city, for the spread of revivals all over the land and world.

It is now a quarter to one o'clock. Time has fled on silver wings... There arose a sailor, now one no more, by reason of ill-health, but daily laboring for sailors. He was converted on board a man-of-war, and he knew how hard it was for the converted sailor to stand up firm against the storm of jeers, and reproaches, and taunts of a ship's crew. "Now I am here," he said, "to represent one who has requested me to ask your prayers for a converted sailor this day gone to sea. I parted from him a little time ago, and his fear is, his great fear, that he may dishonor the cause of the blessed Redeemer. Will you pray for this sailor?" Prayer was offered for his keeping and guidance.

Then came the closing hymn, the benediction, and the parting for twenty-three hours.[5]

Other locals became similarly affected. Slightly northward, the Baptists were reaping such a harvest that their overworked baptisteries forced them to cut through the ice of the Hudson and Mohawk Rivers where they baptized their converts in bone-chilling water.[6] Over 92,000 additions were recorded by Baptist churches in 1858 alone. The Metropolitan Theater in Chicago was packed out with 2,000 people a day. Half of the Atlanta police force had to be laid off because of a reduction in crime.[7] Local merchants literally poured their beer and wine into the streets. The power of God was so strong that even sea captains testified that conviction had broken out on board as their ships neared ports where revival was in progress!

The nation's largest newspapers gave front-page coverage to these supernatural occurrences. The *New York Herald* for March 6, 1858, stated,

"Satan is busy all the morning in Wall Street among the brokers, and all the afternoon and evening the churches are crowded with saints who gambled in the morning."[8] Editor Horace Greeley, of the *New York Tribune*, printed a special revival issue the following month. On November 5, 1857, the press reported that several hundred Canadians came to Christ in Ontario.

While Archbishop Hughes and the St. Leopold Foundation were about to "go off the deep end," Professor Morse had the honor of availing his telegraph services to the revival so that businessmen in various cities could stay abreast of the latest developments. In his work *The Second Evangelical Awakening in America*, J. Edwin Orr summarized "what God *had* wrought":

> The phenomenon of packed churches and startling conversions was noted everywhere. There seemed to be three streams of blessing flowing out from the Middle Atlantic States, one northwards to New England, another southwards as far as Texas, and a third westwards along the Ohio valley. An observer in a leading secular newspaper stated it well when he wrote: "The Revivals, or Great Awakening, continue to be the leading topic of the day...from Texas, in the South, to the extreme of our Western boundaries, and our Eastern limits; their influence is felt by every denomination." Newspapers from Maine to Louisiana reflected his view.... The influence of the awakening was felt everywhere in the nation. It first captured the great cities, but it also spread through every town and village and country hamlet. It swamped schools and colleges. It affected all classes without respect to condition. There was no fanaticism... **At any rate, the number of conversions reported soon reached the total of fifty thousand weekly**, a figure borne out by the fact that church statistics show an average of ten thousand additions to church membership weekly for the period of two years.[9]

Although the prayer revival had momentarily checked Satan's bid for America, "old smutty face" was not about to take things lying down. When the Awakening was at its zenith in 1858, Archbishop Hughes delivered a symbolic counterstroke of defiance by personally laying the cornerstone for the massive St. Patrick's Cathedral on Manhattan's Fifth Avenue, which became the largest Catholic church in the United States. As usual, a measure of clandestine activity was also afoot, Latourette confirming, "In 1857 there was founded at Louvain, in Belgium, an American College in which in the course of seventy-five years over a thousand young Americans were prepared for the priesthood."[10] That same year the Vatican released its first official photographs of the famed *Codex Vaticanus*.

Not only had the Fulton Street Revival brought about the conversion of an exceptional number of immigrants, but it had also been sent as a propitious visitation of grace upon the American people as a whole in preparation for the bloody Civil War years, 1861–1865. Over a million converts coming on the eve of hostilities would go a long way in cushioning the heavy blow. It has been estimated by some that in addition to numerous "Yankee" conversions, one-third of the entire Confederate Army had gotten saved through the immediate and long-range effects of the prayer revival. In his work *Chaplains in Gray,* historian Charles F. Pitts relates how faithful Confederate chaplains sustained the powerful Awakening:

> Through this personal, direct preaching, fervent singing, and ceaseless distribution of literature came the storied great awakening within the Southern armies. Tens of thousands were converted and baptized. From all available records, it appears that the estimates of eyewitnesses were in all probability correct. They were in general agreement that the number of converts reached at least 150,000.[11]

Pitts further points out that the renewed spiritual hunger of the common soldier was abruptly threatened by the Northern monopoly of Bible publishing houses. One desperate rebel wrote, December 1, 1862:

> I am a pore harted sinner and got no chance to be no other way, for I ain't got no Bible. Yankees want us to lose our soles, same as our lifes.[12]

Campaigns were organized among the churches back home to collect Bibles for the troops. The Bibles of fallen soldiers, which had been returned to the families, often were sent back to the front to encourage the living. Pitts describes the eventual, providential solution:

> Having depended entirely on the North for the output of Bibles, the South suddenly found these vital religious supplies cut off. By the help of Southern ingenuity and Northern friends, plates were smuggled in from the North, and preparations were made to print the first Confederate Bibles. In 1861 the initial copies of these Bibles rolled from the presses of the Southwestern Publishing House at Nashville, Tennessee.[13]

"The word of God is not bound."
(II Timothy 2:9b)

XIV

The Wrath of Apollyon

*"Every city or house divided against itself shall
not stand."*(Matthew 12:25b)

PRACTICALLY ALL publicized events that precipitated the War
Between the States were ostensibly related to the slavery issue in
one way or another. A brief review of these salient developments
is in order before considering the standard explanations for the war itself.

Because of the embarrassing reality that slavery had existed in this
country since August, 1619, (a year before the Mayflower Compact) when
the nascent Jamestown settlement was visited by "a dutch man of warre that
sold us twenty Negers,"[1] as well as the fact that it had received more than
a tacit recognition by the U. S. Constitution (see Article I, Section 3), prevailing Northern sentiment called for restricting the "contagion" from
spreading into the territories, rather than eradicating it where it already
existed. This was the official position of Abraham Lincoln as late as 1860[2]:
"I now do no more than oppose the *extension* of slavery."[3] He
acknowledged the underlying motivation of his later Emancipation
Proclamation as being "a fit and necessary war measure for suppressing
said rebellion."[4] Lincoln's incentive was purely *military* in nature:

> Things had gone from bad to worse until I felt we had reached the
> end of our rope on the plan we were pursuing; that we had about played
> our last card, and must change our tactics or lose the game. I now
> determined upon the adoption of the emancipation policy.[5]

In addition to the obvious advantage of an augmented manpower supply, the grandiose "proclamation" also served as a major propaganda ploy to ward off intervention by Great Britain, the South's major trading partner, though strongly anti-slavery in sentiment. This is why the document applied only to slaves being held in *Confederate* states. "Honest Abe's" reprieve did not cover chattel in Kentucky, Maryland or Missouri. Henry Palmerston, prime minister of England, chided Lincoln for undertaking "to abolish slavery where he was without power to do so, while protecting it where he had full power to destroy it."[6]

Furthermore, although it may come as a shock to some, Lincoln was actually more concerned about Negroes entering the territories under *any* conditions, having stated in a Peoria speech in 1854:

> We want them (the Territories) for homes for white people. This they cannot be... if slavery shall be planted within them. Slave states are places for poor people to remove from, not to remove to.[7]

Although many of the South's greatest leaders, such as Robert E. Lee and Stonewall Jackson, perceived slavery to be "a moral and political evil" which would eventually be dissolved by "the mild and melting influence of Christianity,"[8] the recurring petitions for statehood by newly developed territories ensured that the imbroglio would continue to fester. The corollary between westward expansion and slavery was primarily *economic* in nature. Subsisting as an agrarian culture, the South was incapable of supplying itself with the most basic industrial products. In 1860, the North had 110,000 manufacturing plants to the South's 18,000 (with many of the latter requiring the expertise of Northern technicians). The entire Confederacy produced only 36,700 tons of pig iron compared to Pennsylvania's individual tally of 580,000 tons. New York State manufactured finished goods worth nearly $300 million—an incredible *four* times the production of Virginia, Alabama, Louisiana and Mississippi combined.[9]

In view of these drastic disparities, the South found itself in resentful subjection to the Northern industrial establishment. And to make matters worse, this volatile relationship was repeatedly exacerbated by unscrupulous protectionist legislation such as the Tariff of Abominations in 1828. Although Southern congressmen such as John C. Calhoun had succumbed to the shortsighted allurements of protectionism as early as 1816, the record substantiates that the South got the short end of the stick in the overwhelming majority of tariff interference. Though the point may be argued by some, under normal conditions, a protectionist tariff, by its very nature of free market disruption, constitutes a theoretical assault on the fiscal application of individual soul liberty. Consequently, this sectionalized economic intimidation compelled the numerically inferior South to contend for a balance of power in the Senate. Alabama's admission as a slave state in 1819 evened that body at eleven of each.

However, when the Missouri territory petitioned the House of Representatives for consideration as a slave-holding state that same year, James Tallmadge of New York caused a fiasco by offering an amendment prohibiting any further introduction of slaves into the state and requiring all subsequent children of slave parents to be freed at age 25. The amended bill was passed in the House but defeated in the Senate. After a season of intense debate and political maneuvering, including threats of *Northern* secession,[10] the original bill was able to pass both houses the following January, but with a significant stipulation attached.

Known as the Missouri Compromise of 1820, the agreement granted Missouri unfettered slave-holding status as the Union's twenty-third state; however, the "peculiar institution" would be henceforth enjoined in the remaining United States territory north of latitude 36°30'. And just to keep things nice and copacetic, free Maine conveniently "seceded" from Massachusetts to form the offsetting twenty-fourth state. Although this arrangement caused many to be encouraged, an aging Thomas Jefferson wrote, "This momentous question, **like a fire bell in the night,** awakened and filled me with terror," and asserted that he "considered it at once as the knell of the Union."[11] John Quincy Adams noted ominously in his diary, "I take it for granted that the present question is a mere preamble—a title-page to a great, tragic volume."[12]

All was officially quiet on the "western front" for nearly three decades. However, newly acquired lands from the war with Mexico afforded the potential for renewed hostilities, as such territory was technically situated beyond the geographical jurisdiction of the Missouri Compromise. When President Polk requested a bill in 1846 to finance a negotiated peace, David Wilmot, a House Democrat from Pennsylvania, proposed an amendment that "neither slavery nor involuntary servitude shall exist in any part of said territory." After rancorous debate, the Wilmot Proviso was excised from the funding bill, but the nation had become exceedingly agitated once again in the process.

On August 14, 1848, Polk signed a bill excluding slavery from the Oregon Territory, theoretically as a northwest application of 36°30', following the admission of Texas as a slave-holding state three years previously. The discovery of gold in California, also in 1848, brought a rapid increase in population, and by 1850, a state constitution barring slavery had been drafted. As a considerable portion of the land mass was below 36°30', the California petition became an instant political flash point. This was especially so given the nationwide ratio of states at 15 free and 15 slave. This time, it was the tenuous Compromise of 1850 that would postpone the inevitable clash.

Under the proposed legislation of Senator Henry Clay of Kentucky, the Bear Flag Republic would bypass territorial status, entering directly into the Union as a free state, while the Utah and New Mexico territories would be organized according to the popular, or "Squatter," sovereignty thus allowing for the possibility of locally sponsored slavery in the future. Clay's Compromise would also settle the boundary dispute between New Mexico and Texas, abolish the slave trade in the District of Columbia and strengthen the Fugitive Slave Act of 1793. Despite the near deathbed dissuasion of South Carolina Senator John C. Calhoun, the measure was adopted with critical support provided by Daniel Webster of Massachusetts.

Within four short years, however, trouble was brewing once again. This time the controversy was occasioned by intense sectional competition for the nation's first transcontinental rail service. The Southern proposal appeared to be the more expedient routing, as the entire region through which its track would pass was already organized territory, while the land due west of Missouri and Iowa was unorganized and infested with Indians. Senator Stephen A. Douglas of Illinois, an avid supporter of the Union Pacific Railroad, attempted to alleviate this liability by encouraging legislation for the creation of a Nebraska Territory. His efforts met with stiff opposition by Southern lawmakers, as the Missouri Compromise of 1820 had foreordained the proposed territory to a free status, given its location north of 36°30'.

On January 4, 1854, Douglas introduced a Nebraska Bill based on the principle of popular sovereignty as incorporated in the Compromise of 1850. Reasoning that a geographical line had been "superseded" by Clay's reforming measures, Douglas was, in actuality, calling for an indirect repeal of the Missouri Compromise of 1820. The question of slavery in the territories would henceforth be determined by the local inhabitants. Finally, owing to the differences in political and railroad concerns between Iowa and Missouri, the Nebraska area was divided into two smaller territories, one to the west of Missouri to be known as Kansas and the other west of Iowa retaining the name of Nebraska.

With *Uncle Tom's Cabin* in circulation since 1852 and Levi Coffin's Underground Railroad running at full throttle, Congress would take more than 100 days to finally pass the inflammatory Kansas-Nebraska Act. In the aftermath of the bill's passage occurred the greatest partisan realignment in the history of American politics. The Democrats, Whigs and Free Soilers fragmented into Douglas Democrats, Cotton Whigs, Anti-Nebraska Democrats, Conscience Whigs, Free Soilers, Fusion Hard Democrats, Soft Democrats, Temperance, Rum Democrats, Anti-Maine-Law Democrats, Union Maine Law, Adopted Citizen, Know-Nothings and even Know-Somethings. One election in Connecticut drew candidates from 23 different parties.[13]

Over the next six years, one provocative development after another continued to move the nation ever closer to the brink of war. Kansas began her bleeding as pro- and anti-slavery factions flooded the territory in a race for numerical superiority. While scores of settlers were being slain, including the cold-blooded murder of five slavery advocates by John Brown and sons, the "honorable" members of Congress were not exactly setting the best example themselves. Two days after Senator Charles Sumner of Massachusetts excoriated his South Carolina colleague, Andrew Butler, in a speech entitled "The Crime Against Kansas," Butler's infuriated nephew, Congressman Preston Brooks, also of South Carolina, viciously assaulted Sumner in the Senate chamber, literally breaking his cane over the unfortunate man's head.

The explosive *Dred Scott* decision in March, 1857, was countered by the infamous raid of John Brown upon the federal arsenal at Harper's Ferry, Virginia, in October, 1859. After murdering the town's mayor and taking several citizens hostage, Brown's pipe dream of using 1,000 African spears to incite a slave insurrection came to naught as he and his band of 18 fellow visionaries were surrounded in a locomotive roundhouse by the likes of Colonel Robert E. Lee and Lieutenant "Jeb" Stuart. An insightful glimpse into the deranged mind-set of a small, but determined, body of self-righteous belligerents running amuck at that time can be discerned from the eyewitness account of hostage Lewis Washington, a great-grand nephew of the first president, who described the fanatic under fire accordingly: "With one son dead by his side, and another shot through, he felt the pulse of his dying son with one hand and held his rifle with the other, and commanded his men with the utmost composure, encouraging them to be firm and to sell their lives as dearly as they could."[14] Having rejected his counsel's plea of insanity (his wife, two sons and six of his first cousins were judged insane at varying times[15]), John Brown was hanged on October 31, 1859. Thoreau compared the ordeal to Jesus' crucifixion, while the Russian Minister, Edouard de Stoeckl, wrote his government that Brown was being "proclaimed...as the equal of our Savior."[16] The North had found its martyr.

The apex of political sectionalism was realized by the presidential election of 1860. When Northern Democrats at the National Democratic Convention convening in Charleston refused to adopt the resolutions of Southern Democrats protecting slavery in the territories, the Cotton States seceded as a body and called for a new convention in Baltimore on the 18th of June. Virginia and the border states followed shortly thereafter.

What remained of the Charleston convention nominated Stephen A. Douglas of Illinois for president and Benjamin Fitzpatrick of Alabama for vice president. The Southern faction, assembled at Baltimore, decided on John C. Breckinridge of Kentucky for president and Oregon's John Lane for vice president. A third splinter party, calling itself the Constitutional Union, had previously nominated for president and vice president, John Bell of Tennessee and Edward Everett of Massachusetts.

The National Convention of the Black Republican party, convening in Chicago (also in June), adopted a platform declaring freedom to be the "normal condition" of the Territories. Abraham Lincoln of Illinois was the nominee for president and Hannibal Hamlin of Maine the choice for vice president. As predicted, the voting followed strict sectional lines. Lincoln was elected President by having received the entire electoral vote of every free state except for New Jersey. However, the popular vote revealed how splitting their ticket had cost the Democrats a sure victory. Whereas Lincoln received 1,858,200 votes, Douglas garnered 1,276,780; Breckinridge— 812,500 and Bell—753,504. Thus the whole vote *against* Lincoln was 2,824,874, confirming a clear aggregate majority against him of nearly a million votes.

With the South perceiving the proverbial "handwriting on the wall," a decision was made for peaceful secession. On December 20, 1860, South Carolina led the way declaring that the North had elected a man "whose opinions and purposes are hostile to slavery." By February, 1861, Mississippi, Florida, Alabama, Georgia, Louisiana and Texas followed suit, forming the Confederate States of America with Jefferson Davis as its provisional president. (Virginia, Arkansas, Tennessee and North Carolina would follow later.)

At first light on April 12, 1861, as disguised Northern gunboats were steaming to the rescue of Fort Sumter, a Southern artillery emplacement opened fire on the recalcitrant federal garrison. The "irrepressible conflict" was now underway; but *why*?

Although Lee's surrender at Appomattox Courthouse, on April 9, 1865, brought the war to a formal conclusion, over 130 years later, Americans remain hopelessly divided as to the actual *cause* for the conflict itself. For a growing majority in the age of political correctness, the *only* view to hold is that the war was fought to free the slaves. This is the safe position if one wants to avoid being branded as a *racist*. The more pragmatic thinker prefers to view the war as the inevitable clash between the competing economic systems. From this perspective, the War Between the States was, in reality, the "War Between the Cotton Gin and the McCormick Reaper." He might also point out the irony that Eli Whitney was from Massachusetts while Cyrus McCormick was a Virginian. As for the typical American who watches too much television, a dozen reruns of *Gone with the Wind* have convinced him that the war was necessitated by irreconcilable social and cultural differences. And finally, a conservative minority can see no further than a political crisis involving states' rights.

Having given only minimal consideration to these standard theories of *moral, economic, social* and *political* causation, we will now provoke the intellectual community by turning our attention to the all-important *spiritual* explanation for the outbreak of hostilities. The secular "experts" cannot even agree on the correct name for the conflict; author Burke Davis lists 29 different samples.[17] However, a born-again believer has the advantage of interpreting these historical complexities by the illuminating truths of Holy Scripture. Recognizing (as did William Bradford of old) that the Bible identifies Satan as the believer's "ancient foe," we may safely conclude that the nation which has consistently harbored the highest concentration of the world's Christian population would most assuredly be the special object of his intense hatred and ill will. From the sixth chapter of Ephesians, we learn that the devil's kingdom is a highly sophisticated superstructure consisting of *"principalities"* and *"powers."* An allusion to this evil empire is found in the tenth chapter of Daniel where specific demons are presented as being assigned to various nations. Therefore, the paramount question becomes whether or not there is evidence of a pronounced *satanic* involvement in the American Civil War. As the facts will substantiate, the answer is an overwhelming "yes."

I. THE EVIDENCE OF DISORDER

As Scripture declares in I Corinthians 14:33 that *"God is not the author of confusion,"* the initial telltale sign of augmented demonic activity between 1861 and 1865 was the very fact the *United* States would declare war on herself! A Union soldier from Iowa made a grisly discovery on the Allatoona Pass battlefield in October, 1864, reporting:

> When the battle was over one of our boys was found dead facing the enemy who had killed him. Both of them lay with their faces nearly touching, with their bayonets run through each other.[18]

The town of Winchester, Virginia, exchanged hands some 72 times as opposing armies surged to and fro in the northern Shenandoah Valley. During the course of various battles, the bullets themselves appeared to be at war with one another, a soldier at Vicksburg relating, "Rifle balls met in the air and fell to the ground welded together."[19] (General Grant even sent one such pair to Washington.) When Confederate J. N. Ballard took a direct hit in the leg by a Federal bullet, his splintered limb was amputated immediately. Written off as unfit for further action, the undaunted amputee amazed his comrades by hobbling into camp wearing a splendid cork leg he had taken from the body of Union Colonel Ulric Dahlgren who was killed near Richmond.[20]

Confusion reigned as not only fellow Americans, but actual households divided on the field of battle. Historian Burke Davis presents a compelling array of examples. Mary Todd Lincoln had so many relatives fighting for the Confederacy that Senate members of the Committee on the Conduct of the War actually met to consider bringing charges of treason against the First Lady. A surprise appearance by the President himself on behalf of Mrs. Lincoln discouraged any further committee activity. Senator George B. Crittenden of Kentucky had two sons who rose to the rank of major general, one on each side of the conflict, while three grandsons of the deceased Henry Clay fought in blue when four others wore the gray. After a seven-year separation, brothers Henry Hubbard of the First Minnesota and Frederick Hubbard of the Washington Artillery of New Orleans were both wounded at Bull Run and by coincidence placed side by side in a stable serving as a field hospital. Stonewall Jackson's sister, Laura, was a Union sympathizer who vowed to "take care of wounded Federals as fast as brother Thomas would wound them." Commodore Franklin Buchanan, first head of the United States Naval Academy, "jumped ship" to command the *Merrimac* whose battle victims included the U.S.S. *Congress*, on which his brother was an officer. Missouri furnished 39 regiments for the siege of Vicksburg—17 Confederate and 22 Union. And when the U.S.S. *Harriet Lane* was seized during the Confederate shelling and capture of Galveston, Texas, Major A. M. Lea went aboard the stricken vessel with a boarding party only to discover that his own son, a ship's lieutenant, was among the mortally wounded.[21]

The Civil War was also confusing from an *eschatological* view, primarily with regard to Genesis nine. Financing for the North was provided by the Jewish House of Rothschild through their American agent, August Belmont, and for the South through the Erlangers, Rothschild's relatives.[22] Thus we observe the incongruous affiliation whereby *Shemites* supplied the resources for *Japhethites* to slaughter one another on the pretense of freeing *Ham*, with the downsizing of *Japheth* hanging in the balance! The *London Times*, June 23, 1862, pretty well summed up America's disconcerting testimony abroad:

> Whatever may be the result of the civil war in America, it is plain that it has reached a point where it is a scandal to humanity. Utter destruction may be possible or even imminent, but submission is as far off as ever.[23]

II. THE EVIDENCE OF DESTRUCTION

A second, more obvious implication of satanic surreptitiousness can be seen in the horrendous loss of life and property sustained on both sides of the Mason-Dixon line. Appropriately, in the book of Revelation, the Holy Spirit informs us that Satan's title as the angel of the bottomless pit is *Abaddon* in Hebrew and *Apollyon* in Greek, both of which translate as **Destroyer**. (Revelation 9:11)

According to figures supplied from the pension returns of surviving widows, at least 618,000 Americans died in the bloody conflict while some estimates exceed 700,000. By 1864, the war was costing the Union an incredible $3 million per day, with the expense of that year alone exceeding the Federal government's total expenditures from its beginning through 1836. The combined cost for both governments totalled $8 billion.

There were more Americans who lost their lives between 1861 and 1865 than were killed in both World Wars, Korea and Vietnam combined.

Furthermore, the nearly two-thirds of a million fatalities are to be understood against a total population of only 32 million. By comparison, in our second bloodiest conflict, World War II, there were only 250,000 deaths out of a population of 132 million.

However, with Apollyon behind the scene, general figures do not begin to scratch the surface of legitimate suffering and despair. While 67,058 Union soldiers were killed on the field of battle, 43,012 died from related wounds with another 224,586 succumbing to disease. An additional 25,566 were claimed by accidents and miscellaneous causes. Confederate losses have been estimated at 94,000 battle-related deaths with 164,000 additional losses from disease. Commager writes:

> Poor sanitation, impure water, wretched cooking, exposure, lack of cleanliness, and sheer carelessness exposed soldiers on both sides to dysentery, typhoid, malaria, and consumption—the chief killers. Medical services were inadequate and inefficient; hospitals often primitive; nursing at first almost nonexistent though it gradually improved. Care for the wounded was haphazard and callous: after Shiloh and Second Bull Run the wounded were allowed to lie for two or three days on the battlefields without relief. Behind the lines overworked doctors worked desperately in hastily improvised field hospitals. Antisepsis was unknown and anesthetics were not always available; abdominal wounds and major amputations meant probable death. Out of a total of 580 amputations in Richmond in two months of 1862, there were 245 deaths; no wonder a Confederate officer wrote that in every regiment "there were not less than a dozen doctors from whom our men had as much to fear as from their Northern enemies."[24]

As previously mentioned, numbers of amputees declined to retire from combat. Confederate Major General John B. Hood had his left arm incapacitated at Gettysburg and his right leg amputated after the battle of Chickamauga. The determined officer led his men into the battle of Atlanta, strapped in his saddle, wearing a $5,000 French-made cork leg while carrying a spare to boot.[25] (For the record, 8,000 of his men perished in this assault.) The Mississippi state budget for 1865 allocated 20% of its revenue for artificial limbs alone. Prospects such as these led to many a restless night, Corporal Arthur S. Fitch of Company B, 107th New York Infantry writing on the eve of Antietam:

The stillness of the night is broken by the hostile picket shots close to the front. What are the thoughts that fill the minds of the men as they lie there, anxiously awaiting the morning? Who can describe them?[26]

Another arresting statistic involves the mean age of combatants in both armies. Out of a sum total of 2.7 million Federal soldiers, more than 2 million were 21 or younger. Furthermore, 800,000 were 17 or below while 100,000 were 15 or under.[27] Although Confederate figures were usually harder to secure, their percentages were often quite similar. For reasons such as these, the Civil War has also been called, "The Boys' War." Arthur MacArthur of Wisconsin (father of General Douglas MacArthur) was a thrice-wounded colonel by the time he was 18 years of age. E. G. Baxter of Clark County, Kentucky, was a second lieutenant with Company A, 7th Cavalry at age 14. George S. Lamkin of Winona, Mississippi, was severely wounded in the battle of Shiloh at the tender age of 11.[28] When Confederates at Galveston stormed the U.S.S. *Harriet Jones* at dry dock, killing the gallant Captain Wainwright in the process, the ten-year-old son of the slain captain stood at the cabin door with a revolver in both hands maintaining his fire till every bullet was expended.[29] Edward Woods is listed as the youngest person on record to die from gunfire on a Civil War battlefield. The adventurous lad and a friend were souvenir hunting in the Gettysburg battlefield, July 5, 1863, when they became attracted to an abandoned rifle that appeared to be in perfect condition. While looking it over, the older boy accidentally pulled the trigger, killing his *three-year-old* companion in the process.[30]

As the breeding ground for modern warfare, the Civil War produced a chilling list of "firsts" in the killing department. A sample of these inventions would include: repeating rifles and telescopic sights; a workable machine gun; a steel ship with rotating gun turrets and a successful submarine with naval torpedoes; the periscope for trench warfare; land mines and flame throwers; aerial reconnaissance and anti-aircraft fire. In his foreword to G. H. Pember's *Earth's Earliest Ages*, British author G. H. Lang advances the idea that Satan himself may provide the inspiration behind the invention of weapons in general by suggesting a connection between alchemy and chemical warfare: "Is it beyond possibility that some of the modern chemical discoveries, now in use for wholesale massacre, have been revealed diabolically?"[31] Americans were also introduced to the income tax, withholding tax and cigarette tax, as well as the infamous greenbacks, in order to finance these new weapons.

The resulting firepower from such advanced technology had a telling effect on the human anatomy. Davis points out that while the famed Light

Brigade at Balaklava lost 36.7% of its men in their ill-fated charge, 63 Union regiments lost as many as 50% in single battles.[32] Among the 51,112 casualties sustained in the three days of fighting at Gettysburg, the First Minnesota suffered an 82% loss while the 141st Pennsylvania reported a figure of 75.7%. The rotting flesh of 3,000 horses added to the battle's ghastly aftermath. One caravan of jolting wagons removing wounded soldiers from the battlefield stretched for an unbelievable 17 miles through a steady downpour.

During the battle of Resaca, Georgia, a Confederate officer took the trouble to monitor the number of shells careening into his unit. Lieutenant William McMurray of the 20th Tennessee Regiment ascertained that "intervals between shells from Union batteries ranged from three to six seconds, only."[33] At one brief period of only eight minutes during the Federal assault at Cold Harbor, Virginia, over 7,000 men were killed or wounded. Prior to the battle, Union soldiers were seen writing their names on slips of paper and sewing them inside their coats as identification tags. One fatalistic youth made an advance entry in his diary. "June 3. Cold Harbor. I was killed."[34] A Confederate infantryman reported what he witnessed from 30 paces removed.

> The charging column, which aimed to strike the Fourth Alabama, received the most destructive fire I ever saw. I could see the dust fog out of a man's clothing in two or three places at once where as many balls would strike him at the same moment. In two minutes not a man of them was standing. All who were not shot down had lain down for protection.[35]

In one battle along Antietam Creek in Sharpsburg, Maryland, over 26,000 Union and Confederate troops were either killed or wounded, making September 17, 1862, the single bloodiest day in American history—a distinction that has yet to be surpassed. Throughout the six-hour Battle of Antietam, described as "fighting madness," many testified that it was nearly impossible to take a step without treading on a dead or wounded man. Lieutenant Matthew J. Graham, Company H, 9th New York Volunteers wrote:

> I was lying on my back, supported on my elbows, watching the shells explode overhead and speculating as to how long I could hold up my finger before it would be shot off, for the very air seemed full of bullets, when the order to get up was given, I turned over quickly to look at Col.

Kimball, who had given the order, thinking he had become suddenly insane.[36]

A wounded survivor of the 35th Massachusetts Volunteers left a grisly picture indeed.

> The force of a mini ball or piece of shell striking any solid portion of a person is astounding; it comes like a blow from a sledge hammer, and the recipient finds himself sprawling on the ground before he is conscious of being hit; then he feels about for the wound, the benumbing blow deadening sensation for a few moments. Unless struck in the head or about the heart, men mortally wounded live some time, often in great pain, and toss about upon the ground.[37]

As a portion of Stonewall Jackson's artillery was falling back, Robert E. Lee personally urged the men forward. A young private approached him and asked, "General, are you going to send us in again?" Lee looked kindly on the lad and answered, "Yes, my son, you all must do what you can to help drive these people back." The apprehensive Confederate was General Lee's youngest son, Rob.[38]

Whereas the slain in the cornfields at Antietam fell in disciplined rows, all was utter confusion during the three-day Battle of the Wilderness. Desperate soldiers repeatedly lost their footing in the blood-soaked earth as they groped in desperation, Anderson writing:

> Commands got separated, troops shot at friends, and no one knew who—or where—the enemy was. By noon the pandemonium was general. Both armies were facing all points on the compass, and the compass was the only way commanders could locate their men. Dark worse than night—there were not even stars to steer by—turned the Wilderness into a "battle of invisibles with invisibles," said one veteran.
>
> A Federal private remembered that no one "could see the fight fifty feet from him. The roll and crackle of the musketry was something terrible, even to the veterans of many battles. The lines were very near each other, and from the dense underbrush and the tops of the trees came puffs of smoke, the 'ping' of bullets, and the yell of the enemy. It was a blind and bloody hunt to the death, in bewildering thickets, rather than a battle... In advancing it was next to impossible to preserve a distinct line, and we were constantly broken into small groups. The underbrush and briars scratched our faces, tore our clothing, and tripped our feet from under us."[39]

The poor wretches had to contend with forest fires as well!

"The men fought the enemy and the flames at the same time," a Union
private remembered. "Their hair and beards were singed and their faces
blistered. At last, blinded by the smoke and suffocated by the hot breath
of the flames, the whole length of their intrenchments a crackling mass of
fire, they gave way and fell back to the second line of intrenchment. With
a shout the rebel column approached and attempted to seize the abandoned
position. The impartial flames drove them out."[40]

Few battles can be compared to the stark ferocity of Spotsylvania's
Bloody Angle, May 10 and 12, 1864. Describing the area as a "boiling,
bubbling and hissing caldron of death," Lieutenant Stoddart Robertson of
the 93rd New York Regiment gave testimony that "a white-oak tree, twenty-
two inches in diameter was cut down wholly by bullets."[41] Anderson, citing
a survivor:

"The fence rails and logs in the breastworks were shattered into
splinters, and trees over a foot and a half in diameter were cut completely
in two by incessant musketry fire.... We had not only shot down an army,
but also a forest. The opposing flags were in places thrust against each
other, and muskets were fired with muzzle against muzzle. Skulls were
crushed with clubbed muskets, and men stabbed to death with swords and
bayonets thrust between the logs in the parapet which separated the
combatants. Wild cheers, savage yells, and frantic shrieks rose above the
sighing of the wind and pattering of the rain, and formed a demonical
accompaniment to the booming of the guns...."
During momentary lulls, each side screamed at the other to surrender.
When a small group of Rebels held out a trembly white handkerchief, their
comrades shouted, "Shoot them fellows! Shoot them fellows!" and brought
them down along with the surrender flag. Crouching in the ditch,
Confederates reached up and grabbed musket muzzles and held them aloft
until they had been fired, then pushed their own weapons above the
embankment and pressed triggers with their thumbs. Muskets fouled by
rain-wettened powder were fitted with bayonets and tossed as spears
across the breastworks which ever after would be known as the "Bloody
Angle."
Men in the front ranks leapt onto the embankment and fired rifles in
one another's faces, then reached backward for freshly loaded weapons.
"As those in front fell, others quickly sprang forward to take their places."
Confederate bodies rolled into the ditch and were pressed into the mud by
soldiers who trampled to the front. "The bullets seemed to fly in sheets."

Rank after rank of Federals was "riddled by shot and shell and bayonet thrusts, and finally sank, a mass of torn and mutilated corpses; then fresh troops rushed madly forward to replace the dead, and so the murderous work went on." It went on all afternoon. It was still going on as darkness gripped the Bloody Angle.[42]

Of the estimated 10,920 Union casualties at Spotsylvania, the pathetic desperation of a single dying Federal, abandoned to his fate in the foreboding no man's land, best illustrates the utter futility of the war as a whole. Anderson writing:

> It was with horrified sympathy that the men in the new Confederate trenches watched the solitary Union soldier left to die in no-man's-land each day raise himself to a sitting position, and weakly holding onto the barrel of his musket, tentatively try to bash his own head in. He always failed. Each day he made fewer attempts. Finally, he didn't try at all.[43]

When one realizes that this same unnamed wretch who apparently beat his own brains out over 130 years ago was also some poor mother's son and probably a husband and father as well, a deeper pathos for the ultimate cost of combat is attained. Consider the following letter of Asey Ladd, an innocent P.O.W., about to be punished in retaliation for Confederate military activities:

St. Louis, Mo.
October 29, 1864

Dear Wife and Children:
    I take my pen with trembling hand to inform you that I have to be shot between 2 & 4 o'clock this evening. I have but few hours to remain in this unfriendly world. There is 6 of us sentenced to die in [retaliation] of 6 union soldiers that was shot by Reeves men. My dear wife don't grieve after me. I want you to meet me in Heaven. I want you to teach the children piety, so that they may meet me at the right hand of God. I can't tell you my feelings but you can form some idea of my feeling when you hear of my fate.
    I don't want you to let this bear on your mind anymore than you can help, for you are now left to take care of my dear children. Tell them to remember their dear father. I want you to go back to the old place and try to make a support for you and the children. I want you to tell all my friends that I have gone home to rest. I want you to go to Mr. Conner and tell him to assist you in winding up your business. If he is not there get Mr.

Cleveland. If you don't get this letter before St. Francis River gets up you had better stay there until you can make a crop, and you can go in the dry season.

It is now half past 4 AM. I must bring my letter to a close, leaving you in the hands of God. I send you my best love and respect in the hour of death. Kiss all the children for me. You need have no uneasiness about my future state, for my faith is well founded and I fear no evil. God is my refuge and my hiding place.

Good-by Amy.
Asey Ladd[44]

The official record states the half-truth that Private Ladd "died while prisoner of war." Unfortunately, nightmares such as these were the norm from 1861-1865. The Christian family of Christianburg, Virgina, lost 18 different members throughout the bloody conflict. Isadore Guillet, a captain in the Confederacy, was fatally shot while riding the *same* horse on which three of his brothers were previously killed. In the battle of Gettysburg, twin brothers from Company C of the Fifth Texas Regiment were literally fighting side by side. When one of them took a fatal hit from a Federal marksman, the other twin caught him and "gently laid him on the ground." As the surviving brother began to draw himself erect, he also received a lethal ball and literally dropped across his sibling's withering frame.

The suffering inflicted upon the Flint family of East Hartford, Connecticut, was especially heartrending. In his book *Antietam, the Photographic Legacy of America's Bloodiest Day*, author William Frassanito relates the sad details. Alvin Flint, Sr., was originally from Vermont while his wife, Lucy, was from New Hampshire. A July 23, 1860, census listing the population of his township at 2,951 recorded the members of the Flint household as follows: Alvin, Sr., fifty; Lucy, forty-nine; Alvin, Jr., fifteen; Evaline, thirteen; and their youngest child George, age eleven. All three children were enrolled in school. Alvin, Sr., was listed as a papermaker by trade. By nineteenth-century standards, the Flint family would have been considered middle of lower middle class. At any rate, they constituted an average American family of that time. However, this would all be changed with the outbreak of hostilities.

On October 1, 1861, Alvin, Jr., enlisted with Company D of the 11th Connecticut Volunteers forming at Hartford. He was 17 years of age. While Alvin and his unit were preparing to move out two months later, his beloved mother contracted consumption and died on December 6, 1861. Soon after arriving at the front in North Carolina the following month, Alvin's natural homesickness was intensified by word that his 15-year-old sister, Evaline, had also succumbed to the dreaded disease on January 16, 1862.

Haunted by a household of memories, Alvin, Sr., then approaching 52, began to seriously consider joining the army himself. Apparently his younger son George, only 13 at the time, shared in his father's remorse, for in August, 1862, both enlisted as privates in Company B of the newly formed 21st Connecticut Volunteers. On September 11, 1862, Alvin, Sr., and George were shipped out to a training camp near Washington. Frassanito continues:

> There is no way of determining the extent to which Alvin Flint, Jr., was aware of these latest developments as he waited to go into action at Antietam on the morning of September 17, 1862. In all likelihood he was at least aware of his father's intentions of enlisting. There can be little doubt, however, that among Alvin, Jr.'s, thoughts before advancing with the Eleventh Connecticut against the stone bridge were images of his father and younger brother, memories of his mother and sister—and prayers for his own safe delivery from the battle into which he was about to be thrust.
>
> Sometime during the fifteen-minute charge of the Eleventh Connecticut, Alvin Flint, Jr., was hit by enemy rifle fire. Sprawling to the earth, his body torn and bleeding, the eighteen-year-old private lay within sight of Burnside Bridge for an indefinite time before stretcher-bearers were able to reach him. But by then it was too late, for Alvin Flint, Jr., was dead.[45]

The following month, Alvin, Sr., was sent to Sharpsburg on detached service with the Ambulance Corp. Although the body of his son would be shipped home at a later time, the grieving father was unable to locate Alvin, Jr.'s, grave. Heartbroken and embittered, Alvin, Sr., expressed his feelings in a letter to the editor of the *Hartford Courant*, dated Pleasant Valley, Maryland, October 23, 1862:

> Dear Courant: You doubtless are aware that I have come to the land of Dixie, to engage in this killing business.... We arrived [at Sharpsburg] Saturday night, near what I call "Antie-Dam," where my boy was brutally murdered.... I was leaning upon that dear boy, as a prop in my declining years; but if my life is spared, I shall knock out some of the props that hold up this uncalled for, and worse than hellish, wicked rebellion. Hardly had the sadness of the death of a dear daughter, that I lost last January worn off, when this sad, sad calamity should come upon me.

I went to hear the Chaplain preach; his text was, "How dreadful is this place, it's none other than the house of God and the gate of Heaven." Oh that I could have viewed the text as Jacob did, but to me the place was dreadful in the extreme, where my dear boy had been cut down in a moment with no one to say a word to him about the future. Oh how dreadful was that place to me, where my dear boy had been buried like a beast in the field! Oh could I have found the spot, I would have wet it with my tears! Oh how dreadful was that place to me, where I passed two long, long sleepless nights! Had it not been for this sad calamity, my sleep would have been sweet.

Monday morning we moved back five or six miles this side of Harper's Ferry, and feeling as "Lot" did on fleeing out of Sodom, I did not look behind.

My son was a member of the 11th Conn., and his age was 18.[46]

Unfortunately the story does not end with the decease of Alvin, Jr. By late December, 1862, the 21st Connecticut was encamped at Falmouth, Virginia, along the Rappahannock River near Connecticut-held Fredericksburg. In an outbreak of typhoid fever, Alvin, Sr., died on January 10, 1863, with 13-year-old George following his father five days later. The Alvin Flint family of East Hartford, Connecticut, *no longer existed.*

III. THE EVIDENCE OF DECEPTION

Writing under inspiration, the Apostle John declared of Satan, *"And the great dragon was cast out, that old serpent, called the Devil, and Satan, which **deceiveth the whole world**: he was cast out into the earth, and his angels were cast out with him."* (Revelation 12:9) Not only was the American Civil War a time of disorder and destruction, but it was also a time of pronounced satanic *deception.* That Robert E. Lee could be deprived of his most valued commander, Thomas "Stonewall" Jackson (eulogized by Lee as his own "right arm"), by the freak shooting of a confused Rebel picket, illustrates the overall delusion that prevailed throughout the entire nation, not only during the war years but also to this present time as well.

Perhaps *the* classic example of post-war hallucinogens involves the enduring fame of the "Battle Hymn of the Republic." Because of its flowing religious content, the sacrosanct "Battle Hymn" has become one of America's most inspiring Christian numbers, being found in nearly every denominational hymnbook. However, I have often wondered why the song is also such a favorite among born-again Christians when the author was a liberal, Christ-denying Unitarian feminist. *How's that for delusion?* What could Julia Ward Howe possibly have known about the glory of the Lord? The poor woman thought Christ was born among beautiful lilies and had died to make men holy. The Bible Howe rejected declares that the eternal son of God was born in a *manger* (Luke 2:7) and died so that *men could escape the fiery torments of Hell* (Revelation 20:15). Furthermore, few believers have ever taken the time to read Howe's original poem from which the hymn, perverting Revelation 14, 19 and Isaiah 63, was constructed. Her third stanza was conveniently left out of the final product:

I have read a fiery gospel writ in burnished rows of steel;
"As ye deal with my contemners, so with you my grace shall deal;"
Let the Hero, born of woman, crush the serpent with his heel,
Since God is marching on.[47]

The "good news" of Howe's "fiery gospel" was that the human Jesus was somehow propelling the burnished rows of Northern bayonets and scabbards to crush the Southern serpent—i.e., that "heathen" portion of America that had already produced, among others: **Peyton Randolph**, the first president of the First Continental Congress; **Patrick Henry**, the colonists' key agitator for armed resistance; **Thomas Jefferson**, the author of the Declaration of Independence; **George Washington**, America's victorious commander in chief through the Revolution; and **James Madison**, father of the Constitution and the Bill of Rights. A roll call of chief executives would also reveal that four of the first five, seven of the first ten, and ten of the first sixteen presidents were native-born sons of Howe's illusionary land of vipers. According to this Unitarian agitator, the grace of God was not appropriated through faith in the blood of Jesus Christ, but rather in direct proportion to how many Confederate serpents—"my contemners"—were slashed, stabbed and bayoneted on the field of battle. Could we have expected more from a person who had opened up her own home to the likes of John Brown?

Another female who should have stayed home baking cookies was the celebrated Harriet Beecher Stowe, author of *Uncle Tom's Cabin*. When President Lincoln met Harriet for the first time, he greeted her by saying, "So you're the little lady who started the big war."[48]

Although the exploitation of men and women by their fellow human beings was certainly a repugnant and degrading practice, the subsequent exploitation of the exploitation itself has proven to be a far greater calamity to America via a steady erosion of our historic, constitutional liberties (i.e., through the Fourteenth Amendment, Civil Rights Act, etc.) As the evils of radical reconstruction would later confirm, the slavery issue provided the ideal psychological justification for a multitude of sins. William Darrah Kelley, a liberal congressman from Philadelphia declared rather candidly, "Yes, sneer at or doubt it as you may, the negro is the 'coming man' for whom we have waited."[49] And despite the fact that a great-great-great-grand-nephew of "Uncle Thomas" was able to make it all the way to the United States Supreme Court, a certain slave-era mythology continues to inspire modern civil rights advocates with enough racist propaganda to enslave an entire nation through such ideological buffoonery as affirmative action, "hate-crime" legislation, and nebulous discrimination suits.

Despite the fact that many aspects of the sectional conflict remain open to heated debate, a considerable portion of truth has *"fallen in the street"* (Isaiah 59:14), thereby adding to the general deception of the times. For instance, if Harriet is to be taken seriously, the *average* master whipped and abused his slaves at will. Beyond question, some masters were guilty as charged. However, if the normal planter invested $1,000 to $1,500 for a worker (a small fortune in mid-nineteenth-century dollars), would he be likely to starve or mistreat him? Would such abuse be the exception or the norm? Historian John S. Tilley wrote:

> Fortunately some foreigners visited the South in those days for study of the situation. Buckingham, a distinguished Englishman, wrote that the slaves were as well off as were English servants in the middle rank of life. He found them "well-fed, well-dressed, and easy to be governored."
>
> Just before the outbreak of war, a Northern student, Olmsted by name, traveled through the South to investigate conditions. In 1856 he published a book on the subject. He wrote that the slaves had food and clothing in plenty; that their "health and comfort" were better looked after than was that of many free servants; that as a rule, they were treated with kindness; that frequently their marriage rites were performed in the home of the master by the master's own minister; that in many places owners and slaves worshipped together in the same church; that he heard little "of harshness or cruelty."[50]

Tilley, who earned his master's degree at Harvard, also points out the high percentage of slaves who embraced the Christian faith and asks rhetorically, "Do you think that they would have adopted the religion of masters who were brutal to them?"[51] In any case, the condition of American slaves in general was light-years ahead of life back in Africa (as in Nelson Mandela's "necktie" people).

Returning to the war itself, the modern history book is at odds with the *average* correspondence and/or diary entry belonging to the common foot soldier in either army concerning the all-important underlying motive for battle. Did the average blue or gray believe that he was risking life and limb primarily over the "peculiar institution"? Pulitzer-prizewinning author, James M. McPherson, George Henry Davis Professor of American History at Princeton University, studied the letters and diaries of 374 Confederates and 562 Federals and published a number of unique findings in his volume entitled *What They Fought For, 1861–1865.*

Beginning with the literature of the Southern troops, McPherson relates, "Of 374 Confederate soldiers whose letters and diaries I have read, two-thirds expressed patriotic motives."[52] With only one out of every fifteen Southern whites having ever owned a slave, one can hardly expect that 93% of the Southern population would go to war primarily over a custody battle involving the remaining 7%. Most of Harriet's readers never thought about that. McPherson continues:

> Candid discussions of slavery were the exception rather than the rule. Even in private letters, Confederate soldiers professed more often to fight *for* liberty and *against* slavery—that is, against their own enslavement to the North. "Sooner then [sic] submit to Northern Slavery, I prefer death," wrote a South Carolina captain to his wife in 1862, a phrase repeated almost verbatim by many soldiers.[53]

Other expressions of native sentiment included:

> "We are fighting for matters real and tangible... our property and our homes," wrote a Texas private in 1864, "they for matters abstract and intangible." A Tennessee lieutenant insisted that "the yankees are sacrificing their lives for nothing; we ours for home, country, and all That is dear and sacred."... A young Alabama soldier agreed that, "when a Southron's [sic] home is threatened the spirit of resistance is irrepressable [sic]."[54]

Although the typical, prejudiced intellectual may have convinced himself that "Johnny Reb" was fighting to preserve slavery, "Billy Yank" knew otherwise: " 'They fight like Devils in tophet,' an Illinois sergeant wrote of the Confederates in 1862, because they were 'fighting to keep an enemy out of [their] own neighborhood & protect [their] property.' "[55] McPherson concludes, "Only 20 percent of my sample of 374 southern soldiers explicitly voiced these pro-slavery convictions in their letters."[56]

The numbers were not much different for the Federals. "Of 562 Union soldiers whose letters or diaries I have read, 67 percent voiced simple but strong patriotic convictions and 40 percent went further, expressing ideological purposes such as liberty, democracy...including opposition to slavery."[57] McPherson points out that "a good many soldiers disagreed"[58] with the prospect of emancipation:

> "No one who has ever seen the nigger in all his glory on the southern plantations will ever vote for emancipation," wrote an Indiana private. "If emancipation is to be the policy of this war...I do not care how quick the country goes to pot." An abolitionist clergyman's son in the 12th Maine wrote home from Louisiana in the summer of 1862 that "I do not want to hear any more about negroes when I get home....I have got sick and tired of them...and I shall hereafter let abolition alone....They are a set of thieves...and the boys here hate them worse than they do secesh." An artillery major from New York, a Democrat like so many officers in the Army of the Potomac under McClellan, wrote that if Lincoln caved in to "these black Republicans" and made it "an abolition war[,]...I for one shall be sorry that I ever lent a hand to it....This war [must be] for the preservation of the Union, the putting down of armed rebellion, and for that purpose only."[59]

Should the Indiana private quoted above appear to be a racist for reporting what he *saw*, one should review the post-war observations of the *abolitionists* themselves. Nathaniel Weyl relates:

> Even the luminaries of New England liberalism voiced grave doubts concerning the Negro's potentialities. "The degradation of that black race, though now lost in the starless spaces of the past," wrote Ralph Waldo Emerson, "did not come without sin." Charles Francis Adams, the brother of Henry, characterized the Negroes as a "terrible inert mass of domesticated barbarism." Professor Louis Agassiz of Harvard, considered at the time to be America's leading scientist, deemed social equality "a natural impossibility, from the very character of the negro race...." He added: "While Egypt and Carthage grew into powerful empires and attained a high state of civilization; while in Babylon, Syria, and Greece were developed the highest culture of antiquity, the new race groped in

barbarism and *never originated a regular organization among themselves.*"[60]

The "cruel" Southern taskmasters cannot be blamed for these conditions as they openly prevailed among free blacks in the *North* as well. Should the "Land of Dixie" be castigated for racism when...

> Hatred of the free negroes grew in the North as they became a significant part of the population of the great cities. Although their relative numerical importance dwindled with the rising tide of European immigration, their contribution to pauperism, vice and crime remained too substantial to be overlooked. In 1825, 1,340,000 whites in New York State furnished only 480 convicts, whereas 39,000 Negroes provided 150. In Philadelphia, the Negroes were less than 1/30th of the population, but accounted for more than a third of the inmates of penitentiaries. Again, in Massachusetts, the 1820 Census showed that Negroes formed 1/75th of the general population and furnished one-sixth of its criminals. Thus, the crime rate among free Negroes was about ten times that of whites in Northern cities.
>
> An Ohio investigation of the 7,500 free Negroes there found them to be "ignorant, many of them intemperate and vicious." Instead of farming, they huddled in the cities and tried to live by casual labor... In Cincinnati, Frances Trollope found that the free Negroes "herd together in an obscure part of the city called Little Africa."[61]

A California slogan on the eve of the war stated, "No niggers, slave or free."[62] Consequently, it was the opinion of DeTocqueville that:

> On the contrary, the prejudice of the race appears to be stronger in the states which have abolished slavery, than in those where it still exists; and nowhere is it so intolerant as in those states where servitude has never been known... Not only is slavery prohibited in Ohio, but no free negroes are allowed to enter the territory of that state, or to hold property in it.[63]

This is precisely why Lincoln waited so long to issue his Emancipation Proclamation, and then only as a defensive maneuver, as stated to Navy Secretary Gideon Welles, July 13, 1862, "that it was a military necessity absolutely essential for the salvation of the Union, that we must free the slaves or be ourselves subdued, etc., etc."[64] In the later observation of Woodrow Wilson, "It was necessary to put the South at a moral disadvantage by transforming the contest from a war waged against States fighting for their independence, into a war against States fighting for the maintenance and extension of slavery, by making some move for emancipation as the real motive of the struggle."[65] McPherson adds:

> The proclamation intensified a morale crisis in Union armies during the winter of 1862–1863, especially in the Army of the Potomac... Things were little better in Grant's army on the Mississippi... Desertion rates in both armies rose alarmingly. Many soldiers blamed the Emancipation Proclamation. The "men are much dissatisfied" with it, reported a New York captain, "and say that it has turned into a 'nigger war' and all are anxious to return to their homes for it was to preserve the Union that they volunteered."[66]

A further storm of protest was raised in the Union army, particularly among the officers, at the proposal that freed blacks be drafted, armed and led into combat against their former "oppressors." Garrison writes:

> Brig. Gen. George W. Morgan (West Point, class of 1845) took off his uniform as a protest against an impending shift in national policy.... Maj. Gen. John A. Logan of Illinois once threatened to lead soldiers of midwestern birth back to their homes if blacks were permitted to fight against Confederates.[67]

McPherson relates that a mitigating "factor that converted many soldiers to support of emancipation was a growing conviction that it really did hurt the enemy and help their own side."[68]

However, to gain the ultimate perspective of prevailing satanic deception involving slavery and the Civil War, one need only study the example set by the Union's highest leaders. Ulysses S. Grant's wife Julia owned slaves at the outbreak of the war. These slaves were eventually freed, not by Lincoln's Proclamation, but by the Thirteenth Amendment which was ratified December 18, 1866. According to *The Gray Book* as cited by authors James and Walter Kennedy, Grant's excuse for not freeing his slaves earlier was that **"good help is so hard to come by these days."**[69] So much for the Commander in Chief of Howe's "burnished rows of steel."

As to the personal convictions of the Great Emancipator, we invite Honest Abe to speak for himself. In October 16, 1854, Lincoln acknowledged that the slavery issue was a sticky wickett indeed: "If all earthly power were given me, I should not know what to do as to the existing institution."[70] Calling for a restoration of the Missouri Compromise, he said he hated the spread of slavery not only because of the "monstrous injustice of slavery itself," but also because harboring such an institution in America "deprives our republican example of its just influence in the world—enables the enemies of free institutions, with plausibility, to taunt us as hypocrites."[71] This was certainly an accurate assessment. In another important speech cited by David Donald, Lincoln's moderate "containment only" policy can be clearly seen.

> I hold it to be a paramount duty of us in the free states, due to the Union of the states, and perhaps to liberty itself (paradox though it may seem) to let the slavery of the other states alone; while, on the other hand, I hold it to be equally clear, that we should never knowingly lend ourselves directly, or indirectly to prevent that slavery from dying a natural death.[72]

Finally, in his First Inaugural Address on March 4, 1861, the President-elect reaffirmed his non-abolitionist position:

> I have no purpose, directly or indirectly, to interfere with the institution of slavery in the States where it exists. I believe I have no lawful right to do so, and I have no inclination to do so.[73]

Although this middle-of-the-road position may come as a surprise to the typically uninformed champion of human rights, what Lincoln believed about the race issue itself *would harelip every dog in the county!* In a debate with Stephen Douglas at Charlestown, Illinois, on September 18, 1858, Lincoln disclosed, as cited by Richard Current:

> I will say then that I am not, nor have ever have been in favor of bringing about in any way the social and political equality of the white and black races, [applause]— that I am not nor ever have been in favor of making voters or jurors of Negroes, nor of qualifying them to hold office, nor to intermarry with white people; and I will say in addition to this that **there is a physical difference between the white and black races which I believe will forever forbid the two races living together on terms of social and political equality.** And inasmuch as they cannot so live, while they do remain together there must be the position of superior and inferior, **and I as much as any man am in favor of having the superior position to the white race.**[74]

"What's that?" you say. "I never heard *that* in *my* history class." You don't say!? Try this one on for size. In a speech *to a delegation of free blacks at the White House,* August 14, 1862, Lincoln *really* split some rails:

> **Your race suffers very greatly, many of them, by living among us, while ours suffers from your presence. In a word, we suffer on each side. If this be admitted, it affords a reason at least, why we should be separated.**[75]

What Lincoln was referring to is a subject about which the average American has heard absolutely nothing. The President believed, as did the majority of thinking conservatives, that abolition must be accompanied by *colonization.* Lincoln's speech to the black delegation continues:

> **Why should the people of your race be colonized, and where?** Why should they leave this country? This is, perhaps, the first question for proper consideration. You and we are different races. We have between us a broader difference than exists between almost any other two races. Whether it is right or wrong, I need not discuss; but this physical difference is a great disadvantage to us both, as I think...
>
> **The aspiration of men is to enjoy equality with the best when free, but on this broad continent not a single man of your race is made the equal of a single man of ours....** Go where you are treated the best, and the ban is still upon you. I do not propose to discuss this, but to present it as a fact with which we have to deal. I cannot alter it if I would....
>
> See our present condition—the country engaged in war—our white men cutting one another's throats... and then consider what we know to be the truth. But for your race among us there could not be war.... **It is better for us both, therefore, to be separated.**[76]

Haiti, Panama and Liberia were the leading sites under consideration by the American Colonization Society for resettlement of the Negro population. Rousas J. Rushdoony summarizes:

> The Emancipation Proclamation must be set in this context of colonization hopes. However illusory, they were a long-standing consideration and were legally enacted by Congress. **The Negro was to be emancipated of slavery, and, many hoped and believed, the United States was to be emancipated of the Negro.** As late as March, 1865, a month before his assassination, Lincoln was considering the removal of the entire Negro population from the United States.[77]

Understandably, Lincoln's frankness didn't win him any points with Harriet's bunch. The abolitionist Benjamin F. Wade declared that Lincoln's views on slavery "could only come of one who was born 'of poor white trash.' " Henry Ward Beecher said that the President possessed "not an element of leadership, not one particle of heroic enthusiasm." And Wendell Philips described Lincoln as "a second-rate man" and charged his "slackness" with "doing more than the malice of Confederates to break up the Union."[78]

Whenever the real Abraham Lincoln comes into view, any number of stunned neophytes find themselves wondering why Lincoln *seems* to be talking as though he didn't hold to the panacean "All men are created equal" clause. Do you suppose they ever checked to see what the author of that clause believed? Weyl writes:

> **Jefferson opposed slavery as morally indefensible, but he also opposed the incorporation of the Negro in the American social and political system.** He considered the Negro inferior to other races, but thought that that circumstance should not deprive him of his freedom. He was, throughout his long life, in the politically uncomfortable position of wishing the slaves emancipated, but only on the condition that they be deported *in toto* beyond the present or potential frontiers of the United States. **"Nothing is more certainly written in the book of fate,"** Jefferson wrote in his *Autobiography*, **"than that these people are to be free; nor is it less certain that the two races, equally free, cannot live in the same government."**[79]

The father of the Declaration of Independence believed the dilemma of slavery to be a conflict between justice and self-preservation—justice commanding that all men be free; self-preservation that the whites remain separate. Commenting on the difficult but necessary demands of *emancipation* with *expatriation*, Jefferson wrote:

> But as it is, we have the wolf by the ears, and we can neither hold him, nor safely let him go. Justice is in one scale and self-preservation in the other.[80]

To a nation of politically correct "one-world wannabes" the views of Jefferson and Lincoln would be dismissed as the unenlightened shortcomings of borderline racists and hatemongers. This is why America celebrates the birthday of Martin Luther King, Jr., while the birthdays of George Washington and Abraham Lincoln have been subtly relegated to

Presidents' Day. Although these men were probably unaware of any related Scripture, they were being true to a major Bible principle that is anathema to the New World Order.

Ironically, the passage most frequently cited as justification for race mixing just happens to contain the clearest refutation of the practice itself. The verse is Acts 17:26 and the key to claiming that it says what it doesn't say is to quote only the first half: *"And hath made of one blood all nations of men for to dwell on all the face of the earth."* And because differences in physical characteristics are determined by genes and chromosomes, the word *blood* was conveniently dropped in the *American Standard Version, Revised Standard Version* and *New English Bible*. Thus, "he made of **one** every nation of men to dwell on all the face of the earth." (Revised Version, 1881) However, it is only when the *entire* verse is read that God's original plan for restricted international migration becomes apparent—*"and hath determined the times before appointed, and **the bounds of their habitation.**"* The immediate context of Acts 17:26 goes on to show that the divine purpose for "determining boundaries" was so that men would *"seek the Lord."* (Acts 17:27a) The Creator of all mankind was well aware of the fact that the more lost sinners "come together," the more emboldened they become to reject their need of a divine Saviour. As the stiff-necked descendants of Noah turned to a tower of astrology at Babel (Genesis 11:1–9), America's current infatuation with the Psychic Friends Network is indicative of a growing one-world mind-set. (See Dr. G. A. Riplinger's *New Age Versions* for documentation on the "one" in New Age doctrine.) Incidentally, this is why God's natural aquatic impediment to migration, covering 75% of the planet's surface, will no longer be needed on the sin-purged New Earth: *"and there was no more sea."* (Revelation 21:1c)

IV. THE EVIDENCE OF DIVISION

A fourth unmistakable proof of satanic involvement with the American Civil War was the obvious near-rupture of the Union itself. The Methodist, Baptist and Presbyterian bodies had already divided along sectional lines over two decades earlier. (Genesis 13:7) Although Lincoln's famous "House Divided" address of October 25, 1858, may have constituted an oratorical classic, the arresting truth of Matthew 12:25b applied just the same—*"every city or house divided against itself shall not stand."* At the risk of appearing overly simplistic, the general tenor of events that precipitated the great struggle are not nearly so complex when illuminated by Scripture. If Satan hated the "United" States for being a lighthouse of Christian truth, would he not have stood to gain by a division of the nation?

First and foremost, the devil utilized the fanatical abolitionist to stir up strife that might have otherwise been averted. This is what Lincoln meant by calling Harriet Beecher Stowe "the little lady who started the big war." Although the Northern abolitionist was part of a small minority (frequently attacked in the North itself), his deeds eventually agitated a pronounced Southern majority. Lincoln's reassuring words were basically drowned out by the likes of Nat Turner and John Brown. The Emigrant Aid Company armed free-state settlers in Kansas with a new breech-loading weapon of precision—the Sharps rifle. It was called "Beecher's Bible," being named after the abolitionist minister who recommended its use. William Lloyd Garrison publicly burned a copy of the Constitution, calling it **"a covenant with death and an agreement with Hell."**

Such menacing actions of the lunatic fringe played into the hands of the Southern counterpart of political extremism known as the Fire Eaters. This pro-secessionist faction was representative of the powerful planter aristocracy and wielded an unhealthy and disproportionate influence throughout the Land of Cotton. The majority of these Southern elite affiliated with either the Episcopal or Presbyterian churches.[81] The phrase, "Rich man's fight and poor man's war" is a throwback to this cultural inequity. Yet, most of the South reacted with indignation to Northern demands for instantaneous emancipation without *financial remuneration.* After all, the slaves had been purchased up North initially. By 1860 there were in the South some 3.5 million slaves for whom the Southern people had paid Northern flesh markets multiplied millions of dollars. Jefferson had personally calculated that the bill to buy all the slaves and ship them to Africa would have approached $900 million.[82]

It would appear, therefore, that the South had received enough abolitionist provocation to justify a peaceful secession. Had not the President-elect said on an earlier occasion, "Any people, anywhere, being inclined and having the power, have the right to rise up and shake off the existing Government, and form a new one that suits them better"?[83] However, as we all know, the God of Providence ruled otherwise. At the critical Battle of Antietam, Robert E. Lee's famous lost order (Special Order #191), containing confidential information regarding the impending engagement, was found by an alert Union soldier as it lay on the ground wrapped with three cigars in a small parcel. The Army of Northern Virginia never fully recovered from the costly "draw" that followed, sustaining 13,724 casualties in a single day of fighting. It was as Lincoln said in his Second Inaugural Address:

> Neither party expected for the war the magnitude or the duration which it has already attained ...Both read the same Bible and pray to the same God, and each invokes His aid against the other...The prayers of both could not be answered. That of neither has been answered fully. The Almighty has His own purposes. "Woe unto the world because of offenses; for it must needs be that offenses come, but woe to that man by whom the offense cometh."
>
> If we shall suppose that American slavery is one of those offenses which, in the providence of God, must needs come, but which, having continued through His appointed time, He now wills to remove, and that He gives to both North and South this terrible war as the woe due to those by whom the offense came, shall we discern therein any departure from those divine attributes which the believers in a living God always ascribe to Him?[84]

ROME BACKS CONFEDERACY

Although the post-war trauma of radical reconstruction and the Fourteenth Amendment vindicated much of the South's pre-war paranoia, the Lord in His wisdom could see the greater danger that secession would have imposed. Something worse than Jefferson's "wolf" was lurking in the shadows, ex-"Father" Charles Chiniquy writes:

> Rome saw at once that the very existence of the United States was a formidable menace to her own life. From the very beginning she perfidiously sowed the germs of division and hatred between the two great sections of this country and succeeded in dividing the South from North on the burning question of slavery. That division was her golden opportunity to crush one by the other, and reign over the bloody ruins of both, a favored, long-standing policy. She hoped that the hour of her supreme triumph over this continent was come. She ordered the Emperor of France to be ready with an army in Mexico ready to support the South, and she bade all Roman Catholics to enroll themselves under the banners of slavery by joining themselves to the Democratic party. Only one bishop dared to disobey.[85]

Avro Manhattan expands on this "divide-and-conquer" papal stratagem:

> It was clearly in the interest of the Catholic Church, then, to intervene in the American Civil War. A territorial split into two separate, sovereign nations would have likewise halved the Protestant establishment....
>
> Examined within its historical context, the Church's grand strategy will thus be seen to be quite logical. When the Spanish empire had collapsed, the ecclesiastical monopoly of the Catholic Church in those lands formerly under the rule of Spain, collapsed with it. The Church's monolithic influence, which had stretched from the tip of South America to the northernmost point of California, was fragmented. Catholic hegemony was likewise fractionised and enfeebled, both denominationally and politically.
>
> The same formula would have applied to Protestant America, if the South were victorious in the Civil War. The diminution of U.S. stature would have spelt the automatic diminution of American Protestantism. This in its turn would have permitted the potential expansion of Catholicism in two smaller countries where Protestantism would no longer suffocate a young Catholic Church.[86]

A second motive for Rome's pro-Southern sentiment involved the political climate in the Western Hemisphere as a whole. As with the various democratic awakenings in Europe (1815–1848), the glow of United States liberty was also a constant inspiration to the Pope's benighted inhabitants in Latin America. Manhattan writes:

> The Civil War, the greatest disaster to befall the young American nation, was greeted with rejoicing at the Vatican. This for various motives. Among the most prominent: the great Protestant country, the contaminator of the Western Hemisphere, would disintegrate, divide into two or more States, and hence lose the fascination it exerted over Latin America; the war would strengthen the hand of the conservative elements and crush the liberals. The victory of the Southern States, and all that for which they stood, including the retention of slavery, would have consolidated conservatism throughout the Americas. There was nothing the Vatican wanted more.
>
> Owing to these and various other reasons, therefore, the Vatican saw in the outbreak of the American Civil War a manifest help of Divine Providence. *Civilta Cattolica*, then the official mouthpiece of the Vatican, had no doubts whatsoever about it. In addition to which it rejoiced that the U.S. at long last was broken and undone. To quote only one of the many joyous declarations: "...by manifest *Providence, that immense Babylon*

[the U.S.A.], founded on the principles of the revolution, is broken up and undone."[87]

To note a specific example of Vatican concern, the American government, led by Abraham Lincoln, had formally recognized the embattled Mexican regime of Benito Juárez while other nations, mainly at the direct instigation of Pius IX, acknowledged Maximilian of *Austria* (Remember the St. Leopold Foundation?) as Emperor of Mexico. Referring to Vatican plans for a Catholic-American empire in Mexico, Manhattan writes:

> As long as Lincoln and his federal government existed, the scheme was in deadly danger. Consequently Lincoln and the cause for which he stood had to go. For had he emerged the winner, he would not only have endangered the whole scheme of the Mexican Empire, but, by supporting progressive elements in other American countries, would have released tremendous latent forces throughout Latin America, to the further loss of the economic and political stranglehold of Catholicism in those countries. In these circumstances it became the urgent task of Vatican diplomacy to wreck Lincoln's government in the hour of its most dire peril.[88]

The Vatican's desire for a disruption of the American Union was actually put in motion as early as the *Dred Scott* case of 1857. In the **explosive wording** of Chief Justice Roger Taney, of Maryland, Negroes "had for more than a century before been regarded as beings of an inferior order" and "had no rights which the white man was bound to respect." He believed this opinion was "fixed and universal in the civilized portion of the white race."[89] Speaking only of the constitutional legitimacy of the decision and not its morality, Robert Bork assessed the insightful ruling as "the worst constitutional decision of the nineteenth century," and asserted that it "remained unchallenged as the worst in our history until the twentieth century provided rivals for that title."[90] Bork was also of the opinion that the *Dred Scott* case precipitated the war itself, writing:

> The ruling in *Dred Scott* at once became an explosive national issue. As historian Don Fehrenbacher noted, Taney had ruled "in effect that the Republican party was organized for an illegal purpose....No doubt it contributed significantly to the general accumulation of sectional animosity that made some kind of national crisis increasingly unavoidable." There is something wrong, as somebody has said, with a judicial power that can produce a decision it takes a civil war to overturn.[91]

In 1864, the Washington press eulogized the deceased judge with the words, "The Hon. old Roger B. Taney has earned the gratitude of the country by dying at last."[92] However, this was certainly not the opinion of the Vatican State, for Roger Taney, United States attorney general (1831–33), secretary of state (1833–34), and chief justice of the United States Supreme Court (1836–64), *was also a loyal son of the Roman Catholic Church!*

As to the Vatican's modus operandi of disrupting Lincoln's administration, Manhattan writes:

> It could do it by pursuing simultaneously several tactics: *(a)* by undermining his cause within his own rank and file, via American Catholics; *(b)* by undermining his cause in the eyes of world diplomacy; and *(c)* by actively helping his enemies. Vatican machinations against the U.S.A. at this most critical period of American history, although almost unnoticed, could nonetheless have had the most fateful results, as it combated Lincoln on all fronts.[93]

The Catholic Church in the South had the obvious advantage of rebelling in the open. Although the meager population of 1,367,000, or 4.8% of the region's inhabitants led one Jesuit author to describe the Southeastern quarter of the United States as "a Catholic Sahara," Rome's faithful few made a significant contribution that was certainly disproportionate to their numbers.

One of the most controversial topics of Civil War debate concerns the initial firing on Fort Sumter. Did the South Carolinians "jump the gun" as many Northern historians contend? Do you suppose it was just a *coincidence* that Brigadier General Pierre G. T. Beauregard, the Confederate commander at Charleston who directed Captain Charles Lee to commence firing on Sumter, just happened to be *another* Roman Catholic? The former superintendent of the United States military academy also held the Southern distinction of having produced the official Battle Flag of the Confederacy. And then there was Beauregard's significant rout of the Federals at Manassas in the opening battle of the war. According to historian Burke Davis, it was Rose O'Neal Greenhow, former queen of Washington society turned Confederate spy, who played a key role in the Southern victory at Bull Run:

> Her great coup gave the Confederates accurate word of Union army movements before the Battle of Bull Run/Manassas. She sent a message through the lines rolled in the hairdo of pretty Betty Duvall, one of her

agents, telling General Beauregard that the Union troops were marching.... A few days later Mrs. Greenhow added details, predicting the route of march of General Irvin McDowell's men. She did much to help the South win the first great battle.[94]

Rose was *also* a Roman Catholic. And for that matter, so was Robert Ould, head of the Confederate Secret Service, as well as the Assistant Secretary of War. Of the 362 leading Southerners named in the *Biographical Dictionary of the Confederacy*, a total of 32, or just under 9%, was listed as belonging to the Church of Rome. This figure was nearly *twice* their actual ratio to the Southern population as a whole. Furthermore, of the nine denominations listed—Baptist, Catholic, Christian, Episcopal, Jewish, Methodist, Methodist Episcopal, Presbyterian and Quaker—only three, the Episcopal, Methodist and Presbyterian, were better represented numerically. The "Catholic contribution" included: eleven generals, led by Beauregard and James A. Longstreet (the latter having converted after the war), Alpheus Baker, Harry Hays, Louis Hébert, Paul Hébert, Francis Nicholls, Franklin Gardner, William Preston, Walter Stevens, John Walker and William Whiting; one admiral, Raphael Semmes (of the famous Confederate cruiser *Alabama*); eight members of the Confederate Congress, Alexander DeClouet, David Carrol, John Perkins, Jr., Thomas Semmes, Ortho Singleton, William Smith, Edward Sparrow and Charles Viller'e; and three foreign diplomats, Juan Quintero, Pierre Soul'e and Thomas Devine (the latter having helped draw up the Constitution). Even Jefferson Davis was not unaffected by Romish influence. Although nonaffiliated with any denomination until embracing the Episcopal faith after the war, Davis did attend a Roman Catholic boarding school in Kentucky from ages eight through eleven. Author Cass Canfield states, "The three years he spent at the Saint Thomas Aquinas school made him very sympathetic toward Roman Catholicism, so much so that he came close to adopting the faith."[95] Finally, there is strong evidence that the very name "Dixie" has a direct Catholic connection. Davis relates:

> Unlike many Southern banks, the prospering Creole financial houses of New Orleans dealt at par; their notes were traded at face value, and no deductions were made or asked in the brisk trade which came downriver into the gay Louisiana city.
> The most popular of these bank notes was a ten-dollar bill. Its French heritage was clear in the cheery legend on each corner: "Dix." To unlettered tradesmen, stevedores and boatmen, these bills were only

"Dixies," and as their soundness became known in the great river basin, the lower South became "Dixieland," and the term was familiar on the exotic landscape of the waterway and its commerce.[96]

This bit of trivia becomes more meaningful when one learns that 808,690 Catholics, or 59% of the Church's total Southern membership, were found to reside within a 150-mile arc spreading out north and westward of New Orleans. General Pierre Gustave Toutant de Beauregard was a *Cajun*!

The majority of Catholic prelates in the 11 Southern dioceses were openly supportive of the Confederacy. Such men would include Bishops Quinlan (Mobile), McGill (Richmond), Elder (Natchez), Verot (Savannah), Martin (Natchitoches), Whelan (Nashville), Whelan (Wheeling) and Lynch (Charleston). Catholic author Benjamin Blied summarizes, "It is clear, then, that the bishops of the south were not unionists, but defenders of the rights of states and abettors of the confederacy."[97] And believe it or not, it was "Father" Abram Ryan, a chaplain for the Confederacy, who composed the patriotic poems, "Conquered Banner" and "The Sword of Robert E. Lee."

According to another Catholic authority, John Cogley, author of *Catholic America,* the anti-Union sentiment of Southern Catholics had a pronounced effect on their Northern counterparts:

> American Catholic opinion at the time was being formed in the slave-owning states, where the best-educated Catholics resided. These opinion molders, according to Orestes Brownson, the leading Catholic journalist of the time, were "intensely Southern in their sympathies" and "bitterly hostile to New England, or to Yankees." Brownson claimed that through them the Southern attitude was "diffused through the entire Catholic body even in the New England States themselves."[98]

James A. McMaster, Catholic editor of the New York *Freeman's Journal,* was especially vehement against Lincoln and his administration, declaring in an editorial of June 8, 1861:

> Let those heed it who, one year ago, scoffed when we said that the election of Lincoln would cause civil war! We say, now, that if there be not conservatism enough in the country to stop and to rebuke the course of Lincoln and his Cabinet, we will have a bloody revolution and anarchy, resulting in a military despotism, with a different man from Lincoln at its head. We speak what we see and know. Our conscience forces us to speak, whether it please or offend.[99]

McMaster's words must have offended a few folks, as his paper was shut down the following August, at which time he was also arrested and imprisoned in Fort Lafayette for nearly six weeks.

The easiest way for Northern Catholics to give subtle support to the Confederacy was to either *defend* or *dodge* the issue of slavery. Catholic author Robert Leckie states, "Catholic teaching on slavery was that it was a social evil but not necessarily a moral one."[100] In reference to only a *general* rebuke of slavery by Gregory XVI in 1839 which made the American institution "conspicuous by its absence," Leckie wrote, "Nevertheless, the church's position was ambiguous at best and evasive at worst."[101] The fact that Ursuline nuns and Jesuit priests owned slaves in the United States (not to mention the multiplied thousands held in Vatican bondage throughout South America) only added to this standard Catholic equivocation.

However, Catholic apologists are quick to point out the many patriotic remarks of various Northern prelates as well as the heroic exploits of Catholic Federals in battle, normally of Irish descent. What they don't like to discuss is the myriad of *motives* behind such words and deeds, which rarely have anything to do with a genuine love *for* America. For instance, when one realizes that such radical societies as the *Fenian Brotherhood* kept America's Irish acutely aware of the intense anti-British sentiment that prevailed back home, a totally different perspective is presented. The Catholic writer Blied confirms, "Many Irish soldiers in the northern army were ardently hoping to humiliate Britain by humbling her protégé, the south, and to aid their emerald fatherland."[102] This is primarily a reference to the integral economic relationship between Southern cotton and British textile mills. Also, a number of Confederate ships including the *Alabama* were built in British shipyards. Referring to a key leader of the Fenians, Blied adds, "As soon as the civil war broke out O'Mahoney [John O'Mahoney] began to recruit soldiers for the union army, realizing that thereby he would ultimately have at his disposal trained men to use against the hereditary oppressor."[103]

Other Northern immigrants were lured into the "cause" by the appealing *Homestead Act* which was conveniently passed in 1862. Furthermore, the Irish as a whole were resentful of the prospect of competing with blacks in the workplace, whether slave or free. Archbishop Hughes and other leaders were also well aware that their Church was already highly suspect due to the lingering influence of the nativist movement. And, of course, any good Catholic was allowed to fib (tell a white lie) under "extenuating circumstances," the Vatican theologian Liguori confirming, "It is a certain and a common opinion amongst all divines that for a just cause it is lawful to use equivocation (deception)... and to confirm it (equivocation) with an oath."[104]

There were, however, numbers of renegade Catholics who basically didn't give a flip what their church said about anything. A good many survivors of the potato famine had the character to trade legitimate loyalty for a full stomach. Despite his Catholic christening and fanatically papist wife, General William Sherman *despised* the Church of Rome. He pretty much wiped out the parish belonging to the notoriously pro-Confederate Patrick Lynch, bishop of Charleston.

In the fall of 1861, Lincoln put Hughes on the spot by requesting that he represent the United States abroad to dissuade European intervention on behalf of the Confederacy. French troops were already in Mexico while English forces had been deployed to Canada. The crafty prelate agreed to go but not as an official representative of the American government. The Jesuit historian Hennesey confirms what we would expect: "Major papal officials were cool to the northern cause."[105] "Father" Hennesey also acknowledged the existence of a diplomatic communiqué from British agent Odo Russell who informed the foreign office on July 30, 1864, of an audience with Pius IX, who "would not conceal from me the fact that all his sympathies were with the Southern Confederacy and he wished them all success."[106] Hughes' own report to the Secretary of State was equally pessimistic: "There is no love for the United States on the other side of the water."[107]

And in a tactical counterstroke that is rarely mentioned in history textbooks, Russia's Tsar Alexander II notified Lincoln that he was willing to align his troops with the North. The Russian-born historian, Carl Wrangell-Rokassowsky, confirmed:

> Paragraph 3 of the instructions given to Admiral Lessovsky by Admiral Krabbe, at that time Russian Secretary of the Navy, dated, July 14, 1863, ordered the Russian Fleet, in case of war, to attack the enemies' commercial shipping and their colonies so as to cause them the greatest possible damage. The same instructions were given to Admiral Popov, Commander of the Russian Asiatic Fleet.[108]

Although Protestant Britain was willing to compromise ideologically to secure vital economic interests, Russia's support of the North was consistent with her perennial estrangement from Rome. In reference to the Baltic Fleet anchored at Alexandria, Virginia, in 1863, Griffin writes: "The presence of the Russian Navy helped the Union enforce a devastating naval blockade against the Southern states which denied them access to critical supplies from Europe."[109]

On October 18, 1862, a theoretically neutral Pius IX took a significant poke at Lincoln in a pair of letters sent to Hughes and Archbishop John Odin of New Orleans. Coming to the rescue as "the administrator and the Vice-regent of Him who is the Author of Peace," Pius ordered his shepherds to convey his wishes to Washington, D.C.:

> Apply all your study and exertion with the people and the **chief ruler** [Lincoln], to restore forthwith the desired tranquillity and peace...Neither omit to *admonish*, and exhort the people *and their supreme ruler, even in our name*...We are confident [he wrote] that they would comply with our *paternal admonition*.[110]

Although neither archbishop felt "led" to personally admonish President Lincoln, the pontiff's warning was "promulgated among the laity and created much indignation throughout the North."[111] However, Manhattan writes:

> The real significance of the Pope's "admonition" to Lincoln, however, cannot be properly understood until it is remembered that no such words were addressed to Lincoln's opponents. The pope never sent his "paternal admonition" to the Confederate Government. This owing to one simple reason, that the Vatican was in the closest and friendliest relations with it.[112]

Something else that is generally missed by the casual observer is that the Pope's "desired tranquility and peace" *in the fall of 1862* could only be orchestrated by a formal Northern recognition of the Confederate States of America!

A trickle-down effect of this subtle correspondence rattled Lincoln's cage. Manhattan relates what took place the following summer:

> In another instance of the Church's effort to artfully aid the South, the hierarchy was active, *sub rosa*, in the mobilisation of American Catholics against the military machine of the North. This was done by organising the great Draft Riots in New York.
>
> Being the master of indirect, covert manipulation, the Church employed racial and other factors to achieve its objectives. Here it promoted the real or imagined grievances of the Irish by mobilising them against conscription of men deemed necessary for the urgent strengthening of the Union forces.

It is significant that it took the Catholic Church, on the spot, only ten days after the Battle of Gettysburg (from July 13 to July 17, 1863) to attempt to sabotage the North in order to help the Confederates with whom the Vatican was openly sympathising.[113]

Davis gives us the following highlights of the "standard" Catholic riot:

They burned the draft office on Broadway and a dozen more buildings. They looted and burned several homes of wealthy families on Lexington Avenue, burned a Methodist Church, a Negro orphanage, stores, factories, and saloons where they were refused free liquor.

A young Negro was hanged on Clarkson Street, and men danced and sang around him while a fire roasted his flesh. At least thirty Negroes were shot, hanged or stamped to death...Numbers of policemen were wounded and a few killed. The mob grew until it was estimated at between 50,000 and 70,000 people...Many volunteer officers fell under rifle and shotgun fire from windows on upper floors of buildings...

Pitched battles continued. Strong parties of soldiers, policemen, and firemen were defeated. A Marine detachment was driven off by a mob on Grand Street...at Thirty-fourth Street and Second Avenue, 300 policemen with two field guns stood off a mob of 10,000, finally clearing the area.[114]

Horace Greeley, editor of *The New York Tribune*, chided Hughes to control "his people." The aloof Archbishop responded that he was no "head constable," but finally agreed to address the mob after *two* days of violence. "They call you rioters, but I cannot see a rioter's face among you,"[115] he declared unashamedly from the balcony of his official residence. All this means is that he probably had his fingers crossed behind his back. (See Liguori.) Property damage was estimated at $1.5 million with casualties exceeding 1,000.

However, the "timing" of this Catholic rampage, coming in the aftermath of Gettysburg, effected considerable tactical repercussions for the Army of the Potomac. Henry Commager wrote, "This was equivalent to a Confederate victory, for Meade's army was so weakened by detachments for guard duty in Northern cities, that he was unable to take the offensive against Lee after Gettysburg."[116] Yet, according to the majority of Civil War authorities, Meade should never have allowed "Bobby Lee" to escape in the first place. Lee had ordered the now-infamous Pickett's Charge against the strong remonstrance of Longstreet. And for the third time in as many days, "Pete's" unheeded advice cost Lee dearly.

After Pickett's division was decimated on the slopes of Cemetery Ridge, Lee attempted a hasty retreat back to Virginia, but a swollen Potomac refused to cooperate. For many days Lee's forces remained stuck on the wrong side of the river, dreading Meade's inevitable coup de grâce. However, for some "strange" reason, Meade was a no-show and Lee finally escaped, causing Lincoln to bemoan, "Our army held the war in the hollow of their hand, and they would not close it."[117] In what was undoubtedly the turning point of the war, a two-sided "coincidence" would decide the day. Had Longstreet's counsel prevailed, Lee might have gone on to Washington; had Meade seized the moment, the Confederacy would have been shattered. Although perplexing on the surface, the actions of both generals were at least consistent with their *religious* convictions. The Southern Longstreet and the Northern Meade were *both* Roman Catholics!

With "victories" such as Gettysburg costing 23,000 casualties, Lincoln grew increasingly dependent upon foreign manpower. William Seward, secretary of war, soberly acknowledged, "The immigration of a large mass from Europe would of itself decide the contest."[118] In a bold move to mitigate this advantage, Jefferson Davis turned to the Vatican. The Confederate president commissioned Colonel Dudley Mann, then in Brussels, to secure an audience with the Pope. On November 11, Mann presented an official letter to the papal secretary, Cardinal Antonelli. Davis biographer Hudson Strode writes:

> Davis's early years in a Catholic boys' school in Kentucky had given him a profound respect for the Roman Catholic Church, and his regard shone through in the document. Addressing the Pope as "Very Venerable Sovereign Pontiff," Davis thanked him for his peace exhortation to the Catholic clergy in America. He assured His Holiness that the Southern people, "threatened even on their own hearths with the most cruel oppression and terrible carnage," fought "merely to resist the devastation of our country... and to force them to let us live in peace under the protection of our own institutions and under our laws."
>
> To Cardinal Antonelli, Mann disclosed the real purpose of his visit. "But for the European recruits received by the North" he said, "The Lincoln Administration, in all likelihood would have been compelled some time before to retire from the contest." The continued destruction of life, he suggested, was the result of beguiling Catholic Irishmen and South Germans from their homes "to take up arms against citizens who had never harmed or wronged them in the slightest degree."[119]

Cardinal Antonelli replied that the sentiments expressed in his letter were "entirely in accordance with the disposition and character of the august head of the Catholic Church."[120] Two days later, Mann was received in private audience by the pontiff who *appeared* "visibly moved" by the Confederate crisis. On December 23, 1863, in his own handwriting, Pius IX addressed himself to **"The Illustrious and Honorable Jefferson Davis, President of the Confederate States of America."** Originally in Latin, the English translation as listed in the Official Naval Record reads as follows:

ILLUSTRIOUS AND *HONORABLE SIR*: Health! We have received with all fitting kindness the gentlemen sent by *Your Excellency* to deliver us your letters bearing date the 23rd of September last. We certainly experienced no small pleasure when we learned from the same gentlemen and the letters of *Your Excellency* with what emotions of joy and gratitude toward us you were affected, *illustrious* and *honorable sir,* when you were first made acquainted with our letters to those reverend brethren, John, archbishop of New York, and John, archbishop of New Orleans, written on the 18th of October of last year, in which we again and again urged and exhorted the same reverend brethren that, as behooved their distinguished piety and their episcopal charge, they should most zealously use every effort in our name also, to bring to an end the fatal civil war that had arisen in those regions, and that those people of America might at length attain mutual peace and concord, and be united in mutual charity. And very grateful was it to us, *illustrious* and *honorable sir,* to perceive that you and those people were animated with the same feelings of peace and tranquility which we so earnestly inculcated in the letters mentioned as having been addressed to the aforesaid reverend brethren. And would that other people also of those regions, and their rulers, seriously considering how grievous and mournful a thing is intestine war, would be pleased with tranquil minds to embrace and enter upon counsels of peace. We indeed shall not cease with most fervent prayer to beseech and pray God, the omnipotent and all-good, to pour out the spirit of Christian charity and peace upon all those people of America and deliver them from the evils so great with which they are afflicted.

And of the most merciful Lord of compassion himself, we likewise pray that He may illumine *Your Excellency* with the light of His grace, and may conjoin you in perfect love with ourself.

Given at Rome, at St. Peter's, December 3d, in the year 1863, and of our Pontificate the eighteenth.

Pius P.P. IX[121]

Cutting through all the pontifical "hot air," the reader will note that Pius specifically addressed Davis as the *President of the Confederate States of America*. Because any pope is a consummate chameleon, Pius was not about to *officially* commit himself to either side, but was willing to pass along an "inferential recognition" in the words of Secretary of State Benjamin. Copies of this letter were quickly circulated among the Irish on both sides of the Atlantic. In a letter to Mann, Secretary Benjamin related, "The President has been much gratified at learning the cordial reception which you received from the Pope and the publication of the correspondence here has had a good effect."[122]

Although some would play down the significance of this backhanded endorsement, President Lincoln was not one of them, stating, "This letter of the Pope has entirely changed the nature and the ground of the war."[123] Secretary Seward spoke in a similar vein:

> "The design of this quasi-recognition of Mr. Davis, who is thrice addressed as 'Illustrious and Honorable President' is manifest," he declared. "It is a last effort to get up some feeling against the North among the Catholics and to use perhaps the influence of the Holy Father to stop his Irish votaries from volunteering."[124]

As the Pope's recognition of "President Davis" became known among the Northern Irish, a substantial increase in Irish desertions was observed. Although disputed by Catholic writer Theodore Maynard, some estimates were put as high as 72%.[125]

Throughout these years of *disorder, destruction, deception* and *division*, Abraham Lincoln often looked to Heaven for strength and direction. Although Mrs. Lincoln stated that her husband never belonged to any one particular denomination, even the official *American Catholic Historical Researchers* (as cited by Blied) acknowledges, "Mr. Lincoln's father, Thomas Lincoln, was a Baptist, according to the best authorities, and Lincoln attended the church of that denomination in his early years in Indiana."[126] He also attended the Presbyterian church while in Washington. It is the opinion of several Christian historians that the President became a born-again believer at the time of Gettysburg. Despite the pressures and demands of political office, Lincoln's basic sincerity shines through many of his letters and private musings as the war took its terrible toll. On one occasion he wrote, "I am satisfied that when the Almighty wants me to do, or not to do, a particular thing He finds a way of letting me know it." [127] Johnson elaborates:

> He thus waited, as the Cabinet papers show, for providential guidance at certain critical points of the war. He never claimed to be the personal agent of God's will, as everyone else seemed to be doing, but he wrote, "If it were not for my firm belief in an overruling providence, it would be difficult for me, in the midst of such complications of affairs, to keep my reason in its seat. But I am confident that the Almighty has His plans and will work them out, and they will be the wisest and the best for us." When asked if God was on the side of the North, he replied, "I am not at all concerned about that, for I know the Lord is always on the side of right. It is my constant anxiety and prayer that I and this nation should be on the Lord's side." Hence his determination throughout to do the moral thing, as he put it, "I am not bound to win, but I am bound to be true. I am not bound to succeed, but I am bound to live up to the light I have."[128]

As the Lord would have it, the President met Reverend Charles Chiniquy in 1856 when Lincoln was still an attorney. The reader will recall that Chiniquy was a Catholic priest in Canada who eventually found the Saviour and became a Presbyterian minister. His credentials as the leading force of the Canadian Temperance Movement are impressive. The city of Montreal presented him with a gold medal inscribed, "TO FATHER CHINIQUY, APOSTLE OF TEMPERANCE" on one side, and "HONOR TO HIS VIRTUES, ZEAL AND PATRIOTISM" on the other. The Canadian Parliament voted him an Address and £500 as a token of the nation's gratitude. Even the Protestant *Independent Order of Rechabites of Canada* honored the Catholic priest for his battle with the liquor traffic.[129]

In 1851, Pius IX selected Chiniquy to lead a colonization project into the heart of the Mississippi Valley. By the fall of that year, 5,000 French Catholics aided him in establishing the village of St. Anne near Kankakee, Illinois. Jealous of Chiniquy's accomplishments, Bishop O'Regan of Chicago directed certain unscrupulous associates, in 1856, to charge him with slandering the bishop, whereupon the defendant engaged the legal services of Abraham Lincoln. The wicked allegations were subsequently dismissed and a warm friendship was forged between Chiniquy and Lincoln.

Throughout Chiniquy's inglorious career as a priest, he had studied his Bible and grown increasingly troubled with the errors of Romanism. Finally, under vigorous cross-examination by the bishop of Dubuque and a Jesuit priest, "Father" Chiniquy became "Brother" Chiniquy in April of 1858, later writing:

> In that instant, all things which, as a Roman Catholic, I had to believe to be saved—the chaplets, indulgences, scapularies, auricular confession, invocation of the Virgin, holy water, masses, purgatory, etc., vanished from my mind like a huge tower, when struck at the foundation, and crumbles to the ground. Jesus alone remained in my mind as the Saviour of my soul.[130]

When the converted priest returned to St. Anne, the power of the Holy Ghost fell upon his precious flock. News of the awakening attracted over 100 ministers of various denominations to witness the holy scene for themselves. On the 15th of April, 1860, Chiniquy presented the Presbyterian church of the United States with nearly *2,000* converts, including himself, who were subsequently received into full communion with that body.[131]

Later the same year, Chiniquy's worst fears were confirmed concerning his venerable friend: "At the end of August, I learned from a Roman Catholic priest, whom, by the mercy of God, I had persuaded to leave the errors of popery, that there was a plot among them to assassinate the president, I thought it was my duty to go and tell him what I knew."[132] Chiniquy's autobiography goes on to relate how Lincoln was not surprised by this warning, as White House security had already confirmed a Jesuit connection to the previous assassination threats in Baltimore while he was en route to the February Presidential Inauguration. Lincoln was also quite impressed with Professor Morse's exposé of the St. Leopold Foundation.

The President then asked if Chiniquy could explain why a number of Democratic newspapers were circulating erroneous reports that he had been baptized a Roman Catholic. Chiniquy informed him that he was being specifically targeted for assassination as an apostate Catholic. Although such a scenario may appear incredible to one unfamiliar with the voluminous history of Vatican treachery, it is unfortunately all *too* accurate, as even the writings of the pope will confirm: "The killing of an heretic was no murder." (Gregory VII, *Jure Canonico*)[133] Lincoln acknowledged the historical consequences of Chiniquy's assessment, stating:

> If I were fighting against a Protestant South, as a nation, there would be no danger of assassination. The nations who read the Bible fight bravely on the battlefields, but they do not assassinate their enemies. The pope and the Jesuits, with their infernal Inquisition, are the only organized

powers in the world which have recourse to the dagger of the assassin to murder those whom they cannot convince with their arguments or conquer with the sword.[134]

While the existence of such rumors purporting Lincoln's Catholicity was acknowledged by *The American Catholic Historical Researcher* in 1905, less than 20 years after Chiniquy's account, the deceitful editor postdated the story's inception to 1869[135] in an attempt to discredit Chiniquy. Fortunately, another Catholic writer, Dr. Benjamin J. Blied, messed up things by citing two earlier examples of the same rumor. Referring to one, Abbot Wimmer of Pennsylvania, Blied stated, "Later in 1861 he relayed the following information to Munich: 'It is surprising that the president of the United States is a Catholic, but only a bad one.' "[136] Concerning a eulogy that was written for the slain president by a certain Father Weninger and printed in the *Berichie* of the St. Leopold Society, he says, "Weninger next put forth the opinion that Lincoln had been baptized a Catholic and reared as such in his youth but that he had drifted from the faith when he moved from Kentucky to Illinois."[137]

On April 14, 1865, John Wilkes Booth fired a single shot into the brain of Abraham Lincoln while he was attending Ford's Theater in Washington. Mrs. Lincoln recalled his last words:

> He said he wanted to visit the Holy Land and see those places hallowed by the footprints of the Saviour. He was saying there was no city he so much desired to see as Jerusalem. And with the words half spoken on his tongue, the bullet of the assassin entered the brain, and the soul of the great and good President was carried by the angels to the New Jerusalem above.[138]

The *facts* made public during the conspiracy trial are as follows: The meeting place of the assassins, referred to by President Johnson as "The nest where the egg was hatched,"[139] was owned by Mary Surratt. Should we be surprised that Mrs. Surratt was a fanatical Roman Catholic? On the very day after the murder she was heard to say, "The death of Abraham Lincoln is no more than the death of any nigger in the army."[140] The sworn affidavits confirm that her residence at 561 H Street, Washington, D.C., was a common rendezvous of numerous priests in the city.

Mrs. Surratt's son, John, had been studying for the priesthood. Following the assassination, an underground railroad of Catholic priests smuggled him all the way to the Vatican via Montreal and Liverpool. When John was finally captured and extradited to the States for trial, he was wearing the papal uniform of the 9th Company of the Zouaves.

Michael O'Laughlin, who was supposed to murder General Grant, was also a Roman Catholic. John Lloyd, the man who hid Booth's carbine, was a Catholic. Although Booth's companion, David Herold, professed to be a Protestant, McCarty states that he was a "graduate of Jesuit College at Georgetown."[141] The doctor who set Booth's broken leg, Samuel Mudd, was a Catholic. Even Richard Garrett, the owner of the tobacco barn where Booth was shot, was a Catholic.

John Wilkes Booth and George Atzerodt, though nominal Protestants (Booth's parents were Episcopalian), frequently attended mass at St. Mary's, St. Patrick's or St. Aloysian's Catholic Churches. A few hours before his death, Booth wrote, "I can never repent; God made me the instrument of His punishment."[142] He died with the Catholic medal, "Agnus Dei" (Lamb of God), around his neck.

As this provocative chapter is drawn to a conclusion, a final witness bearing impeccable credentials is called forth to silence the skeptic and stir the indifferent. Brigadier General Thomas M. Harris U.S.V. was one of the seven generals and two colonels who comprised the 1865 military commission that tried and condemned the conspirators in the assassination of Abraham Lincoln. These men were described by the fallen president's secretaries, John G. Nicolay and John Hay, as "officers not only of high rank and distinction, but of unusual weight of character."[143] One of these, General Lew Wallace, went on to author the novel *Ben Hur*. General Harris was an accomplished physician.

After a thorough investigation of the evidence at hand, General Harris published his findings in an explosive volume entitled *Rome's Responsibility for the Assassination of Abraham Lincoln*. Among other subjects previously discussed in *What Hath God Wrought!*, Harris concurs with: Rome's infiltration through immigration,[144] Reverend Chiniquy's integrity[145] and the pope's letter to Jeff Davis which triggered a 72% desertion rate among the Irish;[146] concluding "every citizen who is loyal to the Roman Catholic Church is an enemy to our government."[147] The general believed that:

> It is clear that *Rome* is rapidly *getting control of all the sources of power in the United States*, both in civil and military affairs; that she is doing so in pursuance of a well considered and wisely laid plan, and *for the very purpose of subverting our government.*[148]

As to the blame for the assassination itself, Harris writes:

> The *Jesuit* plans with the utmost art and cunning, unhampered by any moral restraints, and always with the utmost secrecy; and carries out his plans in the dark. We think, however, that in this case, we have succeeded in tracing him through all the devious wanderings of his dark and slimy path, and, in fixing upon him the responsibility for the assassination of President Lincoln.[149]

After presenting his case, General Harris concludes:

> Thus the history of this great crime reveals to us *Rome's responsibility for the assassination of Abraham Lincoln,* not as an individual man, however much of personal hatred on the part of the Jesuits might have led them to plan for his death, but as the head of the nation they desired to destroy.[150]

While under a two-year house arrest at Ft. Monroe, Jefferson Davis spent Christmas of 1866 opening presents with his wife Varina by his side. The thoughtfulness of an old supporter especially brightened his day; Strode relates:

> Outstanding among the gifts to the ex-President from strangers was a large inscribed photograph of Pius IX. At the bottom was written in Latin: "Come unto me all ye that labor and are cast down; and I will refresh you." **About a carved decoration at the top of the wooden frame hung a chaplet [crown] of thorns woven by the Pope's own fingers**. The signature of Pius was attested under the seal of Cardinal Barnado. Sympathetic attention from as far away as Rome and from such an illustrious source was gratifying indeed.[151]

> "If the American people could learn what I know of the fierce hatred of the priests of Rome against our institutions, our schools, our most sacred rights, and our so dearly bought liberties, they would drive them out as traitors."
>
> – Abraham Lincoln, 1864[152]

XV

A Costly Mistake

> *"Knowledge puffeth up."* (I Corinthians 8:1b)

I N THE POPE'S initial correspondence to Jefferson Davis, December 3, 1863, he assured the Confederate president of his continuous prayer that the American people be delivered from *"the evils so great with which they are afflicted."* The novice would assume that Pius had in mind the normal "evils" of war-related calamities. Nothing could be further from the truth.

Any doubt as to the Vatican's intense hatred of American liberties was removed in December, 1864, by the Pope's wild-eyed pronouncement known as the *Syllabus of Errors*. Issued as a supplement to the encyclical *Quanta cura*, it was addressed to the bishops of the Roman Catholic Church (including those in the United States) and basically listed the Pope's personal condemnation of the world's 80 worst heresies.

A mini-sample would include the following: Under the heading, "INDIFFERENTISM, LATITUDINARIANISM," Proposition 15 condemns the principle that *"every man is free to embrace and profess that religion which, guided by the light of reason, he shall consider true."* And belonging to this same class, Proposition 18 denounces the principle that *"Protestantism is nothing more than another form of the same true Christian religion, in which form it is given to please God equally as in the Catholic Church."*

Under the class, "ERRORS CONCERNING THE CHURCH AND HER RIGHTS," Proposition 24 condemns the tenet that *"the Church has not the power of using force, nor has she any temporal power, direct or indirect."*

In the sixth category entitled, "ERRORS ABOUT CIVIL SOCIETY, CONSIDERED BOTH IN ITSELF AND IN ITS RELATION TO THE CHURCH," Proposition 55 attacks that principle of government which provides that *"the Church ought to be separated from the State, and the State from the Church."*

The tenth and concluding heading of papal despicability involves "ERRORS HAVING REFERENCE TO MODERN LIBERALISM." Among these, Proposition 77 anathematizes the idea which asserts that *"in the present day it is no longer expedient that the Catholic religion should be held as the only religion of the state, to the exclusion of other forms of worship."*

Proposition 78 condemns the principle of toleration which follows the recognition of other religions besides the Roman Catholic Church: *"Hence it has been wisely decided by law, in some Catholic countries, that persons coming to reside therein shall enjoy the public exercise of their own peculiar worship."*[1]

Although the average American Catholic was never made aware of these embarrassing disclosures, the *Syllabus* was officially sanctioned by the forty bishops and seven archbishops in attendance at the *Second National Council of Roman Catholic Hierarchy in the United States* which convened in Baltimore, October, 1866. Consequently, should the Pope cast a "Bull" at the United States, his American flocks would have to back him, *or else!* The pastoral letter issued by the council dogmatically enjoined that obedience to the civil power of government "must always be exercised according to God's law."[2]

Former secretary of the navy Thompson illuminates the hidden repercussions of the *Syllabus* for America:

> In this extraordinary document it is asserted, with dogmatic brevity and terseness, that it does not appertain "to the *civil* power to define what are the rights and limits within which *the Church* may exercise authority;" that its authority must be decided upon by itself, that is, by the pope, and exercised *"without the permission and assent of the civil government;"* and that, "in the case of conflicting laws between the two powers," the laws of *the Church* must prevail over those of *the State.* Here, every thing is plain—nothing equivocal. The subordination of the State to the Church, and the substitution of the papal hierarchy for the people in enacting and

enforcing such laws as the pope may think necessary for the Church, are distinctly and emphatically asserted.

It requires no pause for reflection to see how directly a "Catholic system" of government, thus constructed, would conflict with the existing civil institutions of the United States. Nor do we need a prophet to tell us that the establishment of such a system here would be followed by their immediate destruction. To permit a church—*any* church—to decide upon the validity or invalidity of our laws after their enactment, or to dictate, beforehand, what laws should or should not be passed, would be to deprive the people of all the authority they have retained in their own hands, and to make such church the governing power, instead of them.[3]

In the process of time, the U.S. State Department began to grow exasperated with these Vatican shenanigans. Sustained papal sympathies for the Confederacy, the portentous *Syllabus* and a half dozen Catholic assassins finally led to the official breaking of diplomatic ties with the "Holy See" in 1867. (The full American legation at the Vatican had been installed by President Polk in 1847.) Although the Pope's desire for a severed Union had not been realized, the ensuing years would give him plenty about which to shout, despite some temporary setbacks for his own Church in the South.

RADICAL RECONSTRUCTION

The surest evidence that a legitimate Southern apprehension concerning impending Northern aggression had precipitated formal secession can be seen by the events which transpired between 1865 and 1867. Abraham Lincoln's last speech on April 11, 1865, was an appeal for a compassionate reconstruction policy. As early as December 8, 1863, the President had promised full executive recognition for any state which could induce at least 10% of its voting populace to take an oath to support the Constitution and abide by federal laws and proclamations regarding slaves. The Johnson-Sherman articles of surrender reflected "malice toward none and charity for all"; the paroled soldiers and officers of the Confederacy would be henceforth unmolested and exempt from Federal prosecution.

Following the President's assassination, Andrew Johnson strove to promote his predecessor's views. With four Southern states already reconstructed under Lincoln, the new chief executive appointed provisional civil governors in the remaining seven states, enjoining them to summon state constitutions. While the new state governments were being assembled,

Johnson commissioned a delegation of observers to report on Southern attitudes and conditions. The consensus of their findings was that the former Confederates had "accepted defeat" in the overwhelming majority. "I am satisfied that the mass of thinking people in the South accept the situation of affairs in good faith," wrote General Grant to his superior. "Slavery and State rights they regard as having been settled forever by the highest tribunal—arms—that man can resort to."[4]

The accuracy of this assessment was corroborated in an eloquent letter drafted by Virginia attorney Alexander H. H. Stuart on behalf of General Robert E. Lee and also signed by Wade Hampton and 30 additional Confederate leaders. A "leaf" from this Southern "olive branch" reads as follows:

> Whatever opinions may have prevailed in the past with regard to African slavery or the right of a State to secede from the Union, we believe we express the almost unanimous judgment of the Southern people when we declare that they consider these questions were decided by the war, and that it is their intention in good faith to abide by that decision...
>
> The great want of the South is peace. The people earnestly desire tranquility and restoration of the Union. They deplore disorder and excitement as the most serious obstacle to their prosperity. They ask a restoration of their rights under the Constitution. They desire relief from oppressive misrule. Above all, they would appeal to their countrymen for the re-establishment, in the Southern States, of that which has justly been regarded as the birth-right of every American, the right of self-government. Establish these on a firm basis, and we can safely promise, on behalf of the Southern people, that they will faithfully obey the Constitution and laws of the United States, treat the negro populations with kindness and humanity and fulfill every duty incumbent on peaceful citizens, loyal to the Constitution of their country.[5]

When the members-elect from the reconstructed states arrived for the convening of Congress on December 4, 1865, the Republican caucus ordered the clerks of both houses to omit their names when reading the roll call. With the upholding of this unethical maneuver by a simple majority vote (the Southerners obviously not voting), the Southern legislators were deprived of their duly elected seats.

A joint committee of 15 radical Republicans ostensibly complained that the Negro was being deprived of his civil rights by a series of labor-related *Black Codes*. General Sherman was one of the few leaders with a grasp on reality, declaring,

No matter what change we may desire in the feelings and thoughts of the people South, we cannot accomplish it by force.... You can hardly yet realize how completely this country has been devastated, and how completely humbled every man of the South is.[6]

Whereas Lincoln and Johnson held that the Southern states had never been out of the Union and thereby were entitled to normal constitutional relations with the Federal government, fanatics such as Thaddeus Stevens of Pennsylvania and Charles Sumner of Massachusetts countered that they had, in fact, committed political suicide and were consequently under the exclusive jurisdiction of Congress. Stevens brazenly declared, **"We shall treat the South as a defeated enemy."**[7] As such, the Pennsylvania lawmaker viewed his sectional rivals as "conquered provinces" which *might* be upgraded to territories in order to "learn the principles of freedom and eat the fruit of foul rebellion."[8]

Although excluded from federal representation in violation of Article V of the Constitution, which reads, "No state, without its consent, shall be deprived of equal suffrage in the Senate," as well as by Article I, Section 2, which enjoins each state to have at least one representative in Congress, the reconstructed state governments continued to function at the local level. When this "rump" Congress proposed the Thirteenth Amendment on February 1, 1865, banning slavery, the "unruly" Southern states joined their Northern counterparts in a smooth ratification process.

However, when the radical Republicans showed their hand by proposing the controversial Fourteenth Amendment on June 16, 1866, the Southern states were no longer in a conciliatory mood. For one thing, Congress could never have garnered the two-thirds vote required by Article V for submission of the amendment for ratification had the Southern states been seated. It was rightly surmised that the subtle prohibition of "nor shall any State deprive any person of life, liberty or property without due process of law" would subject all future state legislation to the scrutiny and caprice of an expanded federal judiciary. Orville Browning, a Northern senator from Illinois, and a member of Johnson's Cabinet, warned, "Be assured that if this new provision be engrafted in the Constitution, it will, in time, change the entire structure and texture of our government, and sweep away all the guarantees of safety devised and provided by our patriotic sires of the Revolution."[9]

With 37 states in the Union at this time, at least 28 would have to ratify the "illegally" proposed amendment to make it a part of the Constitution. On the first go-around, only 21 states voted "yea." The amendment was rejected by the ten Southern states of Texas, Arkansas, Virginia, North Carolina,

South Carolina, Georgia, Alabama, Florida, Louisiana and Mississippi (Mississippi's rejection arriving late), as well as by Kentucky, Maryland and Delaware. Three states did not vote: Iowa, Nebraska and California.[10] Furthermore, Oregon, Ohio and New Jersey later decided to rescind their initial ratification.

Although he had lost the vote fair and square, Thaddeus declared in a speech to Congress,

> The punishment of traitors has been wholly ignored by a treacherous Executive and a sluggish Congress. To this issue I desire to devote the small remnant of my life...Strip a proud nobility of their bloated estates...reduce them to a level with plain republicans; send them forth to labor and teach their children to enter the workshops or handle a plow, and you will thus humble the proud traitors.[11]

Senator Stevens never did explain how this same cream-puff, genteel nobility managed to beat the stuffing out of the Union Army until finally being overcome by attrition. *The Dictionary of American History* cut through his self-righteous rhetoric by declaring, "Historians now recognize that there was an **economic** motive in Radical policy, for their control of the National Government favored northeastern manufacturing and financial interests against those of the West and South."[12]

The Southern states were promptly informed that ratification of the Fourteenth Amendment would now be the sine qua non (price of admission) back into the Union. Kennedy points out the stark hypocrisy of this new Republican mandate:

> The North, in 1866, removed the Southern States from the Union. This was the same North that in 1861 refused to allow the South to secede from the Union. This same North now declared the Southern States to be non-states. To get back into the Union (that originally the South did not want to be a part of anyway, and from which it had previously been denied the right to secede), it was required to perform the function of a state in that Union, while still officially no longer a part of the Union, by ratifying an amendment that previously as states in the Union it had legally rejected![13]

After 750,000 Americans forfeited their lives to prevent the South from peacefully seceding, these same Southern states were flippantly informed that they were not a part of the Union after all!

To help the Southerners "see the light," Stevens and company railroaded the first of three Reconstruction Acts on March 2, 1867. The states that were previously judged "reconstructed enough" to ratify the Thirteenth Amendment, would now be dissolved by Congressional fiat. The South was subsequently re-invaded and divided into five military districts with a commander of the rank of brigadier general, or higher, in each locale. Senator Doolittle of Wisconsin declared, "The people of the South have rejected the constitutional amendment, and therefore we will march upon them and force them to adopt it at the point of the bayonet, and establish military power over them until they do adopt it."[14]

Civilians would be henceforth tried by martial law, despite the fact that the United States Supreme Court had already ruled in the *Milligan* case three months earlier that "military courts were unconstitutional except under such war conditions as might make the operation of civil courts impossible."[15] Historian James Truslow Adams also noted that, "There was even talk in Congress of impeaching the Supreme Court for its decisions!"[16]

Furthermore, Southern whites who had aided the Confederacy were disenfranchised *from* voting while the freedmen *were* granted suffrage, despite the fact that Northern blacks were *not* so privileged.

Although President Johnson vetoed the Reconstruction Act, declaring, "I cannot reconcile a military jurisdiction of this kind with the Constitution,"[17] the Stevens-dominated Congress overrode his veto that very day. (Johnson would later avoid being impeached himself over a petty technicality by the thin margin of a single vote.) Navy Secretary Gideon Wells called it "a terrific engine...a governmental monstrosity."[18] General Schofield wrote Grant from the South about the "absolute unfitness of the negroes as a class," and their belief that freedom means "they are to live in idleness and be fed by the government."[19] Even Governor Oliver Morton, who had defeated the Copperhead movement in his native Indiana, declared that it was "impossible to conceive of instantly admitting this mass of ignorance to the ballot."[20] And for the record, good ol' Thaddeus "His-truth-is-marching-on" Stevens was in perfect agreement with these "racist" views. After all, didn't he want to *punish* the South?

> In my county, there are fifteen hundred escaped slaves. If they are specimens of the negroes of the south, they are not qualified to vote.[21]

The brief era of carpetbag-Negro rule in the South did not make for many precious memories. "Such a Saturnalia of robbery and jobbery," wrote Lord Bryce concerning these times, "has seldom been seen in any civilized country, and certainly never before under the forms of free self-govern-ment."[22] Weyl summarizes this dispensation of Northern revenge:

> While most of these state regimes were white-dominated none could have long survived without the regimental Negro vote. The classic instance of Negro rule in the South is the Reconstruction governments of South Carolina during 1868–74. These regimes were characterized by unabashed corruption combined with monumental ignorance. To the white citizenry of South Carolina, they were remembered not only as institutionalized theft, but as collective degradation.
>
> During these six years there was universal Negro suffrage in the Palmetto State and colored voters decisively outnumbered white. Thus in 1872, the South Carolina Legislature had 94 Negro as against only 30 white members....
>
> For six years "corruption and dishonesty ran riot" and no bill could be passed without bribing the legislature. Negro members of the House furnished their private lodgings and bought themselves flashy jewelry at public expense. State funds were used to furnish a brothel for the salons. When a Negro member lost $1,000 betting on a horse race, he was reimbursed by the Legislature... The furniture which the Legislature bought for itself and its members cost $200,000 and was appraised in 1877 at $17,715.[23]

James S. Pike of Maine, a pre-war abolitionist and devoted Republican, visited South Carolina in 1873 and got the shock of his sheltered life, Weyl writing:

> "It is the spectacle of a society suddenly turned bottomside up," he wrote of the legislature. "The wealth, the intelligence, the culture, the wisdom of the State" had been cast aside for "the most ignorant democracy that mankind ever saw....It is the dregs of the population habilitated in the robes of their intelligent predecessors and asserting over them the rule of ignorance and corruption.... It is barbarism overwhelming civilization by physical force... At some of the desks sit colored men whose types it would be hard to find outside the Congo... "
>
> Pike was struck by "the endless chatter," the "gush and babble," the guffawing, grimacing and horseplay of the Negro legislators, their endless repetitions and incoherence. "Their struggles to get the floor, their bellowings and physical contortions, baffle description.... The Speaker threatens to call **'the gemman'** to order. This is considered a capital joke and a guffaw follows. The laugh goes round and then the peanuts are cracked and munched faster than ever."[24]

THE FOURTEENTH AMENDMENT

Although such degradation surely added insult to injury, the real problem with radical reconstruction concerned our subsequent loss of constitutional freedoms. By July 20, 1868, the newly constituted state governments, *minus the white voters*, "enacted," (rather than "ratified") the Fourteenth Amendment. Ohio, Oregon and New Jersey had attempted to rescind their original ratifications but were denied that constitutional right. In the New Jersey resolution withdrawing its consent to the amendment's adoption, paragraph 15 declares,

> It imposes new prohibitions upon the power of the State to pass laws, and interdicts the execution of such parts of the common law as the national judiciary may esteem inconsistent with the vague provisions of the said amendment, made vague for the purpose of facilitating encroachments upon the lives, liberty, and property of the people.[25]

Paragraph 16 exhibited a portentous warning against a future omnipotent Supreme Court: "It enlarges the judicial power of the United States so as to bring every law passed by the State...within the jurisdiction of the Federal tribunals."[26]

Attorney John W. Whitehead gives us a twentieth-century assessment:

> Understanding the Fourteenth Amendment is necessary because the Supreme Court has been enabled by utilization of the amendment to nationalize the Bill of Rights. Such usage shows how, instead of being a restriction on the federal government, the Bill of Rights has become a tool for furthering centralization of all governmental power in Washington, D.C.[27]

For example, should your state or mine pass a law restricting adult bookstores within a certain distance of a church or school, "Joe Pervert" can now appeal to the appropriate federal circuit court judge that his constitutional right to "liberty" is being deprived. Thanks to the Fourteenth Amendment, any liberal federal judge can cancel out the local convictions of an entire state! No wonder David Lawrence, writing in *U.S. News and World Report*, called the illegal ratification of the Fourteenth Amendment "The Worst Scandal in Our History."[28] Or, as historian James Kennedy put it, regarding the original concept of "government by the consent of the governed,"— "One might say that it too is 'gone with the wind.' "[29]

Now, as this book professes to be a *biblical interpretation of American history*, I would like to suggest a *spiritual* explanation for this costly mitigation of American freedom, and perhaps for even the war itself. Of course, *"the natural man receiveth not the things of the Spirit of God: for they are foolishness unto him: neither can he know them, because they are spiritually discerned."* (I Corinthians 2:14) But to the sensitive believer God says, *"He that hath an ear, let him hear what the Spirit saith unto the churches."* (Revelation 3:13)

The central thesis of this work is that the Spirit's promise of an "open door" made to the first-century church in Philadelphia (Revelation 3:7, 8) had a later and greater historical fulfillment in eighteenth-century America, as evidenced by the unprecedented religious liberties bestowed upon the New Testament church by the glorious First Amendment. It is no coincidence that our nation's Liberty Bell, bearing the inscription from Leviticus 25:10, *"Proclaim liberty throughout all the land,"* just happens to reside in that *other* City of Brotherly Love!

However, the Scripture is clear that this marvelous promise was not extended to a lazy church, but rather to an exhausted body of contending believers: *"For thou hast a little strength, and hast kept my word, and hast not denied my name."* (Revelation 3:8c) As the gaols of Virginia exacted a similar toll on Baptist preachers more than 16 centuries later, it was given to one of their own, Reverend John Leland, to be the providential liaison between the Lord and James Madison for the actual securing of our precious Bill of Rights.

The Holy Spirit further assured the *Philadelphia* Christians that no mere human could shut a door which He Himself had opened. If and when it would ever close, the fingerprints of Christ would be found on the knob. The formula for freedom, therefore, is a simple one: *to whatever degree the local New Testament church keeps the **Word**, the Lord will keep the **door**!*

Recognizing that the door of our constitutional liberties was partially closed by the unlawful ratification of the Fourteenth Amendment in 1868, we can be assured that the church of Jesus Christ must have made the first move by messing with "the Book." The historical confirmation is startling!!

According to *A Brief History of English Bible Translations* by Dr. Lawrence Vance, there were *38* different attempts to overthrow the King James Bible between 1653 (*A Paraphrase and Annotations Upon All the Books of the New Testament* by Henry Hammond) and 1867 (*The Holy Scriptures* by the Mormon, Joe Smith). While most of these perversions were made in England, others like Charles Thompson's *The Holy Bible*

Containing the Old and New Covenant (1808), were produced in America. Some were done by sincere, but misguided, Christians like *The Webster Bible* (1833), and John Wesley's *Explanatory Notes on the New Testament* (1755). The majority were translated by liberals and cultists. Collectively, they were not worth the dynamite needed to blow them up. However, one translation proved far more troublesome than the other 37 combined.

AMERICAN BIBLE UNION VERSION

The fateful American Bible Union Version was commissioned in 1850 and begun in 1852. The more influential New Testament portion was completed in 1864; the Old Testament was finished in 1912. As this translation was primarily the work of American scholars, the resultant momentum from a venture which appeared to be so prestigious proved to be the catalyst for the abominable British Revised Version committee of 1871–1881 led by the apostate duumvirate of Brooke Westcott and Fenton Hort. Armitage wrote that the Union Version "so completely revolutionized public opinion on the subject of revision that a new literature was created on the subject, both in England and America, and a general demand for revision culminated in action on that subject by the Convocation of Canterbury in 1870."[30] One of the leading translators on this diabolical committee acknowledged, "We never make an important change without consulting the Union's version."[31]

The American Bible Union Version barely outlived its translation. (Had *you* ever heard of it before?) Still, its long-range effects for evil have proven incalculable. The New Testament portion of the Revised Version invaded the United States in 1881 with the Old Testament arriving four years later. Together they altered the King James Bible in over 36,000 places! Despite the fact that this generic British production went belly-up as well, practically all of the English translations in the twentieth century have been patterned after the Revised Version and especially its underlying Greek text, known as the *Nestle's* text.

That the Fourteenth Amendment afflicted our Constitution *only four years after the American Bible Union Version was completed* is a point of great significance. However, the fact that this translation was published in the United Sates did not constitute justification, in and of itself, for a divine reduction of American liberties. The biblical principle is that God would keep the door open so long as His *New Testament churches* kept the Word! Historically speaking, the hinges never even creaked when Alexander

Campbell's Church of Christ translation arrived in 1826, calling itself *The Sacred Writings of the Apostles and Evangelists of Jesus Christ.* The same is true of the 1808 American edition of the Presbyterian *Family Expositor: a Paraphrase and Version of the New Testament.*

Well, the sad fact of the matter was that the notorious American Bible Union Version was, in reality, the work of a misguided *Baptist* mission board (by the same name) which was organized at the *Baptist Tabernacle* on Mulberry Street, New York, on June 10, 1850, for the express purpose of producing an *immersionist* version (i.e., John the "Immerser," etc.). The leading force behind this proposed revision was the celebrated Baptist egghead, Reverend Spencer H. Cone, D.D. The intellectual "Dr." Cone actually had quite a few hang-ups with the Authorized Version beyond the "baptizo" question. An excerpt from the second article of the Union's constitution reads accordingly:

> The more accurately a version is brought to the true standard, the more accurately will it express the mind and will of God... In the consideration of this subject some have endeavored to poise the whole question of revision upon the retention or displacement of the word "baptize." But this does great injustice to our views and aims. For although we insist upon the observance of a uniform principle in the full and faithful translation of God's Word, so as to express in plain English, without ambiguity or vagueness, the exact meaning of baptizo, as well as of all other words relating to the Christian ordinances, *yet this is but one of numerous errors, which, in our estimation, demand correction.* And such are our views and principles in the prosecution of this work that, if there were no such word as "baptize" or baptizo in the Scriptures, the necessity of revising our English version would appear to us no less real and imperative.[32]

Now what kind of a way was this for Dr. Cone and company to talk about the Bible that had been used to lead them to Christ in the first place? Critics of the AV's transliterated *baptize* frequently trace the word's origination to either a doctrinal bias on behalf of the translators or a political intimidation on behalf of the King. In his work, *Textual Criticism: Fact and Fiction*, Dr. Thomas Cassidy cites Dr. Larry Pettegrew, Professor of Historical and Systematic Theology at Detroit Baptist Theological Seminary as stating:

> There are some poor translations in the King James Version. When the Anglicans translated the Greek word, "baptizo," for example, they

were afraid to translate it as "immerse." So they simply transliterated it as "baptize." Most Bible-believing Baptists would consider that a mistake.[33]

According to *The Oxford English Dictionary*, the English verb *baptize* was already in use as early as the eleventh century, having been adapted from the French *baptise-r,-izer* (which had in turn been adapted from the Latin *baptīzā-re* from the Greek βαπτίζειν). The earliest usage of *baptize* in English literature is found in 1292, [34] almost a century before Wycliff's epoch translation of the Bible in 1382 and *over three centuries before Hampton Court.* This was also the case in the next six major English translations. Conversely, when the English word *immerse* made its first appearance much later in 1605, it had a different meaning than it does today. Then it was the evolving: "To cause to enter; to involve, include; to merge, to sink." The accepted definition, "To dip or plunge into a liquid; to put overhead in water, etc.; *spec.* to baptize by immersion," did not appear until 1613, *two years after the Authorized Version was completed!*[35] Oxford's primary translation was more than adequate (and certainly superior to the 1605 definition of *immerse*):

> *To immerse in water, or pour or sprinkle water upon, as a means of ceremonial purification, or a token of initiation into a religious society, especially into the Christian church; to christen.*[36]

For the record, Dr. Cone, like John Wilkes Booth and Pope John Paul II, was a professional actor in his earlier years. Although the Princeton-trained Cone knew better, he basically acknowledged that he had pursued the seedy career because he didn't possess the intestinal fortitude *(guts)* to resist the lights.

> In a moment of desperation I adopted the profession of an **actor**. It was inimical to the wishes of my mother, and in direct opposition to my own feelings and principles. But it was the only way by which I had a hope of extricating myself from my pecuniary embarrassments.[37]

Thus, a simple background check on the first Baptist to lead a serious movement to overthrow the AV 1611 (his *personal* translation was completed in 1850) reveals the following. For seven long years, Spencer Cone violated his conscience for filthy lucre's sake by performing in fictitious roles to the ego-swelling applause of the heathen world. As far as I can tell, these are the ideal qualifications for a professional Bible corrector in any age: a *seared conscience*, a *proud spirit*, a *theatrical air*, and a *weakness for the almighty dollar.*

One of Cone's intellectual cronies was a certain Dr. Horatio B. Hackett. Here we have another example of a Baptist who got carried away with his education *only 60 years after the Philadelphia door was opened.* "Hacking" away at the Holy Bible, Horatio declared:

> It is admitted that the received English version of the Scriptures is susceptible of improvement. During the more than 200 years which have passed since it was made, our means for the explanation, both of the text and the subjects of the Bible, have been greatly increased. The original languages in which it was written have continued to occupy the attention of scholars, and are now more perfectly understood. Much light has been thrown upon the meaning of words. Many of them are seen to have been incorrectly defined, and many more to have been rendered with less precision than is now attainable. The various collateral branches of knowledge have been advanced to a more perfect state. History, geography, antiquities, the monuments and customs of the countries where the sacred writers lived, and where the scenes which they describe took place, have been investigated with untiring zeal, and have yielded, at length, results which afford advantages to the translator of the Scriptures at the present day, which no preceding age has enjoyed. It is eminently desirable that we should have in our language a translation of the Bible conformed to the present state of critical learning.[38]

Although the Baptist leadership split along sectional lines over slavery, they were apparently united on attacking the King James Bible. The Bible Revision Association was organized in 1852 at Memphis, Tennessee, to assist in the revision of the American Bible Union. This society later relocated to Louisville, Kentucky, and confined its operation to the Southern states. A short list of participating Southern Baptist "scholars" would include Drs. S. W. Lynd, D. R. Campbell, W. Cary Crane, John L. Dagg, Samuel Baker, J. R. Graves and N. M. Crawford.[39]

Brethren, if the presence of a single backslidden preacher could jeopardize an entire crew of otherwise innocent heathen (*"For I know that for my sake this great tempest is upon you."* Jonah 1:12b), is it unreasonable to assume that Apollyon was "permitted" to scourge America from 1861 to 1865 in consequence of a concerted Baptist effort between 1852 and 1864 to discard the King James Bible? (See also Genesis 30:27; 39:23.) Did not the worldly-wise Andrew Jackson even have more sense than that, having declared in 1845, "That book, Sir, is the Rock upon which our republic rests"?

I am well aware that the "professional" historian would recommend me to the nearest funny farm, but then he would also scoff at II Samuel 24:10, 15:

> *And David's heart smote him after that he had numbered the people. And David said unto the LORD, I have sinned greatly in that I have done: and now, I beseech thee, O LORD, take away the iniquity of thy servant; for I have done very foolishly ... So the LORD sent a pestilence upon Israel from the morning even to the time appointed: and there died of the people from Dan even to Beersheba* **seventy thousand** *men.*

What would a historiographer know about such things? And then there was that loss of freedom in 1868. Should we be surprised that Thaddeus Stevens declared unashamedly, "I was raised a **Baptist** and adhere to their belief"?[40]

Fortunately, the "common" Baptists were not impressed with the intellectual achievements of the American Bible Union, Armitage writing, "While many men of learning and nerve espoused the movement, a storm of opposition was raised against it from one land to the other."[41] I found it rather interesting that the nineteenth-century scholar ridiculed the humble Bible believer then with the same rhetoric that is employed today: "Many others also talked as much at random as if they feared that the book which they hinted had come down from heaven in about its present shape, printed and bound, was now to be taken from them by force."[42]

As there are plenty of dysfunctional Baptist scholars around today who likewise take delight in attacking the Monarch of Books, the words of Thomas Armitage are worth reviewing. Referring to the "storm of opposition," he wrote: "Every consideration was presented on the subject but the main thought: that the Author of the inspired originals had the infinite right to a hearing, and that man was in duty bound to listen to his utterances, all human preference or expediency to the contrary notwithstanding."[43]

Well, the verdict of the Author was an umistakable thumbs-down. Writing twenty-one years later (1907), the notoriously liberal Baptist historian, Henry C. Vedder, was forced to concede:

> **The project of circulating a denominational version of the Scriptures in English has been tested once for all and proved to be a**

disastrous failure. The version was successfully made and possesses many merits, but it could not be circulated; Baptists could neither be forced nor coaxed to use it. They were greatly the losers and are still by reason of this apathy, but we must take the facts of human nature as we find them; and one fact now unquestioned is that the attachment of English-speaking Christians to the version of the Scriptures endeared to them by long use and tender association has proved to be too strong for the successful substitution of any other.[44]

This admission on Dr. Vedder's part smacks of blatant humanism. *Vedder* was the "loser" for attributing the leadership of the Holy Spirit (John 16:13) to "human nature." Should we have expected any better from an apostate who considered "the idea of sacrificial expiation made by the innocent for the guilty" as "especially repugnant to our best ethics"?[45] Beale adds that Vedder also called the Old Testament sacrificial system "too revolting, too stupidly absurd, to be worthy of serious refutation."[46] Thus we see the connection between one's willingness to deny the Word *and* the Lord's name. (Revelation 3:8)

PHILIP SCHAFF

That Dr. Cone's pipe dream was completely lacking in Holy Spirit leadership can be seen by his selection of Dr. Philip Schaff as one of the project's final editors. Schaff was just about the most liberal theologian in the United States at this time. In fact, you might say that he was a "heresy specialist" as he was literally exported from Germany for the express purpose of polluting American seminaries.

Most of my readers have at least heard of the German school of higher criticism and its historic attacks upon the Word of God and orthodox theology in general. What is not so widely known is that this scientific disorder did not originate with German rationalists, but rather, with Jesuit theologians. The first scholar to employ "scientific methods" to the so-called textual and literary problems of the Bible was a Catholic priest, Richard Simon (1638–1712). *The Concise Oxford Dictionary of the Christian Church* states, "He is generally regarded as the founder of Old Testament criticism."[47] Another personality connected with the Catholic foundation for textual criticism was "Father" Jean Mabillon (1632–1707). *Oxford* bills him as "the most erudite and discerning of all *Maurists* (a Benedictine order)."[48] The Catholic physician/theologian Jean Astruc (1684–1766) was the next "critic" on the scene who decided that two different men wrote the Pentateuch.

Because Germany had given birth to the Reformation, the land of Luther was the first nation to be invaded by the Catholic higher critics. A Jesuit school in Rome, *Collegium Germanicum*, was founded for the training of "missionaries" to Germany. "Father" Johann Mohler (1796–1838), professor of history and theology at Tubingen and Munich (the "German Rome"), was the moving force at this time.

Clinging to the destructive tenets of higher criticism, one apostate Lutheran after another began questioning the "scientific accuracy" of the Holy Bible. A short list of such pro-Vatican liberals would include: Ferdinand Christian Baur (1792–1860); Wilhelm Martin Leberecht DeWett (1780–1849); Johann Gottfried Eichhorn (1752–1827); Heinrich Georg August Ewald (1803–1875); Heinreich Friedrich Wilhelm Gesenius (1786–1842); Johann Gottfried Herder (1744–1803); Herman Hupfeld (1796–1866); Gotthold Ephraim Lessing (1729–1781); Johann David Michaelis (1717–1791); Herman Samuel Reimarus (1694–1768); Frederich Daniel Ernst Schleiermacher (1768–1834); David Fredrick Strauss (1808–1874); and Julius Wellhausen (1844–1918).

This was the theological environment that produced Dr. Philip Schaff. Wilkinson writes, "On the eve of his leaving Germany, many Protestant leaders of the new German theology rejoiced with Dr. Schaff over his call to America."[49] The apostate Dr. Dorner, one of Schaff's numerous mentors, coached him accordingly, "Especially do I ask you to give attention to the Trinitarian and Christological controversies."[50]

No sooner had Schaff assumed his duties as professor of church history and biblical literature at the Theological Seminary of Mercersburg, Pennsylvania, than he was tried for heresy after delivering his opening address entitled "The Principles of Protestantism." Wilkinson, citing *The Life of Schaff*: "The address involved the church irreversibly in the doctrinal agitation which went on within its pale for a quarter of a century."[51] Riplinger notes that Schaff's own son acknowledged, " 'The people asso-ciated all manner of doctrinal evil with [him]' and referred to him as a 'traitor.' " With reference to Schaff theology, David Schaff wrote, "[I]t was at that time considered by most [Christians] in the United Sates dangerous and by many heretical."[52]

By the time Cone and his Baptist confederates had engaged Dr. Schaff's expertise for their epic American Bible Union Perversion, their hero's heresy was already established as the "Mercersburg Movement." A converted

Catholic priest testified that "the professors of Mercersburg were insidiously instilling Romanizing poison in their classroom teachings."[53]

It was no accident that Westcott and Hort selected Dr. Schaff to head up both the Old and New Testament RV *Advisory* Committees in the States. At that time, 1870, Schaff had already been chased out of Mercersburg by infuriated parents and had fled to New York's Union Theological Seminary, declaring it to be "so liberal as to allow for all my dissenting views on these and other points."[54] He quickly gathered together a host of like-minded heretics opposed to what he called, **"the moonshine theory of the inerrant apostolic autographs."**[55]

The kindred spirit between Schaff and the apostate revisors commissioned by the Convocation of Canterbury (Westcott and Hort) was occasioned by the subtle reintroduction of Romanism within the Church of England known as the *Oxford Movement,* or *Tractarianism.* With Martin Luther rolling over in his grave, Jesuit agents had begun their insidious infiltration of Britain's intellectual community.

In the spirit of Archbishop William Laud, the leading culprits in this endeavor were Edward Bouverie Pusey (1800–1882) and Frederick Denison Maurice (1805–1872). From his position as Regius Professor of Hebrew at Oxford and Canon of Christ Church, Pusey sought to restore High Church polity and such Romish doctrines as auricular confession and transubstantiation. Frederick Maurice was professor of theology at King's College until he was expelled for denying an eternal Hell in his *Theological Essays* (1853). He was later "picked up" by Cambridge University and installed as Knightsbridge Professor of Moral Philosophy!

One of the better-known Jesuit plants of this period was "Cardinal" John Henry Newman (1801–1890). His followers, such as Frederick William Faber (1814–1863), had labeled the preaching of fellow Englishmen like William Booth, George Whitefield and John Wesley as "detestable and diabolical heresy." Of course, their influence had also spread to English politics. The *Emancipation Act* of 1829 made it legal for Roman Catholics to become elected to Parliament. Finally, after years of spreading pro-Vatican propaganda within the Church of England, the Oxford professor finally "jumped ship" and returned to Rome where he was given a Cardinal's hat in 1879. The sad part of the story is that within a year of his exodus, *over 150 deceived clergy and laymen also crossed over to join him.*

To be familiar with this survey of nineteenth-century apostasy within the Church of England is to understand the mind-set of the forces who clamored for and participated in the Revision Committee of 1871–1881. Men such as

Archbishop Richard Trench and other Vatican sympathizers labored for a decade to replace the readings of the King James Bible with those of the Jesuit *Douay-Rheims* version.

The Catholic most responsible for directing Protestant aggression against the Authorized Version was Cardinal Nicholas Patrick Stephen Wiseman (1802–1865). While rector of the English College at Rome, he studied under Cardinal Angelo Mai (1782–1854), prefect of the Vatican library and celebrated editor of *Codex Vaticanus*. Wiseman himself was described as "a textual critic of the first rank."[56]

WESTCOTT AND HORT

The chief translators of the Revision Committee were Drs. Brooke Foss Westcott (1825–1901) and Fenton John Anthony Hort (1828–1892). If these men believed what they professed to believe, they are both in the fires of Hell. According to their own writings, as preserved in their own biographies, as edited by their own sons, *neither man had an orthodox bone in his body*.

A few of Dr. Hort's pronouncements would include: "Mary-Worship and Jesus-Worship have very much in common";[57] "Baptism assures us that we are children of God";[58] "I am not able to go as far as you in asserting the absolute infallibility of a canonical writing";[59] "But the book which has most engaged me is Darwin...my feeling is strong that the theory is unanswerable";[60] and "Now if there be a devil."[61] Then there is the classic of all times—"The fact is, I do not see how God's justice can be satisfied without every man's suffering in his own person the full penalty for his sins."[62]

Not to be outdone in the heresy department, Dr. Westcott's frothings include: "I never read an account of a miracle but I seem instinctively to feel its improbability";[63] "I reject the word infallibility—of Holy Scripture overwhelming";[64] "Oh, the weakness of my faith compared with that of others! So wild, so skeptical am I. I cannot yield";[65] "But there are many others who believe it possible that the beings of the unseen world may manifest themselves to us in extraordinary ways";[66] and finally, "No one now, I suppose, holds that the first three chapters of Genesis, for example, give a literal history—I could never understand how anyone reading them with open eyes could think they did."[67]

One of the clearest signs of papal affinity with Westcott and Hort was their shared abhorrence for democracy as a whole. While Hort said,

"I...cannot say that I see much as yet to soften my deep hatred of democracy in all its forms,"[68] Westcott declared, "I suppose I am a Communist by nature."[69] And without any question whatsoever, both men, like "His Holiness," hated the United States of America, Hort announcing:

> **I care more for England and for Europe than for America, how much more than for all the niggers in the world!** and I contend that the highest morality requires me to do so. Some thirty years ago Niebuhr wrote to this effect: Whatever people may say to the contrary, **the American empire is a standing menace to the whole civilization of Europe**, and sooner or later one or the other must perish. Every year has, I think, brought fresh proof of the entire truth of these words. American doctrine...destroys the root of everything vitally precious which man has by painful growth been learning from the earliest times till now, and tends only to reduce us to the gorilla state. The American empire seems to me mainly an embodiment of American doctrine, its leading principle being lawless force. Surely, if ever Babylon or Rome were rightly cursed, it **cannot be wrong to desire and pray from the bottom of one's heart that the American Union may be shivered to pieces.**[70]

Throughout the decade-long revision, Westcott and Hort basically utilized two corrupt Greek manuscripts, codices *Vaticanus* (B) and *Sinaiticus* (א), to alter the *Textus Receptus,* the underlying Greek text for most of the King James Bible, in over 5,000 particulars. The reader can draw his own conclusions as to the merits of these two "ancient treasures." While *Vaticanus* was found in the **Pope's library**, *Sinaiticus* was discovered in a monastery **trash can**. As the two false witnesses at Jesus' trial gave conflicting testimony, א and B disagree with one another in 3,036 instances in the four Gospels alone! By contrast, the *Textus Receptus* is comprised of over 5,000 manuscripts with an agreement factor of approximately 90%.

Codex Vaticanus has 589 peculiar readings that are not found in any manuscript on earth, affecting 858 words; *Sinaiticus* has 1,460 similar readings affecting 2,640 words. Codex א has the scribbled corrections of ten different revisors throughout, with Dean Burgon relating, "On many occasions 10, 20, 30, 40 words are dropped through very carelessness. Letters and words, even whole sentences, are frequently written twice over, or begun and immediately cancelled."[71] Should the critic attempt to defend the scribes of א and B by alluding to the "adverse working conditions of primitive times, blah, blah, blah," it should be noted that the unsaved Masoretic scribes of the Middle Ages were allowed to make only *two* mistakes when transcribing an entire Old Testament. If a third error was discovered at Malachi 4:6, the entire manuscript would be destroyed.[72] (i.e., "Three strikes; you're *out!*")

The main reason for Westcott and Hort's "preference" of *Vaticanus* and *Sinaiticus* over the *Textus Receptus* is because these manuscripts represent the textual foundation for the Roman Catholic Bible; why else would they have been chosen? Wilkinson writes:

> Because of the changes which came about in the nineteenth century, there arose a new type of Protestantism and a new version of the Protestant Bible. This new kind of Protestantism was hostile to the fundamental doctrines of the Reformation. Previous to this there had been only two types of Bibles in the world, the Protestant, and the Catholic. Now Protestants were asked to choose between the true Protestant Bible and one which reproduced readings rejected by the Reformers.[73]

THE REVISED VERSION

When the New Testament of the Revised Version was finally released on May 17, 1881, there was great rejoicing within the ranks of Roman Catholicism. Cardinal Wiseman saw the "new Protestant" version as a vindication of the Catholic Douay-Rheims Bible.

> When we consider the scorn cast by the Reformers upon the *Vulgate*, and their recurrence, in consequence, to the Greek, as the only accurate standard, we cannot but rejoice at the silent triumph which truth has at length gained over clamorous error. For, in fact, the principal writers who have avenged the *Vulgate,* and obtained for its critical preeminence, are Protestants.[74]

The "Very Reverend" Thomas S. Preston of St. Ann's Roman Catholic Church in New York shared the identical sentiments:

> The brief examination which I have been able to make of the Revised Version of the New Testament has convinced me that the Committee have labored with great sincerity and diligence, and that they have produced a translation much more correct than that generally received among Protestants. It is to us a gratification to find that in very many instances they have adopted the reading of the Catholic Version, and, have thus by their scholarship confirmed the correctness of our Bible.[75]

Bishop Tobias Mullen of Erie, Pennsylvania, wrote:

> It must be admitted that either the Revisers wished to withdraw
> several important passages of the Holy Scripture from Protestants, or that
> the latter, in their simplicity, have all along been imposed upon by King
> James' translators, who, either through ignorance or malice, have inserted
> in the Authorized Version a number of paragraphs which were never
> written by an apostle or other inspired author.[76]

The finished product altered the King James Bible in over 36,000
places. Many of the changes were unbelievably horrendous. The *Dublin
Review* in July, 1881, predicted, "The New Version will be the death knell
of Protestantism."[77]

I TIMOTHY 3:16

*"And without controversy great is the mystery of godliness: **God** was
manifest in the flesh."*   (King James)

"And without controversy great is the mystery of godliness; **He** who was
manifested in the flesh."   (Revised Version)

II TIMOTHY 3:16

*"**All scripture** is given by inspiration of God."*   (King James)

"**Every scripture inspired of God** is also profitable."   (Revised Version)

I CORINTHIANS 5:7

*"For even Christ our passover is sacrificed **for us**."*   (King James)

"For our passover also hath been sacrificed, even Christ."
                                                            (Revised Version)

JAMES 5:16

*"Confess your **faults** one to another."*   (King James)

"Confess therefore your **sins** one to another."   (Revised Version)

II TIMOTHY 2:15

*"**Study** to shew thyself approved unto God, a workman that needeth not to be ashamed, **rightly dividing** the word of truth."*

(King James)

"Give diligence to **present thyself** approved unto God, a workman that needeth not to be ashamed, **handling aright** the word of truth."

(Revised Version)

Then, there was Dean Burgon's pet peeve concerning the butchery of the Lord's Prayer in Matthew's Gospel. By removing the Doxology— *"For thine is the kingdom, and the power, and the glory, for ever, Amen."*—and substituting "evil one" for evil, the revisors have actually inserted **Satan** into the Lord's Prayer! Imagine beginning such a sacred reading with "Our Father" only to conclude it with the "Evil One"! I guess that's not bad for a pair of liberals who didn't even believe in a literal devil to begin with.

Finally, there was the "bone" of appreciation that was tossed to the American Baptists for having provided the initial inspiration for revision through their "defuncto" Union Version of 1864. Armitage relates:

> Much as Dr. Trench was disquieted about the word "immerse" being "an interpretation" and "not a translation of " *baptizo,* he was not content to let the word "baptize" rest quietly and undisturbed in the English version, when compelled to act on honest scholarship, but inserted the preposition *"in"* as a marginal "interpretation" of its bearings, baptized "in water."[78]

Thus, although the RV's rendering of Mark 1:8 retained the word *baptize* (as found in the AV)—"I indeed have baptized you [4] with water"— the difference became the little marginal indicator [4] next to the word *with*. A glance to the margin reveals the "payoff " —"or, *in.*" What this translates to according to a *spiritual* application of Revelation 3:8 is that a back-slidden minority of egotistical, pseudo-intellectual, Baptist Bible correctors wound up selling our states' rights for the pottage of a single, two-letter word—"in." Thus, for the Baptists to gain *their* two letters, America had to forfeit one mighty important word of her own in the process. As Carl Sandburg noted, before the Civil War our country was referred to in all treaties as "the United States *are*"; after Appomattox, the proper reference became "the United States *is*."[79]

Armitage adds the sober postscript that by 1883,

> the Bible Union was much embarrassed by debt, when it was believed that the time had come for the Baptists of America to heal their divisions on the Bible question, to reunite their efforts in Bible work, and to leave each man in the denomination at liberty to use what English version he chose.[80]

These were noble words but it would take some time to undo the damage. Numbers of God's people had their confidence shaken in the King James Bible. Vedder comments:

> Owing to the increasing infrequency of revivals, and the decline of the older evangelism, the majority of the converts are now received into the churches through the Sunday-school and the young people's society; the conversion of adults becomes with every decade increasingly rare.[81]

And don't you know that the Vatican was more than ready to exploit the weakness? For instance, now you are familiar with the background behind the brash pronouncement of Archbishop John Hughes in 1850 regarding the Vatican's goal of converting all of America to Catholicism. You will recall that the American Bible Union was established only five months earlier and only a couple of miles from the Archbishop's parish. If the local New Testament churches were willing to declare war on their own Bible, *why shouldn't the enemy go on the offensive as well?*

CATHOLIC EXPANSION

By the year 1870, the Catholic population in America was estimated to be about 4,504,000, or roughly 4,186,000 *higher* than the figure was in 1830 when Professor Samuel F. B. Morse sounded the alarm. Dr. Morse went to be with the Lord on April 2, 1872. As the immigration figures confirm, he died a vindicated *prophet* and *patriot*. Among his many posthumous honors, the legislature of the state of New York (being in session at the time) received the following communication from Governor John T. Hoffman on April 3:

The Telegraph to-day announces the death of its inventor, Samuel F. B. Morse. Born in Massachusetts, his home has for many years of his eventful life been in New York. His fame belongs to neither, but to the country and the world; yet it seems fitting that this great State, in which he lived and died, should be the first to pay appropriate honors to his memory. Living, he received from governments everywhere more public honors than were ever paid to any American private citizen; dead, let all the people pay homage to his name. I respectfully recommend to the Legislature the adoption of such resolutions as may be suitable, and the appointment of a joint committee to attend the funeral of the illustrious deceased.

–John T. Hoffman[82]

No doubt the godly Dr. Morse would have rather preferred that the New York legislature honor his memory by heeding his admonition concerning unchecked immigration. Over 600,000 Catholics entered the United States throughout the 1870's, bringing the total Catholic population to a staggering 6,259,000 by 1880. An additional 1,250,000 immigrants arrived during the following decade, raising the figure in 1890 to 8,909,000. Another 1,250,000 came in through the last decade, closing out the century with a total American Catholic population of 12,041,000.[83] This figure constitutes a **3,690% increase** since the St. Leopold Foundation was organized in 1830.

Whereas the pre-Civil War immigrant was generally either German or Irish, the later waves of arrivals throughout the Industrial Revolution hailed from numerous countries, especially in southern and eastern Europe. Such nations included Italy, Poland, Czechoslovakia, Sweden, Denmark, Norway, Great Britain, Russia, Greece, Austria-Hungary and even China and Japan.

Most of us have grown up with a warm feeling in our hearts toward the sacrosanct Statue of Liberty. However, what "the Lady" has represented through the years is *the* very danger Thomas Jefferson and other Founding Fathers had warned us about. *"Give me your tired, your poor, Your huddled masses yearning to breathe free, The wretched refuse of your teeming shore... "* may sound sentimental, but has anyone stopped to think about just what caused those deplorable conditions to exist in the first place? The "gift," (or was it a *Trojan Horse*) came from *Catholic* France, where *her* "huddled masses" have been known to pay homage to *"another* Lady" by the name of *Mary*. Why have we imported the bondage of Romanism to the shores of a free nation? Did not Jefferson give clear warning?

They will bring with them the principles of the governments they leave, imbibed in their early youth... These principles, with their language, they will transmit to their children. In proportion to their numbers, they will share with us the legislation. They will infuse into it their spirit, warp and bias its directions, and render it a heterogeneous, incoherent, distracted mass.[84]

Contrary to popular opinion, Thomas Jefferson never envisioned America as being a great melting pot of humanity, but rather warned of a "heterogenous, incoherent, distracted mass." Even the Catholics knew this to be true. Author John Tracy Ellis in *American Catholicism* cites Russell Blankenship: "The melting pot merely obscures, it never obliterates traces of racial elements."[85] The Bible puts it even more plainly than that: *"O thou man of God, there is death in the pot."* (II Kings 4:40b)

The special prayer at the October 28, 1886, inauguration ceremony of *The Statue of Liberty Enlightening the World*, given by the Reverend Richard S. Storrs, included the words, "It is in Thy favor, and **through the operation of the Gospel of Thy grace,** that cities stand in quiet prosperity."[86] As we have already seen, the "huddled masses" arrived with a *works* salvation, and their priests made sure they *remained* as "huddled masses" beyond the reach of the Gospel. The problem has never been with the Catholic *people*, but rather with their Church's "doctrines of devils." (I Timothy 4:1) (While doing research for this book, I visited the library at the University of Notre Dame in South Bend, Indiana, and met some of the nicest Catholic lay people in the world.) Separating the *Catholic* from *Catholicism* for the sake of eternity is the all-important issue.

PAPAL INFALLIBILITY

With his strategic flock in faraway America growing larger every day, Pius IX received a convenient "word of knowledge" that was certain to help draw the reign of blind submission even tighter in the future. However, "His Holiness" would have to decipher the revelation posthaste as General Raphael Cardonia's Italian army of "backslidden" freedom fighters was about to descend upon the Eternal City.

In 1869, the Pope summoned all his prelates to the First Vatican (Twentieth General) Council to discuss a little "business." The bottom line was that Pius figured out that he was probably *infallible* when he spoke "ex-cathedra," i.e., on key doctrinal matters. (A good example would be his

December 8, 1854, pronouncement of *The Immaculate Conception of the Blessed Virgin Mary*, which recognized the sinlessness of "God's mother," etc.; see Mary's opinion of this infallible decree in Luke 1:47.)

Although Pius had the thing pretty well figured out, a number of his bishops didn't see it that way. A preliminary straw poll taken in secret tabulated 88 nays, 65 yeas with 80 abstentions. The American bishops were particularly uncomfortable about the spot in which such a doctrine would place them back home. After a little pontifical politicking within the Jesuit-controlled proceedings, 410 bishops petitioned Pius to "go for it," while 162 urged caution. On the eve of the final vote, 55 American bishops skipped town rather than tell the "infallible" Pope that he was wrong.

On July 18, 1870, "Pio Nono" proclaimed the dogmas of papal jurisdictional primacy and infallibility. A total of 25 American prelates voted yes while two voted no. The carefully worded decree read as follows:

> We teach and define that it is a dogma divinely revealed that the Roman Pontiff, when he speaks *ex cathedra*, that is, when in discharge of the office of pastor and doctor of all Christians, by virtue of his supreme Apostolic authority, he defines a doctrine regarding faith and morals to be held by the universal Church, by the divine assistance promised him in blessed Peter, is possessed of that infallibility with which the divine Redeemer willed that His Church should be endowed for defending doctrines regarding faith and morals, and that therefore such definitions of the Roman Pontiff are irreformable of themselves, and not from the consent of the Church.[87]

Though the wording was quite impressive, there was nothing said about the approximately two million historical problems with this decree, such as the eleventh-century "misunderstanding" when three different "infallible" pontiffs all claiming to be numero uno at the same time hurled anathemas at one another till King Henry III gave them all the royal boot. The same is true of the "great schism" in 1378 which lasted for 50 years. In yet another case, Pope Eugene IV (1431–47) condemned Joan of Arc to be burned alive as a witch while another infallible "His Holiness," Benedict IV, declared her a saint in 1919.

There was also the time in 897 when Stephen VI brought formal charges against one of his predecessors, Pope Formosus. The defendant had to be exhumed from the pontifical cemetery in order to stand trial. After being found guilty of all the ecclesiastical offenses with which "*Its* Holiness" was charged, the corpse was stripped of its vestments; what was left of the three fingers on the right hand were chopped off and the remains were thrown into the Tiber River. As to which one of the these two pontiffs was infallible, your guess is as good as mine.

Although these contradictions were conveniently avoided, everyone was clearly assured that they would *go to Hell* if they didn't buy the program: "But if any one—which may God avert—presume to contradict this our definition: let him be anathema."[88]

The disgruntled within the ranks eventually got in line, "but not," according to Hennesey, "without considerable soul searching." Jesuit author F. X. Weninger helped matters by putting the jelly on the bottom shelf: "Yes, the Catholic world at large, without any difference of nationality, hemisphere, or zone, acknowledges also in our times, by an interior conviction of faith, the apostolic see as the highest tribunal on earth in matters of faith, and the Roman pontiff to be the infallible teacher of the faithful peoples on the globe."[89]

Baltimore's James Cardinal Gibbons assured the nation's Roman Catholics that

> the present illustrious Pontiff is a man of no ordinary sanctity. He has already filled the highest position in the Church for upwards of thirty years, "a spectacle to the world, to angels, and to men," and no man can point out a stain upon his moral character...
>
> The revealed word of God is the constitution of the Church. This is the *Magna Charta* of our Christian liberties. The Pope is the official guardian of our religious constitution, as the Chief Justice is the guardian of our civil constitution.
>
> When a dispute arises in the Church regarding the sense of Scripture, the subject is referred to the Pope for final adjudication.[90]

Concerning Pius having a "moral character," "Reverend Jim" forgot to tell his readers that the Vatican Council had to "close 'er down" early, as the pontiff's own Italian parishioners occupied Rome on September 20, 1870. To play it safe, "His Holiness" went into a self-imposed exile within the protective walls of *Castel Sant'Angelo* until he finally kicked the bucket in 1878. *The Oxford Dictionary of the Popes* adds, "This affection, however, did not prevent the anticlerical Roman mob... from holding up the procession accompanying his body from its provisional resting-place in St. Peter's to S. Lorenzo fuori le Mura, and attempting to fling it into the Tiber."[91]

Secretary Thompson was not the least bit impressed with all the "pontifical platitudes," writing in 1878:

> The decree of papal infallibility was a severe blow at the cause of personal as well as political freedom; and by now consenting to make it the chief corner-stone of their ecclesiastical polity, they avow their readiness beforehand to acquiesce in whatsoever shall be demanded of them, no matter how enormous it may be and to what degree of humiliation it may reduce them.[92]

And as to the inherent dangers to American freedom, he added,

> From both these classes—both priests and laymen—the pope exacts implicit obedience, without inquiry or any appeal to their own reason. If it shall be yielded by the Roman Catholic population of the United States, and if it is really the design that the papal exactions shall be carried to the extent of interfering with their obligations as citizens, there is no difficulty in seeing that they may be ultimately led into an attitude of antagonism to our form of government. At this point lies the danger most seriously to be apprehended by the people of the United States—a danger which underlies many, if not all, of the questions by which the nation is periodically excited. While we may not now be able to anticipate the precise time or form of its appearing, we should not be unprepared to meet it, if, by any possibility, it shall be hereafter precipitated upon us.[93]

MOODY & SAM JONES

Thus we see that the post-Civil War era was indeed a time of great peril for the United States of America. While the South was being re-invaded by *carpetbaggers*, the North was under siege by *Catholics*. Radical reconstruction and spiraling immigration threatened America with more harm than was inflicted by the war itself.

The greatest cause for alarm, however, was that the twofold crisis was being fostered by an intellectual repudiation of the King James Bible by the leading Baptist scholars of that time. It is true that, in most cases, the average Baptist layman was not "smart" enough to realize he needed an improved Bible; therefore, the Lord was willing to continue using His people in significant ways. For instance, it was a Baptist minister, Reverend Francis Bellamy, who composed our sacred *Pledge of Allegiance* to the flag in 1892.

Nevertheless, the Bible's integrity had been questioned, and the Holy Spirit was not about to allow this challenge to go unanswered.

To afflict the Northern eggheads, a teenage shoe clerk with a fifth-grade education was raised up in the center of New England's intellectual community, while a reclaimed drunken attorney got the heavenly nod for the cream of Southern society. Dwight Lyman Moody (1837–1899) and Samuel Porter Jones (1847–1906) were about to show America just how powerful the old AV 1611 was after all.

Neither of the two would have been viewed as average, even in the kindergarten years. At the age of five, Sam was selected by the older students of the Oak Bowery, Alabama, public school to participate in their commencement exercises. The closing line of his memorized speech was quite a showstopper: "In coming years and thundering tones the world shall hear of Sam P. Jones!"[94] Likewise, when Dwight was only five, he was able to visit his grandmother on one occasion by talking the stagecoach agent into selling him a 10¢ ticket for half-price by promising to ride on the luggage rack. (Of course, this was a "major inconvenience" for a lad so young.) And for his half-fare return, the broke but resourceful entrepreneur picked a bouquet of fresh flowers and successfully offered them to the other agent in lieu of a nickel.[95]

After establishing a successful law practice in the state of Georgia, Sam succumbed to alcoholism and quickly sank to the bottom. He was sobered up by the death of his Christian father and accepted Christ as his personal Saviour in a revival meeting conducted in his grandfather's Methodist church. Sam preached his very first sermon exactly one week later, using Romans 1:16 as his text.

Dwight lost his own father at the tender age of four and later quit school after the fifth grade to help the family make ends meet. Whereas "Dr." Cone turned to acting, Moody chose to support his mother by *working* for a living. Moody's two uncles offered him a position in their Boston shoe store on the condition that he attend Sunday school and church. Moody selected the Mt. Vernon Congregational Church pastored by Ed Kirk, a former associate evangelist for Charles G. Finney. (Revelation 14:13c) When seated in Ed Kimball's young adult class, the unlearned visitor elicited considerable laughter by thumbing through Genesis after the teacher had announced a text in John. Kimball later won his 17-year-old pupil to Christ in the back room of the shoe store where Moody worked. Three weeks after he was saved, Moody applied for church membership but failed the examination interview. In answer to the question, "What has Christ done for you, and for us all, that especially entitles Him to our love and obedience?" Dwight replied, "I think He has done a great deal for us all, but I don't know of anything He has done in particular."[96] He passed on his second attempt ten months later.

Although different from one another in many ways, both men had the same calling—*to demonstrate the power of the Old Black Book!* And yet, their very uniqueness was in itself the ultimate manifestation of biblical potency. While Sam started out as a Methodist circuit rider, Dwight relocated to Chicago and began a Sunday school mission among the city's street urchins. Both men were spiritual workaholics. In back-to-back revivals in St. Louis and Cincinnati, Sam preached 250 sermons in little more than two months. Dwight earned his nickname of "Crazy Moody" by making as many as 200 visits in a single day. He also thought nothing of "bribing" his "Sabbath school scholars" to attend services by rewarding them with gifts ranging from caged squirrels to new suits of clothing. (John 6:26)

As already mentioned, each man was a designer model in the hand of the Master. Not only did they thoroughly understand their purpose, but they persevered with manly resoluteness. With the majority of his meetings conducted in the Bible Belt, the "Hellfire-and-Damnation" Jones rarely preached on Heaven. When a certain committee complained that they had brought him to town to preach to sinners but that he ended up preaching at them, Sam replied, "Never mind, I will get to the sinners. I never scald hogs until the water is hot."[97] Another time when asked why he didn't attack the Catholics, he answered, "When I get through with the Methodists, it's bed-time."

The *Cartersville American* paid the following tribute to Sam's amazing individuality:

> Sam Jones is the greatest revivalist the South has ever produced. I never saw his equal. There is something very wonderful about the man. He can jump on a dry goods box on the public square and commence preaching, and in five minutes every barkeeper and street loafer in town will be listening. He can go to the darkest corner of Pickens County and the most ignorant man in the congregation will understand and appreciate his sermon. He can stand up before the finest city church, before the most intelligent audience and hold them spellbound by his eloquence. He can appear before a mixed audience in a theater and silence the hissing tongues and the loud laugh by the simple story of the cross. "I have known him since he was a wild, rude, dissipated boy on the streets of Cartersville. Before he professed religion and commenced to preach, he was as common as any boy I know. He has loomed into importance as an evangelist and revivalist until he stands now second only to Talmage and

Moody. He is a pale-faced, square-built, dark-skinned man, and would not attract the second glance from a casual observer. But when he speaks he catches the ear of everybody, and touches the heart of every listener. He is strikingly original, and his imagination is rich and fertile, his illustrations are forcible and pointed, his language is terse and strong, his appeals are touching and pathetic, and his powers of endurance beyond anything I ever saw." So talked a gentleman in the presence of the editor... We are proud of Sam Jones, not only because he is a Cartersville man, but because he is a true man, an earnest preacher and a friend to humanity. His mission on earth is a grand one, and grandly does he fill it.[98]

Sam had little patience with "culture vultures." Following his first campaign in Nashville, the high-society crowd confirmed that the feeling was mutual. An excerpt from the *Union* editorial stated:

If Mr. Jones's style and language suit the good people of our city, then we can no longer rightfully maintain our boast that Nashville is the "Athens of the South"... We have as much culture, refinement and esthetic taste in Nashville as any city of its size in the Union, and that this so-called reverend gentleman should be permitted to say such things in our leading pulpits, and then be invited to come again, amazes us beyond expression.[99]

Sam's basic "problem" was that he couldn't stand *hypocrites*. The Honorable Tim Watson was an eyewitness to a Jones meeting in Thompson, Georgia:

How he did peel the amen corner. How he did smash their solemn self-conceit, their profound self-satisfaction, their peaceful co-partnership with the Almighty, their placid conviction that they were trustees of the New Jerusalem. After awhile with solemn, irresistible force he called on these brethren to rise in public, confess their shortcomings, and kneel for Divine grace. And they knelt. With groans, and sobs, and tears, these old bellwethers of the flock fell on their knees and cried aloud in their distress.

Then what? He turned his guns on us sinners. He abused us fore and aft. He gave us grape and canister and all the rest. He abused us and ridiculed us, he stormed at us and laughed at us, he called us flop-eared hounds, beer kegs, and whiskey soaks. He plainly said that we were all hypocrites and liars, and he intimated somewhat broadly, that most of us would steal.

After the meetings the community settled back to business, but it has never been the same community since. Gambling has disappeared, loud profanity on the streets was heard no more, and the bar-rooms were run out of the country.[100]

If "Reverend" Jones were alive today, do you think he would get many speaking invitations? Do you suppose Pat Robertson would want to interview him on the 700 Club? In *The Life and Sayings of Sam P. Jones*, written by his wife, Mrs. Jones informs us that her husband once stirred the community of West Point, Georgia, to revival by having his door-to-door visitation teams (consisting only of Sam, the host pastor and two elderly ladies) greet the unsuspecting residents with the blunt announcement, **"You are going to hell."**[101]

On another occasion, the mayor of Palestine, Texas, was so offended when Sam exposed the corruption in his administration that he literally attacked the evangelist at the local train depot. In a telegraph message to his wife, Sam related:

> Mrs. Sam P. Jones, Cartersville, Ga.:
>   The one-horse mayor of Palestine, Texas, tried to cane me at the train this morning. He hit me three times. **I wrenched the cane from him, and wore him out.** I am well. Not hurt. Will lecture to-night at LaGrange.
>
>   Sam P. Jones[102]

When the Catholic media magnate, William Randolph Hearst, distorted Sam's remarks in *The Examiner*, the evangelist blasted "Patty's Papaw" accordingly. With Hearst's reporters seated before him, Sam retorted:

> You little sap-headed reporters, with eyes so close together that you can see through a keyhole with both of them, are sent here at night to take down my sermons; now, if you can't report them as I deliver them, you stay away from here.[103]

After certain reporters said that the press had made Sam Jones, the preacher replied, "Then let them make another one!"

The first time Moody heard his Southern counterpart preach, he was dumbfounded by his fearless manner and wrote him as follows:

> Dear Brother Jones: God has given you a sledgehammer with which to shatter the formalism of the church, and to batter down the strongholds of Satan. The good Spirit is helping you mightily to use it. God bless you.
>
>   D. L. Moody[104]

Whereas the colorful Jones rarely preached on Heaven, D. L. Moody rarely preached on Hell. Unlike Sam's Bible-Belt listeners, it was Dwight's special mission to take on the immigrants. Having known only religious fear and superstition, thousands of Roman Catholic hearts were melted by Moody's constant theme of the love of God. And yet, like Sam, Dwight was also one of a kind, Barlow writing:

> Occasionally there emerges a man out of the ranks of those soul-winning worthies called evangelists of whom it can rightly be said: "When God made him, He created a new mold and then broke the mold." This is altogether true of Dwight Lyman Moody. You can only explain this evangelist who shook two continents for Christ (America and Europe)—and who was one of God's greatest and the churches' chiefest evangelists; and who was one of the times' supremest soul winners—by saying, "But God."
>
> For if anyone ever appeared to be less qualified for the evangelist's office, it was D. L. Moody. He was unschooled (he quit after six years); he was unconventional (he refused ordination and rejected being called by any title except "Mr. Moody."); he was unseemly in appearance ("he was short, heavy looking—nearly three hundred pounds—[a] commonplace man without grace of look or gesture"); he was unpolished and ungrammatical in his preaching ("his words rushed from his bearded face like a torrent; often two hundred and thirty per minute...short staccato sentences; imperfect pronunciation. Spurgeon said, 'The only man I ever knew who said "Mesopotamia" in one syllable;...many "ain'ts" and "have gots" ' ").[105]

Moody was destined to butt heads with eggheads throughout his long and fruitful ministry. Will Moody wrote of his father's earliest attempts at public speaking:

> It is of interest in this connection to know that when he first rose to speak in prayer-meeting one of the deacons assured him that he would, in his opinion, serve God best by keeping still! Another critic, who commended his zeal in filling the pews he had hired in Plymouth Church, suggested that he should realize the limitations of his vocation and not attempt to speak in public. "You make too many mistakes in grammar," he complained. "I know I make many mistakes," was the reply, "and I lack a great many things, but I'm doing the best I can with what I've got." He paused and looked at the man searchingly, adding with his own irresistible manner: "Look here, friend, you've got grammar enough—what are you doing with it for the Master?"[106]

Both men were challenged to reach their full spiritual potential by listening to another man of God. From the lips of Reverend Simon Peter Richardson, Sam heard the liberating words, "The preacher is not a vessel, not a slave, but a king and his throne is the pulpit."[107] For Dwight, it was the life-changing statement uttered in Dublin, in 1867, by Evangelist Henry Varley that, "The world has yet to see what God will do with and for and through and in and by the man who is fully and wholly consecrated to Him."[108] Moody vowed to himself, "By the grace of God, I'll be that man."

SANCTIONED FROM ON HIGH

However, the significant common denominator for both preachers was their shared contempt for dry orthodoxy and a total reliance upon the precious Holy Bible. Sam would frequently say, "I despise theology and botany, but I love religion and flowers."[109] Mrs. Jones recalled her husband's first year in the ministry:

> The time between his conversion and the meeting of the annual conference was spent in earnest prayer, deep meditation and constant Bible study. Here he laid the foundation for his great ministry...He stored his mind with God's Holy Word, and became charged with its peculiar power. His wonderful memory retained the Scriptures that he learned in those early days, which served him to his last hours. He had a wonderful knowledge of the Bible, and Scripture was ever fresh in his mind. Some of the most beautiful and striking illustrations that Mr. Jones used in his preaching were taken from the Bible. His delineations of Bible characters were the most effective of any illustrations he used.[110]

For the record, Sam Jones was talking about the King James Bible, not the American Bible Union Version! Sam was often heard to say, "I'd rather study my ABC's in Heaven than my Greek and Hebrew in Hell!"

With the right Bible in hand, Sam's meetings were absolutely phenomenal! In 1884, a revival in Chattanooga yielded 1,000 decisions for Christ. Notable crusades in 1885 included: St. Joseph, Missouri (2,200 converts); Birmingham, Alabama (1,800 converts); and St. Louis, Missouri (1,600 converts).

In 1884, 13 pastors united to sponsor a Sam Jones revival in Memphis, Tennessee, the same city where Dr. Cone's Southern cronies had organized the Bible Revision Association in 1852. Thousands upon thousands continued to pack the Court Street Presbyterian Church, the largest auditorium of any kind in the city. Over 1,000 souls came to Christ during this five-week campaign.

The following year (1885), the ministers in Nashville erected a tent seating 6,000 and watched Sam *pack it out four times a day for over thirty consecutive days!* The "early" meeting was held at 6:00 a.m. It has been estimated that nearly 10,000 decisions for Christ resulted from that month-long revival. The city's entire population was only 50,000.

Six months later, Sam conducted a crusade in Cincinnati, considered to be the most wicked and obstinate city to which he had been called to labor. At the conclusion of his five-week Holy Ghost revival, the *Cincinnati Enquirer* reported:

> Never before was such a religious awakening known in Cincinnati...Conversions have been many...It was generally known that yesterday was the last day of his stay here, and every one who had heard him wanted to hear him again...Early in the afternoon policemen were stationed at the doors to control the crowd. For a time the street was completely blocked...It is not an extravagant estimate to say that fifty thousand people sought admission to Music Hall last night...
>
> At seven o'clock Elm Street from Twelfth to Fourteenth Streets was one surging black sea of humanity—the locked out. That no one was crushed to death is a miracle. There were at least forty thousand people around Music Hall...
>
> Mr. Jones drove up to the hall a little after seven o'clock, and, with the aid of a stalwart policeman, entrance was forced part of the way, when finally the policemen took him up on their shoulders and carried him to the entrance of the building...Facing the vast audience [of 10,000], he said: "I thank God the gospel of Jesus Christ can outdraw anything in Cincinnati."[111]

It was during this Cincinnati crusade that Moody heard Sam preach for the first time. The two became good friends, with Sam once remarking, "The difference between Mr. Moody and myself is this: Mr. Moody is like Peter, I am like Sam Jones."[112]

Mrs. Jones wrote, "Mr. Moody, with his usual sagacity, saw the needs of Chicago, as perhaps no other man did, and induced Mr. Jones to turn his steps hither, and begin this work."[113] Reporting on the spring crusade, the April 5, 1886, *Tribune* stated:

The great five-weeks' revival meeting with the Southern evangelist, Sam Jones, as the central and animating figure, is over. The finish was reached in a veritable blaze of glory... The audience last night was large... There must have been fully nine thousand people packed away in the building... There was scarcely breathing, much less standing-room... A careful estimate places the number of people turned away at about ten thousand... The meetings in the Casino during the past five weeks have been attended by nearly two hundred and sixty thousand persons, all of whom have been handled without trouble, disturbance or accident of any kind... Half an hour was spent with about a hundred penitents in the inquiry room. Thus closed the great meeting in Chicago.[114]

While the Lord used Sam primarily in the post-Reconstruction South, D. L. Moody was the greater bomb, being dropped on both sides of the Atlantic. The intelligentsia of the local New Testament church had decided that the Holy Spirit was finished with the "flawed" AV 1611. An evangelist sporting only a fifth-grade education was about to pay his respects to Dr. Cone, Phil Schaff and the other highbrow Bible correctors.

When a liberal minister declared that the story of Jonah and the whale was a myth, newspaper reporters asked Moody for his opinion. His four-word reply was telegraphed across the country: "I stand with Jonah."[115] Commenting on the Bible's supernatural preservation, he stated, "Infidels cast it overboard, but it will always swim to the shore." Moody was never so egotistical as to elevate his own intellect above the Word of God, declaring:

> If you ask, do I understand what is revealed in Scripture, I say no, but my faith bows down before the inspired Word, and I unhesitatingly believe the great things of God even when reason is blinded and the intellect confused.[116]

Of course, when Moody testified that his faith bowed down before "the inspired Word," he wasn't talking about a bunch of writings which no longer existed on the planet. Will Moody, quoting his father:

> It is a singular fact that few men, otherwise well educated, are acquainted with the English Bible. I can secure a hundred men who can teach Greek and Latin well where I can find only one that can teach the Bible well.[117]

Unlike the Greek scholar Schaff, Moody chose to build his ministry on the *English* Bible. Whereas Vedder had lamented, "The conversion of adults becomes with every decade increasingly rare," Moody was able to reap a mighty harvest because he had faith in the English Bible he was preaching: *"For this cause also thank we God without ceasing, because, when ye received the word of God which ye heard of us, ye received it not as the word of men, but as it is in truth, the word of God, which effectually worketh also in you that believe."* (I Thessalonians 2:13) William E. Dodge, a long-time friend of Mr. Moody, declared:

> But a stronger and greater influence was his beginning in the study of the English Bible. He devoted himself to an intense study of it, and from it got two things: In the first place, he gained that clear-cut, plain, simple Anglo-Saxon of the King James version, that gave him such an immense power over people everywhere. In the second place, he gained an arsenal and armament of promise and warning, which he used through all his life with such magnificent power. There was something wonderful about his simple directness. I could give by the hour instances of the clear way in which he went directly to a point.[118]

Because the American Bible Union Version was a product of the "Big Apple," it was fitting that Mr. Moody should receive his anointing in that same locale. After losing most of his facilities in the 1871 Chicago fire, the undaunted preacher journeyed to Wall Street to secure the necessary finances to rebuild. Pollock informs us that Mr. Moody got more than he expected:

> In broad daylight he walked down one of the busiest streets, Broadway or Fifth Avenue, he scarcely remembered which, while crowds thrust by and the clop-clink of cabs and carriages was in his ears and the newsboys shouted. The last chain snapped. Quietly, without a struggle, he surrendered. Immediately an overpowering sense of the presence of God flooded his soul. "God Almighty seemed to come very near. I felt I must be alone." He hurried to the house of a friend nearby, sent up his card, and brushed aside an invitation to "come and have some food." "I want to be alone. Let me have a room where I can lock myself in."
> His host thought best to humor him. Moody locked the door and sat on the sofa. The room seemed ablaze with God. Moody dropped to the floor and lay bathing his soul in the Divine.[119]

Moody's own words were as follows:

> I was crying all the time that God would fill me with His Spirit. Well, one day, in the city of New York—oh, what a day!—I cannot describe it,

I seldom refer to it; it is almost too sacred an experience to name. Paul had an experience of which he never spoke for fourteen years. I can only say that God revealed Himself to me, and I had such an experience of His love that I had to ask Him to stay His hand. I went to preaching again. The sermons were not different; I did not present any new truths, and yet hundreds were converted. I would not now be placed back where I was before that blessed experience if you should give me all the world—it would be as the small dust of the balance.[120]

The previous year, Mr. Moody "drafted" the talented Ira Sankey to become his soloist and congregational song leader. While doing picket duty on a moonlit night during the Civil War, the "Yankee Sankey" was miraculously delivered from certain death when he began to sing, "Saviour, Like a Shepherd Lead Us." A Confederate sniper who had Sankey in his sights was so moved by the singing ("...be the guardian of our way...", etc.), that he lowered his rifle and disappeared into the shadows.[121]

In 1873, Moody and Sankey departed for Westcott and Hort country. England's Christians would also receive a propitious object lesson concerning their "archaic" Authorized Version. Dr. Reese relates some of their exploits over the next two years:

> They spent two weeks in Dundee and then began the Glasgow, Scotland crusade... These meetings soon moved into the 4,000 seat Crystal Palace and after three months climaxed with a service at the famed Botanic Gardens Palace. Moody was unable to even enter the building surrounded by 15,000 to 30,000 people, so he spoke to them from a carriage and the choir sang from the roof of a nearby shed...
>
> Now Ireland was calling... A great climactic service was held... on October 8, in the open air with thousands attending. One final service was held October 15 with admission by ticket only. Tickets were given only to those who wanted to be saved. 2,400 came.
>
> Next it was Dublin... The Exhibition Hall seating 10,000 was filled night after night with an estimated 3,000 won to Christ.
>
> Back in England on November 29, the Manchester crusade was held... As many as 15,000 were trying to gain admission for a single service... Bingley Hall seated only 11,000 but crowds of 15,000 came nightly... Then on the south side of London he spoke for several weeks in the Victoria Theatre until a special tabernacle seating 8,000 was constructed on Camberwell Green where he finished his five month crusade.[122]

The discerning student will note that these sensational meetings (1873–1875) were occurring simultaneously with the blasphemous Revision Committee of 1871–1881. Dr. Hort just had to check things out for himself. Observe his uppity disdain for the Christ-like simplicity of Moody's person:

> Think of my going with Gray yesterday afternoon to hear "Moody and Sankey" at the Hay Market. I am very glad to have been **but should not care to go again.** All was much as I expected, except that the music was inferior, and altogether Sankey did not leave a favorable impression. Moody had great sincerity, earnestness and good sense, with some American humor which he mostly keeps under restraint, but in matter is quite conventional and common place.[123]

It is rather humorous that despite Hort's highbrow description of Moody's manner as "common," his message was convicting enough to send the "good doctor" running—"but [I] should not care to go again." And of course, it was the preaching of the "corrupt" AV 1611 that so unnerved Professor Hort!

The attendance figures from Mr. Moody's closing services in London would have rattled any dry scholar—Agricultural Hall, 60 meetings attended by 330,000; Bow Road Hall, 60 meetings attended by 600,000; Camberwell Hall, 60 meetings attended by 480,000. **In all, 285 meetings were attended by over 2.5 million people!** Not bad for a Bible in need of revision!

After two years in the United Kingdom, Moody and Sankey returned to America in the wake of favorable press reviews. Moody knew his mission, stating, "Water runs down hill, and the highest hills in America are the great cities. If we can stir them we shall stir the whole country."[124] The Northern Baptists were in for the shock of their lives; Dr. Reese states:

> His first city-wide crusade in America was in Brooklyn beginning October 31, 1875 at the Rink, seating 7,000. Only non-church members could get admission tickets as 12,000 to 20,000 crowds were turned away. Some 2,000 converts resulted.
>
> Next came Philadelphia starting on November 21 with nightly crowds of 12,000. On January 19, 1876 President Grant and some of his cabinet attended. Total attendance was 1,050,000 with 4,000 decisions for Christ.
>
> Next it was the New York crusade running from February 7 to April 19, 1876. The meetings were held in the Great Roman Hippodrome on Madison Avenue, where the Madison Square Gardens now stands. Two large halls gave a combined seating attendance of 15,000. Moody had just

turned 39 for this crusade. Some 6,000 decisions came as a result of his ten-week crusade. Three to five services a day were held with crowds up to 60,000 daily.

The Chicago crusade started October 1, 1876 in a 10,000 seat tabernacle, closing out on January 16, 1877. The sixteen week crusade was held with estimates being from 2,500 to 10,000 converts...

The Boston crusade was held January 28 to May 1, 1877 in a tabernacle seating 6,000. 1877–78 saw many smaller towns in the New England states being reached. 1878–79 saw Baltimore reached in 270 preaching engagements covering seven months.[125]

Although loved by the common man, Mr. Moody was the liberals' worst nightmare. The humanist Walt Whitman traveled from his home in Camden, New Jersey, to hear Mr. Moody in Boston. The effeminate poet must have really been shaken, writing:

> Having heard Moody I am satisfied
> But I shall not come to him to be saved.
> He is not my idea of a Saviour.
> I do not believe in him
> Nor his God
> Nor his method of swaying sinners
> nor his stories which sound like lies.
> I, Walt, tell him he is an ignorant charlatan,
> a mistaken enthusiast,
> and that Boston will ere long desire him to *git*.[126]

Fortunately, Walt didn't know what was happening. While the renowned Thomas Orchestra gave a benefit concert for the "Old South" Fund, the hall was reported to be half empty, while 6,000 heard Moody and Sankey.[127]

By this time, Dr. Philip Schaff was getting on in years. As is often the case with apostates, Schaff grew wackier as he neared the end of the trail. In addition to being an avowed liberal theologian, he was also a semi-private devotee of Eastern mysticism. Riplinger points out that Schaff's colleagues at the University of Berlin called him "the theological mediator between East and West."[128] Schaff himself had chided Christians, saying, "They vainly imagine that they have a monopoly on truth."[129]

In 1893, the World's Fair was held in Moody's Chicago from May 7 to October 31. Of particular interest to Schaff was the ecumenical "Parliament of World Religions" exhibit, described by its promoters as "Babel...the actual beginning of a new epoch."[130] Citing *Neely's History of the Parliament of Religions*, Riplinger writes, "It was the first occasion since the tower of Babel to proclaim, 'The Brotherhood of Man,' '[T]he unification of the world in things of religion,' and 'the coming unity of mankind.' "[131]

With constant references to the "recognition of a new age," or the "transforming touch of the new age," a sample of the many lecture titles would include: "Christian and Hindu Thought" (Rev. Hume); "Synthetic Religion" (Kinza Hirai); "Plea for Toleration" (Dr. Field); "Universal Brotherhood" (Prince Wolkonsky); "The good in All Faiths" (Dr. Hugenholtz); "The Ultimate Religion" (Bishop Keane); "Need of a Wider Concept of Revelation" (J. E. Carpenter); "Buddha, The World's Debt to" (H. Dharmapala); "Islam, The Spirit of " (Mohammed Webb) and "Shinto" (Bishop of Japan).[132]

For the record, Schaff called this assemblage of religious perversion "the sum of my life and my theological activity." As America's leading apostate, he was honored to add his personal endorsement, writing, "I give you, with pleasure, the liberty of using my name in the list of those who recommend the holding of an international and interdenominational religious congress."[133] Wilkinson points out that Schaff "was so happy among the Buddhists, Confucianists, Shintoists, and other world religions, that he said he would be willing to die among them."[134]

By contrast, while Schaff was "meditating with the mystics" in the Parliament of Religions, D. L. Moody and a host of soul winners were laying siege to the fairground and its environs with *125* daily Gospel meetings! Describing the World's Fair as "the opportunity of a century," Moody was also burdened for the international religionists in attendance, his son relating:

> Chicago at all times is a cosmopolitan city, and this was, of course, especially apparent during that notable season. Strangers from all parts of the world came by the thousands, and it was Mr. Moody's purpose, as far as possible, to reach all people and all nations.[135]

Whereas the "esteemed" chairman of the American Revision committee expressed his willingness to "die *among* them," Moody used a *King James Bible* to inform the same of One Who had *already* died *for* them! Dr. Reese relates that "1,933,210 signed the guest register of the Bible School."[136] An eyewitness account describes an exhilirating Sunday morning service on the fairground:

The surroundings were the usual circus furniture— ropes, trapezes, gaudy decorations, etc., while in an adjoining canvas building was a large menagerie, including eleven elephants. Clowns, grooms, circus-riders, men, women, and children, eighteen thousand of them, and on a Sunday morning, too! Whether the Gospel was ever before preached under such circumstances I know not, but it was wonderful to ear and eye alike.

When that mighty throng took up the hymn, "Nearer, my God, to Thee," a visible sense of awe fell upon the multitude. After an hour of singing and prayer Mr. Moody rose to preach, his text being, *"The Son of Man is come to seek and to save that which was lost."* The Spirit of God was present. The hush of Heaven was over the meeting.[137]

Moody was probably unaware of America's approaching midnight hour and the role that his fellow World's Fair attendee would play in its encroachment. Schaff's Old and New Testament committees had forwarded a minimum of recommendations to Chairman Ellicott's attention. With the May, 1881, publication of the Revised Version in England, the United States team entered into its agreed-upon waiting period of *20 years* before releasing their own product—the American Standard Version (ASV)—to the American market in 1901. (Apparently, profit was more important than recommended improvements.)

It was during this interim that Dr. Schaff would have viewed "Crazy Moody's" tireless soul-winning marathon. With his life's work behind him, Schaff's desire to die among the "gurus" was realized that same year when he beat them all to their shared fate of a Christ-rejecter's Hell. In this case, the 11 circus elephants that "heard" Moody preach showed more sense than the renowned seminary professor!

By the time of Moody's death on December 22, 1899, the humble evangelist had preached to over 100 million people! And yet, the full significance of this astounding figure can be gained only by considering that the combined population of America and Great Britain (including Wales) was approximately 62 million in 1870 and 108 million in 1900. According to Dr. Paul Tan, Billy Graham's entire evangelistic team addressed only 53,561,970 listeners over a comparative period of time (1947–1977), when the world's population was considerably higher.

Seven years before he went to his reward, Dwight received a special gift from the widow of another giant for God. Although Charles Hadden Spurgeon had always preached from the AV 1611, he did, on rare occasions, succumb to the spirit of his age by referring to certain "improved" renderings, etc. As if to symbolize Mr. Moody's lifetime achievement of restoring confidence in the King James Bible *by producing over 1 million conversions*, the widow of the Prince of Preachers sent Dwight the following hallowed memento:

Mr. D. L. Moody, from Mrs. C. H. Spurgeon.
In tender memory of the beloved one gone home to God. This Bible has been used by my beloved husband, and is now given with unfeigned pleasure to one in whose hands its service will be continued and extended.
S. Spurgeon.
Westwood, London, Nov. 20, 1892.[138]

"Whatever the prejudiced may say against him, the honest-minded and just will remember the amazing work of this *plain man*."[139]

New York Times
3 March 1889

XVI

Murder, Inc.

> *"They that forsake the law praise the wicked: but such as keep the law contend with them."* (Proverbs 28:4)

THE HEADLINES OF the *Cartersville News* for October 16, 1906, sent shock waves throughout the community: "Rev. Sam P. Jones, the great evangelist, is dead. He died on Monday." Death had come suddenly and unexpectedly for the 58-year-old preacher as he was returning home by train from a revival in Oklahoma City, Oklahoma. The cause was thought to be heart failure, superinduced by an attack of acute indigestion.

While only a single person is believed to have attended the interment of Karl Marx, the *socialist*, over 30,000 grieving mourners filed past the remains of Sam Jones, the *evangelist*, as his body lay in state in the center of the capitol building in Atlanta. One woman took a final look at the man of God and fell to the floor crying, "Oh, I can't stand it!" She was dead within the hour.[1]

As a special tribute to the departed soul winner, his Nashville memorial service on October 28 was transformed into a revival meeting. Dr. R. A. Torrey closed the occasion with an earnest appeal to the unconverted to receive Christ, stating:

> It was my privilege to speak the closing words at a memorial service in Northfield, Mass., of the late Dwight L. Moody. It is now my privilege to speak the closing words at the memorial service of another great

evangelist. Sam Jones is now on the other side of the river saying to all the unsaved of Nashville, "Come over here."

While thousands in this city yielded to his appeals during his ministry, there are others who resisted his tender entreaties, but now his voice is calling louder than it ever did before in this tabernacle. I don't believe that Mr. Jones would feel that this service was complete unless an opportunity was given to accept Christ, and I am going to ask those of you who will become Christians to rise to your feet.[2]

That Dr. Torrey was invited to bring the concluding remarks at *both* memorial services is significant. For the Christian who shares God's exalted view of Scripture (Psalm 138:2), the passing of these two mighty evangelists marked the end of one era and the beginning of another—the line of demarcation being a belief in the *preserved* Word of God. Whereas Moody had declared, "I stand with Jonah," Sam added,

> I would have believed it just the same if it had said that Jonah swallowed the whale. I've got no better sense than to believe the Bible. Call me a fool for it, and I'm a happy fool. I believe every word in the Bible. **I accept everything between the lids of the Book.** I have good reasons for my faith.[3]

The reader will note that Sam's faith was not centered on the Bible's miracles, but rather on the Bible itself. And because Sam had never attended seminary (i.e., "hadn't been *messed* with"), the only Bible in which he had any confidence was a book that he could hold in his hand—one that had "lids."

> God Almighty was four hundred years getting up **this Book** and every want of the universe can be supplied out of **this Book**. If I had the billions of men of earth before me I would refer them to **this precious Book**. Here's a blessed balm for every wound, a cure for every ill. Thank God for **this precious Book,** divinely written and divinely given to save the world.[4]

But not just *any* English translation would do. It was a *King James* Bible that had delivered Sam from his drunkenness and that was "reason" enough for him to believe it. According to Dr. Lawrence Vance, a total of 28 different Bibles and New Testaments were produced during the evangelist's lifetime alone.[5] Seeing the handwriting on the wall, Sam declared, "We preachers do not any longer speak with authority."[6] With the spirit of revision in the air, he warned,

> The great curse of the world to-day is not out of the church, but in it. I know I touch upon ground that may bring out resentment, but, brethren, the harder and louder I say this the more I resemble my Divine Master... Every denunciatory sentence He uttered was to the church, to the members of the church...I can stand a railroad humbug, a business humbug, a newspaper humbug, but God deliver me from a religious humbug.
>
> I believe it was at Princeton that some young fellows tried to fool a professor who was a bugologist and knew bugs from creation down. They made up a bug from the head, wings, feet and legs of different bugs, and taking it to him, said, "What kind of a bug is this?" He replied, "Why, that's a humbug."
>
> Now, take the hands of a swindler, the head of a keen trickster and the mouth of a saint, put them together and you have the biggest kind of a humbug.[7]

As noted in a previous chapter, one of the biggest religious humbugs of the nineteenth century was Dr. Philip Schaff, chairman of the 1901 ASV Committee. Why else would an apostate who was comfortable with everything from Buddhism to Catholicism recommend the same Gospel message preached by D. L. Moody? Speaking of his father, David Schaff wrote:

> He gave his encouragement by word and presence to the meetings held on a large scale in New York in 1876, under the leadership of Moody and Sankey. Of them he used to say, "It is a sin to act or speak against such a religious revival, perhaps the greatest the world has seen since Wesley and Whitefield. It is the best refutation of infidelity, and shows what power the simple Gospel story of sin and grace still has."[8]

If Phil *really* meant what he said, why did he sanction over 36,000 changes in the English translation used by Moody to bring about this wonderful revival? Although Schaff had the "mouth of a saint," he also had the "head of a keen trickster." As Sam reiterated, "I always did have a hatred for shams and humbugs and cheats, and of all the humbugs that ever cursed the universe, I reckon the religious humbug is the humbuggiest."[9]

However, though Dr. Schaff was an apostate humbug, he wasn't stupid. His praise of Moody's work would leave the door open to influence the evangelist's intellectual protégé, R. A. Torrey. (*"A flattering mouth worketh ruin."* Proverbs 26:28b)

R. A. TORREY

Because of his faithful track record in personal soul winning, Dr. Torrey's disastrous endorsement of the corrupt Revised Version (1881) made him the outstanding pawn of Satan's revisionist forces. The first president of Moody Bible Institute should have known better. By the year 1881, approximately *90* different translations and paraphrases had already challenged the King James Bible, beginning with Henry Hammond's *A Paraphrase and Annotations Upon All the Books of the New Testament* in 1653 (not to mention an additional *65* by the year of Torrey's death in 1928). Did Dr. Torrey *really* think the RV and ASV would unseat the Monarch of Books?

Secondly, Dr. Torrey had already witnessed the power of the King James Bible since his first encounter with D. L. Moody in 1878. One could say that Torrey had a job in the first place because his boss kept producing the converts in need of training.

The problem was that Dr. Torrey started running with a crowd that cared only about defending the *autographs*. Dr. James M. Gray, a close friend of Dr. Torrey and future dean of Moody Bible Institute, declared:

> Let it be stated further in this definitional connection, that the record for whose inspiration we contend is the original record—the autographs or parchments of Moses, David, Daniel, Matthew, Paul or Peter, as the case may be, and not any particular translation or translations of them whatever.[10]

Another factor which helps explain Torrey's preference for the RV was his dangerous academic sojourn in Germany in 1882–83. While studying in the Lutheran universities of Leipzig and Erlanger, his faith in the Word of God was shaken. Dr. Reese writes:

> As a brilliant student he made great progress in school. Early in his studies he was a pronounced higher critic, but ere he had completed them, he was convinced of the falsity of his views and swung gradually back to old conservative doctrines, reversing the usual trend because of Europe's emphasis on higher criticism.[11]

While Mr. Moody was still alive, Dr. Torrey's earliest books were found to contain numerous citings from the Revised Version. On the title page for *How to Obtain Fullness of Power*, 1897, we read, "Strengthened with **power through** his Spirit in the **inward** man."—Ephesians 3:16, RV[12] In his famous sermon entitled *Ten Reasons Why I Believe the Bible Is the Word of God*, Torrey quotes the RV rendering in John 7:17, "If any man **willeth to** do his will, he shall know of the teaching, whether it be of God, or whether I speak from myself."

However, with the death of his beloved mentor in 1899, Torrey would begin to cry, "Where is the Lord God of Moody?" On December 23, 1901, Torrey and his wife left for a revival tour throughout Asia and the South Pacific. Would you like to know which Bible he used when he was halfway around the world? Although his *mind* led him to embrace Westcott and Hort textual theory, his *heart* knew better when the salvation of lost souls was at stake.

When a Brahmin priest in Madura declared that worshipers bowing before the various Hindu shrines would gain eternal rewards, Dr. Torrey instantly replied, *"But as many as received him, to them gave he **power** to become **the sons** of God."* (John 1:12a)[13] Torrey didn't feel "led" to quote the RV's worthless, "But as many as received him, to them gave he **the right** to become children of God."

Another indication that Torrey chose to use Moody's "mantle" when push came to shove can be gleaned from those who benefitted from his sermons. One of the pastors and committee members from the city of Launceston (Tasmania) wrote:

> It seemed as though one could hear the impact, the thud of some truth, as it got home...People actually came to believe, before he finished, that he thought a quotation from Isaiah or John or Paul, or any of the inspired writers was sufficient warrant for deciding the gravest questions of life, and for doing so at once, without one moment's delay....
>
> **He just pinned us down to the Bible we had been reading all our lives**, as though the Bible settled it, and there was an end of it. This making of Scripture the **ultimate** and **final authority** of all matters of conduct, without any appeal from Scripture to the **scholars**, or to recent thought, or to the modifications which modern exegetes had introduced, was done with such cool nerve and overmastering conviction that it was simply staggering.[14]

However, for the ultimate insight as to which Bible got the job done, why not let Dr. Torrey testify for himself ? Speaking before a welcome-home meeting in Chicago described as "one of the largest crowds in the history of the Windy City," the enlightened Dr. Torrey proclaimed:

> **You, who think we need a new Bible, something better than the Bible, the old Bible, an expurgated Bible, take heed to our experiences. Eighteen months of preaching its Gospel, thirty thousand men and women won to Christ, proves that the Bible, the old Bible, is what the world needs, what the twentieth century needs.**[15]

How could *any* Bible believer improve on such a powerful statement? It is a shame, however, that Dr. Torrey did not stick to his own admonition. Habits can be hard to break, especially when one's peers are involved. Torrey's literary works continued to endorse the "expurgated" Revised Version. The godly educator represents a good illustration of Job 32:9a, *"Great men are not always wise."*

FUNDAMENTALISM

Thus, we discern that with the Homegoing of D. L. Moody and Sam Jones, the *old-time religion* passed off the scene as well. The new movement led by Torrey's intellectual contemporaries came to be known as *Fundamentalism.* The standard definition for this "militant" term, as given by David Beale's *In Pursuit of Purity,* is the "unqualified acceptance of and obedience to the Scriptures."[16]

As we have already seen, however, the only Scriptures recognized by this new movement as the believer's final authority unfortunately *no longer existed* (like John MacArthur, Jr.'s, view of Christ's shed blood at Calvary). And to complicate matters further, because the common man continued to embrace the "archaic, Elizabethan English," as found in the King James Bible, *fundamental* pastors had to conceal their inner convictions that the *new* "Bibles" were really superior to the Authorized Version. Dr. Louis Talbot, the first president of BIOLA, wrote:

> For **public** reading and worship, so do I **prefer** the King James Version. And nothing in all the English language can compare with it for beauty and majesty and dignity of style. It is still the Bible of the people. It is familiar to most Christians, and therefore **desirable** for **public**

reading, **to avoid confusion.** Those are the reasons why I **use** it in the church services....

Yet...since that date, many valuable manuscripts, versions, and archeological discoveries have become available to scholars; and...these devout, scholarly men...have been able to improve on the accuracy of an English translation here and there...

Accordingly, the **American Standard Version** and the **English Revised Version**, which are **practically** the same in **most** respects, are the **most accurate** translations in our English language.[17]

While the perceived enemy of Fundamentalism was supposed to be German rationalism (Baur, Rauschenbusch, Schleiermacher, etc.), it apparently never dawned on anyone that the acclaimed revisions were themselves the product of German apostasy. Arthur Westcott confirmed that, as early as 1861, his father was charged with being "unsafe" and of *"Germanizing."*[18] Like the man in Amos 5:19 who eluded the lion and bear from without only to be bitten by a serpent in his own house, Dr. Torrey repudiated the higher criticism that had swayed him overseas, only to succumb to the venom of Philip Schaff (RV and ASV), the humbuggiest of all German heretics—right in the good old USA.

Most of Dr. Torrey's fundamental peers were Presbyterians such as J. Wilbur Chapman, William Bierderwolf, T. Dewitt Talmage, Louis Talbot, C. I. Scofield, B. B. Warfield, G. Gresham Machen, and William Moorehead (a great-uncle to actress Agnes Moorehead), with an occasional Reformed Episcopalian like James M. Gray thrown in for good measure. A short list of prominent Baptist fundamentalists would include A. T. Pierson, A. J. Gordon, William Bell Riley, T. T. Shields, John Roach Straton, R. T. Ketcham, Lee Scarborough and the incomparable J. Frank Norris.

Although the emerging party line of Fundamentalism continued to develop around the sacrosanct autographs, old timers such as Dr. W. B. Riley found it hard to abandon the "Old Black Book." In his 1917 work, *The Menace of Modernism*, Riley declared, "The King James Version was absolutely inerrant."[19]

Apart from their on-again, off-again shortsightedness concerning the Bible issue, most of these early fundamentalists were good and godly men. And yet, this very testimony made them the ideal couriers for error, as a "lie" passed along by an R. A. Torrey would be harder to catch than one propagated by CFR member, Dr. Reinhold Niebuhr.[20] (Acts 17:11)

However, Beale points out that the "Revision became somewhat of a dead issue very quickly, since the King James Version maintained its popularity over the new version by a great margin."[21] What this militant author is trying to say is that the official version of "Historic Fundamentalism" *flopped* big time! R. A. Torrey even outlived the ASV by four years. (The ASV went bankrupt in 1924.)

The reason why advocates of the Authorized Version often appear to have a bad attitude concerning the subject of Bible revision is because the unscrupulous "scholars' union" continues to disavow the historical record. According to Dr. Vance, approximately *311* different Bibles, New Testaments and paraphrases have surfaced through 1991 and some of the brethren have the audacity to accuse "King-James-only" people of *dividing the body?!*

Now, of course, there would be a stiff price to pay for repudiating the AV 1611. Speaking of codices ℵ and B, Dean John William Burgon, the outstanding conservative scholar of nineteenth-century Anglicanism, had warned his own nation: "Those two documents are caused to cast their sombre shadows a long way ahead and to darken all of our future."[22] Though the sun never set on the British empire in Burgon's day, an English embracing of the Revised Version triggered a spiritual eclipse that has lasted over a hundred years: tribal spears from the Boer War; mustard gas and V2 rockets from World Wars I and II; the sinkings of the *Lusitania* and *Titanic*; socialism and Fabianism; tabloids; punk rockers; IRA bombings; three-day work weeks; Charles and Di's divorce; and *a present national church attendance of only three percent!*

A similar pattern of moral decline and accompanying judgment occurred throughout the United States as well. Larson's *An Encyclopedia of the Cults* states, "Spiritualism was introduced to England and Germany in the 1850's, and **in the United States mediums flourished during the years 1880–1920.**"[23] According to the National Spiritualistic Association, its ranks have swelled to 160 United States "congregations."

America's century of Bible revision literally brought her from the "Gay 90's" to the "*Gay* 90's." Hollywood's first movie was released in 1911, only a decade after the ASV arrived. Over 200,000 Americans died in World War I, with hundreds of returning doughboys being quarantined in New York for syphilis. A deadly influenza epidemic (pestilence) killed an additional 500,000 Americans at home in a single year (1918–1919). Newspapers and magazines began to replace God's Word as the primary reading material in the home. Radio drove the wedge still deeper. The one-room schoolhouse was supplanted by the progressive education of pragmatist

John Dewey. The Roaring 20's ended with the Great Depression. And following an invasion of African music, the songs of Zion were successfully challenged by the blues, jazz, ragtime and the big band sound. Frederick Allen summarizes the sad condition of America's youth:

> The dresses that the girls—and for that matter most of the older women—were wearing seemed alarming enough. In July, 1920, a fashion-writer reported in the *New York Times* that "the American woman...has lifted her skirts far beyond any modest limitation," which was another way of saying that the hem was now all of nine inches above the ground....
>
> The current mode in dancing created still more consternation. Not the romantic violin but the barbaric saxophone now dominated the orchestra, and to its passionate crooning and wailing the fox-trotters moved in what the editor of the Hobart College *Herald* disgustedly called a "syncopated embrace." No longer did even an inch of space separate them; they danced as if glued together, body to body, cheek to cheek....
>
> Supposedly "nice" girls were smoking cigarettes—openly and defiantly, if often rather awkwardly and self-consciously. They were drinking—somewhat less openly but often all to efficaciously... and going out joyriding with men at four in the morning....
>
> Fathers and mothers lay awake asking themselves whether their children were not utterly lost; sons and daughters evaded questions, lied miserably and unhappily, or flared up to reply rudely that at least they were not dirty-minded hypocrites, that they saw no harm in what they were doing and proposed to go right on doing it.[24]

Allen further points out that the grown-ups were not exactly setting the best examples themselves:

> A fertile ground was ready for the seeds of Freudianism...Sex, it appeared, was the central and pervasive force which moved mankind.... The first requirement of mental health was to have an uninhibited sex life. If you would be well and happy, you must obey your libido....
>
> Finally, as the revolution began, its influence fertilized a bumper crop of sex magazines, confession magazines, and lurid motion pictures, and these in turn had their effect on a class of readers and movie-goers who had never heard and never would hear of Freud and the libido. The publishers of the sex adventure magazines, offering stories with such titles as "What I Told My Daughter the Night Before Her Marriage," "Indolent Kisses," and "Watch Your Step-Ins," learned to a nicety the gentle art of arousing the reader without arousing the censor....

Within a very few years, millions of American women of all ages followed the lead of the flappers of 1920 and took up smoking.... A formidable barrier between the sexes had broken down.... Of far greater significance, however, was the fact that men and women were drinking together. Among well-to-do people, the serving of cocktails before dinner became almost socially obligatory. Mixed parties swarmed up to the curtained grills of speakeasies and uttered the mystic password and girls along with men stood at the speakeasy bar with one foot on the old brass rail.[25]

LAWLESSNESS

However, in keeping with our central thesis relating America's unprecedented freedom to her fidelity to the King James Bible, the paramount sign of divine chastisement was evidenced by *a sharp increase of domestic lawlessness.*

On Friday, September 6, 1901, President William McKinley was gunned down by a Polish anarchist named Leon Czolgosz while attending the Pan American Exposition in Buffalo, New York. Before expiring on September 14, the godly McKinley comforted his sorrowing wife with the words, "God's will, not ours, be done!"[26]

Was it mere coincidence that President McKinley was shot only *11* days after Thomas Nelson published the American Standard Version? If so, it was the *third* coincidence in a row. Abraham Lincoln was in the White House when the Baptists released their infamous American Bible Union Version, while President James Garfield was shot by Charles Guiteau on July 2, 1881, only *46* days after the Revised Version was published. *That's some coincidence*—**three attacks on the King James Bible followed by three presidential assassinations!**

As usual, Satan was the ultimate triggerman, waging war against the world's premier Christian nation. John Dillinger (1902–1934) terrorized the Midwest, robbing banks and killing 16 people before he was finally shot by FBI agents. George "Baby Face" Nelson (1908–1934) also robbed banks and murdered several persons including three FBI agents. It took 16 slugs to kill him. George "Machine Gun" Kelly (1897–1954) died in Alcatraz. Bonnie Parker (1911–1934) and Clyde Barrow (1909–1934) perished in a hail of 187 bullets; at the time of their deaths, Clyde was driving in his socks and Bonnie was eating a sandwich. Mrs. Arizona Donnie Clark Barker (1872–1935), affectionately known as "Ma Barker," reared four bank-robbing, murdering sons—Arthur (1899–1939), Fred (1902–1935), Herman

(1894–1927) and Lloyd (1896–1949). Ma and Fred eventually got blown away at Lake Weir, Florida, after a 45-minute gun battle with FBI agents.

The criminal activity in America's cities far surpassed the havoc being caused by independent bank robbers and murderers in the nation's rural areas. The greatest wave of domestic violence in United States history was brought about by the twentieth-century phenomena known as ORGANIZED CRIME. **For some strange reason, it has rarely dawned on the average American (even, sad to say, on the average Christian) that the traditional Mafia, Syndicate, Cosa Nostra, etc., operating in the United States has been approximately *99% Roman Catholic in membership!***

Practically all of these moral problems can be traced to the unheeded warning of Thomas Jefferson that immigrants would flood America with "unbounded licentiousness." By 1900, the Catholic population in the United States had become 12,041,000 or 15.78%. During the following decade that figure climbed to 16,336,000 and by 1920, it was approximately 20 million or 18.76%. **By 1946, America's 24,402,224 Roman Catholics constituted the nation's largest denomination.**[27]

In 1946 the Church's various religious orders included 28,980 ordained priests, 6,721 Brothers and 139,218 Sisters with the hierarchy consisting of 5 cardinals, 22 archbishops and 136 bishops. At this time the Catholic Church owned, controlled and supervised a grand total of 11,075 educational establishments providing Catholic instruction to 3,205,804 young people. Also included in these figures were 769 colleges and universities and 193 seminaries.[28]

The population of every major American city today is predominantly Roman Catholic. Our largest airports are even named after prominent Catholics—Kennedy, LaGuardia, O'Hare, Dulles, Logan (and let's not forget the "Duke"—John Wayne Airport in Orange County, California). The St. Leopold Foundation had done its job well. And, of course, while all of this was going on, God's people were debating the merits of the King James Bible!

As to the "spiritual vibrancy" of America's Roman Catholics, words fail to convey their sad, benighted condition. With the Holy Bible off-limits, Catholics were taught to take their problems to an endless number of saints dealing in their own particular areas of expertise. A sample would include: for arthritis, St. James; dog bites, St. Hubert; blindness, St. Raphael; cancer, St. Peregrine; eye disease, St. Lucy; throat disease, St. Blase; foot disease,

St. Victor; headaches, St. Denis; heart trouble, St. John of God; sterility, St. Giles; and insanity, St. Dympna.

Other "heavenly specialists" could render assistance with such problems as: lightning storms, St. Barbara; beer drinking, St. Nicholas; domestic animals, St. Anthony; fire, St. Lawrence; floods, St. Columban; old maids, St. Andrew; pregnant women, St. Gerard; to have children, St. Felicitas; to obtain a husband, St. Joseph; to obtain a wife, St. Anne; to find lost articles, St. Anthony; and to apprehend thieves, St. Gervase.

Just about any Catholic in good standing had a special patron saint looking after his welfare. These intercessors are also remembered on their special days of the year: actors, St. Genesius (August 25); architects, St. Thomas (December 21); astronomers, St. Cominic (August 4); athletes, St. Sebastian (January 20);[29] etc.

THE ROMAN CATHOLIC BROTHERHOOD

Whenever a soul-winning Christian could get a Catholic to listen long enough to hear about the new birth, the local priest would always assure his shell-shocked parishioner that John 3:3 and 5 are references to Roman Catholic baptism (sprinkling). Cardinal Gibbons wrote in 1897:

> The Church teaches that Baptism is necessary for all, for infants as well as adults, and her doctrine rests on the following grounds: Our Lord says to Nicodemus: "Amen, amen, I say to thee, unless a man be born again of water and the Holy Ghost, he cannot enter into the kingdom of God."[30]

Therefore, according to the supposedly infallible teachings of Rome, every Catholic who has been sprinkled as an infant becomes a born-again Christian. And according to the pope, they are all members of the body of Christ. Should we laugh or cry? Because a bunch of spineless politicians ignored the warnings of President Jefferson, Professor Morse, General Lafayette, Secretary Thompson and Reverend Chiniquy, America received a religious facelift of catastrophic proportions.

How's *this* for *"a called-out assembly of born-again Christians"*? Anthony Joseph "Big Tuna" Accardo, James "Jimmie the Monk" Allegretti, Albert "Lord High Executioner" Anastasia, Donald "The Wizard of Odds" Angelini, Joseph "The Animal" Barboza, James "King of the Bombers" Belcastro, Joseph "Joe Bananas" Bonanno, William "Willie the Rat"

Cammisano, Vincent "Mad Dog" Coll, Frank "Three Fingers" Coppola, Salvadore "Big Nose Sam" DeStefano, John "No Nose" DiFronzo, Jimmy "Jimmy the Weasel" Fratianno, Carmine "The Cigar" Gulante, Joseph "Crazy Joe" Gallo and Benny "Benny the Meatball" Gamson.

And then we have: Mike "Mike the Devil" Genna, Michael "The Pope" Greco, Johnny "Two Gun" Guardino, Vincent "The Saint" Inserro, John "Honest John" Kelly, Paul "Needlenose" Labriola, Angelo "The Hook" La Pietra, Frank "Dago Frank" Lewis, James "Blackie" Licavoli, Carmine "The Doctor" Lombardozzi, Joseph "Big Joe" Leonardo, Jack "Machine Gun" McGurn, John "Eat-'Em-Up" McManus, Nicholas "Nicky Cigars" Marangello, Vincent "Little Vince" Meli, Salvatore "Sally the Shiek" Mussachio, Dominick "Sonny Black" Napolitano, Frank "The Enforcer" Nitti, John "The Ape" Pacelli, Carmine "The Snake" Persico, Joseph "The Olive Oil King" Profaci, Anthony "Tony Pro" Provenzano, Thomas "Crunch" Ronzulli, Joseph "Joe Bono" Riccobono, Alfredo "The Blind Pig" Rossi, Benjamin "Lefty" Ruggiero, Ignazio "Lupo the Wolf" Saietta, Anthony "Fat Tony" Salerno, Anthony "Tony the Ant" Spilotro, Louis "Louie The Fox" Taglianetti, Philip "Chicken Man" Testa, Joseph "Lead Pipe" Todaro, John "Terrible John" Torrio and last but not least, Nicholas "The Choir Boy" Viana.[31]

Doesn't that list of "Christian brethren" remind you of the Pilgrim fathers? It kind of makes you want to sing "Blest Be the Tie that Binds" (and then *throws you into a lake*). In addition to being "born-again Christians," all 50 of these professional killers were members of the Roman Catholic Church. There wasn't a Baptist in the bunch.

Most authorities trace the name *Mafia* back to a thirteenth-century Sicilian resistance movement against invading French armies. MAFIA was originally an acronym for "Morte alla Francia Italia Anela!" (Death to the French is Italy's cry!) The contemporary euphemism, *Cosa Nostra,* introduced by Joseph Valachi during his 1963 Senate testimony, loosely translates to "Our Thing" (like a Catholic Bible study group, etc.)

According to the *World Encyclopedia of Organized Crime,* a Mafia initiation ceremony is conducted as follows:

> The initiate's trigger finger is cut. Blood is then drawn from the wound and a holy card with an image of the family's **patron saint** is burned. According to secret FBI recordings made in Connecticut, in 1989, the oath is as follows: "I (NAME GIVEN) want to enter into this organization to protect my family and to protect my friends. I swear not to divulge this secret and to obey with love and omerta. As burns this saint

so will burn my soul. I enter alive into this organization and leave it dead."[32]

The earliest Mafia enclave in the United States began in the late 1880's in the heavily populated Catholic city of New Orleans. The main "Christian" activity was known as the "Black Hand" (extortion rings), with the two main competing families being the Provenzanos and the Matrangas. When an exceptionally dedicated police chief by the name of David Hennessey declared war on their illegal activities, he was gunned down on October 15, 1890, by several shotgun blasts at point-blank range.

Nineteen Mafia "brothers" were subsequently indicted for Hennessey's murder. The trial was a joke. Most of the 60 potential witnesses were threatened, intimidated or bribed. Numbers of the jurors were tampered with as well. Despite the overwhelming evidence, 16 of the defendants were acquitted with the jury "unable" to reach a verdict on the remaining three. However, before the killers could be released, an angry throng gathered around a New Orleans attorney by the name of W. S. Parkerson.

> "When courts fail, the people must act!" he shouted. "What protection or assurance of protection is there left us when the very head of our police department, our chief of police, is assassinated in our very midst by the Mafia society, and his assassins again turned loose on the community?..."
> Then, with a booming voice, Parkerson asked: "Will every man here follow me and see the murder of Hennessey vindicated? Men and citizens of New Orleans follow me!"[33]

Parkerson and 60 other prominent citizens promptly led a mob of *thousands* to the local jail. Two of the mafiosi were hung from lampposts. Seven others were executed by firing squad in the courtyard, while two others were riddled by bullets as they attempted to hide in a doghouse. The corpses were then hung from trees.

Unfortunately, most American cities were not blessed with such men as Hennessey or Parkerson. (See O. J. Simpson murder case.) Organized crime would soon rule the land. In Kansas City, Missouri, the rackets were controlled by gangsters Johnny Lazia, Frank "Chee Chee" De Mayo and later, Vincenzo Carollo and Charles Binaggio (all Roman Catholics). Over in St. Louis, John and Vito Giannola and Alphonse Palizzola (more "born-again" Catholics) ran the operation. Philip Bruccola was a prominent boss in Boston, while Daniel O'Leary and Philip Testa pioneered Mafia operations in Philadelphia. Santo Trafficante was the Florida boss, while Frank Balistrieri became the top man in Milwaukee.

The two rival "assemblies" in Chicago were led by Johnny Torrio and Dion O'Bannion. When O'Bannion drafted some new muscle, Polish Catholics George "Bugs" Moran and Hymie Weis (Earl Wajcieckowski), Torrio decided to secure some of his own reinforcements. Alphonse "Scarface" Capone, 21-year-old lieutenant of New York's Five Points Gang, was his man.

In less than three years, Torrio and Capone were making $100,000 a week. By 1924, they decided to remove the competition. On November 4, Dion O'Bannion was "whacked" in his own florist shop, and the war was under way. On the day of the funeral, 26 truckloads of flowers valued at $50,000 followed the hearse. One arrangement, a basket of roses, was labeled, "From Al."

Within days a hit squad missed Capone by minutes. Torrio was shot down while on a shopping spree with his wife; he survived the attack but spent 16 days in the hospital. On his release, John called it quits, describing Chicago as "too violent." At age 26, Al Capone had inherited the Torrio empire.

The mayhem continued. Eight carloads of "Christians" made a daylight "visit" on Capone's Cicero headquarters, the Hawthorne Inn. Over 5,000 bullets were fired by the "brethren." On October 11, 1926, Weiss was machine-gunned to death on the steps of Holy Name Cathedral. The gunfire was so intense that it blew away several words in the cornerstone of the cathedral. Bugs Moran was now the last of Capone's rivals.

Finally, on February 14, 1929, "Big Al" perpetrated the infamous St. Valentine's Day Massacre by utilizing a team of hit men disguised as police officers. Seven members of the Bugs Moran gang were "eliminated" inside a garage at 2122 N. Clark Street. Over 500 "born-again" Catholics had died in the "religious" war.

Capone was now king of the Windy City. He had 10,000 speakeasies buying six barrels of beer a week at $55 a barrel, for a weekly total of $3.3 million. They also purchased two cases of liquor a week at $90. With vice, gambling and other rackets, Al was pulling in a modest $6.5 million a week![34] The high-profile hood was forced to travel in a $20,000 steel limousine equipped with a rotating gun turret. A personal bodyguard of 18 thugs accompanied him everywhere. ("I Need Thee Every Hour," etc.) His "army" consisted of 700 hardened gangsters. In the end, it was a simple IRS audit and a tiny needle that dethroned America's public enemy number one.

Indicted for failing to pay his income taxes between 1925–1929, Capone's only defense was that he didn't think he had to pay taxes on money obtained from illegal operations.

After serving eight years in Alcatraz, Capone was released on "good behavior" and retired to his Palm Island, Florida estate. The only problem was that Al was going insane due to a lingering syphilitic condition. It seems that he was well aware of his disease from the onset (contracted from a teenage prostitute) but had refused the standard penicillin cure because he was afraid of needles. He died a raving lunatic on January 25, 1947, and was buried in Chicago's Roman Catholic Mt. Olive Cemetery. (Fearing grave robbers, Mrs. Mae Capone later had the body reburied in a secret plot in Mt. Carmel Cemetery.)

Although Frank "The Enforcer" Nitti and, later, Anthony "Big Tuna" Accardo would continue to guide the Capone empire, the real action would be henceforth in New York City. The "old school" leadership of the New York mob had been split by two "born-again" Roman Catholics, Salvatore Maranzano and Joseph "The Boss" Masseria. Another "born-again" Roman Catholic, Charles "Lucky" Luciano, sided with Maranzano and arranged for the assassination of Masseria. The hit was carried out by Albert "Lord High Executioner" Anastasia, Joseph "Joey" Adonis and Benjamin "Bugsy" Siegel at a Coney Island Restaurant on April 15, 1931. Lucky's alibi was that he was in the restaurant's washroom at the time of the shooting.

Shortly thereafter Luciano learned that Maranzano was planning to hit him. Lucky decided to beat him to the punch. On September 10, 1931, four men dressed as New York police officers entered Maranzano's real estate offices in the Eagle Building on Park Avenue. Salvatore was shot and stabbed to death accordingly.

Having been arrested at age 10 for shoplifting, the sixth-grade dropout Luciano was now the undisputed *capo di tutti capi* (boss of bosses) for the "Big Apple." His main lieutenants were a pair of Jewish killers, Meyer Lansky and "Bugsy" Siegel and the standard supply of "born-again" Catholics—Joey Adonis, Albert Anastasia, Frank "The Prime Minister" Costello and Vito "Don Vitone" Genovese.

These New York hoods were really a fine group of "Christian brothers." For instance, many of their "born-again" hit men would lace their bullets with garlic to induce gangrene in their victims. Cigarette butts and chain saws were often used effectively to elicit certain facts while questioning a "fellow believer." And while most bodies were weighted down with chains or cement and tossed into a river, Joseph Bonanno perfected the "Mafia coffin," also known as a "Double Decker." Carl Sifakis wrote, "The mourning family of the deceased is not even aware that their beloved one is sharing his final burial place with a hit victim, and the pallbearers are simply impressed with the apparent weight of quality wood used for the coffin."[35]

About this time, a real "scuzz ball" by the name of Arthur "Dutch" Schultz returned to the New York scene after an extended absence due to income tax litigation. With Lucky in the driver's seat, Dutch wisely resumed his racketeering operations from Newark, New Jersey. Although Schultz was eventually granted a piece of the action, he made the mistake of planning a hit on the district attorney, Thomas Dewey, who was at that time beginning to investigate the Dutchman's activities. Lucky reminded everyone that it was against his "Christian" ethics to "whack" people *outside* of the family. Consequently, Shultz and several of his bodyguards were blown away at the Palace Chophouse in Newark on October 23, 1935.

Ironically enough, Dewey came after Luciano the following year on a trumped-up charge of running a prostitution ring. Despite the shaky testimony of several dubious witnesses, Lucky was convicted of compulsory prostitution and given 30 to 50 years. After serving nearly ten years in the Clinton State Prison at Dannemora, New York, he was paroled and subsequently deported back to Sicily. When Lucky boarded the ship bound for Italy, he was escorted by three female companions and carried $1 million in cash on his person. Lucky's "luck" eventually ran out when he keeled over with a heart attack in Naples on January 26, 1962. In keeping with his wishes, the body was returned to New York for interment in St. John's Catholic Cemetery in Queens.

Through the years New York's Mafia operations have been governed by five separate crime families of "born-again" Catholics: the Gambinos, the Colombos, the Bonnanos, the Lucheses and the Genoveses. "Murder, Inc." was established as a special Mafia assassination squad. The group was so violent that its own "High Priest," Albert Anastasia, was "whacked" in 1957 as he reclined in a barber chair in New York.

As I stated in an earlier chapter, it was not my lot to grow up on "Walton's Mountain." In the providence of God, I was born and reared in the atmosphere of New York Mafia activity. My father was a "connected guy" who alternated between bookmaking and collections. We lived on the upper east side of Manhattan known as Yorkville. My first address was 323 East Seventy-eighth St. (between First and Second Avenues). In August of 1972, four businessmen were drinking in the Neapolitan Noodle Restaurant on Seventy-ninth Street (also between First and Second Avenues) when they were all summarily executed by an imported hit man from Las Vegas. His target had been four members of the Colombo family. He simply hit the wrong targets. (A trip to the confession booth would fix things fine.)

In my early teenage years, I lived on First Avenue, just off the corner of Eighty-sixth Street, also in Yorkville. According to FBI agent Joseph D. Pistone in his book, *Donnie Brasco—My Undercover Life in the Mafia*, "One of the first places I frequented [to initiate Mafia social contacts] was Carmello's, a pleasant restaurant at 1638 York Avenue, near Eighty-sixth Street and the East River."[36] This was only *one* block from my residence. Agent Pistone's five-year infiltration from 1976 through 1981 brought about over 100 Mafia convictions through the now-famous *Pizza Connection* trials (named for the string of pizza parlors fronting for heroin trafficking).

Thus, we see that the Roman Catholic Mafia of "born-again" killers has ruled the rackets of every major American city since the days of Prohibition. The syndicate, more than any organization on earth, is responsible for the dope, pornography, liquor, gambling and prostitution that has practically destroyed our nation. Doesn't it seem a little strange that *one* "church" has continued to dominate the membership rosters of organized crime in the United States? In his work *American Culture and Catholic Schools,* Emmett McLoughlin remarks concerning the attitude of the Roman Catholic Church toward the Mafia:

> Its leaders, the cardinals and bishops, are conspicuously silent in the face of the Roman Catholic Sicilian Mafia's complete defiance of decency and morals in the promotion of prostitution, narcotics, gambling, and labor racketeering in America. The same bishops and archbishops who vociferously condemn a young Catholic girl for entering a beauty contest say nothing about the traffic in narcotics and whoredom so long as good Catholics run the business.[37]

And if all these "born-again" thugs are in Heaven, —*who in the world* is in the *other* place?

BOB JONES, SR.

With Dr. Torrey's generation of sincere but misguided intellectuals establishing a pattern of critiquing the King James Bible (while standing for the "historic fundamentals" of the faith, etc.), the Lord found it necessary to reach back into the "sticks" once again. With the Mafia running loose, America was not about to be rescued by the Greek department at Princeton University promoting the American Standard Version.

On a farm in Skipperville, Alabama, on October 30, 1883, a weary mother of ten entered into the jaws of death yet again to deliver a baby boy named Bobby. It would not take long for the lad's unusual spiritual endowments to be manifested. At age 11, Bob Jones accepted Christ as his personal Saviour in a country Methodist church, south of Brannon Stand. The following year, the boy preacher held his first *serious* revival meeting at the Mt. Olive Church in Brannon Stand. According to the local newspaper, there were *60* conversions in the one-week meeting.[38]

When Bob was 13, he started his first church and pastored the congregation of 54 members for over a year. At 16, he became a Methodist circuit rider and assumed the spiritual responsibility for five different churches.

Two weeks before Mr. Moody's death, Bob entered Southern University (later renamed Birmingham Southern) in Greensboro, Alabama. The aspiring preacher boy kept his heart warm by speaking somewhere every weekend and with good results. He would often say that while others spent their time reading books, he was busy reading people.

Bob married Mary Gaston on June 17, 1908, and continued holding revivals throughout the South. Like Dwight Moody and Sam Jones, Bob Jones didn't have any more sense than to preach out of the AV 1611 either. In a later campaign in Montgomery, Alabama, he said:

> The king of Judah hated God, His Book and His minister. When the Book, so tediously prepared, every word written by hand, was handed him, he took his penknife, cut it into shreds and burned it. Jeremiah's God lives and His Book lives.
>
> Voltaire made the prediction that in one hundred years nobody would believe the Bible. The century has long passed, and the printing presses find it difficult to supply the ever-increasing demand for God's Book. Men with their penknives and all the methods of destruction their wicked hearts can devise, are trying to destroy the Book; but their efforts will prove vain.[39]

You may rest assured that "The Book" Bob Jones had in mind when he made reference to "The Book" was "The Book" that he had in his hand at the time. And, brother, did he *ever* know how to use it! In a "sermonette" in St. Petersburg entitled "The Outstanding Sins of America," he said:

There are many frizzly headed high school girls who can give your boys lessons in cursing. There are more women swearing today than ever before. There is no danger of a Blue Sunday, but you are about to have a Red Sunday. The bootlegger spits on the Stars and Stripes and tramples the Constitution under his feet. If I were prosecuting attorney, I would prosecute these poker-playing women. There was a time when a bad woman was kicked out of society, but now you elect her president of your club. Folks are pleasure-wild in this country.[40]

While Torrey's sincere but misguided crowd of Bible-critiquing intellectuals were busy erecting the fundamentalist movement, Jones was endeavoring to reestablish the *old-time religion*. It was the recurring theme of his preaching. In a message delivered at the Moore Avenue Baptist Church in Anniston, Alabama, he thundered:

"I think that America has more church members, less spirituality, and more immorality in supposedly decent circles than ever in the history of the country," he said. "We have lost our sense of sin. What this country needs is about twelve months of Hell-fire-damnation preaching, to let people know that sin is sin. There is in America today no dominant prophetic voice."[41]

That last statement of Dr. Bob's is quite profound. The twentieth century in America has been earmarked by a growing number of preachers who have ignorantly repudiated their King James Bibles. Such an evil was foreseen by the revisors themselves, Dr. Hort writing, "It is, one can hardly doubt, the beginning of a **new period** in Church history."[42]

The nineteenth and twentieth centuries divide like the books of Joshua and Judges. Before the RV and ASV arrived, God's men had a *central authority*—the AV 1611. With the passing of D. L. Moody and Sam Jones, the church figuratively entered into the era of Judges where there has been no "king" (as in "King" James Bible) in the land. Consequently, America's Christians have been doing that which is right in their *own* eyes. In a *Moody Monthly* article entitled "Which Translation Is Best for Me?" John Kohlenberger concludes: "In fact there is no 'best' translation...No translation is perfect, but most are 'for the greatest part true and sufficient.' So the question is not, 'Which Bible is best?' But which of the many good translations is best *for you?*"[43]

With few exceptions, the last of the big-name evangelists who experienced a measure of genuine, regional revival were men who were born on the other side of the American Standard Version (1901). Note the scriptural precedent: *"And the people served the LORD all the days of Joshua, and all the days of the elders that outlived Joshua, who had seen all the great works of the LORD, that he did for Israel."* (Judges 2:7)

By attacking America's sins with the right Bible, the fiery evangelist drew large crowds in countless cities. When he held a 1915 crusade in Hartford City, Indiana (population 7,000), over 4,000 people attended the closing service, with 1,000 having to be turned away. The local churches reported 2,400 additions while 16 saloons had to shut their doors.

Crowds of 6,000 heard Dr. Bob in his 1921 campaign in Montgomery. In St. Petersburg, Florida, that same year, the 5,000-seat auditorium was packed out twice a day. Attendance during the six-week crusade in Zanesville, Ohio, reached 20,000 daily, with 4,000 conversions. Over 15,000 people packed the opening service for the 1917 meeting in Grand Rapids, Michigan, with another 3,000 being turned away. When Bob gave the opening altar call, 568 persons came forward.

One of Dr. Bob's more unusual meetings was his 1916 crusade in New York City. This campaign proved to be quite the learning experience for both the country preacher and city pagans alike. There was no question about the fact that New York was certainly not the Bible Belt. There were no attendance figures listed for this crusade in *Builder of Bridges*. Dr. Bob was well aware that New York was Satan's greatest stronghold in America. In one service he stated bluntly, **"The only difference I could see between New York and Hell was that New York was completely surrounded by water."**[44] The major newspaper headlines let it all hang out:

> "NEW YORK WOMEN ON ROAD TO RUIN—LURE MEN TO TREAD IT WITH THEM, SAYS REV. BOB JONES." Another stated, "TANGO AND BATHING SUITS SHOW PREACHER BOB JONES A NEW FIELD FOR HELL FIRE." Again, "COCKTAILS, DANCING AND CIGARETTES ARE MILESTONES ON WOMEN'S PRIMROSE PATH, DECLARES EVANGELIST, WHO THINKS THEIR CLOTHES ARE MORE IMMODEST THAN EVE'S FIG LEAVES."[45]

In one of the more bizarre episodes of the crusade, a special reporter from *The World* took Dr. Bob on a never-to-be-forgotten tour of the city's most notorious underworld sites. In 1916, Paul Kelly was the Boss of New York's infamous Five Points "youth group" consisting of 1,500 "born-again" thugs. Two of Paul's exceptional "youngsters" were 17 year olds, Salvatore Luciana and Alphonse Caponi. A portion of the reporter's account is as follows:

Dr. Bob made a tour of tango tea emporiums, lobster palaces and cabaret restaurants where New York's very latest in rollicking wickedness was set out for his view.... After an afternoon and evening of taxicabbing from one dancing place to another; after seeing some seven thousand New Yorkers at their favorite pastime; after visiting resorts underground, places at the street level and roof gardens, Mr. Jones was quite clear as to what ails New York. **"Your city is dancing on the brink of Hell."**

Dr. Jones goes on to say "... If men would call looseness by its name; if women would recognize that, as never before, they are devoting themselves to the low art of sex appeal, your hundreds of tango teas, cabaret restaurants and dance halls would go out of business tonight.

"I suppose the people will call me a crank for saying all this. But they called Jesus a crank... and the Old Testament prophets were known as the pessimists of their time. New York wouldn't stop this side of Hell and damnation if someone didn't come here and shout a plain warning now and then...

"Certainly the New Yorker is an artist at making vice simple, easy and attractingly disguised. I'd like to see a million mothers and fathers in this town suddenly awaken to what is happening and drag their sons and daughters away from these shameless places. A good spanking would bring home to a lot of these youngsters how far they have one-stepped from the paths of maidenly modesty and youthful cleanliness...

"Drink and dance; dance and drink. That's their merry round to the devil. I had rather have a young daughter of mine drink arsenic than cocktails.... I'm a Southerner, born and bred, and my respect for real women is second to none, but I am bound to say the fault of this modern wickedness lies with the women, and it is upon the woman that the wrath of God is going to be visited."[46]

Unlike the New York of Moody's 1875 Crusade, the 1914 version was so overrun with "born-again" Catholic mafiosi that the city paid little attention to Dr. Bob's warning of judgment. However, that fateful underworld tour left a lasting impression upon the man of God. On December 1, 1926, groundbreaking ceremonies were conducted for *Bob Jones College*. In its heyday (i.e., before Bob, Jr., "carpeted the sawdust trail"), thousands of preacher boys were trained to do battle with the devil.

When Dr. Bob paid another visit to the "Big Apple" in February of 1937, *Time* magazine took notice:

One of Manhattan's most oddly located churches is Calvary Baptist, a stronghold of pure Fundamentalism in West 57th Street within denouncing distance of bars, smart shops, noisy apartment hotels, racy night clubs...Calvary is seldom without a guest evangelist who fills its auditorium...Last week...news hawks turned up at Calvary to hear a visiting Tennessee preacher, Rev. Dr. Robert Jones...One of Tennessee's fifty colleges is....Bob Jones College...Alabama-born Bob Jones... founded his institution a decade ago in northern Florida, planning it as a college for preserving the Bible and the "old time decencies"...Today he has four hundred students.[47]

At the time of this visit (1937), the New York mob was in a temporary state of disarray. Dutch Schultz had been "laid off " only two years earlier, followed by Lucky Luciano's imprisonment in 1936. When Bob Jones preached at Calvary Baptist Church, a 17-year-old juvenile by the name of John Grady was somewhere in the general vicinity, but he did not attend the services. However, one of Dr. Bob's preacher boys by the name of Dr. Randy Carroll later pastored the Marcus Hook Baptist Church in Lynwood, Pennsylvania. On Sunday, August 25, 1974, Pastor Carroll used a King James Bible to preach another New York Catholic down the aisle. The young man was John Grady's son, *Bill*.

BILLY SUNDAY

A second man raised up by the Lord to attack the sins of America was Reverend William Ashley Sunday, better known as "Billy" Sunday. Billy was born in a two-room log cabin in Ames, Iowa, on November 19, 1862. (Note the pre-ASV "Joshua" time zone.) His father, a private in the Union army, died the following month from a disease contracted on the battlefield.

After passing his formative years in the Soldiers' Orphan Home in Glenwood, Iowa, Billy eventually settled in Marshalltown where he got a job in the local furniture store. He soon began to excel on the town baseball team and was subsequently "discovered" and recruited by A. C. Anson of the Chicago Whitestockings. In his seven professional seasons (five with Chicago and one each with Philadelphia and Pittsburgh), Billy was known for his speed. He was the first player in baseball history to round the bases in 14 seconds. He could also run the 100-yard dash in 10 seconds flat.

In the fall of 1887, Billy was recruited by the Lord Jesus Christ. Years later, he recalled:

Twenty-seven years ago I walked down a street in Chicago in company with some ball players who were famous in this world...and we went into a saloon. It was Sunday afternoon and we got tanked up and then went and sat down on a corner....

Across the street a company of men and women were playing on instruments—horns, flutes and slide trombones—and the others were singing the gospel hymns that I used to hear my mother sing back in the log cabin in Iowa and back in the old church where I used to go to Sunday school.... I sobbed and sobbed and a young man stepped out and said, "We are going down to the Pacific Garden Mission. Won't you come down to the mission?"

I arose and said to the boys, "I'm through. I am going to Jesus Christ. We've come to the parting of the ways," and I turned my back on them. Some of them laughed and some of them mocked me; one of them gave me encouragement; others never said a word.

Twenty-seven years ago I turned and left that little group on the corner of State and Madison Streets and walked to the little mission and fell on my knees and staggered out of sin and into the arms of the Saviour.[48]

The year was 1887 and the new convert was 25 years of age. After joining the Jefferson Park Presbyterian Church in Chicago, Billy married Helen Amelia Thompson. In 1891, he retired from professional baseball to work for the YMCA. Three years later, he began assisting J. Wilbur Chapman in tent revivals. When Dr. Chapman returned to the pastorate, "Billy" and "Ma" launched out on their own.

His first revival in Garner, Iowa, January 8–17, 1896, resulted in 268 conversions. After a while, large wooden tabernacles had to be constructed to accommodate the crowds. Billy would have sawdust spread on the ground and then invite prospects to "hit the sawdust trail" at the sermon's close. He would also greet each convert personally with a handshake (as many as 84 per minute).

As the sensational evangelist was likely to do anything in the course of his sermon, from sliding across the platform to smashing chairs, the crowds continued to come. (Some have estimated that he walked a mile over his platform during each sermon.[49]) From 1908–09, campaigns in various Midwestern cities harvested 35,000 souls. One six-week crusade in Portsmouth, Ohio, in 1910 saw 5,224 people "hit the trail." In his 1912 meeting in Wilkes-Barre, Pennsylvania, 16,584 persons (or 25% of the population) came to Christ, while Billy's six-week stay in Beaver Falls, Pennsylvania (Joe Namath's hometown), resulted in 6,000 decisions for Christ—an incredible 50% of that community's total population.

Billy's track record of conversions was truly phenomenal: Wheeling, West Virginia, 8,300; New Castle, Pennsylvania, 6,683; Toledo, Ohio, 7,686; South Bend, Indiana (Notre Dame country), 6,398; Johnstown, Pennsylvania, 11,829; Columbus, Ohio, 18,137; McKeesport, Pennsylvania, 10,022; Springfield, Ohio, 6,804; Erie, Pennsylvania, 5,312; Pittsburgh, Pennsylvania, 26,601.

The indefatigable evangelist attributed his fruitful ministry to the power of the Holy Bible, declaring, "I believe that the man who magnifies the word of God in his preaching is the man whom God will honor."[50] His biographer, William T. Ellis, wrote:

> Billy Sunday does not create a cult: he simply sends people back to **the Bibles of their mothers.**... The work of Billy Sunday is not done with a convert until he has inspired that person to a love and loyalty for the **old Book.**[51]

When Billy Sunday spoke about *the* "Old Book," you can rest assured he was not referring to either the autographs or the contemporary translations of his day. *The New Testament in Modern Speech* by Richard Weymouth (1903), *The Holy Bible in Modern English* by Ferrar Fenton (1903), *The Corrected English New Testament* by Samuel Lloyd (1904) and *The Holy Bible; An Improved Version* by the American Bible Union (1912) constitute but a sample of the 64 generic perversions that appeared throughout his ministry. Every time Billy Sunday preached the Gospel, a King James Bible lay open on the pulpit to Isaiah 61:1. He would often say,

> Here is a book, God's Word, that I will put up against all the books of all the ages. **You can't improve on the Bible.** You can take all the histories of all the nations of all the ages and cut out of them all that is ennobling, all that is inspiring, and compile that into a common book, but you cannot produce a work that will touch the hem of the garment **of the Book I hold in my hand.**... And so this old Book, which is the Word of God, the Word of Jesus Christ, is the book I intend to preach by everywhere.[52]

With the right Bible "in hand," Billy early declared war on the liquor industry. His message, "Get on the Water Wagon," was a revivalist classic and normally lasted an hour and forty minutes. Referring to the hellish traffic, he would say,

I tell you it strikes in the night.... It attacks defenseless womanhood and childhood. The saloon is a coward. It is a thief... it robs you of manhood and leaves you in rags and takes away your friends, and it robs your family. It impoverishes your children and it brings insanity and suicide.

It will take the shirt off your back and it will steal the coffin from a dead child and yank the last crust of bread out of the hand of the starving child.... It will steal the milk from the breast of the mother and leave her with nothing with which to feed her infant. It will take the virtue from your daughter....

It is the dirtiest, most low-down, damnable business that ever crawled out of the pit of hell. It is a sneak, and a thief and a coward.[53]

The crowds were often moved to tears as Billy told it like it was:

In a Northwest city a preacher sat at his breakfast table one Sunday morning. The door-bell rang; he answered it; and there stood a little boy, twelve years of age. He was on crutches, right leg off at the knee, shivering, and he said, "Please, sir, will you come up to the jail and talk and pray with papa? He murdered mama. Papa was good and kind, but whiskey did it, and I have to support my three little sisters. I sell newspapers and black boots. Will you go up and talk and pray with papa? And will you come home and be with us when they bring him back? **The governor says we can have his body after they hang him.**"

The preacher hurried to the jail and talked and prayed with the man. He had no knowledge of what he had done. He said, "I don't blame the law, but it breaks my heart to think that my children must be left in a cold and heartless world. Oh, sir, whiskey did it."

The preacher was at the little hut when up drove the undertaker's wagon and they carried out the pine coffin. **They led the little boy up to the coffin, he leaned over and kissed his father and sobbed, and said to his sister, "Come on, sister, kiss papa's cheeks before they grow cold."** And the little hungry, ragged, whiskey orphans hurried to the coffin, shrieking in agony.

Police, whose hearts were adamant, buried their faces in their hands and rushed from the house, and the preacher fell on his knees and lifted his clenched fist and tear-stained face and took an oath before God, and before the whiskey orphans, that he would fight the cursed business until the undertaker carried **him** out in a coffin.[54]

According to the late Senator Shepherd, author of the Eighteenth Amendment (Prohibition), the Billy Sunday Campaigns were the main cause for the saloons up North closing their doors. (The Baptist evangelist Mordecai Ham was the primary deterrent to booze in the South.)[55] Over 2 million people attended Billy's January 3–March 20, 1915, crusade in Philadelphia. Three years after Bob Jones, Sr., "sowed the seed," Billy reaped a harvest in his 1917 New York City campaign of over 100,000 conversions.

J. FRANK NORRIS

The third prophet of providence to cross into the twentieth century was the man destined to reestablish America's Baptist churches as the leading force for righteousness up to, and including, the present time. J. Frank Norris was born on September 8, 1877, in Dadeville, Alabama. In the year 1888, the family moved to a farm near Hubbard City, Texas, where his father, Warner, fought a losing battle with poverty and alcohol. At age 13, Frank Norris was converted in an old-fashioned Methodist revival and later immersed by Reverend Catlett Smith, pastor of the Hubbard Baptist Church. As young Frank came up out of the baptismal waters, Pastor Smith prayed, "Lord, **take** him, **break** him, and **make** him."[56] In later years Norris would add, "I have been willing for the taking and the making, but I must confess that I have never been willing for the breaking."[57]

Having surrendered to the ministry, Frank was ordained in 1899, and pastored the Baptist church in Mt. Calm, Texas, while also attending Baylor University. On May 5, 1902, he married Lillian Gaddy. Dr. Norris graduated with honors from Baylor in May of 1903, and subsequently earned a master's degree in theology in 1905 from Southern Baptist Seminary in Lousiville, Kentucky.

It would be the unique call of J. Frank Norris to oppose both the sin of his time as well as the gross apostasy within his own denomination. His tireless crusade would birth the Independent Baptist movement in America, but not without experiencing the pangs of prolonged hard labor.

While pastoring the McKinney Avenue Baptist Church in Dallas (1905–1907), Dr. Norris purchased the *Baptist Standard* and used this influential paper to oppose racetrack gambling and the Southern Baptists who supported the same.

In September of 1909, Dr. Norris was called to the First Baptist Church of Fort Worth. A discerning layman by the name of J. T. Pemberton made a prophetic warning to the backslidden congregation:

This church is not in condition for his type of ministry. If he comes there will be the all-firedest explosion ever witnessed by any church. We are at peace with the world, the flesh, and the devil and with one another. **This fellow carries a broad axe and not a pearl handle knife.** I just want to warn you. But now since you have called him, I am going to stay by him.[58]

After a two-year "get-acquainted" period, Norris declared war on Fort Worth's underworld, beginning with the notorious Hell's Half-Acre, where over 700 women of ill repute[59] entertained clients ranging from insignificant cowboys to Butch Cassidy and the Sundance Kid.[60] To complicate matters, a leading member of First Baptist Church owned and rented out property to these sinful enterprises.

In January, 1912, shots were fired into the pastor's study, narrowly missing their intended victim. On another occasion, a stranger brandishing a pistol accosted Dr. Norris with the words, "I'm going to kill you," whereupon the man of God replied, "I don't have time to talk with you," and went on his way. (Proverbs 28:1) When Norris erected a tent in downtown Fort Worth, the city's mayor, W. D. Davis, had the fire department cut it down. (Norris later led the mayor to Christ.)

The First Baptist Church was destroyed in February with Norris being indicted for the arson. Although a first attempt to burn the parsonage as well was foiled by Mrs. Norris, a second effort succeeded on March 2. The jury rendered a "not guilty" verdict on April 25, 1912. Shortly afterward, the Lord pronounced judgment on the real culprit. The district attorney who had been a tool of the liquor interests was violently killed when his Cadillac collided with a streetcar. Dr. Entzminger writes:

> There was a half quart bottle of liquor broken and it was sitting straight up on the pavement, and it had a lobe of brains in it. **This bottle of liquor and brains was carried to Dr. Norris and he took it to the pulpit and preached a sermon on it the next Sunday night on the text, "The Wages of Sin Is Death."**
>
> Of course it created a sensation. Norris was severely criticized. Some women fainted in the audience. And some men did too. You talk about "Great Fear coming upon every soul!" It scared me almost to death. He fought on. He preached on.[61]

Dr. Norris often said, "I have never started a fight, but I have been around when a few were finished."[62] The *Fort Worth Star* once remarked that the Eleventh Commandment in Fort Worth was, "Thou shalt not mess with J. Frank Norris." Thousands of precious souls were reached for Christ under the ministry of this courageous Baptist preacher. Jack Dempsey Floyd, the nine-year-old son of gangster Charles "Pretty Boy" Floyd, was saved and baptized on June 17, 1934.[63] On June 5, 1938, Dr. Norris baptized 50 converts in the Detroit River, and then burned the Nazi and Communist flags to the applause of 30,000 spectators.[64] The most famous rodeo star in the world, Jack "Red" Thompson, was immersed with his wife on November 28, 1944, as his favorite horse, "Hog-Eyes," observed the proceedings.

One of the preacher's greatest trophies was William (Bill) Blevins who had organized the Retail Liquor Dealers Association of Texas and led in a plot to kill their ministerial nemesis. Fortunately, the Holy Spirit got to Bill first, who later testified after 40 years in the saloon business:

> I was heartily in favor of taking him out and so was everybody else... I believe the hand of God interfered... and since I could not put him out of business, I decided to join him. I came to the church, walked down to the front and got down on my knees and he got down with me on his knees and put his arms around my shoulders while I prayed... the prayer "God be merciful to me, a sinner," and He heard me and this man that I so hated... baptized me and I am now past my 80th milestone and in the course of nature will precede him to the other shore, and when I get there I am going to hunt up the Superintendent of that fair land and make two requests of Him.
>
> First I want Him to let me know the day that Frank comes, and second, I want Him to let me off that day that I may be standing down at the beautiful gate and be the first to put my arms around him as the man who led me to Christ, by whose grace I am saved.[65]

While keeping the pressure on the liquor traffic, Norris also began exposing evolution and post-millennialism at Baylor University. The leadership within the Southern Baptist Convention referred to Norris as their "tormentor." Dr. George W. Truett would only acknowledge Norris as "*that man* in Fort Worth."[66] Dr. J. L. Ward, president of Decatur Baptist College, blared on the radio, "I expect to look over the parapets of heaven and see Frank Norris frying in the bottomless pits of hell."[67]

A third target of J. Frank Norris was the Roman Catholic Church. His stand was so strong that his reputation often preceded him. Once, while preaching in New York City's Calvary Baptist Church in 1923, he was nearly heckled down by a visiting delegation of Catholic women.

The greatest crisis in the life of Dr. Norris occurred on July 17, 1926. The mayor of Fort Worth, H. C. Meacham, showed open favoritism to the Catholic Church by purchasing a piece of their land in excess of its true market value. Norris responded from the pulpit, "I don't believe that it is the proper thing for Mr. Meacham...to take $152,000 of the taxpayer's money of Ft. Worth and give it to a Roman Catholic School...in order to benefit Mr. Meacham's business."[68] The mayor's secular business was the Meacham Dry Goods Co. Six employees who attended First Baptist Church were summarily dismissed after the message by Dr. Norris. The next Sunday night (July 11, 1926), Norris brought another "sermonette" entitled "Six Members of First Baptist Church, Fired by L. B. Haughey." (Haughey, a Roman Catholic, managed the store for Mayor Meacham.)

The following Saturday afternoon, Dexter Elliott Chipps, another Roman Catholic and a friend of Meacham, walked into the office of Dr. Norris and made several threats of violence. The mayor would later attest under oath, "I sent D. E. Chipps to the office of J. Frank Norris to kill him."[69] Dr. Entzminger writes:

> Before Norris knew it Chipps kicked the door open... The night watchman of the church always left his gun in... the pastor's office for safe keeping... Norris sought to quiet Chipps and succeeded for a moment... Norris was standing with his back against his desk and had his hand on the gun and did everything he could to avoid trouble... Chipps went out into the hallway and ... whirled around and started back into Norris' office and said, so the testimony shows, "I will kill you, you blankety, blankety, blank!" And quick as a flash, it was over.[70]

Another Norris associate, Tatum Ray, adds:

> In the small sweltering church study three bullets entered the massive body of Chipps that fateful afternoon. The man staggered a few feet forward and fell dying from the impact of the gray forty-five which the preacher pointed at him. In quick confused complexity the whole thing was over. Only the story remained to be told. The life of one man was gone, the life of the other never to be the same.[71]

A crooked grand jury declared on July 29, 1926, that J. Frank Norris did "unlawfully and with malice aforethought, murder and kill one D. E. Chipps."[72] While practically every Catholic church in the area contributed funds for the prosecution, a prayed-up Dr. Norris carried his worn leather-bound Bible to the courtroom each day. Finally, a verdict of "not guilty" was declared; once again, the preacher had prevailed.

It was no coincidence that Dr. Norris had been "turning up the heat" against the "born-again" Catholic gangsters at the time of the Chipps attack. Ray declares:

> ...by the spring of 1926, he associated bootlegging with the growth of "Catholicism" as well as the "corrupt city officials." He preached on the subject, "Shall Catholics and Bootleggers Elect the next United States Senate?"
>
> Weekly his pulpit was dedicated to the stormy impact of his sensationalism, "Roman Catholics vs. Protestantism, that's the issue of Tarrant County today," he would cry as he promised his crowd his loyalty to defend the truth for which the Puritans died against the danger of the Catholic persecution. And he always advertised and then printed his sermons under such titles as "Shall Roman Catholics Rule Tarrant County Today?" "Knights of Columbus Try to Bluff Norris," "Roman Catholics plan high broadcasting system to make United States a Catholic country."[73]

When the Democratic National Convention met in Houston, Texas, in 1928, Al Smith was nominated to oppose the Republican, Herbert Hoover. Ray writes:

> Few men personified the contempt of the Fundamentalist more than Alfred E. Smith. Smith's story was "an American success story," having risen from New York's lower East Side to become four times Governor of his home state, he had labored to assume the role of a "Progressive and friend of the little man," **yet, Al Smith was a devout Roman Catholic,** an outspoken opponent of prohibition, and a reputed friend of Tammany Hall.[74]

Following his retirement from politics, Smith became president of the Empire State Building. My father worked for Smith at this time performing a number of personal duties from buying his cigars to taking Mrs. Smith shopping. *Because Smith was the first Roman Catholic to run for president,* America's Bible-believing citizenry was up in arms over his candidacy. Dr. Norris traveled far and wide stumping the state for Herbert Hoover, declaring, "The question of the campaign is Al Smith and his record...his saloon record, his record as an assemblyman, his vote for and in defense of gambling, prostitution and liquor."[75]

Moreover, J. Frank Norris was perceptive enough to understand the *real* danger of a Smith presidency. Ray confirms:

> He talked about the Roman hierarchy, about the persecution of the dark ages, and the candidate's persistent personal liaison to the dictorial authority in Rome. Holding his Bible high above his head, he would shout, "**This Book** tells me where I came from and where I am going. **This Book** of my mother's and yours.
>
> "Thirty presidents have bent forward and kissed **this precious Book** when they were sworn into the office of sacred trust, and now, in your lifetime and in mine, there are those who would snatch it away, and substitute **another Bible, a different Bible, a foreign Catholic Bible.**"[76]

When the election was held in November, Texas broke with political tradition and voted Republican. Herbert Hoover subsequently defeated Smith in a landslide victory. Dr. Norris called the outcome "the greatest moral victory in the history of America."[77] He later accepted an invitation to Hoover's inaugural ceremony in Washington, D. C.

Although America was firmly in the grip of organized crime, preachers such as Bob Jones, Billy Sunday and J. Frank Norris did what they could to stem the evil tide. Although Al Capone went to Hell (despite the fact that he was a "born-again" Catholic), his personal chauffeur, George Meyers, was able to "beat the rap." After serving 30 years in Leavenworth, Alcatraz and Sing Sing, the man known as Al Capone's "Devil Driver" placed his trust in Jesus Christ as his personal Saviour.

It was my pleasure to talk with Mr. Meyers on a number of occasions. He told me that he once heard Billy Sunday in New York and went away thinking he was "crazy." But in time, the seed took root, and George was born into the family of God. (Isaiah 55:11) At my request, he even called my unsaved father and witnessed to him over the telephone.

In our next chapter, we will examine the most dangerous mafia of all—the only *legal* mafia in America.

XVII

The Legitimate Mafia

> *"For the love of money is the root of all evil."*
> (I Timothy 6:10a)

A MONG SEVERAL OUTSTANDING biographies of Dr. R. A. Torrey, Roger Martin writes in *Apostle of Certainty*:

> The train chugged slowly, wending its way up the heavily-forested Blue Ridge Mountains...Presently...the train came to an abrupt halt, some 1,700 feet high, in the picturesque little Pennsylvania village of Montrose...The view from the top of the little hill was breathtaking. The rolling hills and rugged but scenic forests, decorated with autumn colors and bathed in the glow of the setting sun, prompted an enthusiastic, "This is the most beautiful site for a Bible conference I have ever seen." Dr. Torrey knelt with MacInnis in prayer, and made a quick decision to purchase the property.[1]

Dr. Torrey began his Montrose Bible Conference the following summer of 1908. Commenting on the emerging, interdenominational Bible conference movement as a whole, Beale writes:

> With more and more Americans traveling each summer to popular **resorts**, a growing number of Bible conferences began **competing with tourist camps and resort hotels for the patronage of vacationing Fundamentalists.** From the Montrose summer gatherings in the Pennsylvania mountains to the Boardwalk Bible Conference in Atlantic City, the movement swept America with **a unique vacation package.** It

was a blend of **resort-style recreation**, the old-fashioned camp meeting, and Bible teaching by outstanding Fundamentalist leaders.[2]

While a group of sincere but misguided ASV-espousing, inter-denominational Christians ("Fighting Fundamentalists") began laying the foundation for our present "Heritage-Park-USA" generation by reaching out to the "vacationing fundamentalists" of their day, *another* train car rolled ominously down the tracks. The date was November 22, 1910. Like Dr. Torrey, the occupants of that other coach had a real estate purchase in view, though somewhat larger than the Montrose Conference Grounds. G. Edward Griffin describes the intriguing scenario as follows:

> The New Jersey railway station was bitterly cold that night. Flurries of the year's first snow swirled around street lights.... It was approaching ten P.M., and the station was nearly empty...
>
> In their hurry to board the train and escape the chill of the wind, few passengers noticed the activity at the far end of the platform. At a gate seldom used at this hour of the night was a spectacular sight. Nudged against the end-rail bumper was a long car that caused those few who saw it to stop and stare. Its gleaming black paint was accented with polished brass hand rails, knobs, frames, and filigrees. The shades were drawn, but through the open door, one could see mahogany paneling, velvet drapes, plush armchairs, and a well stocked bar.... Other cars in the station bore numbers on each end to distinguish them from their dull brothers. But numbers were not needed for this beauty. On the center of each side was a small plaque bearing but a single word: ALDRICH.[3]

Rhode Island Senator Nelson Aldrich was one of the most powerful men in Washington at that time. As both chairman of the National Monetary Commission and an investment associate of J. P. Morgan, Aldrich was the undisputed political spokesman for big business. (His son-in-law was John D. Rockefeller, Jr., and his grandson, Nelson Rockefeller, would later become vice president of the United States.) Griffin continues:

> When Aldrich arrived at the station, there was no doubt he was the commander of the private car. Wearing a long, fur-collared coat, a silk top hat, and carrying a silver-tipped walking stick, he strode briskly down the platform with his private secretary, Shelton, and a cluster of porters behind them hauling assorted trunks and cases.
>
> No sooner had the Senator boarded his car when several more passengers arrived with similar collections of luggage. The last man

appeared just moments before the final "aaall aboarrrd." He was carrying a shotgun case.

While Aldrich was easily recognized by most of the travelers who saw him walk through the station, the other faces were not familiar. These strangers had been instructed to arrive separately, to avoid reporters, and, should they meet inside the station, to act as though they did not know each other. After boarding the train, they had been told to use first names only so as not to accidentally reveal each other's identity....

Back at the main gate, there was a double blast from the engine's whistle. Suddenly, the gentle sensation of motion; the excitement of a journey begun. But, no sooner had the train cleared the platform when it shuttered to a stop. Then, to everyone's surprise, it reversed direction and began moving toward the station again. Had they forgotten something? Was there a problem with the engine?

A sudden lurch and the slam of couplers gave the answer. They had picked up another car at the end of the train. Possibly the mail car? In an instant the forward motion was resumed, and all thoughts returned to the trip ahead and to the minimal comforts of the accommodations.

And so, as the passengers drifted off to sleep that night to the rhythmic clicking of steel wheels against rail, little did they dream that, riding in the car at the end of their train, were seven men who represented an estimated one-fourth of the total wealth of the entire world.[4]

The six other passengers aboard the Senator's private car were: Abraham Piatt Andrew, assistant secretary of the United States Treasury; Frank A. Vanderlip, president of the National City Bank of New York (the nation's most powerful bank at that time) representing William Rockefeller and the international investment banking firm of Kuhn, Loeb & Company; Henry P. Davison, senior partner of J. P. Morgan Company; Charles D. Norton, president of J. P. Morgan's First National Bank of New York; Benjamin Strong, head of J. P. Morgan's Banker's Trust Company; and, most important of all, Paul M. Warburg, a partner in Kuhn, Loeb & Company, representing the all-powerful Rothschild banking dynasty in England.

Just before pulling into Raleigh, North Carolina, the train stopped in the switching yard and a track crew quickly disconnected the last coach. When passengers stepped onto the terminal platform only moments later, their train looked exactly as it had when they boarded the previous evening.

Within an hour, the "special" car was reconnected to another train, bound for Georgia. After stops in Atlanta and Savannah, the Senator's party disembarked in the sleepy little town of Brunswick, situated on the Atlantic seaboard. Following a transfer to the local dock, the elite group of financiers was ferried to their secretive, final destination—**Jekyll Island**. A handful of curious onlookers were informed that the Senator's guests were in town for a little duck hunting. (Remember the shotgun case?)

What transpired over the next few days at J. P. Morgan's private hunting lodge would ultimately change the course of human history. Far from duck hunting, the seven financial conspirators were in town to draft the basic plan for what has come to be known as the *Federal Reserve System*. Because it is neither Federal nor in possession of *any* reserves, author G. Edward Griffin called it "The Creature from Jekyll Island."

The first substantive news leak was occasioned by an article in a 1916 edition of *Leslie's Weekly* written by B. C. Forbes, who later founded *Forbes* magazine.

> Picture a party of the nation's greatest bankers stealing out of New York on a private railroad car under cover of darkness, stealthily hieing hundreds of miles South, embarking on a mysterious launch, sneaking on to an island deserted by all but a few servants, living there a full week under such rigid secrecy that the names of not one of them was once mentioned lest the servants learn the identity and disclose to the world this strangest, most secretive expedition in the history of American finance.
>
> I am not romancing. I am giving to the world, for the first time, the real story of how the famous Aldrich currency report, the foundation of our new currency system, was written.[5]

Mr. Rush Limbaugh likes to poke fun at informed patriots who attempt to expose the *real* conspirators within our crumbling republic. Holding to a less-than-positive view of the "Fed" makes me a "kook," according to Limbaugh. The charismatic talk-show host is either ignorant or in somebody's back pocket. At any rate, the "kooks" *who were there* certainly knew what had taken place. In the official biography of Senator Aldrich, written by Nathaniel Wright Stephenson, we read:

> In the autumn of 1910, six men [in addition to Aldrich] went out to shoot ducks. That is to say, they told the world that was their purpose. Mr. Warburg, who was of the number, gives an amusing account of his feelings when he boarded a private car in Jersey City, bringing with him all the accoutrements of a duck shooter. The joke was in the fact that he had never shot a duck in his life and had no intention of shooting any.... The duck shoot was a blind.[6]

In the February 9, 1935, issue of the *Saturday Evening Post*, an article appeared by Frank Vanderlip, another one of Limbaugh's "kooks." In it, he said,

> Despite my views about the value to society of greater publicity for the affairs of corporations, there was an occasion, near the close of 1910, when I was as secretive—indeed, as furtive—as any conspirator....I do not feel it is any exaggeration to speak of our secret expedition to Jekyll Island as the occasion of the actual conception of what eventually became the **Federal Reserve System**....
>
> The servants and train crew may have known the identities of one or two of us, but they did not know all, and it was the names of all printed together that would have made our mysterious journey significant in Washington, in Wall Street, even in London. Discovery, we knew, simply must not happen, or else all our time and effort would be wasted. If it were to be exposed publicly that our particular group had got together and written a banking bill, that bill would have no chance whatever of passage by Congress.[7]

Up until the twentieth century, Satan's main attacks against the local, New Testament church, especially in the United States, have come through Roman Catholicism. That the Catholic Church has become the largest denomination in America is consistent with the Bible's prediction of an end-day, one-world religion. However, the same Bible warns of a one-world government as well. The Creature from Jekyll Island constitutes the twentieth-century origins of this final New World Order. Should a Christian be surprised by such "negative" developments if he also believes that the rapture is around the corner?

Furthermore, the rise of the Federal Reserve System itself was made possible by a vacillating generation of "vacationing fundamentalists" and has continued to serve as a rod of divine judgment upon the nation as a whole. The Bible is quite clear in this matter of monetary chastisement. Speaking of Old Testament Israel, Moses declared: *"The LORD shall open unto thee his good treasure, the heaven to give the rain unto thy land in his season, and to bless all the work of thine hand: and thou shalt lend unto many nations, and thou shalt not borrow. And the LORD shall make thee the head, and not the tail...if that thou hearken unto the commandments of the LORD thy God."* (Deuteronomy 28:12, 13c)

Consequently, when the people of God decided to forget their heavenly benefactor, the body parts became juxtaposed: *"But it shall come to pass, if thou wilt not hearken unto the voice of the LORD thy God, to observe to do all his commandments and his statutes which I command thee this day... The stranger that is within thee shall get up above thee very high; and thou shalt come down very low. He shall lend to thee, and thou shalt not lend to him: he shall be the head, and thou shalt be the tail."* (Deuteronomy 28:15, 43, 44)

With a current national debt of over $5 trillion (not to mention the additional multiplied trillions in *consumer* and *corporate* debt), two things are certain: the "Fed" is a *joke*, and America has lost her "most favored nation" status with Jehovah. (Psalm 33:12) For the sin of rejecting the AV 1611, the blessings of financial freedom are no longer present, as *"the borrower is servant to the lender."* (Proverbs 22:7)

Now before examining the Federal Reserve System in more detail, a brief overview of the banking industry as a whole and the subject of money in particular is in order. Generally speaking, money may be defined as anything of intrinsic value that is accepted as a *medium of exchange.* Griffin points out that there are four types of money: *commodity, receipt, fractional* and *fiat.*[8]

Commodity money is the most primitive (or basic) type of the four, serving originally in the form of barter. ("I'll give you ten of my bananas for one of your blankets," etc.) In the process of time, particular commodities, normally foodstuffs, livestock or produce, became the medium of exchange. (1 banana = 1 bushel of wheat; 1 blanket = 20 bushels of wheat, etc.)

Later, when man learned to refine crude ores, the metals themselves began to serve as the most practical and commonly accepted medium of exchange. Eventually, the gold coin became the standard metal of choice.

With the earliest mention of gold being in Genesis 2:11 (4,000 B.C.), economists attribute the metal's enduring popularity (see Revelation 21:15) to three cardinal attributes. In addition to its proven *durability* and relative *scarcity*, a supply of gold *cannot be easily expanded.* Contrary to paper currency ("funny money"), which can be created in minutes on government printing presses, gold must be laboriously mined from the earth. Interestingly, the gold coin with the longest record of accepted credibility was the *Byzantine* soldis or bezant, which paralleled the circulation of the *Textus Receptus*, 490–1453 A.D.

Receipt money became the second type of exchange, evolving as a convenient resource to hauling one's private supply of gold everywhere. Goldsmiths built sturdy vaults and rented out storage space to local merchants and consumers. (Nehemiah 3:32) When coins were placed in these vaults, the warehouseman would issue a "receipt of deposit," guaranteeing that the gold could be withdrawn at any time.

Initially, the only person who could present the receipt for withdrawal of the coins was the owner himself. Eventually, however, it became customary for the owner to simply endorse his receipt to a third party who could, upon presentation, make the withdrawal as well.

Finally, this system was streamlined by the issuance of a series of smaller receipts adding up to the same deposit total with each slip having printed across the top: "Pay to the Bearer on Demand." Thus, an owner who deposited $100 in gold coin could request ten $10 receipts (as opposed to a single $100 receipt) so as to facilitate third-party endorsements.

As the general population came to trust the local goldsmiths to do exactly what they pledged—to guard their *complete* deposits—and *nothing more*, the smiths' receipts became accepted as a secondary medium of exchange. Although the paper itself was useless, what it represented (i.e., the 100% gold backing in the vault) was quite valuable.

The first banks came into existence when goldsmiths opted to expand their storage services by loaning out *their own gold* to prospective clients (i.e., the income that was earned from guarding their customers' gold deposits). The bankers' "personal" loans would then be paid back with interest known as *usury*. A local economy could run smoothly so long as the banker retained his personal integrity. However, if the trusted loan officer (or "shark") began thinking about all of the dust accumulating on his depositors' coins, financial disaster was imminent.

Fractional money became the mysterious methodology of unscrupulous bankers who couldn't resist the temptation to loan out their clients' gold without the depositors' knowledge. (Joshua 7:21) Having loaned all of their own gold, bankers made the astute observation that few of their depositors ever wanted to remove *all* of their coins simultaneously. Consequently, as net withdrawals rarely exceeded 15% at any one time, it appeared perfectly safe (not to mention profitable) to lend up to 80% or even 85% of their depositors' coins.

When the borrowers received their loans (i.e., the *fractional* loans comprised of someone else's deposits), they usually put the gold right back in the vault for safekeeping, preferring paper money to bulky coins like everyone else. The web would begin to get tangled as the receipts issued to these *borrowers* were just as "official looking" as the receipts issued to the initial *depositors*! Both parties wound up having a legal claim to the same gold!?

Of course, at this point, the certificates were no longer 100% gold-backed. Unknown to the gullible public, the certificates were reduced to a backing of only 54% (100 units of gold divided by 185 certificates equals .54). There were now 85% more receipts than coins. Thus, the banks created 85% more money and funneled it into circulation through their unsuspecting borrowers.[9] *This creation of new money is the essence of* **inflation** (i.e., the total money supply is *inflated* with additional money). As there are now more dollars competing for the same goods and services, prices will increase accordingly. Griffin writes:

> These facts became the arcane secrets of the profession. The depositors were never encouraged to question how the banks could lend out their money and still have it on hand to pay back on an instant's notice. Instead, bankers put on great airs of respectability, stability, and accountability; dressed and acted serious if not stern; erected great edifices resembling government buildings and temples, all to bolster the false image of being able to honor their contracts to pay *on demand*.[10]

Fiat money constitutes paper money that is no longer backed by any gold whatsoever. As fractional money has never been anything else but fiat money in transition, the latter represents the ultimate abuse of the former. The second characteristic of fiat money is that it must be *forced* upon a people as legal tender. When governments issue fiat money, they always decree its supreme legitimacy under pain of fine or imprisonment.

History shows that most fiat money is created during times of war. Griffin continues:

> Wars are seldom funded out of the existing treasury, nor are they even done so out of increased taxes. If governments were to levy taxes on their citizens fully adequate to finance the conflict, the amount would be so great that many of even its most ardent supporters would lose enthusiasm. By artificially increasing the money supply, however, the real cost is hidden from view. It is still paid, of course, but through inflation, a process that few people understand.[11]

In addition to the funding of wars, governments also inflate the money supply to offset trade deficits and/or to balance the budget. Money that is artificially created always leads to inflation, and inflation constitutes the ultimate *hidden tax*.

> Fiat money is the means by which governments obtain instant purchasing power without taxation. But where does that purchasing power come from? Since fiat money has nothing of tangible value to offset it, government's fiat purchasing power can be obtained only by subtracting it from somewhere else. It is, in fact, "collected" from us all through a decline in *our* purchasing power. It is, therefore, exactly the same as a tax, but one that is hidden from view, silent in operation, and little understood by the taxpayer.[12]

Referring to those worthless continentals created by a panicked Congress to help finance the American Revolution, Thomas Jefferson wrote:

> Every one, through whose hands a bill passed, lost on that bill what it lost in value during the time that it was in his hands. This was a real tax on him; and in this way the people of the United States actually contributed those…millions of dollars during the war, and by a mode of taxation the most oppressive of all because the most unequal of all.[13]

By May, 1781, the continental had ceased to circulate as money and was convertible at anywhere from 400 to 1,000 continentals for a single gold or silver dollar. Is it any wonder that our Founding Fathers wrote their painful lessons of fiat money into the nation's Constitution? Article 1, Section 10 reads, *"No state shall… make anything but gold and silver coin a tender in payment of debts."*

It was Ludwig von Mises who stated, "Government is the only agency that can take a useful commodity like paper, slap some ink on it, and make it totally useless."[14] Daniel Webster adds, "Of all the contrivances for cheating the laboring classes of mankind, none has been more effective than that which deludes them with paper money."[15]

Thus we can see that a moral argument exists for a gold standard in opposition to fiat money. Representatives Ron Paul and Lewis Lehrman summarize:

> A monetary standard based on sound moral principles is one in which the monetary unit is precisely defined in something of real value such as a precious metal. Money that obtains its status from government decree alone is arbitrary, undefinable, and is destined to fail, for it will eventually be rejected by the people….

Inflation, being the increase in the supply of money and credit, can only be brought about in an irredeemable paper system by money managers who create money through fractional reserve banking, computer entries, or the printing press. Inflation bestows no benefits on society, makes no new wealth, and creates great harm; and the instigators, whether acting deliberately or not, perform an immoral act. The general welfare of the nation is not promoted by inflation, and great suffering results.

Gold is honest money because it is impossible for governments to create it. New money can only come about by productive effort and not by political and financial chicanery. Inflation is theft and literally steals wealth from one group for the benefit of another....

No wealth is created by paper money creation... Legally increasing the money supply is just as immoral as the counterfeiter who illegally prints money.

Gold money is always rejected by those who advocate significant government intervention in the economy. Gold holds in check the government's tendency to accumulate power over the economy. Paper money is a device by which the unpopular programs of government intervention, whether civilian or military, foreign or domestic, can be financed without the tax increases that would surely precipitate massive resistance by the people....

It is not surprising, then, given this background, that the Congress of 1792 imposed the death penalty on anyone convicted of debasing the coinage. Debasement, depreciation, devaluation, inflation—all stand condemned by the moral law. The present economic crisis we face is a direct consequence of our violations of that law.[16]

For the record, anyone with a King James Bible could have learned this cardinal doctrine from a reading of the second chapter of Daniel. There, the Scriptures teach that mankind moves downward, not upward. The image in Nebuchadnezzar's dream had a head made of **gold** followed in levels of degeneration, by a breast and arms of **silver**, a belly and thighs of **brass**, legs of **iron** and feet of **iron** mingled with **clay**. Daniel two is anathema to the evolutionist.

FEDERAL RESERVE SYSTEM

With this brief history of money behind us, we may now review the events which precipitated the formation of the Federal Reserve System. To understand the Federal Reserve, one must understand the basic structure of a *central* bank, which is nothing more than a government-sponsored monopoly or banking cartel. The Bank of England was chartered in 1694 to institutionalize fractional-reserve banking. The end result of this unholy alliance (and all central banks that followed) was always fiat banking (massive amounts of paper money with no gold backing). Griffin writes:

> As the world's first central bank, it introduced the concept of a partnership between bankers and politicians. The politicians would receive spendable money (created out of nothing by the bankers) without having to raise taxes. In return, the bankers would receive a commission on the transaction—deceptively called interest—which would continue in perpetuity. Since it all seemed to be wrapped up in the mysterious rituals of banking, which the common man was not expected to understand, there was practically no opposition to the scheme. The arrangement proved so profitable to the participants that it soon spread to many other countries in Europe and, eventually, to the United States.[17]

Students of history will detect the augmented pace of European warfare since the arrival of central banks and fiat money: The War of the League of Augsberg, 1689–1697; The War of Spanish Succession, 1702–1713; The War of Jenkin's Ear, 1739–1742; The War of Austrian Succession, 1744–1748; The French and Indian War, 1754–1763; The War Against Revolutionary France, 1793–1801; and the Napoleonic Wars, 1803–1815.[18] Throw in two wars with America, the War of Independence and the War of 1812, and we find that England was at war a total of 63 years between 1689–1815. This works out to *one* year in combat out of every *two*, thanks to the availability of "funny money."

Of the various central bankers, the House of Rothschild eventually became the most powerful financial dynasty in all of Europe. In the early part of the eighteenth century, an unassuming goldsmith by the name of Amschel Moses Bauer migrated from eastern Europe to Frankfurt, Germany. He then opened a countinghouse. Over the door, he placed a red shield adorned with the Roman eagle as his official sign.

Amschel died in 1755, leaving behind an only son, Amschel Mayer, age eleven. The orphan had learned much about the banking business by the time of his father's death. Within only a few years, the boy was employed as a clerk at the Oppenheimer Bank. After a while, Amschel took control of his father's old business, known as the Red Shield firm. *Roth Schild* is German for red shield, and Mayer later decided to change his name to Rothschild.

With the birth of five sons of his own, he added five arrows in the eagle's talons on the family's red shield and Roman-eagle emblem. To make a long story short, these same five arrows eventually took control of the entire banking industry of Europe. The clan of Rothschild central bankers spread out as follows: Amschel II, Frankfurt; Salomon, Vienna; Nathan, London; Karl, Naples; and son number five, Jakob (or James), Paris.

While these jackals were pioneering the world's first international network of central banks by getting one warring nation after another in their debt, the "old man" boasted ominously, "Let me issue and control a nation's money and I care not who writes the laws."[19] James Perloff interprets, "Who cares if the government is running things, if you run the government?"[20] In his biography, *The Rothschilds, a Family Portrait*, Frederic Morton concludes that "those five incredible sons...conquered the world more thoroughly, more cunningly and much more lastingly than all the Caesars before or all the Hitlers after them."[21] For reasons such as these, Thomas Jefferson once remarked, "A private central bank issuing the public currency is a greater menace to the liberties of the people than a standing army."[22]

In 1848 James Rothschild (Paris) sent his own son, Alphonse, to the United States to evaluate the possibility of establishing a direct Rothschild representative. After an extended visit, Alphonse wrote home:

> The country possesses such elements of prosperity that one would have to be blind not to recognize them....I have no hesitation in saying that a Rothschild house, and not just an agency, should be established in America.[23]

American-born (though European-schooled) J. Pierpont Morgan, Sr., replaced the German, August Belmont (born August *Schoenberg*), as the premier but covert Rothschild agent in the United States. Although a friendly competitor at first, Morgan "found his calling" when his London-based firm was saved from financial ruin in 1857 by the Rothschild-controlled Bank of England. George Wheeler writes:

> Part of the reality of the day was an ugly resurgence of anti-Semitism....Someone was needed as a cover. Who better than J. Pierpont Morgan, a solid, Protestant exemplar of capitalism able to trace his family back to pre-Revolutionary times?[24]

Rothschild associates, Paul and Felix Warburg, migrated to the United States from Germany in 1902. Shortly after arriving, the siblings became partners in America's most powerful banking firm, Kuhn, Loeb & Company. The head of Kuhn, Loeb was Jacob Schiff, whose family ties with the Rothschilds went back over a century. While Paul married Nina Loeb, daughter of founder Solomon Loeb, Felix wed Frieda Schiff, Jacob's daughter.

In 1907, Paul Warburg began writing and lecturing on the need for major bank reform at an annual salary of $500,000. Warburg complained that the American monetary system was crippled by its dependency on gold and needed an *elastic* money supply that could be artificially expanded or contracted to accommodate the fluctuating needs of commerce.

By a strange coincidence, the Panic of 1907 occurred the same year. Those in the know pointed the finger at Morgan for spreading rumors about the insolvency of The Knickerbocker Bank and The Trust Company of America. Writing in the April 25, 1949, edition of *Life* magazine, historian Frederick Lewis Allen reported:

> Oakleigh Thorne, the president of that particular trust company, testified later before a congressional committee that... it was the [Morgan's] "sore point" statement alone that had caused the run on his bank... the Morgan interests took advantage of the unsettled conditions during the autumn of 1907 to precipitate the panic, guiding it shrewdly as it progressed so that it would kill off rival banks and consolidate the preeminence of the banks within the Morgan orbit.[25]

The next player on the field was Rhode Island Senator Nelson Aldrich, known as "Morgan's floor broker in the Senate." After the Panic subsided, Aldrich was appointed by the Senate to head the National Monetary Commission. Gary Allen writes, "Although he had no technical knowledge of banking, Aldrich and his entourage spent nearly two years and $300,000 of the taxpayers' money being wined and dined by the owners of Europe's central banks as they toured the Continent 'studying' central banking."[26]

Shortly after the Congressman's return, that fateful duck hunting trip at Jekyll Island took place. Because of his vast expertise, Paul Warburg became the dominant force throughout the sessions. Griffin summarizes:

> What emerged was a cartel agreement with five objectives: stop the growing competition from the nation's newer banks; obtain a franchise to create money out of nothing for the purpose of lending; get control of the reserves of all banks so that the more reckless ones would not be exposed to currency drains and bank runs; get the taxpayer to pick up the cartel's

inevitable losses; and convince Congress that the purpose was to protect the public.[27]

As a throwback to the Fabian crest, Warburg and company would insure that their Creature appeared as a wolf in sheep's clothing. Griffin adds, "For purposes of public relations and legislation, they would devise a name that would avoid the word *bank* altogether and which would conjure up the image of the federal government itself."[28] Do you suppose that there are two Americans out of a hundred who realize that the **Federal** Reserve System is **not an agency of the United States government?** Do you believe there are two Americans out of a hundred who know that the Federal **Reserve** System has *no* reserves whatsoever? Do you think two Americans out of a hundred are aware that the Federal Reserve **System** has never submitted to a single credible audit?

Anthony Sutton, a former research fellow at the Hoover Institute for War, Revolution and Peace, one-time professor of economics at California State University, Los Angeles, and author of 20 research works (another one of Rush Limbaugh's "kooks"), wrote:

> Warburg's revolutionary plan to get American Society to go to work for Wall Street was astonishingly simple. Even today,... academic theoreticians cover their blackboards with meaningless equations, and the general public struggles in bewildered confusion with inflation and the coming credit collapse, while the quite simple explanation of the problem goes undiscussed and almost entirely uncomprehended. **The Federal Reserve System is a legal private monopoly of the money supply operated for the benefit of the few under the guise of protecting and promoting the public interest.**[29]

The first draft of the Federal Reserve Act was called the Aldrich Bill, though it was actually written by Frank Vanderlip and Benjamin Strong under the guidance of Paul Warburg. Because Senator Aldrich was known to be a spokesman for big business, the bill came under intense fire by a number of conservative legislators. Five-term Minnesota Congressman Charles Lindbergh, Sr., warned:

> The Aldrich Plan is the Wall Street Plan. It is a broad challenge to the government by the champion of the money trust. It means another panic, if necessary, to intimidate the people. Aldrich, paid by the government to represent the people, proposes a plan for the trusts instead.[30]

Not only was the Aldrich Bill dying in committee, but President Taft, normally a Republican advocate of big business, refused to champion the push for a central bank. The Money Trust decided on a bold counterstroke.

WOODROW WILSON

Woodrow Wilson became the president of Princeton University in 1902. Cleveland Dodge and Cyrus McCormick, directors of Rockefeller's National City Bank, were university trustees and largely responsible for Wilson's appointment. Ferdinand Lundberg, in *America's Sixty Families*, declared:

> For nearly twenty years before his nomination Woodrow Wilson had moved in the shadow of Wall Street...Dodge and McCormick... constituted themselves his financial guardians...In 1902 this same group arranged Wilson's election as president of the university.[31]

Following the cue of his benefactors, Wilson set his sights on Pennsylvania Avenue, H. S. Kenan writing:

> Woodrow Wilson, President of Princeton University, was the first prominent educator to speak in favor of the Aldrich Plan, a gesture which immediately brought him the Governorship of New Jersey and later the Presidency of the United States. During the Panic of 1907, Wilson declared that: "all this trouble could be averted if we appointed a committee of six or seven public-spirited men like J. P. Morgan to handle the affairs of our country."[32]

To ensure that their Democratic dupe would defeat the incumbent Taft, Morgan's people persuaded Teddy Roosevelt to split the Republican vote as the "Bull Moose" candidate on the Progressive party ticket. The election of 1912 was a classic example of power politics and voter deception. While Felix Warburg was dutifully contributing to the Republican war chest, his brother, Paul, and Jacob Schiff were privately contributing to Wilson's campaign. Yet another Kuhn, Loeb partner, Otto Kahn, supported Roosevelt.

The outcome of the election was exactly as the bankers had anticipated; Wilson won with only 42% of the vote. The inside joke was that "Wilson was elected by Teddy Roosevelt."

As the record would later show, Woodrow Wilson was the consummate political puppet. The man who guided him from the Democratic convention to the presidency was the infamous Colonel Edward M. House. (Fittingly, House did not serve in the military; his title was strictly "honorary.") Of course, the "Colonel" was a key insider for the Money Trust. In *The Intimate Papers of Colonel House,* Professor Charles Seymour refers to House as the "unseen guardian angel" of the Federal Reserve Act.[33] Biographer George Viereck adds, "The Schiffs, the Warburgs, the Kahns, the Rockefellers, and the Morgans put their faith in House."[34]

The degree to which Colonel House dominated Wilson's every move is quite a bizarre scenario in itself. An admiring biographer, Arthur Smith, writing in 1918, says that House held "a power never wielded before in this country by any man out of office, a power greater than that of any political boss or Cabinet member."[35]

Calling House the "Chief Magistracy of the Republic," "Super ambassador" and "The pilot who guided the ship," biographer Viereck wrote:

> For six years two rooms were at his disposal in the North Wing of the White House.... In work and play their thoughts were one. House was the double of Wilson. It was House who made the slate for the Cabinet, formulated the first policies of the Administration and practically directed the foreign affairs of the United States. We had, indeed, two Presidents for one![36]

At Wilson's first Cabinet meeting, Franklin K. Lane introduced himself, saying, "My name is Lane, Mr. President. I believe I am the Secretary of the Interior."[37]

According to Rush Limbaugh, concerned Americans who wonder about these clandestine activities are a bunch of deluded "kooks." Suppose we let the President speak for himself:

> **Mr. House is my second personality. He is my independent self. His thoughts and mine are one. If I were in his place I would do just as he suggested....If anyone thinks he is reflecting my opinion by whatever action he takes, they are welcome to the conclusion.[38]**

To gain the confidence of his electorate, Wilson hypocritically declared:

> There has come about an extraordinary and very sinister concentration in the control of business in the country.... The growth of our nation, therefore, and all our activities, are in the hands of a few men.... This

money trust, or as it should be more properly called, this credit trust... is no myth.[39]

However, Wilson was also quick to "wash his hands" of the ungodly matter, hiding behind the guise of *ignorance*:

> The greatest embarrassment of my political career has been that active duties seem to deprive me of time for careful investigation. I seem almost obliged to form conclusions from impressions instead of from study.... I wish that I had more knowledge, more thorough acquaintance, with the matters involved.[40]

Under the Colonel's guidance, the old Aldrich Bill was given cosmetic surgery and reemerged as the Democratic Glass-Owen Bill. Aldrich, Vanderlip and other high-profile Republican banking advocates put on a pretense of opposing the legislation. Charles Lindbergh wasn't fooled, however, and fought The Creature from Jekyll Island to the finish. In July, 1913, the Minnesota congressman introduced a resolution calling for an investigation of the House Committee on Banking and Currency. Unfortunately, the proposal was defeated by New York Congressman John T. Fitzgerald.

For the record, Fitzgerald was a rabid Roman Catholic who would later join forces with another Catholic House member, Boston's James A. Gallivan, in an attempt to overthrow our constitutional guarantee of a free press. On March 27, 1916, Gallivan introduced the following bill:

> Be it enacted by the Senate and House of Representatives of the United States of America, in Congress assembled, that the Postmaster General shall make the necessary rules and regulations **to exclude from the mails those publications, the avowed and deliberate purpose of which is to attack a recognized religion,** held by the citizens of the United States or any religious order to which citizens of the United States belong.[41]

When a number of prominent citizens assembled in the Haverhill, Massachusetts, city hall on June 4, 1916, to protest the postal bill, a mob of 10,000 Irish Catholics stormed city hall and the police station, wreaking havoc until suppressed by the local militia.

It should come as no surprise that the Vatican would highly favor the crippling Federal Reserve Act. As stated earlier in this chapter, the last days of planet Earth will be dominated by a one-world church *and* a one-world government. Besides, even the Vatican could use a loan now and then. When Carl von Rothschild was received by Pope Gregory XVI on January 10, 1832, the pontiff wisely extended his *hand* to be kissed, rather than the customary *toe*, and pinned the order of St. George on the lapel of the "Kosher Baron."[42] (In 1870, the Vatican floated a loan of 200,000 scudi from Rothschild.[43])

The father of the famous American aviator, Charles Lindbergh, was wise to dangers from both the bankers and the Vatican. Citing the *Catholic Bulletin*, a St. Paul weekly, Lindbergh biographer Bruce Larson writes: " 'Lindbergh's assumption that there was a close alliance between the Roman church and big business was misguided,' said the *Bulletin*, and it summarized his position as 'unmistakable evidence of anti-Catholic prejudice, based, as usual, upon misinterpretation of history.' "[44]

The courageous congressman introduced a resolution in July, 1916, requesting a "true and impartial investigation" concerning charges brought by the Free Press Defense League of Kansas against the Vatican for "carrying out the conspiracy to bring the United States of America under the complete domination of the Pope of Rome and the Catholic hierarchy."[45] Needless to say, Lindbergh had his hands full fighting a losing battle to save American liberties.

When the Federal Reserve Act was released from the joint House and Senate conference committee on December 22, 1913, Lindbergh issued his final warning that the bill "established the most gigantic trust on earth."[46] As Congress was preoccupied with the approaching holiday recess, the ungodly measure quietly passed through the House by a vote of 282 to 60 and with a margin of 43 to 23 in the Senate. President Wilson signed the Act into law the next day. Griffin wrote, "The Creature had swallowed Congress."[47]

WORLD WAR I

With the unconstitutional surrender over America's entire monetary system, the remainder of the century would be a downward slide at best. The graduated income tax was also dumped on the American people in 1913. How convenient! Yet, a far greater debacle was approaching.

The first world war did not begin in 1914, but rather in 1054 when the Vatican lost Russia and the Balkans along with Greece. What the Roman Catholic nephew of the Roman Catholic Austrian emperor, Franz Joseph, was doing, flaunting his royal person along the border of Greek Orthodox Serbia, made about as much sense as David Duke taking a walk through Harlem. The bottom line was that 10 million killed and 20 million wounded became the human cost involved in the four-year attempt by the Roman Catholic House of Hapsburg (*the* ruling family in Europe for over 600 years) to "reclaim" the wandering orthodox nations back to the fold of Holy Mother Church.

The cost in money was where the international bankers came in. When the central banks of England and France went dry, their government heads turned to Morgan for relief. John Moody wrote in 1919, "Not only did England and France pay for their supplies with money furnished by Wall Street, but they made their purchases through the same medium."[48] The Morgan firm became the largest consumer on earth, spending nearly $10 million per day on behalf of the Allies. Griffin wrote, "Each month, Morgan presided over purchases which were equal to the gross national product of the entire world just one generation before."[49]

However, Wall Street started to get a little shaky when the newly invented German U-boats began wreaking havoc on British shipping. A total of over 5,700 Allied ships were sunk between 1914 and 1918. Three hundred thousand tons of cargo went to the bottom weekly. British Foreign Secretary Arthur Balfour would later write, "At that time, it certainly looked as though we were going to lose the war."[50] Historian Robert Ferrell confirmed, "The Allies approached the brink of disaster, with no recourse other than to ask Germany for terms."[51]

In light of such developments, the sale of Allied war bonds plummeted, jeopardizing lucrative commissions. Furthermore, if Britain and France came to terms, the old bonds would go into default, costing Morgan's cronies millions. Direct financial aid from the United States Treasury was prohibited by then-current neutrality treaties. The only way for Morgan's loans to be salvaged was to incite America's entrance into the war. United States ambassador Walter Page sent a telegram to the State Department declaring,

> I think that the pressure of this approaching crisis has gone beyond the ability of the Morgan Financial Agency for the British and French Governments.... The greatest help we could give the Allies would be such a credit... Unless we go to war with Germany, our Government, of course, cannot make such a direct grant of credit.[52]

The American public wanted no part in a European conflict. Wilson had been reelected on the campaign theme, "Because he kept us out of war."

Nevertheless, Colonel House negotiated a secret agreement with England and France in early 1915, pledging United States intervention on behalf of the Entente powers.

The Colonel got things moving by conning the pacifist Wilson into believing that a global government ensuring a stable peace could be attained by America's involvement in the war. Griffin wrote, "One of the strongest bonds between House and himself was their common dream of a world government."[53]

However, conning the American people would require a great deal more imagination. House realized that if the "enemy" could be provoked into attacking the United States, public sentiment would be incensed. Winston Churchill, First Lord of the Admiralty, understood this strategy, stating, "The maneuver which brings an ally into the field is as serviceable as that which wins a great battle."[54]

The "maneuver" chosen by Winston was a deadly ploy indeed. Under what was called "Cruiser Rules," English and German warships extended a mutual courtesy to each other's unarmed merchant ships, which gave their crew members the chance to abandon ship before being sunk. In October, 1914, Churchill issued orders that British ships should no longer heed U-boat orders to halt and be searched. If they were carrying armaments (which many of them were known to do), they were to engage the enemy, ramming the sub, if possible. Such a policy forced the U-boats to remain submerged and to sink, without warning, whatever ships were suspicioned.

Churchill's justification for this cold-blooded strategy was incredible. In a letter to Board of Trade president Walter Runciman, dated February 12, 1915, *only three months before the Lusitania incident,* the First Lord declared, "It is most important to attract neutral shipping to our shores, in the hope especially of embroiling the U.S. with Germany."[55] Churchill later expanded on this clause in his 1923 work, *The World Crisis.*

> The first British countermove, made on my responsibility,... was to deter the Germans from surface attack. The submerged U-boat had to rely increasingly on underwater attack and **thus ran the greater risk of mistaking neutral for British ships and of drowning neutral crews** and thus embroiling Germany with other Great Powers.[56]

The threat to innocent lives was further increased by the covert operations of Morgan's own shipping cartel; Griffin writing, "He quickly learned the profitable skills of war-time smuggling."[57]

THE LUSITANIA

The *Lusitania*, a massive British luxury liner owned by the Cunard Company (a Morgan competitor), was secretly refurbished as an *armed auxiliary cruiser* (as logged in *Jane's Fighting Ships* and the British publication, *The Naval Annual*).[58] Even Bailey and Ryan concede, "One of the many ironies of the *Lusitania* case is that the arming or potential arming of ordinary passenger or merchant ships led directly to the German policy of torpedoing such vessels without warning."[59]

Unbeknownst to her endangered passengers, the *Lusitania* regularly carried a substantial cargo of wartime armaments in violation of existing neutrality laws. After several close calls with pursuing German U-boats, the captain of the *Lusitania*, David Dow, resigned on March 8, 1915, stating he was no longer willing "to carry the responsibility of mixing passengers with munitions or contraband."[60]

In the closing weeks of April, 1915, a substantial payload was smuggled aboard the *Lusitania* which included 600 tons of the explosive pyroxyline, 6 million rounds of ammunition and 1,248 cases of shrapnel shells. When the German embassy in Washington filed a formal complaint in view of existing neutrality laws, the American officials denied any knowledge of such cargo.

As a final effort to avoid disaster, the German government placed an ad in dozens of East Coast newspapers warning Americans not to book passage on the *Lusitania*:

NOTICE!

TRAVELLERS intending to embark on the Atlantic voyage are reminded that a state of war exists between Germany and her allies and Great Britain and her allies; that the zone of war includes the waters adjacent to the British Isles; that, in accordance with formal notice given by the Imperial German Government, vessels flying the flag of Great Britain, or of any of her allies, are liable to destruction in those waters and that travellers sailing in the war zone on ships of Great Britain or her allies do so at their own risk.

IMPERIAL GERMAN EMBASSY,
Washington, D.C., April 22, 1915.

Although the ad did appear in a number of papers,[61] some authorities contend that it was suppressed in many others.[62] (Part of the disagreement may be traced to the time span between the original date requested for publication, April 23—a full week before the sailing date, and the last-minute run by others, such as the May 1 publication by *New York World.*)

According to Simpson, George Viereck, the editor of a German-owned newspaper, obtained a personal audience with Secretary of State, William Jennings Bryan, who subsequently assured him that he would endeavor to persuade the President to issue a renewed public warning. With reference to the President, Simpson wrote, "He did nothing, but was to concede on the day he was told of her sinking that this foreknowledge had given him many sleepless hours."[63]

On May 1, the *Lusitania* left New York harbor with orders to rendezvous with the British destroyer, *Juno,* just off the coast of Ireland. Griffin relates the tragic developments:

> In truth, the *Juno* had been called *out* of the area at the last minute and ordered to return to Queenstown. And this was done with the full knowledge that the *Lusitania* was on a direct course into an area where a German submarine was known to be operating.
>
> To make matters worse, the *Lusitania* had been ordered to cut back on the use of coal, not because of shortages, but because it would be less expensive. Slow targets, of course, are much easier to hit. Yet, she was required to shut down one of her four boilers and, consequently, was now entering submarine-infested waters at only 75% of her potential speed.[64]

Authors Bailey and Ryan (*The Lusitania Disaster*) dispute Simpson's account of the *Juno's* involvement.[65] However, Commander Joseph Kenworthy, one of the naval intelligence officers in the high-command map room on that fateful day, left the room in disgust, later writing, "The *Lusitania* was sent at considerably reduced speed into an area where a U-boat was known to be waiting and with her escorts withdrawn."[66] Griffin adds:

> Colonel House was in England at that time and, on the day of the sinking, was scheduled to have an audience with King George V. He was accompanied by Sir Edward Grey and, on the way, Sir Grey asked him: "What will America do if the Germans sink an ocean liner with American passengers on board?"
>
> As recorded in House's diaries, he replied: "I told him if this were done, a flame of indignation would sweep America, which would in itself probably carry us into the war." Once at Buckingham Palace, King George also brought up the subject and was even more specific about the possible

target. He asked, "Suppose they should sink the *Lusitania* with American passengers on board."[67]

Four hours after this conversation on May 7, 1915, a single torpedo struck the *Lusitania*, triggering a second, internal explosion moments later. The mighty vessel sank in less than 18 minutes. Of the 1,195 persons who lost their lives, 195 were Americans.

Colonel House telegrammed Wilson immediately: "Our action in this crisis will determine the part we will play when peace is made, and how far we may influence a settlement for the lasting good of humanity."[68]

Although Winston Churchill may not have been *directly* responsible for the *Lusitania* sinking (as many writers contend), his bellicose maritime policies were designed to occasion eventual disaster. The *Lusitania's* 1,195 victims were probably more than he had bargained for.

As expected, public outcry was loud and sustained. Wilson and the press continued to fan the flames of jingoism. Finally, on April 16, 1917, Congress caved in and declared war on the Axis powers. Eight days later the War Loan Act was passed, extending $1 billion in immediate credit ("funny money") to the Allies.

By the time the war was over, a total of $9.466 million had been "loaned." According to Ferdinand Lundberg, "the total wartime expenditure of the United States government from April 6, 1917, to October 31, 1919, when the last contingent of troops returned from Europe, was $35.413 billion."[69] Most of this passed through Morgan's operation.

The Creature from Jekyll Island conveniently "created" the money that was given to England and France so they could continue repaying the American banks. Unfortunately, the ordinary citizen got stuck with the bill. Between 1915 and 1920, the nation's money supply "inflated" from $20.6 billion to $39.8 billion, causing a reduction in purchasing power by almost 50%.[70] (This was in addition to the new income tax.)

Years later, columnist Edith Kermit Roosevelt, granddaughter of former president Theodore Roosevelt, would aptly label the power mongers of the so-called "Eastern Establishment" as the **"Legitimate Mafia."**

A little over a month before the signing of the armistice on November 11, 1918, a solitary, born-again Christian from the hills of Tennessee caused quite a stir in the battle of the Argonne Forest. Described by General "Black Jack" Pershing as "the outstanding civilian hero in the World War,"[71] Corporal Alvin Cullum York single-handedly killed 28 German soldiers, captured 35 machine guns, and, with the assistance of half a dozen dough-boys, "rounded up" 132 prisoners—*all to the glory of God!* When Colonel Richard Wetherill exclaimed to York, "It is not human for a man to do what you have done," the humble mountaineer simply replied, "I believed in God, and I done know He watched over me."[72]

This incident marked one of the few bright spots in the otherwise dreadful debacle—30 million casualties and $400.8 trillion in property damage, "over *there*."

XVIII

CFR, FDR, WW II, IMF, UN

> *"The kings of the earth set themselves, and the rulers take counsel together, against the LORD, and against his anointed."* (Psalm 2:2)

THERE ARE ONLY two ways in which world history can be interpreted: the *accidental* theory (big bang, evolution, etc.) and the *conspiratorial* theory. To give credence to the latter is to be branded with the lunatic fringe. (See: Institute of Advanced Conservative Studies' "Kook Test.") In his work, *The Nature of the American System,* Rousas Rushdooney writes:

> In the eyes of most intellectuals, the hallmark of intellectual acceptability is to view history as the outworking of impersonal forces and factors, whereas the epitome of absurd, irrational and even dangerously reactionary thinking is to regard history as in any sense *conspiracy*. Such a view is primitive and naive; it is a form of belief in the devil, we are told.
>
> It is best, at this point, to call attention to the common dictionary definitions, in the Merriam-Webster Dictionary, Second Edition, of conspiracy, which means (1) a "combination of men for an evil purpose; an agreement between two or more persons to commit a crime in concert, as treason; a plot"; (2) "Combination of men for a single end; a concurrence, or general tendency, as of circumstances, to one event; harmonious action"; (3) *"Law.* An agreement, manifesting itself in words or deeds, by which two or more persons confederate to do an unlawful act, or to use unlawful means to do an act which is lawful; confederacy." It is

at once obvious that, in all three senses, conspiracy exists, and that, in the second sense it is present in all kinds of organizations and institutions....

History, therefore, is not the outworking of impersonal forces but a personal conflict between the forces of God and anti-God, Christ and anti-christ, with the ultimate victory assured to God and His Christ. The Bible as a whole presents a view of *history as conspiracy*, with Satan and man determined to assert their "right" to be gods, knowing, or determining, good and evil for themselves (Genesis 3:5). From beginning to end, this is the perspective of Scripture, and only a wilful misreading of it can lead to any other position.[1]

According to Rushdooney, the conspiracy view of history is summarized in Psalm 2, the Old Testament psalm most frequently quoted in the New Testament: "The whole world is seen as organized against the Lord in deliberate opposition to His rule, for David sees, not himself, but the Lord Messiah as the true king."[2]

The Creature from Jekyll Island was just the beginning of latent conspiratorial activities in the United States. Rushdooney, citing Coogan, "With the Federal Reserve Act, the very evils criticized were quickly enthroned so that it could be said, 'Banking, as it is conducted today, is actually a conspiracy operating against society.' "[3]

As the book of Genesis reveals the precise design of an Almighty Creator, history records the subsequent attempts by Lucifer to destroy that creation with equal calculation and precision. Thus, the evil in any generation can be ultimately ascribed to Satan's master conspiracy *"against the LORD, and against his anointed."* The individual "participants" (dupes of the devil) seldom see their roles in this bigger picture.

Similarly, the average Christian rarely comprehends the myriad of present-day conspiracies, while the few who do understand generally react in a non-scriptural manner. (Billy Sunday's revivals doubled as recruiting campaigns, the hellfire evangelist thundering out divine wrath upon "Kaiser Bill," rather than the Rothschilds.) Because most believers have been influenced by the "positive" agenda of twentieth-century American society (i.e., "Something good is going to happen to you"), conspiracy theories are shunned for their *negative* content. (II Timothy 3:1) This "ostrich" approach was anticipated in II Timothy 4:3: *"For the time will come when they will not endure sound doctrine."*

When a percentage of Christians do learn about these machinations, they either become pessimistic in their service for God ("Oh, what's the use!"), or optimistic in a new-found calling to help extricate America from tyranny (Moral Majority, John Birch Society, etc.).

As the theological discipline of a moderate dispensationalism confirms that every period of human stewardship has ended (and will continue to end) in total failure, the Bible believer's response to a forecast of fatalistic reality should be to allow such negatives to perfect his *soberness* and *vigilance*. (I Peter 5:8) If times of persecution have historically worked to purify the church ("the blood of the martyrs is the seed of the church"), why wouldn't the reality of *approaching* persecution do the same? (Ecclesiastes 1:18) Our present chapter will survey the conspiracies which preceded World War II, with special attention being given to the Vatican's role in that bloody conflict.

THE ROUND TABLE

In 1870, a wealthy British socialist by the name of John Ruskin was appointed professor of fine arts at Oxford University. Ruskin advocated placing control of the state (as well as the economy) into the hands of a ruling elite, writing, "My continual aim has been to show the eternal superiority of some men to others, sometimes even of one man to all others."[4]

A powerful movement born during this time was the English socialist society known as *Fabianism*. Whereas the communist believed in over-throwing capitalism through violent revolution, Fabians preferred to achieve the same goals through propaganda and legislation. To accentuate the importance of gradualism, they adopted the turtle as the symbol of their movement. The three leading Fabians in the movement's formative years were Sidney and Beatrice Webb and George Bernard Shaw. At the Webb House in Surrey, England, the following lines from Omar Khayyam appear across a stained-glass window:

> *Dear love, couldst thou and I with fate conspire*
> *To grasp this sorry scheme of things entire,*
> *Would we not shatter it to bits, and then*
> *Remould it nearer to the heart's desire!*

Beneath the line, *"Remould it nearer to the heart's desire,"* the mural depicts Shaw and Webb striking the earth with hammers. A second line reads, *"Pray Devoutly, Hammer Stoutly."* The most subtle message, however, is the Fabian crest which appears between Shaw and Webb—*a wolf in sheep's clothing!*

One of Professor Ruskin's most devoted students was a man by the name of Cecil Rhodes (1853–1902). With financial support from Lord Rothschild and the Bank of England, Rhodes went on to monopolize the diamond mines of South Africa and even became prime minister of the Cape colony from 1890–1896. Rhodes had a personal fortune of at least a million pounds sterling a year (then about five million dollars). He used the greater part of this fortune to advance the socialistic agenda of his Oxford mentor. After his death, the prestigious Rhodes scholarships were founded to perpetuate the English ruling class tradition.

First and foremost, Cecil Rhodes was an impassioned advocate of the coming *New World Order.* According to biographer Sarah Millin, "The government of the world was Rhodes' simple desire."[5] On February 5, 1891, Rhodes organized a highly secretive society to promote global socialism. The core group was known as the "Circle of Initiates," and included such high-rollers as Lord Rothschild, Arthur (Lord) Balfour, (Sir) Harry Johnston, Albert (Lord) Grey, Reginald Baliol Brett (Lord Esher), Alfred (Lord) Milner and William T. Stead.[6] The outer circle originally called the "Association of Helpers," later became known as "The Round Table."

As the historical record confirms, this original band of conspirators eventually exported their clandestine activity to the United States of America where a handful of "insiders" currently exert enormous influence on both domestic and international policy.

The definitive reference work on the history of this diabolical order is entitled *Tragedy and Hope* by the late Dr. Carroll Quigley. Another one of Limbaugh's "kooks," Dr. Quigley was professor of history at the Foreign Service School of Georgetown University where President Clinton attended his lectures. (Georgetown University is one of the largest Jesuit schools in America; Professor Quigley was a member of the Roman Catholic Church.)

Dr. Quigley held memberships in a variety of academic organizations, such as the American Association for the Advancement of Science, the American Anthropological Association and the American Economic Association. He was also a frequent lecturer for such elitist groups as the Brookings Institution, the United States Naval Weapons Laboratory, the Industrial College of the Armed Forces and the Smithsonian Institute.

When Dr. Quigley wrote his 1,300-page tome, it was not intended for the masses, but rather for the professional academician. It was to this select readership that Professor Quigley divulged the time-honored secrets of the Round Table groups. Quigley's credibility for accuracy was reinforced by the uncanny fact that he declared his own personal affinity for their agenda of global domination. He wrote:

> **There does exist, and has existed for a generation, an international Anglophile network which operates, to some extent, in the way the radical Right believes the Communists act.** In fact, this network, which we may identify as the **Round Table Groups**, has no aversion to cooperating with the Communists, or any other groups, and frequently does so.
>
> **I know of the operations of this network because I have studied it for twenty years and was permitted for two years, in the early 1960's, to examine its papers and secret records.** I have no aversion to it or to most of its aims and have, for much of my life, been close to it and to many of its instruments....
>
> In general my chief difference of opinion is that it wishes to remain unknown, and I believe its role in history is significant enough to be known.[7]

As certain right-wing organizations became aware of Quigley's disclosures, an increased demand for *Tragedy and Hope* (by conservatives) triggered a conspiracy of its own. In a personal letter dated December 9, 1975, Quigley wrote:

> Thank you for your praise of *Tragedy and Hope*, a book which has brought me headaches *as it apparently says something which powerful people do not want known*. My publisher stopped selling it in 1968 and told me he would reprint (but in 1971 he told my lawyer that they had destroyed the plates in 1968). The rare-book price went up to $135 and parts were reprinted in violation of copyright.[8]

In another personal letter expressing frustration with the publisher, Quigley wrote:

> They lied to me for six years, telling me they would reprint when they got 2,000 orders, which could never happen because they told anyone who asked that it was out of print and would not be reprinted.
>
> They denied this to me until I sent them Xerox copies of such replies in libraries, at which they told me it was a clerk's error. In other words, they lied to me but prevented me from regaining publication rights....I am now quite sure that *Tragedy and Hope* was suppressed.[9]

What had Professor Quigley written that caused such a stink within the Eastern "Establishment" (Edith Roosevelt's "Legitimate Mafia")? For starters, he exposed the primary role of the international bankers:

> In addition to these pragmatic goals, the powers of financial capitalism had another far-reaching aim, nothing less than to create a world system of financial control in private hands able to dominate the political system of each country and the economy of the world as a whole. This system was to be controlled in a feudalist fashion by the central banks of the world acting in concert, by secret agreements arrived at in frequent private meetings and conferences.[10]

Quigley then goes on to remind his readers that the *real* power brokers are rarely in the forefront:

> It must not be felt that these heads of the world's chief central banks were themselves substantive powers in world finance. They were not. Rather, they were the technicians and agents of the dominant investment bankers of their own countries, who had raised them up and were perfectly capable of throwing them down.
>
> The substantive financial powers of the world were in the hands of these investment bankers (also called "international" or "merchant" bankers) who remained largely behind the scenes in their own unincorporated private banks. These formed a system of international cooperation and national dominance which was more private, more powerful, and more secret than that of their agents in the central banks.[11]

THE BOLSHEVIK REVOLUTION

The mass of covert activity perpetrated by these international scoundrels is truly incredible. While President Wilson was campaigning to "make the world safe for democracy" by committing American boys to the "war to end all wars," the Bolshevik Revolution in Russia was being planned and financed by Round Table kingdom builders. The conquest of Russia was seen as the first phase toward total global domination. In the February 3, 1949, issue of the *New York Journal American*, Jacob Schiff's grandson, John, was quoted by columnist Cholly Knickerbocker as saying that his grandfather had contributed nearly $20 million for the triumph of Communism in Russia.[12]

In his work, *Czarism and Revolution*, author Arsene de Goulevitch, an eyewitness of the Bolshevik revolt, said, "In private interviews I have been told that over 21 million roubles [sic] were spent by Lord [Alfred] Milner in financing the Russian Revolution."[13] (Milner had succeeded Cecil Rhodes as the head of the Round Table upon the latter's death in 1902.) Another English financier indicted by Goulevitch was Sir George Buchanan, the British ambassador to Russia at the time. For American and British citizens to be indirectly aiding the Axis powers by undermining Tsarist Russia was tantamount to treason. This is what Professor Quigley meant by Round Table groups "cooperating with Communists." With America's entrance into the war constituting surety for Wall Street loans, the Allies could "afford" to lose Mother Russia for her vanguard role in the greater New World Order.

The way in which the Round Table agents from America entered Russia at this time was even more ingenious than the Jekyll Island "duck hunt." Ever since 1910, J. P. Morgan was the heaviest contributor to the faltering American Red Cross. Professor Sutton wrote, "The Red Cross was unable to cope with the demands of World War I and in effect was taken over by these New York banks."[14] Can you guess what happened next? Perloff writes:

> In the summer of 1917, to the city of Petrograd—nerve center of the Russian Revolution—came one of the strangest Red Cross missions in history. It consisted of fifteen Wall Street financiers and attorneys, led by Federal Reserve director William Boyce Thompson, plus a small contingent of doctors and nurses. The medical team, discovering that they were but a front for political activities, returned home in protest after one month. The businessmen remained in Petrograd.
>
> The mission supplied financing, first for the socialist regime of Alexsandr Kerensky, and then for the Bolsheviks who supplanted him. In his biography of William Boyce Thompson, Hermann Hagedorn produced photographic evidence that J. P. Morgan cabled Thompson $1 million through the National City Bank branch in Petrograd—the only bank in Russia the Bolsheviks did not nationalize.[15]

For the record, an article in the *Washington Post* of February 2, 1918, confirmed, "William B. Thompson, who was in Petrograd from July until November last, has made a personal contribution of $1,000,000 to the Bolsheviki for the purpose of spreading their doctrine in Germany and Austria."[16] "Capitalizing" on their close friendships with Trotsky and Lenin, Morgan's Red Cross "volunteers" obtained profitable business concessions from the new government which returned their initial investment several times over. (See Reuters article in *Chicago Tribune*, May 23, 1996, Section 1, page 27, column 6: "WWII data link firms to Nazis; Paper trail of shame for banks, Red Cross.")

Over half a century later, Chase Manhattan Bank advertised in several newspapers across the nation, "From 1 Chase Manhattan Plaza to 1 Karl Marx Square, we're international money experts with a knack for making good sense out of confusing East-West trade talk."[17] Something has gone terribly wrong when the American taxpayer has to spend over $100 billion a year on defense to protect himself from 150 Soviet weapon systems which utilize United States technology![18] Professor Sutton concludes, "There has been a continuing, albeit concealed, alliance between international political capitalists and international revolutionary socialists—to their mutual benefit."[19]

COUNCIL ON FOREIGN RELATIONS

The Paris Peace Conference of 1919 resulted in the Versailles Treaty which required Germany to pay the Entente powers severe war reparations. At the conference, President Wilson introduced his pipe dream for peace, known as the Fourteen Points—the last *point* calling for a "general association of nations." (Get the *point*?) Ray Stannard Baker, Wilson's official biographer, confirmed what few people knew, "practically nothing— not a single idea—in the Covenant of the League was original with the President."[20] Perloff says, "It was Colonel House who had written the Covenant."[21] The Colonel's biographer, Charles Seymour, wrote that Wilson "approved the House draft almost in its entirety, and his own rewriting of it was practically confined to phraseology."[22]

In 1917, House brought about a hundred power mongers to a special New York meeting called, "The Inquiry." After developing the "plans for peace," approximately 20 of these "inquirers" went with Wilson to Paris, including House and Paul Warburg. Although the European nations were ready to join, the United States Senate balked at ratification. The average American was still smarting over 336,000 native casualties. The majority were convinced that George Washington had been right after all.

While Colonel House and "The Inquiry" delegates were still in Paris, word reached them of a probable Senate rejection. The internationalists concluded that America would not abandon her sovereignty unless something was done to create a different climate of opinion. During a dinner at the Majestic Hotel on May 30, 1919, it was resolved that an "Institute of International Affairs" would be formed with two central branches—one in Great Britain and the other in the United States. The English group became known as the Royal Institute of International Affairs (RIIA). Its leadership was controlled by members of the London-based Round Table.

On July 29, 1921, the American branch became incorporated in New York as the *Council on Foreign Relations* (CFR). Professor Quigley comments on this Round Table expansion:

> At the end of the war of 1914, it became clear that the organization of this system had to be greatly extended. Once again the task was entrusted to Lionel Curtis who established, in England and each dominion, a front organization to the existing local Round Table Group. This front organization, called the Royal Institute of International Affairs, had as its nucleus in each area the existing submerged Round Table Group.
>
> In New York it was known as the Council on Foreign Relations, and was a front for J. P. Morgan and Company in association with the very small American Round Table Group.[23]

In 1922, the Council stated its own policy as follows:

> The Council on Foreign Relations aims to provide a continuous conference on the international aspects of America's political, economic and financial problems....It is *simply* a group of men concerned in spreading a knowledge of international relations, and, in particular, *in developing a reasoned American foreign policy.*[24]

Others looking in from the outside offer a more critical appraisal. Historian Arthur Schlesinger, Jr., described the CFR as a "front organization" for "the heart of the American Establishment."[25] In his work, *The Best and the Brightest*, David Halberstam labeled it, "the Establishment's unofficial club."[26] Yet, the CFR is rarely assailed by investigative reporters as its ranks include top executives from the *New York Times*, the *Washington Post*, the *Los Angeles Times*, the *Knight* newspaper chain, NBC, CBS, *Time, Life, Fortune, Business Week, U.S. News and World Report* and many, many others (171 organizations and associations, according to John F. McManus[27]).

Headquartered in the elegant Pratt House at 58 East Sixty-eighth Street in New York City, the CFR claimed 3,066 members as of June, 1994. Membership is by invitation only. The cardinal doctrine espoused by the

CFR is the pressing need for a one-world government. Although the Council claims to be pluralistic, even the liberal *New York Times* conceded that the group has "a uniform direction."[28] This predominant focus of the CFR can be easily determined by examining back issues of their official publication *Foreign Affairs*. Called by *Time* magazine "the most influential periodical in print,"[29] the saying goes that "if you want to know what the U. S. government will be doing tomorrow, just read *Foreign Affairs* today."[30] An article in the *second* issue in December, 1922, declared:

> Obviously there is going to be no peace or prosperity for mankind so long as it remains divided into fifty or sixty independent states...Equally obviously there is going to be no steady progress in civilization or self-government among the more backward peoples until some kind of international system is created which will put an end to the diplomatic struggles incident to the attempt of every nation to make itself secure... The real problem today is that of world government.[31]

A 1944 CFR publication, *American Public Opinion and Postwar Security Commitments*, acknowledged that the traditional American was still opposed to a globalistic society:

> The sovereignty fetish is still so strong in the public mind, that there would appear to be little chance of winning popular assent to American membership in anything approaching a super-state organization. Much will depend on the kind of approach which is used in further popular education.[32]

In 1959, the Council issued a position paper entitled *Study No. 7, Basic Aims of U.S. Foreign Policy* proposing that the United States "build a new international order." The recommended steps were as follows:

> 1. Search for an international order in which the freedom of nations is recognized as interdependent and in which many policies are jointly undertaken by free world states with differing political, economic and social systems, and including states labeling themselves as "socialist."

> 2. Safeguard U.S. security through preserving a system of bilateral agreements and regional arrangements.

> 3. Maintain and gradually increase the authority of the U.N.

    4. Make more effective use of the International Court of Justice, jurisdiction of which should be increased by withdrawal of reservations by member nations on matters judged to be domestic.[33]

Writing in a 1974 *Foreign Affairs* article entitled "The Hard Road to World Order," Richard N. Gardner complained, "We are witnessing an outbreak of shortsighted nationalism that seems oblivious to the economic, political and moral implications of interdependence." His strategy recommended that "an end run around national sovereignty, eroding it piece by piece, will accomplish much more than the old-fashioned frontal assault."[34]

Finally, in the fall 1984 *Foreign Affairs*, Kurt Waldheim, former secretary-general of the United Nations and former Nazi, wrote, "As long as states insist that they are the supreme arbiters of their destinies—that as sovereign entities their decisions are subject to no higher authority—international organizations will never be able to guarantee the maintenance of peace."[35]

The most dangerous aspect of the CFR is that it furnishes the personnel for most upper echelon positions within the United States government. Pulitzer prizewinner Theodore White (Limbaugh "kook") wrote that the Council's "roster of members has for a generation, under Republican and Democratic administrations alike, been the chief recruiting ground for cabinet-level officials in Washington."[36]

Calling the Council a "school for statesmen," Joseph Kraft wrote in the July, 1958, *Harpers*, "It has been the seat of...basic government decisions, has set the context for many more, and has repeatedly served as a recruiting ground for ranking officials."[37] David Halberstam concludes sardonically, "They walk in one door as acquisitive businessmen and come out the other door as statesmen-figures."[38]

The historical record speaks volumes. Through 1988, 14 secretaries of state, 14 treasury secretaries, 11 defense secretaries and scores of congressmen and other federal department heads have been members of the CFR. It was George Wallace who said there wasn't a dime's worth of difference between the Democrat and Republican parties. Every four years, Americans basically get to choose between one-world Democrats and one-world Republicans. In 1952 and 1956, CFR Adlai Stevenson opposed CFR Eisenhower. In 1960, it was CFR Kennedy vs. CFR Nixon. When the conservative wing of the GOP nominated Barry Goldwater in 1964 over the ultimate Council member, Nelson Rockefeller, the CFR press took care of Barry in no time.

In 1968, CFR Nixon was pitted against CFR Humphrey. The 1972 "contest" featured CFR Nixon against the CFR McGovern. CFR Ford opposed TC (Trilateral Commission) Jimmy Carter in 1976. (Carter eventually joined the CFR.) Four years later, "smiling" Jimmy was unseated by Ronald Reagan, the "Maverick" (professional actor). Although not a member of the CFR, Reagan chose for his running mate George Bush, a former director for *both* the Council and the Trilateral Commission. The President's transition team included 18 CFR agents. *By mid-1988, 313 CFR members were officiating within the Reagan-Bush administration.*[39]

When the dynamic duo took over in 1981, the accumulated national debt amassed over the nation's 200-year history stood at $935 billion. Four months before the end of Reagan's presidency, the debt had tripled to $2.572 trillion!! During those eight years, the United States went from being the world's largest creditor nation to becoming its largest debtor nation. (Remember the immutable warning in Deuteronomy 28:44?)

In 1988, George "New World Order" Bush defeated CFR Dukakis only to be ousted by CFR Bill Clinton in 1992. (Believe it or not, Marion Barry does not appear on the present CFR membership.)

Two of the more outspoken critics of the CFR have been Edith Kermit Roosevelt and North Carolina Senator Jesse Helms. The granddaughter of Theodore Roosevelt unmasked the Council's strategy, writing in 1961:

> What is the Establishment's view-point? Through the Roosevelt, Truman, Eisenhower and Kennedy administrations its ideology is constant: That the best way to fight Communism is by a One World Socialist state governed by "experts" like themselves. The result has been policies which favor the growth of the superstate, gradual surrender of United States sovereignty to the United Nations and a steady retreat in the face of Communist aggression.[40]

Speaking before the Senate in December, 1987, Jesse Helms declared:

> The viewpoint of the Establishment today is called globalism. Not so long ago, this viewpoint was called the "one-world" view by its critics. The phrase is no longer fashionable among sophisticates; yet, the phrase "one world" is still apt because nothing has changed in the minds and actions of those promoting policies consistent with its fundamental tenets.

Mr. President, in the globalist point of view, nation-states and national boundaries do not count for anything. Political philosophies and political principles seem to become simply relative. Indeed, even constitutions are irrelevant to the exercise of power....

In this point of view, the activities of international financial and industrial forces should be oriented to bringing this one-world design—with a convergence of the Soviet and American systems as its centerpiece—into being.[41]

FDR AND THE GREAT DEPRESSION

In the election of 1920, the American people voiced their disdain for Wilson and his beleaguered administration by sending Warren Harding to the White House with over 60% of the vote. Harding was followed by fellow Republicans Calvin Coolidge in 1924 and Herbert Hoover in 1928. Although these men made their mistakes, none shared the Executive Mansion with any "second personalities." The nation was prospering and at peace, which meant that Wall Street was unhappy. Another "Wilson" had to be found.

Although Franklin Delano Roosevelt may have been touted as the "champion of the little guy," his blue blood and the socialistic mess he created prove otherwise. The Roosevelt family had been involved in banking since the eighteenth century. Franklin's uncle, Frederic Delano, was on the original board of the Federal Reserve. His education was also just right—Groton and Harvard.

In 1928, millionaire John Raskob, vice president of both DuPont and General Motors, became chairman of the Democratic National Committee and drafted Roosevelt for the governorship of New York—the traditional stepping-stone to the presidency. Two months previously, FDR had sent the right signals to Wall Street with his July article in *Foreign Affairs*:

The United States has taken two negative steps. It has declined to have anything to do with either the League of Nations or the World Court.... The time has come when we must accept not only certain facts but many new principles of a higher law, a newer and better standard in **international** relations.[42]

That FDR was just another puppet of the international bankers was affirmed by no less an authority than his own son-in-law, Curtis Dall

(Limbaugh "kook"). In his book entitled *FDR: My Exploited Father-In-Law*, Dall wrote:

> For a long time I felt that FDR had developed many thoughts and ideas that were his own to benefit this country, the U.S.A. But, he didn't. Most of his thoughts, his political "ammunition," as it were, were carefully manufactured for him in advance by the CFR-One World Money group. Brilliantly, with great gusto, like a fine piece of artillery, he exploded that prepared "ammunition" in the middle of an unsuspecting target, the American people—and thus paid off and retained his internationalist political support.[43]

With the passage of the Federal Reserve Act, Senator Lindbergh had warned the American people, "From now on, depressions will be scientifically created."[44] Between 1920 and 1929, three distinct boom-and-bust cycles were orchestrated by the FED. When the "Creature" artificially raised interest rates, prices tumbled; when rates were lowered, inflation cursed the land. Griffin points out how America's curse was England's gain:

> After the war was over, the transfusion of American dollars continued as part of a plan to pull England out of depression. The methods chosen for that transfer were artificially low interest rates and a deliberate inflation of the American money supply. That was calculated to weaken the value of the dollar relative to the English pound and cause gold reserves to move from America to England. Both operations were directed by Benjamin Strong and executed by the Federal Reserve. It was not hyperbole when President Herbert Hoover described Strong as "a mental annex to Europe."[45]

Since borrowing is what causes money to be created under fractional reserve banking, low interest rates from 1920–1929 led to a 61.8% expansion of the nation's money supply. This availability of "easy money" triggered an unhealthy surge of speculation by crazed investors. The "Establishment" press fueled the frenzy with stories of great riches to be made in the stock exchange.

By the spring of '29, the trap was just about set. In March of that year, Paul Warburg issued a discreet warning to certain connected insiders, "If the orgies of unrestrained speculation are permitted to spread, the ultimate collapse is certain not only to affect the speculators themselves, but to bring about a general depression involving the entire country."[46] What this translated to was, "Get out of the stock market fast." Men like John D. Rockefeller and Joseph P. Kennedy were only too happy to oblige.

While the privileged few were abandoning ship, Paul's buddy, Benjamin Strong, president of the Federal Reserve Bank of New York, was assuring the masses:

> The very existence of the Federal Reserve System is a safeguard against anything like a calamity growing out of money rates....In former days the psychology was different, because the facts of the banking situation were different. Mob panic, and consequently mob disaster, is less likely to arise.[47]

To comprehend the Crash of '29, one must be familiar with a practice known as broker "call loans." Perloff writes:

> It must be understood that an expedient existed on the New York exchange called a "24 hour broker call loan." In those days, one could purchase stock on extensive credit. He could lay down, say, $100, and borrow $900 from a bank through his broker, to purchase $1000 in securities. If the stock increased just ten percent in value, he could sell it, repay the loan, and walk away with his original investment doubled.
>
> The only problem was that such a loan could be called at any time— and if it was, the investor had to pay it off within twenty-four hours. For most, the only way to do so was to sell the stock. One can imagine the impact on the market if a great multitude of these loans were called simultaneously.[48]

In the *United States' Unresolved Monetary and Political Problems*, William Bryan explains what took place on that fateful day, October 24.

> When everything was ready, the New York financiers started calling 24 hour broker call loans. This meant that the stock brokers and the customers had to dump their stock on the market in order to pay the loans. This naturally collapsed the stock market and brought a banking collapse all over the country because the banks not owned by the oligarchy were heavily involved in broker call claims at this time, and bank runs soon exhausted their coin and currency and they had to close. The Federal Reserve System would not come to their aid, although they were instructed under the law to maintain an elastic currency.[49]

Prices tumbled as 13 million shares exchanged hands. However, the worst was yet to come. On Tuesday, October 29, the bottom dropped out as

16 million shares were dumped at almost any price imaginable. Over $3 billion in wealth disappeared along with millions of investors.

No less a personage than the chairman of the House Banking Committee, Louis McFadden, conceded:

> It [the Depression] was not accidental. It was a carefully contrived occurrence.... The international bankers sought to bring about a condition of despair here so that they might emerge as rulers of us all.[50]

FDR's son-in-law, Curtis Dall, a syndicate manager for Lehman Brothers, was on the floor at the time of the crash. Concurring with McFadden, he declared, "Actually, it was the calculated 'shearing' of the public by the World-Money powers triggered by the planned sudden shortage of call money in the New York money market."[51]

In his book *The Great Crash, 1929,* Harvard professor John Kenneth Galbraith (Limbaugh "kook") confirmed that Winston Churchill appeared in the visitors' gallery during the height of the panic.[52] Perloff states, "It has been said that Bernard Baruch brought him there, perhaps to show him the power of the international bankers."[53]

While some investors were jumping out of windows or selling apples on the streets, others were counting their profits. Having gotten out in the nick of time, Morgan's cronies reaped the further benefit of buying up the plummeted stock at pennies on the dollar.

As expected, the press blamed President Hoover for the crash. Rather than stimulate growth and recovery, the FED contracted the money supply by more than one-third during the remainder of Hoover's term, thus ensuring that the nation's banks continued to fail. Consequently, the GOP was out; FDR was in.

President Roosevelt wasted little time in settling his *own political* debts. In the first year of his administration, formal diplomatic ties were established with the Soviet Union. ("Colonel" House was still around.)

Under Hoover's presidency, the 1928 series Federal Reserve Note made a commitment to redemption in gold:

> THE UNITED STATES OF AMERICA WILL PAY TO THE BEARER ON DEMAND TEN DOLLARS. **REDEEMABLE IN GOLD** ON DEMAND AT THE UNITED STATES TREASURY.

On April 5, 1933, after only one month in office, FDR outlawed private ownership of gold coins and bullion. Under threat of fine and/or imprisonment, hardworking Americans were ordered to exchange their real worth for "funny money" at the arbitrarily set rate of $20.66. By 1935, when the confiscated gold had been transferred to the newly constructed facility at Fort Knox, the official price of the precious metal was conveniently raised to $35 an ounce.

Note the sleight of hand in FDR's 1934 series Federal Reserve Note:

THE UNITED STATES OF AMERICA WILL PAY TO THE BEARER ON DEMAND TEN DOLLARS. **REDEEMABLE IN LAWFUL MONEY** AT THE UNITED STATES TREASURY.

When suspicious citizens sent these bills to the United States Treasury for exchange in "lawful money," the government merely sent them other Federal Reserve notes of equal value, bearing the same inscriptions. Thus one piece of green paper with printing on it became equal in value to similar pieces of paper.

In 1963, the Treasury decided to end the charade to avoid any further embarrassment. Since that year, Federal Reserve notes merely state:

THIS NOTE IS LEGAL TENDER FOR ALL DEBTS PUBLIC OR PRIVATE.

Nobel-prizewinning economist, Milton Friedman (you guessed it—*another* Limbaugh "kook"), points to the sad delusion of the American public:

Each accepts them [the pieces of paper] because he is confident others will. The pieces of green paper have value because everybody thinks they have value, and everybody thinks they have value because in his experience they have had value.[54]

Of course, the gold would have to go if Roosevelt was going to save America through his panacean New Deal programs. The myriad of tri-lettered socialistic agencies should have been called the New *Debt*. After three preceding Republican administrations had lowered the $25 billion post-war national debt to $16 billion, FDR's handouts sent the figure to $48 billion by 1939—an increase of 300%!

Roosevelt's inaugural year in office was also marked by the repeal of Prohibition via the Twenty-first Amendment, ensuring a nation of drunks. Joseph P. Kennedy would make his millions in the liquor industry.

What a start: diplomatic ties with Russia, rampant socialism, no more gold, but all the booze you could drink—*yet the worst was still to come!*

WORLD WAR II

The rise of Adolph Hitler and the Second World War would have never occurred but for the timely intervention of two subtle collaborators—American industry and the Vatican State.

In his documented work *Wall Street and the Rise of Hitler*, historian Anthony Sutton proves that World War II was not only inevitable, but extremely profitable for a select group of financial insiders. On October 19, 1936 (three years after Hitler came to power), the American ambassador to Germany, William Dodd, wrote FDR from Berlin:

> Much as I believe in peace as our best policy, I cannot avoid the fears which Wilson emphasized more than once in conversations with me, August 15, 1915, and later: the breakdown of democracy in all Europe will be a disaster to the people. But what can you do? At the present moment more than a hundred American corporations have subsidiaries here or cooperative understandings.
>
> The DuPonts have three allies in Germany that are aiding in the armament business. Their chief ally is the I.G. Farben Company, a part of the Government which gives 200,000 marks a year to one propaganda organization operating on American opinion.
>
> Standard Oil Company (New York sub-company) sent $2,000,000 here in December 1933 and has made $500,000 a year helping Germans make Ersatz gas for war purposes; but Standard Oil cannot take any of its earnings out of the country except in goods. They do little of this, report their earnings at home, but do not explain the facts.
>
> The International Harvester Company president told me their business here rose 33% a year (arms manufacturer, I believe), but they could take nothing out. Even our airplanes people have secret arrangement with Krupps. General Motor Company and Ford do enormous businesses here through their subsidiaries and take no profits out. I mention these facts because they complicate things and add to war dangers.[55]

In his personal diary, Dodd noted that he had queried a corporate attorney, "Why do the International Harvester people continue to manufacture in Germany when their company gets nothing out of the country and when it has failed to collect its war losses?"[56] These momentary losses may have puzzled Dodd and even appeared foolish; however, "Big Business" didn't get big by being foolish. International Harvester was well aware that investment in Nazi Germany would yield a nice "harvest" *once an international war was underway!*

Although the Treaty of Versailles had imposed a heavy reparations burden on defeated Germany, Morgan and company were only too happy to arrange convenient financing. Under the Dawes and Young Plans, between 1924 and 1931 Germany paid the Allies approximately 36 billion marks, while American banks loaned 33 billion marks back to the "Fatherland." Professor Quigley points out, "It is worthy of note that this system was set up by the international bankers and that the subsequent lending of other people's money to Germany was very profitable to these bankers."[57] Thus, with a net reparations outflow of only 3 billion marks annually, Germany could well afford to ready herself for a second try at conquering the world. Quigley adds,

> With these American loans, Germany was able to rebuild her industrial system to make it the second best in the world by a wide margin, to keep up her prosperity and her standard of living in spite of the defeat and reparations, and to pay reparations without either a balanced budget or a favorable balance of trade.[58]

Hitler's key German-American Wall Street connections were Hjalmar Horace Greeley Schacht and Ernst Sedgewick Hanfstaengl, otherwise known as "Putzi." Schacht was employed by Equitable Trust, one of the many firms controlled by Morgan. "Putzi" was a cousin of Civil War general John Sedgewick and became an intimate friend of Roosevelt and Hitler alike.

The man most responsible for transforming United States capital and imported technology into a booming German industry was Hermann Schmitz. In 1925, Schmitz created the massive I. G. Farben Chemical cartel by merging together the Bayer, Agfa, Hoechst, Badische Anilin, Weiler-ter-Meer and Griesheim-Elektron chemical companies.[59] Twenty years later, Schmitz and numerous Farben directors would be tried at Nuremberg for war crimes.

On the eve of World War II, the I. G. Farben Company was the largest chemical conglomerate in the world. Described as a "state within a state,"

Senator Homer T. Bone remarked to the Senate Committee on Military Affairs, June 4, 1943, "Farben was Hitler and Hitler was Farben."[60] Max Warburg, brother to Felix and Paul, sat on the Farben *Aufsichsrat*, the supervisory board of directors. (Paul was also on the board of American I.G., Farben's wholly owned United States subsidiary.)

How important was I. G. Farben to Hitler's war-making capabilities? A post-war investigation by the U.S. War Department concluded:

> Without I. G.'s immense productive facilities, its intense research, and vast international affiliations, Germany's prosecution of the war would have been unthinkable and impossible; Farben not only directed its energies toward arming Germany, but concentrated on weakening her intended victims, and this double-barreled attempt to expand the German industrial potential for war and to restrict that of the rest of the world was not conceived and executed "in the normal course of business." The proof is overwhelming that I. G. Farben officials had full prior knowledge of Germany's plan for world conquest and of each specific aggressive act later undertaken.[61]

Due to massive American bond issues, I. G. Farben eventually acquired a participation and managerial influence in some 380 other German firms, as well as 500 additional foreign concerns. Hitler's "pride and joy" owned its own electric power plants, iron and steel units, banks, research units and dozens of commercial enterprises.

In addition to Wall Street cash, good old "Yankee know-how" gave Nazi Germany her ultimate opportunity to wage war on America and her allies. (Total United States casualties including the Pacific theater—322,000 dead, 800,000 wounded.) Professor Sutton provides a classic example of traitorous American ingenuity:

> For instance, in 1934 Germany produced domestically only 300,000 tons of natural petroleum products and less than 300,000 tons of synthetic gasoline; the balance was imported. Yet, ten years later in WWII, after transfer of the Standard Oil of New Jersey hydrogenation patents and technology to I. G. Farben (used to produce synthetic gasoline from coal), Germany produced about 6½ million tons of oil—of which 85 percent (5½ million tons) was synthetic oil using the Standard Oil hydrogenation process.[62]

The process for manufacturing tera-ethyl lead, essential for aviation fuel, was also imported from Standard Oil as was the ability to produce synthetic rubber. In fact, American technology perfected nearly every aspect of Hitler's war machine. Dow Chemical provided large supplies of magnesium for incendiary bombs and miscellaneous explosives. General Electric was responsible for the cartelization of the German electrical industry. Morgan-controlled International Telephone and Telegraph (I.T.T.) made several substantial cash payments to Heinrich Himmler during the war to protect its investment in Focke-Wolfe, an aircraft manufacturing firm producing fighter planes used against the United States.[63]

One of the more macabre advances in the Farben cartel was the invention, production and distribution of the Zyklon B gas used in Nazi concentration camps. Zyklon B was pure Prussic acid, a lethal poison manufactured by I. G. Farben Leverkusen and marketed from the Bayer sales office through Degesch, an independent license holder. Throughout the war, Degesch produced enough gas to liquidate 200 million humans.[64]

The case of father-and-son team Henry and Edsel Ford is a story in itself. On December 20, 1922, the *New York Times* reported that automobile manufacturer Henry Ford was financing Hitler's nationalist and anti-Semitic campaigns in Munich.[65] Sutton writes, "At the outbreak of the war Ford-Werke placed itself at the disposal of the Wehrmacht for armament production."[66] French Ford was able to produce 20 trucks per day for Nazi troop transport. The *New York Times* reported that Hitler felt so warm and cuddly about Henry that

> the wall behind his desk in Hitler's private office is decorated with a large picture of Henry Ford. In the antechamber there is a large table covered with books, nearly all of which are a translation of a book written and published by Henry Ford.[67]

As a token of the Führer's esteem and gratitude, in August, 1938, Henry Ford received the Grand Cross of the German Eagle, a Nazi medal for distinguished foreigners. The *New York Times* reported the occasion as the first time the decoration had been awarded in the United States. The gala affair was the automaker's 75th birthday.

Following a storm of protest, the money-hungry hypocrite responded:

> My acceptance of a medal from the German people [said Ford] does not, as some people seem to think, involve any sympathy on my part with naziism. Those who have known me for many years realize that anything that breeds hate is repulsive to me.[68]

THE VATICAN AND HITLER

While American capitalists were investing in Adolph Hitler for the prospects of lucrative wartime profits and eventual global control, the Holy See likewise chose to endorse the Führer for a number of self-serving motives. First and foremost was the Vatican's apprehension of expanding Communist influence in western Europe. Having been estranged as a wayward daughter since 1054 was bad enough, but now the "child" was grown, Red and after her mother's billions. A crop of homespun "religious" Fascists became the expedient alternative (lesser of two evils) to encroaching Russian Communism.

In February, 1929, the Vatican State was formally recognized by Benito Mussolini, dictator of Italy, through the infamous Lateran Treaty. El Duce affirmed, "We recognize the pre-eminent place the Catholic Church holds in the religious life of the Italian people—which is perfectly natural in a Catholic country such as ours, and under a régime such as is the Fascist."[69] The Concordat required a mutual pledge of support from "His Holiness," Pius XI, who acknowledged Mussolini as "a man of Providence," and declared, "We believe we have thereby given God to Italy and Italy to God."[70]

With her home front secure, the Vatican set out to acknowledge another loyal son of the Church. In September, 1919, a discharged Corporal Hitler visited the "Leiber" room of the Sternecker-Bräu Café and joined the D.A.P. (German Workers' Party). After a long and bitter struggle, Adolph Hitler was appointed chancellor of Germany on January 30, 1933, by President Hindenburg, at the personal recommendation of Papal Chamberlain, Franz Von Papen.

However, to assume full dictatorial power, Hitler would require a two-thirds majority in the Reichstag (the lower chamber of the federal parliament of Germany)—a percentage he did not command at that time. *No problem:* Hitler simply had Hermann Goering and "Putzi" (his and FDR's mutual Wall Street contacts) torch the Reichstag on February 27, 1933, so the blame could be placed on the Communists.[71]

When the Reichstag reassembled in the Kroll Opera House, March 23, there were 81 less "Commie" delegates on hand to oppose the aspiring chancellor. The key maneuver that put Hitler over the top, however, was the critical endorsement of the official Roman Catholic "Center Party" (Zentrum) led by Dr. Ludwig Kaas and former chancellor, Bruening. The grateful dictator stated that same day, "Just as we see in Christianity the unshaken foundation of the moral life, so it is our duty to cultivate friendly relations with the Holy See and to develop them."[72]

On May 17, Hitler summoned the Reichstag once again and obtained a resolution, subscribed not only by the Nazis, the German Nationalists and the Social Democrats, but by the Catholic party also, to the effect that, "These representatives of the German people...place themselves unitedly behind the Government."[73] Democracy was out; a Roman Catholic *maniac* was in. Hans Kerll, Minister of Ecclesiastical Affairs of the Third Reich, declared (as quoted by André Guerber):

> Just as Christ gathered together his twelve disciples in a single cohort faithful to the point of martyrdom, so we are witnesses of an identical spectacle. **Adolph Hitler is in truth the Holy Spirit.**[74]

A few years ago while flying home from a speaking engagement outside of Syracuse, New York, I found myself seated next to an elderly Catholic priest. In the course of our conversation, he informed me that as a layman in the American military, he had served as personal bodyguard to Justice Robert Houghwout of the United States Supreme Court, chief prosecutor at the post-war Nuremberg trials. As my own particular "clerical garb" did not reveal that I was a "fellow reverend," I immediately began to question the former military policeman about the little-known Vatican-Berlin alliance.

My first question dealt with the embarrassing fact that Hitler, Mussolini, Franco, Himmler, Hess, Goering, Goebbels and several thousand other goose-stepping Fascists were, like their Mafia brethren, "born-again" Catholic Christians, according to the tenets of Roman Catholic theology. When I asked my traveling companion why these individuals were never officially excommunicated from the "One True Apostolic Church," etc., he replied that ordinarily, a Catholic will be excommunicated only for breaking a specific law of the Church—like having an abortion.

When I asked whether the murder of 6 million Jews was at least *as* "bad" as *one* abortion, he pointed to Hitler's overt atrocities as proof that the Führer couldn't possibly have been in good standing with his church, thus negating the need for excommunication. (Pretty slick, huh?)

About this time he interjected, "You ask a lot of questions," to which I replied, "Yes." I then asked him to explain why the Pope signed a concordat with Hitler in 1933, considering how wicked he was, etc. After confessing that he didn't know very much about "that concordat," he then attempted to change the subject by asking me what *I* did for a living. With a twinkle in my eye, I responded, *"I'm your worst nightmare—*an Independent Baptist preacher!" For some strange reason, he spent the rest of the flight in the rear of the cabin chatting with a beautiful woman half his age. (He said she was a member of his parish.)

If the good "father" had hung around, I would have also asked him to explain why the Vatican used the Mafia (with the CIA's blessing) to smuggle Nazi war criminals to South America and elsewhere.[75] In light of the Pope's unquestioned endorsement of Hitler's regime, I would have also liked to ask him why the chief prosecutor expressed his personal "gratitude to the Vatican for making available to the Nuremberg trials documents touching upon the charges of persecution of religion in Germany and Nazi-occupied countries."[76]

In the summer of 1933, Hitler and the Vatican did in fact sign a very significant concordat. As a payoff for dissolving their own Zentrum party, the Vatican gained the "religious" ascendancy over everybody else. This was quite a deal considering that only 36% of Germany's population was Catholic, Manhattan writing:

> The Vatican had now reached the principal aims of the Catholic Church in Germany—the disappearance of a Republic, the destruction of a democracy, the creation of absolutism, an intimate partnership of Church and State, in a country where more than half the population was Protestant.[77]

In appreciation for having made her a full partner with the State, the Catholic Church asked God's richest blessing on the Nazi Reich, a prelate announcing:

> On Sundays and Holy days, special prayers, conforming to the Liturgy, will be offered during the principal Mass for the welfare of the German Reich and its people, in all episcopal, parish and conventual churches and chapels of the German Reich.[78]

Throughout the months and years that followed, thousands of political detractors were jailed and/or killed, the press was restrained and the schools were commandeered by Nationalist instructors. Hitler's crackdown was so severe, he even arrested 8,000 Catholic monks and brothers for sodomy.[79]

According to Hitler, it was the Jesuit order that taught him how to crack heads in the first place. Edmond Paris writes:

"I learned much from the Order of the Jesuits," said Hitler... "Until now, there has never been anything more grandiose, on the earth, than the hierarchical organisation of the Catholic Church. I transferred much of this organisation into my own party."[80]

Paris also confirms that *Mein Kampf* was in actuality written by a Jesuit, Father Staempfle, and merely signed by Hitler. Another Hitlerian, Walter Schellenberg, former chief of the Nazi counter-espionage, revealed:

The S.S. organisation had been constituted, by Himmler, according to the principles of the Jesuits' Order. Their regulations and the Spiritual Exercises prescribed by Ignatius of Loyola were the model Himmler tried to copy exactly... The "Reichsfuhrer SS"—Himmler's title as supreme chief of the SS—was to be the equivalent of the Jesuits' "General" and the whole structure of the direction was a close imitation of the Catholic Church's hierarchical order.[81]

Of course, while Adolf was wreaking havoc in Germany, the American people were being kept in the dark. Believe it or not, *Time* magazine (CFR) voted Hitler "Man of the Year" for 1938.

POPE PIUS XII

As Nazi terrorism intensified, Pius XI became increasingly pressured by negative world opinion. When word leaked out that the pontiff was planning to release a public denunciation of both Mussolini and Hitler on the 12th of February, 1939, "His Holiness" up and died only *48 hours before the scheduled pronouncement!*

The new pope was Eugenio Maria Giuseppe Giovanni Pacelli, former secretary of state under Pius XI. Cardinal Pacelli became Pius XII on the second of March. Having served as papal nuncio in Munich and Berlin (1919–1930), Pacelli was referred to as the "German pope." A stalwart ally of Hitler, Pius XII literally became *the* man of the hour. Alexandre Lenôtre wrote, "Germany is, in his eyes, called upon to play the role of the 'sword of God,' of the secular arm of the Church."[82]

Pius learned of Hitler's plan to invade Poland as early as April 24, 1939.[83] Convinced that the demise of a Catholic nation was necessary for the ultimate conquest of Marxist Russia, Pius gave Hitler his blessing (i.e., his promise that he would keep his pontifical mouth *shut*—a promise which he kept). Consequently, on September 1, 1939, Poland was overrun with the power of *blitzkrieg* (lightning warfare). Britain and France declared war two days later. Colonel Joseph Beck, Polish Minister for Foreign Affairs (1932–1939), acknowledged:

> The Vatican is one of those mainly responsible for my country's tragedy. I realized too late that we had been pursuing our foreign policy in the sole interests of the Catholic Church.[84]

Not only did the Pope fail to condemn any of Hitler's territorial aggression or war-related atrocities, especially the horrific death camps, but in some respects, he more than surpassed his partner in crime. The Catholic bloodletting in Yugoslavia is an excellent case in point. Reference works such as *The Vatican's Holocaust* by Avro Manhattan and *Convert... or Die!* by Edmond Paris present the documented evidence that the Catholic Church liquidated over *800,000* orthodox Serbians in Croatia, Yugoslavia, during the years 1940–1945. That totals out to *40 times the fatality count of the Inquisition and the St. Bartholomew's Day Massacre combined!*

The next time some bigoted Catholic tries to dismiss his murderous heritage as a "thing of the past," ask him to explain: 250 peasants buried alive in the Serbian district of Bjelovar;[85] 2,000 children gassed in the death camp at Bosanska Gradiska;[86] a father and son crucified together and then burned in their own home in Mliniste;[87] mothers and children (as young as three) impaled on the same stake in Gorevac;[88] a mother forced to hold the basin which caught the blood of her four sons as their throats were slit in Kosinj;[89] an expectant mother having her unborn child cut out of her womb and replaced by a cat in the death camp at Jasenovac;[90] 1,360 prisoners having their throats cut in a single night by one guard during a sadistic throat-cutting contest (also at Jasenovac);[91] not to mention dismemberments;[92] beheadings;[93] crowns of thorns;[94] "graviso" knives for specialized throat cutting;[95] necklaces of human tongues and eyes;[96] the confining of prisoners to rooms filled with blood to the ankles;[97] and ten thousand other atrocities condoned by the Roman Catholic Archbishop Aloysius Stepinac who prayed at the opening of the Croatian Parliament in February of 1942, for "the Holy Ghost to descend upon the sharp knives of the Ustashi (Catholic guerrilla army)."[98]

With the war underway, Pius decided to cover himself by continuing to court FDR's favor. The two had first met back in October, 1936, when Cardinal Pacelli "dropped in" less than a month before Roosevelt's bid for reelection. Secret negotiations between FDR and the new pope continued over the next few years. On June 16, 1939, the Rome correspondent for the *New York Times* sent a dispatch from the Vatican declaring that, "Steps to bring relations between the Holy See and the United States on a normal diplomatic footing are expected to be taken soon by Pope Pius XII."[99] Cardinal Enrico Gasparri arrived in New York on July 29 and spent three days with Cardinal Spellman to prepare "the juridical status for the possible opening of diplomatic relations between the State Department and the Holy See."[100]

Fortunately, an exchange of diplomats could not be attained without the formal sanction of Congress. And such an approval was highly unlikely due to the anti-United States rantings of numerous American priests. One Jesuit paper declared:

> How we Catholics have loathed and despised this.... civilization which is now called democracy... to-day, American Catholics are being asked to shed their blood for that particular kind of secularist civilization which they have heroically repudiated for four centuries.[101]

By 1933, "Father" Charles Coughlin was attracting a weekly radio audience of over 40 million people across America. Declaring that "the German war is a battle for Christianity,"[102] the pro-Hitler Coughlin announced from his tiny parish in Royal Oak, Michigan:

> We predict that... the National Socialists of America, organized under that or some other name, eventually will take control of the Government on this continent... We predict, lastly, the end of Democracy in America.[103]

Unable to restore diplomatic relations through congressional approval, the crafty Roosevelt decided to appoint his own *personal* ambassador to the Vatican. In December, 1939, Mr. Myron Taylor, a millionaire, high *Episcopalian* (a Catholic who flunked Latin) became the nation's first presidential ambassador to the Holy See. ("See" it coming?)

AMERICA ENTERS THE WAR

Less than two weeks after Hitler's invasion of Poland, Hamilton Fish Armstrong, editor of *Foreign Affairs*, and Walter Mallory, the CFR's chief executive director, consulted in Washington with Assistant Secretary of State

George Messersmith. They very "graciously" proposed that the Council "assist" the State Department with its war-time policy and post-war planning through study groups and timely recommendations. Messersmith, a CFR member himself, granted their request.

This unconstitutional rapprochement became known as the War and Peace Studies Project and was underwritten by the Rockefeller Foundation. Working in secret, they held 362 meetings and prepared 682 papers for FDR and the State Department.[104] The council's predilection for war was evidenced by a media blitz in 1940 asserting that "the United States should immediately declare that a state of war exists between this country and Germany."[105]

However, as in the case of WWI, the majority of Americans were adamantly opposed to participation in another European conflict. A Gallup poll put the figure at 83%. Once again, a dramatic scenario would be needed to alter public opinion.

Despite official United States neutrality, and without Congressional approval, FDR got the ball rolling by shipping 50 destroyers to Britain. With the passage of the Lend-Lease Act, American ships were ordered into the U-boat-infested war zone.

CFR-State Department policy also called for provoking the Japanese government. Secretary of War Henry Stimson (who was *also* a Council member) wrote in his diary, "We face the delicate question of the diplomatic fencing to be done so as to be sure Japan is put into the wrong and makes the first bad move—overt move."[106] Another entry reads, "The question was how we should maneuver them [the Japanese] into the position of firing the first shot."[107]

The Council's War and Peace Studies Project "recommended" a trade embargo against Japan and FDR subsequently complied. Japan's American assets were also frozen and the Panama Canal closed to its shipping. Finally, on November 26, 1941, the United States government sent the Emperor an ultimatum demanding their withdrawal of all troops from China and Indochina, thus abrogating, in effect, their treaty with Germany and Italy. The proud Nipponese were being backed into a dangerous corner.

At approximately 7:53 a.m. on December 7, 1941, Captain Mitsuo Fuchida radioed Admiral Naguma—"Tora, Tora, Tora!" The repeated code word, translated *"Tiger, Tiger, Tiger!"* actually meant, "We have succeeded in surprise attack." Less than two minutes later, 43 Japanese fighters, 40 torpedo planes, 49 high-level and 51 dive bombers screamed across Pearl

Harbor, Hawaii, raining death and destruction on the United States Pacific Fleet. In the brief span of 30 minutes, America lost 8 battleships, 3 cruisers, 4 other vessels, 188 planes and 2,403 men, nearly one-half of whom died on the *Arizona*. The wounded numbered almost 1,200.

At 8:20 p.m. EST, members of the Cabinet began arriving at the White House for an emergency meeting. As they assembled around the President's desk in the Oval Office, Roosevelt told what he knew and answered a few questions. Finally, Texas Senator Tom Connally got around to asking America's Chief Executive what everyone else was already pondering. His face purple, Connally sprang to his feet, banged the desk and shouted, "How did they catch us with our pants down, Mr. President?"[108]

On the following day, Roosevelt addressed a joint session of Congress with the now-famous words: "Yesterday, December 7, 1941—**a date which will live in infamy**—the United States of America was suddenly and deliberately attacked by the naval and air forces of the Empire of Japan." Although his words were dramatic enough to elicit a 388 to 1 vote for a declaration of war against Japan, FDR had *still* not answered Senator Connally's question.

Over half a century has passed and two "twists of fate" have emerged concerning that infamous date. After the war, Captain Fuchida ("Tora, Tora, Tora!") was summoned to Tokyo by General Douglas MacArthur to appear before a special military commission for questioning. Several days later, while heading to the train station for his return trip home, Fuchida was stopped by a born-again Christian who handed him a Gospel tract containing the personal testimony of Jacob DeShazer, a United States airman. (DeShazer had been shot down over Burma while flying in General Doolittle's famous squadron.) Not only did Fuchida read the tract and trust Jesus Christ as his personal Saviour, but he also went on to become a missionary in his native Japan. (The German counterpart to Captain Fuchida's experience was the miraculous conversion of Luftwaffe Colonel Werner Moelders, ace of all German aces and holder of his country's highest award for her fighters—the Knight's Cross of the Iron Cross, with Oak Leaves and Diamonds.[109])

Things did not go as well for FDR, however. Over the years a number of books have documented the fact that Roosevelt and a circle of advisers had *definite foreknowledge* of the "surprise" attack on Pearl Harbor. Of these, the most recent and authoritative is *Infamy: Pearl Harbor and Its Aftermath* (1982) by Pulitzer prizewinner John Toland. A brief summary of the salient developments follows.

American military intelligence had cracked the various wireless codes Tokyo used to communicate with its embassies. Consequently, all Japanese diplomatic communiques were decodable in 1941, allowing the President and his Cabinet to stay abreast of the enemy's every move. In the weeks preceding the attack, intercepted messages confirmed that spies in Hawaii were informing Tokyo of the exact layout of American ships docked in Pearl Harbor. Collectively, the information pointed to an attack on or about December 7th.

Although some of these important signals were ignored or lost in bureaucratic red tape, enough of the facts got through to FDR that by the evening of December 6th, he declared to his chief adviser, Harry Hopkins, "This means war."[110]

The *problem* was that no one alerted the American officers at Pearl Harbor, apart from a general warning issued on November 27 to the commanders in the Philippines, Hawaii and the Panama Canal that weakening negotiations with Japan *could* erupt in hostilities. ("JAPANESE FUTURE ACTION UNPREDICTABLE BUT HOSTILE ACTION POSSIBLE AT ANY MOMENT."[111]) Pearl Harbor commanders, Admiral Husband E. Kimmel and General Walter Short, were not informed concerning the numerous subsequent updates which pointed specifically to a Hawaiian assault.

For starters, a Japanese book entitled *The Three Power Alliance and the U.S.-Japan War*, by Kinoaki Matsuo, published in October, 1940, specifically predicted an attack on Pearl Harbor. In a chapter entitled "The Japanese Surprise Attack Fleet," we read the amazing declaration:

> It is our considered observation and sincere belief, December is the month of the Japanese attack and the SURPRISE FLEET is aimed at Hawaii, perhaps the first Sunday of December....
> No matter how you feel toward our work, will you please convey our apprehension and this information to the President and to the military and naval commanders in Hawaii.[112]

As if to add insult to injury, the Italian magazine *Oggi* published an article in Rome on October 24, 1941, also predicting a Japanese naval attack on the Hawaiian Islands.[113] Both of these off-the-wall eye-openers were forwarded to Maxwell Hamilton of the State Department on December 4th by Kilsoo Haan, an agent for the Korean People's League, along with a precise warning from the Korean Underground that the Japanese would strike Pearl Harbor that coming weekend.[114]

In the fall of 1941, British double agent Dusko Popov, code-named "Tricycle," had given the FBI a detailed plan of the Japanese mission against Pearl Harbor which he had obtained from the Germans.[115]

About this same time, the S.I.S. (The United States Army Signal Intelligence Service) had decrypted a message from Tokyo to Consul General Nago Kita in Honolulu, dividing the waters of Pearl Harbor into five sections and asking for the exact locations of Kimmel's warships and carriers.[116] Three other similar messages indicating unusual interest in Pearl Harbor were also intercepted. One instructed Ensign Takeo Yoshikawa, a naval spy posing as one of Kita's assistants, to report all ship movements "twice a week."[117] None of these developments was sent to Admiral Kimmel.

While the Japanese strike force, *Kido Butai*, was steaming eastbound toward Hawaii, the Matson liner *Turline* was approaching the same destination from the opposite direction. On December 1, a seasoned radio operator by the name of Leslie E. Grogan began picking up "weird" signals northwest by west of Hawaii, a peculiar area for traffic that time of year. Grogan noted the most important particulars of the Japanese signals that continued for 48 hours. The entire report was turned over to the Intelligence Office of the Fourteenth Naval District in Honolulu on December 3.[118]

These exact signals were also detected by Lieutenant Ellsworth A. Hosner at the Intelligence Office of the Twelfth Naval District in San Francisco. Hosner confirmed that the main wire services—RCA, Globe Wireless, Press Wireless and Macay—were all picking up the strange Japanese signals northwest by west of Pearl Harbor. Captain Richard T. McCollough, Chief of Intelligence, surmised that it could be the missing Japanese Fleet.[119] Admiral Kimmel was never informed.

Across the Pacific in Bandoeng, Java, the Dutch army intercepted a Japanese message from Tokyo confirming a scheduled attack on Hawaii. The signal for the final go-ahead would come from Tokyo in the form of a weather broadcast over Radio Tokyo. General Hein Ter Poorten, commander of the Netherlands East Indies Army, hand delivered the vital information to American Brigadier General Elliott Thorpe.[120] On December 4th, Chief Warrant Officer Ralph T. Briggs was on duty at Station M, the navy's East Coast intercept installation. Just before dawn, he made the electrifying detection from the Tokyo weather report—*Higashi no kaze ame*: "East wind, rain"—meaning "WAR WITH AMERICA."[121]

Space does not permit a detailed account of the many sobering facts contained in Toland's definitive work spanning 366 pages. On December 3rd, FBI agent Robert L. Shivers informed Police Lieutenant John A. Burns, head of the Honolulu Espionage Bureau, "We're going to be attacked before the week is out."[122] Late that night Barnet Nover, associate editor of the *Washington Post*, was informed by a British official that an attack was surely on the way. A pair of Japanese carriers had been spotted north of the Marshalls.[123] And in one of Toland's stranger accounts, Captain Johann E. Ranneft, naval attaché of the Netherlands, was shown a particular set of coordinates on a wall map and informed matter-of-factly, "This is the Japanese task force proceeding east."[124] The date was December 2.

Even radio-television commentator and best-selling author Paul Harvey got in on the action, relating that from 1931, "For ten years, every graduating naval cadet in Japan was asked the same question: 'How would you carry out a surprise attack on Pearl Harbor?' "[125] According to *More of Paul Harvey's The Rest of the Story*, the actual invasion route successfully followed by the *Kido Butai* in 1941 was the very route taken by United States Admiral Harry Yarnell in 1932, who decided to demonstrate the vulnerability of Pearl Harbor by slipping in two aircraft carriers undetected. The Japanese naval attachés in Honolulu were so impressed with the mock invasion that they sent all the details to Tokyo. Harvey concluded, "Almost a decade before the attack on Pearl Harbor, *we* showed the Japanese how!"[126]

The subsequent investigations ordered by FDR were nothing more than a giant whitewash; files were confiscated, evidence disappeared, key witnesses were censored and several prominent officials suddenly developed "amnesia." Predictably, Admiral Kimmel and General Short became the fall guys. However, not everyone was willing to look the other way. The distinguished Admiral William F. "Bull" Halsey wrote Kimmel, "As you know I have always thought and have not hesitated to say on any and all occasions, that I believe you and Short were the greatest military martyrs this country has ever produced, and that your treatment was outrageous."[127]

Noting that only a month before the invasion, Secretary of the Interior Harold Ickes recorded in his diary, "For a long time I have believed that our best entrance into the war would be by way of Japan,"[128] author John Toland drew the obvious inference: "The first bomb dropped on Oahu would have finally solved the problem of getting an America—half of whose people wanted peace—into the crusade against Hitler."[129] It was his conclusion that keeping "Kimmel and Short and all but a select few in ignorance" ensured "that the Japanese would launch their attack."[130]

Although Toland implicated Roosevelt in the disaster, he was willing to give him the benefit of the doubt, surmising that the President probably believed "any enemy naval task force would be destroyed before it neared Pearl Harbor."[131]

CONCLUDING DEVELOPMENTS

With America's entrance into the war, the end result was never *really* in doubt. The fact that all but two of the battleships sank in Pearl Harbor (the *Arizona* and *Oklahoma*) were later salvaged[132] was an omen of United States military capabilities. However, thousands of young American lads would have to shed their blood so that Wall Street could maximize their profits from 1941 to 1945.

Dan Smoot, a former FBI agent and assistant to J. Edgar Hoover, confirmed that the foreign ministers of Great Britain, Russia and the United States had been planning the partitioning of post-war Germany as early as October, 1943.[133] Of course, the *real* planners were found within the War and Peace Studies Project. In the closing days of World War II, America's occupation of Berlin was perceived as a critical priority. Even Roosevelt went on record as stating, "We may have to put the United States divisions into Berlin as soon as possible, because the United States should have Berlin."[134] Yet the historical record reveals a different scenario, Smoot writing:

> Our Ninth Army could have been in Berlin within a few hours, probably without shedding another drop of blood; but General Eisenhower [CFR] suddenly halted our Army. He kept it sitting idly outside Berlin for days, while the Russians slugged their way in, killing, raping, ravaging. We gave the Russians control of the eastern portion of Berlin—and of *all* the territory surrounding the city.[135]

As the Yalta Conference would later show (February 4–11, 1945), many additional concessions were yet to be made to "Uncle Joe" Stalin. The CFR was now in control of the United States State Department. It was James Warburg (CFR), son of the late Paul Warburg (CFR), who arrogantly told a Senate committee, "We shall have world government whether or not you like it—by conquest or consent."[136]

A year before the fall of Berlin (July, 1944), another "duck-hunting trip" was held at the Mount Washington Hotel in Bretton Woods, New Hampshire. That historic gathering of CFR globalists gave birth to twin "creatures"—*The International Monetary Fund* and its sister organization, *The International Bank for Reconstruction and Development*, commonly called the IMF and the World Bank. Thanks to a treacherous band of American politicians, the CFR would now have all the money it required to fund the New World Order. And as the United States would "naturally" provide the majority of these "loans" (i.e., 100% giveaways to a myriad of socialistic governments), the national debt was guaranteed to escalate into infinity. Griffin comments on this subtle transfer of assets:

> The method by which world socialism was to be established was to use the World Bank to transfer money—disguised as loans—to the governments of the underdeveloped countries and to do so in such a way as to insure the demise of free enterprise. The money was to be delivered from the hands of politicians and bureaucrats into the hands of other politicians and bureaucrats. When the money comes from government, goes to government, and is administered by government, the result will be the expansion of government.[137]

The CFR's final directive called for the long-awaited revitalization of Wilson's League of Nations. On June 26, 1945, representatives from 50 nations convened in San Francisco (how appropriate) for the historic signing of the United Nations charter. The United States delegation was stacked with 43 Council members. The secretary-general of the conference was United States State Department official Alger Hiss, a member of the CFR and *a secret Soviet agent!* Other high-level American Communists who served as delegates included: Noel Field, Harold Glasser, Irving Kaplan, Nathan Gregory Silvermaster, Victor Perlo, Henry Julian Wadley, and Harry Dexter White.[138] (Remember Quigley's quote about the Round Table groups cooperating with Communists?)

William Jasper summarizes the "net worth" of the United Nations' 47-year reign of evil:

> What the historical record shows, and what is essential for all people of good will to understand, is that the United Nations is completely a creature of the Council on Foreign Relations and was designed by that organization eventually to become an instrument for an all-powerful world government.[139]

As this chapter draws to its conclusion, the reader is directed to a final illustration of where humanity is headed under the New World Order. World

War II was supposedly started because Poland lost her sovereignty after the German invasion. Over 40 million deaths later (6,028,000 of whom were Poles), Poland was handed over to a dictator who made Hitler look like a Sunday school teacher.

> *"And the last state of that man*
> *is worse than the first."*
> (Matthew 12:45b)

XIX

Rosie, Elvis and Billy

> *"Love not the world, neither the things that are in the world.*
> *If any man love the world, the love of the Father is not in him."*
> (I John 2:15)

A WATERSHED IS a high point or ridge which divides the flow of drainage water into separate directions. Thus far we have examined four watersheds or high points in American history. On one side of these points, events flow in a certain direction while on the other side, they course in quite another. These four watersheds of American history are: the American Revolution, the Civil War, the Federal Reserve Act and the New Deal.

While the Revolution transformed British subjects into Americans, the United States "are" became the United States "is" at Appomattox. The aftermath of Jekyll Island created an illegal banking monopoly, thus ensuring a perpetual national debt. The ensuing Great Depression and FDR's socialistic "Band-Aids" reduced the rugged individualist to "Buddy, can you spare a dime?"

The fifth and most significant watershed in American history is World War II. The defeat of Polish cavalry units initiated the conflict; mushroom clouds over Hiroshima and Nagasaki concluded the same. In his editorial for the August 18, 1945, *Saturday Review* entitled "Modern Man Is Obsolete," liberal author Norman Cousins declared, "The new age [that began on August 6, 1945] would change every aspect of man's activities, from machines to morals, from physics to philosophy, from politics to poetry."[1]

On the surface, things appeared wonderfully optimistic for the "Baby Boomer" generation. In the wake of unprecedented post-war prosperity, the nation's churches were experiencing a steady rise in attendance, contrary to the normal pattern. (Matthew 6:24) For the year 1940, approximately 49% of the population attended church weekly. By 1950, the figure had increased to 55%. In 1960, it stood at an all-time high of 69%. Religious contributions kept pace with a record $3.4 billion in 1957, enabling many denominations to build larger and more elaborate sanctuaries for worship.

However, "all that glitters is not gold." In his lecture series, "The Almost Chosen People; Religion, Culture and Public Life in the U.S.," delivered in October, 1994, at the J. P. Morgan Library in New York, British historian Paul Johnson states:

> At the same time, however, the detachment of American popular religion from its doctrinal basis continued. Ordinary churchgoers for instance, showed themselves less and less inclined to read the New Testament. Religion seemed to be less and less about suffering and repentance, and more and more about happiness.[2]

As we shall presently see, the so-called post-war revival era was nothing more than a movement of modern "churches" hustling religious dope to a new generation of materialistic parishioners.

The "spiritual" steroids which produced this unnatural *boom* also brought about the inevitable *bust* (Benny Hinn, Reverend Ike, Shirley MacLaine, Psychic Friends Network, Stallone Solution, etc.). Johnson continues:

> Until the second half of the 20th century religion was held to be, by virtually all Americans, irrespective of their belief or non-belief, to be not only a desirable, but an essential, part of the natural fabric. This was a salient, and in many ways, unique American characteristic which struck European observers as remarkable...
>
> American religion, by which I mean the universally accepted moral theology derived from an ecumenical version of Protestantism, was identified first with Republicanism and then with Democracy, so as to constitute the American way of life, the set of values and the notions of private life and civic behavior which Americans agreed to be self-evidently true and right.
>
> In consequence, those who preached these values from the pulpits or who most clearly, even ostentatiously upheld them from the pews were acknowledged to be among the most valuable citizens in the country.

Hence, as deTocqueville observed, there was no such thing as anti-clericalism in America; whereas in Europe, religious practice and fervor were often, even habitually, seen as a threat to freedom. In America they were seen as its underpinning. In Europe religion was presented, at any rate by the majority of intellectuals, as an obstacle to progress; in America, as one of its dynamics.

This huge and important difference between European and North American attitudes is now becoming blurred and, perhaps, is in the process of disappearing altogether. It is one way, I suppose, in which America is losing its uniqueness, is ceasing to be "the city on the hill," the "promised land" and is becoming a nation like any other. Americans themselves no longer feel that they are the chosen people, or even the "almost-chosen people," as Lincoln put it, but are simply a normal people, no better, no worse, not essentially different from any other.[3]

As the local, New Testament churches in any nation constitute the all-important salt of cultural preservation (Matthew 5:13), an appreciable decline in spiritual vibrancy will ensure a commensurate decay in society as a whole. Though a secularist, Johnson provides an exceptional analysis of the modus operandi employed by effective church-state mutualism:

> The notion of rights is essentially political and secular. The securing of individual rights, compatible with social cohesion, is the whole art of politics. And the quest for rights is a secular activity precisely because the non-religious approach sees the human being as autonomous with purely social obligations.
>
> But equally, it is impossible for any religious philosophy to be rights based. Strictly speaking, no being has rights except God. Human beings merely have duties to God and to each other and the function of a church is to teach them and endeavor to enforce them....
>
> The historic American religious consensus...was based upon an unspoken assumption that duties were wide ranging and imperative. Congress and the courts could properly concentrate on enforcing rights because the churches, and the ardent men and women who composed them, could safely be left to ensure that all were aware of their duties too, and perform them.
>
> Once the stress on duties ceases to be sufficiently powerful, or ceases to operate at all among large sections of society, then a rights-based public philosophy tends to break down because there are more human rights, real or imaginary, than there is justice available to satisfy them. When the element of duty is subtracted from the drive for rights, the result is merely a conflict of rights.[4]

What Johnson was basically saying is that government works best when churches persuade their parishioners to be more duty-conscious and less rights minded. Or, as John Adams wrote:

> Our constitution was made only for a moral and religious people. It is wholly inadequate for the government of any other.[5]

The bottom line is that something terrible has happened to the church of Jesus Christ in the second half of the twentieth century. Therefore, to understand the general demise of America from 1960 to the present, one must first identify the specific foundation of spiritual apostasy laid between 1945 and 1959. The remainder of this chapter will highlight the particulars of this catastrophic defection.

THE ADVENT OF MATERIALISM

In the post-war years, three distinct factors brought about a total transformation in the quality of everyday American life. The first of these steps was taken by "Big Brother," courtesy of The Creature from Jekyll Island. The "G.I. Bill" was designed to reintegrate returning American servicemen into society without disrupting the overall economy. While the Veteran's Administration Loan Act procured billions in "funny money" for low-interest, new-home mortgages, additional grants were extended to provide free college tuition as well.

The second of these post-war resources was made available by the lending institutions themselves in the form of "easy credit" (more funny money). Financial advisor Larry Burkett writes, "Perhaps the most significant economic change of the second half of the twentieth century was the discovery of instant prosperity (called credit) by millions of American families."[6] In addition to home mortgages and short-term car loans, Diners Club became the nation's first credit card in 1950, followed by American Express and Bankamericard in 1958.

The third reason for America's enhanced standard of living also provides an explanation for an apparent spiritual paradox. On the basis of Proverbs 14:34a (*"Righteousness exalteth a nation"*), and Psalm 33:12a (*"Blessed is the nation whose God is the LORD"*), a skeptic would be within his rights to demand a scriptural reconciliation of America's post-war technological advances with her overt wickedness as a people.

The answer to this puzzling dilemma can be found in another pair of conditional promises: Genesis 12:3 and Psalm 122:6. Over 4,000 years after God promised Abram, "I will bless them that bless thee," the U.S. State Department finally did something right for a change by being the first government to extend formal diplomatic recognition to the Sovereign State of Israel. On May 14, 1948, as the outgoing British high commander stepped on board a ship of the Royal Navy, the long-standing British Mandate came to an official end. Zionist David Ben-Gurion immediately proceeded to the main library in Tel-Aviv where the proclamation for statehood was read somewhere between 12:00 and 2:00 p.m. local time. Within two hours (approximately 7:00 a.m. EST), President Harry S. Truman officially acknowledged the Jewish state.

Whereas FDR had been decidedly anti-Semitic and anti-Zionist, Truman became the unwitting agent of divine providence for the reestablishment of God's chosen people in their promised land. It also just so happens that Dr. J. Frank Norris sent a lengthy correspondence to Truman on October 2, 1947, explaining his own theological and political position regarding the question of Jewish autonomy and what the attitude of the United States government should be concerning this matter. His concluding line read, "The time has come, and long past, when the United States should keep its promise and take a firm stand for law and order in that land that gave the world its Bible and Saviour."[7] Notwithstanding the evils perpetrated by various Jewish bankers, the alliance was a wise move in view of Psalm 122:6: *"Pray for the peace of Jerusalem: they shall prosper that love thee."* By the way, have you ever noticed anything unusual in the spelling of Israel's capital, JERUSALEM? (Have you ever counted the number of letters in the name of this fruit-bearing city?)

As the tender fig tree began to draw nourishment from America, the sprouting of her leaves (Matthew 24:32) ensured reciprocal blessings on her otherwise backslidden benefactor. It was no coincidence that within a month of Truman's directive, an official United States Air Force release acknowledged that Captain Charles Yeager had broken the sound barrier in a rocket-powered Bell X-1 at 35,000 feet. (The flight itself had occurred the previous October.) Nor was it a coincidence that same year when H. L. Johnson announced the discovery of a new hydrogen rocket fuel capable of sending men to the moon.[8] (Daniel 12:4)

A steady flow of unprecedented technological breakthroughs, medical advances and product inventions proceeded to keep the American people in a state of perpetual stupefication. A short list of post-war gadgets, foodstuffs and improvements would include: automatic clothes driers, instant potatoes and electric blankets (1946); Almond Joys, RediWhip and Minute Maid orange juice (1947); Nestlés Quik, garbage disposals, Scrabble, auto air conditioners, Michelin radial tires, Honda motorcycles, Porsches and McDonalds (1948); Sara Lee cheesecake, Pillsbury "Bake-offs," Revlon's "Fire and Ice," Volkswagens and pizza (1949); the first kidney and aorta transplants, Miss Clairol, Minute Rice, Corning Ware and "Peanuts" (1950); Univac computers, sugarless chewing gum, Dacron suits, automatic garage door openers and power steering (1951); heart-lung machines, plastic artificial heart valves, Holiday Inns, mechanical lawn mowers, 16 mm home movie projectors, the H-bomb and *Mad* magazine (1952); the first successful open-heart surgery, Corvettes and burglar alarms (1953); Salk's polio vaccine, the first atomic-powered submarine, Levi's faded blue denims, frozen TV dinners and Shakey's Pizza (1954); electric stoves, Ann Landers and Colonel Sanders' Kentucky Fried Chicken (1955); Midas Mufflers, Comet, Imperial margarine, disposable Pampers and Ford convertibles (1956); ICBMs, Darvon and electric typewriters (1957); Explorer I, bifocals, Cocoa Puffs and Pizza Hut (1958); and, last, but not least, heat-seeking missiles, cruise control, the Pioneer IV space probe and hypnosis sanctioned by the A.M.A. (1959).[9]

According to II Timothy 3:4, end-day inhabitants will be *"lovers of pleasures more than lovers of God."* Baby boomers set the pace for "playing" with a host of toys and novelties, not the least of which would include: erector sets and roller derbies (1949); square dancing and the mambo (1950); vibrating mattresses (1951); flying saucer watching and stamp collecting (1952); drag races and 3-D cinerama (1953); Bermuda shorts, bingo and roller-skating marathons (1954); raccoon coats, cruising, Disneyland, and stuffing people into telephone booths (22) and Volkswagens (40), and 3.8 million golf players on 5,000 courses (1955); 7,000 drive-in theaters (1956); pogo sticks, Silly Putty, bowling and frisbee throwing (1957); waterskiing and hula hoops—with one ten-year-old child setting a record at 3,000 spins (1958); and finally, go-carts and parachute jumping (1959).[10]

We've all heard the expression, "An idle mind is the devil's workshop." A plethora of damaging reading material also found its way into the homes of post-war America. Some of the worst would include: *The Common Sense*

Book of Baby and Child Care by Benjamin Spock (1946); *Existentialism* by Jean-Paul Sartre (1947); *Sexual Behavior in the Human Male* by A. C. Kinsey (1948); *Catcher in the Rye* by J. D. Salinger (1951); *Christ and Culture* by Reinhold Neibuhr (1952); *Children Are Bored on Sunday* by Jean Stafford, *Science and Human Behavior* by B. F. Skinner, *Sexual Behavior in the Human Female* by Alfred Kinsey and *The Natural Superiority of Women* by Ashley Montague (1953); *Lord of the Flies* by William Golding (1954); *Lolita* by Vladimir Nabokov, *The Life and Work of Sigmund Freud* by Ernest Jones and *Black Power* by Richard Wright (1955); *A Walk on the Wild Side* by Nelson Algren and *Peyton Place* by Grace Metailous [6 million copies in the first six months] (1956); and *Breakfast at Tiffany's* by Truman Capote (1958).[11]

Hollywood continued to set the pace for "sin in the cinema." *The Bells of St. Mary's* starring Bing Crosby and Ingrid Bergman was released in 1945 and quickly became the greatest Roman Catholic propaganda film of all time. Other pro-Vatican releases would include *Boys Town; Angels with Dirty Faces; The Fighting 69th; The Fighting Sullivans; The Hunchback of Notre Dame; Knute Rockne, All American; The Adventures of Robin Hood; The Cardinal; The Nun's Story; Lilies of the Field; The Song of Bernadette; The Miracle of Our Lady of Fatima; Little Caesar; The Godfather; Rosemary's Baby; The Omen; The Exorcist* and one of the most appealing snow jobs of all—*The Sound of Music.*

A slate of Catholic worldlings like Frank Sinatra, Dean Martin, Rock Hudson, John Wayne, James Cagney, Mickey Rooney, Pat O'Brien, Spencer Tracy, Desi Arnaz, Bing Crosby, Danny Thomas and hundreds of others went on to lead the entertainment industry in pumping out plenty of trash through the nation's neighborhood theaters. Don Ameche was a member of my local parish and attended Mass on a regular basis. Cary Grant converted to Catholicism the year before his death.

Over 60 million people per week were attending such satanic productions as: *From Here to Eternity* (1953); *Dial M for Murder* and *The Wild One* (1954); *Rebel Without a Cause* and *Guys and Dolls* (1955); *Bus Stop* and *High Society* (1956); *Peyton Place, The Prince and the Show Girl* and *God Created Women,* starring Brigitte Bardot (1957); *Gigi* and *Cat on a Hot Tin Roof* (1958); and finally, *On the Beach, La Dolce Vita, Pillow Talk* and *Some Like It Hot,* starring Marilyn Monroe (1959). Incidentally, one report found that Beverly Hills, California, the home of Hollywood stars, has more psychiatrists per square mile than any other community in the world—193 shrinks—one for every 171 residents.[12]

As we have all learned by now, the invention of television has proven to be the leading cause of satanic mind control in the latter half of the twentieth century. *Faraway Hill,* starring Flora Campbell, debuted in 1946 becoming America's first televised daytime soap opera. *TV Guide* went on the stands in 1953. By 1956, 20,000 television sets were being sold per day. Approximately 90% of American homes owned at least one unit by 1960.

A study conducted in 1950 revealed that the average child was watching 27 hours of television per week (42 hours per week by 1959). Another report confirmed that the nation's illiteracy rate reached a new high of 3.2% in 1950. That same year, Boston University president Daniel Marsh predicted, "If the television craze continues with the present level of programs, we are destined to have a nation of morons."[13]

An eerie sign of the times was revealed in yet another survey in 1950. A Columbia University Press editor conducted a poll of the nation's libraries to determine the most boring books in America. First place honors went to John Bunyan's immortal classic, *Pilgrim's Progress,* followed by *Moby Dick* and Milton's *Paradise Lost.*[14] This author sees a spiritual correlation to the fact that Americans consumed 320 million pounds of potato chips and 750 million pounds of hot dogs that same year (foodstuffs unavailable to the imprisoned *Baptist* John Bunyan, who in 1678 penned his classic allegory on crumpled milk bottle tops).

ROSIE THE RIVETER

The post-war years also witnessed a drastic change in the character of America's women. The first bikinis made their shocking appearance on the nation's beaches as early as 1948. While "lady" wrestlers started climbing through the ropes in 1949, female college students began throwing their unmentionables out the windows to lustful young males below.

The beginning of the end for traditional American femininity occurred during the war years when housewives, mothers and single women entered the grimy factories to perform industrial jobs. The May 29, 1943, cover of the *Saturday Evening Post* featured Norman Rockwell's new American superwoman—"Rosie the Riveter." The song by the same name related:

Everyone stops to admire the scene.
Rosie at work on the B-19.
She's never twittery, nervous or jittery,
Rosie, Rosie the Riveter.
What if she's smeared full of oil and grease,
Doing her bit for the old lend lease,
She keeps the gang around,
They love to hang around,
Rosie, Rosie, Rosie, the Riveter.

Old timers will confirm that many a factory hand would "love to hang around Rosie" for *other* reasons as well. An influx of lonely women at the traditionally all-male workplace resulted in disastrous moral consequences. Kelli Peduzzi, author of *America in the 20th Century*, writes:

> Despite the traditional underpinnings, government propaganda did create a completely new image of the American woman in the popular press: She was now a working woman. She wore overalls, sported a welding torch, and carried a lunch box. The famous cover of the *Saturday Evening Post* featuring Norman Rockwell's Rosie the Riveter on May 29, 1943, instantly spoke what no number of slogans could say. Rosie was capable and tough, yet cheerful, well groomed, and all American.
>
> Images like Rosie's spewed forth from Hollywood in the form of womanpower campaign films such as *The Glamour Girls of 1943*, onto magazine and pulp fiction covers, and into popular songs such as "Swing Shift Maisie," "Rosie the Riveter," "The Lady at Lockheed," and "We're the Janes Who Make the Planes." Billboards, posters, even underwear displays in department stores touted the theme of the working woman.[15]

American women were *literally* wearing the pants in the family, Peduzzi confirming, "The sales of women's pants in 1942 were five times greater than in the preceding year."[16] (Deuteronomy 22:5) The *Minneapolis Tribune* for August 25, 1942, asked forebodingly:

> WAACS and WAVES and women welders...Where is it all going to end?...Is it hard to foresee, after the boys come marching home and they marry these emancipated young women, who is going to tend the babies in the next generation?[17]

Although numbers of "Rosies" were more than happy to exchange their riveting guns for vacuum cleaners by war's end, far too many had become infatuated with their paychecks to ever return to normalcy. By 1954, 21 million of the nation's 64 million workers were women (twice as many as 1940). Day care centers and disposable Pampers entered the national vocabulary. (II Timothy 3:3)

This is not to imply that the typical working woman was striving to satisfy her own particular monetary goals. For many households, two paychecks made more sense than one; at least if you wanted to "keep up with the Joneses" (another concept of the post-war years). Between 1950 and 1960, the number of American home owners increased by 9 million. Modest dwellings could be purchased for $6,000 with low-interest loans available for veterans. Over 58 million automobiles were manufactured during the same period. Approximately 458 billion miles were driven in 1950 alone. The Federal Interstate Act of 1956 added 40,000 miles of interstate highways to accommodate the additional vehicles. For the record, by 1950, the "new" Americans were also ingesting 1.2 million pounds of tranquilizers per year. (i.e., "Friendly" Bob Adams isn't so friendly when you can't make the monthly payments.)

The critical 14-year, post-war foundation period itself, 1945 to 1959, divides with a "Rubicon River" experience at the halfway point of 1952. For seven long years (1945–1952), the gods of materialism had laid siege to America. Although their temptations were mighty, the spiritual testimony of the nation's Christian population still held the ultimate power of influence. (Matthew 5:13-16)

A host of Baptist churches fought hard to retain the old-time religion. (Ephesians 4:27) The preacher who had occupied the most prominent leadership role through the first half of the century was Dr. J. Frank Norris. Among his many supernatural feats, Dr. Norris simultaneously pastored for 14 years two of America's largest churches, which were 1,300 miles apart— First Baptist Church of Fort Worth, Texas, and Temple Baptist Church of Detroit, Michigan. However, time was catching up to the grizzled veteran. Homer Ritchie, the immediate successor to Dr. Norris, writes:

> Norris' weakened physical condition at age 73, was observable to all by early 1951. He shifted his feet slowly along as he walked; sickness, age, emotional experiences, arduous travel, hard work, and controversies had all taken their toll. He depended more and more on associates to carry on his work.[18]

Any fear that Dr. Norris had grown soft on Catholicism, due to an unwise audience with Pius XI in 1937 (a purely fact-finding mission, as were his other interviews with Mussolini and Churchill), were put to rest later that year, Ritchie writing:

> In early November, he fired a broadside at President Harry Truman whom he forthrightly declared had violated the United States Constitution by appointing an ambassador to the Vatican in Rome. He further accused Truman of playing politics with the Pope and Catholics to gain votes.[19]

On August 19, 1952, Dr. Norris flew to Jacksonville, Florida, to speak in a youth camp at Keystone Heights. Dr. Ritchie drove him to the airport and noted, "He boarded the plane wearing two different colored socks on his feet and with only a few dollars in his pocket."[20] After the evening service, the young people gathered around him and sang "Onward, Christian Soldiers" and "God Be With You 'Til We Meet Again." Wearied by his long trip, Dr. Norris retired early. Shortly after midnight the noble man of God suffered a severe heart attack and expired at 1:55 a.m.

The death of Dr. J. Frank Norris marked *the spiritual* watershed of the century. The "last days" of the last days were now upon the churches. Although a multitude of spiritual pastors were still on the scene, Dr. Norris was one of the few remaining titans who *"had seen all the great works of the* LORD, *that he did for Israel."* (Judges 2:7b)

As if to picture the dark days ahead, a number of evil milestones were reached during the year of Dr. Norris' death. The apostate National Council of Churches published their blasphemous Revised Standard Version in 1952 which became the top-selling nonfiction release for the next three years. Norman Vincent Peale released his perverted *Power of Positive Thinking.* The United Nations took up its permanent residence on New York City's East River Drive (thanks to an $8.5 million "donation" to U.N. Secretary General Trygvelie by John D. Rockefeller II).

Other foreboding highlights of the year included the world's first sex change (in Denmark); George Jorgensen, age 26, became Christine (Remember Bonnie Sue?). And speaking of perverts, the Liberace Show premiered on national television while the Roman Catholic Bishop Fulton Sheen received an Emmy for his "Life Is Worth Living" broadcast. And finally, Hank Williams' "Your Cheatin' Heart" proved to be one of the year's hottest songs!

Dwight Eisenhower (CFR) defeated Adlai Stevenson (CFR) in the 1952 presidential election, 33 million votes to 27 million. As to the potential for moral leadership by these two professional politicians, Stevenson said, "Some of us worship in churches, some in synagogues, some on golf courses," while Ike was more serious, declaring, "Our government makes no sense unless it is founded in a deeply felt religious faith and **I don't care what it is.**"[21]

The remaining seven years of the decade were filled with numerous sinful developments. *Playboy* magazine debuted in 1953 featuring Marilyn Monroe in the first issue. Circulation would reach 1.1 million by 1960. In 1962, a Unitarian minister, John A. Crane, delivered a "sermon" about *Playboy,* which Hugh Hefner loved to quote:

> *Playboy* comes close now to qualifying as a movement, as well as a magazine. It strikes me that *Playboy* is a religious magazine. It tells its readers how to get into heaven. It tells them what is important in life, delineates ethics for them, tells them how to relate to others, tells them what to lavish their attention and energy upon, gives them a model of the kind of person to be. It expresses a consistent world view, a system of values, a philosophical outlook.[22]

With Marilyn as their guide, a steady stream of "sex goddesses" began their strut across the silver screen: Gina Lollabrigida (1954); Natalie Wood (1955); Kim Novak (1956); Sophia Loren (1957) and Brigitte Bardot (1958). As if to foreshadow the coming brand of carnal, Hollywood Christianity (Pat Boone, Johnny Cash, Roy Rogers and Dale Evans, etc.), Jane Russell professed to being born again in 1950, declaring of the Heavenly Father, "He's a livin' doll."[23] After "growing in grace" for three years, Miss Russell appeared in the 1953 movie, *Gentlemen Prefer Blonds.*

The greatest revolution in American morals was caused by the fifties phenomenon known as "rock and roll." David Wright relates:

> Imagining the 1950s without rock 'n' roll is to visualize a construction site without noise. Yet, before the middle of the decade, there was very little rock, and the music itself went by several names. To middle-class parents, it might be called "boogie-woogie" or "race music," terms covering anything played or sung with vitality by African-Americans on a few big-city AM radio stations. To blacks themselves, it was known as R & B—rhythm and blues. Religious blacks might recognize traces of gospel music. To rural, southern white people, it could be called country swing. And to northern vocalists, who substituted their voices for

instruments, it was doo-wop. It went by almost as many names as it had origins.

Rock music captured the hearts of millions of young people in 1954 and 1955, with hits from Bill Haley and the Comets such as "Shake, Rattle and Roll" and "Rock Around the Clock."

Little Richard, Johnny Ace, Johnny Otis, and groups such as Hank Ballard and the Midnighters, the Platters, Clyde McPhatter and the Drifters, and Billy Ward and the Dominoes produced music that was simply too vibrant to keep off the airwaves.

White-owned radio stations—and almost all were white owned—tried to satisfy teens with wimpy rock ballads, such as Eddie Fisher's "Dungaree Doll" or Kay Starr's "Rock and Roll Waltz." But the kids knew the difference. Overnight, rock was everywhere.[24]

Other rock perverts included Chuck Berry ("Maybellene"), Fats Domino ("Blueberry Hill") and Jerry Lee Lewis, cousin to Evangelist Jimmy Swaggart ("Whole Lot of Shaking Going On"). Dick Clark kept the fires burning with his sensual "American Bandstand" which premiered in 1957. Little Richard ("Good Golly, Miss Molly") gave everybody a scare when he caught a vision of Hell in 1958 and quit show business to become a "preacher." However, he was back on stage in no time.

Throughout this evil era of American history, Christians found themselves being drawn to *"the kingdoms of the world, and the glory of them"* (Matthew 4:8b) just like anyone else. (James 1:14) *Pilgrim's Progress* had been voted the most boring book in the land ("convicting" was probably more like it). The nation's churchgoers wanted more tranquil literature, especially with the threat of nuclear war hanging over their heads. Satan was only too happy to oblige with best-sellers such as, *Peace of Mind* by Joshua Liebman (1946); *Guide to Confident Living* by Norman Vincent Peale (1948); *Peace of Soul* by Bishop Fulton Sheen (1949); *Power of Positive Thinking* by Norman Vincent Peale (1952); and *The Art of Loving* by Erich Fromm in 1956.

The "rocking fifties" also marked the final assault against "the Old Black Book," the AV 1611. As previously noted, the Revised Standard Version topped the charts for best nonfiction in 1952, 1953 and 1954. Eighteen other "the Books" were released before the end of the decade, including *The New Testament in Modern English* by J. B. Phillips in 1958 and *The Holy Bible: The Berkley Version in Modern English* by Gerrit Verkuyl in 1959. (Another 25 perversions would arrive in the sixties, followed by 26 more in the seventies, and 25 more in the eighties.)

One of the earliest professing Christians to "cross over to the other side" was the celebrated Buddy Holly. In his earlier years, Buddy and his family attended the Tabernacle Baptist Church of Lubbock, Texas. Two of "Brother" Holly's "greatest" hits were "Peggy Sue" and "That'll Be the Day." No doubt there would have been more, but the 22-year-old backslider died in a fiery plane crash on February 3, 1959, along with Richie Valens and the "Big Bopper." (Ecclesiastes 7:17)

THE "KING"

According to the late Buddy Holly, "Without Elvis, none of us could have made it" (whatever *that* meant), while Bruce Springsteen added, "That Elvis, man...wrote the book."[25] The name *Elvis* is supposedly derived from the Norse, *Alviss* meaning *all wise*. A survey of the entertainer's life would challenge the fulfillment of this lofty nomenclature.

Elvis Presley was definitely different. After Ed Sullivan commented sanctimoniously that he "wouldn't touch Elvis with a long pole," the variety show host had to eat crow as the singer's popularity continued to soar. Ed booked Elvis for three appearances on the show and paid him an incredible $50,000. After Elvis sang four songs on the final appearance, January 6, 1957, Sullivan came on stage to "honor" his guest: "I wanted to say to Elvis Presley and the country that **this is a real decent fine boy**, and we've never had a pleasanter experience on our show with a big name than we've had with him."[26]

Ed Sullivan was a ratings-conscious hypocrite! If he *really* felt Elvis was a "real decent fine boy," why did he instruct his cameraman that Elvis be filmed only from the waist up to avoid broadcasting his provocative gyrations? Fans did not "hear" Elvis; they *experienced* Elvis! But *what* exactly was Elvis?

The answer to this question constitutes a politically correct time bomb. Dewey Phillips was the first deejay to take a chance with the newcomer. According to Latham, "Dewey thought the young people of America were ready for a singer who sounded *black* but looked *white*."[27] What the listeners of WHBQ Memphis "experienced" in July of 1954 was a "white man's voice singing Negro rhythm."[28] Joe Esposito, one of Elvis' closest friends, wrote:

> When Elvis was growing up, Memphis venues presented segregated shows, one for whites and one for "coloreds." Elvis attended those shows

and learned a great deal. Even his dress style—the collar turned up in back, for instance—reflected the happening Beale Street esthetic. Elvis merged that hip African-American influence with white youth's burgeoning craze for such screen idols as Marlon Brando and James Dean, who personified their own alienation. Movies like *The Wild One* and *Rebel Without a Cause* captured the vague but powerful yearnings of an entire generation. At the time, the aura of volatile unpredictability and sexuality that surrounded those singers and actors was social dynamite.[29]

Elvis himself later confessed:

> I dig the real low-down Mississippi singers, mostly Big Bill Broonzy and Big Boy Crudup, although they would scold me at home for listening to them. "Sinful music," the townsfolk in Memphis said it was. Which never bothered me.[30]

Elvis Presley was used by Satan to introduce America's white youth to the jungle music of Ham (Exodus 32:17,18) and when this "social dynamite" exploded, it blew what was left of "Pilgrim's Pride" to smithereens. In his preface to *The Elvis Reader*, Mojo Nixon wrote:

> Never underestimate the effect Elvis had in his first ten years. Forget about the fat Vegas Elvis at the end and remember that ONE OUT OF THREE AMERICANS SAW ELVIS ON "ED SULLIVAN" IN 1956! And to paraphrase Texas songwriter Butch Hancock, **Elvis wiped out four thousand years of Judeo-Christian uptightness about sex in fifteen minutes of TV. The King shook the fig leaf away and the kids on "The Donna Reed Show" would soon find themselves high as a kite and fornicating in the mud at Woodstock.**[31]

Given the amount of moral damage inflicted throughout his career, not to mention his own sustained indulgences, a person would naturally assume Elvis to be one of the biggest heathens of all time. This, however, was not the opinion of the many Christian leaders who had an opportunity to speak with Elvis in person.

Evangelist Dr. Carl Hatch told this author that he met Elvis at a gospel quartet concert and spoke with him on a number of subsequent occasions. Dr. Hatch relates that Elvis gave a clear testimony of having trusted Jesus Christ at an Assembly of God revival when he was 13 years of age. Elvis detected a genuine spirit of compassion on the part of Dr. Hatch and requested that the man of God keep him in his prayers. An occasional written correspondence would include the plea, "Don't give up on me." It was the opinion of Dr. Hatch that Elvis fit the profile of a backslider.

Dr. Jack Hyles, pastor of First Baptist Church of Hammond, Indiana, once had an impromptu, 30-minute conversation with Elvis in a Dallas hotel lobby. When Dr. Hyles asked him if he knew where he was going when he died, the "King" answered in the affirmative, sharing the same testimony that he gave Carl Hatch. Dr. Hyles then asked Elvis why he was living such a worldly lifestyle. The entertainer replied by comparing his extravagant suit and limousine to the plain attire and automobile of Dr. Hyles. He told the preacher that he was tired of all the rules and simply wanted to be free.

In addition to his personal testimony, Elvis exhibited a number of characteristics consistent with the lifestyle of a modern-day prodigal. His well-known penchant for gospel music continued to the end of his life. (Ephesians 5:19) Many of his background singers were traditional gospel groups such as the Jordanaires, the Imperials and the Stamps Quartet. All three of his Grammy Awards were for gospel numbers: "How Great Thou Art" (1967—studio cut); "He Touched Me" (1972—album) and "How Great Thou Art" again (1974—live concert performance). The majority of his own private record collection was gospel. Few professional performers (Mick Jagger, Elton John, Michael Jackson, etc.) have expressed any affection for Bible-based lyrics.

His favorite gospel song, "How Great Thou Art," was normally included in his concert repertoire. And yet, the very title and theme of this hymn clashed violently with the singer's own accepted industry title—The "King" —yet another telltale sign of a carnal believer. (*"A double minded man is unstable in all his ways."* [James 1:8])

The most conspicuous difference between Elvis and the Hollywood scene was that despite his overt sensuality ("Ah act the way ah feel"), he just never seemed to fit in with the crowd. Actor Ed Asner appeared in two movies with Elvis—*Kid Galahad* and *Change of Habit*. In a letter to a fan, he remembered Elvis as "a very polite, proper young man—friendly in some ways, but I remember that he was rather shy and did not hang around with the cast or crew too much."[32] Veteran actress Barbara Stanwyck had a similar recollection from her role as co-star in *Roustabout*:

> He was a wonderful person to work with. He asked for nothing. So many people expect the other—swelled head and all that. So did I, frankly. But it was not the case. Elvis was a fine person. His manners are impeccable, he is on time, he knows his lines.[33]

Dr. Dallas Dobson, pastor of the giant Riverview Baptist Church in Pasco, Washington, met Elvis on two occasions when he was a policeman in Mississippi. Dr. Dobson gave Elvis a lift in his squad car when the singer's Cadillac broke down. It was his distinct recollection that Elvis was the consummate gentleman.

This unnatural "goodness" (unnatural in the entertainment industry) led Elvis to be generous to a fault. Not only did he more than care for his parents and immediate relatives, but he constantly lavished his male entourage (known as the "Memphis Mafia") with extravagant gifts valued in the thousands of dollars. When Elvis purchased the 160-acre Circle G Ranch in Mississippi, he also bought 30 new Ford Rancheros so his boys could go joy-riding with him.

Elvis also gave consistently to just about anyone he met. In January 1976, he gave away three Cadillacs and two Lincoln Continentals to people he met on a skiing trip in Vail, Colorado. Joe Esposito, the man who knew him best, wrote:

> When I first met him, I thought Elvis was generous because he needed to buy friends, that his bursts of generosity were a way to shake off loneliness. But now I think differently. Elvis didn't pass out money just to massage his ego. **He got a genuine thrill from making people happy, and he was always a bit amazed at the public's reaction to his presence.** He couldn't resist testing it every so often. Elvis wanted to make a difference in people's lives, especially his fans, to whom he was always grateful. He often said that if it weren't for them, he would still be driving a truck.[34]

The saddest evidence that points to the distinct possibility that Elvis was a backslidden Christian was his total inability to enjoy life itself. Because he chose to live in the hog pen, he lost track of his Father's forgiveness. (Luke 15:21) If Elvis did get saved as a boy, the sins of manhood destroyed his spiritual comprehension. *"But he that lacketh these things is blind, and cannot see afar off, and hath forgotten that he was purged from his old sins."* (II Peter 1:9) On one occasion he remarked to Esposito:

> I think there is only one God, but different people worship Him in different ways. Who's to say who's right and who's wrong? I think everyone is right if they just believe in God.[35]

Without the leadership of the Holy Spirit, Elvis naturally became his *own* final authority. Esposito writes:

> He analyzed the Bible sentence by sentence to form his own interpretations, then preached to us his findings. The word "Israel," he'd intone with great authority, really meant "is real." He'd pause dramatically, two fingers poised in a karate posture in the listener's face. "God's name is really 'hallowed'," he'd say without the trace of a smile, "because it says hallowed be thy name."[36]

As the years went by Elvis started mixing his preaching sessions with dope parties. Esposito relates:

> Elvis loved playing games like policeman, fireman and spy, and now his favorite was "master instructing the multitudes." He'd gather his friends and whichever girls were around and read from the Bible and preach. One late night, about fourteen people were in the Palm Springs house. We'd all been smoking grass, laughing and talking, when Elvis turned the conversation to religion. He had smoked a lot of marijuana by then. He asked us to turn off the television and began preaching.
>
> Every time he made what he considered a key point, he waved a cane he was using as his staff, then paused to gaze portentously at us before picking up the thread of his theme. At one point, he looked at the Bible he was holding, then exclaimed, "You gotta hear this!" One of the guys groaned under his breath, "Oh, no, not again!" But Elvis was oblivious, pacing the room as he read aloud: "Verily I say onto [sic] you, except ye be converted and become as little children, ye shall not enter the kingdom of Heaven...But whoso shall offend one of these little ones which believe in me, it were better for him that a millstone were hanged about his neck, and that he were drowned in the depth of the sea!" At this point, Elvis leaped onto the coffee table. He pointed the cane skyward and still clutching the Bible, improvised: "And Jesus said, 'Woe ye [expletive]!' " With that, we all fell out laughing, including Elvis, once he'd realized what he'd said. Everyone was rolling on the floor. Someone lit up another joint and that was the end of Bible class for that night.[37]

When Elvis wasn't "exegeting" the Bible, he was dabbling in various Eastern religions. Some of his favorite books included: *Siddartha* by Hermann Hesse; *The Prophet* by Kahil Gibran; *Autobiography of a Yogi* by Paramahansa Yogananda and *The Life and Teachings of the Master of the Far East* by Baird Spalding.

Elvis continued to pursue the strangest "spiritual" pursuits. At one point he thought that he could even heal the sick, Latham and Sakol writing:

> When members of his entourage were hurt he would lay his hands on the injured area and explain that the pain would soon leave their bodies and pass into his fingertips. In their desire to please Elvis most of them would quickly agree that they were getting better.[38]

Elvis also believed in a myriad of metaphysical powers. Esposito writes:

> He made us all lie on our backs and gaze up at the clouds.... "See that cloud? I'm going to make it move," he'd announce. Sure enough, eventually it would move. Elvis thought it was his mystical powers, not the wind.[39]

Such practices led to other weird habits. Elvis liked to take his dates to the local morgue to check out dead bodies. For some reason, he rarely took a bath. According to his personal physician, Dr. George Nichopoulous, he would sponge himself off but didn't want to get wet all over.[40] Elvis would stay awake all night and "attempt" to sleep during the day. He also was a chronic sleepwalker. A tabloid story that seemed to exemplify the extent of his eccentricities appeared in *The Sun* in mid-1988. According to "reliable sources," the Russians found and photographed an eight-foot statue of Elvis on Mars![41]

If Elvis was in fact a backslidden, born-again believer, he represents both the ultimate example of a shipwrecked life, as well as the spirit of apostate, materialistic Christianity in the last days. It is rather ironic that Elvis believed that he had an unknown spiritual mission in life, Esposito writing:

> As I got to know him better, I realized that he did have a sense of being anointed somehow. Why me? He constantly asked himself and others. The question would bother him more and more as time passed.[42]

Although we can never be sure about his personal salvation, there is no doubt that his bizarre lifestyle constitutes *the* classic object lesson concerning the momentary pleasures of sin. (Hebrews 11:25) The only "anointing" Elvis may have had in this life was to show the world in no uncertain terms that *"sin, when it is finished, bringeth forth death."* (James 1:15b)

The perfect verse to depict the day-to-day experiences of the "King" of rock and roll is found in Ecclesiastes 2:10a where another king confessed, *"And whatsoever mine eyes desired I kept not from them, I withheld not my heart from any joy."* Esposito describes a typical "night out with the boys":

> We often ended an evening by renting the Memphian Theater after midnight in order to avoid autograph seekers and fans. The first time I went, I noticed Elvis took his seat, and everyone sat behind him, never in front. We could just walk up to the refreshment counter and order what we wanted. Elvis took care of the tab, which averaged about four hundred dollars a night. He loved movies and watched his favorites over and over, reciting all the dialogue with the actors.
>
> Other nights he rented the roller rink or Liberty Land, the local amusement park, and we rode the different amusements—especially the bumper cars—for six or seven hours until dawn. He was making up for lost time, two years in Germany and an entire childhood.
>
> **Whatever Elvis wanted to do, he did. Whatever he wanted to buy, he bought.** We were our own crowd, and together we enjoyed movies, the bumper cars at the amusement park, and roller skating at the rink. We returned to Elvis's childhood with him, and as his playmates, we had a great time fulfilling the fantasy of a childhood that should have been.[43]

Elvis certainly had it all! As to personal attractiveness, America's females rated him the most handsome "hunk" alive. The star stood just a hair over six feet, and his normal weight was around 180 pounds. His blue eyes were framed with long lashes. Esposito recalls his earliest impressions:

> Seeing Elvis Presley in the flesh was a jolt. On the strength of his physical presence alone, he commanded the room. He was the best-looking man I'd ever seen, startlingly handsome, with classical, chiseled features and an undefinable quality that distinguished him from everyone else. He grew up around black children, and perhaps that influence gave him a stance like that of no white man I'd ever seen. He walked differently, kind of hip and relaxed. He had that snarl to his lip and an infectious laugh.[44]

In addition to his outstanding physical features, Elvis was also blessed with one of the greatest singing voices in history. Elvis had an incredible *93* singles and *46* albums that went gold. His fourth and fifth gold hits, "Hound Dog" and "Don't Be Cruel," were rated in 1988 as the most popular jukebox records of all time.

The combination of the two nearly made Elvis "King of the Planet." According to a research project in the early 1970's, Elvis was second only to Chinese leader Mao Tse-tung as the most recognized person on earth![45] Biographer Albert Goldman adds that, at the time of the entertainer's death in 1977, Elvis' was the second-most commonly reproduced face in the world; the first was Mickey Mouse.[46]

By every industry standard, Elvis Presley ("the backslidden Christian") was the undisputed "King" of worldly entertainment. In 1945, Frank Sinatra was making a cool $13,500 per week. The "Chairman of the Board" didn't think too highly of Elvis, stating, "His kind of music is deplorable, a rancid-smelling aphrodisiac." On another occasion, he called rock and roll "the most brutal, ugly, degenerate, vicious form of expression it has been my displeasure to hear."[47] However, by 1960, Frank was forced to eat some of Ed Sullivan's "crow leftovers" as the singer's "deplorable" popularity became too hard to resist. On March 21, 1960, Elvis was the featured guest on a Frank Sinatra television special called "Welcome Home, Elvis" broadcast from Miami Beach's Fontainebleau Hotel. For a six-minute appearance during which Elvis sang only two songs, "Fame and Fortune" and "Stuck on You," the "King" was paid $125,000. (He also sang two duets with his host.)

Citing Elvis biographer Jerry Hopkins, Latham and Sakol estimate the "King's" lifetime gross earnings at $18,000,000,000!![48] (That's right—9 zeros!) On January 14, 1973, "Elvis Aloha from Hawaii" was beamed by the Intelsat IV communications satellite at 12:30 a.m. (Honolulu time) to approximately 1 billion people in 40 countries, including Japan, South Korea, South Vietnam, Thailand, Australia, New Zealand, the Philippines and even Communist China! That's not too shabby for an ex-truck driver from Mississippi.

When the Beatles were asked what they most wanted to see during their first-ever tour of the United States, they replied, "Elvis." On August 27, 1965, the "Fab Four" paid a visit to Elvis at his leased Italian-style villa at 525 Perugia Way in the Bel Air section of Los Angeles. John Lennon confessed that the Beatles all felt nervous:

> This was the guy we had all idolized for years—from way back when we were just starting out in Liverpool. He was a legend in his own lifetime, and it's never easy meeting a legend for the first time.[49]

This historic audience with the "King" almost bombed as the "mopheads" were collectively paralyzed by his person. Elvis eventually broke the ice by protesting in tones of mock disgust, "Look, guys, if you're just going to sit there and stare at me, I'm going to bed."[50] Everyone relaxed and an impromptu jam session was soon underway. Lennon would later acknowledge:

> Nothing really affected me until I heard Elvis. If there hadn't been an Elvis, there wouldn't have been the Beatles.[51]

Being the "King" basically meant that Elvis could have anything he wanted. His nickname, "E," should have stood for "extravagance." With money to burn, Elvis bought everything from dune buggies to jet airplanes. In one month alone, Elvis purchased 33 automobiles, more than one per day. Most of the people who worked for "E" eventually received a new Mercedes-Benz as a gift.

The "King" also had some really royal robes. His famed, custom-made gold lamé suit cost $10,000. Many of his elaborate jumpsuits were even given names such as Inca Gold Leaf, Sundial, Burning Flame, Blue Aztec, Mad Tiger, American Eagle, Red Lion, Blue Rainbow and the King of Spades. He also sported an 11-carat diamond ring.

After the birth of his daughter, Elvis purchased a Convair 880 from Delta Airlines for $1 million and named it the *Lisa Marie* in honor of his newborn. (The nation's air traffic controllers nicknamed the *Lisa Marie* as "Hound *Dawg* One.") According to Latham and Sakol:

> The plane required a crew of four, including a stewardess to look after the passengers. The private bedroom featured a queen-sized bed and had its own bathroom with gold-plated fixtures and a shower. At the dining room table, surrounded by eight chairs, full meals were served that were cooked in the galley, where the coffeemaker was always kept running. The conference room had four television sets and there were seven telephones aboard the plane. Elvis liked to call the plane his "penthouse in the sky."[52]

The famed Graceland mansion was purchased in 1957 for $100,000. Originally situated on 13½ acres in what was then the unincorporated town of Whitehaven, it was later annexed by the city of Memphis. The stretch of Highway 51 South passing in front of the mansion was later renamed by the city—Elvis Presley Boulevard.

While Elvis "touched up" the front of Graceland with a number of stately white pillars and the famous wrought iron gates ornamented with guitars and musical notes, his parents added a vegetable garden and chicken coop in the backyard. The interior sported red, pink and purple color schemes with an abundance of velvet, mirrors and deep shag carpeting. Gold trim was de rigueur without. My readers will note yet another subliminal "spiritual" suggestion in the very name of *Grace*land.

While Solomon's harem consisted of 700 wives and 300 concubines, the "King" of rock and roll appears to have had only one spouse while entertaining another 999-plus paramours. Esposito writes:

> Elvis never saw one woman at a time, even during his marriage to Priscilla. Three or four was the average figure. One might be in the air on her way in, crossing flight paths with another on her way out. A third woman would be with Elvis in his hotel suite, with perhaps a fourth on hold in a room a few floors below.[53]

Elvis started "courting" his future wife, Priscilla Ann Beaulieu, when she was only *14* years old. When the teeny-bopper moved into Graceland three years later, she enrolled in the Immaculate Conception Roman Catholic High School as a second-semester junior. While Priscilla was busy doing homework, her famous beau was frequently "entertaining." Even after their Camelot-style wedding on May 1, 1967, the "King" continued to lead an outrageous double life.

A short list of the star's leading "ladies" would include: Natalie Wood, Hope Lange, Tuesday Weld, Barbara Leigh, Raquel Welch, Ann Margaret, Ursula Andress, Mary Ann Mobley, Cybil Shepherd, Barbara Eden and Mary Tyler Moore. By the world's standards, Elvis won the war of egos with Frank Sinatra by not only having a liaison with the "Chairman's" daughter, Nancy, but with his fianceé, Juliet Prowse, as well.[54]

In addition to their shared lifestyle of carte blanche self-gratification, Solomon and his twentieth-century protegé also experienced the inevitable spiritual vacuum. The "King" may have worn a gold *chai* on a chain around his neck (the Hebrew word for *life* and also a letter of the Hebrew alphabet), but his experience was that of his 977 B.C. forerunner: *"I have seen all the works that are done under the sun; and, behold, **all is vanity and vexation of spirit."** (Ecclesiastes 1:14)

In a scenario that he understood all too well himself, Beatle John Lennon said of Elvis:

> The king is always killed by his courtiers. He is overfed, over-indulged, overdrunk to keep him tied to his throne. Most people in the position never wake up.[55]

After "playing the fool" for years, Priscilla moved out of Graceland on February 23, 1972, in order to continue an affair of her own with Mike Stone, her personal karate instructor. The Presleys were legally divorced on October 11, 1973. On the recommendation of John Travolta, Priscilla and daughter Lisa attempted to "find themselves" in the "church" of Scientology. Following her own failed marriage to fellow Scientologist Danny Keough, Lisa Marie went on to marry Mike Jackson, a backslidden Jehovah's Witness. This marriage also ended in divorce. So much for Elvis the "family man."

Over the years Elvis had taken pride in the official Presley logo, "TCB" ("Taking Care of Business") with a lightning bolt underscoring the initials. The insignia was placed everywhere from the gold medallions worn by the "Memphis Mafia" to the tail of the *Lisa Marie*. Priscilla's exit in 1973 began to change all of that in short order.

The first time Elvis experimented with prescription drugs was in 1959 when he used the amphetamine, Dexedrine, to stay awake during all-night Army maneuvers. Other medications followed throughout his entertainment career as numerous physical disorders increased, particularly with his colon. The abuse of barbiturates and tranquilizers to relieve hypertension and insomnia only added to his pharmacological condition. This legal dope addiction accelerated after the "King's" divorce. Esposito confirmed that "three packets containing about four or five [sleeping] pills each...was normal for Elvis...to put him out."[56] Latham and Sakol add:

> It was revealed that in the last seven months of his life Elvis had been prescribed more than five thousand pills (although there is evidence that some of these pills may have been taken by members of his entourage rather than by Elvis himself), and at the time of his death there were ten different medications in his body.[57]

Already a perpetual prisoner of his legendary fame, the drugged-up "King" suddenly began putting on the pounds (as high as 260) and even started losing his hair. As the end drew near, the man who told the preacher that he had left the church to gain his freedom did not so much as own the rights to his own good looks! Latham and Sakol write:

By the end of his life, Elvis Presley didn't even own the rights to his own face. In the 1970s, Colonel Tom Parker set up a record label called Boxcar, based in his hometown of Madison, Tennessee (near Nashville). Originally, the company was to have been a joint venture with Elvis that would extend to issuing records by new young performers. As it turned out, Elvis's only real involvement with Boxcar came on August 15, 1974, when he signed an agreement that transferred all of his commercial rights to the corporation, giving the Colonel the lion's share of the profit from his own personality. **Until a court decision in the 1980s changed the situation, Colonel Parker controlled all licensing agreements and all rights to the image of Elvis.**[58]

The "King's" last recording session took place in the late spring of 1977, just months before his death. During the session he remarked to his producer, Felton Jarvis, *"I'm sort of getting tired of being Elvis Presley."*[59] The sad truth of the matter is that Elvis had no one to blame but himself.

The last gold singles of his career (his 92nd and 93rd) recorded in 1977 were suitably entitled, "Way Down" and "My Way." (*"A man's pride shall bring him low."* [Proverbs 29:23a]) The last concert Elvis gave was at the Market Square Arena in Indianapolis on June 26, 1977 (non-taped). According to the resident "Elvisologist" at Graceland (as related to me over the telephone), it is generally believed that Elvis departed from his traditional finale, "Can't Help Falling in Love," closing both the concert and his public career with the appropriate testimonial—"My Way."

Perhaps the most crushing blow of all came only two weeks before his final curtain call. After having received thousands upon thousands of dollars' worth of extravagant gifts and other expressions of affection from Elvis, three of his closest lifetime companions, Red West, Sonny West and Dave Hebler, published a shocking "tell-all" exposé of their benefactor's drug-related digression entitled *Elvis: What Happened?*

At approximately 10:00 A.M. on August 16, 1977, Elvis and his final flame, Ginger Alden, were in bed at the Graceland mansion when he suddenly got up and said, "I'm going into the bathroom to read a book so the light doesn't bother you."[60] Ginger then replied, "Don't fall asleep." The last words of Elvis Aaron Presley, the undisputed "King" of rock and roll, were as follows: "Okay, I won't."[61]

The Bible says in Galatians 6:7 and 8,

"Be not deceived; God is not mocked: for whatsoever a man soweth, that shall he also reap. For he that soweth to his flesh shall of the flesh reap corruption; but he that soweth to the Spirit shall of the Spirit reap life everlasting."

The words, *"Be not deceived, God is not mocked"* mean that God would be subject to ridicule if a Christian could lead a sinful life and avoid eventual chastisement. (See also Hebrews 12:7.) After damning an entire generation of young people, the time had come for the "King" to meet the *"King of kings."* (I Timothy 6:15)

However, it would not be right for Elvis to depart this life in any normal way. (See Numbers 16:29, 30.) Another generation was in need of a pungent illustration that "kings" have to "pay the piper" like anyone else; *"When the scorner is punished, the simple is made wise."* (Proverbs 21:11a) On the strength of Proverbs 21:12a which states, *"The righteous man wisely considereth the house of the wicked,"* I invite America's Christian young people into the *"bathroom* of the wicked," for it was there that the "King" was *dethroned* while "taking care of business."

Ginger awoke at around 2:20 p.m. and discovered Elvis' body on the bathroom floor. Responding to cries for help over the intercom, Joe Esposito describes what he encountered:

> I scaled the stairs and rushed into the bathroom to find Elvis on the floor. **He had been sitting on the toilet and had fallen face forward at a slight angle, onto his knees. He seemed to have either passed out or died sitting on the toilet, then just keeled over, because he was frozen in that position, on his knees.** He was wearing gold-colored silk pajama tops, and the blue bottoms were bundled around his feet. **His face was smashed into the thick carpeting, his nose flattened to one side,** and he appeared more bloated than usual, as if he'd choked. His eyes were closed. **A book he'd just received from his barber and friend, Larry Geller,** *The Scientific Search for the Face of Jesus***, was still clutched in his hand.**[62]

*"That at the name of Jesus **every** knee should bow."*
(Philippians 2:10a)

BILLY GRAHAM

The Elvis Presley estate continues to generate profits in the millions as his mesmerized devotees refuse to get on with their lives. Many are even convinced that the "King" is still alive. Mojo Nixon writes, "Our culture loves to pretend that death doesn't happen, and when the point man for postwar liberation goes down the tubes, the collective anguish and denial is amazing."[63]

If Elvis had indeed trusted Jesus as a youth, his backslidden life would personify the new breed of materialistic Christians likewise intent on "taking care of business." It is no coincidence that John's epistle to lukewarm Laodicea follows his letter to the church at Philadelphia; the resultant blessings of the former age having led to the avarice of the latter— *"Because thou sayest, I am rich, and increased with goods, and have need of nothing; and knowest not that thou art wretched, and miserable, and poor, and blind, and naked."* (Revelation 3:17) In contrast to the church of "brotherly love," the word *Laodicea* just happens to mean *rights of the people* (as in *"every man did that which was right in his own eyes."* [Judges 21:25b]).

By the mid-1950's, therefore, a growing number of apostate believers were longing for a return to Egypt. (Numbers 11:5) All they lacked was a qualified hireling to lead them. Having noted this distinct shift in wind direction, former Hellfire-and-damnation evangelist, Billy Graham, offered his services for the journey. His southern drawl and Bible-Belt roots would make him a natural for the job. (II Timothy 3:5)

Billy Graham was saved in his hometown of Charlotte, North Carolina, in 1934 under the barn-storming preaching of Baptist evangelist Mordecai Ham. After graduation from high school in 1936, Billy enrolled in Bob Jones College (BJC) in Cleveland, Tennessee. (Bob Jones College later relocated in Greenville, South Carolina, as Bob Jones University.) Billy's immediate clash with the school's discipline and authority set the pace for his lifetime penchant for ministerial compromise. In his acclaimed biography, *A Prophet with Honor*, author William Martin reveals:

> At the end of the summer, Frank Graham drove Billy and the Wilson brothers down to Tennessee to enroll in Bob Jones College. **As soon as they spied out the land, Billy and Grady began figuring ways to conquer it.** In his first foray into politics, he plotted with Grady to "take over the freshman class!" His plan was simple: "I'll nominate you for president, then you nominate me for vice-president." His rousing

nominating speech propelled Grady into office as planned, but when the new president took the chair, he no longer had the opportunity to nominate his friend, and Billy got no office. **From this botched beginning, the rest of the semester when downhill.**[64]

If Billy were to provide the "spiritual" leadership for the "E" generation, he would have to exhibit a number of compatible qualities. (Amos 3:3) As the initial exodus was attained by following a *lawgiver* (Numbers 21:18), the surest way back to Egypt would be via a *lawbreaker.* Another Graham biographer, Marshall Frady, concedes:

> Billy still had about him that quality of an unsubdued and jubilant child of nature. Jimmie Johnson submits, **"He was a totally liberated personality**....His room was never orderly, he just never seemed conscious of such things. He ate a lot of grapefruits up there—he would suck them like oranges, and then just pitch them into the corner... **"He never liked discipline, he never liked to be told what to do,"** says one of his contemporaries there. "He was just still unsurrendered up there. Especially in his unruly, headstrong, going-to-get-the-best-out-of-life nature."[65]

Billy himself would later acknowledge:

> **I never did fit in.**...I couldn't believe the rules there. It shocked me. There were demerits for just about everything, including what they called "loitering in the hall."[66]

(If I may reiterate, were it not for Dr. Randy Carroll's willingness to keep those very same rules, this author would probably still be a Hell-bound Roman Catholic.)

As with Elvis and his "Memphis Mafia," the flashy-dressing freshman learned to glean security from an entourage of his own, later to be known as "The Team." Frady (citing Johnson) continues:

> Billy was no genius, by any stretch of the imagination. Yet he had a—a magic about him. I was—we were all—charmed by his youthful nature. He was just a tall jaunty young man with a loose careless way about him, and he always had a large group of fellows around him, everywhere he went.
>
> As one Bob Jones stalwart puts it, "He just had too much charisma for one body. He was charming, overwhelming, irresistible.[67]

During the Christmas break, Billy visited Florida Bible College, outside of Tampa. Martin writes of his four-day stay: "Billy fell in love with Florida, whose warm climate and lakes and palm trees and flowers seemed paradisiacal in contrast to the wintry cheerlessness at Bob Jones."[68] Delaying his departure to the end of the school year, Billy received enticing letters from Wendell Phillips, who had transferred between semesters. Referring to Phillips, Martin relates:

> Within a few days, he was writing letters in which he described Florida Bible Institute as a Shangri-la where students free from stifling regulations could pluck luscious temple oranges from trees right outside their dormitory windows and could swim and play golf all year round.[69]

Billy left BJC for Florida the following year. Although the new school was not as lax as Phillips had intimated, Billy would later acknowledge, "I was really just a glorified tourist who was taking a few Bible courses."[70] After his graduation in 1940, Billy went on to Wheaton College for some additional "broadening and deepening." While there, his involvement with Youth for Christ eventually helped launch his career in evangelism.

Throughout his formative years in evangelism, Billy took a hard-line fundamentalist position and thus enjoyed the backing of such patriarchs as W. B. Riley, Bob Jones, Sr., John R. Rice and others. While Dr. Rice made him a board member at *The Sword of the Lord*, an ailing Dr. Riley appointed the 29-year-old evangelist president of his Minneapolis-based Northwestern Schools, consisting of a Bible School, a seminary and a brand-new liberal arts college.

As his crowds continued to grow, Billy frequently reaffirmed his commitment to fundamentalist values. He sent Dr. Bob Jones, Sr., a steady flow of gushy letters ("Be assured of my love and loyalty to you," 1/16/47, etc.). On one occasion he "boldly" asserted, "The reason communism is making inroads in the world today is that somewhere along the line the people who were supposed to live Christian lives **compromised** their beliefs."[71] By the turn of the decade, the *real* Billy Graham was about to emerge.

In preparation for a return to the *"land of Ham"* (Psalm 106:22), Billy's endorsement of the Hamite Revised Standard Version in 1952 sent shockwaves through the fundamentalist ranks. (It would be many years before a significant number of fundmentalists would espouse a consistent King James-only position themselves.)

As a further sign that he was veering to the left, Billy also began to accept speaking invitations at liberal seminaries such as Colgate Rochester Divinity School and New York's Union Theological Seminary.

Billy finally tested the waters of cooperative evangelism with his 1954 crusade in Harringay, England. On Saturday, May 22, the Greater London Crusade reached its climax with 120,000 people filling Wemberly Stadium to overflowing. As a payoff for these astounding figures, numbers of liberal theologians were allowed to sit on the platform with the renowned American evangelist. In an article printed in the *Banner of Truth*, London, England, Michael Boland wrote:

> It is quite likely that not one of them shared Dr. Graham's belief in the plenary, verbal inspiration of the scripture. Most of them would not believe in eternal punishment. Some would repudiate the penal and substitutionary view of the Atonement. The Archbishop of Canterbury and Dr. Payne were prominent members of the Ecumenical Movement, working for reunion with Rome.[72]

As to the motive behind such liberal support, Boland confirms that "it was not to redress the balance in their theology, as Dr. Ferm suggests, but to fill their churches."[73] The Harringay experiment initiated the practice whereby converts were directed to "the church of the seeker's choice" (i.e., "have it your way," etc.).

Billy's final break with Fundamentalism was occasioned by his infamous 1957 crusade at Madison Square Garden. The gargantuan meeting (involving over 1,400 churches from 40 different denominations) was sponsored by the Protestant Council of Churches in New York City, which is the local affiliate of the National Council of Churches, which in turn is the affiliate of the World Council of Churches. The notorious liberal, Henry P. Van Dusen, president of Union Theological Seminary, was a member of the sponsoring committee. Other liberals, such as Robert T. McCraken, successor to Harry Emerson Fosdick, were seated on the platform and even led in prayer. When the meeting was over, the "converts" were scattered in every direction. Over 300 cards were given to Norman Vincent Peale's apostate Marble Collegiate "Church." A book could be written on this crusade alone!

Dr. Bob, Sr., could see that Billy was beginning to "look to the lights," writing:

I personally think that it was at this point the devil took Billy up on a high mountain and showed him the kingdom of this world, and how popular he would be. Whether it was the height that made him dizzy, the excitement of what the world had to offer, or the thought that he could win great numbers to the Lord, I believe that at this point Billy sold out true evangelism; and instead of doing the good he might have done, he set in motion the wheels that would harm generations to come.[74]

When Billy was approached by various fundamental leaders, he turned a deaf ear to their appeals. However, before he was able to conduct his next ecumenical fiasco, the 1958 Cow Palace Crusade in San Francisco, the Lord sent Billy a special messenger of his own. In the spirit of Balaam and his donkey, the San Francisco *News* for October 21, 1957, ran the following UPI dispatch:

Evangelist Billy Graham was to be taken to the hospital today after a painful battle with a "big, mean tremendous old ram" that was guarding his two ewes. Saturday afternoon Graham entered the sheep pen on his mountain farm to pick an apple off a tree in the pen. He intended to give the apple to the ram. Instead, the ram butted Graham from behind, knocking him down a 50-foot incline, and then butted him twice more. Graham picked up an ax and fended the ram off until he could scramble over a fence. Graham, suffering an injured knee and cuts and scratches, lay in bed all day yesterday lamenting the fact, "I kept turning the other cheek to that old ram."[75]

Unfortunately, Billy shook it off and proceeded, over the next 35 years, to embarrass the Church of Jesus Christ in one disaster after another. His 1978 crusade in Las Vegas was a classic. In his better days, Graham had enough sense to declare:

There is something alluring about getting something for nothing. I realize that. And that is where the **sin** lies. Gambling of any kind amounts to "theft" by permission.[76]

When a Las Vegas television interviewer asked Graham point blank, "Is gambling sinful?" the chameleon evangelist completely avoided the issue and replied, "Almost everything we do is gambling, but the greatest gamble of all is when we gamble our souls in our relationship with God."[77]

Behind the pulpit, Graham told his listeners exactly what they wanted to hear: "I did not come to Las Vegas to condemn Las Vegas. We came to preach the good news that God wants to love you."[78]

Billy's buddy, Johnny Cash, appeared on the program nightly. One evening he related how a blackjack dealer declined to get saved because he didn't think he could "live it" with the job that he had. Johnny reflected, "You know, that might be trying to do God's thinking for Him, 'cause I believe the Lord would love to have a Christian blackjack dealer in this town."[79]

The bottom line was that *everybody* loved Billy because he wouldn't condemn their sin. In 1976 he defended fellow "Baptist" Jimmy Carter's admission that he enjoyed an occasional highball. In 1972 he laughed it up between Johnny Carson and Ed McMahon on the "Tonight Show." In 1983 he appeared on George Burns' "80th Anniversary in Show Business Special" to help "roast" the Hell-bound star of the Hollywood movie, *Oh, God.*

By the way, with reference to that last statement about George Burns being headed for Hell, another reason Billy is appreciated so much is because he doesn't believe in the same kind of Hell that Jesus did. (Luke 16:24) To keep those cards and letters coming in, Billy told *Time* magazine on November 15, 1993, what he had often stated before:

> The only thing I could say for sure is that hell means separation from God. We are separated from his light, from his fellowship. That is going to be hell. **When it comes to a literal fire, I don't preach it because I'm not sure about it.** When the Scripture uses fire concerning hell, that is possibly an illustration of how terrible it's going to be—not fire but something worse, a thirst for God that cannot be quenched.[80]

Now you know why Billy Graham has been listed in Gallup's "Ten Most Admired Men in the World" poll for over 33 consecutive years (more than any other person). Furthermore, on May 2, 1996, President Bill Clinton bestowed upon Billy the coveted Congressional Gold Medal, the highest honor a civilian can receive. Dr. Bob Jones, Sr., used to say that a man will always be promoted in proportion to the degree that he is able to be controlled. (Have you ever heard Billy Graham attacked by the press?)

Those who would defend Billy Graham, especially with respect to his ecumenical crusades, frequently attempt to draw parallels to the ministries of great evangelists of yesteryear. One such endeavor was *Cooperative Evangelism* by Robert O. Ferm, Th.D., subtitled *Is Billy Graham Right or Wrong?*

Along with other old-time revivalists, D. L. Moody and Billy Sunday were cast as prototypes of Graham's watered-down, Laodicean ministry. Among several perceived similarities, Moody was cited for having outfoxed the local parish priest into calling off the Irish gangs that were harassing his Sunday school work[81] and for avoiding an open denunciation of Catholicism when holding his Dublin crusade in a city that was over 85% Roman Catholic.[82]

When dealing with Billy Sunday, the author draws a lot of conclusions on hearsay and secondhand reports: "At the close of the New York campaign he is *reported* to have said."; "Here it is quite *evident* that Billy Sunday accepted the cooperation of liberals."; "Members of the committee were *evidently* not entirely without reproach."; and, *"Evidently* he continued to throw all responsibility upon the local churches without making any discrimination between their denominational affiliations."[83] With respect to Billy Sunday's New York crusade, Ferm boldly asserts that a number of decision cards (only 5% of the crusade total), "were sent to the Roman Catholic Church...Hebrew synagogues...and...to Christian Science Churches."[84] The author provided *zero* documentation for this charge.

While space does not permit a response to everything Ferm has alleged (and whoever said Moody, Sunday and the others had flawless ministries in the first place?), the following seven *dissimilarities* between Billy Graham and the "old-school" evangelists are worthy of note.

1. Not one of the revivalists selected by Dr. Ferm was a member of a local New Testament church. While Moody was a Congregationalist and Sunday a Presbyterian, Billy Graham *started out* as a Baptist. Graham had more light than his predecessors. *"For unto whomsoever much is given, of him shall be much required."* (Luke 12:48b)

2. Similarly while Sunday was a high school dropout and Moody failed to finish grade school, Graham attended three different Bible colleges and sat at the feet of Bob Jones, Sr. Who taught Moody and Sunday about scriptural separation? (Acts 4:20; 18:25; 19:2; Galatians 6:6; and II Timothy 2:2)

3. To whatever degree Ferm's six Protestant evangelists may have been guilty of ecumenical compromise, their shortcomings were certainly the exception while Graham's have been the rule.

4. When Edwards, Wesley, Whitefield, Finney, Moody and Sunday conducted revival meetings, the communities were never the same again. Need I say more? (I Kings 18:24)

5. While Graham's predecessors exalted the King James Version, Billy has endorsed nearly everything from the Revised Standard Version to the Living Bible. "The Living Bible communicates the message of Christ to our generation."[85]

6. Billy Graham has openly and consistently courted the favor of Rome. While Moody didn't attack the Pope in his Dublin crusade, he didn't praise the scoundrel either. Even Ferm (citing J. Wilbur Chapman) acknowledged, "Indeed, so deep was the encroachment of the revival upon the Roman Catholic population, that Cardinal Cullen felt himself called upon to interdict the attendance of his flock upon the Protestant meeting."[86] When a Catholic priest asked John Wesley where *his* religion was *before* the Reformation, the no-nonsense Methodist replied, "In the same place your face was before you washed it—*behind the dirt.*"

7. Finally, the ministry of Billy Graham has been earmarked by compromise throughout. Was Billy Sunday's "Booze Sermon" compatible with Graham's defense of Jimmy Carter's highballs? Did Edwards and Graham believe in the same *kind* of Hell? Would John Wesley have advocated born-again blackjack dealers? Can you visualize Johnny Carson and Ed McMahon looking into the eyes of Charles G. Finney? Do you suppose Whitefield would have sung the praises of George Burns? *Give me a break!*

Ferm called Billy's meetings "a series of great crusades unprecedented in the annals of Christian evangelism."[87] In another place he said, "The revival of mass evangelism is one of the most encouraging and challenging signs of our times" and "It is a day of great crusades, of daring planning, and of abundant reaping."[88] The readers will note that these idealistic assessments were made in 1958. Another Baptist evangelist by the name of

Lester Roloff rightly surmised the results of Graham's "abundant reaping" by describing latter-day America as "an insane asylum run by the inmates."

About this time a sincere but misguided Christian will invariably ask, "What about all those souls that were saved under Billy's preaching?" Dr. Bob, Sr., would often give the following analogy:

> Suppose I have a beautiful garden, and you are a fruit gatherer, and you tell me that you will gather my fruit. I go away on a trip. You gather the fruit and pile it in the corner. It looks good. But when I go out into my orchard, I find that my trees are ruined. The limbs are broken, there is damaged bark on the trunks, and the roots are damaged and exposed. My trees begin to die, and there is no more fruit. That is the harm that Billy is doing future evangelism.[89]

The greatest harm Evangelist Dr. Billy Graham has done to the vineyard of Jesus Christ has been his open embracing of Roman Catholicism on multiple occasions. Billy could never say enough good things about the "Vicar of Hell." In 1980, he described Pope John Paul II as the "Builder of Bridges" (also the title of the biography of Dr. Bob Jones, Sr., published 11 years earlier) and "the greatest religious leader of the modern world, and one of the greatest moral and spiritual leaders of this century."[90]

Likewise the Hell-bound Roman hierarchy was only too glad to return the compliments. With reference to Billy's approaching area crusade, Boston's Richard Cardinal Cushing said that it would "surely be of great importance for many Christians in the Greater Boston area" so as to "lead many to the knowledge of Our Lord."[91] (Who does he think he's kidding?) The hypocrite also assured his flock that Graham's message **"is one of Christ crucified, and no Catholic can do anything but become a better Catholic from hearing him...I'm one hundred percent for Dr. Graham."**[92]

Billy surely didn't have any problems with the Cardinal's summation that his crusades made Catholics *more* Catholic. In the January, 1978, issue of *McCall's* magazine, the one-time Baptist evangelist remarked, **"I've found that my beliefs are essentially the same as those of orthodox Roman Catholics."**[93]

In 1977 Billy and "the team" were found "taking care of business" on the campus of Notre Dame University! Do you suppose Luther, Hus or Tyndale would have received similar invitations?

However, for the worst sellout of all, we must return to the prophet's own country. (John 4:44) On November 21, 1967, Baptist Billy Graham was awarded an honorary degree of Doctor of Humane Letters (D.H.L.) by the Roman Catholic Belmont Abbey College in Belmont, North Carolina. Beside himself with excitement, Billy noted the significance of the occasion—**"a time when Protestants and Catholics could meet together and greet each other as brothers, whereas 10 years ago they could not."**[94] The proud honoree also joked, "I'm not sure but what this could start me being called 'Father Graham.' "[95]

Billy's final assurance that his Catholic listeners had nothing to worry about was: **"The gospel that built this school and the gospel that brings me here tonight is still the way to salvation."**[96]

What a performance!! What a guy!! America's favorite "reverend"!! In 1990, Dr. Graham may have received his most coveted honor of all—the privilege of becoming the 1,000th celebrity to receive a star on the Hollywood Walk of Fame. A reporter noted that he was "the first of his profession to be so honored!" Were John the Baptist alive today, they'd put him *in* the cement!

> *"Woe unto you, when all men*
> *shall speak well of you!"*
> (Luke 6:26a)

XX

Cold War Years

> *"But evil men and seducers shall wax worse and worse,*
> *deceiving, and being deceived."* (II Timothy 3:13)

ISTORIANS HAVE REFERRED to the post-Yalta era of tense, atomic-age diplomacy as the Cold War years. The collective, salient policies employed throughout this period have moved the United States ever closer to a crescendo of globalistic enslavement.

As evidenced in the previous chapter, the gradual surrender of America's sovereignty has been in direct proportion to a commensurate apostasy within the Body of Christ. (II Thessalonians 2:3) Enamored by a myriad of materialistic temptations (Revelation 3:17), the Laodicean Christian is oblivious to those First Amendment prerequisites pioneered by his Philadelphia forefathers—*"Thou hast a little strength, and hast kept my word, and hast not denied my name."* (Revelation 3:8c) Pleasure has replaced persecution, revision has undermined the Word and ecumenical evangelism has denied the Name. Once again, "religion begat prosperity, and the daughter devoured the mother."

Although a current pro-Israel policy may account for certain technological "blessings," our national moral demise is reflective of a terribly backslidden church. When several football stars were discovered to be among the 90 West Point cadets expelled in 1951 for cheating, the army coach remarked, "God help this country if we don't play football."[1] (II Timothy 3:4)

Another army man by the name of Douglas MacArthur had a different perspective:

History fails to record a single precedent in which nations subject to moral decay have not passed into political and economic decline. There has been either a spiritual awakening to overcome the moral lapse, or a progressive deterioration leading to ultimate national disaster.[2]

With the passage of the infamous Civil Rights Act of 1964, the door of American liberty was closed and *bolted*, the old-time religion exchanged for a New World Order!

VATICAN-WASHINGTON ALLIANCE
1945–1958

A casual student of history would identify the United States and the Soviet Union as the principal antagonists of the Cold War era. Although this would be *militarily* correct, British historian Avro Manhattan reminds us of the ultimate international aggressor:

> The Vatican is a superpower. On a par with the USA and Soviet Russia. Indeed, since at times it can act as a formulator of the policies of both, it can be reckoned as the paramount superpower of our times.
>
> Its adherents, a massive portion of mankind, nearing a billion, can be made to operate in every corner of the world. Sixty million within the USA herself.
>
> This is done via religion. Since the religious credence of individuals cannot be assessed in times of political, economic and military parlance, the Vatican's might, appears unreal and insubstantial. Behind its intangibility, however, its power is real, tangible and concrete.
>
> For its potential hostility or support can benefit, neutralize, or damage the world strategies of both the Soviet Union or of the USA. Indeed it can destabilize the political and military balance of both. This is so, since the Vatican has a world strategy, world objectives and world interests inter-twining with those of its two rivals. And since its global operations can either harmonize or can oppose those of the USA and or Russia, it follows that more often than not, it is convenient for them to coordinate theirs with those of the Vatican.
>
> When seen in this light, therefore, the Vatican is a superpower in its own right. Indeed, because of its duality as a political and as a religious centre [sic], it can outbid the other two... Thus, whereas, the USA has a mere 250 million citizens and the Soviet Union about 300 million, the

Vatican, via the Catholic Church, can influence, between 800 and 1000 million Catholics.

These, unlike the citizens of the other two superpowers, who are strictly confined within physical and political barriers, have no frontiers whatsoever. They are posted within the USA, Soviet Russia, and within hundreds of other countries, and can be made to operate, independently of their own administrations, governments or regimes.[3]

Therefore, to properly interpret international affairs between 1945 and 1990, one must recognize how the Papacy has chosen to interact with the American and Soviet governments. In his acclaimed volume, *The Vatican Moscow Washington Alliance*, Manhattan illuminates this triad of diplomatic machination:

As the White House in Washington is the symbol of the U.S., and the Kremlin in Moscow of the Soviet Union, so the Vatican in Rome is that of the Catholic Church. While the first is identified with the economic dynamism of the West, and the second with the revolutionary dogmas of Marxism, the third is the political facet of a religion claiming to be the only repository of truth. Because of that, the Vatican will side with one or the other, or indeed with anybody else, as long as it can further its own influence.

The pattern has been one of historical consistency. Early in this century, for instance, it sided with the Empires of Monarchical Europe; after World War I, it sustained the Fascist Dictatorships; following World War II, it fanned the Cold War by supporting the U.S. against Soviet Russia; after the Viet Nam War, it sided with Soviet Russia against the U.S. In the eighties it has struck another working partnership with the U.S.[4]

Following the collapse of Nazi Germany, "His Holiness" Pius XII harnessed the services of influential American Roman Catholics to continue the Vatican's ideological offensive against the Soviet Union. In light of Stalin's increasing atrocities, an anti-Soviet, Vatican-Washington Alliance served as a mutually beneficial propaganda ploy. However, whereas the "Holy Father" was committed to Russia's complete annihilation (and subsequent forced religious conversion) the CFR-dominated State Department was never inclined to go that far. Rather than "bomb the commies," Round Table elitists preferred to exploit the situation by protracting and sublimating "Red Scare" sentiment as a means of fostering their own globalistic agenda.

TRUMAN
1945–1952

The alliance got off to a positive start in 1947 with the lucrative European Recovery Program (ERP), better known as the Marshall Plan (named after President Truman's secretary of state, General George C. Marshall). Originally promoted as a humanitarian undertaking, the massive foreign aid package ("funny money giveaway") gained needed grass roots momentum when its purported anti-Communist merits were promulgated. The eventual cost to the American taxpayer for this CFR bailout of Catholic Europe was a staggering $43 billion. Professor Hans Sennholtz described it as a "windfall for socialism."[5]

The next Council project was the establishment in 1949 of the North Atlantic Treaty Organization (NATO). After Winston Churchill delivered a speech at Fulton, Missouri, in 1946, many American citizens became alarmed at his imagery of a sinister "Iron Curtain." Few, however, remember the solution which he proposed—a "fraternal association of English-speaking peoples."[6] Although promoted as an anti-Communist coalition, NATO was in reality just another step toward a coming New World Order. Shortly after America's entry into NATO was ratified by the United States Senate, CFR member Elmo Roper (future treasurer for the Atlantic Union Committee) wrote in a pamphlet entitled "The Goal Is Government of All the World,"

> But the Atlantic Pact (NATO) need not be our last effort toward greater unity. It can be converted into one more sound and important step working toward world peace. It can be one of the most positive moves in the direction of One World.[7]

James Perloff relates how the Council's use of anti-Communist rhetoric was geared to dismantle American sovereignty. (Remember the Fabian turtle?):

> Within the North Atlantic context, both the Marshall Plan and NATO may be understood as facets of the attempt to use the threat of Soviet Communism to push America and Europe into a binding alliance, as a halfway house on the road to world order. The Marshall Plan created the economic footing for this alliance, while NATO represented the military component.[8]

FATIMIZATION

While the U.S. State Department *appeared* committed to an aggressive, anti-Soviet contrivance, the "Holy See" decided to facilitate matters by employing a public relations scam of its own. Pius believed that a third world war was necessary to reclaim backslidden Russia for Catholicism. In order to prepare several million Catholics for their impending crusade, the pontiff resuscitated a papal con game that had proved beneficial in World War II. Pius would remind his superstitious parishioners that the Virgin Mary herself had assured the church of Russia's ultimate conversion.

The charade began back in 1917 (the year of the Bolshevik Revolution) when "Our Lady" suddenly "appeared" to three illiterate children in the desolate locale of Fatima, Portugal. To validate her apparition, the Jesuit priest H.S. DeCaires (authorized by the archbishop of Dublin in 1946), assured the faithful that

> The sun became pale, three times it turned speedily on itself, like a Catherine wheel... At the end of these convulsive revolutions it seemed to jump out of its orbit and come forward towards the people on a zig-zag course, stopped, and returned again to its normal position.[9]

Manhattan sardonically notes, "The fact that the other two thousand million human beings the world over never noticed the sun agitate, rotate and jump out of its orbit did not bother the Catholic Church in the least."[10]

Mary's "message" to little Lucia (later to be "Sister Lucia") and her companions was intended for the Pope to bring about "the consecration of the World to her Immaculate Heart" to be followed by "the consecration of Russia." The Virgin guaranteed in no uncertain terms, "The Holy Father will consecrate [Catholicize] Russia to me."[11]

When the word got out, pilgrims by the millions began converging on Fatima (six million by 1928). In 1925, "Our Lady" was good enough to bring baby Jesus along to say a few words. Dave Hunt cites the blasphemous account in *Lucia Speaks: The Message of Fatima According to the Exact Words of Sister Lucia:*

> On the 10th of December, 1925, the Most Holy Virgin Mary appeared to Lucia, with the **Child** Jesus by Her side, elevated on a cloud of light. Our Lady rested one hand on Lucia's shoulder, while in the other hand She held a heart surrounded with sharp thorns. At the same time the **Child** Jesus spoke: "Have pity on the Heart of your Most Holy Mother. It is

covered with thorns with which ungrateful men pierce it at every moment, and there is no one to remove them with an act of reparation."[12]

In 1938, on the eve of World War II, a papal nuncio was dispatched to Fatima where a throng of 500,000 Mary-worshipers heard an updated version of the original appearance. Apparently Lucia had forgotten about a separate set of three secrets which Mary had given her specifically for Pius. Thereupon, in June of 1938, she revealed the contents of two of the great secrets. The first was a vision of Hell, and the second was a reiteration that Soviet Russia would be converted to Roman Catholicism. The third was sealed in an envelope and put into the custody of an ecclesiastical authority not to be revealed until 1960. I can still remember hearing a Catholic nun inform our second-grade class that Pius had "trembled with fear and almost fainted with horror"[13] when he read the final message. (We never *did* hear what it said.) By way of a personal testimony to the lingering power of Mariolatry, I can also recall, as a 21-year-old adult, having made a special "pilgrimage" to my childhood parish church for the sole purpose of lighting a candle (with a 25¢ donation in the box) before a statue of Mary to entreat her favor for a promotion I was seeking while employed with British Airways.

Whether Sister Lucia was in on the hustle or got conned herself by a seducing spirit posing as Mary, the ploy brought about the intended results. As the war got under way, thousands of duped Catholics, including many from America, joined the Nazi armies and went directly to the "Russian front." For some strange reason, Mary never showed up to explain why her Catholic champion, Adolph, fell short at consecrating Russia to her heart.

By 1945, it was time to give the Fatima fraud another go. On this attempt, the Pope would pull out all the stops. An American priest sculpted a life-size statue of the Immaculate Heart of Mary based upon the detailed instructions of Sister Lucia. In 1946, the graven image (Exodus 20:4) was crowned before more than a million devotees. The crown, weighing 1,200 grams of gold, had 313 pearls, 1,250 precious stones and 1,400 diamonds. Pius was extremely emotional and assured the crowd that the Lord's promises would be fulfilled.

> "Be ready!" he warned. "There can be no neutrals. Never step back. Line up as crusaders!"[14]

What happened next is almost too hard to believe. Confirming that truth is certainly stranger than fiction, the statue of Mary was subsequently dispatched on a global "goodwill" pilgrimage to stir up religious fervor against the Soviet Union. Rome's dumb idol was officially received by the foreign governments of 53 nations in Europe, Asia, Africa, the Americas and Australia. In 1950, the "Madonna Tour" came to an end in Moscow where "Our Lady," accompanied by her papal escort, "Father" Arthur Brassard, was formally greeted by Admiral Kirk, the American ambassador. After a minimum of small talk, Mary was solemnly placed in the church of the foreign diplomats for an obvious, subliminal message: "To wait for the imminent liberation of Soviet Russia."[15]

By this time the frightful American-Russian atomic race was well under way. A growing lobby of bellicose Roman Catholics, both secular and sacred, continued to fuel the national hysteria. On August 6, 1949, Catholic Attorney General MacGrath addressed the national Knights of Columbus (Vatican SS) convention in Portland, Oregon, where he urged his fellow knights to "rise up and put on the armor of the church militant in the battle to save Christianity"[16]—"Christianity" of course meaning the Catholic Church. "Father" Walsh, Jesuit vice president of Georgetown University (Carroll Quigley, Bill Clinton, etc.), assured the nation that "President Truman would be morally justified to take defensive measures proportionate to the danger"[17] which, of course, meant the use of the atom bomb.

During this period, "His Holiness" was holding talks with a variety of prominent international leaders of the non-Communist world. America was no exception. To cite but one example, Manhattan notes that during a single day in June, 1949, Pius received *five* United States generals in successive audiences: General Mark Clark, wartime commander of the U.S. Fifth Army in Italy and subsequent field officer in the Korean conflict; Lieutenant General J. Cannon, commanding general of the U.S. Air Force in Europe; Major General Robert Douglas, chief of staff of the U.S. Armed Forces in Europe; Major General Maxwell Taylor, Deputy Commander, European Command; and Lieutenant General Geoffrey Keyes, commanding general of the U.S. forces in Austria.[18]

However, as the plot began to thicken, Pius discerned that the American State Department (CFR) was not fully committed to a Russian invasion. Even the Round Table elitists were smart enough to appreciate the potential devastation of nuclear weapons. To have a new world order, you have to have a world. As Allan King, Jr., wrote in *Foreign Affairs* in 1957:

> Moreover, we must be prepared to fight limited actions ourselves... And *we must be prepared to lose limited actions...* Armed conflict can be

limited only if aimed at limited objectives and fought with limited means. If we or our enemy relax the limits on either objectives or means, survival *will* be at stake, whether the issue is worth it or not.[19]

This was nothing new; popes had been "bucked" in the past. As the "woman" (Vatican whore) is seen to ride the "beast" (antichrist's Revived Roman Empire) at the start of the tribulation period (Revelation 17:3) only later to be thrown and burned by the same (Revelation 17:16), a number of influential Catholics decided to "mount" the system.

James Forrestal, Truman's secretary of defense, was one of the most tragic, highly placed victims of the Cold War. At times it can be difficult knowing whether the anti-establishment position of high-profile American Catholics is generated by legitimate patriotism or Vatican manipulation. (A failure to make this distinction is the primary shortfall of the otherwise conservative *John Birch Society* which employs numerous Roman Catholics.) The Catholic Forrestal stunned many Round Table insiders with the extent of his anti-Communist, crusading bravado, stating:

> Consistency has never been a mark of stupidity. If the diplomats who have mishandled our relations with Russia were merely stupid, they would occasionally make a mistake in our favor.[20]

President Truman fired his outspoken secretary in March, 1944. However, Forrestal remained a paranoid dupe of the Vatican. On one occasion, upon hearing a civilian aircraft overhead, he dashed along a Washington street shouting, "The Russians have invaded us."[21] Apparently, Forrestal's *real* enemies were Stateside. Perloff relates:

> Forrestal then planned to buy the *New York Sun* and convert it into an anti-Communist citadel—an undertaking sure to mean steamy revelations about Washington. He never had the chance. Five days after his dismissal, he was taken to Bethesda Naval Hospital (for "fatigue"), where he was heavily drugged and held incommunicado for seven weeks. All visitors except immediate family were denied. Forrestal's diaries—undoubtedly explosive—were meanwhile confiscated by the White House.
>
> His priest, Monsignor Maurice Sheehy, finally prevailed upon Navy Secretary John Sullivan to authorize his release. On May 22, 1949, Forrestal was scheduled for discharge. But at 2 AM that morning, he *fell* from a window near his sixteenth-floor room. *His bathrobe cord was found knotted around his neck.* The death was declared suicide. Forrestal's brother Henry called it murder. The tragedy, subsequent cover-up, and

contradictions in the "suicide" verdict were canvassed by Cornel Simpson in his 1966 book *The Death of James Forrestal.*[22]

The following month, Francis Matthews, a fanatical Roman Catholic, was appointed secretary of the navy. On the morning he took the oath of office, Matthews, his wife and their six children attended Mass and received Holy Communion ("ate Jesus") in the chapel of the naval station in Washington, D.C.[23]

KOREAN WAR
1950–1953

On June 25, 1950, the world heard the distressing news that an army from North Korea had suddenly burst into South Korea and apparently was destroying everything before it. Korea had been divided across the middle, along latitude 38° north, prior to the end of World War II—the northern part to be occupied by Russia and the southern part by the United States.

While America's born-again believers were busy singing, "Take Me Out to the Ball Game," the "woman" and the "beast" were fighting over the world. "His Holiness" struck the first blow through Navy Secretary Matthews. Truman's latest Cabinet appointee was not your average Roman Catholic. Francis Matthews was the Supreme Knight of the Knights of Columbus, chairman of the National Catholic Community Service and the Pope's privy chamberlain.

On August 25, 1950, Secretary Matthews shocked the international community with a speech he delivered in Boston calling upon the United States to *launch an attack upon Soviet Russia.* The move, he said, would make the American people **"the first aggressors for peace."** Manhattan relates:

> In case his advocacy had been misunderstood, or had not been taken in all seriousness, Mr. Matthews elaborated his idea with an explanation that made his meaning unmistakable: "To have peace," he said, "we should be willing to pay any price—even the price of instituting a war... They would brand our program as imperialist aggression...we could accept that...with complacency, for in the implementation of a strong affirmative peace-seeking policy, though it cast us in a character *new to a true democracy—the initiator of a war of aggression*—would win for us

a proud and popular title—we would become *the first aggressor for peace.*"[24]

The speech created an immediate global sensation. There were hurried denials. President Truman authorized the State Department to censure Matthews' jingoism with the following brusque response: "The U.S. does not favour instituting a war of any kind."[25] Dr. Philip Jessup, American ambassador-at-large and leading State Department adviser, bluntly declared, "Dropping atomic bombs on the Soviet Union now is not the way we act. It is not the way America does things."[26]

However, Pius was determined to keep the pressure on. George Craig, of the Catholic-dominated American Legion, publicly asserted that the United States should start World War III "on our own terms."[27] Catholic theologians were quick to assuage any premeditated guilt. "The use of the atom bomb is not forbidden,"[28] declared "Father" Francis Connell, C.S.S.R. Professor of *Moral* Theology at the Catholic University of Washington. "Father" Walsh added, "Neither reason nor theology nor morals require men or nations to commit suicide by requiring that we must await the first blow from a power with no moral inhibitions."[29]

Three months after Secretary Matthews' controversial remarks, the Pope dropped his *own* bomb by announcing to the world (through Cardinal Tedeschini's October disclosure at Fatima) that he, too, had received a surprise visit by "Our Lady." In his address to one million Fatima cultists, the Cardinal declared with emotion that

> another person has seen this same miracle...He saw it outside Fatima...Yes, he saw it years later. He saw it at Rome. The pope, the same our Pontiff, Pius XII...yet he saw it.[30]

Cardinal "Teddy" then gave the all-important particulars:

> On the afternoon of October 30th, 1950, at 4 p.m....the Holy Father turned his gaze from the Vatican gardens to the sun, and there...was renewed for his eyes the prodigy of the Valley of Fatima.[31]

The Pope's official testimony was then read to the gasping pilgrims:

> Pope Pius XII was able to witness the life of the sun (author's reminder: a huge burning sphere 866,000 miles in diameter)....under the hand of Mary. The sun was agitated, all convulsed, transformed into a

picture of life...in a spectacle of celestial movements...in transmission of
mute but eloquent messages to the Vicar of Christ.[32]

As to the "inspiration" behind the vision, Manhattan refers elsewhere to
"the immense amount of drugs that had sustained him [Pope Pius XII] for
years, possibly the real cause of many hallucinations, promptly accounted as
'miracles' by his admirers."[33] (i.e., too many "zig-zag papers" led to a *zig-
zag* in the sun, etc.)

Be that as it may, the Catholic press turned the latest papal con job into
renewed credibility. Only one week after the Pope's shocking disclosure, the
American people heard an even more unsettling pronouncement:

> Nomination sent to the Senate on October 20, 1951: General Mark W.
> Clark, Army of the United States, to be Ambassador Extraordinary and
> Plenipotentiary of the United States of America to the State of Vatican
> City.[34]

Not only would the Catholic Clark command the American forces in
Korea, but he would also be the nation's official ambassador to Rome—a
relationship expressly forbidden by the United States Constitution. (Notice
how the door continues to close a little more all the time?)

In the face of a Protestant backlash, Francis Cardinal Spellman of New
York, the leading Roman Catholic in America, issued the following
statement:

> I am pleased at the action of President Truman in appointing an
> Ambassador to the Holy See. Certainly the United States and the Holy See
> have identical objectives of peace and it is most logical therefore that there
> should be a practical exchange of viewpoints in the search for this peace
> so devoutly desired by all peoples and especially "little peoples."
>
> I am also very pleased that President Truman has appointed to this
> post a distinguished, able and patriotic American as is General Mark
> Wayne Clark whose contributions to our country both as a military and
> civic leader have been outstanding.[35]

As if to add insult to injury, Cardinal Spellman would later be made
Vicar General of all United States armed forces, frequently referring to
American GI's as "Soldiers of Christ."[36]

The final Vatican scheme to induce an attack against Soviet Russia
concerned a rather bizarre edition of *Collier's* magazine (also in October,
1951) which specifically predicted an American invasion for 1952. (Do you

recall the significance of *that* year?) Over 4 million copies of this special issue, numbering 130 pages, flooded the bookstalls of America and Europe alike.[37]

By now the main entrance at the Vatican was a revolving door of military powers. Manhattan writes:

> Simultaneously with all these sinister events, a gloomy world press reported that the head of all the American and European armed forces, General Eisenhower, had arrived in the Holy City, preceded and followed by the Foreign, economic and war ministers of twelve European nations, meeting in Rome to organize the "anti-Russian military front." General Eisenhower informed the war ministers of the twelve nations that they had met to rearm the West as fast as possible, because of the imminence of a new Dark Age and of a "new barbaric invasion," the very words used by Pope Pius XII.
>
> Their task? The prompt organization of an American-led European Army of forty fully-armed fighting divisions by 1952 and of one hundred by 1953, the very same dates when *Collier's* special issue had so confidently predicted the invasion and occupation of Russia would take place.
>
> General Omar Bradley, Chairman of the U.S. Joint Chiefs of Staff, meanwhile was received in audience by Pius XII (end of November, 1951) followed shortly afterwards (December 6, 1951) by Field Marshall Lord Montgomery, Deputy Supreme Commander of Allied Forces in Europe.
>
> Sundry Army, Navy and Air Force saturation-bombing experts from Spain, France, England and, above all, the U.S., continued to be granted audiences by His Holiness, Pius XII. To read the official lists of war leaders visiting him at this period is like reading a list of war leaders going to be briefed at a global super-Pentagon.[38]

The "heat" in Truman's "kitchen" was approaching downright uncomfortable, the President writing on December 9, 1951:

> There are a few misguided people who want war to straighten out the present world situation... We had conference after conference on the jittery situation facing the country. I have worked for peace for five years and six months, and it looks like World War III is near.[39]

However, despite these many desperate attempts by the "Vicar of Christ" to incite a third world war, the "golden rule" of the Round Table ultimately prevailed (whoever has the *gold* makes the *rules*). From a New World Order perspective, much more could be gained over the long haul (Fabian turtle) if a distinct Communist threat were sustained.

The unscrupulous military policies employed during the Korean War would set the pace for the remainder of the century. For the first time in our nation's history, American GI's fought under a UN flag (even though they supplied 90% of the manpower). The fact that the Constitution had restricted declarations of war to Congress was nullified by the recently ratified UN charter.

Another oddity of the "conflict" was that Russia could have used her superpower veto to restrict America's military intervention, but did not. Why would the Soviets pass up a legitimate opportunity to protect their surrogate operation in Korea? Perloff writes, "This raises the possibility that their 'blunder' was intentional."[40]

No less strange than the Russian conduct was the State Department's prosecution of the war. American soldiers were expected to fight according to unprecedented restrictions and guidelines (i.e., no more "all's fair in love and war," etc.). Among the many foreboding fiascos, the hindering of General Douglas MacArthur was unlike anything in America's military history. To halt the advance of the Chinese Communists across the Yalu, MacArthur had ordered the river's bridges bombed. Within hours, his order was countermanded by General Marshall. Perloff cites MacArthur's response:

> I realized for the first time that I had actually been denied the use of my full military power to safeguard the lives of my soldiers and the safety of my army. To me, it clearly foreshadowed a future tragic situation in Korea, and left me with a sense of inexpressible shock.[41]

American pilots were forbidden to hit supply targets beyond the Yalu or pursue Chinese MIG's when they retreated beyond the border. General Lin Piao, commander of the Chinese forces, later acknowledged:

> I never would have made the attack and risked my men and my military reputation if I had not been assured that Washington would restrain General MacArthur from taking adequate retaliatory measures against my lines of supply and communication.[42]

Concerning the evils of "bureaucratic containment," even General Clark testified that it was "beyond my comprehension that we would countenance a situation in which Chinese soldiers killed American youth in organized, formal warfare and yet we would fail to use all the power at our command to protect those Americans."[43]

In April, 1951, President Truman fired General MacArthur for the "crime" of being one of the few men with enough guts to protest the horror of "limited war." Perloff notes that within 48 hours, 125,000 telegrams were sent to the White House in protest of the firing. MacArthur returned home to the greatest ticker tape parade in United States history.

The sinister role played by the CFR in Korea can be illustrated by the words of Council member Adlai Stevenson in the lead article for the April, 1952, edition of *Foreign Affairs*:

> The burden of my argument, then, based on the meaning of our experience in Korea as I see it, is that we have made historic progress toward the establishment of a viable system of collective security.[44]

EISENHOWER
1952–1960

Dwight D. Eisenhower was elected the nation's thirty-third president in 1952 on the campaign slogan, "I like Ike." Ike certainly didn't like the American people though, as his cumulative spending deficits were nearly *five* times greater than Harry Truman's.[45] Ike was a CFR member and so were the key men of his administration. (Remember that the covert activities of the *Cold War* era were precipitated by the carnal Christianity of a *lukewarm* church. [Revelation 3:16])

That Eisenhower had some pretty good connections may be surmised by his rapid rise to power. For instance, in 1941, Ike was a tenderfoot lieutenant colonel who had never seen a day of battle in his life; two years later, he was a four-star general and supreme commander of Allied forces in Western Europe! After the war, he returned home to become United States chief of staff. Despite his lack of academic credentials, he was made president of Columbia University. Eisenhower biographer Stephen Ambrose unravels the mystery: "The elite of the Eastern Establishment moved in on him almost before he occupied his new office."[46] After joining the CFR and working on the editorial board of *Foreign Affairs*, Ike was appointed supreme commander of NATO in 1950. Two years later, he was president of the United States of America.

It was during the early years of the Eisenhower Administration that a new league of international conspirators was formed. Because the first meeting that brought American and European globalists together was held in 1954 in the Bilderberg Hotel in Oosterbeek, Holland, the meetings have come to be known as *Bilderberg* Meetings (the groundwork being started in 1952.[47]) In his work, *The Bilderbergers Unmasked*, Dr. Joe Boyd writes:

> The Bilderbergers are a group of people from all over the world who attend international meetings to discuss and plan the course and progress of the one-world Marxist government. They include government leaders, rich bankers, scholars, businessmen, military leaders, publishers, intellectuals, and other outstanding figures of many walks of life. They are definitely leftist and are of the Socialist-Communist ilk.[48]

Bilderberg meetings are held once a year in various countries and are 100% secretive. The American press is barred and invited participants are not even allowed to bring a tape recorder to the conference. According to Dr. Boyd's research, past Bilderberger attendees have included: David and Nelson Rockefeller, **Edmund de Rothschild**, Henry Kissinger, William F. Buckley, Robert S. McNamara, Zbigniew Brzezinski, George W. Ball, Gerald Ford, Frank Church, J. William Fulbright and **Notre Dame president, Reverend Theodore M. Hesburgh, who is also a member of the CFR**.

Dr. Boyd provides the Round Table connection:

> How much influence does the conspiratorial CFR (Council on Foreign Relations) have in the Bilderberg organization? **More people attend from the Council on Foreign Relations than from any other place or organization in the world.** In one meeting, "of the nineteen listed American representatives, twelve were members of the Council on Foreign Relations. The Bilderbergers are dominated by the CFR." (Liberty Lobby, p. 43.)[49]

With the death of Joseph Stalin in 1953, the Vatican's anti-Soviet crusade became seriously undermined. "Uncle Joe" had been the consummate "boogie man," while Nikita Khrushchev was perceived as the antithesis of the deceased tyrant.

At this critical juncture, the Pope's hope fell on an American Catholic by the name of Joseph R. McCarthy. Like Secretary Forrestal, McCarthy not only hated Communists, but uncooperative Council adherents as well. In his *New York Times* article on the CFR, Anthony Lukas wrote:

> Though his nominal targets were Communists in Government, by the fifties few Communists retained important positions, and as McCarthy bulled ahead it became clear that his real target was the Eastern Establishment, which had run the nation's foreign policy for decades...
>
> McCarthy never explicitly attacked the Council (as he did the closely allied Institute of Pacific Relations). But many of those he denounced were or had been Council members: Frederick Vanderbilt Field, Alger Hiss, Lauchlin Currie, Owen Lattimore, Philip Jessup, Charles Bohlen and Dean Acheson.[50]

According to Ike's biographer, Stephen Ambrose, the President "was determined to destroy McCarthy."[51] Predictably, Cardinal Spellman was one of the Senator's most credible defenders, stating in a press conference, August 3, 1953:

> There are three things I will say about Senator McCarthy. He was a Marine, and having been with the Marines myself, the fact that a man was a Marine places him very high in my book as regards patriotism. He is against Communism and he has done and is doing something about it. He is making America aware of the danger of Communism. He has been elected Senator from his native State, and no one is known better than by his neighbors. I am willing to accept the verdict of the citizens of Wisconsin concerning Senator McCarthy.[52]

Perhaps the strongest evidence that a generation of materialistic Christians had turned their country over to Satan can be seen by Eisenhower's appointment of siblings, John Foster Dulles as secretary of state and Alan Dulles as CIA director. As if to illustrate Jeremiah 16:18a, *"And first I will recompense their iniquity and their sin double; because they have defiled my land,"* both of these appointed *"higher powers"* (Romans 13:1) were loyal CFR members *and* fanatical Roman Catholics!!

The Dulles brothers were career Council participants. While John was a founding member who wrote articles in *Foreign Affairs* from the outset, Alan joined in 1926 and later became that body's president. In addition to being an in-law of the Rockefellers, John's elitist connections also included the chairmanship of the Rockefeller Foundation and the Carnegie Endowment for International Peace.

Their outspoken views on the merits of globalism were widespread and many. The CIA director forecasted:

> There is no indication that American public opinion, for example, would approve the establishment of a super state, or permit American membership in it. In other words, time—a long time—will be needed before world government is politically feasible... [T]his time element might seemingly be shortened so far as American opinion is concerned by an active propaganda campaign in this country.[53]

With reference to the UN's evolutionary role in world affairs, John Dulles wrote in his book, *War or Peace*:

> The United Nations represents not a *final* stage in the development of world order, but only a primitive stage. Therefore its primary task is to create the conditions which will make possible a more highly developed organization.[54]

In a controversial speech before the regional meeting of the American Bar Association at Louisville, Kentucky, in 1952, Secretary Dulles presented the CFR's anti-constitutional philosophy:

> Treaties make international law and also they make domestic law. Under our Constitution, treaties become the supreme law of the land. They are, indeed, more supreme than ordinary laws for congressional laws are invalid if they do not conform to the Constitution, **whereas treaty law can override the Constitution.** Treaties, for example, can take powers away from the Congress and give them to the President; they can take powers from the States and give them to the Federal Government or to some international body, and they can cut across the rights given the people by their constitutional Bill of Rights.[55]

Note how far America has drifted from the days of Thomas Jefferson, who warned:

> I say the same as to the opinion of those who consider the grant of the treaty-making power as boundless. If it is, then we have no Constitution.[56]

Exactly where the brothers' loyalty to Council directives ended and devotion to "Holy Mother" Church began is impossible to say with clarity. The point is that freedom-loving American people were the losers either way. (Thanks to Billy Graham Christianity.) In the final analysis, it would appear that the Vatican held a slight edge over the Catholic brothers. (Incidentally, John's son eventually became a Jesuit priest.)[57]

The United States secretary of state and CIA director conducted so much business at Cardinal Spellman's New York office that the prelate's residence became known as the "Little Vatican." The so-called Hungarian Revolution of 1956 (engineered by the CIA) was seen as a necessary first step for a land invasion of Soviet Russia. The Pope's handpicked dictator, Cardinal Joseph Mindszenty, was driven into Budapest escorted by three Hungarian tanks.[58] When a Russian "anti-Revolution" task force showed up and crushed the uprising with ease, "Reverend Joe" seemed to disappear into thin air. He was later discovered hiding in the American Legation facilities at Budapest. Protected by diplomatic immunity, the Catholic cardinal celebrated Mass at an altar bedecked with American flags.[59] His self-imposed exile on American "soil" lasted for over 12 years.

At the height of the Hungarian insurrection (1956), Secretary Dulles made a shocking disclosure to both the *London* and *New York Times*, which summarily reported: "Mr. Dulles admitted that the USA had on three occasions in the past eighteen months come closer to atomic war... than was imagined."[60] The *London Times* described the affair as "what almost amounts to a crusade of Christendom."[61]

The most outrageous foreign interference of all occurred only weeks before the 1960 American-Soviet summit meeting in Paris. With Ike and Nikita scheduled for tense, face-to-face peace talks (i.e., with "Russia's consecration to Mary's heart" about to be put on hold, etc.), a "CIA" spy plane suddenly came streaking across Russian air space out of nowhere. The U-2 was shot down and its pilot, Gary Powers, was captured and sentenced to ten years in prison for espionage.

Having been denied access to Disneyland was bad enough, but a spy plane buzzing around was more than the Russian premier could take. Khrushchev denounced the American "banditry" and reveled in his propaganda triumph. A. J. Liebling described the administration's posturing in the *New Yorker*. "After denying we did it, admitting we did it, denying Ike knew we did it, admitting Ike knew we did it, saying we had a right to do it and denying we were still doing it, we dropped the subject."[62] In his farewell address, Eisenhower wearily cautioned:

> We must guard against the acquisition of unwarranted influence... by the military-industrial complex. The potential for the disastrous rise of misplaced power exists and will persist.[63]

Thanks to the traitorous activities of the Catholic Dulles brothers, the Cold War would continue.

VATICAN-MOSCOW ALLIANCE
1958–1978

In the meantime in October, 1958, "His Holiness," Pius XII, had died and gone to Hell. (Luke 16:23) Predictably, the world press eulogized the old reprobate as the "Prince of Peace." Representatives from 54 countries attended his final requiem with the United States delegation being led by none other than Secretary of State Dulles. (John would join his friend the following year.)

The passing of Pius proved to be a diplomatic time bomb for the State Department (CFR) as the new pope, Eugenio *Maria* Giuseppe Giovanni Pacelli, and most recently, Cardinal Roncalli, otherwise known as John XXIII would be decidedly pro-Red throughout his five-year, caretaker pontificate.

A rabid socialist at heart, John was the outspoken antithesis of his crusading predecessor. As if to illustrate the sweep of coming reforms, his first official act as pope was to evict the German nun who had been Pius' personal "housekeeper" for 30 years.

As the "new" woman in the city of "seven mountains" (Revelation 17:9), John chose to dismount the bucking U.S.A.-CFR beast and team up with the old Russian bear for a while. (Ezekiel 38:2) (As the Soviet hierarchy remains beholden to the international bankers, as does the United States, the true interworkings of global relationships admittedly becomes increasingly complex as we approach the rapture. [*"But evil men and seducers shall wax worse and worse, deceiving, and being deceived."* (II Timothy 3:13)])

Although corrupted and controlled by the Eastern Establisment, the United States was still the world's predominant Christian nation. It was John's view that no self-respecting Catholic pope should be caught aligning the "Holy See" with a Bible-believing people. From 1958 onward, atheistic Russia was to be the preferred ideological bedfellow. (Luke 23:12)

Cardinal Spellman was the first American prelate to be informed that he would no longer be welcomed at the Vatican. This was a heavy blow to the U.S. State Department as Spellman had been the linchpin for the Washington-Vatican Alliance. The banished cardinal suffered a "political apoplexy" when John conversely rolled out the red carpet for Alexei Adzhubei, editor of *Izvestia* (the official organ of the Soviet Communist party), yet far more significantly, the son-in-law of Premier Nikita Khrushchev himself.[64] The times, they were a-changin'.

Pope John was so radical that even "Our Lady" got the pontifical boot! Under his sudden rapprochement with Soviet Russia, the fanatical Fatima Cult would have to hit the road. The gruff 77-year-old Pope simply informed the Portuguese hierarchy to drop at once *"La pulcinellada"* (Venetian slang for leg pulling or burlesque).[65] To this day, the Catholic world has yet to learn the content of Mary's third secret.

One of John's more practical moves was to lift the ban of excommunication imposed by Pius on Catholics who voted for Communist candidates. The tacit dogma was that Catholicism was now compatible with socialism and even Communism. Indeed, the *London Times* surmised the pontiff's actions as "ready to carry out an uninhibited approach...towards the Soviet Union."[66] Manhattan summarizes the new Vatican-Moscow Alliance:

> As a practical proof of the genuineness of his policies, Pope John declared again and again that his pontificate would be characterized by official tolerance towards Communism, in general, and by an increased acceptance of a "modus vivendi" with Soviet Russia in particular. This, not only with regard to ideological problems, but also when dealing with religious-historical ones, like that related to the renewal of the relationship between the Catholic and the Russian Orthodox churches.
>
> After having made that clear, to both the U.S.A. and Soviet Russia, then he added that from 1958, that is from his election, onwards, far from supporting any U.S.A. war schemes, he, Pope John, would sabotage all their operations, should such operations have been conducive to the outbreak of another world war. Soviet Russia and the U.S.A. knew that Pope John meant what he said, and readjusted their policies accordingly. The birth of the Vatican Moscow Alliance had become a milestone in the relations of the Vatican with Soviet Russia and her Commissars. Washington had been relegated second to no-one as a centre [sic] of mischief and the potential trigger of World War III.[67]

In addition to his political reforms, Pope John also called for the historic second Vatican Council, which met from October, 1962, through December, 1965. The story has been told how, during an interview, John had opened the window of his study, explaining that the purpose for Vatican II was to permit a new and refreshing wind to blow through the stuffy edifice of the

Church. Manhattan writes, "The chief purpose of the Council, he said, was to bring Roman Catholicism into tune with the times."[68] This "new and refreshing wind" was the beginning of the Ecumenical Movement.

KENNEDY
1960–1963

Two years after the Vatican-Moscow Alliance was forged, the American people committed the unpardonable sin of electing their first Roman Catholic president. The United States would pay a high price for this deplorable repudiation of its traditional Christian heritage.

John F. Kennedy was the son of a one-time bootlegger who made it to the top of his "profession" by producing a nation of pitiful whiskey orphans. Joe Kennedy's blood money fulfilled the vision of Archbishop Hughes that an Irish Catholic would one day sit in the White House.

The President's penchant for immorality has been exceeded only by the likes of Bill Clinton and Wilt Chamberlain. (His middle initial—"F"— could have stood for *fornicator*.) Kennedy's illicit affairs ran the gamut from Marilyn Monroe (whom he shared with little brother Bobby) to the girlfriend of Chicago mobster, Sam "Momo" Giancana. It is believed by many that Kennedy even had the CIA hire the "born-again" Giancana to whack "fellow believer" Fidel Castro. Handsome and charismatic, the youngest Chief Executive in history, John "F" Kennedy was the epitome of his "Rosie-Elvis-Billy"-era constituents.

America's first Catholic president appears to have been a more direct agent of Satan (John 13:27) rather than a total pawn of either the CFR or Cardinal Spellman. Contemporary authorities depict the maverick profligate as frequently resisting the "woman" and "beast" alike. While Manhattan writes, "Once president, however, he had been sufficiently astute not to succomb [sic] to the intrigues of the Catholic hierarchy,"[69] Perloff summarizes Kennedy as "A man with an independent streak, he was apparently never a true 'insider.' "[70] (It is believed, however, that Kennedy claimed to be a CFR member when he was in the Senate.[71])

Be that as it may, the Kennedy Administration was still overrun with the standard percentage of Council personnel. A short list would include: Dean Rusk, secretary of state; John McCone, CIA director; Douglas Dillon, secretary of the treasury; McGeorge Bundy, national secretary adviser; Walt Rostow, deputy national security adviser; Roswell Gilpatric, deputy secretary of defense; Paul Nitze, assistant secretary of defense; George Ball, under secretary of state; Henry Fowler, under secretary of the treasury; Arthur Schlesinger, Jr., special assistant to the President; Jerome Wiesner, special assistant to the President; Averell Harriman, assistant secretary of state for Far Eastern affairs; Angier Duke, chief of protocol; and John McCloy, chief of U.S. Disarmament Administration.

Harvard professor John Kenneth Galbraith stated, "Those of us who had worked for the Kennedy election were tolerated in the government for that reason and had a say, but foreign policy was still with the Council on Foreign Relations people."[72]

Notwithstanding the macho image Kennedy gained from the Cuban missile crisis (occasioned in the first place by the Bay of Pigs fiasco and only eventually brought to an end by the rarely publicized, concessive dismantling of United States warheads in England, Italy and Turkey), the President's brief administration did much to erode American liberties.

In 1961, Kennedy presented his plan for national disarmament to the United Nations; it was entitled *Freedom from War: The United States Program for General and Complete Disarmament in a Peaceful World.* Also known as Department of State Publication 7277, it called for a three-stage program for the *gradual* (Remember the turtle?) transfer of United States arms to the United Nations. During Stage II (the stage America is currently in) the document requires: "The U.N. Peace Force shall be established and progressively strengthened." Such will be accomplished "to the end that the United Nations can effectively in Stage III deter or suppress any threat or use of force in violation of the purposes and principles of the United Nations."[73] This insidious policy concludes, "In Stage III progressive controlled disarmament...would proceed to a point where no state would have the military power to challenge the progressively strengthened UN Peace Force."[74]

Freedom from War was superseded in April, 1962, by another pipe dream called *Blueprint for the Peace Race: Outline of Basic Provisions of a Treaty on General and Complete Disarmament in a Peaceful World.* Its third stage also called for the strengthening of the UN Peace Force "until it had sufficient armed forces and armaments so that no state could challenge it." (Kennedy would find out how peaceful the world *really* was on November 22, 1963.)

With reference to the perpetuation of these treasonous policies by subsequent administrations, Gary Allen wrote:

While the newspapers and TV have prattled endlessly about disarmament, nary a word has been said about the other side of the coin: all such proposals call for *arming* the United Nations! This apparently is the best-kept secret since the formula for Coca-Cola.[75]

And as if all this wasn't bad enough, under the UN charter, any United Nations "peace" force would be commanded by the under secretary-general for political and security council affairs. Would you believe that *fourteen of the fifteen secretaries who have held this position since 1946 have been citizens of the USSR?* (Dragoslav Protitch of Yugoslavia held the post from 1954–1957.)

On February 16, 1961, Kennedy signed ten radical executive orders giving the president of the United States complete dictatorial control over the lives of American citizens, to be used "in any time of increased international tension or economic or financial crisis." These directives, to be implemented through the Office of Emergency Planning are as follows: Executive Order 10995 confiscates all communications; 10997, electric power, petroleum, gas, fuel and minerals; 10998, food reserves and farms; 10999, means of transportation, control of highways and seaports; 11000, drafts all citizens into work forces under government supervision; 11001, health, welfare and educational functions; 11002, registration of citizens by postmaster general; 11003, control of airports; 11004, takes over housing and finance authorities, designates areas to be abandoned as "unsafe," establishes new location for populations, relocates communities, and builds new housing; and 11005, railroads, inland waterways and public storage facilities. Executive Order 11051 delegates all such crisis coordination to the Office of Emergency Planning within the jurisdiction of the White House.

Though such actions may appear wildly autocratic at first, the President was only exploiting a deplorable situation that began with Franklin Roosevelt. In March, 1933, FDR prevailed upon Congress to *suspend the Constitution* (a "temporary departure from that normal balance of public procedure") in order "to wage war against **the emergency**" (the "Great Depression"). Consequently, House Resolution 1491 was passed on March 9, 1933:

> *Be it enacted by the Senate and House of Representatives of the United States of America in Congress assembled,* That the Congress hereby declares that a serious emergency exists and that it is imperatively necessary speedily to put into effect remedies of uniform national application.[76]

As the perceived original state of emergency has *yet* to be rescinded, the Constitution of the United States has literally been adrift for over 60 years. President Kennedy wasn't the only scoundrel who knew how to "work the system." The foreword to Senate Report 93549, published in 1973, reads in part:

> Since March 9, 1933, the United States has been in a state of declared national emergency. In fact, there are now in effect four presidentially proclaimed states of national emergency: In addition to the national emergency declared by President Roosevelt in 1933, there are also the national emergency proclaimed by President Truman on December 16, 1950, during the Korean Conflict, and the states of national emergency declared by President Nixon on March 23, 1970, and August 15, 1971.
>
> These proclamations give force to 470 provisions of Federal law. These hundreds of statutes delegate to the President extraordinary powers, ordinarily exercised by the Congress, which affect the lives of American citizens in a host of all-encompassing manners. This vast range of powers, taken together, confer enough authority to rule the country without reference to normal constitutional processes.[77]

Kennedy's traitorous executive orders were eventually superseded by the ungodly *Federal Emergency Management Agency* (FEMA), between 1978 and 1979.

VIETNAM
1962–1973

America's decade-long "undeclared" war in Vietnam is a good illustration of our nation's rapid deterioration as a constitutional republic. Although the fighting would be greatly escalated under the Johnson and Nixon Administrations, President Kennedy did his part by sending the South Vietnamese military advisers, well-armed helicopters and other sophisticated weapons. The international bankers were back in business once again.

The Vietnam War represents yet another grave watershed in the history of America. No single event has generated more social transformation. Sadly, however, most of this transition has been ugly—a reflection of the war itself.

Like the "police action" in Korea (33,529 U.S. casualties), the war in Vietnam was fought according to "rules of engagement." American troops were not allowed to fire at the Vietcong unless fired upon. Vehicles more than 200 yards off the Ho Chi Minh Trail could not be bombed. North Vietnamese MIG's could not be attacked if spotted on a runway—only if airborne. Surface-to-air missile sites could not be bombed while under construction—only after they were operational.

When the nightmare of Vietnam was finally over, the patriotic spirit of America had been broken. Flag burnings, demonstrations and anarchy replaced motherhood and apple pie as the nation's cultural staples. Norman Rockwell's days were numbered. The devil was having a field day.

America's tragic involvement with the nation of South Vietnam began with John Foster Dulles and Francis Cardinal Spellman. Like most any international problem, the war in Indochina was precipitated by the "Holy See." After the Geneva Conference artificially divided Vietnam into North and South in 1954, the U.S. State Department (John Dulles, Catholic, CFR) and the CIA (Alan Dulles, Catholic, CFR) helped depose Emperor Bao Dai and installed a wild man by the name of Ngo Dinh Diem as Prime Minister. The new president promptly appointed his own brother, Ngo Dinh Nhu, chief of the Can Lao movement, the fearsome South Vietnamese Secret Police. Should we be surprised that the brothers *were fanatical Roman Catholics?*

Brother number three, Ngo Dinh Thuc, was the Catholic archbishop of the province of Thuathien. Yet another, Ngo Dinh Can, governed central Vietnam as a warlord from the town of Hue while the fifth brother, Ngo Dinh Luyen, ruled the province of the Cham minorities.

The obvious problem with this Vatican pentagram was that the population of South Vietnam was approximately 85% *Buddhist*—not *Catholic.*

One of the least understood causes for America's entry into the Vietnam War was the nationwide turmoil caused by a rabid Roman Catholic dictator attempting to forcefully convert 10 million Buddhists to "Our Lady." As a generation of shocked Americans discovered on the evening news, numbers of Buddhist monks would rather burn themselves alive than switch to Catholicism. Between 1955 and 1960, at least 24,000 "dissenters" were wounded, 80,000 executed or otherwise murdered and 275,000 detained or interrogated during Diem's religious reign of terror. Eventually about 500,000 Buddhists were sent to either concentration or detention camps.[78] Manhattan writes:

The Catholic state-machinery of suppression became so overpowering and ruthless that the U.S. had to protest, privately and officially, the barefaced religious character of Diem's Catholic policy.... It took tremendous personal courage to prepare oneself for death by fire in order to uphold one's own religious belief. The self-immolation of Buddhist monks and nuns helped to revive the religiosity of millions of Buddhists, who became determined to resist the unjust laws of the Diem government.[79]

President Diem and his brothers remained committed to their holy crusade. Buddhist temples were closed. The best jobs and political appointments were reserved for Catholics. Mobs of papists were continually set on Buddhist worshipers. Manhattan reports what Americans rarely ever heard on CBS, NBC or ABC:

In the case of President Diem, when he put Catholicism first, he alienated not only the vast majority of South Vietnamese masses, but even more dangerous the greatest bulk of the South Vietnamese army, who on the whole had supported him politically. It was this, the potential and factual endangering of the anti-communist front upon which Diem's policy had stood, that finally set into motion the U.S. military intervention, with all the disastrous results which were to follow.

Although Diem remained as the U.S. political protégé, by pursuing a policy inspired by his own personal religious zeal, and by disregarding certain diplomatic and political interests interconnected with the general military strategy of the U.S., he had endangered a whole policy in Southeast Asia. This became even more obvious, not only because of the exceptional restlessness which he provoked throughout the country, but above all, because his religious persecutions had seriously imperiled the effectiveness of the army.

It must be remembered that the vast majority of the South Vietnamese troops were made up of Buddhists. Many of these, upon seeing their religion persecuted, their monks arrested, their relatives in camps, had become despondent, and indeed, mutinous. There were increasing cases of absenteeism, desertions, and even rebellions. The overall result of this was not so much that the religious war was incapacitating the Diem's regime itself, but even worse, that the military calculations of the U.S. were being seriously imperiled.[80]

In retrospect, such a pulverizing of anti-Communist resistance by a Catholic-led administration would have been in keeping with the Vatican-Moscow Alliance. "His Holiness" Pope John XXIII was not about to lose any sleep over the forthcoming slaughter of American youth in the rice paddies of Vietnam.

When public opinion eventually forced President Kennedy to choose between supporting the interests of his church or promoting his own political career, Jack wisely chose the latter. Consequently, the first "born-again" Roman Catholic president of the United States put a contract on the first "born-again" Roman Catholic president of South Vietnam. On November 2, 1963, the CIA "whacked" Diem along with his sibling gestapo chief, Ngo Dinh Nhu.

Less than three weeks later, Kennedy got "hit" himself. (Matthew 26:52) Debate has raged for years as to who *really* pulled the trigger on that fateful morning in Dallas. Some contend that it was Castro's men, while others think it may have been Sam Giancana, as Attorney General Bobby Kennedy promptly dropped his Mafia investigations after John's untimely death.The majority, however, attribute his assassination to the CIA or other corrupt insiders. (Nineteen key witnesses to what *really* happened died under mysterious circumstances within *two* years.)

Of course, a Christian with a King James Bible will always have a discerning edge on the secular historian. My opinion is that the Lord God Almighty put his *own* contract on the fornicating Roman Catholic president. Remember the historical record—*three* attacks on the Word of God followed by *three* presidential assassinations? Do you suppose the June 17, 1963, Supreme Court decision to ban prayer and the Bible from America's public schools had anything to do with his death? *"And immediately the angel of the Lord smote him* [King Herod], *because he gave not God the glory."* (Acts 12:23a)

POPE PAUL VI
1963–1978

Five months before President Kennedy's assassination, Pope John XXIII went on to his own reward (Acts 1:25). The new "Vicar of Christ" was another pro-Communist Italian by the name of Giovanni Battista Montini who chose the stage name of Paul VI. For the next 15 years, Pope Paul would expand the Vatican-Moscow Alliance, much to the chagrin of American officials.

"His Holiness" hit the ground running with a number of pontifical "firsts": the first pope to set foot in the Holy Land; the first in history to visit

Australia and India; the first to go to North and South America; the first to visit the heart of Africa *and* the first to *address the United Nations*. From Jerusalem to Yankee Stadium, Paul VI showed an unprecedented commitment to ecumenical shuttle diplomacy.

However, the former Cardinal Montini bewildered his American flock by courting the Communists even more than his aged predecessor had. In his first encyclical, *Ecclesiam Suam*, issued in August, 1964, the pontiff, known as the "Velvet Steamroller," declared, "The Church should enter into a dialogue with the world" since "we do not despair that ideologies [communism] might one day be able to enter into a more positive dialogue with the Church."[81]

This protracted Vatican alliance with Soviet Russia reflected a perceived growth of Communism on one hand and the downsizing of American military capabilities on the other. Manhattan writes, "As the supreme headquarters of a global cold war, which was being lost on all fronts, the United States had become a liability the Church could not afford and an obstacle to the successful prosecution of the new Pontificate."[82]

In anticipation of an ultimate triumph by the Soviet Union, a theological hybrid emerged from the Vatican promoting the spiritual benefits of a "catholicised Communism." Known as *Liberation Theology*, "Christ the King" was subtly replaced by "Christ the *Worker*" and even "Christ the *Liberator*." Murals depicting Jesus Christ wearing coveralls became a common symbol in the world's Communist "parishes." Jesuit priests and Marxist guerillas started going "soul winning" together. Whenever the media would report that some devoted priest or nun had "fallen at their post of duty," the fact that they keeled over with an assault weapon in hand (not to mention half a dozen grenades as well) was conveniently dropped from the copy.

JOHNSON
1963–1968

When surveying the administration of Lyndon Baines Johnson, we see that the bottom truly dropped out of the little that was left of old-time America. JFK's "New Frontier" became LBJ's "Great Society." A new breed of "Americans" became programmed to live from one welfare check to the next.

The Vietnam imbroglio exploded in 1965 with thousands of American boys being sent to their deaths in another no-win undeclared war. During the fighting, Johnson met regularly with an inner circle advisory group that he personally nicknamed "the Wise Men." Twelve of these fourteen "wise guys" were CFR members.

To make matters worse, a "privileged" cartel of United States firms supplied the enemy with their weapons of destruction. Rockefeller got the ball moving by traveling to Moscow in 1964. On September 12th of that year, the *Chicago Tribune* reported:

> David Rockefeller, president of Chase Manhattan bank, briefed President Johnson today on his recent meeting with Premier Nikita S. Khrushchev of Russia. Rockefeller told Johnson that during the two-hour talk, the Red leader said the United States and the Soviet Union "should do more trade." Khrushchev, according to Rockefeller, said he would like to see the United States extend long-term credits to the Russians.[83]

Later, on October 7, 1966 (less than a year before the bloody Tet Offensive), LBJ stated:

> We intend to press for legislative authority to negotiate trade agreements which could extend most-favored-nation tariff treatment to European Communist states...We will reduce export controls on East-West trade with respect to hundreds of non-strategic items.[84]

Three weeks later, the *New York Times* reported on October 27: "The Soviet Union and its allies agreed at the conference of their leaders in Moscow last week to grant North Vietnam assistance in material and money amounting to about one billion dollars."[85]

In an earlier chapter, reference was made to the fact that approximately 150 Soviet weapons systems were manufactured with either U.S. technology, parts, financing or all three. Secretary of the Navy John Lehman told the May 25, 1983, graduating class at Annapolis:

> Within weeks, many of you will be looking across just hundreds of feet of water at some of the most modern technology ever invented in America. Unfortunately, it is on Soviet ships.[86]

Of the many illustrations of America's aid to her enemies that could be cited, the Soviet Union's Karma River truck factory is one of the most infamous. This mammoth facility, spread over 36 square miles along the Karma River, has an annual production output of 100,000 multi-axle 10-ton trucks, trailers and off-the-road vehicles. As late as the year 1987, it was considered to be the largest truck factory in the entire world. Unfortunately, the Karma River facility came into existence via the cooperation of several American manufacturers. A few of these companies exposed by Professor Anthony Sutton would include: Honeywell, Inc.; Swindell-Dresser, Co.; Glidden Machine & Tool, Inc.; Landis Manufacturing Co.; Warner & Swazey Co.; Ingersol Milling Machine Co.; Combustion Engineering, Inc.; National Engineering Company; Holcroft & Co.; and the Gulf and Western Industries, Inc.[87]

Author Gary Allen provides the treasonous inference to any and all Soviet aid provided during the Vietnam War:

> The Viet Cong and North Vietnamese received 85 percent of their war materials from Russia and the Soviet-bloc nations. Since their economies are incapable of supporting a war, the Communist arm of the conspiracy needed help from the Finance Capitalist arm. The United States financed and equipped both sides of the terrible Vietnamese war, killing nearly 55,000 of our own soldiers by proxy. Again, the mass media kept the American public from learning this shocking truth.[88]

While our elected officials were making sure that the enemy had plenty of bullets, they were also working overtime to weaken America's military might. *The Betrayers* co-authors, Phyllis Schlafly (a Roman Catholic) and Admiral Chester Ward, report that from 1961 through 1968, Secretary of Defense Robert McNamara (CFR) was guilty of the following:

> [McNamara] reduced our nuclear striking force by 50%, while the Soviets had increased theirs by 300%... caused the U.S. to lose its lead in nuclear delivery vehicles... scrapped ¾ of our multimegaton missiles... cut back the originally planned 2,000 Minutemen to 1,000... destroyed all our intermediate and medium-range missiles... cancelled our 24-megaton bomb... scrapped 1,455 of 2,710 bombers left over from the Eisenhower Administration... disarmed 600 of the remaining bombers of their strategic nuclear weapons... [McNamara has] frozen the number of Polaris subs at 41, refusing to build any more missile-firing submarines... refused to allow development of any new weapons systems except the TFX (F-111)... [and] cancelled the Skybolt, Pluto, Dynasoar and Orian missile systems.[89]

REPORT FROM IRON MOUNTAIN
1963–1966

As a New World Order disciple, McNamara envisioned an age when war would be no more, as political interdependence and global disarmament would theoretically eliminate potential belligerents. However, a peaceful world without the Prince of Peace is a misnomer. (Remember November 22, 1963?) McNamara was aware that the masses are more easily managed under war-time conditions or even under the threat of war. When citizens fear invasion and conquest, they will always endure the bureaucratic infringements of their own governments. Furthermore, war can be used to stimulate passion and patriotism.

Therefore, if society would be stabilized in the coming millennium, a substitute for war would have to be discovered in order to maintain this passive submission. To find such a solution, the Department of Defense, under Secretary McNamara, commissioned the prestigious Hudson Institute in 1963 to produce a think-tank study on the problem. The Hudson Institute, situated at the base of Iron Mountain in Croton-on-Hudson, New York, was founded and directed by Herman Kahn, formerly of the Rand Corporation and a CFR member. Kahn's eggheads were agreed that what they were looking for would have to: "(1) be economically wasteful, (2) represent a credible threat of great magnitude, and (3) provide a logical excuse for compulsory service to the government."[90]

The controversial *Report from Iron Mountain* was subsequently released in 1966. After considering a number of psychological diversions, from alien invasions to "blood games" (intensified sports violence—i.e., "Ultimate Fighting Challenge," etc.), the Hudson Institute decided on the issue of *environmentalism.* Griffin writes:

> The final candidate for a useful global threat was pollution of the environment. This was viewed as the most likely to succeed because it could be related to observable conditions such as smog and water pollution—in other words, it would be based partly on fact and, therefore, be credible. Also, predictions could be made showing end-of-earth scenarios just as horrible as atomic warfare. Accuracy in these predictions would not be important. Their purpose would be to frighten, not to inform.... The masses would more willingly accept a falling standard of living, tax increases, and bureaucratic intervention in their lives as simply "the price we must pay to save Mother Earth."[91]

When a copy of the *Report from Iron Mountain* was leaked to the press, the government claimed it was a hoax. Dr. John Kenneth Galbraith, well-known historian and professor at Harvard, vouched for its authenticity and testified that he was originally invited to participate in the study. Galbraith wrote:

> As I would put my personal repute behind the authenticity of this document, so would I testify to the validity of its conclusions. My reservations relate only to the wisdom of releasing it to an obviously unconditioned public.[92]

An official excerpt from the controversial Iron Mountain report reads as follows:

> When it comes to postulating a credible substitute for war...the "alternate enemy" must imply a more immediate, tangible, and directly felt threat of destruction. It must justify the need for taking and paying a "blood price" in wide areas of human concern. In this respect, the possible substitute enemies noted earlier would be insufficient. One exception might be the environmental-pollution model, if the danger to society it posed was genuinely imminent....
>
> It may be, for instance, that gross pollution of the environment can eventually replace the possibility of mass destruction by nuclear weapons as the principal apparent threat to the survival of the species. Poisoning of the air, and of the principal sources of food and water supply, is already well advanced, and at first glance would seem promising in this respect; it constitutes a threat that can be dealt with only through social organization and political power...
>
> However unlikely some of the possible alternative enemies we have mentioned may seem, we must emphasize that one *must* be found of credible quality and magnitude, if a transition of peace is ever to come about without social disintegration. It is more probable, in our judgment, that such a threat will have to be invented.[93]

Now you know where "Save the Whales" originated. This is why Vice President Gore wrote a comic book entitled *Earth in the Balance*. Since the publication of this report in 1966, other fear tactics have been concocted such as overpopulation, drug abuse and crime waves.

The *Club of Rome* is yet another clique of international conspirators who annually release end-of-the-world scenarios based on predictions of famine and overpopulation. Comprised of such personalities as Sol Linowitz,

Harland Cleveland, Clairborne Pell and former president Jimmy Carter, the Club recommends birth control and euthanasia as part of their apocalyptic panacea.

CIVIL RIGHTS ACT
1964

As previously mentioned, America's most costly repudiation of Almighty God occurred on June 17, 1963, when the United States Supreme Court declared that the Bible and prayer were no longer welcome in the nation's public schools. (Luke 8:36) After all, the Christians themselves had shown little respect for the precious Word of God. "Funny Bibles" continued to roll off the press: New World Translation (1961); the Amplified Bible (1965); Jerusalem Bible (1966); New Scofield Reference Bible (1967); New English Bible (1970); New American Standard Bible (1971); The Living Bible (1971); Cotton Patch Version (1973); Good News Bible (1976); New International Version (1978); Reader's Digest Bible (1982); New King James Version (1982); International Children's Bible (1986); Easy-to-Read Version (1986); New Revised Standard Version (1989); the 21st Century King James Version (1991); and another 65 perversions—just since 1960.

With the expulsion of Jesus Christ under the Kennedy Administration, the door of American liberty was finally closed—*never to open again!* Two months later, another fornicator by the name of Michael (Martin) Luther King, Jr., proclaimed, "I have a dream." King's dream became America's nightmare on June 24, 1964, with the passage of the infamous Civil Rights Act. **A self-righteous pharisaical crusade against racial injustice would now supersede the Gospel of the Lord Jesus Christ as the primary religious concern in America.**

Because 999 out of every 1,000 Americans (saved and lost alike) are addicted to television, and therefore rarely if ever do any serious reading, the myriad of evil ramifications from the Civil Rights Act are not even remotely perceived. Regarding this totalitarian Act, John C. Satterfield (past president of the American Bar Association) warned, "It will completely destroy democracy as outlined in the Constitution...it is uncontrolled federal executive power.[94]...Six members of the House Judiciary Committee signed that statement. The protest ended with the notation that the Civil Rights Act of 1964 is 'a blueprint for total regimentation.' "[95]

In essence, the Civil Rights Act was the devil's final assault on the historic Baptist distinctive of individual soul liberty. With one stroke of the pen, Americans lost their rights to free association, private clubs, free speech, and the right to protect their private property from deadbeats, perverts and criminals.

For instance, if you have a business which you purchased with your own hard-earned money, and some queer with an earring applies for a job, you cannot reject his application on the basis of his "sexual orientation." If you do, the filthy Sodomite can sue you. The same standard applies to an apartment you may choose to rent out. If, in your personal opinion (whether or not based on past experience), you decline to take a chance on an applicant of *any* particular color or ethnic background, you will also be fined and threatened with jail. The bottom line is that you've lost your God-given freedom to *discriminate* with your own investment capital. And, as a growing number of successful reverse discrimination suits (triggered by insane affirmative action rulings) has revealed, the Civil Rights Act is really only concerned with the perceived injustices perpetrated against African-Americans. Do you detect a racial bias in the name "National Association for the Advancement of *Colored* People"? Should the occasion arise, do you suppose the media would give equal time to the inception of a sister organization called the "National Association for the Advancement of *White* People"?

As they say, "The proof of the pudding is in the eating"; one need only examine what is left of the public schools and America in general to confirm what is wrong with the Civil Rights Acts of 1964. And yet, the very discussion of these "sensitive" **FACTS** is considered politically incorrect and borderline hate crime behavior. However, as *"the righteous are bold as a lion"* (Proverbs 28:1b), I make no apologies for declaring the truth. It is a matter of public record that, in every imaginable category, America's ultimate moral decline began with kicking the Bible *out* (1963) and bussing the minorities *in* (1971). According to David Barton in *America: To Pray? or Not to Pray?* the top public school problems *before* 1963 were listed as: (1) Talking, (2) Chewing gum, (3) Making noise, (4) Running in the halls, (5) Getting out of turn in line, (6) Wearing improper clothing and (7) Not putting paper in the wastebaskets. *Since* 1963, the leading offenses have been: (1) Rape, (2) Robbery, (3) Assault, (4) Burglary, (5) Arson, (6) Bombings, (7) Murder, (8) Suicide, (9) Absenteeism, (10) Vandalism, (11) Extortion, (12) Drug abuse, (13) Alcohol Abuse, (14) Gang Warfare,

(15) Pregnancies, (16) Abortions and (17) Venereal diseases.[96] (Now *that's* what I would call being insensitive!)

Try these statistics on for size. The birthrate for unwed mothers 15 to19 years of age in 1963 was about 15 births per 1,000 girls. In 1993, the figure was 44 per 1,000. Teenage pregnancy overall increased 400% since the Civil Rights Act. Each day, 2,756 teens become pregnant and 1,340 babies are born to teen mothers.[97]

The rate in 1963 for the sexually transmitted disease of gonorrhea was 14 cases per 100,000 population. In 1993, it was approximately 54 per 100,000. Over three million teens a year now become infected with one of the more than two dozen STDs.[98]

Only 3% of 15 year olds in 1963 engaged in premarital sex, while the rate for 1987 was 28% (an approximate increase of 1,000%). Sexually active eighteen year olds went from 23% in 1963 to over 70% in 1987. Currently, 8,441 teenagers become sexually active each and every day.[99]

Rape arrests for ages 13 to 18 were listed as slightly over 240 per 100,000 in 1965. In 1992, the figure was pushing 360. Aggravated assault arrests for ages 13 to18 in 1965 were 550 per 100,000, while in 1992 they were 2,300 per 100,000. Murder arrests went from 35 per 100,000 in 1965 to approximately 140 per 100,000 in 1992.[100]

With America's youth "on the ropes," the so-called "British Invasion" brought the Beatles, Rolling Stones, Herman's Hermits and other foreign perverts to our groaning shores. An insignificant item appearing in a 1960 edition of the *New York Times* puts things in their proper *spiritual* perspective: "The Fulton Street prayer meetings, held during the noon hour for the past 103 years, have been shut down."[101]

Following the Civil Rights Act of 1964, America "evolved" into a jungle society. *The Columbia Chronicles* (Lois and Alan Gordon) document the fruit ("cultural highlights") of Billy Graham's ecumenical revivals: America's first topless and bottomless go-go girls in San Francisco, 276 million gallons of alcohol consumed, and the debut of the Hell's Angels (1964); miniskirts, "Flower Power," "Soul Music," the Grateful Dead opening in San Francisco, and 4,000 arrested with 35 deaths in Watts rioting (1965); "Black Power," strobe lights, psychedelic posters, Jimmy Hendrix, "Flower Children," LSD, Ouija boards and Tarot cards (1966); coed college dorms, and America's first rock festival in Monterrey, California (1967); *Hair* and 100 black riots in America's major cities (1968); Ted Kennedy and Mary Jo Kopechne, Janis Joplin and Woodstock and *Penthouse* magazine (1969).

The 1970's begin with *Jesus Christ Superstar*, no-fault divorce in California, lesbian Billy Jean King earning $100,000 and April 22 proclaimed as Earth Day (1971); capital punishment ruled unconstitutional, and the Watergate break-in (1972); "Pet rocks," 50 rock stars earning 2 to 6 million dollars per year and *Roe v. Wade* (1973); girls entering Little League and 1,543 streakers expressing themselves at the University of Georgia (1974); satellite television, cable arrives and Rolling Stones tour grosses $13 million (1975); Patty Hearst busted for bank robbery (1976); Supreme Court rules spankings in public schools unconstitutional, and 400,000 teenage abortions (1977); 1,137,000 unmarried couples living together and gambling legalized in New Jersey (1978); 11 people crushed to death at a Who concert and divorce rate experiences a 69% increase over the previous decade (1979).

Rounding out the first 20 years following the "glorious" Civil Rights Act, we have: 1 million teenage pregnancies, 43 million Americans admitting to trying drugs at least once, Mark David Chapman shooting John Lennon, "Who Shot J.R.?" and the national divorce rate peaking at one in every two marriages (1980); Pacman, Dr. Ruth's sex-talk radio show, the first test-tube baby, MTV on 250 cable stations, and Elizabeth Taylor splits from husband number seven—Senator John Warner (1981); AIDS arrives, Jane Fonda's aerobic video and 4,000 Moonies married at Madison Square Garden (1982); Calvin Klein and Dial-a-Porn (1983); Jesse Jackson and Louis Farrahkan upset the Jews, male bunnies at Playboy Club, Vanessa Williams poses for *Playboy* and Mike Jackson's hair catches on fire during a Pepsi commercial (1984).

While all of this perversion was occurring, Americans were pre-occupying themselves with pleasure, primarily in the area of professional sports. (II Timothy 3:4) And, as Satan is no fool, some of the greatest legends of all times have been "born-again" Roman Catholics. In addition to the "Fighting Irish" of Notre Dame (Knute Rockne, Paul Hornung, Joe Montana, Terry Hanratty, John Lujack, etc.), other notable American icons have included: Rocky Marciano, Babe Ruth, Vince Lombardi, Joe DiMaggio, Yogi Berra, Roger Staubach, Carl Yastrzemski, Joe Namath, Tommy Lasorda, Joe Garagiola, Mario Andretti, Don Shula and hundreds of others.

Dr. Paul Lee Tan provides a conclusive picture of our present, decadent society:

> Illustrative of the change and decay in the world around us is the difference of emphasis between the first telegraph message sent by Samuel Morse and the first still picture transmitted by satellites. "The first telegraph message sent by Inventor Samuel Morse over a 40-mile line between Washington and Baltimore was 'What hath God wrought?' [In March] the first still picture ever transmitted via two satellites, Lani Bird II and Early Bird, was sent more than 7,000 miles between Honolulu and London." The picture? Swedish Crown Prince Carl Gustaf together with a coed in a bikini on the beach at Waikiki.[102]

NIXON
1968—1974

Richard M. Nixon (CFR) was elected president primarily as a reaction *against* Lyndon Johnson (CFR). Hubert Humphrey (CFR) had been LBJ's vice president. Like his presidential mentor of eight years, Nixon was another "My Fair Lady" CFR project. A small town lawyer in 1946, Nixon suddenly becomes the vice president of the United States of America only six years later.

After losing the presidential race to Kennedy, as well as a bid for the governorship of California, Nixon moved to New York for a Council sabbatical. Dick literally moved into the same apartment building owned by Nelson Rockefeller, who also lived there as well. (My father held a security position in this building at the same time and saw both men regularly.)

Richard Nixon put up his "For Sale" sign by writing an article in the October, 1967, *Foreign Affairs* entitled "Asia After Vietnam." Nixon wrote of the Asian disposition "to evolve regional approaches to development needs and to the evolution of a new world order."[103] (And most Christians thought George Bush originated this term.) Richard Nixon was in the White House the following year.

The "presidential payoff" was the appointment of more than 110 CFR members to important government positions. The most significant Council plant was Nixon's "choice" for national security adviser, Dr. Henry Kissinger. Perloff citing J. Robert Moskin:

It was principally because of his long association with the Rockefellers that Henry Kissinger became a force in the Council. The *New York Times* called him "the Council's most influential member," and a Council insider says that "his influence is indirect and enormous—much of it through his Rockefeller connection."[104]

The high point of the Nixon era was probably the Apollo XI mission in July, 1969. However, while Neil Armstrong was taking his "one small step for mankind," over half a million American GI's were wandering around in Vietnam. On April 30, 1970, Nixon escalated the fighting into neutral Cambodia. In conjunction with the fantasy—"Peace with honor,"— American boys were *still* being slaughtered when the Watergate scandal preempted Nixon's presidency.

It was during the Nixon years that yet another globalistic agency was born—the *Tri-Lateral Commission*. By the turn of the decade, David Rockefeller was convinced that the UN could not pull the world's nations together in one swoop. Therefore, it was decided to do so in stages through the *Tri*-Lateral Commission; the "Big 3" being North America, Western Europe and Japan. This newest "creature" was hatched July 23 and 24, 1972, at the Tarrytown, New York, estate of David Rockefeller. (The North American Free Trade Agreement [NAFTA] and the General Agreement on Tariffs and Trade [GATT] are two notable products of this stratagem.)

While the Vietnam and Watergate fiascos were highly visible, Nixon's underhanded policies concerning the nation's gold reserves were not as readily detected by the American public. At the end of World War II, Fort Knox contained the largest gold hoard in the history of the world. Total United States reserves exceeded 26,000 metric tons, or 701.8 million ounces—a staggering 69.9% of the world's supply. But today, the General Accounting Office admits that only 24 million ounces of pure gold—909 tons remain in the vaults of Fort Knox (less than 3.5% of United States holdings in 1949).[105] A steadily weakening dollar due to nonstop inflation led foreign governments to exchange their American dollars for gold. As the low price of $35 per ounce was artificially maintained by the Treasury Department, gold continued to move out of the country. And remember, Americans were not allowed to get in on the gold sales—only foreigners.

By 1971, the coffers were so low that "Tricky Dicky" shocked the world by declaring that America would no longer honor its promise to foreign holders of dollars to redeem those dollars in gold. By "closing the gold window" on August 15, 1971, President Nixon acknowledged to the international community that the United States Treasury was officially bankrupt. By 1991, the International Monetary Fund (IMF), the financial right arm of the United Nations, was the largest known holder of gold bullion—3,539 short tons (compared to only 1,017 United States and 754 Japan).[106]

For what it's worth, when Mrs. Louise Auchincloss Boyer, a grand-daughter of Colonel Edward House and executive assistant to Nelson Rockefeller, was about to implicate her employer for the missing gold at Fort Knox, she suddenly "fell" out of the window of her tenth-floor apartment at 530 East Eighty-sixth Street (my old neighborhood). Her death, like that of Secretary Forrestal, was ruled a probable *suicide*.[107]

FORD
1974–1976

A nonentity.

CARTER
1976–1980

A *greater* nonentity.

VATICAN-WASHINGTON ALLIANCE
1978–

Paul VI kicked the bucket on August 6, 1978. What happened next is *really* spooky. When the late Pope's followers' campaign for another pro-Russian pontiff became deadlocked with a faction in league with the CIA, the stalemate was broken with the election of a neutral candidate, Cardinal Luciani, patriarch of Venice. When Luciani was asked in Latin, "Do you accept your election as Supreme Pontiff which has been canonically carried out?" the astute "victim" astonished the officiating cardinals by replying, "May God forgive you for what you have done in my regard."[108] Thirty-three days later, Pope John Paul I (Luciani) died "mysteriously" in his sleep.

Actually, John Paul I was supposed to have checked out sooner. A couple of weeks earlier, the Russian Orthodox Metropolitan Nikodim, archbishop of Leningrad and Novograd, made an official visit to the Vatican.

When Nikodim was invited to join John Paul for some coffee, the unfortunate Metropolitan picked up the Pope's cup by mistake. One sip and he was "out of here." Manhattan writes, "He clutched his chest with both hands, emitting a choking grunt, then crashed on the floor, toppling backwards, with a thud."[109]

Conversely, John Paul I "passed away" in private. There was no autopsy. A team of embalmers showed up out of nowhere almost immediately after being summoned by Cardinal Villot at approximately 6:10 a.m.! The corpse was a mess—bulging eyes, distorted jaw, a horrendous grimace, etc. Finally, the pontiff's personal housekeeper, Sister Vincenza, the one who discovered the crime, vanished into thin air, never to be heard from again.[110]

During John Paul's "temporary reign," the CIA had intensified their lobbying efforts. This time, the KGB-backed coalition would lose. Accordingly, one of the shortest papal administrations in history was followed by an equally record-setting reelection process. On this occasion, it was the Polish Cardinal Karol Wojtyla who became Pope John Paul II on October 16, 1978.

Wojtyla's primary support had come from the American Cardinals Cody (Chicago), Cooke (New York) and Krol (Philadelphia). Now that their pro-U.S.A. candidate was the new "His Holiness," it was time to celebrate. After the Pope made his first balcony appearance to the faithful (as a layman, Wojtyla had been a professional actor), he approached Cardinal Villot and astounded several nearby cardinals by asking "whether the champagne was now available?"[111] Manhattan continues:

> Cardinal Villot, far from having been surprised at the unusualness of the request, there in the very heart of the Vatican, smiled, nodding with approbation, after which he made a discreet signal to somebody.
>
> Almost instantly nuns appeared, seemingly from nowhere [like John Paul I's embalmers], carrying trays with glasses and bottles of champagne on them. Most Cardinals stared at the nuns, and even more at the bottles, not knowing what to make of it. **The more so, since the nuns were carrying not one single bottle, but dozens of them.**
>
> Several frowned, others looked openly puzzled, not knowing what was happening. Bottles of champagne? What was the idea? Was it meant to be a champagne celebration for the papal election? There, in the very heart of the Vatican, in the presence of the new Pope? If so, who had given the order? Whose idea had it been?... How come that there had been brought so many champagne bottles? Who had ordered such great quantity?...

Many of them, after a while, in fact, had accepted their glasses, and had drunk. Some even toasted, led by Cody, Wysznski and Villot. Several, however, remained puzzled. **How had it been possible for anyone to have guessed that the new elected Pope was eventually to ask immediately, not for one bottle but for three crates of champagne?**

The question was of deep significance, since it implied the reality of a plotting conspiracy, which had more depth than at first anticipated...

Within a few minutes after the glasses had been emptied, they were filled again, by the eager giggling nuns. As the operation proceeded, it soon turned into a veritable champagne party. The new Pope, far from confining himself to offering one single glass, after having drunk his first one, himself took hold of a magnum of champagne and uncorked it, with the professional ease and efficiency of a waiter, filling the empty glasses of the nearest Cardinals. While doing so, he signalled others to do the same. The nuns looked in amazement, as did the most conservative Cardinals. Nobody had ever seen anything like it...

The new Pope continued to pour out more and more champagne to anyone with an open glass. At one moment, he filled that of Cardinal Krol, patting him on the back. "I must return to Philadelphia," he then told him, "so that you and I can sing together again." Krol drank, toasting the invitation. "Welcome, welcome, any time."

The words were heard by Cardinal Cooke, who, half jokingly asked Krol to sing. Krol asked, "Here? Now?" "Yes," said Cooke. "Here and now!" After drinking more champagne, Krol then began to sing, at first low keyed, then even louder. The chattering Cardinals listened, surprised, then became silent, not knowing what to make of it.

After a long pause, during which astonishment mixed with embarrassment, was sensed by all, several Cardinals joined in and sang with Krol, lifting their glasses as the new Pope continued to pour more champagne into the empty ones...

Porcine Cody became even more expansive, and asked Krol to sing a special called "The Mountaineer." "It is his Holiness' favourite,"... Krol started to sing again, this time in Polish. **The Cardinals applauded, while Krol looked questionably at the new Pope, who started once more to pour champagne into the glasses of the nuns themselves.**

"Sing it again," then he told Krol. "Sing it again and I will join you." Some of the Cardinals were delighted. Others seemed almost ready to join in with the two. Krol, after another drink, began to sing louder than before. The new Pope did the same, singing in tune with Krol in his baritone voice. After singing for a while in a kind of duet, finally the two lifted their glasses in a mutual toast....

Suddenly Krol, who perhaps had drunk more than was good for him, embraced the new Pope, with whom he started to babble at

machine gun speed in Polish, about something or other.... A spectacle to remember.[112]

REAGAN
1980—1988

The first target of the renewed Vatican-Washington Alliance was the Communist bloc in Eastern Europe. Enter Lech Walesa, *Solidarity* and the subsequent liberation of Poland. For his part in the transformation, the "Holy Father" took a "hit" from KGB Chief Yuri Andropov on May 13, 1981, but lived to tell about it.

As the attempted assassination had occurred on the anniversary of "Our Lady's" appearance at Fatima, May 13, 1917, Pope Paul attributed his deliverance to the Virgin's intercession. He later had a special message embroidered in Latin on the inside of his papal robes—*totus tuus sum Maria*—"Mary, I'm all yours."[113]

A year before the shooting, Ronald Reagan became the nation's thirty-ninth chief executive. While the western world reacted with euphoria at the sudden prospect of a real and lasting peace, one patriotic American wasn't buying it. Dr. Lawrence Patton McDonald, a United States Senator from Georgia as well as a medical surgeon, knew all too well what a generation of television addicts did not—that America had just as many enemies within as she had without. As chairman of the John Birch Society, Senator McDonald not only fought the Communists, but was Washington's most outspoken critic of trade and technology transer to the USSR. In the foreword to Gary Allen's book, *The Rockefeller File,* Congressman McDonald condemned "the drive of the Rockefellers and their allies to create a one world government, combining super-capitalism and communism under the same tent."[114] Apparently, someone felt that the good doctor knew too much. On September 1, 1983, the probing senator, along with 269 passengers and crew, on Korean Airlines Flight 007 en route from Alaska to Seoul, were blasted from the skies by a missile fired from a Soviet Interceptor. The Russian fighters had trailed the commercial airliner for two hours and could have fired only with top clearance from Moscow.

With JFK having set a new religious precedent, numerous Catholics were given prominent positions within the Reagan Administration, such as: Alexander Haig (CFR), secretary of state; Nicholas F. Brady (CFR) secretary of the treasury; William Casey (CFR), CIA director; Donald Regan (CFR), chief of staff; Robert McFarlane (CFR), Richard Allen, and Judge William Clark, national security advisers; Vernon Walters, ambassador-at-large; Jeane Kirkpatrick (CFR), United States ambassador to the UN; Raymond J. Donovan and Ann Dore McLaughlin, secretary of labor; William J. Bennett and Lauro F. Cavazos, secretary of education; Margaret M. Heckler, secretary of health and human services.

By this time there were also 12 Catholic governors and 129 Catholics in Congress. (This number grew to 141 in 1993, more than double the second-place United Methodist total of 65.) There were also thousands of additional Roman Catholics in the FBI, CIA, Pentagon and even the Supreme Court.

From a purely biblical perspective, the most significant action of President Reagan was his satanic rapprochement with the "Holy See." On December 14, 1981, Reagan picked up the White House telephone and conducted a ten-minute conversation with Pope John Paul II. Manhattan states: "The casualness of the direct talk between Pope and President revealed not only the operational intimacy of the two leaders, but exposed also the tip of a submerged political iceberg whose massiveness had not as yet been fully assessed by the U.S."[115]

"His Holiness" *granted* the American president a special audience in the Vatican Library (one-time home of *Codex Vaticanus*) on Monday, June 7, 1982. The two "former actors" talked in private for 50 minutes about the Polish situation. In a *Time* magazine article, February 24, 1992, entitled "The Holy Alliance," reporter Carl Bernstein quotes Reagan's first national security adviser, Richard Allen (Roman Catholic), as stating, "This was one of the great secret alliances of all time."[116] Bernstein continues:

> At their first meeting, Reagan and John Paul II discussed something else they had in common: both had survived assassination attempts only six weeks apart in 1981, and both believed God had saved them for a special mission. "A close friend of Ronald Reagan's told me the President said, 'Look how the evil forces were put in our way and how Providence intervened,' " says Pio Cardinal Laghi, the former apostolic delegate to Washington. According to National Security Adviser Clark, the Pope and Reagan referred to the "miraculous" fact that they had survived. Clark said the men shared "a unity of spiritual view and a unity of vision on the Soviet empire: that right or correctness would ultimately prevail in the divine plan."[117]

In the months and years ahead, the two governments (U.S.A. and "Holy See") developed a cozy relationship. "Anything that we knew that we thought the Pope would not be aware of, we certainly brought it to his attention," says Reagan. "Immediately." On one occasion, when United States Ambassador-at-Large Vernon Walters (Roman Catholic) questioned a particular stratagem, Archbishop Pio Laghi (apostolic delegate) related afterwards, "I told Vernon, 'Listen to the Holy Father. We have 2,000 years experience at this.' "[118]

Noting that Reagan's diplomatic team was comprised of devoted Roman Catholics, the *Time* correspondent added:

> They regarded the U.S.-Vatican relationship as a holy alliance: the moral force of the Pope and the teachings of their church combined with their fierce anticommunism and their notion of American democracy. Yet the mission would have been impossible without the full support of Reagan, who believed fervently in both the benefits and the practical applications of Washington's relationship with the Vatican. One of his earliest goals as President, Reagan says, was to recognize the Vatican as a state "and make them an ally."[119]

In April of 1984, Ronald Reagan (one-time darling of the Moral Majority) did that very thing by appointing a Roman Catholic proselyte, William S. Wilson, official United States Ambassador to the "Holy See." With the Vatican's reciprocity, the formal exchange of ambassadors revived an unholy alliance that had been dead for over a century. Manhattan concludes, "But the exchange was an equally important event in the Catholicization of the U.S. making the Catholic Church a special religious-diplomatic-political entity operating in the very heart of the U.S."[120]

The following month, Reagan and the Pope met again, this time on American turf. The historic linkage took pace in Alaska's Fairbanks International Airport, May 2, 1984, as the two leaders were coming and going—the President from China and John Paul to the Far East. (This was the Pope's second Alaskan visit, making him a "sourdough.") With Reagan at his side, the international gangster addressed a throng of well-wishers:

> It gives me great pleasure to visit Alaska once again, and from this northern state to send a greeting of special warmth and affection to all the citizens of the United States of America... Today I am here in person, to give you the assurance that I have not forgotten you. Even when I am

miles away, I hold the people of Alaska and those of the whole United States, close to my heart. I do not forget you, for we are linked together by bonds of friendship, of faith, and of love....

As I stated at the beginning of this year in my message for the world day of peace, if men and women hope to transform society, they must begin by changing their own hearts first. Only with a "new heart" can one rediscover clear-sightedness and impartiality with freedom of spirit, the sense of justice with respect to the rights of men, the sense of equality, **with global solidarity between the rich and the poor**, mutual trust and fraternal love...

May God grant you the strength to express this harmony in your own lives, in your relationship with others. May he give you the courage to share generously and selflessly the blessing that you yourselves have received in abundance.

God bless America![121]

After his spiel, the Pope and Reagan were escorted to an airport conference room where they discussed "global" hunger and disease for 30 minutes. Upon the President's return to Washington, White House spokesman Larry Speakes related that Reagan and the Pope were like two "old friends" during their meeting in Fairbanks.

In the process of time, the Cold War was ostensibly concluded. The Berlin Wall came tumbling down, and the USSR appeared to disintegrate before our very eyes. With the exception of a few "minor" obstacles (AIDS, dope, crime, famine, the ozone level, etc.), the Millennium is now supposed to be around the bend. Or *is* it?

While preaching in Fairbanks in 1993, I called the operations manager of the Fairbanks International Airport to request permission to visit the conference room where the meeting between Reagan and the Pope had been held. (The room is normally reserved for the Governor and his staff.)

A security guard escorted me to the site, unlocked the door, and waited outside while I wandered around the macabre sanctum, alone with my thoughts. Looking at Old Glory, I pondered how much longer she could possibly wave. When I exited the room, I couldn't help noticing the subliminal message in the title order attached to the plaque on the outside wall—"Pope & President Conference Room."

> *"And the woman which thou sawest is that great city,*
> *which reigneth over the kings of the earth."*
> (Revelation 17:18)

XXI

The Great Apostasy

> *"For that day shall not come, except there come a falling away first."* (II Thessalonians 2:3b)

THE CHILDREN OF Issachar were described in I Chronicles 12:32a as being *"men that had **understanding of the times**, to know what Israel ought to do."* Given the widespread deception that Jesus said would usher in the end times (Matthew 24:24), today's Christians are in dire need of Bible-based discernment. *"Beloved, believe not every spirit, but try the spirits whether they are of God: because many false prophets are gone out into the world."* (I John 4:1)

When the Christians at Thessalonica were deceived into believing they were already in the tribulation period, Paul assured them, *"That day shall not come, except there come a **falling away** first, and that man of sin be revealed, the son of perdition."* (II Thessalonians 2:3b) The expression "falling away" is a translation of the Greek word ἀποςταςια, from which we get our English word *apostasy*. The commonly accepted definition for *apostasia* is "defection from truth."

As the aged apostle was preparing "to be offered," he penned a closing outline for this approaching storm of unbelief.

> *I charge thee therefore before God, and the Lord Jesus Christ, who shall judge the quick and the dead at his appearing and his kingdom; Preach the word; be instant in season, out of season; reprove, rebuke, exhort with all longsuffering and doctrine. For the time will come when they will not endure sound doctrine; but after*

their own lusts shall they heap to themselves teachers, having itching ears; And they shall turn away their ears from the truth, and shall be turned unto fables But watch thou in all things, endure afflictions, do the work of an evangelist, make full proof of thy ministry. (II Timothy 4:1-5)

Paul's first charge to young Timothy was to *"preach the word."* Implied in this command is the all-important concept of "final authority." Timothy was instructed to *"preach **the** word,"* not "any number of reliable translations," etc. The reader will note further that Timothy was admonished to ***"preach** the word."* Teaching is *not* preaching. (I Timothy 4:11) Exegeting is *not* preaching. Sharing is *definitely* not preaching. *Preaching* is preaching! Someone has defined preaching as employing "the excited voice."

After challenging Timothy to maintain a consistent temperament—*"be instant in season, out of season"*— Paul reminded his *"son in the faith"* (I Timothy 1:2a) that he would have to get tough with unruly members. Obviously, Paul did not have a PMA (positive mental attitude), as his threefold directive was two-thirds *negative—"reprove, rebuke, exhort."* This ratio is identical to the formula given Jeremiah when he was confronting apostate Israel—*"to root out, and to pull down, and to destroy, and to throw down, to build and to plant."* (Jeremiah 1:10)

Although the *length* of the church age was not made known to Paul, the Holy Spirit did reveal the *carnal conditions* that would prevail at the end. Deceived by their own lusts, a generation of materialistic Christians, no longer willing to *"endure sound doctrine,"* would exchange *preachers* for *teachers*—turning *"their ears from the truth"* and being *"turned unto fables"* in the process. (Refer to the following chapter.)

This very scenario was foreshadowed in the truth of Matthew 6:24:

No man can serve two masters: for either he will hate the one, and love the other; or else he will hold to the one, and despise the other. Ye cannot serve God and mammon.

Here our Saviour categorically declares that no human can submit to God and money simultaneously. All men—whether saved or lost—must choose between the two. It is no coincidence that our present "Bible-of-the-Month Club" generation just happens to coincide with an unparalleled age of materialism. To put it another way, America's Bible selection increases with her standard of living. Appreciating the reason for this will explain the growing animosity toward the King James Bible.

As *"no man can serve two masters,"* the Christian who decides to sell out for mammon becomes incapable of submission to God. He who willfully succumbs to the cares of this world and the deceitfulness of riches could not submit to God if he wanted to.

Once the apostate "goes for the gold," his singular, face-saving profile becomes unmistakable: *"Having a form of godliness, but denying the power thereof."* (II Timothy 3:5a)

Because the "rich young rulers" of our day have become spiritually incapacitated, they will not embrace a Bible that lays exclusive claim to the English-speaking world. Instead they will take cover behind the assurances of Christian scholarship that one conscientious translation is as good as the next. They'll embrace *anything* but a dreaded submission to *one* Book.

When this concept of materialistic paralysis is comprehended, several other theological maladies are found to be related. For instance, consider the doctrine of the local church. Because of his aspiration to build "bigger barns," the end-day materialist will inevitably seek membership in the non-obligatory "invisible church." When he decides to visit around (having grown bored "fellowshipping" with "invisible" church members), he will be sure to avoid any church where the pastor is in charge, gravitating instead to an elder-board structure (i.e., no final authority in the pulpit).

Although his first-century ancestor could submit to *his* pastor's authoritative, *"Wherefore my sentence is..."* (Acts 15:19), today's temporal-minded religionist can only complain about "legalism." And, of course, the host of miscellaneous, non-denominational "Agape Chapels," "Family Centers," etc., will always be preferred to the restrictive and reproachful tag of *Independent Baptist.* (Hebrews 13:13)

With an outward demeanor projecting a mere *"form of godliness,"* lifestyle evangelism and Lordship salvation are right around the corner. After all, "if He's not Lord of all, then He's not Lord at all," etc. Carnal Christians wouldn't think of "confronting" a total stranger with the Gospel. (Acts 8:30)

And as materialistic Christians cannot submit to spiritual authority, they dead sure won't tolerate some "uncouth, leather-lunged *preacher* letting it rip" during the Sunday morning "worship hour." Who cares what the Bible says? *"Cry aloud, spare not, lift up thy voice like a trumpet, and shew my people their transgression, and the house of Jacob their sins."* (Isaiah 58:1)

Rather than embrace prophets proclaiming heavenly ultimatums (*"Thus saith the Lord,"* etc.), end-day worldlings have opted to *"heap to themselves teachers, having itching ears."* (II Timothy 4:3b) To accommodate this growing need for ministerial hirelings (John 10:13), a host of cultured, smooth-talking "Bible teachers" have reported for duty, specializing in "sermonettes for Christianettes who smoke cigarettes"—America's *pulpit* ministries being reduced to *puppet* ministries in the process.

Most of these "reverends" such as John MacArthur, Jr., "Chuck" Swindoll, James Kennedy, M. R. DeHaan II and others do not fly the *Baptist* standard. (Charles Stanley is a *Southern* Baptist.) Some, like Harold Camping ("Thank you for calling and sharing, and shall we take our next call, please"), are *way* out in left field. According to "Weird Harold," president of Family Stations, Inc., in Oakland, California, the Lord was supposed to have returned in 1994.

As a man's teeth will appear more yellow when his face is covered with shaving cream, one need only hear the fire-breathing radio sermons of Baptists Oliver B. Green ("save the soul nearest Hell") and Lester Roloff ("living by faith") to appreciate the consummate wimpiness of today's so-called "electronic shepherds." Neither man wasted five minutes "sharing" the word; they *preached* it! (In the "Greek," they "dumped the whole load.") The same could be said for Dr. Harold Sightler's Bright Spot Hour versus WMBI's namby-pamby "radio pastor," Donald Cole. Although Drs. Green, Roloff and Sightler are all with the Lord, they are *still* outpreaching today's exponents of "FM Christianity." (Revelation 14:13)

The way in which Satan uses these so-called "teaching ministries" ("havens of rest" for unsubmissive apostates) to beguile unsuspecting members of local New Testament churches is really quite ingenious. The confusion always begins when some naive Christian innocently tunes in to a broadcast and hears a "helpful lesson" on some relevant topic. Invariably the local pastor will be asked, "What could possibly be wrong with a ministry that feeds the sheep?"

Apart from the major doctrinal problems espoused by various non-denominational ministries concerning Lordship salvation, hyper-Calvinism, elder rule, modern Bible translations and even the blood of Jesus Christ (specifically, its *present* whereabouts), two very subtle snares are rarely, if ever, discerned by the rank-and-file members of local Baptist churches.

Any average radio "Bible study" may contain a measure of scriptural truth (though the trend is toward *psychoseduction*). Yet, because the devil is so slick, the ultimate problem is not with what the "radio pastor" *does* say, but with what he does *not* say! Realizing that his listeners (the folks who send in the cash) are no longer willing to *"endure sound doctrine,"* "Dr. Messemup" is not about to declare *"all the counsel of God."* (Acts 20:27)

How often do you hear a radio Bible study about the *"vengeance of eternal fire"* (Jude 7), the Vatican as the *"MOTHER OF HARLOTS"* (Revelation 17:5), the *"abomination"* of men wearing earrings or women wearing pants (Deuteronomy 22:5), the *"shame"* of a man wearing long hair or a woman wearing short hair (I Corinthians 11:5-7), the immodesty of mixed swimming (I Timothy 2:9), the loss of testimony in a mother working outside the home (Titus 2:5), credit-card mania (Romans 13:8), unrestrained "boob tube" viewing (Psalm 101:3) and a host of many other *"sound doctrines."* If holding to Bible-based standards makes me a legalist (despite the fact that *legalism* is a *works* salvation [Galatians 2:16]), then I will gladly bear this unscriptural term of reproach. And yet, the truth is that *everyone* has standards. What self-respecting pastor would let a *naked* person sit in his service? Some of us just have more *guts* than others.

A second point of deception concerns the teaching mode itself. The Bible clearly states that a pastor is to teach the Word. (I Timothy 4:11; 6:2) However, as in the case with what was *not* being taught, the problem isn't with teaching per se, but with a pastoral ministry that is *exclusively* given to teaching. Who could read the Bible and fail to see that a pastor is *also* told to *"command"* (I Timothy 4:11) and *"exhort."* (I Timothy 6:2) "Teaching" ministries are in vogue because "exegeting" and "fit throwing" ("th'o'in' a fit" in "Southern") don't mix in today's modern society. Again, who cares what the Bible says? According to *Strong's Concordance*, there are 178 Scripture verses where the words *teach, teacher, teachest, teacheth* or *teaching* are found. Similarly, there are another 153 references where the words *preach, preached, preachest, preacheth* or *preaching* are used. The two disciplines go together and cannot be divided.

BILL HYBELS

Now because the wages of lust is *more* lust (Proverbs 27:20), Laodicean religionists have even become dissatisfied with the laid-back teaching ministries of West Coast theologians. Therefore, something *new* had to be created. In 1975, a 24-year-old pussyfooter by the name of Bill Hybels brought historic Christianity to an all-time low by starting the Willow Creek

Community Church in South Barrington, Illinois, with a **neighborhood survey**. In a 1995 ABC special entitled "In the Name of God," Hybels acknowledged to Peter Jennings:

> When we were going to start Willow Creek I didn't know this community at all, so I and three others went door to door for a month and we just asked people, "Do you actively attend a local church?" If they said, "Yes," we said, "Good for you, keep going!" If they said, "No, we don't attend a local church," then we just asked the simple question, "Would you tell us why you stopped going?"[1]

Peter Jennings then commented:

> What Bill Hybels learned is that people didn't like **old-fashioned sermons**, and they were bored by **traditional church music**. Which is why Willow Creek today is specifically user-friendly.[2]

Even the secularist Jennings had enough sense to spot the heathen atmosphere of Willow Creek, stating to Bill, "It didn't feel to me at all religious to be in the —what? auditorium, sanctuary, umm, it's really more like a theater. Is that intentional?" Without flinching, Hybels replied, "Yes—it is because, uh, one of the things that we're really about as a church is to try to help non-churched people, feel, umm, that they can investigate Christianity in sort of a **neutral setting**."[3] Where is the scriptural precedent for such nonsense? A *neutral* setting? Like in Exodus 32:26 and 27?

> *Then Moses stood in the gate of the camp, and said, **Who is on the LORD'S side? Let him come unto me.** And all the sons of Levi gathered themselves together unto him.*
> *And he said unto them, thus saith the LORD God of Israel, Put every man his sword by his side, and go in and out from gate to gate throughout the camp, and slay every man his brother, and every man his companion, and every man his neighbour.*

Neither *"cold nor hot"* is more like it. What else could you have expected from one of Bill Clinton's personal spiritual advisers? *"Can two walk together, except they be agreed?"* (Amos 3:3)

The nonspiritual atmosphere at Willow Creek was also apparent to another reporter who stated in the *U.S.A. Weekend*:

To attract churchgoers today, you've got to please the consumers. That means high-tech entertainment. Day care. Self-help groups. No pleas for money. **No Bible-thumping.**

Happy customers from California to Maryland are eating up "fast-food religion" this Easter. Pastor Bill Hybels' answer for getting 30- and 40-year-olds into the tent: Marketing. **Ask consumers what they want, then let them (as they say at Burger King) have it their way.**[4]

The article's description of the Willow Creek ministry included:

A slick, show-biz service where drama and soft rock are served up on a stage washed in pink and blue spotlights. A soft-sell sermon is delivered.[5]

The hypocritical Hybels then had the gall to tell Jennings:

Well, I get uncomfortable when people mix too much of spirituality and business, because fundamentally we're not selling a product—we're really not. Fundamentally, we're proclaiming the message of Amazing Grace.[6]

Jennings also brought his camera crew to the workplace of one of Hybels' church members. The satisfied "consumer" proclaimed:

It doesn't bother me at all if they use, uh, marketing techniques to get me to go there. Uh, it gets me there, and I hear the message then. And I appreciate that they're making it easy for me. **I like things that are easy** [laughter].

It's like going to a movie, umm,... only better. They have songs that I like. They, uh, have dramas with real actors, and it *is* **slick**, and it makes me want to come back and hear more. The more I hear, then, the more I learn and the better Christian, then, I'll be.[7]

Alert to any opportunity to discredit the Lord Jesus Christ, Jennings made sure his cameraman caught "Brother John" *puffing on a cigarette* while giving his testimony.

When attempting to justify all of the compromise orchestrated by his staff of 167 (which includes professional musicians, producers, directors and technicians), Bill got a tad bit "teary-eyed," relating to Peter:

A few days ago I was with a man who was in **spiritual process** [chic 90's term] and he said, "So explain to me again, what does it mean to be a Christian?"

Now I have a choice to make at that moment. He's asking *the* central question of the universe. Am I going to use words and ideas that make me sound *smart*, or am I going to communicate the core of the Christian message in a way that he can understand?

And, when you have enough relationships with people whose eternity is hanging in the balance, and when you know they have families and children who are looking up to them for spiritual direction, you just want to make it clear.[8]

Because Hybels is smooth, he leaves you with the impression that these are the only two alternatives from which a "burdened" pastor can choose— "words and ideas" that make the pastor sound "smart," *or* Willow Creek's brand of high-tech Hollywood Christianity. Do you suppose Bill and his team ever heard of the *Holy Spirit*? (Acts 19:2) How about the "option" mandated by Scripture?

> *For after that in the wisdom of God the world by wisdom knew not God, it pleased God by the **foolishness of preaching** to save them that believe.* (I Corinthians 1:21)

As a non-convicting "Christianity" is so appealing to Laodiceans, Jennings' report noted that approximately 800 other "churches" nationwide are loosely federated with Hybels' mess through the Willow Creek Association. Pastor Wesley Dupin of the Daybreak Community Church in rural Michigan declared:

> It's not all church—it's not all gloom and doom, and all of you take your Bible now—let's open the hymnal and let's just *bore* each other. Let's show them we can also have **fun** and that can be *very* controversial...I think Jesus Christ would use similar methods if He were here today...I think you have to do some Madison Avenue, and I don't think that's a bad word. McDonald's has done it for years. They're smart.[9]

Now we are looking at "Have it your way" Christianity *and* "You deserve a break today" Christianity. Sounds like *junk food* to me!

Pastor David Guerrin from the Ridge Point Community Church, also in western Michigan, told Jennings:

The forms that are traditionally associated with the church are so incongruent with the world that we live in. I mean you step through a time warp in terms of the forms that you see.

The danger is always that we will *so* accommodate ourselves to the culture in which we find ourselves that the message *will* be watered down. We'll give in to modernity.

The key to avoiding that is to determine ahead of time what are the non-negotiables. I mean, what are the hills that you'll die on? Let's determine those up front and let's do everything we can to protect and preserve those. **As for the rest, that's all negotiable.**[10]

My Bible says to hold "all" on the hills: *"Neither give place to the devil."* (Ephesians 4:27) Pastor Dave is full of prunes!

In his closing remarks, Peter Jennings did a little preaching of his own: "Finally, the challenge is this: As these churches *try* to attract sellout crowds, *are* they in danger of selling out the Gospel?"[11]

While Hybels and his satellites are helping materialistic Americans to salve their consciences by keeping them strung out on religious dope, another confederation of apostates is working to perfect the end-day ecumenical movement with the pope as its head.

As these various para-church "ministries" are examined, one will detect the presence of at least three common denominators. First, each movement has a particular *moral* crisis in view, whether involving abortion, the home, or the nation as a whole. Next, those who volunteer for these crusades are assured that they *can* make a difference in "bringing America back to God." And finally, due to the need for political clout, conservative "Christians" of *all* faiths (including Roman Catholics, Mormons, Jews and Charismatics) must lay aside their "minor" theological differences and work *together* to help save America.

Although this sounds nice and patriotic on the surface (like the "Battle Hymn of the Republic" and the Statue of Liberty, etc.), it doesn't line up with the Holy Scriptures. When the liberal King Ahab conned King Jehoshaphat into yoking up with him to fight a *common* enemy, the "crusade" ended in disaster ("Jumpin' Jehoshaphat," etc.). After the rout, the Lord sent a messenger to his naive servant:

> *And Jehu the son of Hanani the seer went out to meet him, and said to king Jehoshaphat, **Shouldest thou help the ungodly, and***

*love them that hate the LORD? therefore is wrath upon thee from
before the LORD.* (II Chronicles 19:2)

Because America's Christians have become so addicted to money and
pleasure, they have become *"blind, and cannot see afar off."* (II Peter
1:9a, b) This is why the church at Laodicea was counseled to *"anoint thine
eyes with eyesalve, that thou mayest see."* (Revelation 3:18c) As an entire
generation of lukewarm believers casually flip through any number of
generic New Age versions, their collective unwillingness to endure sound
doctrine has spelled ICHABOD over the church in America. (I Samuel 4:21)

By way of illustration, Baptist preachers (nor any other born-again
believers, for that matter) have no business kneeling in front of abortion
clinics beside Roman Catholic priests! II Corinthians 6:14a is *still* in the
Bible! *"Be ye not unequally yoked together with unbelievers."* Post-
millennial pipe dreams like the *Moral Majority* are, in reality, *too* little, *too*
late. America's sin exists because of a half-century of Christians backsliding.
An unequal yoke of heathens and believers is not the Bible blueprint for
moral reform. When Paul shut down the silversmith industry at Ephesus, he
didn't do so with a *Moral Majority*; he did it through a *Soul-winning
Minority!*

> *Moreover ye see and hear, that not alone at Ephesus, but
> almost throughout all Asia, this Paul hath persuaded and turned
> away much people, saying that they be no gods, which are made
> with hands.* (Acts 19:26)

When Sam Jones, Mordecai Ham, Billy Sunday and Bob Jones, Sr.,
cleaned up the communities of their day, they did it through the power of
God! The saloons closed their doors because the customers (and, in some
cases, the owners themselves) had accepted Jesus Christ—*not* because a
coalition of Baptists, Presbyterians, Catholics, Mormons and Jews were
picketing on the sidewalk!

America is in a mess because the Church of Jesus Christ has sold out for
fun and games. And with a new "Bible" coming out every other week, the
prospect of a *national* revival this side of the tribulation period is nonexistent
at best. This is why the *rapture* is called the *"blessed hope"*! (Titus 2:13)
This is also why our Saviour asked, *"When the Son of man cometh, shall he
find faith on the earth?"* (Luke 18:8b)

JERRY FALWELL

One of the saddest losses to the cause of Christ in my lifetime has been the apostasy of Dr. Jerry Falwell. A sincere Independent Baptist pastor for several years, Dr. Falwell eventually made the same mistake as King Jehoshaphat—*he compromised with the devil.*

Although Dr. Falwell began his ministry with the AV 1611, he later endorsed the generic New King James Version (misnomer) published by Thomas Nelson. Also, in a 1991 *Saturday Evening Post* advertisement for the perverted *Living Bible,* he acknowledged:

> The *Living Bible* has ministered to me personally every morning for many years. There is no way I can measure the spiritual contribution the *Living Bible* has made to my ministry.[12]

Without the right Bible for guidance (Psalm 119:105), Dr. Falwell was bound to get off track sooner or later. In April, 1980, he addressed the ecumenical "Washington for Jesus" rally. His fellow speakers included three Roman Catholic priests—John Bertolucci, John Randall and Michael Scanlon—as well as Pat Robertson, Robert Schuller and Jim "PTL" Bakker.[13]

In 1979, Dr. Falwell incorporated the *Moral Majority* and reported to *Christianity Today,* February 21, 1986, that Roman Catholics comprised the largest constituency (30%) of his Baptist-based movement.[14]

David Cloud notes that in the December, 1984, issue of the *Fundamentalist Journal* (Falwell's publication), a Roman Catholic cardinal was given a public forum to tell fundamental Baptists what they needed to hear. Edward Dobson, the *Journal's* editor, stated:

> "What would you say to a Fundamentalist if given the opportunity?" This was the question we recently asked a Jewish rabbi, a Roman Catholic cardinal, an Evangelical leader, and an articulate voice for liberal Christianity...
>
> For too many years, we Fundamentalists have existed in our hermetically sealed world and promoted the attitude that we do not care what anyone else thinks about anything. In this issue of the *Journal*, we venture into new territory and listen to what others say and think about Fundamentalism.
>
> The article by Joseph Cardinal Bernardin is especially interesting. It reflects many of the changes that have occurred in the Roman Catholic

church in recent decades. We view much of that change in a positive light... To Cardinal Bernardin's unique insight into the American Catholic church we say, "gratias."[15]

In the March, 1985, issue of the *Fundamentalist Journal*, Ed Dobson, then vice president of student affairs at Liberty Baptist College, declared, "**Extremists** who declare that the Papacy is of anti-Christ... are **insensitive to others and lack the love of Christ**."[16]

That same year, Catholic Senator Ted Kennedy of *Chappaquiddick* fame was invited to be a guest speaker at Liberty Baptist College and Thomas Road Baptist Church. Cloud writes:

> The Senator announced to the audience of 5,000, "I am an American and a Catholic." He then lectured them on Pope John XXIII's renewal of the gospel call and the voice of Catholic bishops in the U.S.A.
>
> He opened his speech with these words, "I have come here to discuss my beliefs about faith and country, tolerance, and truth in America... I love my country and I treasure my faith."... The Senator was given two standing ovations and was interrupted a dozen times by applause.[17]

In his 1985 *Moral Majority Report*, Dr. Falwell referred to Pope John Paul II and Billy Graham as "great moral and religious leaders."

Finally, as "one good turn deserves another," Cloud notes that the *Fundamentalist Journal* for December, 1986, sported a photo of the *Baptist* pastor speaking to the students at *Notre Dame University*.[18]

In 1988, the coalition-minded Falwell sent a bizarre mailing to numerous religious bookstores advertising a film about "His Holiness," Pope John Paul II. Cloud cites this letter in his work entitled *Flirting with Rome*:

> Dear Christian Bookstore Owner: Pope John Paul II will never become a Baptist, and it is for sure that I will never convert to Roman Catholicism. **However, I have stated often that I believe this Pope is a man of unique character and courage. His consistent stand on moral and social issues has provided the world leadership so desperately needed at this hour.**
>
> Robert Evans is the Cecil B. deMille of this generation. It should be, then, no marvel that Mr. Evans has so perfectly captured the innermost person and principles of John Paul II. When I first watched the "Power of Faith," I was deeply moved. **While the Pope and I have broad doctrinal and theological differences, this man's commitment to the dignity of human life and his strong opposition to tyranny and bigotry provide**

a shining light for the people of our generation who need such reinforcement...I think people from all faiths and walks of life will appreciate this film.[19]

By this time, the ecumenical crowd was taking note of Dr. Falwell's growing apostasy. In an editorial for the January 15, 1988, *Christianity Today*, writer Terry Muck observed:

> Perhaps Falwell's greatest accomplishment, however, was getting Protestants, Catholics, and Jews to work together on common causes. The Moral Majority is a coalition of groups that heretofore had let theological difference's [sic] stand in the way of coordinated activity on shared concerns like abortions and pornography. **It stands as a model of ecumenicity of the best sort**—an agreement to work together on issues without trying to gloss over theological differences.[20]

Not only were the neo-Evangelicals aware of Jerry's compromise, but more significantly, the Vatican was as well! Keith Fournier is the Roman Catholic dean of "evangelism" at the Franciscan University of Steubenville, Ohio. In his book, *Evangelical Catholics*, Fournier acknowledges how apostates like Jerry Falwell are helping to break down the walls of separation between God's people and the Mother of Harlots. With reference to a meeting he attended of the American Congress of Christian Citizens, Fournier states:

> In our meeting room were major evangelical leaders I've admired for years—Dr. Charles Stanley, Dr. Jerry Falwell, Dr. D. James Kennedy, Pat Robertson, and many others. **I found not only a tremendous openness to my presence, but also a growing respect for my church and a thawing in what had been hard ice in the past.** Perhaps the comments of Dr. Falwell were most illustrative.
>
> He told the whole group not even to consider trying to affect public policy with only a narrow evangelical Protestant church coalition. He said that from its inception any such effort must include Catholics and consultation with great churchmen such as Cardinal Law and Cardinal O'Connor. Clearly not backing off one bit from his self-described "narrowness of doctrine," Dr. Falwell showed a refreshing openness.[21]

With the passing of years, Jerry Falwell has continued to stumble down the road of apostasy. When Jim Bakker was exposed, Jerry rode a *water slide* in a publicity stunt to help save the "spiritual" PTL Club.

Currently, Dr. Falwell is courting the Southern Baptists and subtly preparing numbers of naive Independents for a return *back* to the convention's den of iniquity. In the meantime, the Southern Baptist Convention is likewise preparing for a trip of its own, a first-time move toward Roman Catholicism. Cloud writes:

> Three Southern Baptist leaders were part of an ecumenical team of 19 U.S. religious leaders that met with Pope John Paul II [February 1992] to explore possibilities for an international interfaith effort to combat child and hardcore pornography... The group included Catholics, Mormons, Pentecostals and representatives of the NAE and NCC.
>
> The Pope said: "... [T]he unanimous witness of our common convictions regarding the dignity of man, created by God, the followers of various religions, both now and in the future, will contribute in no small measure to the growth of that civilization of love which is founded on the principles of an authentic humanism. I encourage your worthy effort, and I cordially invoke upon all of you the abundant blessing of Almighty God."[22]

Along with Dr. Falwell's rejection of scriptural separation, Lynchburg's Liberty University has totally repudiated the standards of old-time religion as well. In preparation for this chapter, I personally viewed a promotional video of the school and *got the shock of my life in the process!*

The first scene of the presentation is a carnal-looking music group called "New Song" which is really nothing more than "Old Sin." Watching several clips of satanically inspired "Christian rock" on the Lynchburg campus made me want to *vomit!* (Revelation 3:16)

It is precisely due to the *unbelievable* compromise in Christian music promoted by Jerry Falwell, Bill Hybels, Amy Grant, Sandi Patti and hundreds of other traitors that a Pandora's box of the worst "noise" this side of Hell has been opened!

How could a professing patriot like Falwell endorse such trash when today's rock music is so *openly* demonic? It has been my experience from teaching in a Bible college for ten years that young people should be able to find safety in a Christian environment from an atmsophere that could lead to such hellions like KISS ("Kids in Satan's Service"), WASP ("We Are Sexual Perverts") and SLAYER ("Satan Laughs As You Eternally Rot").

While LU's promotional video did not show even a single clip from the Thomas Road Baptist Church, the hellish rock group Black Sabbath conducts public invitations at their concerts for fans to surrender their lives to Satan. You'd think the "educators" at Liberty University would be aware of the demonism in rock music. Twisted Sister sings *"Burn* in Hell"; The Grim Reaper sings *"See You* in Hell"; Onslaught sings *"Power* from Hell"; and AC/DC sings *"Highway* to Hell." To help the young people reach their final destination, Motley Crue sings "Shout at the Devil"; Black Sabbath sings "We Sold Our Soul for Rock 'n' Roll"; and Morbid Angel sings **"Blaspheme the Ghost."** For "inspiration," Sad Iron sings, "We all praise the devil, he's so fine; we'll all praise the devil 'til the day we die." While Morbid Vision's album cover shows three men on crosses with the devil trying to tear the middle victim off his cross, Coven's cover shows a serpent around the body of Jesus, and Satan ready to stab him with a sword. (For the record, there are also plenty of underground satanic videos available where kidnapped children are literally *dismembered* or *burned alive* before the cameras.)

When one of the New Song losers in the LU video yells, "Now let's not forget one of the most important ingredients in college life," a second New Song loser answers, "Food." The first New Song loser corrects him with, "No—**fun**—right guys?" A bunch of worldly looking students reply, "Right!" Then, loser number one says, "Check this out." The names and images of several "Christian rockers" are then flashed across the screen, being introduced as LU regulars: Steven Curtis Chapman, Carman, Clay Cross, 4 Him, Michael W. Smith, The News Boys and Jars of Clay. The male performers who were shown in action had long hair and beards and were wearing shorts. The two losers from "Lynchburg's own" D.C. Talk looked like they were *high*, and the so-called Christian comedian Mark Lowry looked like a doofus ("Greek" word for *idiot*).

One of the *most* important ingredients in college life is supposed to be *fun*?? Do you suppose anyone at the "World's Most Exciting University" has ever read Ecclesiastes 7:4? *"The heart of the wise is in the house of mourning; but the heart of fools is in the house of mirth."* LU's "Spirit of Liberty" philosophy is analogous to the "SPIRIT OF ROCK" culture:

> *Metal on metal*
> *It's the only way*
> *To (expletive) with tomorrow,*
> *Let's live for today!*

So much for Jerry and his "Jesus First" pins. *"For Demas hath forsaken me, having loved this present world."* (II Timothy 4:10a)

JACK VAN IMPE

Dr. Jack Van Impe is another well-known *former* Independent Baptist who sold his birthright for a mess of pottage. (Genesis 25:33) Whereas Falwell compromised over *politics*, Van Impe's "burden" is *prophecy*.

After faithfully serving the body of Christ for many years, Jack and Rexella got in over their heads financially and subsequently felt "led" to find a larger "flock." Evidently it dawned on the "Walking Bible" that Roman Catholics could be intrigued with dramatic end-day scenarios just like anyone else. And, as the checks sent in by Catholic viewers would cash just the same as those mailed in by born-again believers, why not "reach out" ($$$$$) to them as well?

However, there was only one minor problem with the plan. How could Bible prophecy be taught without indicting "His Holiness"? How can one attempt to explain Revelation 17 and 18 without identifying Roman Catholicism as the Mother of Harlots? What Spirit-filled Christian doesn't know that the Vatican will be the focal point of the coming one-world religion of the anti-Christ?

Dr. Van Impe should be aware of the historic Baptist-Protestant position on the Papacy. In Chapter 26, paragraph 4 of the Baptist Confession of 1688, we read:

> The Lord Jesus Christ is the head of the Church, in whom, by the appointment of the Father, all power for the calling, institution, order or government of the Church is invested in a supreme and sovereign manner; neither can the Pope of Rome, in any sense, be head thereof, but is no other than Antichrist, that man of sin and son of perdition, that exalteth himself in the Church against Christ, and all that is called God: whom the Lord shall destroy with the brightness of His coming.[23]

On one occasion when the renowned Baptist pastor, Charles Haddon Spurgeon, read II Thessalonians 2:3, 4 and 8, he exclaimed, "Arrest the Pope on suspicion of being the Antichrist."[24]

The Protestant creeds read similarly. Article 80 of the Episcopalian *Irish Articles* (1615) states:

> The Bishop of Rome is so far from being the supreme head of the universal Church of Christ, that his works and doctrine do plainly discover him to be that "man of sin," foretold in the holy Scriptures, "whom the

Lord shall consume with the spirit of His mouth, and abolish with the brightness of His coming.[25]

Article 6 of the Presbyterian *Westminster Confessions of Faith* and the Congregational *Savoy Declaration*, Chapter 26, paragraph 4 read alike:

> There is no other head of the Church but the Lord Jesus Christ; nor can the Pope of Rome in any sense be head thereof; but it (he) is that Antichrist, that man of sin and son of perdition that exalteth himself in the Church against Christ, and all that is called God [the *Savoy Declaration* adds], whom the Lord shall destroy with the brightness of His coming.[26]

In his précis of J. A. Wylie's 1851 classic, *The Papacy Is the Antichrist*, Dr. Ian Paisley, courageous pastor of the Martyrs Memorial Presbyterian Church in Belfast, Northern Ireland, shares a shocking illustration of pontifical incrimination. Originally noted by Andreas Helvig in his 1612 work, *Roman Antichrist*, Wylie points out the uncanny correlation between the pope's traditional title—VICARIVS FILII DEI (Vicar of Christ), presently appearing on the papal tiara—and the prophecy of Revelation 13:18:

> *Here is wisdom. Let him that hath understanding count the number of the beast: for it is the number of a man; and his number is Six hundred three score and six.*

Paisley cites Wylie:

> Now certain Roman characters have numerical values.
>
> I=1; V=5; X=10; L=50; C=100; D=500.
>
> Now let us count the number of the man at the Vatican. God has told us to do it.

V=5	F= --	D=500
I=1	I=1	E= --
C=100	L=50	I=1
A= --	I=1	
R= --	I=1	
I=1		
V=5		
S= --		
112	53	501 = 666

112   +   53   +   501   =   666

So the numerical value of the Pope's title on his golden crown at his public coronation, namely "VICARIVS FILII DEI" is that remarkable number 666.[27]

If "Brother" Jack and "Sister" Rexella were going to attract Roman Catholic viewers to their prophecy format, they would have to come up with a scam to cover the *man of sin* in the process. And did they *ever*!!

Following the party line of Billy Graham and Jerry Falwell, Van Impe "perceived" that the present pope, John Paul II, is unlike most other pontiffs have been. Yes, siree, our reigning "Holy Father" is quite a "spiritual giant," etc. However, as Jack would tell it, things are not exactly what you would call copacetic back at the Vatican. (Now here's where the *con* comes in.) According to a special Van Impe Ministries video entitled *Startling Revelations: Pope John Paul II*, a conspiracy is presently afoot within the Roman Catholic Church to overthrow poor John Paul II. The bottom line is that the *new* pope will be the end-day false prophet. (So in the meantime, keep those cards and letters coming, etc.)

As to the documentation for this sinister plot, the Van Impes quote extensively from a book entitled *The Keys of This Blood*. And who is the author of this shocking exposé? I quote from the video jacket:

> *Startling Revelations: Pope John Paul II* is based on hundreds of pages of information, in five volumes, penned by the eminent Catholic Theologian, Malachi Martin, a close friend and advisor to the last four popes. Martin is an expert on Catholicism, **a former Jesuit**, and a professor at the Vatican's Pontifical Biblical Institute. His opinions are regarded as authoritative.[28]

Realizing that he had his work cut out for him, Jack began the program by heading off his "insensitive" critics at the pass:

> This is a news program and we take the headlines, analyze them and then try to show you where they're found in the Bible.
> When we quote Pope John Paul II, Martin Luther, John Calvin of the Reform Movement or John Knox of Presbyterianism, **some of you actually write us and get upset.** [Noooo!!]
> Listen, we want to present the news as it is, and I think you're going to find this very informative. You need to hear what Pope John Paul II has to say.[29]

Isn't it amazing how so many people keep telling us that we need to hear what John Paul has to say? Did you catch the part about their being a *news team*—so they don't have to answer for any subliminal heresy they promote in the process of "reporting"?

In all my life I have never seen a **cheesier-appearing** collection of phonies than Jack and Rexella Van Impe, and especially the "spooky"-sounding Chuck Ohman. Some of us were in the world before we got saved and can spot a hustler—secular or religious—a mile away. These apostates are a disgrace to the body of Christ! Just listen to their unadulterated claptrap, Jack stating:

> Here is the book, *The Keys of This Blood*, and on pages 295, 296, 304 and 683, the Pope names the names of the defectors within the church among his bishops. **I don't want to name them on the air, but they're here.**[30]

Since when is a *real* man of God supposed to be afraid of anything? *"The fear of man bringeth a snare."* (Proverbs 29:25a)

After a running commentary with Rexella, interspersed with exhilarating talk about the rapture, Jack begins his dramatic finale ("Cheese City"):

> And Rexella, I want to close this program with the most startling statement anyone will ever hear, and it's page 684 of Malachi Martin's book. And he says there are enough liberals now among the bishops that they can elect a pope who doesn't even believe some of the things the Bible teaches about Christ.
>
> And he says, "When that happens [drama in his voice] Roman Catholics will then have the spectacle of a pope, validly elected who cuts the entire visible body of the Church loose from the traditional unity. The shudder that will shake the Roman Catholic body in that day will be the shudder of its death agony. For its pains will be from within itself, orchestrated by its leaders and its members. No outside enemy will have brought this about. Many will accept the new regime; many will resist; all will be fragmented. There will be no one on earth to hold the fractionating members of the visible Roman Catholic body together as a living compact organization."[31]

After adding, "The Pope says, 'I'm afraid for the future of my church,' " Van Impe winds down his personal remarks with, "What's this all mean?—Jesus is coming! Are *you* saved?"

As the broadcast comes to a close, Rexella reassures one and all, "God's love is the oil that reduces friction. God loves you; so do we. Good night." You have to hand it to "Brother" Jack; that angle was pretty *slick*!

Before moving on to the next religious entrepreneur, I thought my readers could use a dose of *real* spiritual manhood. Martin Luther once said:

> Many think I am too fierce against popery; on the contrary I complain that I am, alas, too mild; I wish I could breathe out lightning against pope and popedom, and that every wind were a thunderbolt... I will curse and scold the scoundrels until I go to my grave, and never shall they have a civil word from me...
>
> For I am unable to pray without at the same time cursing. If I am prompted to say, "Hallowed be thy name," I must add, "Cursed, damned, outraged be the name of papists." If I am prompted to say, "Thy kingdom come," I must perforce add, "Cursed, damned, destroyed must be the papacy."
>
> Indeed, I pray thus orally every day and in my heart, without intermission... I never work better than when I am inspired by anger. When I am angry I can write, pray, and preach well, for then my whole temperament is quickened, my understanding sharpened.[32]

JAMES DOBSON

Psychologist Dr. James Dobson has proven to be one of the most dangerous apostates of all. Dr. Dobson has repeatedly disclaimed any theological credentials, espousing instead the virtues of clinical psychology. A *Focus on the Family* employee wrote:

> Dr. Dobson has made a deliberate decision to direct the attention of our ministry away from matters of biblical interpretation and theology, choosing instead to concentrate our efforts exclusively on family-related topics.[33]

How does one separate "biblical interpretation" from "family-related topics"? *"And, ye fathers, provoke not your children to wrath: but bring them up in the nurture and admonition of the Lord."* (Ephesians 6:4) Dobson prefers the "higher authority" of **psychology** despite the biblical injunction, *"Learn not the way of the heathen."* (Jeremiah 10:2a)

In their acclaimed critique of James Dobson entitled *Prophets of Psychoheresy II*, authors Martin and Deidre Bobgan write:

> Dobson's teachings are psychological in theory and practice. His discussions about the nature of children and adults and how to change behavior come primarily from psychology rather than from the Bible. And in numerous instances, they come from that kind of psychology which is opinion and not science. While he opposes the teachings of some psychologists, he embraces the theories and practices of others. Like most practitioners, he is eclectic in his approach in that he picks and chooses from a variety of theorists. However, his psychology is neither original nor biblically based.[34]

With his promotion of pagan psychology, James Dobson has orchestrated an incredibly subtle assault upon Holy Scripture by introducing an "alternative" authority at best and, more commonly, an inferior one at worst. Bobgan and Bobgan write:

> The heresy is the departure from absolute confidence in the word of God for all matters of life and conduct and a movement toward faith in the unproven, unscientific psychological opinions of men. Thus we call it "psychoheresy."[35]

The fact that Dobson sprinkles a few Bible verses into his program is far worse than if he had opted for a total ban. (Revelation 3:15) When he isn't quoting from (and thereby subliminally recommending to you) any number of heathen or Christian psychologists such as Sigmund Freud, William Glasser, E. L. Thorndike, B. F. Skinner, Stanley Coopersmith and Clyde Narramore,[36] Dobson simply asserts his *own* opinion as final authority. In the great majority of cases, he declines to give a supporting Scripture. The Bobgans point out:

> However, each concession to psychology eats away at total reliance on God and His Word until psychology is no longer a supplement to the Bible, but a supplanter of the Word. Soon the dominant perspective on human nature is psychological rather than biblical.[37]

Not only is *Focus on the Family* casting a shadow over the Bible, but over the New Testament office of pastor as well. A whole generation of Christians is being indoctrinated with the notion that most of their serious emotional disorders require the "expertise" of a *clinical psychologist*. Such old-school remedies as "Quit your meanness" (Reverend Sam Jones) would no longer do in a sophisticated culture.

When I was pastor of the Kootenai County Baptist Church in Post Falls, Idaho, I invited Dr. *Dallas* Dobson, pastor of the First Baptist Church in Pasco, Washington, to speak at our church's Valentine Banquet. Having rented the banquet facilities at the local Holiday Inn, I arranged for the marquee to read, "Kootenai County Baptist Church Welcomes Dr. Dobson." Our church phone literally rang off the hook as area callers assumed that my guest was *James* Dobson, the *psychologist*. When they discovered that it was "only" *Dallas* Dobson, the *preacher*, they lost interest immediately. The fact that Dr. Dobson built the largest Baptist church west of the Mississippi River, running over 2,000 every Sunday, didn't mean a thing. He was "only" a *pastor*.

As in the case of Evangelist Billy Graham, psychologist James Dobson could see which way the wind was blowing. When describing the conditions that would prevail in the last days, the Holy Spirit moved Paul to place *"lovers of their own selves"* at the head of the list. (II Timothy 3:2) Dr. Dobson has chosen to cash in on this spiritual flaw with a threefold message of *self-esteem, self-worth* and *self-acceptance.* He should have named his ministry "Focus on *Self.*" The Bobgans state:

> In the opening chapter of *Hide or Seek* Dobson uses a psychological foundation and framework for defining, diagnosing, and solving problems of living. He describes problems in psychological rather than biblical terms. Then, he analyzes problems according to what parents and society did not provide in terms of so-called needs of the self as proposed by humanistic psychology. His solutions or goals are self-esteem and self-confidence. And the rest of the book is devoted to strategies for overcoming the problem (low self-esteem and inferiority) through building high self-esteem and self-confidence.[38]

According to Dr. James Dobson, psychologist, the whole world is in trouble—not because of the *Adamic nature*—but because of *low self-esteem*:

> The matter of personal worth is not only the concern of those who lack it. In a real sense, the health of an entire society depends on the ease with which its individual members can gain personal acceptance. *Thus, whenever the keys to self-esteem are seemingly out of reach for a large percentage of the people, as in the twentieth-century America, then widespread "mental illness," neuroticism, hatred, alcoholism, drug abuse, violence, and social disorder will certainly occur. Personal worth*

is not something human beings are free to take or leave. We must have it, and when it is unattainable, everybody suffers.[39]

Dobson also teaches that self-esteem is generated by the positive way in which others view our lives. In his book *What Wives Wish Their Husbands Know About Women*, he writes:

> Feelings of self-worth and acceptance, which provide the cornerstone of a healthy personality, can be obtained from only *one* source... Self-esteem is **only** generated by what we see reflected about ourselves in the eyes of other people. It is only when others love us that we love ourselves. It is only when others find us pleasant and desirable and worthy that we come to terms with our own egos.[40]

According to Dobson's humanism, the Apostle Paul must have suffered from some *really* low self-esteem. *"This thou knowest, that all they which are in Asia be turned away from me."* (II Timothy 1:15a) Apparently, the Lord never read Dobson's book either!

> *If the world hate you, ye know that it hated me before it hated you. If ye were of the world, the world would love his own: but because ye are not of the world, but I have chosen you out of the world, therefore the world hateth you. Remember the word that I said unto you, The servant is not greater than his lord. If they have persecuted me, they will also persecute you; if they have kept my saying, they will keep your's also.* (John 15:18-20)

Yet at least Jim practices what he preaches. From all appearances, the *world* really loves Dr. James Dobson. In fact, the El Pomar Foundation in Colorado Springs, Colorado, was so convinced that Dobson's personnel would have a *positive* impact on their community that they gave *Focus on the Family* a cool $4 million to purchase the land on which their headquarters is now located.

> *And, behold, the whole city came out to meet Jesus: and when they saw him, they besought him that he would **depart** out of their coasts.* (Matthew 8:34)

The reason Dobson is embraced by heathen everywhere is because he doesn't tell it like it is! In the first place, they couldn't understand if he did

(II Corinthians 2:14) and in the second, there wouldn't be any more $4 million checks if he switched from psychology back to the Bible. Jim knows that the world can't handle such "therapeutic" themes as: *"Every man at his best state is altogether vanity"* (Psalm 39:5c); *"And without shedding of blood is no remission"* (Hebrews 9:22b); *"The heart is deceitful above all things, and desperately wicked: who can know it?"* (Jeremiah 17:9); *"Not that we are sufficient of ourselves to think any thing as of ourselves; but our sufficiency is of God"* (II Corinthians 3:5); *"To whom God would make known what is the riches of the glory of this mystery among the Gentiles; which is Christ in you, the hope of glory"* (Colossians 1:27) and *"Let us go forth therefore unto him without the camp, bearing his reproach."* (Hebrews 13:13)

Given these multiplied compromises, it should come as no great surprise to my readers that James Dobson is also soft on Roman Catholicism. The November, 1989, issue of *Focus on the Family's Clubhouse* magazine featured a smiling Mother Teresa on the cover with the lead article entitled "Teresa of Calcutta: Little Woman with a Big Heart."[41] **Mother Teresa will split Hell wide open one day if she doesn't get born again like anyone else—*no matter how many Indians she has fed!*** (John 3:3)

An article in the January, 1990, *Focus on the Family Citizen* called Pope John Paul II "the most eminent religious leader who names the name of Christ."[42] In September of that same year, Dobson's picture appeared on the front cover of the Catholic magazine *New Covenant* along with a positive report on *Focus on the Family.*[43]

For the final sellout, the Catholic Franciscan University of Steubenville, Ohio, bestowed an honorary doctorate upon James as a statement of their support for his ministry.[44] Now we have "Father" Billy and "Father" Jimmy! *Gaaagg!*

> *For I will promote thee unto very great honour, and I will do whatsoever thou sayest unto me: come therefore, I pray thee, curse me this people.* (Numbers 22:17)

MISCELLANEOUS APOSTATES

Compromisers such as Bill Hybels, Jerry Falwell, Jack Van Impe and James Dobson have set the pace for an entire generation of spineless rapprochement with the Vatican. Author David Cloud cites Dr. W. A. Criswell, former president of the Southern Baptist Convention and one-time pastor of Evangelist Billy Graham, as stating, **"I don't know anyone more dedicated to the great fundamental doctrines of Christianity than the Catholics."**[45]

When high-profile Baptists like Criswell make these kinds of insane statements, the sky becomes the limit for everyone else. With two Catholic priests seated beside him on the October 17, 1989, "Praise the Lord" program, TBN (Trinity Broadcast Network) president Paul Crouch confessed,

> I'm eradicating the word Protestant even out of my vocabulary... I['m] not protesting anything... [it's] time for Catholics and non-Catholics to come together as one in the Spirit and one in the Lord.[46]

Cloud notes that the February, 1992, issue of the *Bookstore Journal* (the official publication of the Christian Booksellers Association) featured three articles on the subject, "The Catholic Market: Dispelling Myths, Building Bridges."[47] The cover of this issue is highlighted by a large string of *rosary beads*!

Cloud then goes on to expose Hank Hanegraaff and the Christian Research Institute:

> Recently on "The Bible Answer Man" radio program, Norm Geisler declared that the Roman Catholic doctrine of justification by faith was biblical. Luther would be shocked! Christian Research Institute director Hank Hanegraaff (Walter Martin's successor), who was interviewing Norm, agreed... CRI... has even allowed Scott Hahn (another leading Catholic apologist) on "The Bible Answer Man," to promote Roman Catholicism without offering the slightest rebuttal! (*The Berean Call*, April, 1992)
>
> In two CRI Perspective sheets, Christian Research Institute President Hank Hanegraaff makes it clear that he does not believe Romanism is a cult: "While Protestants continue to disagree over the issue, CRI firmly maintains that Roman Catholicism is a religious system which includes both orthodox biblical Christianity and elements of unbiblical or "cultic" doctrine and practice... We acknowledge the presence in Roman Catholicism of many genuine brothers and sisters in the Lord, while also recognizing that many of those within Roman Catholicism worldwide appear to be lost... One thing we are unwilling to do is to misrepresent

Roman Catholicism or to exaggerate its faults. That would be patently unfair, at CRI we've always striven for balance.

Well, in spite of the vast differences between Catholics and evangelicals, I believe our points of agreement provide us with common ground through which we can share and discuss the gospel in love and with understanding.[48]

The religion page of the *Los Angeles Herald Examiner* for September 19, 1987, quotes "Reverend" Robert Schuller as declaring, "It's time for Protestants to go to the shepherd [the pope] and say, '**What do we have to do to come home?**' "[49] At his Crystal Cathedral, March 2-4, 1990, Schuller hosted the charismatic/Catholic-sponsored "6th Annual West Coast Conference on the Holy Spirit." Dave Hunt notes that "the majority of the audience were Roman Catholics, as were about half of the speakers." Schuller announced unashamedly:

> When I had the dream of this cathedral, I didn't want to build it without the blessing of the Holy Father. So I made a trip to Rome and I met with the Pope...I took a picture of the cathedral and I told him I was building this and that [I wanted it to] receive his prayers of blessings. A photograph, of course, was taken of us and I have it hanging on my 12th floor...Then on the 30th anniversary of my ministry here I received the most beautiful full-colored photograph of the Holy Father bestowing his apostolic blessing upon my holy ministry, with a wonderful personal handwritten message.[50]

When it comes to putting up a swanky edifice, Schuller couldn't have picked a better authority than John Paul II. The Pope's "modest" dwelling place (the Vatican Palace) has 900 flights of stairs and more than 1,400 rooms. John's personal penthouse apartment consists of only 19 rooms, lavishly furnished with paneled blond wood, carpeted floors, drapes in gold damask and satin-covered chairs. (The "papal pad" also comes with gold dinner plates and a dozen telephones.)

In the September 6, 1985, issue of *Christianity Today*, we find an amazing editorial by senior editor Kenneth Kantzer entitled "A Man Under Orders." Cloud cites the following excerpt:

> John Paul II's personal appeal to evangelicals cannot be denied. Despite his Mariology, his adamant opposition to contraception, to all

divorce on any grounds, his emphasis on priestly celibacy, his teaching on the role of women (which sometimes comes across as though the only legitimate place of women is in the home), and his strong clericalism, their enthusiasm has not been dimmed.

Their appreciation is based on his strong support of certain fundamental doctrines of biblical faith; his biblical emphasis in which his messages are invariably sprinkled with scriptural teaching; his strong commitment to the family, to a biblical sexual ethics, and to pro-life positions; his insistence upon justice and true freedom of religion everywhere; and his bold stand for the priority of the Christian message over political involvement. **All these endear him to the hearts of evangelicals.**[51]

In another syrupy editorial in the November 7, 1986, *Christianity Today*, Kantzer wrote:

Traditional Roman Catholics are a different matter altogether. They retain much of biblical Christianity and possess qualities that I admire and wish to imitate. For example, I treasure their reverence before God, the dignity of their worship, their faithful attendance at church, their frequent celebration of the Lord's Supper, **their loyalty to the Bible**, their willingness to stand up and be counted for the faith, their skill in the arts and literature, their educational system, their emphasis on sexual purity, and their stand against divorce, abortion, euthanasia and homosexuality....

For the evangelical, the most exciting change in Roman Catholicism is the new freedom for the gospel...the gospel is central to most Catholic charismatics. They have become true evangelicals with varying degrees of concern about bringing their new-found faith into harmony with the church's teaching....

How does all this affect the evangelical? First, we should continue to dialogue. To refuse to dialogue would be to say two things no evangelical wants to say: (1) We are not interested in our Lord's desire to have a united church, and (2) We evangelicals have nothing to learn from anyone....

Second, we can rejoice with the new-found evangelicals in the Roman Catholic church. We can encourage them. **We can learn from them.** We need not attack what we deem to be holdovers from Roman Catholic doctrine, but we can exalt the Lord with them and urge them to join us in testing faith by Holy Scripture....Finally, we can work together on those political and social issues where we are in such strong agreement.[52]

EVANGELICALS AND CATHOLICS TOGETHER
1994

All of this whimpering came to a head on March 29, 1994, when 20 evangelical personalities, together with 20 Roman Catholic leaders, endorsed a blasphemous ecumenical document called *Evangelicals and Catholics Together: The Christian Mission in the Third Millennium*. The *New York Times* release on March 30 read in part:

> They toiled together in the movements against abortion and pornography, and now leading Catholics and evangelicals are asking their flocks for a remarkable leap of faith: to finally accept each other as Christians. In what's being called a historic declaration, evangelicals including Pat Robertson and Charles Colson [one of the chief originators] joined with conservative Roman Catholic leaders today in upholding the ties of faith that bind the nation's largest and most politically active religious groups. They urged Catholics and evangelicals...to stop aggressive proselytization of each other's flocks.[53]

The stated purpose for this traitorous declaration was "to advance Christian fellowship, cooperation, and mutual trust among true Christians in the North American cultural crises and in the worldwide task of evangelism."

The "ECT" document is filled with subliminal suggestions, deceptive pronouncements and blatant lunacy. The opening sentence *infers* that Catholicism is united while Protestantism is fragmented: "We are Evangelical Protestants and Roman Catholics who have been led through prayer, study, and discussion to common convictions about Christian faith and mission." While the "evangelical" wing of Protestantism is noted, no such differentiation is made concerning the Mother of Harlots. To the contrary, one simple statement clearly implies that *all* Roman Catholics are Christians:

> As we near the Third Millennium, there are approximately 1.7 billion Christians in the world. About a billion of these are Catholics and more than 300 million are Evangelical Protestants.[54]

Not only was the first *sentence* a deception, but the first *authority* quoted is John Paul II: "If in the merciful and mysterious ways of God the Second Coming is delayed, we enter upon a Third Millennium that could be in the words of John Paul II 'a springtime of world missions.' *(Redemptoris Missio)*"[55] This wacky concept contradicts the last prayer in the Bible, *"Even so, come, Lord Jesus."* (Revelation 22:20c)

The first *passage* cited is taken from a modern English translation and is horribly misinterpreted: "May they all be one; as you, Father, are in me and I in you, so also may they be in us that the world may believe that you sent me." (John 17:21) Every truly born-again believer becomes one with all believers at conversion: *"For by one Spirit are we all baptized into one body, whether we be Jews or Gentiles, whether we be bond or free; and have been all made to drink into one Spirit."* (I Corinthians 12:13) As far as *practice* is concerned, the Bible gives numerous grounds for division, such as Romans 16:17, I Corinthians 5:9-11 and II Thessalonians 3:14. (The key New-Age word "ONE" is used 36 times in just the first three pages of Colson's document.)

Having given the Baptists credit for pioneering religious liberty, the ECT paper then takes off for an excursion into cloud land:

> Religious freedom is itself grounded in and is a product of religious faith, as is evident in the history of Baptists and others in this country. Today we rejoice together that the Roman Catholic Church—as affirmed by the Second Vatican Council and boldly exemplified in the ministry of John Paul II—is strongly committed to religious freedom and, consequently, to the defense of human rights. Where Evangelicals and Catholics are in severe and sometimes violent conflict, such as parts of Latin America, we urge Christians to embrace and act upon the imperative of religious freedom.[56]

Who ever heard of religious freedom in a Roman Catholic country? The *real* background to the ECT document is the growing exodus of converted Roman Catholics out of the churches in South America. Hunt cites a recent news report:

> Stunned by the staggering growth of evangelical "sects" in Brazil, leaders of the Roman Catholic Church have threatened to launch a "holy war" against Protestants unless they stop leading people from the Catholic fold...At the 31st National Conference of the Bishops of Brazil...Bishop Sinesio Bohn [called] evangelicals a serious threat to the Vatican's influence in his country.
>
> "We will declare a holy war; don't doubt it," he announced. **"The Catholic Church has a ponderous structure, but when we move, we'll smash anyone beneath us."**

According to Bohn, an all-out holy war can't be avoided unless the 13 largest Protestant churches and denominations sign a **treaty**... [that] would require Protestants to stop all evangelism efforts in Brazil. In exchange, he said, Catholics would agree to stop all persecution directed toward Protestants.[57]

Thus, we find the mutual "no soul-winning" pledge in the ECT fairy tale. Since Evangelicals and Catholics are "Christians," they mustn't try to proselytize one another!

In view of the large number of non-Christians in the world and the enormous challenge of our common evangelistic task, it is neither theologically legitimate nor a prudent use of resources for one Christian community to proselytize among active adherents of another Christian community.[58]

Although Martin Luther may have addressed his letters to the pope as "Your *Hellishness*," the ECT document declares "bearing false witness against other persons and communities, or casting unjust and uncharitable suspicions upon them, is incompatible with the Gospel." And according to Colson and his cronies, the insensitive "soul winners" need to seek one another's forgiveness!

In considering the many corruptions of Christian witness, we, Evangelicals and Catholics, confess that we have sinned against one another and against God. We most earnestly ask the forgiveness of God and one another, and pray for the grace to amend our own lives and that of our communities.[59]

Of course, the most outstanding heresy of the document pertains to salvation. How's this for "unity" of doctrine?

For Catholics, all who are validly baptized are born again and are truly, however imperfectly, in communion with Christ. That baptismal grace is to be continuingly reawakened and revivified through conversion. For most Evangelicals, but not all, the experience of conversion is to be followed by baptism as a sign of new birth. For Catholics, all the baptized are already members of the church, however dormant their faith and life....

These differing beliefs about the relationship between baptism, new birth, and membership in the church should be honestly presented to the Christian who has undergone conversion. [Who ever heard of a *Christian* who had *not* undergone conversion?!?] But again, his decision regarding communal allegiance and participation must be assiduously respected.

There are, then, differences between us that cannot be resolved here. But on this we are resolved: All authentic witness must be aimed at conversion to God in Christ by the power of the Spirit. **Those converted— whether understood as having received the new birth for the first time or as having experienced the reawakening of the new birth originally bestowed in the sacrament of baptism**—must be given full freedom and respect as they discern and decide the community in which they will live their new life in Christ. In such discernment and decision, they are ultimately responsible to God, and we dare not interfere with the exercise of that responsibility.[60]

Something tells me that the prophet Samuel wouldn't have signed. How's *this* for respect?

> *Then said Samuel, Bring ye hither to me Agag the king of the Amalekites. And Agag came unto him delicately. And Agag said, Surely the bitterness of death is past. And Samuel said, As thy sword hath made women childless, so shall thy mother be childless among women.* **And Samuel hewed Agag in pieces before the LORD in Gilgal.** *(I Samuel 15:32, 33)*

The religious perverts (as Bob Jones, Sr., would have called them) listed as participants in the heretical Evangelicals and Catholics Together document are as follows: **Mr. Charles Colson**, Prison Fellowship; Fr. Juan Diaz-Vilar, S.J., Catholic Hispanic Ministries; Fr. Avery Dulles, S.J., Fordham University; Bishop Francis George, OMI, Diocese of Yakima (Washington); Dr. Kent Hill, Eastern Nazarene College; **Dr. Richard Land, Christian Life Commission of the Southern Baptist Convention; Dr. Larry Lewis, Home Mission Board of the Southern Baptist Convention**; Dr. Jesse Miranda, Assemblies of God; Msgr. William Murphy, chancellor of the archdiocese of Boston; Fr. Richard John Neuhaus, Institute on Religion and Public Life; Mr. Brian O'Connell, World Evangelism Fellowship; Mr. Herbert Schlossberg, Fieldstead Foundation; Archbishop Francis Stafford, archdiocese of Denver; Mr. George Weigel, Ethics and Public Policy Center; and Dr. John White, Geneva College and the National Association of Evangelicals.

The religious perverts listed as *endorsing the document* are: Dr. William Abraham, Perkins School of Theology; Dr. Elizabeth Achtemeier, Union

Theological Seminary (Virginia); Mr. William Bentley Ball, Harrisburg, Pennsylvania; **Dr. Bill Bright, Campus Crusade for Christ**; Professor Robert Destro, Catholic University of America; Fr. Augustine DiNoia, O.P., Dominican House of Studies; Fr. Joseph P. Fitzpatrick, S.J., Fordham University; Mr. Keith Fournier, American Center for Law and Justice; Bishop William Frey, Trinity Episcopal School for Ministry; Professor Mary Ann Glendon, Harvard Law School; Dr. Os Guinness, Trinity Forum; **Dr. Nathan Hatch, University of Notre Dame**; Dr. James Hitchcock, St. Louis University Boston College; Fr. Matthew Lamb, Boston College; Mr. Ralph Martin, Renewal Ministries; Dr. Richard Mouw, Fuller Theological Seminary; Dr. Mark Noll, Wheaton College; Mr. Michael Novak, American Enterprise Institute; **John Cardinal O'Connor**, archdiocese of New York; Dr. Thomas Oden, Drew University; Dr. J. I. Packer, Regent College (British Columbia); **Rev. Pat Robertson**, Regent University; Dr. John Rodgers, Trinity Episcopal School for Ministry; and Bishop Carlos A. Sevilla, S. J., archdiocese of San Francisco. (These two sets of names released by the "John Ankerberg Show" appear to be an incomplete list, as the signers alone were stated as being 40 in number.)

Understandably, the ECT document created an immediate stir within the body of Christ. To forestall a split among evangelicals, Chuck Colson, J. I. Packer and Bill Bright agreed to meet with John MacArthur, Jr., R. G. Sproul, James Kennedy, John Ankerberg, Joseph Stowell, John Woodbridge and Michael Harton. The powwow was held on January 19, 1995, in the private office of Dr. D. James Kennedy, pastor of the Coral Ridge Presbyterian Church in Ft. Lauderdale, Florida.

The signers were unwilling to either remove their names or alter the text of the ECT document. As an eleventh-hour compromise, they did agree to issue a wimpy "Clarifying Statement," in which they were willing to affirm, among other things:

> Our para-church cooperation with evangelically committed Roman Catholics for the pursuit of agreed objectives **does not imply acceptance of Roman Catholic doctrinal distinctives** or endorsement of the Roman Catholic church system.

> And...

> We understand the statement that "we are justified by grace through faith because of Christ," in terms of the substitutionary atonement and **imputed righteousness of Christ**, leading to full assurance of eternal

salvation; we seek to testify in all circumstances and contexts to this, the historic Protestant understanding of salvation by faith alone *(sola fide).*[61]

Shortly after this second meeting, a five-session forum was conducted at the Coral Ridge Presbyterian Church where John Ankerberg questioned John MacArthur, Jr., R. C. Sproul and the host pastor, James Kennedy, on the ramifications of Evangelicals and Catholics Together with special attention being given to the clarifying statement.

Although these men are to be commended for taking a public stand against Roman Catholicism, a number of serious inconsistencies have mitigated their efforts. To my knowledge, none of them would subscribe to a strong position in favor of the King James Bible. In their book *Protestants and Catholics, Do They Now Agree?* coauthors John Ankerberg and John Weldon quote primarily from the New American Standard Version and the New International Version—"Used by Permission." Thus we observe that a team of modern Protestants is attempting to fight the Vatican with a text rejected by the reformers themselves; the *very* text embraced by the enemy!

Second, while Dr. D. James Kennedy is shown speaking out against ECT, his own track record is laced with ecumenical involvement. Dr. Kennedy was one of the speakers for the April, 1980, "Washington for Jesus" rally where at least two Catholic priests were also on the program. In 1988, he participated in the ecumenical "Congress '88" in Chicago where Joseph Cardinal Bernardin, archbishop of Chicago, brought the opening address. He also joined 60 ministers, including several Catholic priests, at the Lincoln Memorial in Washington, D.C., in July, 1986, for the Coalition on Revival's covenant-signing ceremony.[62] And finally, Dr. Kennedy's Evangelism Explosion training is gladly extended to Roman Catholics! Citing *Biblical Missions,* July/August, 1985, David Cloud relates:

> When asked about this, the senior vice-president of Evangelism Explosion had this to say: "As far as we have been able to ascertain to this date, the Roman Catholics who are being trained in Evangelism Explosion in their respective churches are faithfully declaring the Gospel in its essence."[63]

John MacArthur, Jr., appeared to voice the strongest opposition to the ECT document. However, when the final session was opened to questions and answers, the second question was a showstopper. A man asked:

I come from Brazil, the largest Roman Catholic country in the world. I heard you gentlemen say that what is at stake here is the Gospel. Therefore, aren't those who advocate Lordship Salvation views guilty of the same mistake as Roman Catholics are, by adding works to the Gospel, and therefore denying justification by faith alone?[64]

The effect was as if a *bomb* had gone off in the auditorium. MacArthur's Lordship salvation heresy had already been assailed by fellow evangelicals Charles C. Ryrie (*So Great Salvation*) and Zane C. Hodges (*Absolutely Free*). Ankerberg attempted to reduce the tension with,

MacArthur, we *knew* that question *had* to come up tonight *somewhere*. [Laughter.] Very good. All right, it's time to answer it, John.

Although visibly uncomfortable, MacArthur replied unashamedly:

I've written on that question, haven't I? Look—that is a straw man [heavy breathing]. To say that Lordship Salvation—whatever that term might mean to people—has the connotation that you must believe in Jesus as Lord in order to be saved—I don't know how that all of a sudden became an aberrant view. But somewhere down the path it has become aberrant in some circles to affirm the Lordship of Jesus Christ, in spite of the fact that Paul said you have to confess with your mouth Jesus as Lord in order to be saved.[65]

With Kennedy and Sproul providing moral support, the next ten minutes were given to a defense of Lordship salvation.

During the broadcast it was announced that John White, president of Geneva College, was the only signatory who had removed his name from ECT to date. Ankerberg added that the Clarifying Statement was being forwarded to all of the original signers, and he expressed his confidence that the evangelicals would sign. As of June, 1996, (the time I received the video), 17 months *after* the clarification statement was produced, no further information regarding evangelical endorsements was available from the Ankerberg people. So much for *sola fide*.

Pope John Paul II
Time magazine
"Man of the Year–1994"

XXII

The Promise Keepers

> *"For there shall arise false Christs, and false prophets, and shall shew great signs and wonders; insomuch that, if it were possible, they shall deceive the very elect."* (Matthew 24:24)

A S THE CHURCH age draws to a climactic end, the so-called Promise Keepers movement constitutes the devil's ultimate ecumenical maneuver.

The story goes that University of Colorado football coach Bill McCartney was sharing his "burden" with a friend concerning the need for a specialized ministry for men. Encouraged by his pastor, Reverend James Ryle, McCartney organized a brain trust with several others and Promise Keepers was hatched.

From its inception, the movement has experienced continuous phenomenal growth. In the summer of 1991, the first major Promise Keepers meeting drew 4,200 men. In 1992, there were 22,000 delegates. The following year, over 50,000 Promise Keepers packed into the Folsom Stadium in Boulder, Colorado. The total for 1994 exceeded 300,000. Over 40,000 clergymen attended a special pastors' conference in Atlanta, Georgia, February 13–15, 1996. Another 67,000 Promise Keepers filled Chicago's Soldier Field to overflowing June 28–29, 1996. (As of this writing, a "million man march" on Washington, D.C., is being planned for the fall of 1996.) While McCartney continues to be the focal point of Promise Keepers' momentum, Randy Phillips (another one of Pastor Ryle's parishioners) is the actual behind-the-scenes president of this mammoth organization. The

Promise Keepers' head office receives 10,000 phone calls and up to 5,000 pieces of mail per day.

There isn't enough room left in this volume to adequately explain the satanic components of Promise Keepers conferences. I can barely scratch the surface in one chapter. We can be certain that Lucifer is the *real* founder of Promise Keepers because the format is *so* subtle. The Bible is certainly in favor of Christian men becoming better husbands and fathers. However, to quote the wisdom of Dr. Bob Jones, Sr., "It is never right to do wrong in order to get a chance to do right." The Scripture clearly states, *"To obey is better than sacrifice."* (I Samuel 15:22b)

Following in the tradition of Billy Graham, Jerry Falwell, James Dobson and others, McCartney's crowds have grown in proportion to the amount of Bible doctrine that has been compromised. Promise number six (*"the number of a man"* [Revelation 13:18c]) in the Seven Promises of a Promise Keeper reads, "A Promise Keeper is committed to reaching beyond any racial and denominational barriers to demonstrate the power of biblical **unity**." While Steve Green sang "Let the Walls Come Down," ministers attending the Atlanta clergymen's conference were exhorted to apologize to one another for past "insensitive" remarks.

Unity remains the outstanding dogma of Promise Keepers philosophy. Yet, according to the Bible, unity is based upon what a Christian **believes** in his **mind**: *"That ye stand fast in one spirit with **one mind**"* (Philippians 1:27), *"That ye may with **one mind** and one mouth glorify God"* (Romans 15:6), and *"but that ye be perfectly joined together in the **same mind** and in the same judgment."* (I Corinthians 1:10)

Yet, according to Coach McCartney,

> The church is in bondage to the giant of denominational restrictions and another giant of racial and ethnic boundaries. PK is dedicated to uniting men through vital **relationships**.[1]

These "vital relationships" are *more* than a little weird. Albert Dager comments on the type of encounter groups being introduced into hundreds of local churches by Promise Keeper point men and ambassadors:

> One method of breaking the ice in the Promise Keepers men's groups is to play a game called **"People Bingo."** In this game the men review categories pertaining to certain traits and experiences, and mark a box that contains those elements. They go from man to man asking about those traits and experiences. The first person to complete five in a row in any

direction within a set time wins. The traits and experiences are based upon Robert Hicks's book, *The Masculine Journey*, and many center on the men's sexuality. I call it spiritual voyeurism.

Some of the questions regarding traits and experiences ask if they have been arrested at least once; **if they are wearing boxer shorts or bikini briefs**; if they were neglected or abused by their father; if they have emotional battle scars from a recent family feud; if they had a circumcision, vasectomy or prostate operation.[2]

Can you picture the apostles sitting around and asking one another such junk? Do you think McCartney ever asked his football players what kind of underwear *they* were wearing?

For the record, *real* men (like former all-American Joe Boyd) don't need encounter groups to fulfill their God-given responsibilities. (Lamentations 3:27; Galatians 6:5) And the spiritual encouragement of a friend or two at a time of crisis (Ecclesiastes 4:9, 10) does not constitute group sex therapy.

Other "masculine" topics of discussion include "**When I was potty trained and stopped wetting the bed**," "An unfortunate experience with pornography," "My first really embarrassing moment with a girl" and "The wedding night."[3] (I wonder how the wives of these "Chatty Kathy" Promise Keepers feel about their wedding nights being discussed in public.)

Of course, *sodomites* are drawn to such perversion and the Promise Keepers roll out the "pink" carpet for them. Although any sexual expression apart from the traditional marriage relationship is acknowledged as sinful, this *stated* position is watered down by applying a "politically correct, psychological approach to the subject of homosexuality." *They* say:

> As to homosexuality, Promise Keepers shares the same historical and biblical stance taken by Evangelicals and Catholics—that sex is a good gift from God—to be enjoyed in the context of heterosexual marriage. Promise Keepers also recognizes that homosexuality is a complex and potentially polarizing issue. There is a great debate surrounding its environmental and genetic origins, yet as an organization **we believe that homosexuals are men who need the same support, encouragement and healing we are offering to all men.**
>
> While we have clear convictions regarding the issue of homosexuality, we are **sensitive** to and have compassion for the men who are struggling with these issues. **We, therefore, support their being included and welcomed in all our events.**[4]

Every delegate who attended the Promise Keepers 1993 convention in Boulder, Colorado, received a complimentary copy of the previously mentioned book, *The Masculine Journey: Understanding the Six Stages of Manhood,* by Robert Hicks. Under the heading for Chapter Two, "Creational Male—Adam: The Noble Savage," we are presented with the "wisdom" of Charles Darwin: **"Man with all his noble qualities still bears in his bodily frame the indelible stamp of his lowly origin."**[5] It appears that Bob has some serious hang-ups which he is intent on passing along to the rest of us:

> I believe Jesus was phallic with all the inherent phallic passions we experience as men. But it was never **recorded** that Jesus had sexual relations with a woman. He may have thought about it as the movie *The Last Temptation of Christ* portrays, but even in this movie He did not give in to the temptation and remained true to his messianic course. **If temptation means anything, it meant Christ was tempted in *every* way as we are. That would mean not only heterosexual temptation but also homosexual temptation!** I have found this insight to be very helpful for gay men struggling with their sexuality.[6]

A blasphemous film, *The Last Temptation of Christ* portrayed graphic sexual lust, not merely temptation. Fantasizing about sin goes *beyond* temptation. It is a sin within the heart. According to Hicks, *the Son of God had to deal with the temptation of homosexuality.*

As I said before, Bob has some *real* hang-ups. The Bobgans add:

> Hicks declares: "I believe until the church sees men for what they are, phallic males with all their inherent spiritual tensions, it will not begin to reach men where they are living." In fact, he contends that men's sexual problems (including "sexual addictions," pornography, and adultery) "reveal how desperate we are to express, in some perverted form, the deep compulsion **to worship with our phallus.**"[7]

Speaking of "phallic males," over 600 Roman Catholic priests attended the Atlanta clergymen's conference, which brings us to the ultimate mission of Promise Keepers—*unity with the Vatican*! In the 1994 Seize the Moment Men's Conference in Portland, Oregon, McCartney shouted out:

> Hear Me: **Promise Keepers doesn't care if you're Catholic.** Do you love Jesus; are you born of the Spirit of God?[8]

Being a former Roman Catholic himself, the charismatic McCartney wouldn't *think* of insulting "His Holiness." Christian Van Liefde, "pastor" of St. Hilary Catholic Church in Pico Rivera, California, was quoted in the Saturday, May 6, 1995, *Los Angeles Times* as stating, "Promise Keepers places a very strong emphasis on returning to your own church congregation or parish and becoming an active layman."[9]

In the March 31 issue of *The Tidings*, the official newspaper for the archdiocese of Los Angeles, staff writer Mike Nelson reported, "Promise Keepers is a basic program of evangelization for men of faith, begun among more fundamentalist and evangelical Christian communities, but now being expanded to include Catholic congregations."[10] Van Liefde assured the faithful in the same article,

> There is no attempt at proselytizing or drawing men away from their faith to another church. The primary message of the weekend is turning your life over to Jesus Christ and standing tall as a man of faith.[11]

On a recent ABC news broadcast, Peter Jennings honored Bill McCartney as the program's Personality of the Week. *"Yea, and all that live godly in Christ Jesus shall suffer persecution."* (II Timothy 3:12)

LATTER RAIN

As bad as the preceding PK exposé is seen to be, it pales in comparison with the rarely known background and related future agenda of this diabolical movement.

In the late 1920's and 1930's a wave of esoteric teaching came into vogue, mixing truth with error and relying heavily on allegorical interpretation. Out of this hodgepodge of heresy in the 1940's came the doctrines known as "Latter Rain" (Deuteronomy 11:14) and the "Manifest Sons of God." (Romans 8:19) The cardinal beliefs of these cultists center on God's *restoration* to the end-day church (via his manifest sons) "truth" (latter rain) that was *lost* during the Dark Ages (i.e., the Alexandrian text, etc.).

George Warnock, a Latter Rain spokesman in the 1950's, predicted that the church would experience a 40-year lull followed by a glorious, end-day revival. Known interchangeably as Neo-Pentecostalism or Restoration theology (not to be confused with *Reconstructionism*, a distant cousin), these "doctrines of devils" were initially repudiated by the Assemblies of God denomination in 1948, and again in the 1960's, only to be embraced by the "charis-maniacs" of the 1990's.

UNHOLY LAUGHTER

In 1977, a 33-year-old South African "evangelist" by the name of Rodney Howard-Browne had an encounter with the spirit world (which *he* claimed was God) that left him "intoxicated on the wine of the Holy Ghost." He wrote:

> Suddenly the fire of God fell on me. It started on my head and went right down to my feet. His power burned in my body and stayed like that for three whole days.[12]

When *the Lord's* fire fell on Evangelist Dwight L. Moody, the dedicated soul winner ushered a million souls into the kingdom. The "strange fire" experienced by Browne led the false prophet to testify, "I began to **laugh** uncontrollably and then I began to weep and then speak with other tongues."[13]

While visiting the United States in 1987, Browne prophesied that God would send missionaries to America for a revival of "supernatural signs and wonders." (*"An evil and adulterous generation seeketh after a sign."* [Matthew 12:39a]) He later added that the Lord had handpicked *him* for the job.

In April of 1989, while Browne was conducting a meeting in Albany, New York, a pack of demons took over the service. (*He* claimed it was God.) People started falling out of their seats; some were laughing while others were crying. (I Corinthians 14:33)

After a number of similar "revivals," Rodney hit the big time during a four-week campaign at a "church" in Lakeland, Florida. The 10,000-seat auditorium was nearly filled every night. Visitors hailed from Africa, Argentina and Great Britain. Hundreds fell to the floor laughing their guts out. Henceforth, Browne would be known as the "Holy Ghost Bartender" of "Joel's Bar." (*"And whosoever speaketh a word against the Son of man, it shall be forgiven him: but whosoever speaketh against the Holy Ghost, it shall not be forgiven him, neither in this world, neither in the world to come."* [Matthew 12:32])

THE VINEYARD

About this time, another crackpot minister by the name of John Wimber was experiencing his own "heavenly" revelations. (He claims 27 specific contacts [14]— but who's counting?) Wimber, who at one time wrote musical arrangements for the Righteous Brothers, is currently the senior pastor of Vineyard Christian Fellowship (VCF) in Anaheim, California, and also heads up the Association of Vineyard Churches (AVC) and Vineyard Ministries International (VMI). (I can see Stonewall Jackson rolling over in his grave.) According to "Pastor John," the Lord said,

> I'm going to start it all over again. I'm going to pour out my Spirit in your midst like I did in the beginning.[15]

And then "Pastor John" said,

> But I looked at myself (suffering from cancer), and I'm out of energy. In my spirit I was just murmuring "Oh God, oh God." And at that point (mid January) the Lord gave me a word. I heard myself say: Shall I have this pleasure in my old age? The very words that Sarah **laughingly** said to herself when she overheard the LORD say she was going to have a son from her 90-year-old womb by her 100-year-old husband. (Genesis 18:10). This was a word of life from the Lord, and it touched me deeply.[16]

From here on out, things get "wild and woolly." After Randy Clark, a VCF pastor in St. Louis, got the "holy giggles," another one of Wimber's "preacher boys" by the name of John Arnott experienced the laughing phenomena way up in Toronto, Ontario. Ed Tarkowski wrote in June, 1995:

> Since January 20, 1994, Airport Christian Fellowship, a small Vineyard church in Toronto, has had services six nights a week for the last 10 months that have sometimes lasted until 2:00 a.m. Over 100,000 people have attended, and nearly 40,000 of those have been visitors from all over the world who come for what is being called the "Toronto Blessing."[17]

Absolute pandemonium breaks out at these meetings. One woman (II Timothy 3:6) described *her* experience at a Full Gospel Businessmen's Fellowship banquet in Houston:

The man [the speaker] said, "Well, Jesus, bless Frances!" Down I went faster than you could blink an eye, followed one second later by my precious husband!...I tried to get my hands off of the floor, but nothing happened. I couldn't believe what had happened to me, because it was physically impossible for me to move...

I felt as though someone had given me a divine alka seltzer because way down deep in the very center of my being I began to feel a most peculiar type of "bubbling."...Then it abruptly came out of my mouth in the form of the loudest laugh I have ever heard....No pressure on my mouth could keep the laughing back. I laughed, laughed, laughed and laughed....I stopped laughing just as quickly as I started, and **suddenly I was released from the bed of Holy Ghost glue in which I had been resting.**[18]

JOEL'S ARMY

Now according to Latter Rain theology, the bottom line is that all of this "Holy Ghost laughter" is due to the fact that the church is *pregnant!!* Yes, you heard it right the first time—*pregnant*. While "prophet" Byron Mode of Dallas revealed, "God is romancing his Church, and through the romance he says, 'I'm going to then IMPREGNATE and through the IMPREGNATION will then come NEW BIRTH...,' "[19] the End-time Handmaidens prophecy in October, 1994, adds:

Sarah is a type of the Church. The Church is "withered," and its womb is dried up in many places, but God is sending a revival of joy to awaken and renew the Church so that she can bring forth the "man-child" of joy, even the **army of overcomers** who will go forth in the likeness and image of the Lord in these last days.[20]

Did you catch that last part about an "army of overcomers"? Because Restoration theology teaches that the church has replaced Israel (standard Vatican polity), the heretics frequently wrest Old Testament Scriptures from their hermeneutical context. The "army of overcomers" is a reference to what is known among Latter Rain adherents as "Joel's Army." The following prophetic profile of the *devil's* army at *Armageddon* forms the basis of Wimber's "looney-tune" hermeneutics.

Blow ye the trumpet in Zion, and sound an alarm in my holy mountain: let all the inhabitants of the land tremble: for the day of the LORD cometh, for it is nigh at hand;

A day of darkness and of gloominess, a day of clouds and of thick darkness, as the morning spread upon the mountains: a great people and a strong; there hath not been ever the like, neither shall be any more after it, even to the years of many generations.

A fire devoureth before them; and behind them a flame burneth: the land is as the garden of Eden before them, and behind them a desolate wilderness; yea, and nothing shall escape them.

The appearance of them is as the appearance of horses; and as horsemen, so shall they run.

Like the noise of chariots on the tops of mountains shall they leap, like the noise of a flame of fire that devoureth the stubble, as a strong people set in battle array.

Before their face the people shall be much pained: all faces shall gather blackness.

They shall run like mighty men; they shall climb the wall like men of war; and they shall march every one on his ways, and they shall not break their ranks:

Neither shall one thrust another; they shall walk every one in his path: and when they fall upon the sword, they shall not be wounded.

They shall run to and fro in the city; they shall run upon the wall, they shall climb up upon the houses; they shall enter in at the windows like a thief.

The earth shall quake before them; the heavens shall tremble: the sun and the moon shall be dark, and the stars shall withdraw their shining.

(Joel 2:1-10)

As the church gives birth to little Isaac (meaning "laughter"—Get it?), a mighty revival/harvest is supposed to circle the globe in fulfillment of the Jewish Feast of Tabernacles. (Hang on, it gets crazier—or is it *scarier?*)

When Isaac (the revived church) grows up, he (they) will evolve into Joel's Army of *immortal* super-Christians. And the main function of Joel's Army is to "clean house for Jehovah." Jewel van der Merne (an Assembly of God minister who opposes Latter Rain theology) cites a "prophetic revelation" by some heretic named Glenn Foster:

I have been cleansing the Church. Now I am ready to begin cleansing the nations... The fire that falls first is upon the sacrifice on the altar— that's my Church. Then the fire falls upon the false prophets—that's the government and leadership of the world that rules in cruelty in its own wisdom...This is a special day—an appointed time...Behold, my Jehus [Joel's Army] are ready to receive a fresh anointing. Jehu will replace the rule of Ahab and Jezebel...there is a prophetic word upon the lips of the Elijahs of this hour, which shall feed the flesh of Jezebel to the dogs.[21]

Another "seer" states:

The Lord will raise up a great company of prophets, teachers, pastors and apostles that will be of the spirit of Phinehas...they will be moved by the jealousy of the Lord for the purity of His people...It was said of the Apostle Paul that he was turning the world upside down; it will be said of the apostles soon to be anointed that they will have turned an upside down world right side up. **Nations will tremble at the mention of their names.**[22]

Kenneth Copeland, a redneck apostate, puts the jelly on the bottom shelf:

One of these days, you may just be talking to someone, asking them how things went at church last Sunday, and they may say, Oh it was great! The glory of God was so strong it healed ten cripples, opened the ears of thirty deaf people, cured seven cases of cancer **and killed Brother Bigmouth and Sister Strife**...When the fire of God begins to burn and the rivers of the Spirit start to flow, he'll have to do one of two things: he'll either have to yield to the Spirit and let go of that sin by repenting, or he'll have to resist the flood of God's Spirit and be swept away.[23]

GUESS WHO?

Now for the critical moment of truth—*can you guess the misconstrued identity of Joel's Army*? I'll give you a hint: It has to do with the denominational affiliation of Phillips and McCartney. Their pastor, "Reverend" James Ryle, is the pastor of **Boulder Valley Vineyard Church** and a former associate of Vineyard Ministries founder, **John Wimber**. Jewel van der Merwe writes:

In a recent interview in response to a question as to whether the Promisekeepers could be fulfilling the prophecy in Joel of raising an army, James Ryle answered, "Yes...300,000 men have come together so far this year under Promisekeepers...Never in history have 300,000 men come together except to go to war. **These men are gathered for War.**"[24]

"Pastor" Ryle, who is also on the Promise Keepers Board of Directors, is not exactly what you would call a "spiritual giant." Jewel van der Merwe writes:

> Several years ago he [Ryle] had a vision regarding the "new music" that God was bringing to the church. **In this vision he had the revelation that the Beatles had the anointing for the new music that God wanted to bring forth, but somehow they missed God**—but God is still going to have another chance to bring forth this new music and people will just fall on their faces when they hear this sound.[25]

Tarkowski notes the subliminal indoctrination of Latter Rain heresy in official PK literature:

> Promise Keepers has incorporated key doctrines of the Manifest Sons of God into their material. The February 1995 issue of Suitable Helpers, a newsletter for women participating in Promise Keepers expresses that believers can become Christ Incarnate: "Our Lord is calling out a great host of men ready and willing to become 'Christs' in their homes: Promise Keepers. In grand, bold sweeps, **God has mustered an army.**"[26]

With the Promise Keepers unknowingly poised to become Joel's Army of religious hooligans, televangelist Pat Robertson has committed his media weight to the approaching holocaust. On a broadcast aired October 27, 1994, Robertson's generic sidekick, Ben Kinchlow (the Ed McMahon of Laodicea), asked the CBN president what he thought of a recent "700 Club" special on the laughing phenomena. (Note how the hypocrite tried to cover himself.)

> I applaud it. **But, again, you have to be careful that it doesn't go off into fanaticism**...But we've seen people fall over—absolutely—and all the rest of it. It's just the way it is when God's power is (evident).[27]

So Pat is worried about "fanaticism," is he? How much *crazier* can you get than "professing" Christians testifying about going to "Joel's Bar" so they can fall down laughing into a bed of Holy Ghost glue? (*"Will they not say that ye are mad?"* [I Corinthians 14:23b])

Four months earlier, on June 9, Robertson interviewed a "prophet" named Judson Cornwall. This madman told the audience that a fellow "prophet," Glenn Foster, had a vision of the two of them being *pregnant*. *Supposedly*, the Lord told Glenn:

> I am now impregnating some of my mature, older ministers with truth...I'm choosing my older men because I can trust them to carry that truth to full gestation and have patience to raise it up once it is delivered. **I will visit America one more time, and I will bring forth truth that is not now being taught and you will be part of it.**[28]

The powerful driving force behind the so-called "Religious Right" commented:

> The war's inside of us....If that war gets won, I mean, you're talking about major revival. One more time for America....It's gotta be **now!**[29]

On January 2, 1995, Robertson began to prophesy of a sweeping revival that would take us to the year 2000 A.D.:

> Ladies and gentlemen,...I have been in prayer for the last several days trying to find the mind of the Lord, and I'm relatively encouraged about 1995....**I do think we are entering on the greatest spiritual revival that has ever taken place in the history of mankind. It is going to build in intensity over the next five years**...I believe God is going to send a great revival **in the next five years** that will exceed anything that our minds can conceive. I'm talking about hundreds and hundreds and hundreds of millions of people that will come into the Kingdom, all over the world. It's going to be fabulous.[30]

My readers will note that Robertson's eschatology is identical to the Dominion theology of the Vineyard movement—that a revived end-day Church (Joel's Army) will bring in the Kingdom. Pat continues:

> I do think that the Biblical model is...**first** a revival, an outpouring of His Spirit, **then** a great harvest of souls, and **then** a judgment on the ungodly who broke His covenant and refuse to follow His ways. And so that's coming. It's just a question, it's being delayed for a while till we get the harvest in.[31]

Robertson would put the present generation of professing Christians into a Millennial setting by the year 2000 *without a rapture or tribulation period!* He says the post-revival judgment falls on the *ungodly.* With reference to the first beast of Revelation 13, the King James Bible declares, *"And it was given unto him to make **war** with the saints, **and to overcome them:** and power was given him over all kindreds, and tongues, and nations."* (Revelation 13:7)

The host described in Joel 2:1-11 is the army of the *beast* (Revelation 16:14)! Why would *Zion* "sound an alarm" at the arrival of their Messiah? The "darkness" and "gloominess" described in Joel 2:2 are the same conditions which were forecast in Matthew 24:15-26.

For the record, the *real* Joel's Army mentioned in Joel 2:11 does not show up until the *end* of the tribulation period: *"And I saw the beast, and the kings of the earth, and their armies, gathered together to make **war** against **him that sat on the horse, and against his army.**"* (Revelation 19:19) Someone needs to inform a dizzy church age that the person on the horse is *not* Bill McCartney or Pat Robertson but **Jesus Christ the King!**

This focus on the year **2,000** is a key Latter Rain concept. And because one misappropriation of Scripture is as good as another, not only will the "Church" experience the Old Testament Feast of Tabernacles via her unprecedented "ingathering of souls," but she will *also* celebrate the Year of Jubilee—*in* **2000 A.D.** In his book entitled *The Star of 2000*, Jay Gary, A.D. 2000 Global Service Office Coordinator, fantasizes:

> On the last and greatest day of the Feast of Tabernacles, Jesus "stood and said in a loud voice, 'If anyone is thirsty, let him come and drink' " (John 7:37). Then as well as today, Jesus calls us to experience His jubilee...[Israel's] 50th year was the Jubilee—or the culmination of joy. The entire year was consecrated to making right whatever had gone wrong. **I am convinced that the year 2000 can truly be a Jubilee year for the entire human family.**[32]

Pat Robertson, high potentate of the "Religious Right," couldn't agree more. As early as 1981, Robertson's *Perspective* newsletter contained a section entitled *A Radical Proposal to Halt Inflation.* In it he stated, "If inflation is to be broken, there must be a **cancellation of debt—on a world-wide basis,**" and also, "Every type of debt, secured or unsecured, should be **totally released.**"[33]

JOHN PAUL'S JUBILEE

Now with all this talk about "Joel's Bar" and the "new wine" of joy being passed around, we shouldn't be surprised that John Paul II, good ol' "Tiny Bubbles" himself, would play the lead role in this finale of deception. No "Holy Father" in his right mind would fail to cash in on the propitious turn of a millennium.

The last time such a "golden" opportunity presented itself, Pope Silvester II (999–1003) was the reigning "Vicar of Christ." In the closing months of the tenth century, Silvester exploited the growing paranoia of his superstitious flock by proclaiming that the world would end at the close of the millennium. Manhattan relates:

> Many Roman Catholics, in fact, who until then had ignored Christ's teaching about temporal wealth, now took it in deadly earnest. As the year 1000 drew nearer, they got rid of their possessions with increasing speed. How? By donating them to what they were told was Christ's bride on earth, the Roman Church. And so it came to pass that monasteries, nunneries, abbeys, bishops' palaces and the like bustled with activity. Believers came and went, not only to confess their sins, to repent and to prepare for the end of the world in purity and poverty, but also to donate and give to the Roman Catholic Institution all they had. They gave her their money, their valuables, their houses, their lands. Many of them became total paupers, since what would it avail them to die as the owners of anything when the world was destroyed? Whereas, by giving away everything they were gaining merit in the eyes of the Great Judge!
>
> The Church, via her monastic orders and clergy, accepted the mounting offers of earthly riches. This she did by duly recording them with legal documents, witnesses and the like. Why such mundane precautions? To prove to the Lord on Judgment Day that Smith in England, Schmidt in Germany, Amundsen in Scandinavia, MacLaren in Scotland and O'Donovan in Ireland had truly got rid of their earthly possessions? Not at all! To prove with matter-of-fact concreteness that the possessions of all those who had given were, from then on, the possessions of the papacy.For that is precisely what happened.
>
> When, following the long night of terror on the last day of December 999, the first dawn of the year 1000 lit the Eastern sky without anything happening, many Roman Catholics, whether they believed that the Lord had postponed the Day in response to prayers or that they had made a mistake, gave an audible sigh of relief throughout Christendom. Those who had given away their property made for the ecclesiastical centers which had accepted their "offerings," only to be told that their money,

houses, lands, were no longer theirs. It had been the most spectacular give-away in history.[34]

Meanwhile, back at the ranch, Pope John Paul II himself just *happens* to be calling for a grand, ecumenical Jubilee celebration during the year 2000! With the prospect of bankrupting what is left of Christian America, John will do *his* part for the "sake of humanity," etc. On November 10, 1994, the "Holy Father" released a 72-page letter entitled *The Coming of the Third Millennium: Preparation for the Jubilee of the Year 2000.* Ed Tarkowski cites from this socialistic manifesto:

> From this point of view, if we recall that Jesus came to "preach the good news to the poor" (Mt. 11:5; Lk. 7:22), how can we fail to lay greater emphasis on the church's preferential option for the poor and the outcast?... Thus, in the spirit of the Book of Leviticus (25:8-12), Christians will have to raise their voice on behalf of all the poor of the world, proposing the jubilee as an appropriate time to give thought, among other things, to reducing substantially, **if not canceling outright, the international debt which seriously threatens the future of many nations**... In fact, preparing for the year 2000 has become as it were a hermeneutical key of my pontificate.[35]

With the majority of realistic economists expecting a crash at any moment, a Vatican-sponsored "Jubilee" could conceivably coincide with a Round Table-sponsored United Nations bailout via a cashless, one-world monetary unit known as the *Bancor*, backed by the global assets of the IMF-World Bank conglomerate. (Revelation 13:17) Thus, it would appear that the *corporate* identity of the "beast" ridden by the "woman" in Revelation 17:3 (i.e., the financial base of the Revived Roman Empire) is none other than "The Creature from Jekyll Island" in its fully matured form.

In the *Detroit Free Press* for November 28, 1994, religion writer David Crumm announced:

> In weekend ceremonies at the Vatican, Pope John Paul II called on his new cardinals to work with him on an ambitious plan for world peace that includes meetings of Muslim, Christian and Jewish religious leaders in Bethlehem, Jerusalem and on Mt. Sinai in 1999.[36]

THE AGE OF AQUARIUS

Having inaugurated his "holy pontificate" with a champagne bash, the aging party animal apparently wants to go out with a bang. And because

New Agers have been looking to the year 2000 as the "Dawning of the Age of Aquarius," they are more than welcome to attend as well—the more the merrier! In fact, the "power of God" is supposed to be so overwhelming that a major miracle of reconciliation is being predicted to occur. New Ager Barbara Marx Hubbard describes the impending "Planetary Pentecost":

> The planetary celebration will begin for the birth of humankind in the universe, a blessed Cosmic Child eagerly awaited by the evolved beings through the universe without end. Hallelujah... An uncontrollable joy [Planetary Smile] will ripple through the thinking layer of Earth. The co-creative systems, which are lying psychologically dormant in humanity will be activated. From within, all sensitive persons will feel the joy of the force, flooding their systems with love and attraction.[37]

The final result of both the Latter Rain Tabernacles/Jubilee celebrations *and* the New Age Planetary Pentecost will be the birth of a unified body filled with one spirit of joy and celebration. Hubbard concludes:

> It was a planetary smile—like the smile of a newborn baby.... Now for the first time, we were seeing it together. Ecstatic joy rippled through the planetary body—and through me as one of its billions of members.... I saw it was true. We are being born.... **We are going to be one body, whether we like ourselves or not.**[38]

RETROSPECTION

So there you have it! Coach McCartney's deluded disciples are apparently too busy batting beach balls around the auditorium to realize that their hero's Vineyard roots go a *lot* deeper than the PK's three non-negotiables of *integrity, commitment* and *action.* Somehow they missed Job 14:4, which says, *"Who can bring a clean thing out of an unclean? not one."*

Sadly, any number of these men could reason, "If Promise Keepers is really all that bad, why would godly men like James Dobson, Howard Hendricks, Tony Evans, Bill Gaither and others be lending their enthusiastic support? Hasn't Dr. Joe Stowell, president of the prestigious Moody Bible Institute, personally spoken at more than one Promise Keepers Conference?"

The question arises as to how this unprecedented deception was perpetrated. Ed Tarkowski provides an illuminating perspective:

How did so many Christians come from there to here in so short a time? Looking back, it seems that the Word of Faith and Positive Thinking teachings struck the first spark. These did much to turn hearts to a self-centered life rather than a God-centered one. As hearts glowed with proclamations such as "Every promise in the book is mine," "Claim your inheritance," and "Take the land," Restoration teaching waited for its opportunity.

Then when the Church at large finally realized that a New World Order based on New Age spirituality was planned for our future, Restorationists made their move. For years they'd preached that the Church was to bring in the Kingdom of God, but no one, particularly Evangelicals, had paid attention. Those pesky beliefs about tribulation and rapture had blinded the Church to their truth, but now Christians wanted political rights!

The inheritance promised by Word of Faith teachers coincided nicely with the Restorationist's promise of a Christian Kingdom on earth. "Take the land" was applied to a literal land, and the Christianizing of society and its governments became a real possibility. The emphasis was no longer on the hope of Jesus' coming to save both Israel and the Church. Instead, a united intercessory Church turned to an Old Testament promise made to Israel: "If My people, which are called by My name, shall humble themselves and pray;... I... will restore their land." In all the excitement, the word "revival" was subtly redefined, and hardly anyone noticed.

Finally, after 25 years of incremental change in Church thinking, the Restorationists stood on the revised purpose for revival and announced, "A great move of God is beginning! Revival is here!" The new good news was that God had an endtime army which would march through the land to victory, and each Christian was a potential soldier. And when "the fire fell" through Rodney Howard-Browne and the Toronto Blessing, Christians from all over the world came to Toronto to enlist.

Now the restoration of dominion began to merge with the supernatural potential by the Latter Rain teachings, and revival took on even more meaning. God's Army would be equipped with victory over death, and the Power of Evangelism of Latter Rain would be directed to Restorationism's objectives. Jesus' cross became the symbolic sword of this new gospel and lost even more of its godly meaning. The gospel of sin, Christ's shed blood and the cross, and the promise of His personal, visible return in victory was overtaken by the gospel of revival. Christians from all over the world saw the flames burning bright and were drawn to its light, and a new unity began to arise.[39]

As we gaze in wonderment at the Promise Keepers' "mixed multitude" of neo-Evangelicals, backslidden Baptists, liberal Protestants, Catholic priests, Mormon elders and "sensitive" Sodomites euphorically high-fiving one another in the name of the Lord, Rodney Howard-Browne's allusion to spiritual intoxication is more readily comprehended.

However, the Lord Jesus Christ is *definitely* not the host of this Charismatic wine party. The Saviour specifically **promised** his Apostles in the upper room, *"I will not drink henceforth of this fruit of the vine, until that day when I drink it new with you in my Father's kingdom."* (Matthew 26:29)

Furthermore, Rodney "let-it-bubble-out-your-belly" Howard-Browne is not the "Holy Ghost Bartender" at "Joel's Bar" either; the "joint" is run by a *barmaid*:

> *And the **woman** was arrayed in purple and scarlet colour, and decked with gold and precious stones and pearls, having a golden **cup** in her hand full of abominations and filthiness of her fornication... For all nations have **drunk** of the **wine** of the wrath of her fornication.* (Revelation 17:4; 18:3a)

If there's a *male* pouring drinks at the ecumenical shindig in 2000 A.D., look for a "phallic guy" who works for **THE MOTHER OF HARLOTS.** (Hint: His favorite song is "The Mountaineer.") By the way, when "Joel's Bar" is eventually closed down, the great majority of "inebriated" patrons will find themselves reassembled for a final "get-together"—to drink a *different* wine, from a *different* cup:

> *And the third angel followed them, saying with a loud voice, If any man worship the beast and his image, and receive his mark in his forehead, or in his hand, the same shall **drink** of the **wine** of the wrath of God, which is poured out without mixture into the **cup** of his indignation; and he shall be tormented with fire and brimstone in the presence of the holy angels, and in the presence of the Lamb. And the smoke of their torment ascendeth up for ever and ever: and they have no rest day nor night, who worship the beast and his image, and whosoever receiveth the mark of his name.* (Revelation 14:9-11)

*"I also will **laugh** at your calamity."*
(Proverbs 1:26a)

XXIII

Hold Fast!

> *"Not forsaking the assembling of ourselves together, as the manner of some is; but exhorting one another: and so much the more, as ye see the day approaching."* (Hebrews 10:25)

A S THIS BOOK was going to press, the devil's global extravaganza loomed a mere 3½ years away. With this ominous countdown under way, Roman Catholics, neo-Pentecostals and New Agers prepare to zero in on the "party poopers" (discerning Bible believers) who refuse to go with the flow. (Matthew 24:26) In her book *The Revelation: Our Crisis Is a Birth*, New Age "prophetess" Barbara Marx Hubbard attempts to intimidate the body of Christ:

> Dearly beloved of the **existing churches**, do not reject the saviors of the world, the natural Christs who are springing up among you, as well as among peoples who, though they have not been **institutionalized** as Christians, yet hold God consciousness in their attention at all times.[1]

She then justifies the eradication of whatever narrow-minded riffraff may refuse to heed her warning:

> First you may have to decide to save the child by **destroying those elements which are unhealthy.** If you are a surgeon delivering a child whose umbilical cord is wrapped around his neck, you must operate quickly, or the child will be strangled by the cord that connects him to the past.

The operation to save humanity is also painful. You do not want to kill bodies but to change minds, yet the "good" will also suffer as you eliminate self-centeredness that would destroy the whole body.[2]

In an earlier "vision" at the Toronto Vineyard in 1984, "prophet" Wes Campbell saw the future religious bloodletting as a reenactment of the War Between the States. Is it mere coincidence that the nation's Bible belt is cast once again as the consumate evil? ("His truth is marching on," etc.):

And the church was gathered in a large civil war-type big stately mansion, a big ballroom, and they were dancing. And they were dressed in colorful clothes and happy, and they were moving and they were laughing and they were dancing and they were just having the wonderful party of their life.

And he looked at that and Bob began to laugh and he said "Look at them dance, look at them have fun." And an angel came and said "Wait. Not yet." And then what happened is that strangely in the ballroom, the crowd began to change, and they began to take sides, and they began to have blue coats and gray coats, and in a moment civil war broke out. A bloody civil war broke out. Ryle has had a similar vision. The Lord even showed him how the blue coats stand for the revelatory, the revelation, and the gray for gray matter, man's wisdom. And in this context the north fought the south and the south fought the north, and the south wanted to keep the people enslaved. They wanted their money. They wanted their bodies. They wanted their personhood to keep the system going. And the north said, "No! Freedom! Freedom!"

And they went into a terrific fight, and it was father against son, brother against brother, and a man's enemies were in his own house. And the angel said this: "There won't be a house that escapes weeping." We do not know how long this time of visitation will continue in this capacity. But when the time is up you run with all your might, because as this begins to be known throughout the entire Christian community of the world, there will come a polarization.

And there eventually will become wars. There will be wars in your household. Your own family may not understand what's going on. Your own family may turn against you. That doesn't mean they're evil. That just means as Christians they haven't seen this aspect of the Holy Spirit. 'Cause they're Christians. We're talking about Christians. But the end of the vision was this: that after the time of bloodshed, the Lord was going to heal the breach. And then the harvest will come in.[3]

In addition to these blatant pronouncements, an *"understanding of the times "*(I Chronicles 12:32a) will confirm that America has come a mighty long way from her "Little House on the Prairie" days: phone sex and phone psychics; Dennis Rodman, a.k.a. "The Worm"; Benny Hinn and Benny Hill; "don't ask, don't tell"; virtual reality and computer pornography; Hillary, Chelsea, Socks, Bill and Whitewater; UFO landing strips and the Information Highway; Waco and Ruby Ridge; Mighty Morphin Power Rangers; Rodney King and the Lion King; heavy metal, Michael Jackson, pedophiles and child sacrifice; O. J. Simpson and Jack Kevorkian; microchip monitoring technology; Oprah and Madonna; unisex Little Leagues and female police officers; Jesse Jackson (CFR) and Joseph Cardinal Bernardin (CFR); Janet Reno and federal district court judges; CIA drug trafficking and a nationwide crime epidemic; Chuck Templeton Awards; Free Masonry; "Minister" Louis Farrahkan's ½ Million Man March; George Bush (CFR, TC) and Yale University's Order of Skull and Bones; Hate Crimes, RICO and Tort Law; black helicopters, detention centers and thousands of UN troops on American soil; Dan Rather (CFR), Colin Powell (CFR), Andrew Young (CFR), Dick Cheney (CFR) and Donna Shalala (CFR, TC); Bruce Babbitt (CFR, TC) and Paul A. Volcker (CFR, TC); Justice Sandra Day O'Connor (CFR), Justice Ruth Bader Ginsburg (CFR) and Justice Stephen G. Breyer (CFR); William F. Buckley (CFR), Henry A. Kissinger (CFR, TC), **Newton L. Gingrich (CFR)** and Rush Limbaugh; IRS, BATF, FEMA, ACLU, UNESCO, MTV, NAMBLA, AIDS, Visa, GATT, MJTF, FINCEN, NAFTA, NPR, HIV, NIV, NASV, and Robert Sloan, Jr., president of Baylor University (SBC) performing a jitterbug with his wife, Sue, April 18, 1996, at the first campus dance in the school's 151-year history, approved in a poll by 94% of the student body. (Matthew 14:6)

A black preacher-friend of mine once described the current world scene as "Chaos in the Cosmos."

Things are even getting a bit too rough for America's premier mayor, Marion Barry. "His Honor" dropped out of sight during the first two weeks of May, 1996, to visit rest centers in Maryland and Missouri. The *Chicago Tribune* for May 14, reported:

> Denying he had relapsed into alcohol or drug abuse, Mayor Marion Barry declared himself physically and spiritually fit to resume work after two weeks of rest in seclusion.

With dozens of applauding city officials seated at two long tables before him, Barry said he had abruptly left the financially troubled capital on April 29 because he had detected "telltale signs" of physical and spiritual relapse.

"Each of us is human," he said. "The president takes time off and goes to Camp David and other places. What's the furor over my ability to continue?"...

Looking dapper in a black suit, having shed 22 pounds, the mayor talked mostly about the state of his religious beliefs and spiritual renewal rather than the city's problems.

"I know that many people don't understand why or believe that an elected official should be publicly talking about the holy spirit of God," he said.

"This nation was founded by God-fearing people, men such as Martin Luther King Jr., who have shown us that internal values impact external actions in every area of our lives."

Later, he told the assembly, **"God chose me and God working through the people of Washington placed me in the mayor's office."**

Barry did concede that the city, its finances overseen by a congressionally picked control board, was "in financial distress" and needed to borrow $500 million from the U.S. Treasury.[4]

Mayor Barry isn't the only corrupt politician in Washington who ought to be *thrown in the slammer*! Over the three-day period, June 30–July 1, 1992, Joseph Biden—a **Roman Catholic** congressman from Delaware— delivered a speech in the Senate entitled **"The Threshold of the New World Order."** A few of the excerpts are as follows:

> The full panoply of threats to our future security and prosperity, the proliferation of deadly high-tech weapons, the accelerating degradation of our planetary environment, economic protectionism and unfair competition, overpopulation and migration, narcotics and AIDS all require **global solutions.** [Remember the Report from Iron Mountain?]
>
> Fortunately, the American people comprehend the reality; and precisely for that reason, they expect to see the strong hand of American leadership in world affairs... My answer is that the moment is upon us to define a compelling concept of a **new world order** to commit our selves to it, and to lead the world to its realization.
>
> The imperative to **cooperate** carries with it another imperative; that America lead the world into the **21st century** as boldly as it led the West in a half-century of cold war. In the decisive years ahead—years that will determine the very nature of our planet—**international cooperation** on

the scale necessary will succeed only if the world's preeminent nation assume that mantle of visionary leadership.

But on the eve of the **21st century**, basic facts of life on Earth— alarming facts we may wish to deny but which are undeniable—require us to expand our understanding of security. **Collective security** today must encompass not only the security of nations but also mankind's security in a **global environment**...Militarily, we must think of national defense as relying on strong American Armed Forces, but also, in equal measure, on our ability to generate actions of prevention and response by the entire **world community**.

And most fundamentally, we must now see economics not only as the foundation of our national strength but also as embracing the protection of our **global environment**, for economics and the environment have become inseparable...**The UN Security Council** must reflect the reality of **world power** and the reality of **world problems**; it must comprise those countries with the resources—both material and human—to address the full range of **global security** concerns [i.e., bankrupt what is left of America].

A more pressing need, on which we should act without awaiting the negotiation of membership changes is to further empower the **Security Council** through the standing availability of military forces...To realize the full potential of collective security, we must divest ourselves of the vainglorious dream of a pax Americana [American peace]—and look instead for a means to regularize swift, **multinational** decision and response.

The mechanism to achieve this lies—unused—in article 43 of the **United Nations Charter**, which provided that: "All members undertake to make available to the Security Council, on its call and in accordance with a special agreement or agreements, **armed forces**...necessary for the purpose of maintaining international peace and security."...The time has come; the United States, in conjunction with other key nations, should now designate forces under article 43 of the **United Nations Charter**.[5]

Joe wants to "help" America prepare for the twenty-first century. The fact is, a cartoon in *Mad* magazine contained more truth than was contained in the senator's entire traitorous speech. The scene depicted a frantic bomber pilot clutching the controls of his devastated aircraft. Smoke was billowing from the cockpit. Bullet holes were everywhere. Turning to his bleeding co-pilot, he said, "If you think this is bad, *wait 'til we get out of the hangar!*"

It was precisely due to such calamitous end-time conditions that the Holy Spirit moved the author of Hebrews to write, *"Not forsaking the assembling of ourselves together, as the manner of some is; but exhorting* *one another: and so much the more, as ye see the day approaching."* (Hebrews 10:25)

The Bible teaches that the closer we get to the end, the more faithful we must be to the *"house of God, which is the church of the living God, the pillar and ground of the truth."* (I Timothy 3:15) An important reason for this injunction is found in Matthew 24:12: *"And because iniquity shall abound, the love of many shall wax cold."* While unsaved men have to cope with "Chaos in the Cosmos" (Job 14:1), God would have His children *"exhorting one another."*

Furthermore, it should be obvious by now that the Holy Spirit wasn't talking about "The Church of Your Choice." The central purpose of my book has been to point born-again believers *back* to the local New Testament church, *"and so much the more, as ye see the day approaching." What Hath God Wrought!* was written in defense of the Independent Baptist churches of America. (Jude 3)

If you are a sincere, born-again Presbyterian, you need to get *immersed* and become a sincere member of a local New Testament church. If you are a sincere, born-again Methodist, you need to do the same. (You'll love the doctrine of eternal security.) If you are a saved Roman Catholic, you *definitely* need to dump the Whore and join the ranks of Independent Baptists. If you have found your way into a wishy-washy, non/inter-denominational, "we-don't-stand-for-anything-so-we-will-fall-for-anything" religious social club, you *desperately* need to become an Independent Baptist. And by *all* means, if you are not a member of any denomination, you need to enlist in the only fighting unit that is presented in Holy Scripture.

For those readers who are not actively serving in a soul-winning, sin-fighting, King James Bible-honoring, Hellfire-and-damnation Independent Baptist church, the probable reason would be limited to either an unawareness of the issue (Acts 19:2), an inaccessibility to such a church (Acts 18:2) or an unwillingness to bear the stigma of an Independent Baptist (Hebrews 13:13). The underlying cause for the last reason would be a general unwillingness to live for eternal values. (II Timothy 4:10)

The Lord has a special exhortation for the Laodicean Christian who has been willfully blinded by the *"care of this world and the deceitfulness of riches."* (Matthew 13:22b) Satan personally showed our High Priest the *"kingdoms of the world, and the glory of them"* saying, *"All these things will I give thee, if thou wilt fall down and worship me."* (Matthew 4:8, 9)

Having rejected this temptation in the days of his flesh, the King of Glory declares, *"To him that overcometh will I grant to sit with me in my throne, even as I also overcame, and am set down with my Father in his throne."* (Revelation 3:21)

As to my readers who *are* members of a local New Testament Baptist church, *your* message is a vital one as well. At the onset of the Philadelphia age (1789), Bible-believing soul winners were exhorted to "go out" through the open door of unprecedented religious liberty. Although there were Laodicean-minded believers around at that time, their numbers were negligible in comparison.

However, with the advent of materialism and the resultant modern Bible movement (Rosie, Elvis and Billy), Laodiceans have moved into the *majority*, leaving Philadelphia Christians in the *minority*. The effect on the Great Commission has been devastating. Because a generation of worldly churches have refused to open *their* doors to the Lord Jesus Christ Himself (Revelation 3:20), fewer and fewer Gentiles have been finding their *own* way through the critical *"door of faith."* (Acts 14:27) This resultant loss of salt has in turn led to the closing of the initial, all-important door to America's First Amendment religious guarantees. (Revelation 3:8)

Therefore, the battle orders for the *closing* days of the Philadelphia church age are: *"**Hold** that **fast** which thou hast, that no man take thy crown."* (Revelation 3:11) As more and more traditional liberties are being extinguished, Philadelphia soul winners are finding their activities increasingly restricted. Hence a return to the admonition once given the godly Dark Ages remnant in Thyatira, *"I will put upon you none other burden. But that which ye have already **hold fast** till I come."* (Revelation 2:24b, 25)

This is not to say that the Philadelphia minority should grow lax in their personal soul-winning efforts because a nation of materialistic Gentiles have found their like-minded, backslidden Christian neighbors to be a momentary conscience soother (i.e., "Well, if *that's* what being a Christian is all about—count me out," etc.). To the contrary, in times of apostasy the faithful remnant need to fight all the harder. This is especially true according to the Mosaic code of warfare (as perfected by Gideon in Judges 7:1-7):

And the officers shall speak further unto the people, and they shall say, What man is there that is fearful and fainthearted? let him go and return unto his house, lest his brethren's heart faint as well as his heart. (Deuteronomy 20:8)

The Baptist songwriter, P. P. Bliss, put it this way:

> *See the mighty host advancing,*
> *Satan leading on;*
> *Mighty men around us falling,*
> *Courage almost gone!*
>
> *"Hold the fort, for I am coming,"*
> *Jesus signals still;*
> *Wave the answer back to heaven,*
> *"By Thy grace we will."*

The harvest of the New Testament church has followed the normal threefold stage of ingathering as illustrated by the doctrine of the resurrection. Paul wrote, *"But every man in his own order: Christ the firstfruits; afterward they that are Christ's at his coming"* (I Corinthians 15:23), the resurrection of tribulation saints constituting the gleanings.

Likewise, with respect to the reaping of lost mankind, the firstfruits were gathered between Pentecost and Hampton Court. The main harvest (the era of revivalism) commenced with the 1611 Authorized Version, while conversely, the blatant rejection of the King James Bible for any number of generic challengers has ushered in the final stage of gleanings.

Though incognizant of the need for a "King-James-only" position at the time, a powerful Baptist counterattack of soul winning and church building was launched in the 1960's and 1970's. Much of the inspiration and leadership during this period was provided by Dr. G. B. Vick and the Baptist Bible College of Springfield, Missouri, Dr. Lee Roberson and the Highland Park Baptist Church bus ministry and by Drs. John R. Rice and Jack Hyles through the Sword of the Lord conferences. Unfortunately, as with the short-lived revival under King Josiah (II Kings 22) which merely forestalled Israel's judgment, this hiatus of evangelistic fervor was eventually eclipsed by the advent of the charismatic megachurch movement.

As the sixth and seventh books of the Bible, *Joshua* and *Judges*, parallel the sixth and seventh churches of Revelation, *Philadelphia* and *Laodicea*, we are not surprised to find that the concluding statement of Judges, *"In those days there was no king in Israel: every man did that which was right in his own eyes"* (Judges 21:25) is followed by the beautiful little story of a *Gentile* maiden who faithfully *gleans* in the field. What better place for the the book of Ruth than after the book of Judges?

While the *Orpahs* of this age "go back," *we* must pattern ourselves after Ruth's faithfulness:

> *And Ruth said, Intreat me not to leave thee, or to return from following after thee: for whither thou goest, I will go; and where thou lodgest, I will lodge: thy people shall be my people, and thy God my God.* (Ruth 1:16)

As in the case of Ruth, our gleaning time will also be consummated by a *wedding celebration.* And as the name *Boaz* means *swift in motion,* our Kinsman Redeemer will be sure to retrieve *His* bride *"in the twinkling of an eye."* (I Corinthians 15:52a)

This leads us back to the subject of "doors." Beloved, with the once-open door of religious liberty closed *before* us, be encouraged that *another* door is about to be opened from *above.* The message of "hold fast" will soon be changed to "Come up!"

> *After this I looked, and, behold, a **door was opened in heaven**: and the first voice which I heard was as it were of a **trumpet** talking with me; which said, **Come up** hither, and I will shew thee things which must be hereafter.* (Revelation 4:1)

Amidst the great Laodicean apostasy, Philadelphia Christians are specifically pointed to the blessed hope of His soon-appearing:

> *Because thou hast kept the word of my patience, I also will keep thee from **the hour of temptation**, which shall come upon all the world, to try them that dwell on the earth. Behold, **I come quickly**: hold that fast which thou hast, that no man take thy crown.* (Revelation 3:10, 11)

As the pressure from Joel's Army and any number of other satanic end-day scenarios builds, local church members are to *"comfort one another with these words"*:

*For the Lord himself shall descend from heaven with a shout, with the voice of the archangel, and with the **trump** of God: and the dead in Christ shall rise first: Then we which are alive and remain shall be caught up together with them in the clouds, to meet the Lord in the air: and so shall we ever be with the Lord.* (I Thessalonians 4:16, 17)

Do the words *"and so much the more, as ye see the day approaching"* ring with new meaning?

With so many "Demases" selling out for this present world, it is *imperative* for the Philadelphia believers to stay after souls. To waver is to jeopardize our reward—*"that no man take thy crown."* The Apostle Peter reminds us:

That the trial of your faith, being much more precious than of gold that perisheth, though it be tried with fire, might be found unto praise and honour and glory at the appearing of Jesus Christ. (I Peter 1:7)

Likewise, John the Beloved warns:

And now, little children, abide in him; that, when he shall appear, we may have confidence, and not be ashamed before him at his coming. (I John 2:28)

Paul relates this shame to a dereliction of personal soul winning and missionary support:

Awake to righteousness, and sin not; for some have not the knowledge of God: I speak this to your shame. (I Corinthians 15:34)

The majority of born-again believers are under the impression that the rapture will be the most exhilarating event of their Christian experience. Sporting bumper stickers such as, "Warning, in case of rapture, this car will self-destruct, etc." the prospect of being *"ashamed before him at his coming"* has apparently never dawned on Laodicea. Note the cross reference to I Peter 1:7 and the specific mention of "shame" in our Lord's personal rebuke of His lukewarm church.

> *I counsel thee to buy of me **gold tried in the fire**, that thou mayest be rich; and white raiment, that thou mayest be clothed, and that the **shame** of thy nakedness do not appear; and anoint thine eyes with eyesalve, that thou mayest see.* (Revelation 3:18)

The glow of such heavenly raiment will be in direct proportion to the believer's personal soul winning:

> *And they that be wise shall **shine** as the brightness of the firmament; and they that **turn many to righteousness** as the stars for ever and ever.* (Daniel 12:3)

The average Christian today is so temporal-minded, he doesn't even comprehend the major implication of the rapture itself. It is not insignificant that Laodicea was the only church in Revelation exempted from even a minimal commendation. Modern-day Laodicea constitutes *the* church age which has been blessed with the most *light* (commentaries, tapes, Bible on computer, etc.), *material conveniences* (indoor toilets, Air Jordan gym shoes, etc.) and *protection from persecution* (Bloody Mary, the rack, etc.). In fact, end-day believers are *so* spoiled, *they won't even have to meet the Grim Reaper!* (I Corinthians 15:51)

Yet, in the face of a divine accountability—*"For unto whomsoever much is given, of him shall be much required"* (Luke 12:48)—the "Rosie, Elvis and Billy" generation has produced the *least* amount of fruit! (Matthew 25:25)

So *why* is there a rapture of the body of Christ in the first place? From a dispensational point of view, I Thessalonians 5:9 certainly does apply, *"For God hath not appointed **us** to wrath, but to obtain salvation by our Lord Jesus Christ."* The same could be said for Daniel 9:24, *"Seventy weeks are determined upon **thy** people and upon **thy** holy city."*

However, a desire to shield the last Christian generation from tribulation judgment is not the *exclusive* reason for the translation of the saints. God's children have been suffering torture and martyrdom for 2,000 years. As bad as the time of Jacob's trouble will be, pain is still pain. Personally, if I were a lost man and had to choose between my wife being eaten by a lion or getting hit in the head with a 100-pound hailstone, I believe I'd prefer the latter as a "mercy shot."

A pertinent text which has been overlooked by the "modern exegete" is Matthew 5:13, *"Ye are the salt of the earth: but if the salt have lost his savour, wherewith shall it be salted?* **it is thenceforth good for nothing,** *but to be cast out, and to be trodden under foot of men."*

One of the most obvious reasons for the rapture is because the backslidden church of Laodicea has simply *run out of spiritual gas*—the salt *has* lost its savor!! How many of *your* unsaved relatives (particularly the male side of the family) have gotten under conviction watching Benny Hinn jumping around in his white suit?

Occasionally, it becomes necessary for preachers to explain the untimely death of a brazen backslider by referring to the Bible's *"sin unto death."* (John 5:16) According to a common interpretation, when the living testimony of a wayward Christian becomes more of a hindrance to the Gospel than a help, the Lord may call him Home early. (Ecclesiastes 7:16, 17)

Now what if this same principle were applied to the professing church as a whole within the world's most influential "Christian" nation? How long would the *body of Christ* be allowed to wander around if the *majority* of *its* members were likewise found to be more trouble than *they* were worth? Consider the following testimony of "Brother" Jerry and "Sister" Carol Love in the Bible-Belt state of North Carolina, as printed in the February 20, 1996, *Chicago Tribune*:

> "Naked and Not Ashamed," say Christians
>
> Living up to the Genesis verse "naked and not ashamed" Christian nudists are planning a weekend retreat of hot-tubbing, karaoke and reading Bibles in the buff.
>
> **"We believe you can be a nudist and religious too,"** said Jerry Love, a Methodist who already has booked 60 reservations from around the country for the getaway at his Whispering Pine family nudist resort.
>
> His wife Carol, a **Baptist**, added: "Christians can help to make nudism wholesome, family-oriented fun." Christian nudists say their practice is rooted in Biblical teaching.
>
> The Loves, who said they plan to make the gathering and [sic] annual event, said the conference will give Christian nudists a safe place to share their faith.[6]

The "Loves" are just one more sorry reason why unsaved Americans are less and less interested in entering through their *own* designated *"door of faith."* (Acts 14:27) And when "Gentiles" are no longer willing to comprise the bride (Esther 1:17), the focus shifts to a Jewess (Esther 2:17). Note

Paul's warning to the Gentiles of a potential disenfranchisement in the future:

> *Well; because of unbelief they were broken off, and thou standest by faith. Be not highminded, but fear: For if God spared not the natural branches* [Israel], *take heed lest he also spare not thee.* (Romans 11:20, 21)

Paul goes on to explain that as the Lord turned his attention away *from* rebellious Israel *to* the Gentile nations in the first century, he will one day reverse that very process:

> *Behold therefore the goodness and severity of God: on them which fell, severity; but toward thee, goodness, **if thou continue in his goodness: otherwise thou also shalt be cut off. And they also, if they abide not still in unbelief, shall be graffed in**: for God is able to graff them in **again**.* (Romans 11:22, 23)

Once again, the key admonition to the Philadelphia remnant at the *end* of the Laodicean age is, *"Behold, I come quickly: hold that fast which thou hast, that no man take thy crown."* (Revelation 3:11) Remember that twentieth-century materialism has proven to be the *first* weapon in Satan's 2,000-year-old war against the church to seriously pulverize the majority of born-again believers. What Nero and Bloody Mary could not accomplish ("Faith of our fathers living still, in spite of dungeon, fire and sword"), Visa, Discover and MasterCard have.

Therefore, *if* you will say **"No"** to the temptation of materialism, you will gain a victory for the Master that 99 other Christians were unwilling to attain. If you can hang on till the rapture, you'll be mighty glad that you did. *"Him that overcometh will I make a **pillar** in the temple of my God, **and he shall go no more out**: and I will write upon him the name of my God, and the name of the city of my God, which is new Jerusalem, which cometh down out of heaven from my God: and I will write upon him my new name."* (Revelation 3:12)

You may be doing most of the "heavy lifting" now, but on the other side of I Thessalonians 4:16, Philadelphia soul winners *"shall go no more out"*! Bless God, the "Neo's" will be running the bus routes during the Millennium!!

Finally, as the pastor of a local New Testament church constitutes the highest office in the land, I close this volume with a respectful word of exhortation to God's men. Thank God for faithful pastors; we couldn't make it without them! Every layman should be aware of the shepherd's charge:

> *Take heed unto thyself, and unto the doctrine; continue in them: for in doing this thou shalt both save thyself,* ***and them that hear thee.*** (I Timothy 4:16)

Men of God, *whatever you do,* continue to hold the line, *"in season, out of season"*! Keep the pulpit hot and keep the standard high! Though the human race is clamoring for a *New World Order,* what they *really* need is the *Old-Time Religion,* as our *"God requireth that which is past."* (Ecclesiastes 3:15)

When Satan tries to incite one preacher or camp against another *over nonessentials,* remember our glorious Baptist distinctive of *individual soul liberty.* We don't have to play "People Bingo," but we *can* be found *"exhorting one another, and so much the more, as ye see the day approaching."* **There were no camps in the *gaols*!**

Thank God for the churches which have set the pace for soul winning and foreign missions. Hallelujah for the churches which have fought to maintain our Baptist heritage! And praise the Lord *especially* for the churches which have focused our attention on the King James Bible issue! With John Paul's party just a few years away, we're going to need all the spiritual camaraderie we can muster.

Yet, in the final analysis, every true preacher stands ready to *fight it out alone* if necessary! The aged warrior Paul wrote in his last epistle, *"This thou knowest, that all they which are in Asia be turned away from me."* (II Timothy 1:15) The last book of the Bible was penned by a preacher who testified:

> *I John, who also am your brother, and companion in tribulation, and in the kingdom and patience of Jesus Christ, was in the isle that is called Patmos, for the word of God, and for the testimony of Jesus Christ.* (Revelation 1:9)

While preaching in a Bible conference in the state of Ohio, I heard the host pastor use an illustration which I have never forgotten. He was describing our spiritual warfare amidst the growing apostasy. He said that the hour was late, and the smoke was thick. He described his own uniform as being tattered and torn. His only weapon was a broken saber.

As he continued with this gripping portrayal, my mind raced back to Durant's depiction of Marshal Ney during the rout at Waterloo, who "stood horseless and bewildered, his face blackened with powder, his uniform in rags, a broken sword in the hand that had almost grasped victory."[7]

The man of God concluded his analogy with a dramatic coup de grâce that shook the entire congregation. He stated with all sincerity—"When the Lord Jesus Christ returns at battle's end, I want to be found *swinging my sword in the smoke.*"

> *And when the chief Shepherd shall appear, ye shall receive a crown of glory that fadeth not away.* (I Peter 5:4)

> *Ho, my comrades! see the signal,*
> *Waving in the sky!*
> *Reinforcements now appearing,*
> *Victory is nigh.*

> *See the glorious banner waving!*
> *Hear the trumpet blow!*
> *In our Leader's name we'll triumph*
> *Over ev'ry foe.*

> *Fierce and long the battle rages,*
> *But our help is near;*
> *Onward comes our great Commander.*
> *Cheer, my comrades, cheer.*

> Refrain:
> *"Hold the fort, for I am coming,"*
> *Jesus signals still;*
> *Wave the answer back to heaven,*
> *"By Thy grace we will."*

> *"Occupy till I come."*
> (Luke 19:13b)

Appendix A

HOW SOME BAPTISTS WERE PERSECUTED IN VIRGINIA

A Memorial

AFFERMAN, JOHN; Middlesex . . Cruelly beaten—incapacitated for work.

ALDERSON, JOHN; Botetourt . . . . Jailed for (?).

AMMON, THOMAS; Culpeper . . . . Jailed for preaching.

ANTHONY, JOSEPH; Chesterfield . . . . Jailed for preaching. "Three months."

BAKER, ELIJAH; Accomac . . . . Pelted with apples and stones.

BAKER, ELIJAH; Accomac . . . . Banishment attempted.

BAKER, ELIJAH; Accomac . . . . Jailed for preaching. "Fifty-six days."

BANKS, ADAM; Culpeper . . . . Jailed for (?).

BARROW, DAVID; Nansemond . . . . Ducked and nearly drowned by 20 men.

BARROW, DAVID; Nansemond . . . . Dragged from the house and driven away.

BURRUS, JOHN; Caroline . . . . Jailed for preaching.

CHAMBERS, THOMAS; Orange . . . . Jailed for (?).

CHASTAIN, RANE; Chesterfield . . . . Ordered to leave the county, or go to jail.

CHASTAIN, RANE; Chesterfield . . . . Commanded to take a dram, or be whipped.

CHILES, JAMES; Spotsylvania . . . . Jailed for preaching. "Forty-three days."

CHONING, BARTHOLOMEW; Caroline . . . . Jailed for (?).

CLAY, ELEAZER; Chesterfield . . . . Man rode up to cowhide him—failed.
CLAY, JOHN; (?) . . . . Jailed for preaching.
CORBLEY, JOHN; Culpeper . . . . . . Frequently taken from pulpit—beaten.
CORBLEY, JOHN; Orange . . . . Jailed for preaching.
CORBLEY, JOHN; Culpeper . . . . Jailed for preaching.
CRAIG, ELIJAH; Culpeper . . . . Jailed for preaching. "One month."
CRAIG, ELIJAH; Culpeper . . . Jailed for preaching. "Duration unknown."
CRAIG, ELIJAH; Orange . . . . Jailed for preaching.
"Seventeen or 18 days."
CRAIG, ELIJAH; Orange . . . . Jailed for preaching. "A considerable time."
CRAIG, JOSEPH; Spotsylvania . . . . Apprehended, but escaped.
CRAIG, JOSEPH; Orange . . . . Presented for being absent for church.
CRAIG, LEWIS; Spotsylvania . . . . Indicted, tried, but not imprisoned.
CRAIG, LEWIS; Spotsylvania . . . . Jailed for preaching. "Four weeks."
CRAIG, LEWIS; Caroline . . . . Arrested and required to give bond.
CRAIG, LEWIS; Caroline . . . . Jailed for preaching. "Three months."
CRAIG, LEWIS; Caroline . . . . Carried to Williamsburg on habeas corpus.
DELANEY, JOHN; Culpeper . . . . Jailed for permitting a man to pray.
EASTIN, AUGUSTINE; Chesterfield . . . . Jailed for preaching.
ELKINS, RICHARD; Pittsylvania . . . . Two men started for warrant.
Frightened.
FALKNER, RICHARD; Middlesex . . . . Arrested but released.
FRISTOE, DANIEL; Fauquier . . . . Service interrupted by curses
and silly antics.
FRISTOE, DANIEL; Stafford . . . . Warrant issued but not executed.
FRISTOE, DANIEL; Stafford . . . . Gun presented to his breast.
FRISTOE, WILLIAM; Stafford . . . Application for warrant for him refused.
FRISTOE, WILLIAM; Stafford . . . . Pursued by man with gun, but escaped.
FRISTOE, WILLIAM; Stafford . . . . Taken by a warrant,
went to Philadelphia.
GOOLRICH, JAMES; Caroline . . . . Jailed for preaching.
GREENWOOD, JAMES; Middlesex . . . . Presented for being absent
from church.
GREENWOOD, JAMES; King and Queen . . . . Jailed for preaching.
"Sixteen days."
GREENWOOD, JAMES; Middlesex . Jailed for preaching. "Forty-six days."

HARGATE, THOMAS; Amherst . . . . Jailed for preaching.

HARRISS, SAMUEL; Pittsylvania . . . . . . Mightily opposed and slandered.

HARRISS, SAMUEL; Culpeper . . . . "You shall not preach here."

HARRISS, SAMUEL; Culpeper . . . . Meeting broken up by a mob.

HARRISS, SAMUEL; N. Carolina . . . . Knocked down while preaching.

HARRISS, SAMUEL; Culpeper . . . . Door battered down.

HARRISS, SAMUEL; Culpeper . . . Arrested as a vagabond, schismatic, etc.

HARRISS, SAMUEL; Orange . . . . Pulled down and hauled about
by hair, hand, etc.

HARRISS, SAMUEL; Loudon . . . . Locked up in gaol for some time.

HERNDON, EDWARD; Caroline . . . . Jailed for preaching.

IRELAND, JAMES; Culpeper . . . . Tried to suffocate him with smoke.

IRELAND, JAMES; Culpeper . . . . . Tried to blow him up with gun powder.

IRELAND, JAMES; Culpeper . . . . Tried to poison him. Injured for life.

IRELAND, JAMES; Culpeper . . . . Drunken rowdies put
in same cell with him.

IRELAND, JAMES; Culpeper . . . . Threatened with a public whipping.

IRELAND, JAMES; Culpeper . . . . . . Horses ridden over his hearers at jail.

IRELAND, JAMES; Culpeper . . . . Men made their water in his face.

IRELAND, JAMES; Culpeper . . . . Jailed for preaching. Five months.

IRELAND, JAMES; (?) . . . . Opposition everywhere.

KAUFMAN, MARTIN; Shenandoah . . . . Severely beaten with stick.

KOONTZ, JOHN; Shenandoah . . . . Severely beaten with butt end
of large cane.

KOONTZ, JOHN; (?) . . . . Met in the road and beaten.

KOONTZ, JOHN; (?) . . . . Arrested and started to jail,
but released.

LANE, DUTTON; Lunenburg . . . . "Charged not to come there again."

LANE, DUTTON; Pittsylvania . . . . Endured much persecution.

LANE, DUTTON; Pittsylvania . . . . His mother beaten by his father.

LELAND, JOHN; Orange . . . . Threatened with a gun.

LEWIS, IVISON; Gloucester . . . . "Met with violent opposition."

LEWIS, IVISON; Essex . . . . Arrested but not imprisoned.

LOVALL, WILLIAM; King and Queen . . . . Jailed for preaching.
"Sixteen days."

LUNSFORD, LEWIS; Lancaster

LUNSFORD, LEWIS; Northumberland . . . . His preaching interrupted
by mob violence and legal proscription.
LUNSFORD, LEWIS; Richmond
LUNSFORD, LEWIS; Westmoreland
LUNSFORD, LEWIS; Richmond ... Summoned and required to give bond.
MCCLANNAHAN, WILLIAM; Culpeper . . . . Jailed for preaching.
MAJOR, RICHARD; Fairfax .... Warrants issued but not executed.
MAJOR, RICHARD; Fauquier . . . . Warrants issued at Bull Run—
defended—Giants.
MAJOR, RICHARD; Fauquier . . . . Man went to meeting
determined to kill him.
MAJOR, RICHARD; Fauquier . . . . Mob so outrageous—
nearly pulled to pieces.
MARSHALL, DANIEL; Pittsylvania . . . . "Endured much persecution."
MARSHALL, WILLLIAM; Fauquier ... Arrested but they failed to jail him.
MASH, WILLIAM; Spotsylvania . . . . Jailed for preaching.
"Forty-three days."
MASTIN, THOMAS; Orange . . . . Presented by grand jury.
MAXWELL, THOMAS; Culpeper . . . . Jailed for preaching.
MINTZ, EDWARD; Nansemond . . . . Ducked and driven away
in his wet clothes.
MOFFETT, ANDERSON; Culpeper . . . . Jailed for preaching.
MOORE, JEREMIAH; (?) . . . . Brutally assaulted by a mob.
MOORE, JEREMIAH; Fairfax . . . . Apprehended and carried
before magistrate.
MOORE, JEREMIAH; Fairfax ... Jailed for preaching, perhaps three times.
MORTON, ELIJAH; Orange . . . . Ousted as a Justice
because he was a Baptist.
MULLINS, WILLIAM; Middlesex . . . . Presented for being absent
from church.
MURPHY, JOSEPH; (?) . . . . Carried before magistrate, not imprisoned.
PICKET, JOHN; Fauquier . . . . Great opposition from mobs
and magistrates.
PICKET, JOHN; Culpeper . . . . Misrepresented by Parson
before congregation.
PICKET, JOHN; Culpeper . . . . Jailed for preaching.

PICKET, JOHN; Fauquier ... Jailed for preaching. Three months or more.

PITMAN, HIPKINS; Caroline . . . . Arrested and threatened with whipping.

PITMAN, JAMES; Caroline . . . . Jailed for preaching. "Sixteen days."

PITTS, YOUNGER; Caroline . . . . Arrested, abused and released.

REED, JAMES; (?) . . . . Dragged off stage, kicked and cuffed about.

REED, JAMES; Spotsylvania ... Jailed for preaching. "Forty-three days."

SAUNDERS, NATHANIEL; Culpeper . . . . Summoned to appear
at court for preaching.

SAUNDERS, NATHANIEL; Culpeper or Orange . . . . Arrested and tried,
but acquitted.

SAUNDERS, NATHANIEL; Culpeper . . . . Jailed for preaching.

SHACKELFORD, JOHN; Essex . . . . Jailed for preaching. "Eight days."

SPENCER, JOSEPH; Orange . . . . Jailed for preaching.

SPILLER, PHILIP; Stafford . . . . Jailed for preaching.

STREET, HENRY; Middlesex . . . . Received one lash—
prevented by companions.

TANNER, JOHN; Chesterfield . . . . Jailed for preaching. Gave bond.

TANNER, JOHN; Norfleet's Ferry . . . . Shot with a shotgun.

TAYLOR, JOHN; Hampshire . . . . Suffered the "rage of mobs."

THOMAS, DAVID; Stafford . . . . . Violent opposition—worship prevented.

THOMAS, DAVID; STAFFORD . . . . Ruffians armed with bludgeons
to beat him.

THOMAS, DAVID; Culpeper or Orange . . . . Dragged out amidst
clinched fists, etc.

THOMAS, DAVID; Fauquier (?) . . . . Pulled down while preaching—
dragged out.

THOMAS, DAVID; Culpeper or Orange . . . . Attempt made to shoot him—
battle followed.

"THREE OLD MEN"; Stafford . . . . . . Indicted, fined, but not imprisoned.

TINSLEY, DAVID; Chesterfield . . . . Jailed for preaching.
Four months and 16 days.

TRIBBLE, ANDREW; Orange . . . . Presented for preaching.

WAFORD, THOMAS; Middlesex . . . . Severely beaten with a whip.

WAFORD, THOMAS; Essex . . . . Arrested, searched and released.

WALKER, JEREMIAH; James City . . Opposed by the "Parson and others."

WALKER, JEREMIAH; Chesterfield . . . . Jailed for preaching.

WALKER, JEREMIAH; Chesterfield .... Denied the prison bounds.
WALKER, JEREMIAH; Lunenburg .... Sued in two actions
for baptizing two boys.
WALLER, JOHN; Hanover .... Hauled about by the hair of his head.
WALLER, JOHN; (?) .... Almost rent asunder by friend and foe.
WALLER, JOHN; Caroline .... Jerked off stage—
head beaten against ground.
WALLER, JOHN; Caroline .... Whipped severely by the Sheriff.
WALLER, JOHN; Caroline .... Jailed for preaching. Ten days.
WALLER, JOHN; Essex .... Jailed for peaching. Fourteen days.
WALLER, JOHN; Spotsylvania .... Jailed for preaching. Forty-three days.
WALLER, JOHN; Middlesex .... Jailed for preaching. Forty-six days.
WARE, JAMES; Caroline .... Jailed for preaching. Sixteen days.
WARE, ROBERT; Middlesex .... Presented for not going to church.
WARE, ROBERT; (?) ...... Annoyed by men drinking and playing cards.
WARE, ROBERT; Essex .... Jailed for preaching. Eight days.
WARE, ROBERT; Middlesex .... Jailed for preaching. Forty-six days.
WEATHERFORD, JOHN; Chesterfield .. Jailed for preaching. Five months.
WEATHERFORD, JOHN; Chesterfield .... Denied the prison bounds.
WEATHERFORD, JOHN; Chesterfield .... Hands slashed while preaching.
WEBBER, WILLIAM; Middlesex ..... Jailed for preaching. Forty-six days.
WEBBER, WILLIAM; Chesterfield ... Jailed for preaching. Three months.
WEEKS, ANDERSON; Stafford .... Arrested on a warrant,
but not imprisoned.
WYLEY, ALLEN; Orange .... Jailed for preaching. "For some time."
YOUNG, JOHN; Caroline ...... Jailed for preaching. Five or six months.

Excerpt from pages 516–520
Imprisoned Preachers and Religious Liberty in Virginia
by Lewis Peyton Little

Endnotes

INTRODUCTION

1 Cotton Mather, *The Great Works of Christ in America*, vol. 1 (Carlisle, Pa.: Banner of Truth Trust, 1979), 25.
2 Robert Flood, *The Rebirth of America*, ed. Nancy Leigh DeMoss (Philadelphia, Pa.: Arthur S. DeMoss Foundation, 1986), 151.
3 *Ibid.*, 21.
4 Arnold Dallimore, *George Whitefield*, vol. 1 (Carlisle, Pa.: Banner of Truth Trust, 1989), 400.
5 Mrs. Sam P. (Laura) Jones, *Life and Sayings of Sam P. Jones,* 2d ed., rev. (Atlanta, Ga.: Franklin-Turner Co., Publishers, 1907), 213.

CHAPTER I
America, the Beautiful?

1 Chuck Shepherd, John Kohut, and Roland Sweet, *News of the Weird* (New York: New American Library, 1989), 9.
2 Chuck Shepherd, John Kohut, and Roland Sweet, *More News of the Weird* (NewYork: Penguin Books, 1990), 55.
3 Shepherd, Kohut, and Sweet, *News of the Weird,* 146.
4 Shepherd, Kohut, and Sweet, *More News of the Weird,* 167.
5 Tim Roche and David Barstow, "Pregnant Woman Shoots Her Fetus," *St. Petersburg Times,* 8 September 1994, 1a-1b.

6 Shepherd, Kohut, and Sweet, *News of the Weird*, 9.
7 Shepherd, Kohut, and Sweet, *More News of the Weird,* 117.
8 Shepherd, Kohut, and Sweet, *News of the Weird*, 17.
9 V. Dion Haynes, "Board Blame Girl, 9, Who Is Suing in Classroom Rape," *Chicago Tribune,* 5 January 1995, sec. 2, p. 3.
10 David C. Rudd and Angela Bradberry, "8-Year-Old Shot in 3rd-Grade Classroom," *Chicago Tribune*, 11 March 1992, sec. 2, p. 1.
11 "Boy, 9, Fatally Shoots Off-Duty Cop," *Chicago Tribune,* 30 December 1994, sec. 1, p. 17.
12 Shepherd, Kohut, and Sweet, *News of the Weird,* 52.
13 *Chicago Sun Times,* 25 May 1994, sec. 2c, p. 8.
14 *Chicago Sun Times,* 15 October 1994, p. 4-5.
15 Chuck Shepherd, John Kohut, and Roland Sweet, *Beyond News of the Weird* (New York: Penguin Books, 1991), 81.
16 Shepherd, Kohut, and Sweet, *More News of the Weird,* 51.
17 John Kohut and Roland Sweet, *News from the Fringe* (New York: Penguin Books, 1993), 20.
18 Don Boys, *Liberalism: A Rope of Sand* (Indianapolis, Ind.: Good Hope Press, 1979), 81.
19 Anita Manning, "Pop Culture for College Credit," *USA Today,* 21 December

1994, p. 4(D).

[20] John Williams, "Porno 101," *Reader's Digest*, September 1993, 96.

[21] Kohut and Sweet, *News from the Fringe*, 79-80.

[22] Shepherd, Kohut, and Sweet, *More News of the Weird*, 151.

[23] Paul Lee Tan, *Encyclopedia of 7,700 Illustrations* (Rockville, Md.: Assurance Publishers 1979), 1381.

[24] Police report, anonymous.

[25] Shepherd, Kohut, and Sweet, *More News of the Weird*, 12.

[26] Tan, *7,700 Illustrations*, 415.

[27] Shepherd, Kohut, and Sweet, *More News of the Weird*, 162.

[28] Tan, *7,700 Illustrations*, 156.

[29] P. K. McCary, *Black Bible Chronicles* (New York: African American Press, 1993), 6.

[30] Mike Royko, "Cows in the Green House," *Reader's Digest*, November 1990, p. 62.

[31] Dave Ruben, "Dodo Solution," *Reader's Digest*, April 1992, p.147.

[32] Lisa Schissren, "Bill and Hillary at the Trough," *American Spectator*, August 1993, p. 22.

[33] Shepherd, Kohut, and Sweet, *Beyond News of the Weird*, 112.

[34] *Ibid.*, 10.

[35] Shepherd, Kohut, and Sweet, *News of the Weird*, 135.

[36] *Ibid.*, 70.

[37] "Dahmer Killed in Prison Attack: Strangled and Dismembered 17 Boys and Men and Cannibalized Some of Them," *Chicago Tribune*, 28 November, 1994.

[38] Kohut and Sweet, *News from the Fringe*, 120.

[39] "Advertisement," *The Boston Globe*, 15 May 1994, sec. B, p. 21.

[40] Kohut and Sweet, *News from the Fringe*, 120.

[41] "San Francisco Mourns 10,000th AIDS Death," *Chicago Tribune*, 9 January 1993, sec. 1, p. 4.

[42] John Carlson, "One By One: How AIDS Devastated an Iowa Family," *Des Moines Sunday Register*, 23 January 1994,

sec. A, p. 9.

[43] Shepherd, Kohut, and Sweet, *More News of the Weird*, 174.

[44] Kohut and Sweet, *News from the Fringe*, 11.

[45] Shepherd, Kohut, and Sweet, *News of the Weird*, 101.

[46] Tan, *7,700 Illustrations*, 153.

[47] Shepherd, Kohut, and Sweet, *Beyond News of the Weird*, 224.

[48] John W. Whitehead, *The Stealing of America* (Milford, Mich.: Mott Media, 1977), 43-44.

[49] Tal Brooke, *When the World Will Be As One* (Eugene, Oreg.: Harvest House Publishers, n.d.), 187-188.

[50] Joseph D. Pistone and Richard Woodley, *Donnie Brasco: My Undercover Life in the Mafia* (New York: New American Library, 1987), 198.

[51] "12th Cop Kills Himself in New York," *Chicago Tribune*, 26 December 1994, sec. 1, p. 6.

[52] John Pletz, "Police Billboard Stops Traffic," *The Post Tribune*, 21 October 1994, sec. A, p. 1.

[53] Herb Caen, "Shades of Guilt," *Reader's Digest*, September 1993, 96.

[54] Michael Connelly, "Body of Evidence," *Reader's Digest*, May 1993, 103-4.

[55] Shepherd, Kohut, and Sweet, *News of the Weird*, 66.

[56] Shepherd, Kohut, and Sweet, *Beyond News of the Weird*, 213.

[57] Shepherd, Kohut, and Sweet, *News of the Weird*, 66.

[58] *Ibid.* , 66.

[59] *Ibid.*, 110.

[60] *Ibid.*, 18.

[61] Shepherd, Kohut, and Sweet, *More News of the Weird*, 147-48.

[62] Don Meloy, "Pity the Poor Killer," *Reader's Digest*, September 1992, 23.

[63] Editorial, "Two Muggings," *Reader's Digest*, June 1990, 196.

[64] Charles J. Sykes, *A Nation of Victims* (New York: St. Martin's Press, 1992), 3.

[65] Shepherd, Kohut, and Sweet, *News of the Weird*, 12.

[66] "Meaty Fight: Woman Shoots Son

Over Him," *Chicago Tribune*, 30 November 1991, sec. 1, p. 18.
[67] Shepherd, Kohut, and Sweet, *News of the Weird*, 21.
[68] Shepherd, Kohut, and Sweet, *More News of the Weird*, 195.

CHAPTER II
What's Really Wrong with America?

[1] David Remnick, "The Situationist—Annals of Politics," *New Yorker*, 5 September 1994, 93.
[2] Clyde Haberman and Albin Krebs, "Transsexual on Police," *New York Times*, 2 February 1979, sec. 3, p. 26.
[3] Paul Duggan and Ruben Castaneda, "4 Die in Police Headquarters Shootings," *Washington Post*, 23 November 1994, sec. A, p. 1.
[4] Christopher Hitchens, "Contempt for the Little Colony: How Barry and Bush Run Washington," *Harper's*, October 1989, 70.
[5] Fred Barnes, "National Capitols, National Sham," *Reader's Digest*, November 1989, 108-9.
[6] "The Case of Marion Barry: Political Persuasion and Self-Denial," *USA Today*, September 1990, pp. 88-89.
[7] David Corn, "The Devil Made Him Do It," *The Nation*, 10 September 1990, p. 228.
[8] "Barry Tells National Talk Show Host Sex Was His Downfall," *Jet*, 3 June 1991, 24.
[9] Michael Riley, "I Guess You All Figured That I Couldn't Resist That Lady," *Time*, 9 July 1990, 19.
[10] *Ibid.*
[11] *Jet*, 11 May 1994, 4.
[12] Remnick, "Annals of Politics," *New Yorker*, 5 September 1994, 88.
[13] Maureen Dowd, "Resurrection," *New York Times Magazine*, 11 September 1994, 50.
[14] Hendrik Hertzberg, "Barry's Offensive," *New Republic*, 25 June 1990, 10.

[15] "Bye-Bye, Barry: Washington's Embattled May Call It Quits," *Time*, 25 June 1990, 23.
[16] Michael Kinsley, "Trial by Jury," *New Republic*, 3 September 1990, pp. 6, 12.
[17] Dowd, "Resurrection," 50.
[18] *Chicago Sun Times*, 30 January 1995, p. 6.
[19] *Ibid.*
[20] *Ibid.*
[21] Ray Chamberlin, *Quotes and Quaint Stories of Great Americans* (Cynthiana, Ken.: Privately printed, n. d.), 16.

CHAPTER III
A Nation of Providence

[1] Merrill F. Unger, *Archaeology and the Old Testament* (Grand Rapids, Mich.: Zondervan Publishing House, 1970), 83.
[2] *The Scofield Study Bible*, ed. C. I. Scofield (New York: Oxford University Press, 1945), 16.
[3] Unger, *Archaeology and the Old Testament*, 76.
[4] Rousas J. Rushdoony, *This Independent Republic* (Fairfax, Va.: Thoburn Press, 1978), 93-94.
[5] Daniel J. Boorstin, *The Genius of American Politics* (Chicago: University of Chicago Press, 1953), 47.
[6] *Ibid.*, 50-51.
[7] Peter Marshall and David Manuel, *The Light and the Glory* (Old Tappan, N. J.: Fleming H. Revell, Co., 1977), 81.
[8] *Ibid.*, 83.
[9] *Ibid.*, 100.

CHAPTER IV
Popish Trash

[1] Alexander McClure, *Translators Revived,* with a foreword and update by R. E. Rhoades (Litchfield, Mich.: Maranatha Bible Society, 1858), 16.
[2] William Bradford, *Of Plymouth Plantation: 1620-1647* (New York:

Random House, 1981), 1.

[3] Arthur Fenton Hort, *Life and Letters of Fenton John Anthony Hort*, vol. 1 (London: Macmillan & Co., 1896), 121.

[4] William Manchester, *A World Lit Only by Fire* (Boston: Little, Brown & Co., 1993), 59.

[5] *Ibid.*, 60.

[6] Will Durant, *The Story of Civilization*, vol. 1-8 (New York: Simon & Schuster), About the Author, n.p.

[7] Will Durant, *The Story of Civilization*, vol. 4, *The Age of Faith* (New York: Simon & Schuster, 1950), 780.

[3] *Ibid.*, 4:781-82.

[9] Will Durant, *The Story of Civilization*, vol. 6, *The Reformation* (New York: Simon & Schuster, 1957), 211.

[10] *Ibid.*, 6:212-13.

[11] *Catholic Encyclopedia*, 1912 ed., *s.v.* "Torquemada."

[12] Durant, *The Story of Civilization*, 6:262.

[13] Samuel Eliot Morrison, *Admiral of the Ocean Sea* (Boston: Little, Brown & Co., 1942), 492-93.

[14] Durant, *The Story of Civilization*, 6:265.

[15] Morrison, *Admiral of the Ocean Sea*, 359.

[16] Peter Marshall and David Manuel, *The Light and the Glory* (Old Tappan, N.J.: Fleming H. Revell, Co., 1977), 56.

[17] Christopher Hibbert, *Rome, The Biography of a City* (New York: W. W. Norton & Co., 1985), 135.

[18] Avro Manhattan, *The Vatican Billions* (Chino, Calif.: Chick Publications, 1983), 88.

[19] *Ibid.*, 90.

[20] *Ibid.*

[21] *Ibid.*, 91.

[22] *Ibid.*, 91-92.

[23] *Ibid.*, 92-93.

[24] *Ibid.*, 93-94.

[25] Bernard Brendan, *Pizarro, Orellana, and the Exploration of the Amazon* (New York: Chelsea House Publishers, 1991), 22.

[26] *Ibid.*, 23.

[27] John Hemming, *The Conquest of the Incas* (New York: Harcourt, Brace, 1970), 162.

[28] *Ibid.*, 308.

[29] *Ibid.*, 78.

[30] *Ibid.*, 79.

[31] Bradford, *Plymouth Plantation*, 302-3.

CHAPTER V
Not As Other Men

[1] Paul Lee Tan, *Encyclopedia of 7,700 Illustrations* (Rockville Md.: Assurance Publishers, 1979), 289-90.

[2] M. Stanton Evans, *The Theme Is Freedom* (Washington, D.C.: Regency Publishing, 1994), 189.

[3] *Ibid.*, 188.

[4] William L. Sachse, ed., *English History in the Making*, vol. 1, *Readings from the Sources, to 1689* (Lexington, Mass.: Xerox College Publishing, 1967), 10.

[5] William Bradford, *Of Plymouth Plantation: 1620–1647* (New York: Random House, 1981), 16.

[6] *Ibid.*, 25.

[7] *Ibid.*, 26.

[8] *Ibid.*, 27-28.

[9] *Ibid.*, 34-35.

[10] *Ibid.*, 49.

[11] *Ibid.*, 50.

[12] *Ibid.*, 60.

[13] Peter Marshall and David Manuel, *The Light and the Glory* (Old Tappan, N. J.: Fleming H. Revell, Co., 1977), 117.

[14] Bradford, *Plymouth Plantation*, 66.

[15] Thomas J. Fleming, *One Small Candle* (New York: W. W. Norton & Co., 1964), 85.

[16] Bradford, *Plymouth Plantation*, 69.

[17] *Ibid.*, 69-70.

[18] *Ibid.*, 71.

[19] William J. Federer, *America's God and Country Encyclopedia of Quotations* (Coppell, Tex.: Fame Publishing, 1994), 435-36.

[20] Bradford, *Plymouth Plantation*, 75.

[21] *Ibid.*, 74.

22 *Ibid.*, 77.
33 *Ibid.*
24 *Ibid.*, 77-78.
25 *Ibid.*, 88.
26 *Ibid.*, 79.
27 *Ibid.*
28 Marshall, *Light and Glory*, 187.
29 Lawrence Friedman, *Crime and Punishment in America* (New York: Harper Collins Publishers, 1993), 33.
30 Bradford, *Plymouth Plantation*, 79-80.
31 Eugene Aubrey Stratton, *Plymouth Colony* (Salt Lake City, Utah: Ancestry Publishing, 1986), 21.
32 Bradford, *Plymouth Plantation*, 85.
33 *Ibid.*, 92.
34 Cotton Mather, *The Great Works of Christ in America*, vol. 1 (Carlisle, Pa.: Banner of Truth Trust, 1979), 55.
35 Bradford, *Plymouth Plantation*, 89.
36 *Ibid.*, 100.
37 *Ibid.*, 126.
36 *Ibid.*, 142-43.
39 *Ibid.*, 143.
40 *Ibid.*, 262.

CHAPTER VI
An Efficacious Experiment

1 Albert Henry Newman, *A Manual of Church History*, vol. 2 (Valley Forge, Pa.: Judson Press, 1933), 283-84.
2 James L. Adams, *Yankee Doodle Went to Church* (Old Tappan, N. J.: Fleming H. Revell, Co., 1989), 48.
3 John Christian, *A History of the Baptists*, vol. 2 (Texarkana, Tex.: Bogard Press, 1922), 15.
4 Peter Marshall and David Manuel, *The Light and the Glory* (Old Tappan, N.J.: Fleming H. Revell, Co., 1977), 177-78.
5 M. Stanton Evans, *The Theme Is Freedom* (Washington, D.C.: Regency Publishing, 1994), 193.
6 *Ibid.*, 33.
7 *Ibid.*, 98.
8 *Ibid.*, 99.
9 *Ibid.*, 104.
10 *Ibid.*, 99.
11 *Ibid.*, 103.
12 Christian, *A History of the Baptists*, 2:23-24.
13 Marshall and Manuel, *Light and Glory*, 209.
14 William Bradford, *Of Plymouth Plantation* (New York: Random House, 1981), xvi.
15 Daniel J. Boorstin, *The Genius of American Politics* (Chicago: University of Chicago Press, 1953), 53-54.
16 Marshall and Manuel, *Light and Glory*, 216.
17 David Benedict, *A General History of the Baptists*, vol.1 (Gallatin, Tenn.: Church History Research & Archives, 1985), 378.
18 *Ibid.*, 374.
19 Evans, *The Theme Is Freedom*, 199.
20 Thomas Armitage, *A History of the Baptists*, vol. 2 (Watertown, Wis.: Baptist Heritage Press, 1988), 631.
21 *Ibid.*, 2:621.
22 Rick Drummond, *The Story of American Protestantism*, vol. 2 (Boston: Beacon Press, 1950), 51.
23 Christian, *A History of the Baptists*, 2:29.
24 Armitage, *A History of the Baptists*, 2:627.
25 Bradford, *Plymouth Plantation*, 286.
26 Henry C. Vedder, *A Short History of the Baptists* (Valley Forge, Pa.: Judson Press, 1907), 289.
27 *Ibid.*
28 Armitage, *A History of the Baptists*, 2:639.
29 *Ibid.*, 2:642.
30 *Ibid.*, 2:642-43.
31 *Ibid.*, 2:643.
32 *Ibid.*
33 *Ibid.*
34 Vedder, *A Short History of the Baptists*, 290-91.
35 E. Wayne Thompson and David L. Cummins, *This Day in Baptist History* (Greenville, S.C.: Bob Jones University Press, 1993), 24.
36 *Ibid.*

[37] *Ibid.*, 135.

[38] Armitage, *A History of the Baptists,* 1:vii.

[39] D. B. Ray, *Ray's Baptist Succession* (Parsons, Kans.: Foley Railway Printing Co., 1912), 16.

[40] Christian, *A History of the Baptists,* 2:44.

[41] *Ibid.*, 1:14.

[42] *Ibid.*, 1:28.

[43] Cotton Mather, *The Great Works of Christ in America*, vol. 1 (Carlisle, Pa.: Banner of Truth Trust, 1979), 74.

[44] Armitage, *A History of the Baptists,* 2:620.

[45] Evans, *The Theme Is Freedom,* 188.

[46] *Ibid.*, 197.

[47] Christian, *A History of the Baptists,* 1:17.

[48] *Ibid.*, 1:18.

[49] Armitage, *A History of the Baptists,* 1:350.

[50] Vedder, *A Short History of the Baptists,* 104.

[51] Armitage, *A History of the Baptists,* 1:350-51.

[52] David Benedict, *A General History of the Baptist Denomination in America*, vol. 1 (Gallatin, Tenn.: Church History Research & Archives, 1985), 271.

[53] *Ibid.*, 1:359-60.

[54] *Ibid.*, 1:362.

[55] Thompson and Cummins, *This Day in Baptist History,* 314.

[56] Benedict, *A General History of the Baptist Denomination in America,* 1:374.

[57] *Ibid.*, 1:379

[58] Marshall and Manuel, *Light and Glory,* 207.

[59] Armitage, *A History of the Baptists,* 2:717.

[60] Christian, *A History of the Baptists,* 2:170-71.

[61] *Ibid.*, 2:44.

[62] Benedict, *A General History of the Baptist Denomination in America,* 1:465.

[63] Paul Johnson, *The Almost Chosen People,* tape 1 (San Francisco, Calif.: Laissez Faire Audio, n.d.) audio cassette.

[64] *Ibid.*, tape 1.

CHAPTER VII
Penance or Jesus?

[1] Peter Marshall and David Manuel, *The Light and the Glory* (Old Tappan, N.J.: Fleming H. Revell, Co., 1977), 73-74.

[2] Edmond Paris, *The Vatican Against Europe,* trans. A. Robson (London: Wickliffe Press, 1961), 75.

[3] James S. J. Hennessey, *American Catholics* (New York: Oxford University Press, 1981), 12.

[4] *Ibid.*, 20.

[5] *Ibid.*, 23.

[6] *Ibid.*, 27-29.

[7] *Ibid.*, 29.

[8] Paul Johnson, *The Almost Chosen People,* tape 1 (San Francisco, Calif.: Laissez Faire Audio, n.d.), audio cassette.

[9] Hennessey, *American Catholics,* 56.

[10] Richard B. Morris, *Seven Men Who Shaped Our Destiny* (New York: Harper & Row Publishers, 1973), 186.

[11] Hennessey, *American Catholics,* 63.

[12] *Ibid.*, 57.

[13] John Christian, *A History of the Baptists,* vol. 2 (Texarkana, Tex.: Bogard Press, 1922), 221.

[14] Albert Henry Newman, *A Manual of Church History,* vol. 2 (Valley Forge, Pa.: Judson Press, 1933), 673.

[15] Christian, *A History of the Baptists,* 2:173-74.

[16] *Ibid.*, 2:176.

[17] A. J. Langguth, *Patriots* (New York: Simon & Schuster, 1988), 206.

[18] Lewis Peyton Little, *Imprisoned Preachers and Religious Liberty in Virginia* (Gallatin, Tenn.: Church History Research & Archives, 1987), 392.

[19] Johnson, *The Almost Chosen People,* tape 1.

[20] *Ibid.*

[21] Arnold Dallimore, *George Whitefield,* vol. 1 (Carlisle, Pa.: Banner of Truth Trust, 1989), 230.

[22] *Ibid.*, 1:289-92.

[23] John Pollock, *George Whitefield and the Great Awakening* (Belleville, Mich.: Lion Publishing, 1972), 248.

24 Dallimore, *George Whitefield,* 1:441.
25 *Ibid.,* 1:481.
26 Pollock, *Whitefield and the Great Awakening,* 219.
27 Christian, *A History of the Baptists,* 2:174.
28 Pollock, *Whitefield and the Great Awakening,* 148.
29 Dallimore, *George Whitefield,* 1:439.
30 *Ibid.,* 1:434-35.
31 *Ibid.,* 1:400.
32 Pollock, *Whitefield and the Great Awakening,* 162.
33 Christian, *A History of the Baptists,* 2:179.
34 *Ibid.,* 2:179.
35 Dallimore, *George Whitefield,* 1:533.
36 *Ibid.,* 1:534.
37 *Ibid.,* 1:587.
38 Christian, *A History of the Baptists,* 2:180.
39 *Ibid.,* 2:180-81.
40 Thomas Armitage, *A History of the Baptists,* vol. 2 (Watertown, Wis.: Baptist Heritage Press, 1988), 719-20.
41 E. Wayne Thompson and David L. Cummins, *This Day in Baptist History* (Greenville, S.C.: Bob Jones University Press, 1993), 532.
42 Dallimore, *George Whitefield,* 2:446-47.
43 *Ibid.,* 2:341.
44 Pollock, *Whitefield and the Great Awakening,* 263.
45 Dallimore, *George Whitefield,* 1:542-43.
46 Pollock, *Whitefield and the Great Awakening,* 269-70.
47 *Ibid.,* 270.
48 Dallimore, *George Whitefield,* 2:440.
49 Langguth, *Patriots,* 31.

CHAPTER VIII
Gaols and Grates

1 James L. Adams, *Yankee Doodle Went to Church* (Old Tappan, N.J.: Fleming H. Revell, Co., 1989), 107.
2 Lewis Peyton Little, *Imprisoned Preachers and Religious Liberty in Virginia* (Gallatin, Tenn.: Church History Research & Archives, 1987), 11.
3 *Ibid.,* 28.
4 *Ibid.,* 66.
5 *Ibid.,* 143.
6 *Ibid.,* 296.
7 *Ibid.,* 461.
8 *Ibid.,* 41.
9 *Ibid.,* 45.
10 *Ibid.,* 47
11 *Ibid.,* 148.
12 *Ibid.,* 50.
13 *Ibid.,* 55.
14 *Ibid.*
15 *Ibid.,* 94.
16 *Ibid.,* 97.
17 *Ibid.,* 346.
18 *Ibid.,* 124.
19 William J. Federer, *America's God and Country Encyclopedia of Quotes* (Coppell, Tex.: Fame Publishing, 1994), 289.
20 Little, *Imprisoned Preachers,* 266.
21 *Ibid.,* 312.
22 *Ibid.,* 441.
23 *Ibid.,* 128.
24 *Ibid.,* 229-30.
25 *Ibid.,* 388.
26 *Ibid.,* 168.
27 *Ibid.,* 133.
28 *Ibid.,* 106.
29 *Ibid.,* 167-68.
30 Gordon S. Wood, *The Radicalism of American Revolution* (New York: Vintage Books, 1993), 144.
31 *Ibid.,* 274.
32 *Ibid.,* 372-73.
33 *Ibid.,* 287.
34 *Ibid.,* 289.
35 *Ibid.,* 237-38.
36 *Ibid.,* 339.
37 *Ibid.,* 151.
38 *Ibid.,* 162.
39 *Ibid.,* 163.
40 *Ibid.,* 164.
41 *Ibid.*
42 *Ibid.*
43 *Ibid.,* 188.
44 *Ibid.,* 166.

[45] *Ibid.*, 168.
[46] *Ibid.*, 163.
[47] *Ibid.*, 163-64.
[48] *Ibid.*, 168-69.
[49] *Ibid.*, 179-80.
[50] *Ibid.*, 504-5.
[51] *Ibid.*, 233-34.
[52] *Ibid.*, 419.
[53] *Ibid.*, 130-31.
[54] *Ibid.*, 394.
[55] Thomas Armitage, *A History of the Baptists*, vol. 1 (Watertown, Wis.: Baptist Heritage Press, 1988), 799.
[56] *Ibid.*, 1:352.
[57] *Ibid.*, 1:734.
[58] *Ibid.*, 1:797.
[59] *Ibid.*, 1:797-98.

CHAPTER IX
Free Indeed

[1] Andrea Millen and Rich Millen, *Laissez Faire Books*, August 1995, p. 30.
[2] William J. Federer, *America's God and Country Encyclopedia of Quotes* (Coppell, Tex.: Fame Publishing, 1994), 204-5.
[3] Millen and Millen, *Laissez Faire Books*, 29.
[4] John Eidsmoe, *Christianity and the Constitution* (Grand Rapids, Mich.: Baker Books, 1995), 116.
[5] Federer, *America's God and Country*, 323.
[6] David Barton, *America's Godly Heritage* (Aledo, Tex.: WallBuilder's Press, 1993), 6.
[7] Eidsmoe, *Christianity and the Constitution*, 22.
[8] A. J. Langguth, *Patriots* (New York: Simon & Schuster, 1988), 345.
[9] M. Stanton Evans, *The Theme is Freedom* (Washington, D.C.: Regency Publishing, 1994), 205.
[10] Arnold Dallimore, *George Whitefield*, vol. 2 (Carlisle, Pa.: Banner of Truth Trust, 1989), 497.
[11] *Ibid.*, 2:510.
[12] J. T. Headley, *Chaplains and Clergy of the Revolution* (New York: Charles Scribner & Sons, 1864), 4.
[13] James Adams, *Yankee Doodle Went to Church* (Old Tappan, N. J.: Fleming H. Revell, Co., 1989), 30.
[14] *Ibid.*, 30-31.
[15] Headley, *Chaplains and Clergy*, 4.
[16] *Ibid.*
[17] *Ibid.*
[18] *Ibid.*, 5-6.
[19] *Ibid.*, 6.
[20] Langguth, *Patriots,* 222.
[21] *Ibid.*, 223.
[22] Headley, *Chaplains and Clergy,* 24.
[23] Federer, *America's God and Country*, 38-39.
[24] A. Loyd Collins, *God and American Independence* (Orlando, Fla.: Christ for the World Publishers, 1974), 39.
[25] Langguth, *Patriots,* 239.
[26] Collins, *God and Independence*, 41.
[27] Headley, *Chaplains and Clergy*, 24.
[28] Langguth, *Patriots,* 242.
[29] *Ibid.*, 243.
[30] *Ibid.*, 245.
[31] Collins, *God and Independence*, 43.
[32] Langguth, *Patriots,* 248.
[33] Collins, *God and Independence*, ind.
[34] *Ibid.*, 45.
[35] Langguth, *Patriots,* 250.
[36] *Ibid.*, 276.
[37] Headley, *Chaplains and Clergy*, 83.
[38] *Ibid.*, 84.
[39] *Ibid.*, 84-85.
[40] Collins, *God and Independence*, 45-46.
[41] *Ibid.*, 49.
[42] James Thacher, *Eyewitness to the American Revolution* (Stanford, Conn.: Longmeadow Press, 1994), 26.
[43] Langguth, *Patriots,* 286.
[44] Collins, *God and Independence,* 51-52.
[45] Wendell Evans, Ph.D., Unpublished Prepared Class Notes: Synopsis of American History (Crown Point, Ind.: Hyles-Anderson College, n.d.), 32.
[46] Collins, *God and Independence,* 34.
[47] *Ibid.*, 38.
[48] *Ibid.*, 47.

49 *Ibid.*, 50-51.
50 Eidsmoe, *Christianity and the Constitution*, 116.
51 Headley, *Chaplains and Clergy*, 18.
52 *Ibid.*, 7.
53 Langguth, *Patriots*, 329.
54 *Ibid.*, 374.
55 John Christian, *A History of the Baptists*, vol. 2 (Texarkana, Tex.: Bogard Press 1922), 229.
56 *Ibid.*, 2:229-30.
57 *Ibid.*, 2:228.
58 *Ibid.*, 2:230.
59 *Ibid.*, 2:262.
60 E. Wayne Thompson and David L. Cummins, *This Day in Baptist History* (Greenville, S.C.: Bob Jones University Press, 1993), 242.
61 Langguth, *Patriots*, 372.
62 Catherine Millard, *The Rewriting of American History* (Camp Hill, Pa..: Horizon House Publishers, 1991), 91.
63 Langguth, *Patriots*, 359.
64 Evans, *The Theme Is Freedom*, 243.
65 Daniel J. Boorstin, *The Genius of American Politics* (Chicago: University of Chicago Press, 1953), 93.
66 *Ibid.*, 98.
67 *Ibid.*
68 Eidsmoe, *Christianity and the Constitution*, 418.
69 *Ibid.*, 419.
70 *Ibid.*, 420.
71 Langguth, *Patriots*, 363.
72 Henry F. Woods, *American Sayings* (New York: Essential Books, 1945), 6.
73 Eidsmoe, *Christianity and the Constitution*, 356.
74 Thomas Armitage, *A History of the Baptists*, vol. 1 (Watertown, Wisc.: n.p., 1988), 792.
75 Langguth, *Patriots*, 376.
76 *Ibid.*, 377.
77 Collins, *God and Independence*, 96.
78 Langguth, *Patriots*, 383.
79 Christian, *A History of the Baptists*, 1:225.
80 Langguth, *Patriots*, 384.
81 A. Loyd Collins, *God in American History* (Orlando, Fla.: Christ for the World Publishers, 1969), 40.
82 *Ibid.*
83 Langguth, *Patriots*, 414.
84 Millard, *Rewriting of American History*, 61.
85 Headley, *Chaplains and Clergy*, 58.
86 *Ibid.*, 102.
87 *Ibid.*, 65.
88 Collins, *God in American History*, 47.
89 Headley, *Chaplains and Clergy*, 66.
90 *Ibid.*, 71.
91 Thompson and Cummins, *This Day in Baptist History*, 49.
92 William Cathcort, *Baptist Patriots* (Grand Rapids, Mich.: Guardian Press, 1976), 42.
93 Christian, *A History of the Baptists*, 1:234.
94 *Ibid.*, 1:237.
95 Headley, *Chaplains and Clergy*, 75.
96 *Ibid.*, 75.
97 Thompson and Cummins, *This Day in Baptist History*, 220.
98 Eidsmoe, *Christianity and the Constitution*, 113.
99 Langguth, *Patriots*, 469.
100 *Ibid.*, 471.
101 Collins, *God and Independence*, 120-21.
102 Langguth, *Patriots*, 450-51.
103 Thacher, *Eyewitness to the American Revolution*, 31.
104 Collins, *God and Independence*, 189.
105 Langguth, *Patriots*, 451.
106 Collins, *God in American History*, 51.
107 Thacher, *Eyewitness to the American Revolution*, 283-84.
108 Collins, *God and Independence*, 172-73.
109 Thacher, *Eyewitness to the American Revolution*, 289.
110 Langguth, *Patriots*, 540-41.
111 Collins, *God and Independence*, 187.
112 *Ibid.*, 170.
113 *Ibid.*, 175.
114 Thacher, *Eyewitness to the American Revolution*, 291.
115 Armitage, *A History of the Baptists*,

1:794.
[116] Thompson and Cummins, *This Day in Baptist History*, 327.
[117] *Ibid.*, 237.
[118] James Norwood, Unpublished Prepared Pamphlet, George Washington's Faithful Pastor (n.p., n.p., n.d.), 1.
[119] Thompson and Cummins, *This Day in Baptist History*, 327-28.
[120] Eidsmoe, *Christianity and the Constitution*, 46.
[121] Lewis Peyton Little, *Imprisoned Preachers and Religious Liberty in Virginia* (Gallatin, Tenn.: Church History Research & Archives, 1987), 472.
[122] *Ibid.*, 473.
[123] Thompson and Cummins, *This Day in Baptist History*, 391.
[124] *Ibid.*, 25.
[125] Armitage, *A History of the Baptists*, 1:791.
[126] Eidsmoe, *Christianity and the Constitution*, 107.
[127] Christian, *A History of the Baptists*, 2:273.
[128] Armitage, *A History of the Baptists*, 1:734.
[129] Thompson and Cummins, *This Day in Baptist History*, 26.
[130] Armitage, *A History of the Baptists*, 1:788.
[131] Little, *Imprisoned Preachers*, 492.
[132] *Ibid.*, 492-93.
[133] Eidsmoe, *Christianity and the Constitution*, 107-8.
[134] *Ibid.*, 109.
[135] Don Boys, "Baptists and Freedom," *Common Sense for Today*, May-June 1996.

CHAPTER X
A Turnpike to the Pacific

[1] A. Loyd Collins, *God in American History* (Orlando, Fla.: Christ for the World Publishers, 1969), 55-56.
[2] *Ibid.*, 56.
[3] David Barton, *The Myth of Separation* (Aledo, Tex.: WallBuilder's Press, 1993), 41.
[4] John Eidsmoe, *Christianity and the Constitution* (Grand Rapids, Mich.: Baker Books, 1995), 243.
[5] *Ibid.*, 243.
[6] *Ibid.*, 244.
[7] Barton, *The Myth of Separation*, 104.
[8] *Ibid.*, 23.
[9] John Tracy Ellis, *American Catholicism* (Chicago: University of Chicago Press, 1955), 68.
[10] Eidsmoe, *Christianity and the Constitution*, 92.
[11] *Ibid.*, 274.
[12] John Christian, *A History of the Baptists*, vol. 2 (Texarkana, Tex.: Bogard Press, 1922), 221.
[13] James S. J. Hennessey, *American Catholics* (New York: Oxford University Press, 1981), 62.
[14] *Ibid.*, 62.
[15] *Ibid.*
[16] A. J. Langguth, *Patriots* (New York: Simon & Schuster, 1988), 521.
[17] *Ibid.*, 522.
[18] *Ibid.*, 469.
[19] John Keegan, *A History of Warfare* (New York: Vintage Books, 1994), 348.
[20] James Thacher, *Eyewitness to the American Revolution* (Stanford, Conn.: Longmeadow Press, 1994), 305.
[21] *Ibid.*, 306-7.
[22] Kenneth Scott LaTourette, *A History of Christianity* (New York: Harper & Brothers, 1953), 1009.
[23] Will Durant, *The Story of Civilization*, vol. 10, *Rousseau and Revolution* (New York: Simon & Schuster, 1967), 900.
[24] Samuel Eliot Morrison and Henry Steele Commager, *The Growth of the American Republic* (New York: Oxford University Press, 1962), 356.
[25] Eidsmoe, *Christianity and the Constitution*, 19.
[26] William J. Federer, *America's God and Country Encyclopedia of Quotes* (Coppell, Tex.: Fame Publishing, 1994), 5.
[27] Adrienne Koch and William Peden, *The Life and Selected Writings of Thomas Jefferson* (New York: Random House, 1944), 323.

[28] Keith Hardman, *The Spiritual Awakeners* (Chicago: Moody Press, 1983), 124.

[29] *Ibid.*, 115.

[30] *Ibid.*, 112.

[31] *Ibid.*, 113.

[32] *Ibid.*, 116.

[33] *Ibid.*

[34] *Ibid.*, 141.

[35] *Ibid.*, 132.

[36] *Ibid.*, 131.

[37] Henry C. Vedder, *A Short History of the Baptists* (Valley Forge, Pa.: Judson Press, 1907), 320.

[38] Philip Schaff, *History of the Christian Church*, vol. 8, *The Swiss Reformation* (Grand Rapids, Mich.: Wm. B. Eerdmans Publishing Co., 1910), 491.

[39] Laurence Vance, *The Other Side of Calvinism* (Pensacola, Fla.: Vance Publications, 1991), 9-10.

[40] *Ibid.*, 10.

[41] *Ibid.*, 12.

[42] Vedder, *A Short History of the Baptists*, 239-41.

[43] D. B. Ray, *Ray's Baptist Succession* (Parsons, Kans.: Foley Railway Printing Co., 1912), 17

[44] Vedder, *A Short History of the Baptists*, 251.

[45] *Ibid.*, 231.

[46] *Ibid.*, 321-22.

[47] Arnold Dallimore, *George Whitefield*, vol. 2 (Carlisle, Pa.: Banner of Truth Trust, 1989), 160.

[48] Hardman, *Spiritual Awakeners*, 133.

[49] *Ibid.*, 136.

[50] *Ibid.*

[51] *Ibid.*, 137.

[52] *Ibid.*, 135-36.

[53] Christian, *A History of the Baptists*, 2:359.

[54] *Ibid.*, 2:359-60.

[55] David Benedict, *A General History of the Baptist Denomination*, vol. 1 (Gallatin, Tenn.: Church History Research & Archives, 1985), 164.

[56] *Ibid.*, 1:165-66.

[57] Hardman, *Spiritual Awakeners*, 139.

[58] *Ibid.*, 125.

[59] *Ibid.*, 128.

[60] Carl Sandburg, *Abraham Lincoln: The Prairie Years and the War Years* (New York: Harcourt, Brace & Co., 1926), 83.

[61] *Ibid.*

[62] W. P. Strickland, ed., *Autobiography of Peter Cartwright, The Backwoods Preacher* (New York: Carlton & Porter Publishers, 1857), 205.

[63] *Ibid.*

[64] *Ibid.*, 207-8.

[65] Federer, *America's God and Country*, 412.

[66] *Ibid.*, 413.

[67] *Ibid.*, 411.

[68] Strickland, *Autobiography of Peter Cartwright*, 133.

[69] Federer, *America's God and Country*, 352.

[70] *Ibid.*, 307.

[71] Strickland, *Autobiography of Peter Cartwright*, 192.

[72] *Ibid.*, 192-93.

[73] *Ibid.*, 193-94.

[74] Robert V. Remini, *The Revolutionary Age of Andrew Jackson* (New York: Avon Books, 1977), 32.

[75] *Ibid.*, 34.

[76] Federer, *America's God and Country*, 309.

[77] *Ibid.*, 310.

[78] Ray Chamberlin, *Quotes and Quaint Stories of Great Americans* (Cynthiana, Ky.: Ray Chamberlin, n.d.), 36.

[79] Federer, *America's God and Country*, 312.

[80] *Ibid.*

[81] *Ibid.*, 311.

CHAPTER XI
What Hath God Wrought!

[1] Robert V. Remini, *The Revolutionary Age of Andrew Jackson* (New York: Avon Books, 1977), 174.

[2] *Ibid.*, 172.

[3] E. Wayne Thompson and David L. Cummins, *This Day in Baptist History* (Greenville, S.C.: Bob Jones University

Press, 1993), 87.

[4] John S. Tilley, *Facts the Historians Leave Out* (Montgomery, Ala.: Paragon Press, 1951), 9.

[5] Robert Leckie, *American and Catholic* (New York: Doubleday & Co., 1970), 179.

[6] Virgil W. Bopp, *Confidently Committed* (Grand Rapids, Mich.: Regular Baptist Press, 1987), 112.

[7] A. Loyd Collins, *God in American History* (Orlando, Fla.: Christ for the World Publishers, 1969), 61-62.

[8] Keith J. Hardman, *The Spiritual Awakeners* (Chicago: Moody Press, 1983), 148-49.

[9] Thomas Armitage, *A History of the Baptists* (Watertown, Wis.: Baptist Heritage Press, 1988), 817.

[10] Hardman, *Spiritual Awakeners,* 176.

[11] *Ibid.*

[12] James Gilchrist Lawson, *Deeper Experiences of Famous Christians* (Anderson, Ind.: Warner Press, 1972), 243.

[13] William J. Federer, *America's God and Country Encyclopedia of Quotes* (Coppell, Tex.: Fame Publishing, 1994), 204.

[14] *Ibid.*, 205.

[15] Charles Chiniquy, *50 Years in the "Church" of Rome* (Chino, Calif.: Chick Publications, 1985), 50.

[16] *Ibid.*, 51.

[17] *Ibid.*, 53.

[18] Mitchell Wilson, *American Science and Invention* (New York: Bonanza Books, 1954), 9.

[19] *Ibid.*, 6-7.

[20] *Ibid.*, 37.

[21] *Ibid.*, 3-4.

[22] *Ibid.*, 22.

[23] Paul Lee Tan, *Encyclopedia of 7,700 Illustrations* (Rockville, Md.: Assurance Publishers, 1979), 480-81.

[24] *Ibid.*, 1390.

[25] *Ibid.*, 484.

[26] *Ibid.*, 1023-24.

[27] Ariel Durant and Will Durant, *The Story of Civilization*, vol. 10, *Rousseau and Revolution* (New York: Simon & Schuster,

1967), 507.

[28] Paul Johnson, *The Almost Chosen People*, tape 2 (San Francisco, Calif.: Laissez Faire Audio, n.d.), audio cassette.

[29] Thomas Armitage, *A History of the Baptists*, vol. 2 (Watertown, Wis.: Baptist Heritage Press, 1988), 770.

CHAPTER XII
The Devil's D-Day

[1] Dr. S. Ireneus Prime, *The Life of Samuel F. B. Morse* (New York: Arno Press, 1974), 730.

[2] *Ibid.*, 728.

[3] Samuel F. B. Morse, *Foreign Conspiracy Against the Liberties of the United States* (New York: Arno Press, 1977), 28-29.

[4] Baldwin Ward, *Pictorial History of the World* (New York: Year, n.d.), 432.

[5] Samuel F. B. Morse, *Imminent Dangers to the Free Institutions of the United States Through Foreign Immigration* (New York: Arno Press, 1969), 7.

[6] Morse, *Foreign Conspiracy,* 19-20.

[7] Morse, *Imminent Dangers*, 8.

[8] *Ibid.*

[9] Morse, *Foreign Conspiracy,* 31.

[10] Morse, *Imminent Dangers*, 8.

[11] *Ibid.*

[12] R. W. Thompson, *The Papacy and the Civil Power* (New York: Harper & Brothers Publishers, 1876), 29.

[13] *Ibid.*, title page.

[14] Morse, *Foreign Conspiracy*, 110.

[15] *Ibid.*, 34-35.

[16] Thompson, *The Papacy and the Civil Power,* 91.

[17] Morse, *Foreign Conspiracy,* 41.

[18] *Ibid.*

[19] *Ibid.*, 41-42.

[20] Thompson, *The Papacy and the Civil Power,* 79.

[21] *Ibid.*, 38.

[22] Charles Chiniquy, *50 Years in the "Church" of Rome* (Chino, Calif.: Chick Publications, 1985), 285.

23 Prime, *The Life of Samuel F B. Morse*, 729.

24 John A. Garraty and Peter Gay, eds., *The Columbia History of the World* (New York: Harper & Row, 1972), 798.

25 Morse, *Imminent Dangers*, 14.

26 Chiniquy, *50 Years*, 281-82.

27 John Tracy Ellis, *American Catholicism* (Chicago: University of Chicago Press, 1955), 121.

28 Paul Johnson, *The Almost Chosen People*, tape 2 (San Francisco, Calif.: Laissez Faire Audio, n.d.), audio cassette.

29 Ray Allen Billington, *The Protestant Crusade* (Chicago: Quadrangle Books, 1964), 123.

30 Morse, *Foreign Conspiracy*, 176-77.

31 Morse, *Imminent Dangers*, iv.

32 Billington, *Protestant Crusade*, 35.

33 Morse, *Foreign Conspiracy*, 148.

34 Billington, *Protestant Crusade*, 324.

35 *Ibid.*, 195.

36 *Ibid.*, 324.

37 *Ibid.*

38 *Ibid.*, 196.

39 *Ibid.*, 197.

40 *Ibid.*, 198.

41 Morse, *Imminent Dangers*, 9.

42 Thompson, *The Papacy and the Civil Power*, 106.

43 *Ibid.*, 116.

44 Morse, *Imminent Dangers*, 11.

45 *Ibid.*

46 Billington, *Protestant Crusade*, 120.

47 *Ibid.*, 129.

48 *Ibid.*, 123.

49 *Ibid.*, 44.

50 Ellis, *American Catholicism*, 72.

51 *Ibid.*, 70.

52 Morse, *Foreign Conspiracy*, 53.

53 Billington, *Protestant Crusade*, 53.

54 *Ibid.*, 54.

55 *Ibid.*, 58.

56 *Ibid.*

57 *Ibid.*, 59.

58 *Ibid.*

59 *Ibid.*, 223.

60 Chiniquy, *50 Years*, 37.

61 James Cardinal Gibbons, *The Faith of Our Fathers* (Baltimore, Md.: John Murphy & Co., 1897), 394.

62 Charles Chiniquy, *The Priest, The Woman and The Confessional* (Chino, Calif.: Chick Publications, n.d.), 13.

63 *Ibid.*, 15.

64 Loraine Boettner, *Roman Catholicism* (Philadelphia, Pa.: Presbyterian & Reformed Publishing Co., 1962), 168.

65 *Ibid.*, 39.

66 Chiniquy, *50 Years*, 40.

67 Billington, *Protestant Crusade*, 60.

68 *Ibid.*, 63.

69 *Ibid.*, 67.

70 Morse, *Foreign Conspiracy*, 59.

71 Billington, *Protestant Crusade*, 75.

72 Morse, *Foreign Conspiracy*, 182-83.

73 *Ibid.*, 58.

74 Thompson, *The Papacy and the Civil Power*, 75.

75 Morse, *Foreign Conspiracy*, 64-65.

76 Billington, *Protestant Crusade*, 135.

77 *Ibid.*, 37.

78 *Ibid.*, 43.

79 Gibbons, *The Faith of Our Fathers*, 98, 102-104.

80 Thompson, *The Papacy and the Civil Power*, 76.

81 Billington, *Protestant Crusade*, 143.

82 *Ibid.*, 153.

83 *Ibid.*, 155.

84 *Ibid.*, 157.

85 *Ibid.*, 158.

86 *Ibid.*

87 *Ibid.*, 165.

88 *Ibid.*, 168.

89 *Ibid.*

90 *Ibid.*, 346.

91 *Ibid.*, 351.

92 *Ibid.*, 222.

93 *Ibid.*

94 *Ibid.*, 223.

95 Morse, *Foreign Conspiracy*, 11.

96 Billington, *Protestant Crusade*, 233.

97 Theodore Maynard, *The Story of American Catholicism* (New York: Macmillan Co., 1941), 289.

98 Billington, *Protestant Crusade*, 291.

99 *Ibid.*

100 Chiniquy, *50 Years*, 288.

101 *Ibid.*, 285.

[102] *Ibid.*
[103] Billington, *Protestant Crusade,* 310.
[104] *Ibid.,* 309.
[105] *Ibid.,* 305.
[106] *Ibid.,* 308.
[107] *Ibid.,* 3-4.

CHAPTER XIII
A Spiritual Interlude

[1] George Park Fisher, *History of the Christian Church* (New York: Charles Scribner's Sons, 1887), 580.
[2] R. W. Thompson, *The Papacy and the Civil Powers* (New York: Harper & Brothers Publishers, 1876), 33.
[3] *America's Great Revivals* (Minneapolis, Minn.: Dimension Books, n.d.), 65.
[4] *Ibid.,* 57-58.
[5] *Ibid.,* 59-62.
[6] Edwin Orr, "Potent Answers to Persistent Prayer," *The Rebirth of America,* ed. Nancy Leigh DeMoss, comp. Robert Flood, sec. 1, J (Philadelphia: Arthur S. DeMoss Foundation, 1986), 63.
[7] David O. Beale, *In Pursuit of Purity* (Greenville, S.C.: Unusual Publications, 1986), 15.
[8] Keith J. Hardman, *The Spiritual Awakeners,* (Chicago: Moody Press, 1983), 187.
[9] *Ibid.,* 187-88.
[10] Kenneth Scott LaTourette, *A History of Christianity* (New York: Harper & Brothers, 1953), 1236.
[11] Charles F. Pitts, *Chaplains in Gray* (St. John, Ind.: Christian Book Gallery, 1957), 114.
[12] *Ibid.,* 32.
[13] *Ibid.,* 31.

CHAPTER XIV
The Wrath of Apollyon

[1] Nathaniel Weyl, *The Negro in American Civilization* (Washington, D.C.: Public Affairs Press, 1960), vii.
[2] William B. Heseltine and David Smiley, *The South in American History* (Englewood Cliffs, N.J.: Prentice-Hall, 1960), 276.
[3] Richard N. Current, *The Lincoln Nobody Knows* (New York: Hill & Wang, 1958), 219.
[4] John S. Tilley, *Facts the Historians Leave Out* (Montgomery, Ala.: Paragon Press, 1951), 18.
[5] G. Edward Griffin, *The Creature from Jekyll Island* (Appleton, Wis.: American Opinion, 1994), 379.
[6] Tilley, *Facts the Historians Leave Out,* 19.
[7] Weyl, *The Negro in American Civilization,* 74.
[8] Tilley, *Facts the Historians Leave Out,* 9.
[9] Paul Kennedy, *The Rise and Fall of the Great Power* (New York: Random House, 1987), 180.
[10] Samuel Eliot Morrison and Henry Steele Commager, *The Growth of the American Republic,* vol. 2 (New York: Oxford University Press, 1962), 443.
[11] Samuel Eliot Morrison and Henry Steele Commager, *The Growth of the American Republic,* vol. 1 (New York: Oxford University Press, 1962), 444.
[12] *Ibid.*
[13] Ray Allen Billington, *The Protestant Crusade* (Chicago: Quadrangle Books, 1964), 390.
[14] Morrison and Commager, *The Growth of the American Republic,* 2:660.
[15] Burke Davis, *The Civil War, Strange and Fascinating Facts* (New York: Fairfax Press, 1960), 84.
[16] Rousas J. Rushdoony, *The Nature of the American System* (Fairfax, Va.: Thoburn Press, 1978), 19.
[17] Davis, *The Civil War, Strange and Fascinating Facts,* 79.
[18] Webb Garrison, *Civil War Curiosities* (Nashville, Tenn.: Rutledge Hill Press, 1994), 91.
[19] *Ibid.,* 90.
[20] *Ibid.,* 36.
[21] Davis, *The Civil War, Strange and Fascinating Facts,* 24-28.

22 Gary Allen, *None Dare Call It Conspiracy* (Rossmoor, Calif.: Concord Press, n.d.), 40

23 Garrison, *Civil War Curiosities*, 187.

24 Morrison and Commager, *The Growth of the American Republic*, 2:696.

25 Garrison, *Civil War Curiosities*, 27.

26 Museum Quotations, *Soldiers' Expressions* [The 9th Regiment N.Y. Volunteers] (Sharpsburg, Md.: Antietam National Battlefield, n.d.), 293.

27 Davis, *The Civil War, Strange and Fascinating Facts*, 63.

28 *Ibid.*, 66.

29 Garrison, *Civil War Curiosities*, 96.

30 *Ibid.*, 208-9.

31 Davis, *The Civil War, Strange and Fascinating Facts*, 2.

32 *Ibid.*, 219.

33 Garrison, *Civil War Curiosities*, 203.

34 Nancy Scott Anderson and Dwight Anderson, *The Generals* (New York: Alfred A. Knopf, 1988), 399.

35 *Ibid.*, 400.

36 Museum Quotations, *Soldiers' Expressions*, 293.

37 Museum Quotations, *History of 35th Massachusetts Volunteers* (Sharpsburg, Md.: Antietam National Battlefield, n.d.), 48.

38 Anderson and Anderson, *The Generals*, 270.

39 *Ibid.*, 369-70.

40 *Ibid.*, 375.

41 Garrison, *Civil War Curiosities*, 92.

42 Anderson and Anderson, *The Generals*, 388-89.

43 *Ibid.*, 391-92.

44 James Ronald Kennedy and Walter Donald Kennedy, *The South Was Right* (Gretna, La.: n.p., 1994), 381-82.

45 William A. Frassanito, *Antietam* (New York: Charles Scribner's Sons, 1978), 234.

46 *Ibid.*, 233-34.

47 William J. Federer, *America's God and Country Encyclopedia of Quotes* (Coppell, Tex.: Fame Publishing, 1994), 299

48 *Ibid.*, 575.

49 Rushdoony, *Nature of the American System*, 83.

50 Tilley, *Facts the Historians Leave Out*, 15-16.

51 *Ibid.*, 17

52 James M. McPherson, *What They Fought For, 1861-1865* (Baton Rouge, La.: Louisiana State University Press, 1994), 13.

53 *Ibid.*, 51.

54 *Ibid.*, 18.

55 *Ibid.*, 53.

56 *Ibid.*, 53-54.

57 *Ibid.*, 35.

58 *Ibid.*, 60.

59 *Ibid.*, 60-61.

60 Weyl, *The Negro in American Civilization*, 86.

61 *Ibid.*, 54.

62 Theodore Maynard, *The Story of American Catholicism* (New York: Macmillan Co., 1941), 356.

63 Rousas J. Rushdoony, *This Independent Republic* (Fairfax, Va.: Thoburn Press, 1978), 71.

64 Weyl, *The Negro in American Civilization*, 80.

65 Tilley, *Facts the Historians Leave Out*, 20.

66 Edward McPherson, *Political History of the United States During the Period of Reconstruction April 15, 1865–July 15, 1870* (New York: Dacapo Press, 1972), 63.

67 Garrison, *Civil War Curiosities*, 97.

68 McPherson, *Political History During Reconstruction*, 66.

69 Kennedy and Kennedy, *The South Was Right*, 27.

70 Morrison and Commager, *The Growth of American Republic*, 2:654.

71 Anderson and Anderson, *The Generals*, 152.

72 David Herbert Donald, *Photograph* (New York: Simon & Schuster, n.d.), 134.

73 Rushdoony, *This Independent Republic*, 72.

74 Current, *The Lincoln Nobody Knows*, 233.

75 Weyl, *The Negro in American*

Civilization, 74.
76 *Ibid.*, 76.
77 Rushdoony, *This Independent Republic*, 73.
78 Garrison, *Civil War Curiosities*, 238.
79 Weyl, *The Negro in American Civilization*, 35.
80 *Ibid.*, 50.
81 John B. Boles, *Masters and Slaves in the House of the Lord* (Lexington, Ky.: University Press of Kentucky, 1988), 8.
82 Weyl, *The Negro in American Civilization*, 48.
83 E. A. Pollard, *The Lost Cause* (New York: Gramercy Books, 1994), 86.
84 Federer, *America's God and Country*, 389.
85 Charles Chiniquy, *50 Years in the "Church" of Rome* (Chino, Calif.: Chick Publications, 1985), 291.
86 Avro Manhattan, *The Vatican Moscow Washington Alliance* (Chino, Calif.: Chick Publications, 1986), 337-38.
87 Avro Manhattan, *The Dollar and the Vatican* (Springfield, Mo.: Ozark Books, 1988), 27-28.
88 *Ibid.*, 29.
89 Robert Leckie, *American and Catholic* (New York: Doubleday & Co., 1970), 70.
90 Robert H. Bork, *The Tempting of America* (New York: Simon & Schuster, 1990), 28.
91 *Ibid.*, 34.
92 Garrison, *Civil War Curiosities*, 235.
93 Manhattan, *The Dollar and the Vatican*, 29.
94 Davis, *The Civil War, Strange and Fascinating Facts*, 147.
95 Cass Canfield, *The Iron Will of Jefferson Davis* (New York: Fairfax Press, 1978), 5.
96 Davis, *The Civil War, Strange and Fascinating Facts*, 183.
97 Benjamin J. Blied, *Catholics and the Civil War* (Milwaukee, Wis.: n.p., 1945), 69.
98 John Cogley, *Catholic America* (New York: Dial Press, 1973), 56.
99 John Tracy Ellis, *American Catholics*

(Chicago: University of Chicago Press, 1955), 93.
100 Leckie, *American and Catholic*, 167.
101 *Ibid.*, 168.
102 Blied, *Catholics and the Civil War*, 39.
103 *Ibid.*, 98.
104 Charles Chiniquy, *50 Years*, 54.
105 James S. J. Hennessey, *American Catholics* (New York: Oxford University Press, 1981), 150.
106 *Ibid.*, 156.
107 *Ibid.*, 150.
108 Griffin, *The Creature from Jekyll Island*, 378.
109 *Ibid.*
110 Manhattan, *The Dollar and the Vatican*, 30.
111 *Ibid.*, 31.
112 *Ibid.*
113 Manhattan, *The Vatican Moscow Washington Alliance*, 341.
114 Davis, *The Civil War, Strange and Fascinating Facts*, 114-15.
115 Hennessey, *American Catholics*, 150.
116 Morrison and Commager, *The Growth of the American Republic*, 2:746.
117 *Ibid.*, 768.
118 Maynard, *Story of American Catholicism*, 362.
119 Hudson Strode, *Jefferson Davis, Confederate President*, vol. 2 (New York: Harcourt, Brace & Co., 1959), 501.
120 *Ibid.*
121 Fred C. Ainsworth, Brig. Gen. and Joseph W. Kirkley, *The War of the Rebellion*, ser. 4, vol. 3, (Washington, D.C.: n.p., 1900), 401.
122 Strode, *Jefferson Davis*, 502.
123 Manhattan, *The Vatican Washington Moscow Alliance*, 340.
124 *Ibid.*
125 *Ibid.*, 342.
126 Martin I. J. Griffin, *The American Catholic Historical Researches* (Philadelphia: n.p., 1905), 166.
127 Paul Johnson, *The Almost Chosen People*, tape 2 (San Francisco, Calif.: Laissez Faire Audio, 1995), audio cassette.
128 *Ibid.*

[129] Chiniquy, *The Priest, The Woman and The Confessional,* (Chino, Calif.: Chick Publications, n.d.), 5.

[130] Chiniquy, *50 Years,* 345.

[131] *Ibid.,* 361.

[132] *Ibid.,* 291.

[133] *Ibid.,* 314.

[134] *Ibid.,* 294.

[135] Martin I. J. Griffin, *The American Catholic Historical Researches* (Philadelphia: n.p., 1905), 209.

[136] Blied, *Catholics and the Civil War,* 95.

[137] *Ibid.,* 149.

[138] Federer, *America's God and Country,* 391.

[139] Burke McCarty, *The Suppressed Truth About the Assassination of Abraham Lincoln* (Haverhill, Mass.: Arya Varta Publishing Co., 1924), 109.

[140] Chiniquy, *50 Years,* 310.

[141] McCarty, *The Suppressed Truth,* 135.

[142] Chiniquy, *50 Years,* 310.

[143] William Hanchett, *The Lincoln Murder Conspiracies* (Urbana and Chicago: University of Illinois Press, 1986), 68.

[144] Thomas M. Harris, *Rome's Responsibility for the Assassination of Abraham Lincoln* (Los Angeles: Heritage Manor, 1960), 7-8.

[145] *Ibid.,* 7.

[146] *Ibid.,* 12-13.

[147] *Ibid.,* 6.

[148] *Ibid.,* 7.

[149] *Ibid.,* 21.

[150] *Ibid.,* 29.

[151] Strode, *Jefferson Davis,* 2:302.

[152] Harris, *Rome's Responsibility,* 1.

CHAPTER XV
A Costly Mistake

[1] Anne Fremantle, ed., *The Papal Encyclicals in Their Historical Context* (New York: New American Library, 1956), 145-152.

[2] R. W. Thompson, *The Papacy and the Civil Power* (New York: Harper & Brothers Publishers, 1876), 44.

[3] *Ibid.,* 42-45.

[4] Samuel Eliot Morrison and Henry Steele Commager, *The Growth of the American Republic,* vol. 2 (New York: Oxford University Press, 1962), 26.

[5] Nathaniel Weyl, *The Negro in American Civilization* (Washington, D.C.: Public Affairs Press, 1960), 99-100.

[6] Morrison and Commager, *The Growth of the American Republic,* 2:26.

[7] James Roland Kennedy and Walter Donald Kennedy, *The South Was Right* (Gretna, La.: Pelican Publishing Co., 1994), 171.

[8] Weyl, *The Negro in American Civilization,* 88.

[9] John W. Whitehead, *The Separation Illusion,* (Milford, Mich.: Mott Media, 1977), 73.

[10] Edward McPherson, *Political History of the United States During the Period of Reconstruction April 15, 1865-July 15, 1870* (New York: Dacapo Press, 1972), 194.

[11] Morrison and Commager, *The Growth of the American Republic,* 2:28.

[12] J. George Randall, *Dictionary of American History,* 1940 ed., *s.v.* "Radical Republicanism."

[13] Kennedy and Kennedy, *The South Was Right,* 172-73.

[14] Whitehead, *Separation Illusion,* 74.

[15] David Lawrence, "Worst Scandal in Our History," *U.S. News and World Report,* 26 January 1970, 95.

[16] *Ibid.*

[17] Weyl, *The Negro in American Civilization,* 91.

[18] *Ibid.*

[19] *Ibid.,* 86.

[20] *Ibid.*

[21] *Ibid.*

[22] *Ibid.,* 97.

[23] *Ibid.,* 97-98.

[24] *Ibid.,* 98.

[25] Kennedy and Kennedy, *The South Was Right,* 174.

[26] *Ibid.*

[27] Whitehead, *Separation Illusion,* 73.

[28] Lawrence, "Worst Scandal," *U. S.*

News & World Report, 96.

[29] Kennedy and Kennedy, *The South Was Right*, 171.

[30] Thomas Armitage, *A History of the Baptists*, vol. 2 (Watertown, Wis.: Baptist Heritage Press, 1988), 909.

[31] *Ibid.*, 2:911.

[32] *Ibid.*, 2:907-8.

[33] Thomas Cassidy, *Textual Criticism: Fact and Fiction* (Spring Valley, Calif.: First Baptist Church Publications, 1994), 4.

[34] Armitage, *A History of the Baptists*, 2:940.

[35] *Ibid.*, 2:684.

[36] *Ibid.*, 2:904.

[37] *Ibid.*, 2:905.

[38] *Ibid.*, 2:902.

[39] *Ibid.*, 2:918.

[40] Thomas Fredrick Woodley, *Thaddeus Stevens* (Harrisburg, Pa.: Harrisburg Telegraph Press, 1934), 560.

[41] Armitage, *A History of the Baptists*, 2:908.

[42] *Ibid.*, 2:901.

[43] *Ibid.*, 2:908.

[44] Henry C. Vedder, *A Short History of the Baptists* (Valley Forge, Pa.: Judson Press, 1907), 340-41.

[45] David O. Beale, *In Pursuit of Purity* (Greenville, S.C.: Unusual Publications, 1986), 178.

[46] *Ibid.*

[47] Elizabeth A. Livingstone, ed., *The Concise Oxford Dictionary of the Christian Church* (Oxford, England: Oxford University Press, 1977), 476.

[48] *Ibid.*, 314.

[49] Benjamin G. Wilkinson, *Our Authorized Bible Vindicated* (Payson, Ariz.: Leaves of Autumn Books, 1990), 233-34.

[50] *Ibid.*, 234.

[51] *Ibid.*

[52] G. A. Riplinger, *New Age Bible Versions*, (Ararat, Va.: AV Publications, 1993), 458.

[53] Wilkinson, *Our Authorized Bible Vindicated*, 235.

[54] Riplinger, *New Bible Versions*, 458.

[55] *Ibid.*

[56] Samuel C. Gipp, *An Understandable History of the Bible* (Macedonia, Ohio: Bible Believer's Bookstore, 1987), 93.

[57] Arthur Fenton Hort, *Life and Letters of Fenton John Anthony Hort*, vol. 1 (London: Macmillan & Co., 1896), 49-50.

[58] *Ibid.*, 1:81.

[59] *Ibid.*, 1:421-22.

[60] *Ibid.*, 1: 416.

[61] *Ibid.*, 1:121.

[62] *Ibid.*, 1:120.

[63] *Ibid.*, 1:56-57.

[64] Arthur Westcott, *Life and Letters of Brooke Foss Westcott*, vol. 1 (London: Macmillan & Co., 1903), 207.

[65] *Ibid.*, 1:52.

[66] *Ibid.*, 1:118.

[67] *Ibid.*, 2:69.

[68] Hort, *Life and Letters of Hort*, 2:34.

[69] Westcott, *Life and Letters of Westcott*, 1:309.

[70] Hort, *Life and Letters of Hort*, 1:459.

[71] David Otis Fuller, *True or False?* (Grand Rapids, Mich.: Grand Rapids International Publications, 1973), 77

[72] D. A. Waite, *Defending the King James Bible* (Collingswood, N.J.: Bible for Today Press, 1993), 25.

[73] Wilkinson, *Our Authorized Bible Vindicated*, 244.

[74] *Ibid.*, 227.

[75] *Ibid.*, 229.

[76] *Ibid.*, 227.

[77] *Ibid.*, 230.

[78] *Ibid.*, 911.

[79] Paul Lee Tan, *Encyclopedia of 7,700 Illustrations* (Rockville, Md.: Assurance Publishers, 1979), 1542-53.

[80] Armitage, *History of the Baptists*, 2:912.

[81] Vedder, *A Short History of the Baptists*, 381.

[82] Dr. S. Ireneus Prime, *The Life of Samuel F. B. Morse* (New York: Arno Press, 1974), 744.

[83] Louis Putz, *The Catholic Church, U.S.A.* (Chicago: Fides Publishers Association, 1956), 162.

[84] Samuel F. B. Morse, *Imminent Dangers to the Free Institutions of the*

United States Through Foreign Immigration (New York: Arno Press, 1969), 14.

85 John Tracy Ellis, *American Catholicism* (Chicago: University of Chicago Press, 1955), 51.

86 William J. Federer, *America's God and Country Encyclopedia of Quotes* (Coppell, Tex.: Fame Publishing, 1994), 370.

87 Lorraine Boettner, *Roman Catholicism*, 235.

88 *Ibid.*, 235.

89 Ellis, *American Catholicism*, 127.

90 Gibbons, *The Faith of Our Fathers*, 145-50.

91 J. N. D. Kelly, *The Oxford Dictionary of Popes* (Oxford, England: Oxford University Press, 1990), 310.

92 Thompson, *The Papacy and the Civil Power*, 25.

93 *Ibid.*, 28.

94 Mrs. Sam P. (Laura) Jones and Walt Holcomb, *The Life and Sayings of Sam P. Jones*, 2d ed., rev. (Atlanta, Ga.: Franklin-Turner Co., Publishers, 1907), 47.

95 Will Moody, *The Life of D. L. Moody by His Son* (Murfreesboro, Tenn.: Sword of the Lord Publishers, n.d.), 28.

96 Keith J. Hardman, *The Spiritual Awakeners* (Chicago: Moody Press, 1983), 195.

97 Ed Reese, *The Life and Ministry of Sam P. Jones (1847-1906)*, Christian Hall of Fame Series, no. 4 (Glenwood, Ill.: Fundamental Publishers, 1975), 10.

98 Jones, *Life and Sayings of Jones*, 110.

99 *Ibid.*, 137.

100 Reese, *Sam P. Jones*, 12-13.

101 Jones, *Life and Sayings of Jones*, 89.

102 *Ibid.*, 293.

103 *Ibid.*, 280.

104 *Ibid.*, 187.

105 Fred Barlow, *Profiles in Evangelism* (Murfreesboro, Tenn.: Sword of the Lord Publishers, 1976), 125.

106 Moody, *Life of Moody*, 61.

107 Barlow, *Profiles in Evangelism*, 100.

108 Moody, *Life of Moody*, 134.

109 Jones, *Life and Sayings of Jones*, 86.

110 *Ibid.*, 60.

111 *Ibid.*, 197-98.

112 *Ibid.*, 325.

113 *Ibid.*, 216.

114 *Ibid.*, 218.

115 Moody, *Life of Moody*, 496.

116 John Pollock, *Moody* (Grand Rapids, Mich.: Zondervan, 1967), 300-301.

117 Moody, *Life of Moody*, 497.

118 *Ibid.*, 573-74.

119 Pollock, *Moody*, 90.

120 Moody, *Life of Moody*, 149.

121 Pollock, *Moody*, 80.

122 Ed Reese, *The Life and Ministry of Dwight L. Moody (1837-1899)*, Christian Hall of Fame Series, no. 3 (Glenwood, Ill.: Fundamental Publishers, 1975), 9-10.

123 Arthur Fenton Hort, *Life and Letters of Fenton John Anthony Hort*, vol. 2 (London: Maxmillan & Co., 1896), 207.

124 Moody, *Life of Moody*, 263.

125 Reese, *Moody*, 10-11.

126 Pollock, *Moody*, 199.

127 *Ibid.*

128 Riplinger, *New Age Bible Versions*, 458.

129 *Ibid.*

130 *Ibid.*, 459.

131 *Ibid.*

132 *Ibid.*, 460.

133 *Ibid.*

134 Wilkinson, *Authorized Bible Vindicated*, 248.

135 Moody, *Life of Moody*, 416-17.

136 Reese, *Moody*, 12.

137 Moody, *Life of Moody*, 415-16.

138 *Ibid.*, 447.

139 Hardman, *Spiritual Awakeners*, 207.

CHAPTER XVI
Murder, Inc.

1 Mrs. Sam P. (Laura) Jones and Walt Holcomb, *Life and Sayings of Sam P. Jones*, 2d ed., rev. (Atlanta, Ga.: Franklin-Turner Co., Publishers, 1907), 369.

2 *Ibid.*, 392.

3 *Ibid.*, 449-50.

4 *Ibid.*, 452.

5   Laurence M. Vance, *A Brief History of English Bible Translations* (Pensacola, Fla.: Vance Publications, 1993), 46-54.

6   Jones, *Life and Sayings of Jones*, 459.

7   *Ibid.*, 453-54.

8   David S. Schaff, *The Life of Philip Schaff* (New York: Charles Scribner's Sons, 1897), 280-81.

9   Jones, *Life and Sayings of Jones*, 426.

10   Robert L. Sumner, *Bible Translations* (n.p.: Biblical Evangelist, 1979), 10.

11   Ed Reese, *The Life and Ministry of Reuben Torrey (1856–1928),* Christian Hall of Fame Series, no. 1 (Glenwood, Ill.: Fundamental Publishers, 1975), 6.

12   R. A. Torrey, *How to Obtain Fullness of Power* (Murfreesboro, Tenn.: Sword of the Lord Publishers, n.d.), title page.

13   Roger Martin, *R. A. Torrey, Apostle of Certainty* (Murfreesboro, Tenn.: Sword of the Lord Publishers, 1976), 157.

14   *Ibid.*, 150.

15   *Ibid.*, 164.

16   David O. Beale, *In Pursuit of Purity* (Greenville, S.C.: Unusual Publications, 1986), 3.

17   Sumner, *Bible Translations,* 19-20.

18   Arthur Westcott, *Life and Letters of Brooke Foss Westcott,* vol. 1 (London: Macmillan & Co., 1903), 218.

19   George W. Dollar, *A History of Fundamentalism in America* (Greenville, S.C.: Bob Jones University Press, 1973), 4.

20   William Jasper, *Global Tyranny... Step By Step* (Appleton, Wis.: Western Island Publishing, 1993), 98.

21   Beale, *In Pursuit of Purity,* 82-83.

22   John William Burgon, B.D., *The Revision Revised* (Paradise, Pa.: Conservative Classics, 1883), 312.

23   Bob Larsen, *Larsen's New Book of Cults* (Wheaton, Ill.: Tyndale House Publishers, 1989), 388.

24   Frederick Lewis Allen, *Only Yesterday and Since Yesterday,* vol. 1 (New York: Bonanza Books, 1986), 89-93.

25   *Ibid.*, 1:98-110.

26   Marshall Everett, *The Complete Life of William McKinley and Story of His Assassination,* memorial ed. (n.p.: Historical Press, 1901), 17.

27   Avro Manhattan, *The Vatican and the USA* (London: Watts and Co., 1946), 4-5.

28   *Ibid.*

29   Ralph Woodrow, *Babylon Mystery Religion* (Riverside, Calif.: Ralph Woodrow Evangelistic Association, 1966), 32-33.

30   James Cardinal Gibbons, *The Faith of Our Fathers* (Baltimore, Md.: John Murphy & Co., 1897), 307.

31   Jay Robert Nash, *World Encyclopedia of Organized Crime* (New York: Dacapo Press, 1993), 582-622.

32   *Ibid.*, 490.

33   *Ibid.*, 268.

34   Jackson Morley, *Crimes and Punishment: A Pictorial Encyclopedia,* vol. 1, *Aberrant Behavior* (Paulton, England: B.P.C. Publishing, 1973), 122.

35   Carl Sifakis, *The Mafia Encyclopedia* (New York: Facts on File, 1987), 210.

36   Joseph D. Pistone and Richard Woodley, *Donnie Brasco, My Undercover Life in the Mafia* (New York: New American Library, 1987), 37.

37   Loraine Boettner, *Roman Catholicism* (Philadelphia, Pa.: Presbyterian & Reformed Publishing Co., 1962), 399.

38   R. K. Johnson, *Builder of Bridges* (Murfreesboro, Tenn.: Sword of the Lord Publishers, 1969), 22.

39   *Ibid.*, 130.

40   *Ibid.*, 137.

41   *Ibid.*, 154.

42   Arthur Fenton Hort, *Life and Letters of Fenton John Anthony Hort,* vol. 3 (London: Macmillan & Co., 1896), 139.

43   John R. Kohlenberger III, "Which Translation Is Best for Me?" *Moody Monthly,* May 1987, 17.

44   Johnson, *Builder of Bridges,* 69.

45   *Ibid.*, 68.

46   *Ibid.*, 69-70.

[47] *Ibid.*, 166.

[48] William T. Ellis, *Billy Sunday, The Man and His Message* (Philadelphia, Pa.: John C. Winston Co., 1914), 40-41.

[49] Ed Reese, *The Life and Ministry of Billy Sunday (1862-1935),* Christian Hall of Fame Series, no. 45 (Glenwood, Ill.: Fundamental Publishers, 1975), 7.

[50] Ellis, *Billy Sunday,* 147.

[51] *Ibid.*, 249.

[52] *Ibid.*

[53] *Ibid.*, 101.

[54] *Ibid.*, 113-14.

[55] E. E. Ham, *Fifty Years on the Battlefront with Christ* (n.p.: Old Kentucky Home Revivalist, 1950), 206.

[56] Roy Emerson Falls, *A Biography of J. Frank Norris* (Euless, Tex.: n.p., 1975), 17.

[57] *Ibid.*

[58] *Ibid.*, 31.

[59] E. Ray Tatum, *Conquest or Failure* (Dallas, Tex.: Baptist Historical Foundation, 1966), 125.

[60] Falls, *J. Frank Norris,* 34.

[61] Lewis Entzminger, *The Frank Norris I Have Known for 34 Years* (St. John, Ind.: Christian Book Gallery, n.d.), 112.

[62] Falls, *J. Frank Norris,* 39.

[63] Homer Ritchie, *The Life and Legend of J. Frank Norris* (Fort Worth, Tex.: n.p., 1991), 229.

[64] *Ibid.*, 230.

[65] Entzminger, *The Norris I Have Known,* 132.

[66] Falls, *J. Frank Norris,* 51.

[67] *Ibid.*, 50.

[68] *Ibid.*, 57-58.

[69] J. Frank Norris, *Inside History of First Baptist Church, Fort Worth and Temple Baptist Church, Detroit* (Fort Worth, Tex.: n.p., 1939), 16.

[70] Entzminger, *The Norris I Have Known,* 108-9.

[71] Tatum, *Conquest or Failure,* 221.

[72] *Ibid.*, 227.

[73] *Ibid.*, 215.

[74] *Ibid.*, 247.

[75] *Ibid.*

[76] *Ibid.*, 249.

[77] *Ibid.*, 250.

CHAPTER XVII
The Legitimate Mafia

[1] Roger Martin, *R. A. Torrey, Apostle of Certainty* (Murfreesboro, Tenn.: Sword of the Lord Publishers, 1976), 209.

[2] David O. Beale, *In Pursuit of Purity* (Greenville, S. C.: Unusual Publications, 1986), 91-92.

[3] G. Edward Griffin, *The Creature from Jekyll Island* (Appleton, Wis.: American Opinion, 1994), 3-4.

[4] *Ibid.*, 4-5.

[5] *Ibid.*, 9.

[6] *Ibid.*, 10.

[7] *Ibid.*, 11.

[8] *Ibid.*, 153.

[9] *Ibid.*, 167.

[10] *Ibid.*, 167-68.

[11] *Ibid.*, 160-61.

[12] *Ibid.*, 162.

[13] *Ibid.*

[14] Anthony Sutton, *War on Gold* (Seal Beach, Calif.: '76 Press, 1977), 67.

[15] *Ibid.*

[16] Ron Paul and Lewis Lehrman, *The Case for Gold* (Washington, D.C.: Cato Institute, 1982), 172-76.

[17] Griffin, *Creature from Jekyll,* 183-84.

[18] *Ibid.*, 232.

[19] *Ibid.*, 218.

[20] James Perloff, *The Shadows of Power* (Appleton, Wis.: Western Island Publishers, 1988), 44-46.

[21] Frederick Morton, *The Rothschilds, A Family Portrait* (Greenwich, Conn.: Fawcett Publications, Inc., 1963), 21.

[22] Griffin, *Creature from Jekyll,* 329.

[23] *Ibid.*, 414.

[24] *Ibid.*, 415.

[25] Gary Allen, *None Dare Call It Conspiracy* (Rossmoor, Calif.: Concord Press. n.d.), 44.

[26] *Ibid.*, 46.

[27] Griffin, *Creature from Jekyll,* 23.

[28] *Ibid.*, 17.

[29] *Ibid.*, 22-23.

[30] *Ibid.*, 448.

[31] *Ibid.*, 447.

[32] *Ibid.*, 448.

[33] Allen, *None Dare Call*, 49.

[34] *Ibid.*

[35] Griffin, *Creature from Jekyll*, 457.

[36] *Ibid.*, 45.

[37] Perloff, *Shadows of Power*, 28.

[38] *Ibid.*, 27-28.

[39] Griffin, *Creature from Jekyll*, 456.

[40] *Ibid.*, 459.

[41] Burke McCarty, *The Suppressed Truth About the Assassination of Abraham Lincoln* (Haverhill, Mass.: Arya Varta Publishing Co., 1924), 243.

[42] Morton, *The Rothschilds*, 84.

[43] Avro Manhattan, *The Vatican in World Politics* (New York: Horizon Press, 1949), 24.

[44] Bruce L. Larson, *Lindbergh of Minnesota* (New York: Harcourt, Brace, Jovanovich, 1973), 227-28.

[45] *Ibid.*, 207.

[46] *Ibid.*, 165.

[47] Griffin, *Creature from Jekyll*, 468.

[48] *Ibid.*, 236.

[49] *Ibid.*

[50] *Ibid.*, 238.

[51] *Ibid.*

[52] *Ibid.*, 239.

[53] *Ibid.*, 242.

[54] *Ibid.*, 248.

[55] Thomas A. Bailey and Paul B. Ryan, *The Lusitania Disaster* (New York: Free Press, 1975), 188-89.

[56] Griffin, *Creature from Jekyll*, 249.

[57] *Ibid.*, 246.

[58] *Ibid.*, 247.

[59] Bailey and Ryan, *The Lusitania Disaster*, 10.

[60] Colin Simpson, *The Lusitania* (New York: Little, Brown & Co., 1972), 87.

[61] Bailey and Ryan, *The Lusitania Disaster*, 75.

[62] Simpson, *Lusitania*, 91.

[63] *Ibid.*, 97.

[64] Griffin, *Creature from Jekyll*, 252.

[65] Bailey and Ryan, *The Lusitania Disaster*, 174.

[66] Griffin, *Creature from Jekyll*, 253.

[67] *Ibid.*

[68] *Ibid.*, 257.

[69] *Ibid.*, 259.

[70] *Ibid.*

[71] Tom Skeyhill, *Sergeant York: Last of the Long Hunters* (St. John, Ind.: Christian Book Gallery, n.d.), 225.

[72] *Ibid.*, 223.

CHAPTER XVIII
CFR, FDR, WW II, IMF, UN

[1] Rousas J. Rushdoony, *The Nature of the American System* (Fairfax, Va.: Thoburn Press, 1978), 135-40.

[2] *Ibid.*, 140.

[3] *Ibid.*, 150.

[4] G. Edward Griffin, *The Creature from Jekyll Island* (Appleton, Wis.: American Opinion, 1994), 270.

[5] William Jasper, *Global Tyranny... Step by Step* (Appleton, Wis.: Western Island Publishers, 1993), 53.

[6] Carroll Quigley, *Tragedy and Hope* (New York: Macmillan Co., 1966), 131.

[7] *Ibid.*, 950.

[8] Griffin, *Creature from Jekyll*, 268-69.

[9] *Ibid.*, 269.

[10] Quigley, *Tragedy and Hope*, 324.

[11] *Ibid.*, 326-27.

[12] Griffin, *Creature from Jekyll*, 265.

[13] *Ibid.*, 267.

[14] *Ibid.*, 275.

[15] James Perloff, *The Shadows of Power* (Appleton, Wis.: Western Island Publishers, 1988), 40.

[16] *Ibid.*, 40.

[17] Gary Allen, *The Rockefeller File* (Seal Beach, Calif.: '76 Press, 1976), 119.

[18] Gary Allen, *Say "No!" to the New World Order* (Seal Beach, Calif.: Concord Press, 1987), 106.

[19] Allen, *The Rockefeller File*, 99.

[20] Perloff, *Shadows of Power*, 31.

[21] *Ibid.*

[22] *Ibid.*, 32.

23 Quigley, *Tragedy and Hope*, 951-52.
24 Perloff, *Shadows of Power*, 37.
25 *Ibid.*, 6.
26 *Ibid.*
27 John F. McManus, *The Insiders* (Appleton, Wis.: John Birch Society, 1995), 9.
28 Perloff, *Shadows of Power*, 10.
29 *Ibid.*, 7.
30 *Ibid.*, 9.
31 *Ibid.*, 11.
32 *Ibid.*
33 *Ibid.*
34 *Ibid.*, 12.
35 *Ibid.*
36 *Ibid.*, 7.
37 Allen, *The Rockefeller File*, 55.
38 Perloff, *Shadows of Power*, 7.
39 McManus, *Insiders*, 49.
40 Perloff, *Shadows of Power*, 14.
41 *Ibid.*, 14-15.
42 *Ibid.*, 54.
43 *Ibid.*, 55.
44 *Ibid.*
45 *Ibid.*, 474.
46 *Ibid.*, 496.
47 *Ibid.*, 497.
48 *Ibid.*, 56.
49 *Ibid.*, 56-57.
50 *Ibid.*, 55.
51 *Ibid.*, 56.
52 *Ibid.*, 57.
53 *Ibid.*
54 Anthony Sutton, *War on Gold* (Seal Beach, Calif.: '76 Press, 1977), 90.
55 Anthony Sutton, *Wall Street and the Rise of Hitler* (Seal Beach, Calif.: '76 Press, 1976), 15-16.
56 *Ibid.*, 16.
57 Quigley, *Tragedy and Hope*, 308.
58 *Ibid.*, 308-9.
59 Sutton, *Wall Street and Hitler*, 33.
60 *Ibid.*
61 *Ibid.*, 35.
62 *Ibid.*, 22-23.
63 *Ibid.*, 83.
64 *Ibid.*, 37.
65 *Ibid.*, 90.
66 *Ibid.*, 94.
67 *Ibid.*, 92.
68 *Ibid.*, 93.
69 Avro Manhattan, *The Vatican in World Politics* (New York: Horizon Press, 1949), 117.
70 Edmond Paris, *The Vatican Against Europe* (London: Wickliffe Press, 1988), 75.
71 Sutton, *Wall Street and Hitler*, 118-20.
72 Manhattan, *Vatican in World Politics*, 172.
73 *Ibid.*
74 Paris, *Vatican Against Europe*, 79.
75 Avro Manhattan, *The Vatican Holocaust* (Springfield, Mo.: Ozark Books, 1980), 135-41.
76 Manhattan, *Vatican in World Politics*, 222.
77 *Ibid.*, 177.
78 *Ibid.*, 176.
79 *Ibid.*, 187.
80 Edmond Paris, *The Secret History of the Jesuits* (Chino, Calif.: Chick Publications, 1975), 164.
81 *Ibid.*
82 Paris, *Vatican Against Europe*, 167.
83 Manhattan, *Vatican in World Politics*, 191.
84 Paris, *Vatican Against Europe*, 167.
85 Edmond Paris, *Convert...or Die!*, trans. Lois Perkins (Chino, Calif.: Chick Publications, n.d.), 59.
86 *Ibid.*, 130.
87 Manhattan, *The Vatican's Holocaust*, 52.
88 *Ibid.*, 49.
89 Paris, *Convert...or Die!*, 60.
90 *Ibid.*, 135.
91 Manhattan, *Vatican's Holocaust*, 48.
92 Paris, *Convert...or Die!*, 106.
93 *Ibid.*, 191.
94 *Ibid.*, 106.
95 Paris, *Vatican Against Europe*, 209.
96 Paris, *Convert...or Die!*, 129.
97 *Ibid.*, 189.
98 Manhattan, *Vatican's Holocaust*, 48.
99 Avro Manhattan, *The Vatican and the USA* (London: Watts and Co., 1946), 27.
100 *Ibid.*

[101] *Ibid.*, 21.
[102] Paris, *Secret History of Jesuits,* 159.
[103] Manhattan, *Vatican and USA,* 23.
[104] Perloff, *Shadows of Power,* 64.
[105] *Ibid.*, 66.
[106] *Ibid.*, 66-67.
[107] *Ibid.*, 67.
[108] John Toland, *Infamy: Pearl Harbor and Its Aftermath,* (New York: Doubleday and Company, 1982), 13.
[109] Josh McDowell, *Evidence That Demands a Verdict,* vol. 1 (San Bernardino, Calif.: Campus Crusade for Christ International, 1972), 343.
[110] Toland, *Infamy,* 5.
[111] *Ibid.*, 6.
[112] *Ibid.*, 290.
[113] *Ibid.*
[114] *Ibid.*, 289.
[115] *Ibid.*, 14.
[116] *Ibid.*, 5.
[117] *Ibid.*
[118] *Ibid.*, 279-80.
[119] *Ibid.*, 280-81.
[120] *Ibid.*, 281.
[121] *Ibid.*, 287.
[122] *Ibid.*, 286.
[123] *Ibid.*
[124] *Ibid.*, 283.
[125] Paul Harvey, *The Rest of the Story* (New York: William and Morrow & Co., 1980), 132.
[126] *Ibid.*, 134.
[127] Toland, *Infamy,* 176-77.
[128] *Ibid.*, 318.
[129] *Ibid.*
[130] *Ibid.*
[131] *Ibid.*, 319.
[132] Toland, *Infamy,* 13.
[133] Dan Smoot, *The Invisible Government* (Dallas, Tex.: Dan Smoot Report, 1962), 27.
[134] *Ibid.*
[135] *Ibid.*, 29.
[136] Perloff, *Shadows of Power,* 61.
[137] Griffin, *Creature from Jekyll,* 105.
[138] Jasper, *Global Tyranny,* 47-48.
[139] *Ibid.*, 48.

CHAPTER XIX
Rosie, Elvis and Billy

[1] Kelli Peduzzi, *America in the 20th Century, 1940–1949,* vol. 5 (New York: Marshall Cavendish Corp., 1995), 664.
[2] Paul Johnson, *The Almost Chosen People,* tape 2 (San Francisco, Calif.: Laissez Faire Audio, n.d.), audio cassette.
[3] Johnson, *Almost Chosen People,* tape 3.
[4] *Ibid.*
[5] John Eidsmoe, *Christianity and the Constitution* (Grand Rapids, Mich.: Baker Books, 1995), 381.
[6] Larry Burkett, *The Coming Economic Earthquake* (Chicago: Moody Press, 1991), 54.
[7] Homer Ritchie, *The Life and Legend of J. Frank Norris* (Fort Worth, Tex.: n.p., 1991), 277-88.
[8] Lois Gordon and Alan Gordon, *The Columbia Chronicles of American Life, 1910–1992* (New York: Columbia University Press, 1995), 366.
[9] *Ibid.*, 348-469.
[10] *Ibid.*
[11] *Ibid.*
[12] Paul Lee Tan, *Encyclopedia of 7,700 Illustrations* (Rockville, Md.: Assurance Publishers, 1979), 867.
[13] Gordon and Gordon, *Columbia Chronicles,* 383.
[14] *Ibid.*, 390.
[15] Peduzzi, *America in 20th Century,* 627.
[16] *Ibid.*, 631.
[17] *Ibid.*, 627.
[18] Ritchie, *Life of Norris,* 208.
[19] *Ibid.*, 210.
[20] *Ibid.*, 214.
[21] Gordon and Gordon, *Columbia Chronicles,* 401.
[22] Jane Stern and Michael Stern, *Encyclopedia of Culture* (New York: Harper-Collins Publishers, 1992), 390.
[23] Gordon and Gordon, *Columbia Chronicles,* 390.
[24] Peduzzi, *America in 20th Century,* 836-37.

[25] Marie Cahill, *Elvis* (North Dighton, Mass.: J. G. Press, 1994), 56.

[26] Caroline Latham and Jeannie Sakol, *"E" Is for Elvis* (n.p.: Penguin Group, 1990), 261.

[27] *Ibid.*, 203.

[28] Peter Guralnick, *Last Train to Memphis: The Rise of Elvis Presley* (Boston: Little, Brown Co., 1994), 162.

[29] Joe Esposito and Elena Oumano, *Good Rockin' Tonight* (New York: Simon & Schuster, 1994), 70.

[30] Latham and Sakol, *"E" for Elvis,* 245.

[31] Kevin Quain, *The Elvis Reader* (New York: St. Martin's Press, 1992), xiv-xv.

[32] Latham and Sakol, *"E" for Elvis,* 14.

[33] *Ibid.*, 255.

[34] Esposito and Oumano, *Good Rockin'*, 33.

[35] *Ibid.*, 86.

[36] *Ibid.*, 189.

[37] *Ibid.*, 121-22.

[38] Latham and Sakol, *"E" for Elvis,* 226.

[39] Esposito and Oumano, *Good Rockin'*, 75-76.

[40] Latham and Sakol, *"E" for Elvis,* 203.

[41] *Ibid.*, 169.

[42] Esposito and Oumano, *Good Rockin'*, 35.

[43] *Ibid.*, 55-56.

[44] *Ibid.*, 16.

[45] Latham and Sakol, *"E" for Elvis,* 238.

[46] *Ibid.*, 238.

[47] *Ibid.*, 243.

[48] *Ibid.*, 30.

[49] *Ibid.*, 20.

[50] *Ibid.*

[51] *Ibid.*, 157.

[52] *Ibid.*, 160.

[53] Esposito and Oumano, *Good Rockin'*, 13.

[54] *Ibid.*, 74.

[55] Susan Doll, *Elvis: Portrait of a King* (Lincolnwood, Ill.: Publications International, 1995), 171.

[56] Esposito and Oumano, *Good Rockin'*, 237.

[57] Latham and Sakol, *"E" for Elvis,* 208.

[58] *Ibid.*, 30-31.

[59] *Ibid.*, 271.

[60] Esposito and Oumano, *Good Rockin'*, 237.

[61] Latham and Sakol, *"E" for Elvis,* 155.

[62] Esposito and Oumano, *Good Rockin'*, 238.

[63] Quain, *Elvis Reader*, xiv.

[64] William Martin, *A Prophet with Honor* (New York: William Morrow & Co., 1991), 68.

[65] Marshall Frady, *Billy Graham: A Parable of American Righteousness* (Boston: Little, Brown & Co., 1979), 96-97.

[66] *Ibid.*, 98.

[67] *Ibid.*, 97.

[68] Martin, *Prophet with Honor,* 69.

[69] *Ibid.*, 70.

[70] *Ibid.*, 71.

[71] Cort R. Flint, *The Quotable Billy Graham* (Anderson, S.C.: Droke House Publishers, 1966), 50.

[72] Michael Boland, "Co-operative Evangelism at Harringay," *The Banner of Truth*, iss. 42 (London: England, May/June 1966), 8.

[73] *Ibid.*, 9.

[74] R. K. Johnson, *Builder of Bridges* (Murfreesboro, Tenn.: Sword of the Lord Publishers, 1969), 277

[75] G. Archer Weniger, "Preliminary Considerations for Fundamentalists on the Graham Ecumenical Evangelistic Campaign Scheduled for San Francisco" [April 1958], Oakland, Calif.

[76] Flint, *Quotable Graham,* 79.

[77] Curtis Mitchell, *Billy Graham: Saint or Sinner* (Old Tappan, N.J.: Fleming H. Revell Co., 1973), 105.

[78] *Ibid.*, 116.

[79] *Ibid.*, 114.

[80] Nancy Gibbs and Richard N. Ostling, "God's Billy Pulpit," *Time*, 15 November, 1993, 74.

[81] Robert O. Ferm, *Cooperative*

Evangelism, Is Billy Graham Right or Wrong? (Boston: Little, Brown & Co., 1979), 70.

82 *Ibid.*, 71-72.

83 *Ibid.*, 81-83.

84 *Ibid.*, 84.

85 "Advertisement," *Saturday Evening Post*, March 1991, inside back cover.

86 Ferm, *Cooperative Evangelism*, 71.

87 *Ibid.*, 11.

88 *Ibid.*, 12.

89 Johnson, *Builder of Bridges*, 291.

90 David 0. Beale, *In Pursuit of Purity* (Greenville, S.C.: Unusual Publications, 1986), 264.

91 Martin, *Prophet with Honor*, 309.

92 *Ibid.*, 310.

93 Dave Hunt, *A Woman Rides the Beast* (Eugene, Oreg.: Harvest House Publishers, 1994), 388.

94 Paul Smith, "Belmont Abbey Confers Honorary Degree," *The Gastonia Gazette*, 22 November 1967, n.p.

95 *Ibid.*

96 *Ibid.*

CHAPTER XX
Cold War Years

1 Lois Gordon and Alan Gordon, *The Columbia Chronicles of American Life, 1910–1992* (New York: Columbia University Press, 1995), 399.

2 Dave Hunt, *Peace, Prosperity and the Coming Holocaust* (Eugene, Oreg.: Harvest House Publishers, 1983), 170.

3 Avro Manhattan, *Murder in the Vatican* (Springfield, Mo.: Ozark Books, 1985), 5-6.

4 Avro Manhattan, *The Vatican Moscow Washington Alliance* (Chino, Calif.: Chick Publications, 1986), 11.

5 William Jasper, *Global Tyranny... Step By Step* (Appleton, Wis.: Western Island Publishers, 1993), 244.

6 James Perloff, *The Shadows of Power* (Appleton, Wis.: Western Island Publishers, 1988), 84.

7 *Ibid.*, 85.

8 *Ibid.*, 86.

9 Avro Manhattan, *Vietnam: Why Did We Go?* (Chino, Calif.: Chick Publications, 1984), 27.

10 *Ibid.*

11 *Ibid.*

12 Dave Hunt, *Global Peace and the Rise of the Antichrist* (Eugene, Oreg.: Harvest House Publishers, 1990), 123.

13 Manhattan, *Vatican Moscow Washington Alliance*, 143.

14 Manhattan, *Vietnam*, 30.

15 Avro Manhattan, *The Vatican's Holocaust* (Springfield, Mo.: Ozark Books, 1986), 186.

16 Manhattan, *Vietnam*, 31-33.

17 *Ibid.*, 36.

18 Manhattan, *Vatican Moscow Washington Alliance*, 115-16.

19 Perloff, *Shadows of Power*, 121-22.

20 *Ibid.*, 98.

21 Manhattan, *Vietnam*, 33.

22 Perloff, *Shadows of Power*, 98.

23 Manhattan, *Vietnam*, 33.

24 Manhattan, *The Dollar and the Vatican* (Springfield, Mo.: Ozark Books, 1988), 79.

25 *Ibid.*, 79.

26 *Ibid.*, 50.

27 *Ibid.*

28 *Ibid.*

29 *Ibid.*, 81.

30 Manhattan, *Vietnam*, 40.

31 *Ibid.*

32 *Ibid.*

33 Manhattan, *Vatican's Holocaust*, 200.

34 Robert I. Gannon, *The Cardinal Spellman Story* (Garden City, N.J.: Doubleday & Co., 1962), 173.

35 *Ibid.*

36 Manhattan, *Vietnam*, 71.

37 *Ibid.*, 43.

38 *Ibid.*, 47.

39 *Ibid.*, 50.

40 Perloff, *Shadows of Power*, 91.

41 *Ibid.*, 91.

42 *Ibid.*, 92.

43 *Ibid.*

44 Perloff, *Shadows of Power*, 93.

45 *Ibid.*, 105.
46 *Ibid.*, 101.
47 Joe M. Boyd, *The Bilderbergers Unmasked* (Mt. Salem, W.Va.: Privately printed, 1991), 3.
48 *Ibid.*, 2.
49 *Ibid.*, 33.
50 Perloff, *Shadows of Power,* 106.
51 *Ibid.*, 106.
52 Gannon, *Cardinal Spellman,* 348.
53 Jasper, *Global Tyranny,* 83.
54 *Ibid.*, 87.
55 *Ibid.*, 108-9.
56 *Ibid.*, 101.
57 Manhattan, *Vatican's Holocaust,* 197.
58 *Ibid.*, 194.
59 *Ibid.*, 195.
60 *Ibid.*, 197.
61 *Ibid.*, 199.
62 Edmund H. Harvey, Jr., ed., *Our Glorious Century* (Pleasantville, N. Y.: The Reader's Digest Association, 1994), 295.
63 *Ibid.*
64 Manhattan, *Vatican Washington Moscow Alliance,* 152.
65 *Ibid.*, 144.
66 *Ibid.*, 153.
67 Manhattan, *Dollar and Vatican,* 97.
68 Manhattan, *Vatican Washington Moscow Alliance,* 145.
69 Manhattan, *Dollar and Vatican,* 104.
70 Perloff, *Shadows of Power,* 114.
71 *Ibid.*, 110.
72 *Ibid.*, 111.
73 Jasper, *Global Tyranny,* 13.
74 *Ibid.*
75 Gary Allen, *Say "No!" to the New World Order* (Seal Beach, Calif.: Concord Press, 1987), 146.
76 Gene Schroder, *War and Emergency Powers* (Dallas, Tex.: n.p., n.d.), 59.
77 *Ibid.*, 52.
78 Manhattan, *Vietnam,* 117.
79 *Ibid.*
80 *Ibid.*, 127.
81 Manhattan, *Vatican Moscow Washington Alliance,* 170.
82 *Ibid.*, 77.
83 Perloff, *Shadows of Power,* 123.
84 *Ibid.*, 124.
85 *Ibid.*
86 Allen, *Say "No!" to New World Order,* 97.
87 *Ibid.*, 110.
88 Gary Allen, *The Rockefeller File* (Seal Beach, Calif.: '76 Press, 1976), 110-11.
89 Allen, *Say "No!" to New World Order,* 147-48.
90 G. Edward Griffin, *The Creature from Jekyll Island* (Appleton, Wis.: American Opinion, 1994), 518.
91 *Ibid.*, 522-23.
92 *Ibid.*, 524.
99 *Ibid.*, 523.
94 U.S. Congress, *Document No. 914,* 88th Cong., 1st Sess., 62.
95 *Ibid.*
96 David Barton, *America: To Pray? or Not To Pray?* (Aledo, Tex.: WallBuilder's Press, 1994), 35.
97 *Ibid.*, 28-29.
98 *Ibid.*, 30-31.
99 *Ibid.*, 32-33.
100 *Ibid.*, 36-40.
101 Tan, *7,700 Illustrations,* 1041.
102 *Ibid.*, 1033.
103 Perloff, *Shadows of Power,* 144.
104 *Ibid.*, 145.
105 Bill Still, *On the Horns of the Beast,* (Winchester, Va.: Reinhardt & Still Publishers, 1995), 221-22.
106 *Ibid.*, 233.
107 Still, *Horns of Beast,* 241-43.
108 Avro Manhattan, *Murder in the Vatican* (Springfield, Mo.: Ozark Books, 1985), 116-17.
109 *Ibid.*, 136.
110 *Ibid.*, 160.
111 *Ibid.*, 209.
112 *Ibid.*, 210-14.
113 Hunt, *Global Peace,* 124.
114 Gary Allen, *The Rockefeller File* (Seal Beach, Calif.: '76 Press, 1976), 3.
115 Manhattan, *Vatican Moscow Washington Alliance,* 63.
116 Carl Bernstein, "The Holy Alliance," *Time,* 24 February 1992, p. 28.
117 *Ibid.*, 30.

[118] *Ibid.*, 33.

[119] *Ibid.*, 31.

[120] Manhattan, *Vatican Moscow Washington Alliance*, 68.

[121] "Pope Remembers a Child's Gift," *Fairbanks Daily News-Miner*, 2 May 1984, 3.

CHAPTER XXI
The Great Apostasy

[1] Peter Jennings, *In the Name of God*, produced by Martin Smith, 60 minutes, American Broadcasting Company, 1995, videocassette.

[2] *Ibid.*

[3] *Ibid.*

[4] Cindy Lafavre Yorks, "McChurch," *Daily Courier News, U.S.A. Weekend*, 13-15 April 1990, 4.

[5] *Ibid.*

[6] Jennings, *In the Name of God*.

[7] *Ibid.*

[8] *Ibid.*

[9] *Ibid.*

[10] *Ibid.*

[11] *Ibid.*

[12] "Advertisement," *Saturday Evening Post*, March 1991, inside back cover.

[13] David W. Cloud, *Flirting with Rome*, vol.2, *Key Men and Organizations* (Oak Harbor, Wash.: Way of Life Literature, 1992), 20.

[14] *Ibid.*

[15] *Ibid.*, 21.

[16] *Ibid.*

[17] *Ibid.*, 22-23.

[18] *Ibid.*, 22.

[19] *Ibid.*

[20] *Ibid.*

[21] *Ibid.*, 23.

[22] David Cloud, *Flirting with Rome*, vol. 3, *Southern Baptist Convention* (Oak Harbor; Wa.: Way of Life Literature, 1993), 29.

[23] Ian R. K. Paisley, *Antichrist* (Belfast, Northern Ireland: Martyrs Memorial Productions, n.d.), 14.

[24] *Ibid.*, 20.

[25] *Ibid.*, 13.

[26] *Ibid.*, 14.

[27] *Ibid.*, 67.

[28] Jack Van Impe and Rexella Van Impe, *Startling Revelations: Pope John Paul II* (Troy, Mich.: Van Impe Ministries, n. d.) videocassette jacket.

[29] Jack Van Impe and Rexella Van Impe, *Startling Revelations: Pope John Paul II*, produced by Van Impe Ministries, 60 minutes, n.d., videocassette.

[30] *Ibid.*

[31] *Ibid.*

[32] Will Durant, *The Story of Civilization*, vol.6, *The Reformation* (New York: Simon & Schuster, 1957), 418.

[33] Martin Bobgan and Deidre Bobgan, *Prophets of Psychoheresy II* (Santa Barbara, Calif.: East Gate Publishers, 1990), 146.

[34] *Ibid.*, 10-11.

[35] *Ibid.*, 4.

[36] *Ibid.*, 21.

[37] *Ibid.*, 23.

[38] *Ibid.*, 28.

[39] *Ibid.*, 40.

[40] *Ibid.*, 107.

[41] Cloud, *Flirting with Rome*, 2:19.

[42] Dave Hunt, *Global Peace and the Rise of Antichrist* (Eugene, Oreg.: Harvest House Publishers, 1990), 105.

[43] Cloud, *Flirting with Rome*, 2:20.

[44] *Ibid.*

[45] Dave Hunt, *A Woman Rides the Beast* (Eugene, Oreg.: Harvest House Publishers, 1994), 388.

[46] *Ibid.*, 412.

[47] Cloud, *Flirting with Rome*, 2:16-17.

[48] *Ibid.*, 17.

[49] *Ibid.*, 412.

[50] Hunt, *Woman Rides Beast*, 431.

[51] Cloud, *Flirting with Rome*, 2:25-26.

[52] *Ibid.*, 26-27.

[53] Hunt, *Woman Rides Beast*, 5.

[54] John Ankerberg, *Evangelicals and Catholics Together: The Christian Mission in the Third Millennium* (Chattanooga, Tenn.: Theological Research Institute, 1994), 1.

[55] *Ibid.*

56 *Ibid.*, 4-5.
57 Hunt, *Woman Rides Beast*, 8.
58 *Ibid.*, 7.
59 *Ibid.*
60 *Ibid.*, 7-8.
61 Ankerberg, "Clarifying Statement," *Evangelicals and Catholics Together*, n.p.
62 Cloud, *Flirting with Rome*, 2:30.
63 *Ibid.*, 28.
64 John Ankerberg, *Protestants and Catholics: Do They Now Agree?* produced by John Ankerberg, 60 minutes, 1995, videocassette.
65 *Ibid.*

CHAPTER XXII
The Promise Keepers

1 Ralph Coles, *Ecumenical Confusion in Atlanta* (Oak Harbor, Wash.: Way of Life Organization, n.d.), 2.
2 *Ibid.*, 9.
3 Albert James Dager, "Promise Keepers: Is What You See What You Get?" *Media Spotlight*, July 1995, p. 9.
4 *Ibid.*, 6.
5 Robert Hicks, *The Masculine Journey: Understanding the Six Stages of Manhood* (Colorado Springs, Col.: Navpress, 1993), 31.
6 *Ibid.*, 181.
7 Martin Bobgan and Deidre Bobgan, *Prophets of Psychoheresy II* (Santa Barbara, Calif.: East Gate Publishers, 1990), 5.
8 Dager, "Promise Keepers," 14.
9 *Ibid.*, 16.
10 *Ibid.*
11 *Ibid.*
12 Ed Tarkowski, *Laughing Phenomena: Its History and Possible Effects on the Church* (McKean, Pa.: n.p., 1995), 6.
13 *Ibid.*
14 *Ibid.*
15 *Ibid.*
16 *Ibid.*
17 *Ibid.*, 7.
18 *Ibid.*, 8.
19 *Ibid.*, 11.
20 *Ibid.*
21 Jewel van der Merwe, "Latter Rain and the Rise of Joel's Army," *Discernment*, October-December, 1994, 7.
22 *Ibid.*
23 Tarkowski, *Laughing Phenomena*, 8.
24 van der Merwe, *Discernment*, 7.
25 Tarkowski, *Laughing Phenomena*, 7.
26 *Ibid.*, 43.
26 *Ibid.*, 12.
27 *Ibid.*, 10.
29 *Ibid.*, 11.
30 *Ibid.*, 11-12.
31 *Ibid.*, 13.
32 *Ibid.*, 28.
33 *Ibid.*, 31.
34 Avro Manhattan, *The Vatican Billions* (Chino, Calif.: Chick Publications, 1983), 55-56.
35 Tarkowski, *Laughing Phenomena*, 30.
36 *Ibid.*
37 *Ibid.*, 47.
38 *Ibid.*, 48.
39 *Ibid.*, 15-16.

CHAPTER XXIII
Hold Fast!

1 Ed Tarkowski, *Laughing Phenomena: Its History and Possible Effects on the Church* (McKean, Pa.: n.p., 1995), 27.
2 *Ibid.*
3 *Ibid.*, 21.
4 Glen Elsasser, "Mayor Barry Denies Drug, Alcohol Relapse," Chicago Tribune, 14 May 1996, sec. 1, p. 4.
5 Senator Joe Biden, *The Threshold of the New World Order: The Wilsonian Vision and American Foreign Policy in the 1990's and Beyond* (Maryland Heights, Mo.: Better Books, 1994), 9-63 [typed from the Congressional Record by Jeanne Billingsley, July 1994]
6 Associated Press Release, "Naked and Not Ashamed, Say Christians," *Chicago Tribune*, 20 February 1996, sec. C, 1.
7 Will Durant, *The Story of Civilization*, vol. 11, *The Age of Napoleon* (New York: Simon & Schuster, 1975), 748.

Sources Consulted

BOOKS

ADAMS, JAMES L. *Yankee Doodle Went to Church.* Old Tappan, N.J.: Fleming H. Revell, Co., 1989.

ALLEN, FREDERICK LEWIS. *Only Yesterday and Since Yesterday.* New York: Bonanza Books, 1986.

ALLEN, GARY. *None Dare Call It Conspiracy.* Rossmoor, Calif.: Concord Press, n.d.

_____. *The Rockefeller File.* Seal Beach, Calif.: '76 Press, 1976.

_____. *Say "No!" to the New World Order.* Seal Beach, Calif.: Concord Press, 1987.

AMERICA'S GREAT REVIVALS. Minneapolis, Minn.: Dimension Books, n.d.

ANDERSON, NANCY SCOTT AND DWIGHT ANDERSON. *The Generals.* New York: Alfred A. Knopf, 1988.

ANKERBERG, JOHN AND JOHN WELDON. *Protestants and Catholics: Do They Now Agree?* Eugene, Oreg.: Harvest House Publishers, 1995.

ARMITAGE, THOMAS. *A History of the Baptists.* Vols. 1 & 2. Watertown, Wis.: Baptist Heritage Press, 1988.

AURANDT, PAUL. *More of Paul Harvey's The Rest of the Story.* New York: William Morrow & Co., 1980.

BAILEY, THOMAS A. AND PAUL B. RYAN. *The Lusitania Disaster.* New York: Free Press, 1975.

BARLOW, FRED. *Profiles in Evangelism.* Murfreesboro, Tenn.: Sword of the Lord Publishers, 1976.

BARTON, DAVID. *America: To Pray? or Not To Pray?* Aledo, Tex.: WallBuilder's Press, 1994.

_____. *America's Godly Heritage.* Aledo, Tex.: WallBuilder's Press, 1993.

_____. *Bulletproof George Washington.* Aledo, Tex.: WallBuilder's Press, 1994.

_____. *The Myth of Separation.* Aledo, Tex.: WallBuilder's Press, 1993.

BEALE, DAVID O. *In Pursuit of Purity.* Greenville, S.C.: Unusual Publications, 1986.

BENEDICT, DAVID. *A General History of the Baptist Denomination in America.* Vols. 1 & 2. Gallatin, Tenn.: Church History Research & Archives, 1985.

BILLINGTON, RAY ALLEN. *The Protestant Crusade.* Chicago: Quadrangle Books, 1964.

BLIED, BENJAMIN J. *Catholics and the Civil War.* Milwaukee, Wis.: n.p., 1945.

BOETTNER, LORAINE. *Roman Catholicism.* Philadelphia: Presbyterian & Reformed Publishing Co., 1962.

BOLES, JOHN B. *Masters and Slaves in the House of the Lord.* Lexington, Ky.: University Press of Kentucky, 1988.

BOORSTIN, DANIEL J. *The Genius of American Politics.* Chicago: University of Chicago Press, 1953.

BOPP, VIRGIL W. *Confidently Committed.* Grand Rapids, Mich.: Regular Baptist Press, 1987.

BORK, ROBERT H. *The Tempting of America.* New York: Simon & Schuster, 1990.

BOYD, JOE M. *The Bilderbergers Unmasked.* Mt. Salem, W.Va.: Privately printed, 1991.

BOYS, DON. *Liberalism: A Rope of Sand.* Indianapolis, Ind.: Goodhope Press, 1979.

BRADFORD, WILLIAM. *Of Plymouth Plantation, 1620–1647.* New York: Random House, 1981.

BRENDAN, BERNARD. *Pizarro, Orellana, and the Exploration of the Amazon.* New York: Chelsea House Publishers, 1991.

BROOKE, TAL. *When the World Will Be As One.* Eugene, Oreg.: Harvest House Publishers, n.d.

BURGON, JOHN WILLIAM. *The Revision Revised.* Paradise, Pa.: Conservative Classics, 1883.

BURKETT, LARRY. *The Coming Economic Earthquake.* Chicago: Moody Press, 1991.

CAHILL, MARIE. *Elvis.* North Dighton, Mass.: J. G. Press, 1994.

CANFIELD, CASS. *The Iron Will of Jefferson Davis.* New York: Fairfax Press, 1978.

CARTWRIGHT, PETER. *Autobiography of Peter Cartwright: The Backwoods Preacher.* St. John, Ind.: Christian Book Gallery, 1988.

CASSIDY, THOMAS. *Textual Criticism: Fact and Fiction.* Spring Valley, Calif.: First Baptist Church Publications, 1994.

CATHCORT, WILLIAM. *Baptist Patriots.* Grand Rapids, Mich.: Guardian Press, 1976.

CHAMBERLIN, RAY. *Quotes and Quaint Stories of Great Americans.* Cynthiana, Ky.: Ray Chamberlin, n.d.

CHINIQUY, CHARLES. *50 Years in the "Church" of Rome.* Chino, Calif.: Chick Publications, 1985.

_____. *The Priest, The Woman and The Confessional.* Chino, Calif.: Chick Publications, n.d.

CHRISTIAN, JOHN. *A History of the Baptists.* Vols. 1 & 2. Texarkana, Tex.: Bogard Press, 1922.

CLOUD, DAVID W. *Flirting with Rome.* Vol. 2, *Key Men and Organizations.* Oak Harbor, Wash.: Way of Life Literature, 1992.

_____. *Flirting with Rome.* Vol. 3, *Southern Baptist Convention.* Oak Harbor, Wash.: Way of Life Literature, 1993.

COGLEY, JOHN. *Catholic America.* New York: Dial Press, 1973.

COLLINS, A. LOYD. *God and American Independence.* Orlando, Fla.: Christ for the World Publishers, 1974.

_____. *God in American History.* Orlando, Fl.: Christ for the World Publishers, 1969.

CURRENT, RICHARD N. *The Lincoln Nobody Knows.* New York: Hill & Wang, 1958.

DALLIMORE, ARNOLD. *George Whitefield, The Life and Times of the Great Evangelist of the Eighteenth-Century Revival.* Vols. 1 & 2. Carlisle, Pa.: Banner of Truth Trust, 1989.

DAVIS, BURKE. *The Civil War, Strange and Fascinating Facts.* New York: Fairfax Press, 1960.

DOLL, SUSAN. *Elvis: Portrait of the King.* Lincolnwood, Ill.: Publications International, 1995.

DOLLAR, GEORGE W. *A History of Fundamentalism in America.* Greenville, S.C.: Bob Jones University Press, 1973.

DONALD, DAVID HERBERT. *Lincoln.* New York: Simon & Schuster, 1995.

DRUMMOND, RICK. *The Story of American Protestantism.* Boston: Beacon Press, 1950.

DURANT, WILL. *The Story of Civilization.* Vol. 4, *The Age of Faith.* New York: Simon & Schuster, 1950.

_____. *The Story of Civilization.* Vol. 6, *The Reformation.* New York: Simon & Schuster, 1957.

_____. *The Story of Civilization.* Vol. 11, *The Age of Napoleon.* New York: Simon & Schuster, 1975.

DURANT, ARIEL AND WILL DURANT. *The Story of Civilization.* Vol. 10, *Rousseau and Revolution.* New York: Simon & Schuster, 1967.

EIDSMOE, JOHN. *Christianity and the Constitution.* Grand Rapids, Mich.: Baker Books, 1995.

ELLIS, JOHN TRACY. *American Catholicism.* Chicago: University of Chicago Press, 1955.

ELLIS, WILLIAM T. *Billy Sunday: The Man and His Message.* Philadelphia, Pa.: John C. Winston, Co., 1914.

ENTZMINGER, LOUIS. *The J. Frank Norris I Have Known for 34 Years.* St. John,

Ind.: Christian Book Gallery, n.d.

ESPOSITO, JOE AND ELENA OUMANO. *Good Rockin' Tonight.* New York: Simon & Schuster, 1994.

EVANS, M. STANTON. *The Theme Is Freedom.* Washington, D.C.: Regency Publishing, 1994.

EVERETT, MARSHALL. *The Complete Life of William McKinley and Story of His Assassination.* Memorial ed. N.p.: Historical Press, 1901.

FALLS, ROY EMERSON. *A Biography of J. Frank Norris.* Euless, Tex.: Privately printed, 1975.

FERM, ROBERT O. *Cooperative Evangelism: Is Billy Graham Right or Wrong?* Grand Rapids, Mich.: Zondervan Publishing House, 1958.

FISHER, GEORGE PARK. *History of the Christian Church.* New York: Charles Scribner's Sons, 1887.

FLEMING, THOMAS J. *One Small Candle.* New York: W. W. Norton & Co., 1964.

FLINT, CORT R. *The Quotable Billy Graham.* Anderson, S.C.: Droke House Publishers, 1966.

FLOOD, ROBERT AND NANCY L. DEMOSS. *The Rebirth of America.* Philadelphia, Pa.: Arthur S. DeMoss Foundation, 1986.

FRADY, MARSHALL. *Billy Graham: A Parable of American Righteousness.* Boston: Little, Brown & Co., 1979.

FRASSANITO, WILLIAM A. *Antietam.* New York: Charles Scribner's Sons, 1978.

FREMANTLE, ANNE. *The Papal Encyclicals in Their Historical Context.* New York: New American Library, 1956.

FRIEDMAN, LAWRENCE. *Crime and Punishment in America.* New York: Harper Collins Publishers, 1993.

FULLER, DAVID OTIS, D.D., ed. *True or False?* Grand Rapids, Mich.: Grand Rapids International Publications, 1973.

GANNON, ROBERT I. *The Cardinal Spellman Story.* Garden City, N.J.: Doubleday & Co., 1962.

GARRISON, WEBB. *Civil War Curiosities.* Nashville, Tenn.: Rutledge Hill Press, 1994.

_____. *A Treasury of Civil War Tales.* Nashville, Tenn.: Rutledge Hill Press, 1988.

GIBBONS, JAMES CARDINAL. *The Faith of Our Fathers.* Baltimore, Md.: John Murphy & Co., 1897.

GIPP, SAMUEL. *An Understandable History of the Bible.* Macedonia, Ohio: Bible Believer's Bookstore, 1987.

GRIFFIN, G. EDWARD. *The Creature from Jekyll Island.* Appleton, Wis.: American Opinion, 1994.

GURALNICK, PETER. *Last Train to Memphis: The Rise of Elvis Presley.* Boston: Little, Brown & Co., 1994.

HAM, E. E. *Fifty Years on the Battlefront with Christ.* n.p.: Old Kentucky Home Revivalist, 1950.

HANCHETT, WILLIAM. *The Lincoln Murder Conspiracies.* Urbana and Chicago: University of Illinois, 1986.

HARDMAN, KEITH J. *The Spiritual Awakeners.* Chicago: Moody Press, 1983.

HARRIS, THOMAS M. *Rome's Responsibility for the Assassination of Abraham Lincoln.* Los Angeles: Heritage Manor, 1960.

HEADLEY, J. T. *Chaplains and Clergy of the Revolution.* New York: Charles Scribner, 1864.

HEMMING, JOHN. *The Conquest of the Incas.* New York: Harcourt, Brace & Jovanovich, 1970.

HENNESSEY, JAMES S. J. *American Catholics.*New York: Oxford University Press, 1981.

HESSELTINE, WILLIAM B. AND DAVID SMILEY. *The South in American History.* Englewood Cliffs, N.J.: Prentice-Hall, 1960.

HIBBERT, CHRISTOPHER. *Rome, The Biography of a City.* New York: W. W. Norton & Co., 1985.

HICKS, ROBERT. *Masculine Journey: Understanding the Six Stages of Manhood.* Colorado Springs, Colo.: Navpress, 1993.

HODGES, ZANE. *Absolutely Free.* Grand Rapids, Mich.: Academic Books, 1989.

HORT, ARTHUR FENTON. *Life and Letters of Fenton John Anthony Hort.* Vols. 1 and 2. London: Macmillan & Co., 1896.

HUNT, DAVE. *Global Peace and the Rise of the Antichrist.* Eugene, Oreg.: Harvest House Publishers, 1990.

_____. *Peace, Prosperity and the Coming Holocaust.* Eugene, Oreg.: Harvest House Publishers, 1983.

_____. *A Woman Rides the Beast.* Eugene, Oreg.: Harvest House Publishers, 1994.

JASPER, WILLIAM. *Global Tyranny...Step By Step.* Appleton, Wis.: Western Island Publishers, 1993.

JOHNSON, R. K. *Builder of Bridges.* Murfreesboro, Tenn.: Sword of the Lord Publishers, 1969.

JONES, MRS. SAM P. (LAURA) AND WALT HOLCOMB. *Life and Sayings of Sam P. Jones.* 2d ed., rev. Atlanta, Ga.: Franklin-Turner Co., Publishers, 1907.

KEEGAN, JOHN. *A History of Warfare.* New York: Vintage Books, 1994.

KENNEDY, JAMES ROLAND AND WALTER DONALD KENNEDY. *The South Was Right.* Gretna, La.: Pelican Publishing Co., 1994.

KENNEDY, PAUL. *The Rise and Fall of the Great Powers.* New York: Random House, 1987.

KEYSER, LES AND BARBARA KEYSER. *Hollywood and the Catholic Church.* Chicago: Loyola University Press, 1984.

KOCH, ADRIENNE AND WILLIAM PEDEN. *The Life and Selected Writings of Thomas Jefferson.* New York: Random House, 1944.

KOHUT, JOHN AND ROLAND SWEET. *News from the Fringe.* New York: Penguin Group, 1993.

LANGGUTH, A. J. *Patriots.* New York: Simon & Schuster, 1988.

LARSEN, BOB. *Larsen's New Book of Cults.* Wheaton, Ill.: Tyndale House Publishers, 1989.

LARSON, BRUCE. *Lindbergh of Minnesota.* New York: Harcourt, Brace, Jovanovich, 1973.

LATHAM, CAROLINE AND JEANNIE SAKOL. *"E" Is for Elvis.* New York: Penguin Group, 1990.

LATOURETTE, KENNETH SCOTT. *A History of Christianity.* New York: Harper & Brothers, 1953.

LAWSON, JAMES GILCHRIST. *Deeper Experiences of Famous Christians.* Anderson, Ind.: Warner Press, 1972.

LECKIE, ROBERT. *American and Catholic.* New York: Doubleday & Co., 1970.

LITTLE, LEWIS PEYTON. *Imprisoned Preachers and Religious Liberty in Virginia.* Gallatin, Tenn.: Church History Research & Archives, 1987.

MANCHESTER, WILLIAM. *A World Lit Only By Fire.* Boston: Little, Brown & Co., 1993.

MANHATTAN, AVRO. *Catholic Imperialism and World Freedom.* London: Watts & Co., 1952.

_____. *The Dollar and the Vatican.* Springfield, Mo.: Ozark Books, 1988.

_____. *Murder in the Vatican.* Springfield, Mo.: Ozark Books, 1985.

_____. *The Vatican and the USA.* London: Watts & Co., 1946.

_____. *The Vatican Billions.* Chino, Calif.: Chick Publications, 1983.

_____. *The Vatican in World Politics.* New York: Horizon Press, Inc., 1949.

_____. *The Vatican Moscow Washington Alliance.* Chino, Calif.: Chick Publications, 1986.

_____. *The Vatican's Holocaust.* Springfield, Mo.: Ozark Books, 1986.

_____. *Vietnam: Why Did We Go?* Chino, Calif.: Chick Publications, 1984.

MARSHALL, EVERETT. *Complete Life of William McKinley and Story of His Assasination, Memorial Edition.* n.p.: Historical Press, 1901.

MARSHALL, PETER AND DAVID MANUEL. *The Light and the Glory.* Old Tappan, N.J.: Fleming H. Revell, Co., 1977.

MARTIN, ROGER. *R. A. Torrey: Apostle of Certainty.* Murfreesboro, Tenn.: Sword of the Lord Publishers, 1976.

MARTIN, WILLIAM. *A Prophet with Honor.* New York: William Morrow & Co., 1991.

MATHER, COTTON. *The Great Works of Christ in America*, Vol. 1. Carlisle, Pa.: Banner of Truth Trust, 1979.

MAYNARD, THEODORE. *The Story of American Catholicism.* New York: Macmillan Co., 1941.

MCCARTY, BURKE. *The Suppressed Truth About the Assasination of Abraham Lincoln.* Haverhill, Mass.: Arya Varta Publishing Co., 1924.

MCCLURE, ALEXANDER. *Translators Revived.* Litchfield, Mich.: Maranatha Bible Society, 1858.

MCDOWELL, JOSH. *Evidence that Demands a Verdict.* Vol. 1. San Bernardino, Calif.: Campus Crusade for Christ International, 1972.

MCMANUS, JOHN F. *The Insiders.* Appleton, Wis.: John Birch Society, 1995.

MCPHERSON, JAMES. *What They Fought For, 1861–1865.* Baton Rouge, La.: Louisiana State University Press, 1994.

MILLARD, CATHERINE. *The Rewriting of American History.* Camp Hill, Pa.: Horizon House Publishers, 1991.

MITCHELL, CURTIS. *Billy Graham: Saint or Sinner.* Old Tappan, N.J.: Fleming H. Revell Co., 1973.

MOODY, WILL. *The Life of D. L. Moody.* Murfreesboro, Tenn.: Sword of the Lord Publishers, n.d.

MORRISON, SAMUEL ELIOT. *Admiral of the Ocean Sea.* Boston: Little, Brown & Co., 1942.

MORRISON, SAMUEL ELIOT AND HENRY STEELE COMMAGER. *The Growth of the American Republic.* Vols. 1 & 2. New York: Oxford University Press, 1962.

MORRIS, RICHARD B. *Seven Men Who Shaped Our Destiny.* New York: Harper & Row Publishers, 1972.

MORSE, SAMUEL F. B. *Foreign Conspiracy Against the Liberties of the United States.* New York: Arno Press, 1977.

_____. *Imminent Dangers to the Free Institutions of the United States Through Foreign Immigrants.* New York: Arno Press, 1969.

MORTON, FREDERICK. *The Rothschilds, A Family Portrait.* Greenwich, Conn.: Fawcett Publications, 1963.

NEWMAN, ALBERT HENRY. *A Manual of Church History.* Vols. 1 & 2. Valley Forge, Pa.: Judson Press, 1933.

NORRIS, J. FRANK. *Inside the History of First Baptist Church, Fort Worth and Temple Baptist Church, Detroit.* Fort Worth, Tex.: Privately printed, 1939.

ORLANDI, ENZO. *The Life and Times of Washington.* New York: Curtis Publishing Co., 1967.

PAISLEY, IAN R. K. *Antichrist.* Belfast, Northern Ireland: Martyrs Memorial Productions, n.d.

PARIS, EDMOND. *Convert...or Die!* Translated by Lois Perkins. Chino, Calif.: Chick Publications, n.d.

_____. *The Secret History of the Jesuits.* Translated from the French. Chino, Calif.: Chick Publications, 1975.

_____. *The Vatican Against Europe.* Translated by A. Robson. 2d ed. London: Wickliffe Press, 1961.

PAUL, RON AND LEWIS LEHRMAN. *The Case for Gold.* Washington, D.C.: Cato Institute, 1982.

PEDUZZI, KELLI. *America in the 20th Century, 1940–1949.* New York: Marshall Cavendish Corp., 1995.

PEMBER, G. H. *Earth's Earliest Ages.* Grand Rapids, Mich.: Kregel Publications, 1975.

PERLOFF, JAMES. *The Shadows of Power.* Appleton, Wis.: Western Island Publishers, 1988.

PISTONE, JOSEPH D. AND RICHARD WOODLEY. *Donnie Brasco: My Undercover Life in the Mafia.* New York: New American Library, 1987.

PITTS, CHARLES F. *Chaplains in Gray.* St. John, Ind.: Christian Book Gallery, 1957.

POLLARD, E. A. *The Lost Cause.* New York: Gramercy Books, 1994.

POLLOCK, JOHN. *Moody.* Grand Rapids, Mich.: Zondervan, 1967.

_____. *George Whitefield and the Great Awakening.* Belleville, Mich.: Lion Publishing, 1972.

PRIME, S. IRENEUS. *The Life of Samuel F. B. Morse.* New York: Arno Press, 1974.

PUTZ, LOUIS. *The Catholic Church, U.S.A.* Chicago: Fides Publishers Association, 1956.

QUAIN, KEVIN. *The Elvis Reader.* New York: St. Martin's Press, 1992.

QUIGLEY, CARROLL. *Tragedy and Hope.* New York: Macmillan Co., 1966.

RAY, D. B. *Baptist Succession.* Parsons, Kan.: Foley Railway Printing Co., 1912.

REESE, ED. *Christian Hall of Fame Series.* Vol. 4, *The Life and Ministry of Sam P. Jones, (1847–1906).* Glenwood, Ill.: Fundamental Publishers, 1975.

_____. *Christian Hall of Fame Series.* Vol. 3, *The Life and Ministry of Dwight L. Moody (1837–1899).* Glenwood, Ill.: Fundamental Publishers, 1975.

_____. *Christian Hall of Fame Series.* Vol. 45, *The Life and Ministry of Billy Sunday (1862–1935).* Lansing, Ill.: Fundmental Publishers, n.d.

REMINI, ROBERT V. *The Revolutionary Age of Andrew Jackson.* New York: Avon Books, 1977.

RIPLINGER, G. A. *New Age Bible Versions.* Ararat, Va.: AV Publications Corp., 1993.

RITCHIE, HOMER. *The Life and Legend of J. Frank Norris.* Fort Worth, Tex.: Privately printed, 1991.

RUSHDOONEY, ROUSAS J. *This Independent Republic.* Fairfax, Va.: Thoburn Press, 1978.

_____. *The Nature of the American System.* Fairfax, Va.: Thoburn Press, 1978.

RYRIE, CHARLES. *So Great Salvation.* Wheaton, Ill.: Victor Books, 1989.

SANDBURG, CARL. *Abraham Lincoln: The Prairie Years and the War Years.* New York: Harcourt, Brace & Co., n.d.

SCHAFF, DAVID S. *The Life of Philip Schaff.* New York: Charles Scribner's Sons, 1897.

SCHAFF, PHILIP. *History of the Christian Church.* Vol. 8, *The Swiss Reformation.* Grand Rapids, Mich.: Wm. B. Eerdmans Publishing Co., 1910.

SCHRODER, GENE. *War and Emergency Powers.* Dallas, Tex.: n.p., n.d.

SCOFIELD, C. I., ed. *The Scofield Study Bible.* New York: Oxford University Press, 1945.

SHEPHERD, CHUCK AND JOHN KOHUT AND ROLAND SWEET. *Beyond News of the Weird.* New York: Penguin Books, 1991.

_____. *More News of the Weird.* New York: Penguin Books, 1990.

_____. *News of the Weird.* New York: New American Library, 1989.

SIMPSON, COLIN. *The Lusitania.* New York: Little, Brown & Co., 1972.

SKEYHILL, TOM. *Sergeant York: Last of the Long Hunters.* St. John, Ind.: Christian Book Gallery, n.d.

SMOOT, DAN. *The Invisible Government.* Dallas, Tex.: Dan Smoot Report, 1962.

STILL, BILL. *On the Horns of the Beast.* Winchester, Va.: Reinhardt & Still Publishers, 1995.

STRATTON, EUGENE AUBREY. *Plymouth Colony.* Salt Lake City, Utah: Ancestry Publishing, 1986.

STRICKLAND, W. P., ED. *Autobiography of Peter Cartwright, The Backwoods Preacher.* New York: Carlton & Porter Publishers, 1857.

STRODE, HUDSON. *Jefferson Davis, Confederate President.* Vol. 2. New York: Harcourt, Brace & Co., 1959.

SUMNER, ROBERT L. *Bible Translations.* n.p.: Biblical Evangelist, 1979.

SUTTON, ANTHONY C. *America's Secret Establishment.* Billings, Mont.: Liberty House Press, 1986.

_____. *Wall Street and the Rise of Hitler.* Seal Beach, Calif.: '76 Press, 1971.

_____. *War on Gold.* Seal Beach, Calif.: 76 Press, 1971.

SYKES, CHARLES J. *A Nation of Victims.* New York: St. Martin's Press, 1992.

TARKOWSKI, ED. *Laughing Phenomena: Its History and Possible Effects on the Church.* McKean, Pa.: Privately printed, 1995.

TATUM, E. RAY. *Conquest or Failure.* Dallas, Tex.: Baptist Historical Foundation, 1966.

THACHER, JAMES. *Eyewitness to the American Revolution.* Stanford, Conn.: Longmeadow Press, 1994.

THOMPSON, E. WAYNE AND DAVID L. CUMMINS. *This Day in Baptist History.* Greenville, S.C.: Bob Jones University Press, 1993.

THOMPSON, R. W. *The Papacy and the Civil Power.* New York: Harper & Brothers Publisher, 1876.

TILLEY, JOHN S. *Facts the Historians Leave Out.* Montgomery, Ala.: Paragon Press, 1951.

TOLAND, JOHN. *Infamy: Pearl Harbor and Its Aftermath.* Garden City, N.Y.: Doubleday, 1982.

TORREY, R. A. *How to Obtain Fullness of Power*, Murfreesboro, Tenn.: Sword of the Lord Publishers, n.d.

UNGER, MERRILL F. *Archaeology and the Old Testament.* Grand Rapids, Mich.: Zondervan Publishing House, 1970.

VANCE, LAURENCE. *The Other Side of Calvinism.* Pensacola, Fla.: Vance Publications, 1991.

VEDDER, HENRY C. *A Short History of the Baptists.* Valley Forge, Pa.: Judson Press, 1907.

WAITE, D. A. *Defending the King James Bible.* Collingswood, N.J.: Bible for Today Press, 1993.

WESTCOTT, ARTHUR. *Life and Letters of Brooke Foss Westcott.* Vols. 1 and 2. London: Macmillan & Co., 1903.

WEYL, NATHANIEL. *The Negro in American Civilization.* Washington, D.C.: Public Affairs Press, 1960.

WHITEHEAD, JOHN W. *The Separation Illusion.* Milford, Mich.: Mott Media, 1977.

WILKINSON, BENJAMIN G. *Our Authorized Bible Vindicated.* Payson, Ar.: Leaves of Autumn Books, 1990.

WOODLEY, THOMAS FREDERICK. *Thaddeus Stevens.* Harrisburg, Pa.: Harrisburg Telegraph Press, 1934.

WOODROW, RALPH. *Babylon Mystery Religion.* Riverside, Calif.: Ralph Woodrow Evangelistic Association, 1966.

WOODS, GORDON S. *The Radicalism of American Revolution.* New York: Vintage Books, 1993.

REFERENCE WORKS

ADAMS, JAMES. *Dictionary of American History.* Vols. 3, 4 & 5. New York: Charles Scribner's Sons, n.d.

AINSWORTH, BRIG. GEN. FRED C. *The War of the Rebellion.* Series IV, Vol. III. Washington: n.p., 1900.

CATHOLIC ENCYCLOPEDIA. 1912 ed., *S.v.* "Torquemada."

FEDERER, WILLIAM J. *America's God and Country Encyclopedia of Quotes.* Coppell, Tex.: Fame Publishing, 1994.

GARRATY, JOHN A. AND PETER GAY, EDS. *The Columbia History of the World.* New York: Harper & Row, 1972.

GORDON, LOIS AND ALAN GORDON. *The Columbia Chronicles of American Life, 1910–1992.* New York: Columbia University Press, 1995.

GRIFFIN, MARTIN I. J. *The American Catholic Historical Researches.* Philadelphia: n.p., 1905.

HARVEY, EDMUND H., JR., ed. *Our Glorious Century.* Pleasantville, N.Y.: Reader's Digest Association, n.d.

KELLY, J. N. D. *The Oxford Dictionary of Popes.* Oxford, England: Oxford University Press, 1990.

LIVINGSTONE, ELIZABETH A., ed. *The Concise Oxford Dictionary of the Christian Church.* Oxford, England: Oxford University Press, 1977.

NASH, JAY ROBERT. *World Encyclopedia of Organized Crime.* New York: Dacapo Press, 1993.

MORLEY, JACKSON. *Crimes and Punishment: A Pictorial Encyclopedia.* Vol. 1. *Aberrant Behavior.* Paulton, England: B. P. C. Publishing, 1973.

RANDALL, J. GEORGE. *Dictionary of American History,* 1940 ed., *S.v.* "Radical Republicanism."

SACHSE, WILLIAM L., ED. *English History in the Making.* Vol. 1. *Readings from the Sources, to 1689.* Lexington, Mass.: Xerox College Publishing, 1967.

SIFAKIS, CARL. *The Mafia Encyclopedia.* New York: Facts on File, 1987.

SIMPSON, J. A. AND E. S. C. WEINER. *The Oxford English Dictionary.* 2d ed., Vol. 1. Oxford: Clarendon Press, 1989.

STERN, JANE AND MICHAEL STERN. *Encyclopedia of Culture.* New York: Harper-Collins Publishers, 1992.

TAN, PAUL LEE. *Encyclopedia of 7,700 Illustrations.* Rockville, Md.: Assurance Publishers, 1979.

VANCE, LAURENCE. *A Brief History of English Bible Translations.* Pensacola, Fla.: Vance Publications, 1993.

WAKELYN, JON L. *Dictionary of the Confederacy.* Westport, Conn.: Greenwood Press, 1972.

WARD, BALDWIN. *Pictorial History of the World.* New York: n.p., n.d.

WILSON, MITCHELL. *American Science and Invention.* New York: Bonanza Books, 1954.

WOODS, HENRY F. *American Sayings.* New York: Essential Books, 1945.

PERIODICALS

"ADVERTISEMENT." *The Boston Globe*, 15 May 1994, sec. B, 21.

"ADVERTISEMENT." *Saturday Evening Post,* March 1991, inside back cover.

A.P. RELEASE. "Naked and Not Ashamed, Say Christians." *Chicago Tribune,* 20 February, 1996, Sec. C, 1.

BARNES, FRED. "National Capitol, National Sham." *Reader's Digest*, November 1989, 108-9.

"BARRY TELLS NATIONAL TALK SHOW HOST SEX WAS HIS DOWNFALL." *Jet*, 3 June 1991, 24.

BERNSTEIN, CARL. "The Holy Alliance." *Time*, February 1992, 28.

BOBGAN, MARTIN AND DEIDRE BOBGAN. *Prophets and Psychoheresy II.* Santa Barbara, Calif.: East Gate Publishers, 1990.

BOLAND, MICHAEL. "Cooperative Evangelism at Harringay." *The Banner of Truth.* Iss. 42. London, England: May/June 1966, 8.

"BOY, 9, SHOOTS OFF-DUTY COP." *Chicago Tribune*, 30 December 1994, sec. 1, 17.

BOYS, DON. "Baptists and Freedom." *Common Sense for Today*, May-June 1996.

"BYE-BYE BARRY: WASHINGTON'S EMBATTLED MAYOR CALLS IT QUITS." *Time*, 25 June 1990, 23.

CAEN, HERB. "Shades of Guilt." *Reader's Digest*, September 1993, 96.

CARLSON, JOHN. "One By One: How AIDS Devastated an Iowa Family." *Des Moines Sunday Register,* 23 January 1994, sec. A, 9.

"CASE OF MARION BARRY: POLITICAL PERSUASION AND SELF-DENIAL." *USA Today,* September 1990, 88-89.

CHICAGO SUN TIMES. 25 May 1994, Sec. 2C, 8.

CHICAGO SUN TIMES. 15 October 1994, 4-5.

CHICAGO SUN TIMES. 30 January 1995, 6.

COLES, RALPH. *Ecumenical Confusion in Atlanta.* Oak Harbor, Wash.: Way of Life Organization, n.d.

CONNELLY, MICHAEL. "Body of Evidence." *Reader's Digest,* May 1993, 103-4.

DAGER, ALBERT JAMES. "Promise Keepers: Is What You See What You Get?" *Media Spotlight,* July 1995.

"DAHMER KILLED IN PRISON ATTACK: Strangled and Dismembered 17 Boys and Men and Cannibalized Some of Them." *Chicago Tribune,* 28 November 1994.

DOWD MAUREEN. "Resurrection." *New York Times Magazine,* 11 September 1994, 88.

DUGGAN, PAUL AND RUBEN CASTANEDA. "4 Die in Police Headquarter Shooting." *Washington Post,* 23 November 1994, sec. A, 1.

ELSASSER, GLEN. "Mayor Barry Denies Drug, Alcohol Relapse." *Chicago Tribune,* 14 May 1996, Sec. 1, 4.

GIBBS, NANCY AND RICHARD N. OSTLING. "God's Billy Pulpit." *Time,* 15 November 1993, 74.

HABERMAN, CLYDE AND ALBIN KREBS. "Transsexual on Police." *New York Times,* 2 February 1979, sec. 3, 26.

HAYNES, V. DION. "Board Blames Girl, 9, Who Is Suing in Classroom Rape." *Chicago Tribune,* 11 March 1992, Sec. 2, 1.

HITCHENS, CHRISTOPHER. "Contempt for the Little Colony: How Barry and Bush Run Washington." *Harper's,* October 1989, 70.

JET. 11 May 1994, 4.

KOHLENBERGER, JOHN R. III. "Which Bible Translation Is for Me?" *Moody Monthly,* May 1987, 17-19.

LAWRENCE, DAVID. "Worst Scandal in Our History." *U. S. News and World Report,* 26 January 1970, 95.

LAWSON, CHARLES. "Promise Keepers." *The Lion of Judah,* June 1995, Vol. 1:1.

MANNING, ANITA. "Pop Culture for College Credit." *USA Today*, 21 December 1994, 4(D).

MCPHERSON, EDWARD. *Political History of the United States During the Period of Reconstruction, April 15, 1865–July 15, 1870.* New York: Dacapo Press, 1972.

"MEATY FIGHT: WOMAN SHOOTS SON OVER HAM." *Chicago Tribune*, 30 November 1991, sec. 1, 18.

MELOY, Don. "Pity the Poor Killer." *Reader's Digest,* September 1992, 23.

NORWOOD, JAMES. *George Washington's Faithful Pastor.* n.p., n.p, n.d.

PLETZ, JOHN. "Police Billboard Stops Traffic." *The Post Tribune*, 21 October 1994, sec. A, 1.

"POPE REMEMBERS A CHILD'S GIFT." *Fairbanks Daily News-Miner,* 2 May 1984.

RENNICK, DAVID. "The Situationist—Annals of Politics." *New Yorker*, 5 September 1994, 93.

RILEY, MICHAEL. "I Guess You All Figured That I Couldn't Resist That Lady." *Time*, 9 July 1990, 19.

ROCHE, TIM AND DAVID BARSTOW. "Pregnant Woman Shoots Her Fetus." *St. Petersburg Times,* 8 September 1994, 1a-1b.

ROYKO, MIKE. "Cows in the Green House." *Reader's Digest*, November 1990, 62.

RUBEN, DAVE. "Dodo Solution." *Reader's Digest*, April 1992, 147.

RUDD, DAVID C. AND ANGELA BRADBERRY. "8-Year-Old Shot in 3rd-Grade Classroom." *Chicago Tribune*, 11 March 1992, sec. 2, 1.

"SAN FRANCISCO MOURNS 10,000TH AIDS DEATH." *Chicago Tribune*, 9 January 1993, sec. 1, 4.

SCHISSREN, LISA. "Bill and Hillary at the Trough." *American Spectator*, August 1993, 22.

SMITH, PAUL. "Belmont Abbey Confers Honorary Degree." *The Gastonia Gazette,* 22 November 1967.

"12TH COP KILLS HIMSELF IN NEW YORK." *Chicago Tribune*, 26 December 1994, Sec. 1, 6.

"TWO MUGGINGS." *Reader's Digest*, June 1990, 196.

VAN DER MERWE, JEWEL. "Latter Rain and the Rise of Joel's Army." *Discernment*, October-December 1994.

WILLIAMS, JOHN. "Porno 101." *Reader's Digest*, September 1993, 96.

YORKS, CINDY LAFAVRE. "McChurch." *Daily Courier News, U.S.A. Weekend*, 13-15 April 1990, 4-7.

AUDIO AND VIDEO

ANKERBERG, JOHN. *Protestants and Catholics: Do They Now Agree?* Produced by John Ankerberg. 60 minutes, 1995. Videocassette.

JENNINGS, PETER. *In the Name of God.* Produced by Martin Smith. 60 minutes. American Broadcasting Company, 1995.

JOHNSON, PAUL. *The Almost Chosen People.* 3 audio cassettes. San Francisco, Calif.: Laissez Faire Audio, n.d.

"THE SPIRIT OF LIBERTY." Produced by Liberty University. 12 minutes. n.d. Videocassette.

VAN IMPE, JACK AND REXELLA VAN IMPE. *Startling Revelations: Pope John Paul II.* Produced by Van Impe Ministries. 60 minutes, n.d. Videocassette.

MISCELLANEOUS

BIDEN, SENATOR JOSEPH. *The Threshold of the New World Order: The Wilsonian Vision and American Foreign Policy in the 1990's and Beyond.* Maryland Heights, Mo.: Better Books, 1994.

COLSON, CHARLES. *Evangelicals and Catholics Together: The Christian Mission in the Third Millenium.* rep. by permission by Ankerberg. Chattanooga, Tenn.: Theological Research Institute, 1994.

EVANS, WENDELL L. "Synopsis of American History." n.d. Unpublished lecture notes. Hyles-Anderson College, Crown Point, Ind.

MCCARY, P. K. *Black Bible Chronicles*. New York: African American Press, 1993.

MILLEN, ANDREA AND RICH MILLEN. *Laissez Faire Books*. August 1995. 30.

MUSEUM QUOTATIONS. *Soldiers' Expressions*. Sharpsburg, Md.: Antietam National Battlefield, n.d.

U.S. CONGRESS. *Document No. 914*. 88th Cong., 1st Sess., 62.

WENIGER, G. ARCHER. "Preliminary Considerations for Fundamentalists on the Graham Ecumenical Evangelistic Campaign Scheduled for San Francisco." [April 1958] Oakland, Calif.

Index

Scripture Index